THE STORY OF
POETRY

By the same author

Criticism

Fifty Modern British Poets: an introduction
Fifty English Poets 1300–1900: an introduction
Reading Modern Poetry
Lives of the Poets

Anthologies

Eleven British Poets
New Poetries I and *II*
Poets on Poets (with Nick Rennison)
The Harvill Book of Twentieth-Century Poetry in English

Poetry

Choosing a Guest
The Love of Strangers
Selected Poems

Fiction

The Colonist
The Dresden Gate

Translations

Flower & Song: Aztec Poetry (with Edward Kissam)
On Poets & Others, Octavio Paz

THE STORY OF
POETRY

VOLUME ONE

*English Poets and Poetry
from Cædmon to Caxton*

Michael Schmidt

Weidenfeld & Nicolson

LONDON

For Evelyn Lichtenschopf

First published in Great Britain in 2001
by Weidenfeld & Nicolson

© 2001 Michael Schmidt
The moral right of Michael Schmidt to be identified as the author
of this work has been asserted in accordance with the
Copyright, Designs and Patents Act of 1988.

A CIP catalogue record for this book
is available from the British Library.

ISBN 0 297 64703 2

Typeset by Selwood Systems, Midsomer Norton
Set in Minion
Printed in Great Britain by
Butler & Tanner Ltd, Frome and London

Weidenfeld & Nicolson

The Orion Publishing Group Ltd
Orion House
5 Upper Saint Martin's Lane
London, WC2H 9EA

CONTENTS

An Informal History

Foreword *Reading and Writing*   3

Introduction *Caedmon and Old English Poetry*   7

The L Plate *The Seven Deadly Sins*   15

Beginnings *The Old English Canon*   21

Beowulf   32

It begins again *Richard Rolle of Hampole,*
    Robert Manning of Brunne, John Barbour   39

Tutelary Spirits *Richard II and John Wycliffe*   49

'In stori stif and stronge . . .' *The Gawain Poet*   56

'In englesh forto make a book . . .' *John Gower*   62

Southwark *John Gower, Boethius,* Romance of
    the Rose, *Geoffrey Chaucer*   71

'And as I lay and leaned and looked in the wateres'
    William Langland   79

'Go, litel bok' *Geoffrey Chaucer*   85

Sing cuccu! *Anon*   107

Entr'acte *Charles of Orleans, Thomas Hoccleve,*
    John Lydgate, Juliana Berners   110

'merely written for the people' *Ballads*   119

'Not as I suld, I wrait, but as I couth' *Robert*
    Henryson, William Dunbar, Gavin Douglas,
    Stephen Hawes   126

The Watershed *William Caxton*   138

Anthology

PREFACE   147

OLD ENGLISH   149

1 The Dream of the Rood (translated by Charles Schmidt)
2 The Seafarer (translated by Edwin Morgan)

3 The Wanderer (translated by Edwin Morgan)
4 The Ruin (translated by Edwin Morgan)
5–11 Seven Riddles (translated by Edwin Morgan)
12 from *Beowulf* (translated by Edwin Morgan)

MIDDLE ENGLISH   175

Richard Rolle of Hampole
13 'When Adam delved and Eve span'
14 'Unkind man'
15 'Memento Homo Quod Cinis Es'
16 'Lo lemman sweet'
17 'Three good brothers are ye'
18 'My truest treasure so traitorly taken'

Ballads
19 from *The Ancient Ballad of Chevy Chase*
20 Sweet Willie and Lady Margery
21 Sir Patrick Spence
22 The Wife of Usher's Well
23 Kinmont Willie
24 Riddles Wisely Expounded
25 Robin, the Kitchie-Boy
26 The Nut Brown Maid

Lyrics, Poems of Celebration and of Faith
27 'Green Groweth the Holly'
28 'Blow, northern wind'
29 'You and I and Amyas'
30 'Herefore, and therefore'
31 'Bring us home good ale, sir'
32 'Lenten is come with love to town'
33 'All night'
34 'There is no rose'
35 A Boar's Head
36 'This endris night'
37 'Lullay, my child, and weep no more'
38 Regina celi letare
39 Mother white as lily flower
40 Timor mortis conturbat me

The *Gawain* Poet
41 from *Pearl*
42 from *Gawain and the Green Knight*

William Langland
43 from *Piers Plowman*

a from Prologue
b Passus VII

John Gower

44 from *Confessio Amantis*
a　from Prologue (*1392*)
b　Tale of Florent
c　Deianira and Nessus
d　Pyramus and Thisbe
e　Pygmalion
f　Ceïx and Alceone
g　The Supplication

Geoffrey Chaucer

45 from *The Book of the Duchess*
a　The Dream
b　Lament and Consolation

46 from *The House of Fame*
a　from Proem
b　The Dream

47 from *Troilus and Criseyde*
a　from Book II, Proem
b　from Book II, Criseyde Reflects
c　from Book V, Criseyde's letter and the rest

48 from *The Canterbury Tales*
a　General Prologue
b　The Miller's Tale
c　The Wife of Bath's Tale
d　The Nun's Priest's Tale

49 Merciless Beauty: A Triple Rondel

Charles of Orleans

50 'My ghostly father I me confess'
51 'When I am laid to sleep as for a stound'
52 'But late ago went I my heart to see'
53 'In the forest of noyous heaviness'
54 'I have the obit of my lady dearè'

Thomas Hoccleve

55 Two Rondels
a　To Money
b　Money's Reply
56 from *Thomas Hoccleve's Complaint*
57 from *Ars Sciendi Mori*
58 from *The Regement of Princes*
a　Hoccleve meets and talks with an old beggar
b　Envoy

John Lydgate
59 London Lickpenny
60 from *Life of Our Lady: Book I, The Prologue*
61 The Fifteen Tokens Before the Doom
62 from *The Troy Book: The Envoy*
63 from *The Fall of Princes*
 a   The Dance Macabre: Prologue
 b   The Words of the Translator

James I, King of Scotland
64 from *The Kingis Quair*

Robert Henryson
65 The Tale of the Uponlandis Mouse, and the Burges Mouse
66 *The Testament of Cresseid*
67 A Prayer for the Pest

Gavin Douglas
68 from *Aeneados*
 a   To Know the Translator
 b   General Prologue
 c   from Prologue, Book Seven

William Dunbar
69 'London thou art the Flower of Cities all'
70 from The Two Married Women and the Widow
71 The Thistle and the Rose
72 The Dregy of Dunbar
73 Done is a Battle on the Dragon Black
74 Lament for the Makaris

Stephen Hawes
75 from *The Coercion of Swearers*
76 from *The Example of Virtue*
77 from *The Pastime of Pleasure*
 a   *A Commendation of Gower, Chaucer and Lydgate*
 b   *How Grand Amour went to geometry and what geometry is*

Acknowledgements   475

Bibliography   476

General Index   483

Index of Titles   489

Index of First Lines and Extracts   493

An Informal History

FOREWORD

'In a graveyard in England, I think it was in Bath, I once saw yellow pine-needles nestled into the "runes" of the letters on a fallen gravestone (probably eighteenth century).'

Evelyn Schlag

The Old English word *rún* meant *secret*, or by extension *secret counsel*. In a culture where reading and writing were the exception rather than the rule, where most transactions were carried out in speech and where the poetic tradition was oral, writing was a secret code. Those who possessed it had power. They could scheme among themselves, they could whisper without moving their lips, they could address the gods.[1] Our word *rune* obviously derives from *rún*. In runic communication, the individual letters were called *rünstafas* and the interpretation of the runs of *rünstafas* was called *rædan* (*reading*) in Old English. Odin in the Norse *Edda* sacrificed himself in order to acquire the skill to use runes, unlocking their magic, which was a form of wisdom, to become a 'rune-master'.

The original runes were probably incised in wood, bone or another relatively hard material, and sometimes the incisions were filled in with colour to make them stand out. In Old English the technical expression for engraving or incising was *wrítan*. When we take up pen or biro or patter on a keyboard, *writing*, we are re-enacting a runic discipline. Writing, to begin with, was a way of codifying and keeping knowledge from the people. It was a 'closed book' to all but the initiate. It also had its perils, of course: it preserved words and information which could be stolen and misused. The Druids were forbidden from putting their learning into writing for fear that it would be misappropriated.

A Roman writer in the sixth century described how the Germanic runes were painted on smooth sticks, on ash wood. The beech wood tablet also used for runing was called a *bóc*, and we may regard it as the forbear of the

---

[1] John Amos Comenius comments on how the Indians of America could not understand how a man could manage to convey his thoughts to another man without speech or a messenger, just by sending a piece of paper. (*The Great Didactic* of John Amos Comenius, p. 84).

book, at the same time being grateful for the invention and evolution of paper.

Runic writing was decisively displaced in the ninth and tenth centuries by the Roman alphabet brought in by Irish missionaries. The emergence of an English literature – a written poetry and prose – is inextricably linked with the growth of the Church, the monastic scribal traditions, and the Biblical stories, homilies and patristics that the Church carried in its rather different Irish (in the North) and Roman (in the South) luggage. With the Danish raids on the monasteries, their unsettled survival, and finally their dissolution, countless manuscripts of early provenance were destroyed. Given the vicissitudes of British history and the climate of the British Isles, the miracle is that anything at all survives.

The runes became vestigial but were not entirely lost from memory: a poet might exploit them. The Old English poet Cynewulf worked his name in runic anagram into the concluding lines of *Juliana, Elene, Christ II* and *Fates of the Apostles*. It was a way of personalizing his versions of what was in fact the common property of his church.

Written language, when it moves beyond secrecy and mystery, finds its first use in codifying and setting down what a tribe or a people *need* to know: laws and customs, prayers and rituals, the story of its origins, elements which oral tradition can carry only so far. But a written language can keep secrets even so. The early runic poems were mysterious, and mystery persists in some of the other forms of Old English poetry which survive. The most popular form is the *riddle*, which unlike modern riddles is rooted in word-play, punning and metaphor and closely follows in the Latin tradition of riddling. The word has its origin in *rædan*: to puzzle out the sense, to read. A riddle takes the form of a question and often gives life back to a cliché of expression or feeling. There are ninety-four riddles in the *Exeter Book* (**5–11**). The forty-seventh evokes that voracious little wrecker, the book-moth.

> Moththe word fræt: me thæt thuhte
> *Moth ate word: I that thought*
>
> wrætlicu wyrd,   tha ic thæt wundor gefrægn,
> *a marvellous fate,   when I discovered the wonder,*
>
> thæt se wyrm forswealg   wera gied sumes,
> *that the worm swallowed down   a particular man's words,*
>
> theof in thystro   thrymfæstne cwide
> *thieved in the dark   his glorious quoths*
>
> and thæs strangan stathol.   Stælgiest ne wæs
> *and his powerful truths.   The stealing guest was not*

wihte thy gleawra   the he tham wordum swealg.
a whit the wiser   that he'd swallowed the words.

Aristotle said riddles 'expressed true facts under impossible conditions'. They are often facts true in and true to the language. Mystery and secret have been localized. Cynewulf's runic autographs are riddling in this sense.

Less riddling and mysterious, the *gnomes* were magical because, once heard, they entered memory, never to be dislodged. They are like condensed English epigrams or maxims, short and meaty, expressing a truth generally acknowledged and at their worst tending towards sententiousness. The Roman historian Tacitus records an early Germanic gnome: 'Women must weep and men remember.' Gnomes may have been a popular form: they survive in two of the Old English manuscripts, a string of wise or weary pearls, like the wisdom of Hesiod's *Works and Days*, that come tumbling out helter-skelter, some fresh and striking, some obscure, some merely commonplace. In the *Cotton* manuscript we find a series of gnomic verses that provide a mnemonic catalogue of Church festivals. Among the succinct phrasing, rhyme is heard.

... Wyrd byth swithost.   Winter byth cealdost,
... Fate is strongest.   Winter is coldest,

lencten hrimigost,   he byth lengest ceald,
spring most frost-rimed,   it is longest time cold,

sumor sunwlitegost,   swegel byth hatost,
summer sunbrightest,   heaven is hottest,

haerfest hretheadegost,   hælethum bringeth
harvest [autumn] most glorious,   to men it brings

geares wæstmas   tha the him God sendeth.
the year's fruits   which God sends to him.

The *Sun*'s sub-editors and other tabloid headline writers inherit the gnome.

If riddles are rooted in the classics, proverbs, popular too, are of Biblical pedigree. They tend to be more symmetrically constructed than gnomes and relate to specific ethical or legal themes, hence the care in design. 'Waste not, want not' has an air of homespun authenticity. It is Benjamin Franklin wholesome, reassuringly conventional. The proverb is unlikely to be an original thought; it is more a case of 'what oft was thought but ne'er so succinctly expressed', a morsel of formulaic wisdom. The categories are not pure: the gnome can shade into the proverb, though the riddle keeps itself to itself.

Proverbs work their way into most Old English poems, pithily summarizing the moral intentions of the poet, providing detachable, epigrammatic wisdom. In the Bible, Proverbs is ascribed to King Solomon. King Alfred was carved from similar stone.

INTRODUCTION

> Nu scolon herigean   heofonrices Weard
> Meotodes meahte   and his modgethanc
> weorc Wuldor-Fæder   swa he wundra gehwæs
> ece Drihten,   or onstealde
> He ærest sceop   ielda bearnum
> heofon to hrofe   halig Scyppend
> tha middangeard   moncynnes Weard
> ece Drihten   æfter teode
> firum foldan   Frea ælmihtig
>
> *'Cædmon's Hymn'*

The Venerable Bede accounted it a miracle. The first English poem, or rather, the first English poem that we can date with any accuracy – to about 657 AD – was composed extempore by a working man, a neat-herd,[2] with the collusion of an angel, at the monastery of the Abbess Hild, Streoneshalh (Whitby, Yorkshire).

An illiterate herdsman 'specially distinguished and honoured by divine grace', of uncertain age, but past the first and even the second flush of youth, came to the monastery as a labourer around 657. He died there twenty-three years later, when Bede himself was only seven years old. By the time Bede had become the great teacher and scholar of Wearmouth and Jarrow, the history of the neat-herd was established and legend was beginning to attach to him. Bede names him: he was called Cædmon; and the poem has come to be known as 'Cædmon's Hymn'. It survives in seventeen manuscripts of Bede's *Historia Ecclesiastica Gentis Anglorum* (*Ecclesiastical History*).

Cædmon first sang his hymn only about half a century after King Edwin was converted to Christianity at York by Bishop Paulinus, yet the faith the poem declares seems untroubled and deeply rooted. The poem, too, is deeply rooted, in a tradition of oral poetry that developed from a West Germanic tradition some three and a half centuries older. Recited verse may have been popular; certainly, its audience was not confined exclusively to monks, nuns, clerks or the rich and powerful members of society.

---

[2] Employed in looking after livestock, from bullocks to cows and heifers.

In the evenings at Streoneshalh, to pass the time, farm labourers gathered to play the harp and to sing. Cædmon was new to the monastery, perhaps shy, perhaps stand-offish. In any case, he was in the habit of withdrawing to his sleeping-pallet in the byre, or in the stables, so as not to show himself up. Then one night an apparition in the form of a man – call him an angel – entered his dream. 'Sing me something, Cædmon,' he commanded. 'I cannot sing anything,' Cædmon replied, 'and therefore I came out from this entertainment and retired here, as I know not how to sing.' (All the translations make him speak a pseudo-archaic English, the stiltedness intended to suggest remoteness in time, like the deep varnish encrusting old paintings.) The angel replied, 'Yet you *could* sing.' He said: sing about the Creation and, Bede relates, the words began to flow from Cædmon's lips. In his own Old English, he praised the Creator with his whole heart, and for the first time.

At the next opportunity he took the harp when it came his way and repeated his eloquent song of Creation to his workmates. The supervisor of the labourers overheard him and took the new-fledged poet to the Abbess and her colleagues, who tested him and resolved that his was a gift of divine grace. He was admitted to the monastery as a lay brother.

His poem is a kind of variation on the Lord's Prayer, notable less for its originality than for the strong emphasis of its affirmation. A mute herdsman became, overnight, an eloquent witness. Bede says that once Cædmon's tongue was loosened there was no stopping him; he composed poems out of the first two books of the Bible and on New Testament themes, perhaps dictating them to a monastic scribe ('his teachers wrote down the words from his lips') or simply transmitting them, because they were memorable, directly into the memory of his auditors. Such processes can occur when an oral tradition is still alive. 'He had not, indeed, been taught of men, or through men, to practise the art of song, but he had received divine aid, and his power of song was the gift of God.' We are not allowed to lose sight of his humble, rural origin or of his original vocation as a neat-herd: 'All that he could learn by listening' (for it is doubtful that he learned to read or write) 'he pondered in his heart and, ruminating like some clean beast, he turned it into the sweetest of songs.' Not only was he the first English poet; he was the first *inspired* poet, a Romantic a millennium and a quarter before his time. The phrase 'like some clean beast' is a wonderful characterization, Johnsonian in its patronizing tone and in its accuracy of spirit.

Where was Cædmon from? His name is not English. Is it a corruption of the British *Catumanus*? Was he of Celtic origin? Did his family come from Wales or, like some of the very earliest Christians in England, did his people come originally from Ireland? Did he establish a school of poets at Streoneshalh? We cannot advance beyond conjecture. In the seventeenth century, partly on Bede's authority, Franciscus Junius (François Dujon) attributed to Cædmon major scriptural poems contained in the Bodleian Library manuscript known as Junius XI and dating from around the end of the first millennium, and published them in Amsterdam: *Genesis, Exodus, Daniel*, and the strange anthology-poem *Christ and Satan*, a collection of lyrical variations on and amplifications of key Bible stories, most memorably the Temptation of Christ and the Harrowing of Hell. These poems are no longer considered Cædmon's: scholarship has left them anonymous and all that remains to his credit is the original hymn. Bede remarks, 'Many others, also, in England, imitated him in the composition of religious songs.'

Is this in fact where poetry in English begins, in a kingdom which isn't yet called England, in service of a Church which is more Celtic than Roman, and in an idiom that looks so alien? An English speaker innocent of philology encounters Old English with a sense of shock. It is a foreign language, closer in some respects to German than to the languages and dialects we speak today. It looks hard to pronounce (though it is more phonetic than modern English); there are strange letters: ligatures like æ, and unfamiliar symbols called yoks and thorns which have fallen out of use and are resolved into 'th', 'y' and 'g' in this book. No wonder that, confronted with the tangle that history has made of the roots of our own language, most readers prefer to begin with Middle English, where the difficulties are more tractable.

But Old English is less opaque than it seems at first. With a little effort we can pick out a number of words that are not entirely removed from modern English, and the syntax is simpler than in Latin or German. Here is Cædmon's poem again, not translated but with some of the language adjusted towards modern usage.

Nu [*now*] scolon [*should we*] herigean   heofonrices [*heavenly*] Weard [*Warder*]
Meotodes meahte [*might*]   and his modgethanc
weorc [*work*] Wuldor-Fæder [*?-Father*]   swa he [*he*] wundra [*wonders*] gehwæs
ece Drihten   or onstealde
He [*He*] ærest [*first*] sceop [*shaped*]   ielda bearnum
heofon [*heaven*] to hrofe [*roof*]   halig [*holy*] Scyppend
tha [*then*] middangeard [*middle earth*]   moncynnes [*mankind's*] Weard [*Warder*]
ece Drihten   æfter [*after*] teode
firum foldan   Frea ælmihtig [*almighty*]

Twenty-one words out of forty-two we can – uncertainly – sense ghosting their way through the strange orthography. Given the formulaic repetitions, it is not beyond the skills of even an amateur philological sleuth, with the aid of an Old English dictionary, to come to a translation of sorts, releasing the sense of this early poem without pretending to transpose it into a modern idiom. The world vision, like the language, is strange and can be inferred but not, as Bede says of his Latin version, translated.[3]

Nu scolon herigean   heofonrices Weard
Now we should praise   heaven-reich's Warder

Meotodes meahte   and his modgethanc
the Measurer's might   and the thoughts of his mind

weorc Wuldor-Fæder   swa he wundra gehwæs
work of the Father of Glory   when he of each wonder

ece Drihten   or onstealde
– eternal Lord –   the original made

He ærest sceop   ielda bearnum
He first gave shape   for the bairns of men

heofon to hrofe   halig Scyppend
heaven as a roof   holy Shaper of things

tha middangeard   moncynnes Weard
then middle earth   mankind's Warder

ece Drihten   aefter teode
– eternal Lord –   and afterwards created

firum foldan   Frea ælmihtig
for men the earth   Sovereign almighty

In condensed form, 'Cædmon's Hymn' provides us with a lesson in the forms of Old English verse from the oral tradition. Some of those forms survive and re-emerge, much elaborated, in the Middle English of the fourteenth century in a specifically literary tradition – in the *Gawain* poet's writings and in Langland's *Piers Plowman* for example.

Oral traditions do not always pre-date the use of writing. The ballad tradition in the Scottish Borders, for example, coexists with an abundant literary tradition elsewhere in Britain. Oral traditions are for the most part popular in various ways. The poems are usually accompanied by music. In 'Widsith' and *Beowulf* the *gleeman* or *scop* (a minstrel of some standing, usually attached to a court) sings to a harp. A harp was uncovered in the famous Sutton Hoo excavations. Was this the only instrument used? Was the Germanic round harp common in England? The character of the instrument still rouses debate; in all likelihood a range of instruments was used down the centuries of composition and performance, but as with archaic

---

[3] *Hic est sensus, non autem ordo ipse verborum ... neque enim possunt carmina, quamvis optime composita, ex alia in aliam linguam ad verbum sine detrimento sui decoris ac dignitatis transferri ...*

and classical Greek poetry, the words of the singer were never unaccompanied, and the singer never subsided into mere speech.

The *scop* recited or performed to an audience that was homogeneous in one respect: it had clear formal and narrative expectations. Like all popular cultural traditions, oral poetry is essentially conservative. A story can travel down several generations, or from one language to a cousin language, gathering into its folds new elements, creating the rich texture of actual historical contingencies and the sort of bizarre anachronisms that mark Homer's poems in ancient Greece. Nothing is ever quite lost, even though its sense might be.

Usually the stories told are familiar to the audience. That is part of their attraction. What matters is the telling, the sounds the poet makes, the order in which he (always *he*) recounts the tale. Variation, not novelty, is what matters. Oral poets inherit patterns of exposition, lexical stress, alliteration and assonance which they master through apprenticeship, not as theory but as practice. Audiences are trained painlessly, through the pleasure of listening, and can hear excellence quite as clearly as they hear flaws and lapses. We have a sense that the 'rules' inhere in the poems in the oral tradition, unlike the literary tradition where rules are often defined and can – in the hands of a crude practitioner – mechanically dictate new verse. We can tabulate sound patterns, extrapolate epithets, analyse the poems in various ways, but there is something irreducible in the poetry. And it works best for us, as it did for them, if we read it aloud.

Perhaps the most peculiar aspect of the oral tradition, from the point of view of modern readers, is, *pace* Cædmon, that we do not ask who the *poet* is. A poem is something that grows and changes with performance until at last it is arrested by a scribe and put to parchment, preserved and eventually edited into textual form. But it is different in kind from the poetry of a literary culture in which we can ask what the individual poet's intentions are or were; where we can historicize and interpret in relation to a named individual. Apart from 'Cædmon's Hymn', we cannot date any Old English poem. Each one has elements that we can date, but often those elements are from different periods, the earlier ones preserved in the later recitation and finally in the writing down, the textualizing, of the poem.

What are some of the formal elements that we can expect from Old English oral poetry? When we try to say it aloud, one of the first things we notice about 'Cædmon's Hymn', as it is generally printed nowadays, is a gap in the middle of each line, compelling a strong pause (or *caesura*) that creates a strict rhythmic parallelism between the half lines; taking the poem whole, we see a kind of spine of pauses around which the body of language is articulated. Each half line balances the other half line, and most of the half lines have two strongly accented syllables, so that each line has four strong accents. Within each line, two or usually three of the four accented syllables begin with the same or a similar sound, consonant or vowel, and there are internal echoes which chime or rhyme:

> Nu scolon **he**rigean   **he**ofonrices Weard
> **M**eotodes **m**eahte   and his **m**odgethanc
> **w**eorc **W**uldor-Fæder   swa he **w**undra gehwæs
> **e**ce Drihten   or **o**nstealde
> He **æ**rest sceop   **ie**lda bearnum
> **h**eofon to **h**rofe   **h**alig Scyppend
> tha **m**iddang*eard*   **m**oncynnes W*eard*
> **e**ce Drihten   **æ**fter teode
> **f**irum **f**oldan   **F**rea ælmihtig

Alliteration and assonance are further structural elements. And finally, within this short poem the phrase *ece Drihten* is repeated, like one of the stock epithets in Homer's poems.

We should play the poem one more time, showing where the accents or lexical stresses fall. Unlike Latin poetry, where scansion is in accordance with syllable length rather than accent, in Old as in most Middle and Modern English poetry, metre and rhythm are a matter of stress patterns. Each half line has two, or sometimes three, accented syllables, and a variable number of unaccented syllables.

> <u>Nu</u> scolon <u>he</u>rigean   <u>heo</u>fonrices <u>Weard</u>
> <u>Meo</u>todes <u>mea</u>hte   and his <u>mod</u>geranc
> <u>weorc</u> <u>Wul</u>dor-Fæder   swa he <u>wun</u>dra ge<u>hwæs</u>
> <u>ece</u> <u>Drih</u>ten   or <u>on</u>stealde
> <u>he</u> <u>æ</u>rest sceop   <u>iel</u>da <u>bear</u>num
> <u>heo</u>fon to <u>hro</u>fe   <u>ha</u>lig <u>Scyp</u>pend
> tha <u>mid</u>dangeard   <u>mon</u>cynnes <u>Weard</u>
> <u>ece</u> <u>Drih</u>ten   <u>æf</u>ter <u>te</u>ode
> <u>fi</u>rum <u>fol</u>dan   <u>Frea</u> æl<u>mih</u>tig

What would the fellow farm workers, the monks and the Abbess have admired in this little poem? First, the *weave*, the freedom with which the poet, in a synthetic language dependent less on prepositions than on case endings, can vary the order of the words to fit the rhythmic and alliterative pattern. They would have responded to the parallelisms, now creating apposition, now contrast, and to the way the verb *herigean* ('praise') has four objects. They would have liked the kennings, those compound words like *middangeard* and *heofonrices* and *Wuldor-Fæder,* two literal terms whose marriage is succinct metaphor. Most of all they would have warmed to the source and nature of the poem's celebration: the rustic speaker animated by divine and poetic grace.

Cædmon's nine little lines, standing emblematically at the head of the English – in any event, the Old English – poetic tradition, are a useful key to the poetry of the longest and darkest period of English literature, 650 to the Norman Conquest in 1066, more than four centuries from which the total surviving line-count of verse is about 30,000. That is fewer lines than Chaucer wrote, less than a fifth of what Lydgate wrote. Time, climate, history – eventually the Normans but, before them, invaders from Denmark and elsewhere – were unkind to wandering bards and to the libraries in which their poems were recorded and shelved. Without the conversion of Britain to Christianity and the creation of monasteries, even less poetry would have survived. In Britain as in other spiritually-colonized lands the Church preserved in written form elements of the pre-Christian culture, perhaps for pleasure, but perhaps also in a spirit of colonial anthropology; a knowledge of the prior culture made it easier to work on the spiritual character of a people and to convert them more than superficially to a different faith.

It is likely that some of the writing down of pagan texts was ordered by English abbots who felt an attachment to the old words and forms. Was it sentimentality, a sense of 'identity' with ancestors, or more an excitement at the power of the language and of a vision of the world less regulated, less resolved, a world in which dragons lived, in which exile from the thane was purgatorial, and where the body endured pain and hardship? And yet the poems proved that there was a language to fill the voids and silences, a formed and formal language which the Abbot could understand and which touched him in ways that Latin and scripture could not. In preserving the poems of his language, even if they were gradually embroidered and finally rewoven with Christian patternings, or were awkwardly combined in ways which disrupted or destroyed the ancient narrative line, what the Abbot was preserving was an ingredient that went into the making of himself, of his English monks, and of the English kings and peasants. It was not only a language and its rhythms that sounded in increasingly muffled forms through the repeated scribal transcriptions and adulterations. It was a culture and the identity which that culture defined and called to account. The terms of Cædmon's address to God are not those of an Italian, French or Irish postulant. They belong to an Englishman addressing his thane; an English Christian convert addressing his Lord.

When in 797 the English theologian Alcuin, coadjutor with Charlemagne in educational reforms and finally Abbot of Tours, demanded of Hygebald,

Bishop of Lindisfarne, 'Quid Hinieldus cum Christo?',[4] it was precisely this issue which troubled him. Why did the monks prefer to listen to the recitation of heroic poems during their collations rather than the word of scripture? 'Let the words of God be read at priestly gatherings; there it is proper to listen to a reader, not a cither-player; to hear priests' sermons, not lay songs.'

Yet when it came to religious verse, what did the English poet have to go on? The heroic and elegiac traditions were his antecedents, just as they had been for Cædmon. Even Old English prose can be highly alliterative and contains elements of parallelism and phrasal balance with which the poetry has made us familiar. It is as though the heroic and elegiac verse of the pagan tradition had provided the idiom for the Christian verse, in ways which Alcuin would have found perplexing because inherent in the language itself, its structures and emphases, is a value system not entirely at one – or at-oneable – with the beliefs and themes it is called upon to express. There is, indeed, a very specific and sometimes incongruously odd diction at work, artificial but quite consistent. The kenning is a kind of incorporated riddle, and riddling is a key feature in Old English poetry. The part stands for the whole; the sea becomes 'whale road' and language a 'word hoard', like the treasure guarded by Beowulf's fateful dragon. There are double negative constructions, understatement of various kinds, some ironic in intention, some heroic. There are repetitions of phrases and constructions, variation on specific themes; and rather than development of argument, restatements which alter, though they do not necessarily advance, an idea or an emphasis. Latin and Biblical literature provided themes and models, but the modes of expression, even as they incorporated elements of the authoritative literary and moral classics, did more than translate them.

---

[4] 'What does Ingeld have to do with Christ'? Alcuin had written a Latin elegy on the destruction of Lindisfarne by the Danes four years earlier, one of a series of sackings and destructions down the years (right up to Henry VIII and the dissolution of the monasteries) which deprived us of the bulk of our medieval literary heritage.

THE L PLATE

Nowe spede vs atte oure begynnynge.

from *Mandeville's Travels: a metrical version.*

Like the early farm labourers who listened to Cædmon and the abbots who instructed their scribes to set down the pagan poems they heard, we ought all to be hearers of poems. A poem, especially one indebted to the oral tradition, lies inert on the page, like a musical score, until we animate it. We generally make the poem's noises in our heads, or we speak them aloud to an empty room. What a poem does to a reader's mouth is part and parcel of what it does to a reader's ears: the physiology of reception is something that wide reading and re-reading develop.

Being a general rather than a specialist reader of poetry is a worthwhile liberty. The specialist, in particular the scholar of a period, attains a mastery that serves us in the provision of authoritative texts; we respect and even envy such scholarship. Inevitably, as general readers, we will make errors – of emphasis, fact, interpretation, commission, omission. But on the whole we're the lucky ones. Specialist readers read from their specialism, finding a way through to what they suspect they will find. Philologists, literary historians or theorists have necessary agendas, and poems slot into them. The question in Old English poetry of dialect and linguistic provenance can be fascinating, but at the end of the day there is still the poem to be read; and just as reading is always approximate, so must scholarship be, given the state of the surviving texts and the sparseness of linguistic and historical record.

If *we* stumble across a poem that a specialist has pinned like a butterfly to an argument and we try to unpin it so it can fly again, or so it can die (as some poems ought to do), the specialists will dismiss us as unlicensed readers. They reckon that they alone have the authority to enter the tenth, or the fourteenth, century. And of course they are right. They bring to their reading a wealth of relevant and irrelevant knowledge. Not being specialists, we bring our ignorance; we remain unlicensed. There are some doubtful and some real advantages in our situation. We read a poem, not a text. Poems: no matter how difficult the language seems when it first sneaks up on us, no matter how opaque the allusions or complex the imagery, no matter what privileges or hardships the author experienced or how remote his or her learning is from ours. Poems, because they are there, because they have been written down and later published, because they survive and can be 'accessed', are democratic spaces. Even those poems written in Old and Middle English which at first glance look foreign will yield something to the attentive reader.

Poetry, whether from an oral or a literary tradition, is language that has been deliberately shaped. It communicates by *giving*. It does not conform to a critical code and it does not belong to a particular discipline. The scholarship that surrounds it should be less a palisade preventing access than a bridge through time into it. A poem elicits answering energies from us, if we are not put off by its strange aspect and if we listen closely. Listening closely may involve ingesting additional information along with the poem, in order to hear it properly. Once heard – the prosody clarified, then the vocabulary and syntax teased out – the Old and Middle English poem is as much ours as Shakespeare, or Wordsworth, or Auden are.

We should – as a prerequisite for setting out on our quest for medieval as for modern poetry in English – cultivate 'techniques of ignorance'. The phrase is C.H. Sisson's. We do this in order to find out what is there, not what we – because we have read Seamus Heaney's *Beowulf* or Ezra Pound's 'Seafarer' – expect to find. Acknowledged ignorance is a useful instrument, a way of eluding prejudice, reflex, habitual response. As soon as we are properly ignorant we begin to develop a first rather than a second nature, to question even familiar things in ways that would not have occurred to us before, to hear sounds in poems that eluded our 'trained' ears, and to hear the new sounds that the older Englishes make.

The astute and acid biographer Lytton Strachey declared: 'Ignorance is the first requisite of the historian – ignorance, which simplifies and clarifies, which selects and omits, with a placid perfection unattainable by the highest art.' The task is less to explain than to illuminate. We follow a rough chronology where we can because it is convenient to do so, not because we are historicists; and bright beams of light from the suqs and chapels of the tenth and fourteenth shine into the twenty-first century. As we approach a familiar poet in this story (Langland or Chaucer or Skelton, for example) we may feel anticipation as at reaching a familiar town – and surprise that it is not mapped quite as we expected.

Mercator in 1569 published his famous map projection, a vision of the world as the segmented peel of an orange. It took him a long time to get it right, and it has been subject to adjustment ever since. How to reduce a lumpy sphere to a plane? Was he the first Cubist? At least his plane is a comprehensible, if not immediately recognizable, image of a sphere at a particular time. The task of drawing a map of medieval English poetry is like playing three-dimensional chess: you have the changing character of

English itself, over half a millennium during which poetry was written in a language still gathering into standard forms and then – with the Norman Conquest – forced into a synthesis which altered its fundamental rhythmic and lexical properties. This produced two languages, which are both remote from ours, and each of which is divisible into dialects and subsets that are not always mutually comprehensible.

It is beginning to sound like a terrain accessible only to scholars and specialists with their alpenstocks and climbing gear. We are on the verge of losing the courage we need to proceed. What is required of non-specialists is a sense of adventure, a desire to indulge – in this poetic venture, at least – the Seven Deadly Sins which medieval poets systematically anatomize.

Pride makes us equal with scholars and specialists and careless of their censure. *Lechery* puts us in tune with the varied passions and loves that we encounter in the Middle English poems (in Old English our libido atrophies). We feel *Envy* when a reader who has gone before pre-empts our response; this spurs us on to fresh readings. *Anger* overwhelms us when injustices occur: when a poet is lost for a generation or a century. Why is Charles of Orleans not better loved? Why is Gower so cruelly neglected? Is it necessary to forget Hawes, a great spirit if not a great poet? We experience *Covetousness* when we encounter poets we are prepared to love but their books are unavailable in the shops, so we covet our friends' libraries or the great private collections. *Gluttony* means we will not be satisfied even by a full helping of Gower or Henryson or the whole mess of *Judith*; we feed and feed and still ask for more (though with *Judith* gluttony would be an aberration).

Finally, dear old *Sloth* has us curled up on a sofa or swinging in a hammock with our books piled around, avoiding the day job and the flesh-and-blood lover's complaint.

These are necessary vices, and ones familiar to the poets: the list is found in Langland, Chaucer, Gower, Hoccleve, Lydgate; it survives in the Elizabethans. They knew the vices from the inside, learning them first at church as part of the catechism and then personifying them in cautionary catalogues, devising sub-sets and variations. They knew what was wrong; the devil had the best tunes when there was a devil. We should not imagine that the poets were wholly innocent of the vices they cautioned against. On the contrary, the lavish – even loving – attention they gave to them suggests the kind of commerce they had with them.

* * *

Wars and revolutions *always* come at the wrong time for poetry. Old English had reached a remarkable maturity, sophistication and even stability when the Norman Conquest threw up a terminal obstacle in its path. The big possibilities of Gower, Chaucer and Langland were postponed by history and by the rise of classical humanism. The full-flowering Scottish tradition of Henryson, Dunbar and Douglas was defeated when Scotland was defeated. The French have a lot to answer for, from Norman times onward; the English themselves, Southerners in particular, have a lot to answer for, too. Standardization invariably leads to impoverishment, for a time at least. In the case of Middle English transforming itself into Modern English, that time lasted for just over a century.

Even that statement is only approximately true. We are dealing with a history of exceptions, since the 'standard' or mean of any age or period is mediocre (*aurea mediocritas*, the golden mean). There is no straight line from poem to poem, or from poet to poet; it is all zig-zags, like history. A bad poem can provide the cornerstone for a good one; a good poet can instruct a host of poor imitators. Most occasions are lost in time. If we are to tell the story, we must draw imaginary lines and infer where necessary from the text (perilously assuming that the text has authorial authority even if it was transmitted through the uncertain hands of a series of scribes) occasions, motives, formal intentions. Even so, good poems swim free of their age and live in ours; and if we understand them on their terms rather than conform them to our own, they take on a fuller life, and so do we.

Poems swim free of their age, but it is hard to think of a single poem that swims entirely free of its medium, not just language but language used in the particular ways that mark poetry. Each medieval poet, oral or literary, is made of poems and other literary works from a past that especially engages him and of works by near antecedents and contemporaries that embed themselves in whole or in part in memory and imagination. Some elements stick as phrases, others as misremembered lines. There are also phrases and lines held deliberately hostage, jotted in a notebook for eventual exploitation. Reading Chaucer, we can discriminate between fragmentary allusions – to Dante, Boethius, Virgil and others – that imagining memory provides, and those that come from the hostage list. A distinctive feature of Old and Middle English poetry is that none of the poets is embarrassed about borrowing. The idea of 'plagiarism' has no bearing here. Poetry is an art of adaptation, accretion. Every poet has a hand in another poet's pocket, lifting out small change and sometimes a folded bill. It is borrowing, a borrowing that is paid back by a poem. Notions of copyright and 'moral right' (*droit morale*), of a poet in some way owning his creation, belong to a later, bourgeois age.

Even the most parthenogenetic-seeming poem, even Cædmon's hymn, has a pedigree. The poet may not know precisely a line's or a stanza's parents; indeed, may not be interested in finding them out. Yet as readers of poetry we can come to know more about a poem than the poet does and know it more fully. We know it in its survival, in time. We gain confidence to speak the strange-looking syllables aloud, we gather semantic information and develop instincts, we *read with our ears* and eventually we can hear Chaucer transmuted through Spenser, Skelton through Graves, Dunbar through MacDiarmid, the Border Ballads through Wordsworth, Causley and Hughes.

A medieval poet is a kind of anthologist, by nature or design. The oral poets are anthologists by nature. They receive and enhance a formulaic tradition. We cannot call it a 'literature' because 'literature' implies letters and writing. Figuratively speaking, John Gower and Geoffrey Chaucer lined up the French poems and classical stories they were going to translate or transpose into English; they marked passages to expand or excise. From secondary sources (in memory or on parchment) they culled images, passages, facts, to slot into their new context. Then began the *formal* process, stronger in Chaucer than in Gower, and stronger still in the *Gawain* poet, of making those resources reconfigure for *their* poem. It is here that they began to add something of their own. The scholarly sport of searching out sources and analogues is useful in determining not only what is original in conception, but what is original in mutation or metamorphosis: how the poet alters emphases, changes the colour of the lovers' hair, adjusts motive, enhances evocations, to make a new poem live. Sometimes a poem grows directly out of another, like a branch grafted on to a tree. Henryson's *Testament of Crisseid* (wholly dependent on Chaucer's *Troilus*) is the most compelling example from the medieval period that survives.

Poets grow, poetry grows. The growth of poetry is the story of poems: where they come from and how they change. It begins in the story of language. Where does the English poetic medium begin, what makes it cohere, what impels it forward, what obstacles block its path? The medium becomes an increasingly varied resource; the history of poetry within it is not of the rise and fall of great dynasties. In the fourteenth century, Langland walks the same London streets as Chaucer, though their poetry is different in kind. Dunbar breathed the same London air as Skelton, but their sensibilities (apart from a gift for invective) could hardly be more distinct. The anonymous Border Balladeers were composing and elaborating their ballads while Stephen Hawes was agonizing over English poetry and the awkwardnesses of its transition into what he could not have known was the modern period. To him it felt like an ending.

There is a history of poetry and, within the work of each poet, a history of poems. We have to start with language. And to start with language we must also start with politics. The struggle of English against Latin and then French is the Resistance; the conflict between English and Gaelic, Welsh, Irish and Cornish is a less creditable chapter which begins in literary earnest after the end of the medieval period. At every point there are poems, voiceprints from which we can infer a mouth, a face, a body and a world. It is a world we can enter by listening as we move our lips through the series of shapes and sounds that the letters on the page describe.

BEGINNINGS

Lytel ic wes betwih brothur mine, ond iungra in huse feadur mines.
Pusillus eram inter fratres meos, et adolescentior in domo patris mei.

from the *Mercian Hymns* of the eighth century,
with the ninth-century Latin gloss

The art of English poetry begins after the ebb of empire. In the wake of Rome, a series of small kingdoms re-emerged, at peace and war with one another, and vulnerable to the depredations of the Danes who were much too close and predatory for comfort.

In each little kingdom there were courts, some more sophisticated than others. In each court there must have been entertainers, including minstrels whose job it was to fill the long winter nights with stories, songs and distractions designed to celebrate the household, the lord and his ante-cedents, or simply to amuse. They picked up stories from legend, oral tradition, and when the Christian God arrived, from the Bible and the legends that surrounded its narratives. The tradition was largely non-literary, the *scop* or minstrel carrying in his head, thanks to mnemonic formulae and a formidable skill, lyric and elegiac offcuts as well as 28 ell bolts[5] of language on which he played variations as he sang.

The way in which a poem arrives at a reader has an effect on how it is conceived and composed. The ballad sheet, the illuminated manuscript, the slim volume, the epic poem, the 'representative anthology', the elec-tronic poem or performance piece each make different demands on the poet and have a distinct technology for transmission to their audience or market. Poets of the seventh and even of the eleventh century composed for recitation, not for the page. Their job was to charm the ear and to keep it charmed, in some instances for hours at a time. They strove for clarity and vividness of sense. They accompanied themselves on musical instru-ments of various levels of sophistication. The tools of their trade were not the quill, the pen, the biro, nor did they compose on parchment, paper or keyboard. They had memory and accompaniment and they unfolded poems, by means of voice, on the attentive air. It was poetry's purest ecology.

---

[5] Roll of woven fabric, usually of a definite length.

The poems were infinitely re-usable, never quite the same twice because memory added and removed decoration. The audience responded or lost interest at different points and thus collaborated in the unique experience of recitation. The *scop* was revising every time he re-opened his mouth. An aural scholar comparing two performances of the same poem would have all the problems that a scholar examining different scribal texts might have, but it would have been multiplied by the additional variables that audience and specific occasion provided.

At no stage in the early poetry of English do we find the subjective poet. There are 'personal themes' of loneliness, exile and suffering, but the voice that sings is not self-absorbed or self-obsessed. The bourgeois spirit that enters our poetry with Gower and Chaucer (but not Langland, the *Gawain* poet or the Balladeers) is remote from Old and early Middle English poetry. It simply was not the medium for such subjectivity which, if it existed at all, found its means of expression somewhere else, perhaps in prose, in meditation or devotion. 'Only a poet of experience,' Robert Graves writes, 'can hope to put himself in the shoes of his predecessors, or contemporaries, and judge their poems by recreating technical and emotional dilemmas which they faced while at work on them.'[6] The technical and emotional dilemmas of poets alive in the oral tradition are so remote as to be virtually incomprehensible to most modern poets, including those performance poets who have been heard to affirm that they follow in an ancient tradition of recitation. The difference between the anonymous *scop* and the modern performance-poet goes beyond the anonymity of the former and the manifest subjectivity of the latter. It is a matter of technical subtlety and resource, the difference between a living tradition and an amplified set of conventions rooted in a complex electronic technology. A commercially-designed and directed popular culture cannot be compared with a tradition in touch with an audience: it is a product calculatedly in touch with a market.

William of Malmesbury reports (five centuries after the event) that Aldhelm used to sing songs – ballads, perhaps – on the bridge in order to lure a congregation into his church for the sermon. Oral poetry was popular. It could be a baited lure, or a broad and colourful pathway, into the house of God.

* * *

Here is a riddle. Where does English poetry start? With the Old English chicken or the Middle English egg?

Does it make sense to start a history of English poetry as far back as 657, with Cædmon? The scholar and critic A.R. Waller thought so. 'And from

---

[6] Robert Graves, *Collected Writings on Poetry* (Manchester, 1995). Many of the references to Graves are drawn from that book.

those days to our own,' he wrote almost a century ago, 'in spite of periods of decadence, of apparent death, of great superficial change, the chief constituents of English literature – a reflective spirit, attachment to nature, a certain carelessness of "art", love of home and country and an ever-present consciousness that there are things worth more than death – these have, in the main, continued unaltered.' The changes may appear to us more than superficial and the thematic constants a little more complex, than they seemed to this civilized and comfortably-settled scholar.

Sixty years after Waller, his argument persisted. 'Microcosm and macrocosm, *ubi sunt*, consolation, Trinitarianism – these are but some of the ideas and motifs,' wrote Stanley Greenfield, 'that Old English literature shares with the works of later writers like Donne, Arnold, Tennyson, and Milton.' This is more fanciful and arbitrary, because it pretends to be more specific, than Waller. The later English poets he calls as witnesses answer the four 'motifs' listed, but those motifs, singly or in combination, are characteristic of any European literature – or indeed, of almost any literature we might care to name.

Old English poetry is remote in time and temperament even from Chaucer and Gower, who are only three centuries away, but it does have some affinities with Langland and the work of the *Gawain* poet, with the alliterative verse of Richard Rolle of Hampole and others, and with surviving shreds of popular verse. The spirit of the more secular Old English poetry is not remote from the spirit of the ballads. It would strain credulity to draw the line much further forward, despite echoes and analogies. Gerard Manley Hopkins, Ezra Pound and W.H. Auden undeniably used the old traditions in selective ways for their own ends, generally when they were learning their craft and looking for antidotes to the lazy smoothness of their periods. But to them Old English was a language as alive and foreign as Welsh or Icelandic, a poetic rather than an immediately linguistic or lexical resource, and something to be used analytically and selectively.

All the same, we might as well begin at this beginning, even if it looks like another country altogether, and even if we will need to start again in a few pages, from a rather different point of departure.

Old English poetry was composed in several related dialects, and when it was written down it was often partly transposed from one dialect into another. This is not uncommon with oral literatures. For example, Ionian Greek oral poets 'composed' the *Iliad* and *Odyssey*, probably during the ninth and eighth centuries before Christ. These works were committed to writing between the seventh and sixth centuries. There was a gap of centuries between the events and their composition, and a further gap between their evolving composition and their transcription in Athens under Pisistratus. As a result, throughout the surviving texts there are elements of distortion, 'correction', misunderstanding, interpolation. The written text has been deliberately *stabilized* but the content remains, linguistically and in other respects, quite volatile. Mycenæan elements mingle with material from three centuries after the end of the Mycenæan world (1100 BC); there is ninth and eighth century material. Some of the weapons described are Mycenæan, some are from three centuries later, some from even earlier periods, and some contemporary. As in *Beowulf,* funeral customs are conflated (inhumation and cremation, for example). Narrative matter from an older tradition survives in later poems. In 'Widsith' and 'Deor' there are allusions to Eormenric (d. 375) and Ælfwine (d. 573), and Theodoric. There are also celebrations of heroic actions and conduct – glory, bonds of protection, loyalty etc. – which must have been strictly anachronistic at the time of transcription.

The great Greek epics are cultural amalgams littered with anachronisms, and they are a curious linguistic mix: Peloponnesian, Aeolic, Ionic and Attic elements survive together. This demonstrates the poems' territorial spread, perhaps, their cultural breadth; but also a copyist tradition culminating in Athens. Might it suggest too the development of a deliberately formalized and 'literary' language at the time of transcription, the emergence of a 'decorum'? Or are the Attic elements from the time of the poems' 'final' redaction and the other elements vestiges from its transfer, orally, through time and space westwards to Athens?

It is likely that if one had asked the illiterate Greek singer of tales, or the Old English *scop,* about the actual lines of his poem, or what a particular word might mean, he would have found it difficult to understand the question. He would not have seen the poem in his mind's eye, or heard it in his mind's ear, as a series of discrete lines. It would have existed as phrases rhythmically related, a prosodic flow; and the notion of a word as an entity separable from its context would have been obscure to him. Even in the manuscripts that survive, lineation is not generally marked – the text runs on continuously, like prose – and the caesura is not indicated. The scribes themselves took the parcelling out of the verse for granted.

The language known as Old English consists of a bunch of Germanic first cousin dialects (the second cousins include Old Saxon, old High German, Old Norse and Gothic) which were spoken in England between the fifth century and the Norman Conquest. It arrived with raiding parties from Northern Germany – Angles, Saxons and Jutes – who decided to settle. The Saxons, whose dialect was called West Saxon, took up residence in the South West, the Jutes in the South East where they spoke Kentish, and the Angles, speaking Anglian, north of the Thames. This replicated the language patterns in North Germany itself. Little survives from the early period. It is only in the seventh and eighth centuries that we begin to get a hold on the language, three centuries into its use in Britain. By that time the dialect patterns have developed further. Mercian (spoken between the

Thames and the Humber) is markedly distinct from Northumbrian (north of the Humber), judging from the limited evidence that survives (inscriptions, glosses and three poems). We know most about Mercian and, particularly, West Saxon. Wessex was effectively the cultural centre of the country from the time of Alfred (849–901) to the Conquest. Indeed, most of the surviving literature is preserved in that dialect, even if it was originally produced in another.

The surviving manuscripts, which were all composed within monastic communities, date from around 1000, though many of the poems were composed well before that time. Thanks to the Church's scribal practices, religious elements find a way into secular poems and classical elements find their way into religious and devotional verse. The manuscripts incorporate a cacophony of elements; scholars have the fascinating task of untangling 'authentic' from superadded features.

Most Old English poetry survives in four key monastic 'codices' or manuscripts. We have already glanced at *Junius XI* which contains *Genesis*, *Exodus*, *Daniel* and *Christ and Satan*, so-called 'Cædmonian Poems' which are thought to be of an early date. Then there is the *Vercelli Book*, possibly the earliest codex of all, with twenty-nine pieces, of which the most poetically powerful is 'The Dream of the Rood' (1). There is also *Cotton Vitellius A.xv*, in the British Library, which includes *Beowulf* (12), *Judith* and other material. It was originally two separate codices, but was bound together early in the seventeenth century.

Poetically most important is the amazing *Exeter Book*, presented to Exeter Cathedral by Leofric, the first Bishop of Exeter, who died in 1072. The *Exeter Book* contains the greatest secular and some of the most remarkable religious verse in Old English, including 'The Wanderer', 'The Seafarer', 'The Ruin', 'Widsith', 'Christ' and the riddles. If this codex had perished, the reasons for studying Old English poetry would have been much reduced.

'The Battle of Maldon' is the greatest surviving 'occasional' poem, the occasion itself recorded in the *Anglo Saxon Chronicle* entries for 991. Byrhtnoth's heroic defeat is recounted by one of his followers. The singer places some of the most powerful heroic-elegiac lines in Old English in Byrhtwold's mouth:

Hige sceal the mare,   heorte the cenre,
Courage shall be the more,   heart the keener,

mod sceal the mare,   the ure mægen lytlath.
mood shall the more,   as our might littles.

Her lith ure ealdor   eall forheawen,
Here lies our lord   all hewn to bits,

god on greote...
good man in the grit...

'The Battle of Maldon' is all of a piece. The theme is struggle, unavailing but sustained – like the moral struggle of classic Greek tragedy, but here expressed in action – that we encounter elsewhere in Old English poetry. The oral and literary traditions dovetail in this poem of vivid narrative and elegiac definition.

We should focus on the *Exeter Book* first. Its poems are often described as 'early'. We can pass on then to the small body of wonderful poems from other sources and end with the unavoidable curate's egg of *Beowulf*.

What survives in the *Exeter Book* and the other codices may be corrupt, fragmentary and undependable. But whatever the condition of the text, the poetry is not in any sense primitive or technically unformed. The Anglo Saxon of the tenth century world had moved beyond the seeming spontaneities of Cædmon. A 'plough-lad' not unlike Cædmon may, as Waller suggests, have composed these pre-Christian lines 'when he had drawn his first furrow':

Hal wes thu, folde,   fira modor,
beo thu growende   on godes faethme:
fodre gefylled   firum to nytte

Stopford Brookes translated this archly as:

Hale be thou Earth, Mother of men!
Fruitful be thou in the arms of the god.
Be filled with thy fruit for the fare-need of man!

The later *scop* knew what he had to say and he had the established means of saying it. He invented nothing new in the way of form or story; what was new was the disposition of the elements in particular configurations, the addition of new thematic concerns (religious, for example, or political), and the variation and decoration he achieved.

A *scop* might or might not be learned, but a scribe had to be. Latin and Greek had arrived in Britain with Theodore (originally from Asia), the seventh-century Archbishop of Canterbury, and the Abbot Hadrian (from Africa). Benedict Biscop, Bede's teacher and patron, not only helped establish but stocked the libraries at Jarrow and Wearmouth. Bede's disciple Egbert of York founded its school and decorated its churches. The great Alcuin was able to be educated 'in the cloister school of his native city'. So good was the education that people were sent from the Continent to study in Britain both the classical *trivium* of grammar, logic and rhetoric and the *quadrivium* of astronomy, arithmetic, geometry and music. Alcuin commented on the efficacy of the instruction and the efficiency of the scriptoria where the books were produced. 'The young monks file into the *scriptorium* and one of them is given the precious parchment volume containing a work of Bede or Isidore or Augustine, or else some portion of the Latin Scriptures, or even a heathen author. He reads slowly and clearly at a measured rate while all the others, seated at their desks, take down his words; thus perhaps a score of copies are made at once.' A huge volume of work could be got through in a single scribe's lifetime. Admittedly, after waves of Danish terror had laid England waste from the Humber to the Tyne, the ecclesiastical and educational fabric was rent, and not until Alfred did a whole culture re-emerge. All the same, once the literary culture had been set in motion, it was sometimes able to persist fitfully through the gratuitous, bloody and costly interruptions of the Scandinavian raiders and settlers, and then to flourish.

A century ago it was a convention to divide Old English poetry into two categories: 'national' and 'Christian'. The 'national' arguments for retaining Old English as a compulsory element in the undergraduate university syllabus have lost their force. It is doubtful whether the division was ever more than a political device, making it almost a patriotic obligation upon the student of English literature to start at that remote beginning. It is worth repeating that there was no nation to which the secular poems relate or refer. The idea of a single 'nation' emerged rather later in history than when the so-called 'early national poems' were first composed, at the time of the seven kingdoms. What is more, the poetry that is described as Christian is composed in an idiom, and with formal and thematic traces, of secular and heroic traditions, just as the heroic poems are touched and sometimes deeply marked and marred by Christian elements, whether traditional or scribal it is hard to say. The material regarded as 'national' is often of Teutonic origin in terms of narrative, character and motif.

We can take 'Widsith', probably the oldest substantial English poem to have survived, as an example. It recalls the heroes and barbarous peoples who invaded Italy, and the speaker is rich in heroic tales which will not stand too much historical scrutiny. The poem includes elements of epic and elegy. The kernel of it may be a fourth-century poem by a minstrel who visited the unsettling Gothic court of Eormenric, who died in 375. To this a subsequent poet or poets added later journeys and genealogies, composing towards the end of the seventh century. Accretion, as in a medieval cathedral, *was* the creative process. Time sequence proved unimportant, the question of anachronism hardly arises: events, happenings (especially heroic happenings) have a 'factuality' as concrete in the imagination as that of trees and mountains. A happening is *there* and the past tense is not 'over' except in time. 'Widsith' celebrates the minstrel's own vocation, a wanderer among people and a rememberer of (not a witness to) events and deeds. Given the cryptic, abbreviated quality of certain passages, it is tempting to suggest that the poem represents a kind of prompt-text and that the *scop* would have filled out the rather skeletal story as he performed. English stories and landscapes do not feature either in this or in several other poems in the *Exeter Book*.

Its crucial wealth is to be found in the poems that follow 'Widsith', all of them textually challenging because of corruptions and interpolations and still much argued over by scholars. The forty-two line minstrel's lament 'Deor' is unusual in the surviving canon, one of only two Old English poems (the other is 'Wulf and Eadwacer') with a refrain:

> Thæs ofereode,   thisses swa maeg.
> (*That passed, so may this*).

The refrain gives the poem a stanzaic quality, and the tragic or unhappy stories the poet glances at open out again on the heroic imagination. It is an intriguing poem but unusual rather than outstanding.

'Deor' is followed by one of the great Old English monologues, 'The Wanderer' (3), which tells of the sufferings of a man who has lost his lord, his companions and therefore his identity. The *comitatus* relationship involved the unbreachable mutual loyalty of chief and retainer, so that when the chief died the retainer in a sense perished, like the bereaved Indian wife who would once have committed suttee; but this Anglo Saxon retainer commits poetry instead of hurling himself on his lord's pyre.

'The Wanderer' stands first in a tradition that culminates in poems such as Walt Whitman's 'O Captain, My Captain' and 'When lilacs last'. Solitary, uncompanioned, the poet moves through the unresponsive world and remembers. He dreams of his vanished sense of security and purpose, when he served his lord. Waking, he sees the snow falling and the ashen waves breaking over and over on the shore. The images of things ending and passing create a desolated music. By a simple transposition a monastic scribe could baptize this poem, making the departed lord into Christ and the lamenting poet into the human soul. The Christian interpolations in the poem are light and probably the product of just such a tentative and fortunately uninsistent transposition.[7] The *ubi sunt* motif ('where have they gone?') is most moving on first reading and diminishes on re-reading the poem.

Less subtle is the Christian transformation of the most famous shorter Old English poem, memorably translated by Ezra Pound. 'The Seafarer'

---

[7] Only 'The Battle of Finnsburh' survives as a scribally 'unretouched' or unbaptized 'Germanic lay'. It is not an outstanding poem in any event.

(2) is the same length as 'The Wanderer' and may be read as a dialogue between a wearied old sailor and a younger interlocutor, or as a monologue with a marked change of key halfway through. The reader impatient of the Christian elements can take lines 1–64 as a complete poem, rich in metaphor and powerful in rhythmic movement as the old heart, restless again for travel, comes alive at the prospect. With line 65 the enduring, sinewy sailor seems to collide with a psalmist, and the indomitable durability of endeavour is displaced by a sense of worldly vanity. The second half of the poem is powerful but out of key with the first, an extended grim moral to a short and harshly affirmative tale.

In 'The Wife's Complaint' we hear a female speaker, though her diction and her prosody are indistinguishable from the male speakers' of other poems. Her text is difficult and corrupt. She recalls how her husband has left her and crossed the sea; she has been persecuted by his foes and is in a sort of prison, in a cave under an oak tree, where she can sorrow and lament all day and curse her foes, hoping that one day they may know the agony of exile and solitude. Unlike 'The Wanderer', she is constrained to a single place, but like him her life and identity depend upon a lord whose absence leaves her purposeless and friendless. 'The Husband's Message' (the manuscript is torn and decayed) reads like a direct response to 'The Wife's Complaint'. It is spoken by the 'letter', perhaps a runic stick, that the husband has sent to reassure his wife and invite her to come, when the tide is right, to the new home he has prepared for her. The runic conceit is carried to completion by the mysterious runic riddle with which the poem concludes.

Also seriously torn in the *Exeter Book* is a poem scholars call 'The Ruin' (4), evoking the collapsed buildings and glory of a city. It may well refer to ancient Bath, judging from the springs and baths it remarks on, the wealth and gaiety. The season conspires with the poem's mood. It is tempting to read 'The Ruin' as anticipating Oliver Goldsmith's masterpiece, 'The Deserted Village'.

If we move from the largely secular to the specifically Christian world of poetry, we find that the Christian themes and narratives are treated in much the same style, and with the same diction and form, as the secular and heroic work. If Fate has become Providence, it is more a change of terminology than a transformation of sense. Christ has become King or thane, his Apostles retainers performing feudal functions, but again he speaks and acts less like a Biblical figure than like a leader holding court and doing deeds. We owe Christ fealty: here is feudalism projected on the wide screen of Heaven. Whenever a church appropriates a pagan culture and Christianizes it (as it did in Mexico, Peru and India for example) more of the pagan survives than the priesthood bargains for. So too in Britain.

In Britain, early Christianity had two separate sources and cultures.

St Augustine's missions in the South brought structures and traditions continuous with those of the Continent. This was a vigorous and specifically *Roman* Catholicism. But earlier there had been the Irish or Celtic incursions in the North, where English poetry begins twice over, once in Old English with Cædmon and again with the recrudescence of the vernacular in the fourteenth century and such figures as Richard Rolle of Hampole.

Celtic Christianity was less theologically orientated than the Roman. Aidan, the Apostle of the North, followed the martyr King Oswald and converted 'the rude north Anglian tribes'. Streoneshalh, the Whitby of Cædmonian fame, was governed by Abbess Hild in accordance with Celtic, not Roman, usage. (It is worth remarking the presence of significant women within the spiritual and administrative hierarchy of the Northern church.) If at the Synod of Whitby (664) the unity of the church under Roman rule was conceded, certain features which can be identified as Celtic persisted. 'The Dream of the Rood', the second part of 'The Seafarer' and 'Phoenix' appear much more Celtic than Roman: deep feeling has an absolutely central place. It has been suggested that the Celtic church was organisationally simpler, spiritually more tolerant and alert to actual Christian virtues than to doctrinal orthodoxy and ritual propriety. It was more comprehensible, accessible and therefore congenial to the people. It would be an exaggeration to see in it a kind of ur-Protestantism, making a space for the subjective (on which both elegy and lyric are founded), stressing the relation of the individual questing soul with God ('The Seafarer', 'The Dream of the Rood') and also emphasizing the humanity of Christ, the brotherhood of man, the fellowship of the saints. And yet the contrasting character of the two religious cultures might be regarded as prefiguring a cultural and political divide which has persisted into the present century.

Many of the religious poems consist largely of paraphrase. 'Genesis' is such a poem, structurally curious because in it Lucifer and his cohort of angels fall twice. 'Genesis B' is an Old Saxon interpolation, quoting matter directly from Old Saxon. The connections with the mainland remained strong: Britain had not yet become an island. The poem 'Exodus' is freer and more lively; of the directly Biblical poems it is certainly among the more rewarding.

What survives of secular Old English poetry is uniformly intriguing and some of it can be described as great, holding its own with the mature literatures of Europe at the time. The religious verse is more conventional, with vivid moments and startling variations on familiar themes, but is often less compelling as narrative and as spiritual drama than the prose Homilies. One religious poem, however, is in a class by itself: 'The Dream of the Rood' (1).

It is the first dream vision in English, god-fathering a line that includes massive poems such as Langland's *Piers Plowman*, Gower's *Confessio*

Amantis, all of Chaucer's early vision poems, and much of the less achieved work of the fifteenth century. In 'The Dream of the Rood' the sleeper, oppressed by his own burden of sin, sees the crucifixion. As in a riddle (though we know the answer from the outset), the Rood, the cross itself, speaks its tale of pain, triumph and paradox: now suffering, now glory. When the poet awakes the riddle that has troubled his soul is resolved, he is released from his uncertainty and understands what Christ's sacrifice means in terms of his own, and every believer's, redemption. After Christ's death, He harrowed hell and rose again.

Before the poem was discovered in the *Vercelli Book*, some lines from it had been found carved in Germanic runes (in the Northumbrian dialect, not the dialect of the surviving manuscript) on an ancient stone cross at Ruthwell, near Dumfries, and – attributed to Cædmon – were translated. Later, the poem was more plausibly attributed to Cynewulf, the other great named Old English poet and author of at least four poems, the best of which is 'Elene', about St Helena's quest for the True Cross. But 'The Dream' cannot with authority be removed from that distinguished category of work attributed to Anonymous.

The idiom and values of the heroic pagan tradition here confront the most extreme human deed of all: man's crucifying of the incarnate God and that God's forgiving purpose. Christ is a hero of a new kind, allowing himself to be taken and tortured, showing his might in his will to forgive. Defeated in body, he triumphs in spirit, and that triumph raises us all with it. It is a perfect transposition of heroic values into a new key, a transposition which had eluded other *scops* active with the same tools as 'The Dream' poet. The speaking cross is like the retainer who, to serve his lord, must do unspeakable things which that lord requires. For the poet, the cross's voice is real and potent; it sees the blood congeal in gems and then re-liquify. It feels the flesh and weight of the punished saviour with an intense, almost erotic passion.

Some Old English poetry was composed after the Norman Conquest, 'Durham' for example, an *encomium urbis* or city celebration poem, early in the twelfth century. The city was northern; the Venerable Bede was buried in its cathedral. Norman French progressed unevenly up the island. But the days of Old English were over. Late in the twelfth century, 'The Owl and the Nightingale' typifies the change. It is a *débat* in rhymed octosyllabic verse, the vocabulary – not over-Norman – *courtois* or courtly, the idiom assured and alien to what had been written down before. The poet was a Southerner, Nicholas of Guildford, a priest living in Dorset.

The break – or a break, in any case – was complete.

BEOWULF

'*Hwæt...*'

from *Beowulf*, line 1

Epic and elegy are the chief Old English modes. The elegiac poems are for the most part relatively short, lucid and moving. They are like after-echoes of epic, the song that remains after the deeds are sung; a poetry of individual consequences. The only substantial epic that survives is *Beowulf* (**12**). It contains sufficient passages of elegy for us to wonder whether the elegies themselves survive from larger, lost epics, the unforgettable speeches of forgettable heroes. After *Beowulf* (**12**), the only other bits of Old English epic are a fifty line fragment of *Finnsburgh* and two fragments (thirty-two and thirty-one lines) of *Waldhere*. To these, not much literary importance attaches.

Those of us who were compelled to read Old English at university generally retain warm memories of 'The Wanderer', 'The Seafarer', the lyrics and elegies of the *Exeter Book* and the spirit-rending 'The Dream of the Rood'. We were amused by the *Riddles* and tried our own hands at translating them; we diligently considered the impact of Old English prosody on Pound, Auden and others. But many of us retain dark and even hostile memories of *Beowulf*. That hostility has something at least to do with the poem. The problem was not its length. It just did not seem very *good*, set beside other epic and romance literature.

There was the quality of the narrative itself, its ceremoniousness, the lack of excitement and suspense; and the form in which the poem has survived seems rather a mess despite the best efforts of the scholars to justify or restore it. How is it that Hrothgar's *scop* sings of the Christian creation in a heroic court, but Beowulf enjoys a pagan cremation and funeral? Why are the Christian elements throughout the poem so often awkward and out of place? We have met such incongruities before, but not on the sustained scale of *Beowulf*. It survives in a single tenth-century manuscript: there is nothing against which to cheek it.

Certainly there are poetic and thematic parallelisms within the poem's structure: it opens with Scyld Scefing's funeral rites and ends with Beowulf's own (I hope I have not spoiled the surprise for any new reader); there are elements of 'envelope structure' and deliberate interlacing of motifs and themes. All the same, my jaw dropped when Seamus Heaney published his translation in 1999, and dropped further when his translation became a bestseller. Heaney's *Beowulf* has a force and vigour perhaps in excess of the original, which for me – more than thirty years on, and having read it in American and British universities and discussed it exhaustively in seminars – sat grim and forbidding on the page, like the dragon which inflicted, not a moment too soon, the mortal wounds that brought an operatically protracted death and funeral to the eponymous hero. Having reluctantly roused the dragon, I read the poem in a different spirit today. I also reckon that, single-handedly, Seamus Heaney has revived the seemingly terminal fortunes of Old English as a discipline. It may never again be made compulsory in universities, but – if it is available at all – thanks to his efforts at realization undergraduates may well volunteer for its service, taking, as it were, the thane's penny.

Beowulf has for centuries been a favourite scholarly playground. Sources, analogues, parallels are extensively charted. The classical and Christian elements are considered: are they anachronistic, later interpolations? Or are they part of the essential character of the poem? Is it a transcribed oral composition, or was it rooted in oral tradition and worked up by poets and scribes into its present state? It draws on various historical figures whose actual existence is attested elsewhere: how dependable is it? How remote are the events it recounts from the time of its original composition? History apart, the narrative is based largely on folk tale: 'the Bear's Son' motif; the 'Sandhill' episode of the Icelandic *Grettir Saga*; Germanic legend. Epic resonance is provided by the sixth-century background of Danish Scyldings and Geatish Hrethlings. There is almost nothing of Britain in the first British epic. As the great *Beowulf* editor Fr Klaeber says, 'With the possible exception of the family of Wealhtheow, England is not represented save for the ancient Angle legend of Offa.' Well, it's a start.

Beowulf is a retainer to Hygelac the Geat in the first part of the poem (**12a**); there is an intermission and when the poem recommences (**12b**) it is half a century later and Beowulf has become Geatish King. In his life there is hardship and strife. He fights with three great monsters, the first two – Grendel and his famous Mother – in Denmark, where Beowulf frees Hrothgar's hall Heorot from monster-raids and wins the Danish King's thanks and praise. In the third battle he kills an unnamed dragon that has ravaged his own people, then dies himself.

Two fifths of the poem (about 1300 of the 3183 lines) consist of direct speech, a striking feature given that we tend to think of it as an adventure story. The speech is highly formalized and ritualistic: the verb with which the poet generally introduces a speaker is *matheloda*, 'made a speech'. No one *speaks*, everyone *makes a speech*, and most of the speeches are strophic, unlike the descriptive and action passages where transitions occur within a line. We hear an authentic voice of Old English poetry, but not the authentic voice of the Old English man or woman here; it has been edited out of the text. We witness vivid rituals – funeral rites, ceremonies of thanksgiving – and mighty struggles, but again, they have little direct bearing on the usage of the Anglo Saxon people. Many of the speeches are expressions of Christian belief or sentiment, while the narrative, the customs and ceremonies are largely heathen. However, there are no references to heathen gods or heathen worship. A Christian minstrel or a Christian scribe has clearly been at work. The Christianity is not insistent or doctrinal, but it is sufficient to remove from the poem its supporting religion and ideology.

Hygelac was a real king of the Geats, who fell in battle near the Rhine some time between 512 and 520. Many of the other Swedish notables mentioned were probably historical, like Healfdene the Dane and his descendants. On the other hand, Beowulf and Scyld Scefing may or may not have existed. There is no decisive corroborative account of them and their nature and exploits are on such a scale, and vested with such super-human power, that they tax literal belief. Might Beowulf have been based on Bothvarr Biarki, chief of Hrólfr Kraki's knights (*Hrólfs Saga Kraka*)? Scholars can pose the question and assemble the scant evidence, but the question will remain.

The historical events which can be externally confirmed all cluster around the years 490–525. We can infer, without absolute certainty, that some form of the poem – or the various versions of different minstrels – began to be recited, not in Britain but in Denmark, after 530, and that as time passed it gathered legend, mystery, inconsistency, archaism, and finally Christianity. What we can date is not the poem we have but an oral ur-poem from which it probably evolved.

Originally composed in a northern or midland dialect, *Beowulf* is preserved only in the late West Saxon forms that, as Klaeber says, predominated, 'with an admixture of non-West Saxon, notably Anglian, elements'. The question of linguistic origin is of less concern to us here than the fact that the poem is an amalgam of elements, implying a transposition from the dialect in which it was recited into another, in which it was written down. Certainly, this happened with 'The Dream of the Rood'. Vestiges of suppressed linguistic forms are retained for reasons of prosody, diction or other artistic purpose, or because the scribe slightly misunderstood what was being said, or because he himself used a different dialect or language group from the one he was employed to work in.

The poem may combine four tales of quite distinct origin, brought together under one poetic roof. Beowulf versus Grendel and Beowulf versus Grendel's mother are two distinct but related stories. Then there is the long account of Beowulf's return, and lastly, the tale of his final battle.

Scholarship usually divides the poem into eleven 'chapters' or sections; the story is intermittent, fantastic and ceremonious in equal degrees. In tracing the plot sequentially those 'chapters' fall apart before our eyes. First (**12a**), we witness the funeral ceremony of Scyld Scefing, the Danish King. The body is placed on a ship piled high with arms and treasure and the ship sails away. Then the reigns of Scyld's son and grandson, Beowulf (not our man) and Healfdene, are briskly rehearsed, and we meet King Hrothgar, son of Healfdene. He builds a great festive hall called Heorot. His happiness, his achievement and the peace of his kingdom are destroyed by the monster Grendel (portrayed as Cain's offspring) who attacks at night and eats up as many as thirty knights in a single dinner. He cannot be resisted and the hall stands empty (lines 1–193).

After a dozen years of such ravages, cue Beowulf, nephew of Hygelac and King of the Geats. With fourteen good comrades and true he sets out to help Hrothgar, and, arriving in Denmark, is pointed to Hrothgar's house. Hrothgar remembers that he was close to Beowulf's grandfather. They converse and then feast abundantly. During dinner Beowulf is taunted by Unferth, the King's 'orator', for having failed to win a swimming contest with Breca. Beowulf replies with a different version of the story in which he does win. The Queen (Wealhtheow) fills his cup and he vows to vanquish Grendel or die. Heorot is left to Beowulf and his companions. They sleep. Beowulf arms himself. He resolves not to use his sword (lines 194–665).

Enter Grendel (**12b**), who devours one of Beowulf's comrades. A big fight ensues in which Beowulf pulls off Grendel's arm. The monster, mortally wounded, flees. Beowulf shows off the torn arm and is thanked. Hrothgar rewards him. The King's minstrel during the feast recites the story of Hnaef and Finn. Wealhtheow thanks Beowulf too and gives him a necklace (lines 665–1232).

When everyone is feasted out and tucked up, a more formidable monster arrives: Grendel's mother, bent on revenge. She bears away Aeschere, chief of the King's councillors. Beowulf promises vengeance once again and sets out to follow her. The pool where Grendel's mother lives is overshadowed with trees. It is deep and connects with the sea. Beowulf dives in and finds a cave where he fights with Grendel's mother and kills her with a sword he finds. There, too, he discovers the corpse of Grendel, and cuts off the head as a grim trophy. By the time Beowulf returns (**12c**), his friends have despaired of his survival. Grendel's head is brought to the palace, the King renews his praises and moralizes (a little incongruously) on pride (lines 1233–1784).

Beowulf says his farewells to Hrothgar and goes home. The virtues of Hygd, the young wife of Hygelac, are praised; she is contrasted with Thrytho, Offa's wife, who in youth was murderous. Beowulf reports his exploits to Hygelac. His speech includes something which has only been mentioned briefly before (lines 83–5): the relations between Hrothgar and his son-in-law Ingeld, Prince of Heathobeardan. Ingeld's father was killed by Danes and he is urged to seek revenge. An old warrior keeps egging him on. Beowulf hands over to his king the gifts he received for his labours and Hygelac gives him back a sword and a portion of the kingdom (lines 1785–2199).

Time passes very suddenly and fast. Hygelac perishes; his son Heardred is slain by Swedes. Beowulf ascends the throne and is a great ruler for fifty years. But now he is old, and along comes a fire-spitting dragon to destroy his land and his own home. The dragon was asleep but a runaway slave broke in and stole from its treasure hoard. Beowulf is enraged to have the peace of his kingdom so rudely broken and decides to attack. With its instinct for the anticlimactic, the poem chooses this moment to digress and recount Beowulf's past exploits and how he got (entirely honourably) the throne (lines 2200–2396).

Back in the main narrative, Beowulf draws near the dragon's lair, and as he does so, he reflects upon his family history, provides detail and a host of unpronounceable names and conflicts which can be of limited interest to anyone but Beowulf himself, a passing Geat, a graduate student or a scholar with time to kill. Beowulf instructs his companions (not all as brave as he is) to wait outside and enters the perilous barrow alone. Attacked by the dragon, he discovers that his sword will not even dent its hide. Wiglaf, a doughty comrade, comes to his rescue. Beowulf lands a hit on the dragon's head, his sword breaks, and the dragon gets him by the neck. Wiglaf wounds the foe at last and Beowulf somehow manages to finish it off with a knife. Our hero has, however, been mortally wounded. Wiglaf brings the treasure into the light and Beowulf gives instructions for his funeral, presents Wiglaf with armour and a necklace, and dies (lines 2397–2842).

The story is not quite over. The cowardly knights who ran from the mouth of the lair when they heard Beowulf being drubbed return. Wiglaf gives them a piece of his mind. A messenger brings news and prophesies that without Beowulf the Geats must expect attacks from all sides, from the Franks, the Swedes, and everyone else. This underlines the magnitude of the loss of a great leader: the world itself is altered. The warriors examine the treasure. Wiglaf repeats Beowulf's instructions, the dragon's remains are tossed into the sea, the King's body (despite the Christianizing of the poem) is burnt on a great pagan pyre, then a barrow is constructed over the remains of the pyre and treasure from the dragon's lair is placed in it. The poem concludes with an account of mourning and the proclamation of the King's virtues by twelve warriors who ride ceremoniously around the barrow (lines 2843–end).

There is little narrative flow as such in the poem. As Fr Klaeber remarks, 'Looseness is, in fact, one of its marked peculiarities.' In each fight, the outcome is foretold. Suspense in plot is not to be looked for, and nor is linear progression. Gaps in the narrative may be due to intermittent transmission, or to a failure of the *scop* to join up discrete narrative elements, or to the nature of the narrative customs of the time. It may simply be due to scribal incompetence. Since we have no other English epic with which to compare it, we remain in the dark. When the poet repeats the same material 'from different perspectives', is the repetition intentional or is a scribe struggling to join up different versions? Or has he fallen asleep?

We do not *see* the characters in the poem. They exist only within the actions they commit or in the speeches they make. Because the speeches are formulaic and formalized, it is not, as Ben Jonson would have it, 'Speak that I may see thee.' There is no individuated 'thee' for us to see. But the *scop* does linger on interpretation: what his actors feel, what their actions signify, providing a kind of moral psychology, fascinating in itself, even though it does not give the impression of being *embodied* in a character. Bodies are taken for granted and, given the remoteness and strangeness of the poem, are not 'real' to us. There are few metaphors apart from those embedded, more or less alive, in the kennings. There is no humour, irony or levity to be found. A dogged earnestness is the hallmark.

Critics make much of the poem's drawing of landscape. Geographies have been deduced but again the elements of description are thrifty and for the most part detail is characteristic or generic rather than specific. The exception is Grendel's lake (1357ff), notable as an early example of 'nature poetry'.

Hie dygel° lond	*mysterious*
warigeath wulfhleothu,° windige næssas,	*occupied wolf-lairs*
frecne fengelad,° thær fyrgenstream*	*dangerous fen paths; mountain stream*
under næssa° genipu ni*th*er gewiteth*,	*mist; netherwards goes*
flod under foldan. Nis thæt feor heonon	
milgemearces,° *thæt* se mere stande*th*	*measured in miles*
ofer *th*æm hongia*th* hrinde bearwas,°	*frosted groves*
wudu° wyrtum fæst wæter oferhelma*th**.	*with roots; overshadows*
*Th*ær mæg nihta gehwæm ni*th*wundor seon,	*portents*
fyr on flode. No *th*æs frod leofa*th*	*wise*
gumena bearna, *thæt th*one grund wite.	

As the *scop* says, 'nis *th*æt heoru stow' ('that was not a nice place'). Seamus Heaney's celebrated version makes the place a little more *heoru* than it ought to be because he has chosen an idiom which, though heightened and highly rhetorical in parts, is characteristically familiar rather than rigorously formal. J.R.R. Tolkien, who in imagination fought with Beowulf's foes and understood his victories and heroic defeat, declared that any attempt to translate *Beowulf* should take account of its strictly stylized vocabulary and metre. Had Heaney observed this prudent advice it is doubtful that his version would have been so widely celebrated. The scholarly establishment might frown at its most cherished text being made a bestseller by a poet who breaks the rules; and yet if Old English survives as a semi-popular literary discipline rather than a philological bone-yard, it will be due to the practical advocacy of Heaney, Edwin Morgan, Michael Alexander and other translators who read Old English by the light of the new.

Heaney concedes this frankly: 'deviations, distortions, syncopations and extensions do occur; what I was after first and foremost was a narrative line that sounded as if it meant business and I was prepared to sacrifice other things in pursuit of this directness of utterance.' He also played subversions with his diction, using an Ulster idiom here and there, an Irish word at key points, a colonization of the poem so subtle that he must draw attention to it in his Introduction. On the whole he has given the poem a welcome if uncharacteristic clarity: 'So the Geat people, his hearth-companions, / sorrowed for the lord who had been laid low.'

IT BEGINS AGAIN

Trippe a littel with thy fot
Ant let thy body gon.

from *MS Rawlinson D. 913*[8]

Written language, and scribal language in particular, with its strict disciplines and traditions, tends to be conservative when it is recording facts or texts. The vernacular is codified into verse and prose which aspire not to the fluency of speech but to the authority of formal statement. The written literature of Old English, 'regularized' in the dialect of Wessex, from which most of our surviving texts emanate – even those originally composed in other dialects – does not reflect the diction or rhythm of tenth and eleventh-century discourse or the various idioms of the dwindling oral and popular literature at the time. The apparent linguistic jolt between, say, 'The Battle of Maldon' and 'The Owl and the Nightingale' is not only the result of a radical linguistic transformation; it is in part a change in the dialect of the scribe. One of the fascinations of Middle English, well into the latter half of the fourteenth century, is the variety of dialect and diction. Layamon's *Brut* looks at first more like rough and ready Old than civilized Middle English; the diction and rhyming forms of the *Gawain* poet are geographically, paleographically and culturally remote from Langland's language; and Langland, like Lazarus the beggar, squats resolute and threadbare at Dives's – John Gower's – *almost* entirely familiar gate.

When at the Norman Conquest Wessex lost its ascendancy, three centuries went by before the language began to settle and stabilize into a new literary dialect, a poetic *lingua franca*. The unarguable authority of Chaucer and Gower helped to bring about the re-consolidation. They shared a dialect and a city; their clarity, flexibility and variety of tone and register made them masters to be imitated. In their assimilations and transpositions of the Latin classics, of Italian and French, they gave English a European literature, and at the same time gave Europe an English literature with a distinctive character and culture.

* * *

[8] 'Poems Without Contexts: The Rawlinson Lyrics', J.A. Burrow *Essays on Medieval Literature* p. 26.

Where do we first experience formal language? In many of the same kinds of places that the medieval poets did: in lullaby, nursery rhyme, street rhymes, popular songs, anthems. In church, synagogue, mosque or temple, in hymn and scripture and sermon; in graveyards, on tombstones. Their world was more varied than ours in *shared* linguistic resources.

English poets at the start of the fourteenth century were sung to by their mothers or – orphaned by the Plague – by foster-mothers or relations. They were dragged to church, through churchyards full of individual and mass graves inscribed with scripture, or with Latin verses. Inside, they heard Latin intoned and sang English, French and Latin. There were sermons in English: the priest pointed out stylized mural paintings of religious events on the walls, in the stained glass windows, or at statues and images. Those images expressed a long tradition of symbolism and composition to feed the imagination. Incense clouded up from the censers. The bright images hovered, as if removed, in another, ideal and lavishly illuminated sphere above the reeking congregation. (We can be pretty sure that the congregation did reek.)

In such polyglot[9] churches, where shreds of paganism survived in elaborate ceremonial, the English children who would become poets learned that things could be said in different languages, and that the dialect spoken at home or in the lanes always came last. They learned that there were parallel worlds: the stable Latin world of the scriptures, paintings, windows, statues; and the world in which they lived, where plagues and huge winds and wars erased the deeds of men. Obviously earth was a place of trial, hardship and preparation. When they came to write, it was out of this Manichæan knowledge. *Knowledge*, not belief. Belief came later, when knowledge began to learn its limitation. Belief is an act of spiritual will, born of the possibility of disbelief, with the spirit of the Reformation, which was just beginning to stir, or to revive, in the early fourteenth century. The wisdom of the northern churches in pre-Norman times had touched upon these themes.

Our starting point now is not seven discrete kingdoms. It is England, a 'colonial' culture subject to Norman rules (if not rule), with a Catholic spiritual government answerable to Rome. The people accept the ephemerality of this world along with an absolute promise of redemption for those who observe the letter of the faith. They know that the language of learning is Latin, and the language of power and business Norman French. Their English is a reluctantly-acknowledged cousin. When the Normans took England they saw no merit in the English tongue: it was an aberration

---

[9] Polyglot or 'macaronic': the macaronic poems consisted of a mixture of lines, in English and Latin or in English and French or in English and French *and* Latin, or with Greek included as well. Some poems of this nature survive as Christmas carols, 'O Jesu parvule' for example. Later on, a Latin refrain was sometimes used to give liturgical authority to a poem.

to be attenuated and erased, just as the English later tried to erase Irish and Welsh, Scots Gaelic and Cornish, and later still, to impose English in the colonies. In some respects, they were rather more successful than the Normans.

By the end of the fourteenth century, the time for English had undeniably arrived. The writings of John Gower, Geoffrey Chaucer, William Langland, the *Gawain* poet and the Balladeers were still fresh. An oral tradition was alive in market towns, provincial courts and manor houses. It took much of the century for the language to gather its energies together, but by the end some majestic peaks had risen out of a landscape previously (and subsequently) almost entirely flat.

The turbulent middle of the fourteenth century shook the prejudice against English which even learned Englishmen had felt. The language began to flex its muscles, and not only on the edges of the crowd but in the heart of it, at court and in the Church. Calamity was its patron. The Black Death first reached English shores before John Gower turned twenty, in the twenty-first year of Edward III's reign. In August of 1348 it arrived from France at Weymouth. It devastated Bristol, and in the early part of 1349 overtook London and East Anglia. It was still at large in Scotland and Ireland in 1350. It is hard to imagine what it must have been like (worse than war, where potential victims were pre-selected), to learn each day of dead or dying friends, to see bodies carted through the streets or heaped in a tangled mess at corners.

The Plague was an especially frightening and disgusting illness. It started with hard lumps and tumours, which were followed by scalding fever, and grey patches on the skin like leprosy. Then the cough developed, with blood welling from the lungs. Three days: terror, agony, death. Langland describes it in a passage that Thomas Warton says may have influenced Milton:[10]

Kynde cam aftir, with many kene soris,°	*sorrows*
As Pockes and Pestilences, and moch people shente.°	*destroyed*
So Kynde thorgh corruptions, killid full manye:	
Death cam dryvyng aftir, and al to dust [pashed]	
Kyngs and knyghttes Kaysours, and popis.–	
Many a lovely lady, and lemmanys of knyghttes,	
Swowed° and sweltid* for sorwe of Deathi's dentes.	*swooned; grew faint*

All at once there were not enough peasants to work the soil, servants to tend the house, or priests to administer unction and conduct funeral services. No one was immune. Three archbishops of Canterbury, eight hundred diocese priests in Norwich, and half the monks in Westminster all died in one year.

---

[10] *Paradise Lost* Book II lines 475ff.

Eight *hundred* priests in Norwich! The Church was big, but the Black Death was bigger. Women toiled in the fields. Harvests were left to rust. Parliament was suspended and courts of law were not convened. It was a time of too much loss for sorrow, too much fear for civil strife. There were more dead than graves to bury them in. Corpses were piled in plague pits and covered with lime. If the Plague made a feast of the poor, it was at least democratic. The King's own daughter perished.

Another victim was Richard Rolle of Hampole (**13–18**), a big-hearted anchorite who wrote verse. 'Full dear me think He has me bought with bloody hands and feet.' He was a man of soul, a poet-martyr, who may have translated the Psalms. Unable to put out of his mind the terrible fact of the crucifixion, he repeats his vision of it time after time, with an insistence embodied in the hard rhymes:

> Naked his white breast, and red his bloody side,
> Wan was his fair hue, his woundès deep and wide.
> In five stids° of his flesh the bloodè can down glide.　　　　　*places*
> As streams done on the strand; this pain is not to hide.

Later, in his lyrics, we read:

> White was his naked breast, and red his bloody side;
> Wan was his fair face, his woundès deep and wide.
> The Jewès would not wand° to painè him that tide;*　　　　*refrain; time*
> As streamès doth on strand, his blood can down glide.

It is hard to establish authentic 'texts' by an author unless a number of similar manuscripts survive. Most medieval writers formed schools, which meant that their works were copied, added to and altered. Much has been assigned to Richard Rolle that may not belong to him. Why was he such a mediocre poet, with only occasional astonishing lines and passages? Probably because he lacked a formal imagination and accepted a ready-made mechanical and repetitive rhetoric. Such an approach yields – if any – only local felicities.

The poet was born about 1300[11] at Thornton-le-Dale near Pickering, North Yorkshire. The North of England was still a centre of English writing but it had begun to lose out to the Midlands. Oxford was becoming focal, especially after the foundation of Balliol College around 1263. Rolle's early ability impressed Thomas de Neville, Archdeacon of Durham, and it was he who arranged for him to go to Oxford, paying the fees and expenses. It was usual for boys to go up to Oxford at the age of thirteen. In Rolle's

---

[11] Chaucer died in 1400: it is astounding how poetry developed in a single century.

Oxford, the friars still led exemplary lives. He learned Latin, disliked ordinary philosophical writers and loved scripture above all else. In a different age he might have been a Primitive Methodist.

At nineteen he returned home for the summer vacation anxious about his soul, intending to become a hermit. He made himself a hermit's habit out of two of his sister's dresses and parts of his father's rain-wear. His sister declared him mad and he ran away in his new garb, never to return.

He was recognized, as grace or fortune would have it, by one of his Oxford contemporaries, a son of a local squire called John Dalton whose spouse had spotted the strange young man on his knees at the local church. The next day, Rolle preached. It was the Feast of the Assumption. The sermon moved Dalton to offer his support for the apprentice hermit.

The Dalton family set him up as a hermit on their estate. (Hermits were not unusual in the medieval world: they were licensed and subject to the discipline of bishops.) Rolle never became a priest but he may have been in minor orders. His authority was spiritual: he became a mystic. After some years he moved to a new cell close to Margaret Kirby, a hermit whom he helped to cure – it was thought a miracle – of an hysterical seizure and to whom he dedicated some of his work, including poetry. He wrote for her and other women in English because, generally speaking, women were not taught Latin. This educational oversight was thus a major catalyst in the emergence of our vernacular poetry. Finally, he went on to Hampole, near Doncaster, where Cistercian nuns looked after him. On Michaelmas Day 1349 the Black Death took him. The nuns petitioned for him to be made a saint.

His verses – if they are his – express personal feeling simply. He began in the old alliterative tradition and progressed to rhyme. His followers imitated what was an easy style. What is his, what did he borrow or translate, and what belongs to his follower William Nassyngton? When we think we are admiring Rolle we may actually be reading Nassyngton's imitations (but then there is not much to admire in Rolle or his followers). Already poets, even holy ones, are practising techniques of false attribution, getting their work read by borrowing the authority of a revered name. Publishers began to practise this subterfuge two centuries later, but it is as well to remember that they learned that deception, and others, from poets, and religious poets at that.

Rolle especially loved the Psalms: 'great habundance of ghostly comfort and joy in God comes in the hearts of them that says or sings devoutly the psalms in loving of Jesus Crist.' He wrote a Latin commentary, then another, followed by English versions. It is hard to extrapolate a system of belief from his work, but his doctrine of Love is not like other mystics': he is alive to the world he only half inhabits. The good works a man does in this world praise God. Injustice offends *caritas*, and such acts particularly rile God.

His Latin works display, a friendly critic says, 'more erudition than eloquence'. The surviving verse in English includes a paraphrase of the Book of Job, a Lord's Prayer, seven penitential psalms, and the almost unreadable *The Pricke of Conscience*. It must have been readable once for it has been widely preserved in manuscript. Warton copied it out and said: 'I prophesy that I am its last transcriber'. In seven parts, it treats of man's nature, of the world, death, purgatory, Judgment Day, Hell's torments and Heaven's joys. The verse is awkward to scan: a basic iambic tetrameter measure with six, seven and sometimes (depending on the voicing of the final 'e' and how regular you want the iamb to be) ten syllables to the line, and from three to five stresses. It raises the crucial problem of all the old poems: there is so much variation between manuscripts that it is impossible to say what the poet intended.

Miracles were said to have occurred at Hampole when the nuns vainly nominated Rolle for sainthood. Rome made nothing of this hermit toiling in a remote and harsh language. His fame revived just before the Peasants' Revolt, when Lollard influence was increasing. (Lollard, from *lollen*, to loll or idle, was applied to street-preachers.) Rolle's writings were exploited by reformers, which put him right out of favour with the conservative church establishment. He was a potential saint for a different kind of faith.

Around 1378 his commentary on the Psalms was re-issued with Lollardish interpolations. No one knows who revised it: some point the finger, implausibly, at John Wycliffe. Though not a poet, though his works are as confused in attribution as Rolle's, though he was exploited, celebrated and reviled for centuries after his death, Wycliffe is one of the tutelary spirits presiding over our poetic history. He made it possible not only for King David to sing in English – there were English versions of the Psalter even before Rolle – but for Moses and Isaiah and God to use our vernacular, and for the Bible as a whole to land on English shores in English. Suddenly the language is good enough for Jesus. It has become legitimate.

The Black Death continued its transforming work, returning again and again. 'Servitude was disappearing from the manor and new classes were arising to take charge of farming and trade.' Thus G.M. Trevelyan tells it, making it part of an abstract process, draining it of human anguish and spiritual vertigo. 'Modern institutions were being grafted on to the medieval, in both village and town. But in the other great department of human affairs – the religious and ecclesiastical, which then covered half of human life and its relationships – institutional change was prevented by the rigid conservatism of the Church authorities, although here too thought and opinion were moving fast.' 'Thought and opinion' were provoked by the intransigence of men who governed and profited by the Church. These visionless administrators alienated free spirits and the intellectually dissatisfied.

The voice of Wycliffe begins to become audible. Church corruption is attacked by Chaucer, by Langland, and (more gently) by Gower; but Wycliffe drives it home forcefully from the pulpit and in his writings, to the lay heart, and to the very heart of the Church. The Church is no *more* corrupt than other institutions, but its corruption is privileged, sanctioned and directed from abroad. The laity is more educated than in the times of Anselm and Thomas à Beckett. The church, all the same, prefers to ignore discontent and keep its monopolies and privileges intact.

Customs of fiefdom that constrained peasants on the land and preserved the feudal order of society no longer held. After the Plague, too few men remained to do the work. Survivors began to realize their worth, and then their power. They wanted more than they'd had: mobility, food, even wages. Peasants began to band together, recognizing power in community. The rich grew less secure in privilege. The more philosophical among them sensed that *they* were dependents. Up to a third of the population perished in two years. When the Plague returned in 1361, it was a plague of children. That year cattle suffered a new disease as well. The fever touched souls: many thought God spoke through that fire.

Reformers found a voice. Some spoke English. Before then, nobles and merchants had taught their children French from the cradle: 'and provincial men will liken themselves to gentlemen, and strive with great zeal for to speak French, so as to be more told of' – a kind of social *bona fides*. But under Edward III change began, accelerating under Richard II as John de Trevisa noted in his 1387 translation of Ranulf Higden's universal history, *Polychronicon*: 'This manner was much used before ... and is since then somewhat changed. For John Cornwall, a master of grammar, changed the lore in grammerschool and construction of French into English ... so that now, the year of our Lord a thousand three hundred four score and five, of the second kyng Richard after the Conquest nine, in all the grammarschools of England children leaveth French, and construeth and learneth in English, and haveth thereby advantage in one side, and disadvantage on another. Their advantage is that they learneth their grammar in less time than children were accustomed to do. Disadvantage is that now children of grammarschool conneth no more French than can their left heel, and that is harm for them if they should cross the sea and travel in strange lands ...' The Plague was a catalyst. But transformation was not easy. One version of English could be more remote from another than French was. A northern and a southern man, meeting by chance or for business, would resort to French because their dialects were mutually incomprehensible, as much in diction as in accent. Now English, a bastard tongue, starts to move in the other direction from Latin. Latin broke up, but English began to coalesce. Dialects started to merge into an English *language* when scribes, and later printers, got to work. London usage became the idiom for written transactions. Those who made language public and portable, in the form of broadsheets and books, brought it, and eventually us, together. After a hundred years a young maid of Dundee and an old man of Devizes could hold a kind of conversation, not necessarily in limericks.

Much more than half our vernacular *literature* was northern before that time. Perhaps it still is – except the North has learned to speak more conventionally. English in its youth was hungry. The Normans imposed French but English was voracious even before they came and in the courts of Cnut and Æthelred, when the Conquest was some way off, adjustments took place, influences from the Continent loosening the consonantal knots of a congested Old English idiom. English swallowed French (digestion altered it). The Conquest meant that English in its various forms had to gobble up faster. Still, written texts, being more conservative, lagged behind speech. There is authority in formality, it is a risk to use the language of the day for important matters because it is in flux and you never know which dialect, which bits of new diction or patterns of syntax, will prevail.

John de Trevisa comments in his translation of Higden's *Polychronicon*: 'It seemeth a great wonder how English, that is the birth-tongue of Englishmen, and their own language and tongue, is so diverse of sound in this land', while Norman French, a foreign idiom, is the *lingua franca* of the islands. In Trevisa's own translation, which makes sense when read aloud, Higden writes: 'For men of the est with men of the west, as hyt were vnder the same party of heuene, acordeth more in sounyng of speche than men of the north with men of the south. Therefore hyt ys that Mercii, that buth men of myddel Engelond, as hyt were parteners of the endes, vnderstondeth betre the syde longages, Northeron and Southeron, than Northeron and Southeron vnderstondeth eyther other.' But it's the Southeron idiom that prevails and becomes the written form even for Northeron writers. The Northeron, Higden says, is *scharp, slyttyng,* and *frotyng* – harsh, piercing and grating. Early evidence of an abiding prejudice.

Foreign affairs continued to be conducted during the Plague as if there was no crisis at home. There were skirmishes, battles and wars in France, Spain and Scotland, with cruelty and piracy on every side. There was death by disease and on the field. England was certainly part of Europe. Sick at home, Englishmen went abroad to die or to bring back wealth. They were preparing for their defeat. Edward III died in 1377 and was succeeded by Richard II, a boy who grew to a colourful, corrupt majority. Demands on poor and common people, demands for tax, service, subjection, grew. The Peasants' Revolt had urgent causes, and though it was too early in history for the masses to rise successfully against a king, it was high time – Richard II knew it quite as well as Gower did – for the court and the masters to learn to speak and sing in the language of their people.

Fortunately, there was more to build on than Richard Rolle of Hampole.

There was *Gawain and the Green Knight, Pearl,* the English ballads, lyrics and dozens of vulgar translations of French works. There are poems the scholars will find shelved high up in old houses and churches, or bound in to ancient books, and poems they will never find, as well as elegies, verses of moral precept, religious meditations, lives of saints ... Were they lost because they weren't worth keeping, or because they were so constantly used that they were thumbed to bits? Parchment wasted with the hungry love of reading eyes, recitation, with handing back and forth between poets and scholars and minstrels. Were they lost during the Reformation, when great libraries were burned, or emptied out and sold to the local gentry – as the wicked and wonderful biographer and gossip John Aubrey remembers with pain – to be twisted into plugs for wine-casks, sliced into spills to start fires, or cut into convenient sheets as bog parchment?

Reading English in the first half of the fourteenth century was a furtive activity, frowned on by authority. When Edward III came to the throne English was revalued; from having been the underdog's tongue it became the chosen instrument of Geoffrey Chaucer. Robert Manning of Brunne had used what would become Chaucer's and Gower's tetrameters almost fifty years before – with a mechanical awkwardness which Gower corrected. *Handlyng Sinne* was based on a French work by the English writer William of Wadington, the *Manuel de Pechiez* – a book Gower also used. Manning explained his purpose in his *Chronicle of England,* completed in 1338:

Haf I all in mine English laid	
In simple speechè as I couthe,°	*could*
That is lightest in mannès mouthe.	
I made noght for no discours,	
Ne for no seggers, no harpours,	
But for the love of simple men	
That strangè English can not ken;	
For many it ere that strange English	
In rhyme wate never what it is,	
And but they wist° what it meante,	*knew*
Ellis me thought it were alle schente.°	*destroyed*

The lines are end-stopped, little breathless runs. One can respond to them in a spirit of historical gratitude, but their value is local. It is crude stuff; the language is not up to much, but it starts clearing a space. The same is true of the Scot John Barbour's vast limping history *The Bruce,* begun in 1372, where the lines do not pause but halt on a proud and assertive (if sometimes approximate) rhyme, often achieved with great violence to the word order. The poet – like the Old English historians, a man of the cloth,

Archdeacon of Aberdeen – promises history rather than fable, and verse serves its oldest function of chronicling:

> Storys to read are delatibill°   *delightful*
> Suppose that thai be nocht but fable,
> Then should storys that suthfast° wer   *truth*
> And thai war said in gud maner
> Have doubill plesance in hearyng...

The 'doubill plesance' is, he assures us, first the 'carpyng', the hearing aloud or recitation. The second is the pleasure we derive from hearing true things. How true are these things? The Bruce and his trusty mate James Douglas exist in a world of romance only just coloured by history, culminating in Bannockburn and a Scottish nation. 'A! Freedome is a noble thing!' Thus, without systematic alliteration and in a thoroughly Continental spirit, Barbour took the Matter of Scotland and prepared a somewhat rocky way for the great voices that follow. Scots still have his book in their library of classics, though I suspect few actually read it, apart from school children who have their 'distinctive heritage' rammed down their throats, and politicians of the new Scotland when they are looking for authoritative quotes.

TUTELARY SPIRITS

'... Seketh Seynt Truthe, for he may save yow alle.'

Piers Plowman, B version, V, 57

Opposite John Wycliffe, England's first European mind, stands Richard II, the other presiding genius of this history. On an impulse he commanded Gower to write in English. He was King when modern (which we call Middle) English poetry decisively came of age; after his reign, again a shadow fell.

But first to Wycliffe. Our poetry starts when God and King David, the priest of Ecclesiastes and the narrator of Job, Jesus and St Paul begin to speak English without apology. Rolle and the early Bible translators deserve some credit: it was they who first tutored the Word. Reformers and prophets helped locate our distinctive voice. It was Wycliffe who laid the foundation for the English radical traditions, both liberal and revolutionary. The light and shadow of his thought play over the work of Gower and Chaucer, and especially of Langland. He is still spiritually and intellectually alive in the age of Milton, and just audible even in Shelley. He is not forgotten until our radicalisms become secular and Marx displaces a long Christian Socialist and Utopian tradition with materialist literalism.

Wycliffe was born in Yorkshire in 1320. Little is known of his career until 1360 when he is described as 'Master of Balliol' at Oxford. He received ecclesiastical preferments and in 1374 accepted the living of Lutterworth and held it until his death in 1384. His spiritual disciple Jan Hus and Arundel, an Archbishop of Canterbury, affirm from different perspectives that Wycliffe translated the Bible himself. Arundel writes to the Pope: 'The son of the Old Serpent filled up the cup of his malice against Holy Church by the device of a new translation of the Scripture into his native tongue.' In justifying the translation Wycliffe refers to the York Mystery Plays, which he may have seen in his youth, and in which the Lord's Prayer and other Biblical matter was rendered in English. In *De Veritate Sacrae Scripturae* he argues that scripture is the crucial fact, against which tradition has no weight. His sobriquet was *Doctor Evangelicus*, and he asked why there was no English Bible when other languages already had the Book. His desire to see it translated was consistent with his desire to disperse poor priests throughout England: they should be able to preach from a Bible their congregations would understand.

With the passage of time, Wycliffe grew combative. His detractors say he was frustrated in preferment within the hierarchy; but his advocates maintain that he was righteous in civic and spiritual wrath. 'False peace is grounded in rest with our enemies when we assent to them without withstanding; and sword against such peace came Christ to send.' Whether he had a direct hand in it or not, he certainly encouraged work on an English Bible and inspired its completion. The institutions of the Church needed to be tested regularly against the word of scripture, which laymen had a right to read in their own language. 'It seemeth first that the wit of God's law should be taught in that tongue that is more known, for this wit is God's word. When Christ saith in the Gospel that both heaven and earth shall pass, but His words shall not pass, he understandeth by His words His wit. And thus God's wit is Holy Writ, that may on no manner be false. Also the Holy Ghost gave to apostles wit at Wit Sunday for to know all manner languages, to teach the people God's law thereby; and so God would that the people were taught God's law in diverse tongues. But what man, on God's behalf, should reverse God's ordinance and His will?'

He was patronized by John of Gaunt, the King's uncle, and became deeply involved in political controversies. Employed to negotiate with Pope Gregory XI in 1374, he witnessed a corrupt papacy at first hand. Why should a pope have the right to make levies in an England already crippled by taxation to finance wars? Why should a pope appoint foreigners to English benefices? His stance was popular. By means of teaching, sermons and writings, and through his connections and travels, he developed influence at home and abroad. Early on he wrote about 'dominion', following Richard FitzRalph, Archbishop of Armagh, whose line was that the world belongs to God, our 'capital lord', and that only righteousness can justify property: if the Church abuses its property or its power, the state must take away its endowments.

And if the state commits abuses? The answer is not far to seek. All secular and ecclesiastical authority derives from God and is forfeit if it is wrongly used. Pope, king, priest, feudal lord: each ought to be subject to this precept. Wycliffe's expression is coarser than FitzRalph's; it is that of a man who accepts and espouses, rather than teases out, a doctrine. His writings spread from the pulpit and the lecture hall, and were put to use. He vehemently attacks worldliness and venality, in court and church. In 1377, at the height of his popularity, when he was summoned before the Bishop of London to answer charges of improper teaching, street riots on his behalf ended the court session. The Pope charged him with heresy, a heresy compounded in 1380 by his work on the Bible. Scholars say we have to accept that no English writings can authoritatively be attributed to Wycliffe. But equally no one can prove that he *didn't* write them. No doubt parts were added, as they were to Rolle; certainly, substantial parts were faked. But Wycliffe's spirit informs much of it, and it is consistently the spirit of a man gifted with clarity, anger and radical grace.

In 1381, with riots against a poll tax and tax collectors set upon in many English towns, radicals were not popular with the authorities. The Peasants' Revolt against the new tax and the 1351 Statute of Labourers frightened court and Church alike. Resistance to popular demands (which were outlandish only in being popular and underwritten by the threat of violence) hardened. The Kentish rebels chose Wat Tyler as their leader – and there can be more than one perspective on him. Essex and Kentish rebels entered London. A 'Letter to the Peasants of Essex' was circulated, in which John Ball combines prose and rough verse. The letter is written in an English remote from that of the court, but not from the alliterative traditions of Old English. It is touched with the sense of radical fraternity implied in some readings – or misreadings – of Wycliffe:

> Iohon Schep, som tyme Seynte Marie priest of York, and now of Colchestre, greteth wel Iohan Nameles, and Iohan the Mullere, and Iohon Cartere, and biddeth hem that thei bee war of gyle in borugh, and stondeth togidre in Godes name, and biddeth Peres Plowman go to his werk, and chastise wel Hobbe the Robbere, and taketh with yow Iohan Trewman, and alle hiis felawes, and no mo, and loke schappe you to on head, and no mo.
> Iohan the Mullere hath ygrounde smal, smal, smal;
> The Kynges sone of heuene schal paye for al.
> Be war or ye be wo;
> Knoweth your freend fro your foo;
> Haueth ynow, and seith 'Hoo';
> And do wel and bettre, and fleeth synne,
> And seketh pees, and hold you therinne;
> and so biddeth Iohan Trewman and alle his felawes.

Read aloud, the oddnesses of spelling and word-order evaporate. It *looks* very old. But it dates from 1381, more than a decade after Chaucer's *The Book of the Duchess*, with its classical allusions, conventionalized landscape and remoteness from a recognizable England, was written. And it mentions Piers the Plowman, a character out of Langland, or plucked by Langland from popular lore.

Wat Tyler arrived in a poorly defended London. Richard II was holed up in the Tower. On 14 June Simon of Sudbury, Chancellor and Archbishop of Canterbury, was beheaded by the mob. The next day Richard summoned Tyler and his Kentishmen to Smithfield to parley, where, in the King's presence, Tyler was stabbed by William Walworth, Mayor of London.

Leaderless, the rabble dispersed, and it was only a matter of time before the King repealed the concessions he had made under duress. Nevertheless, radical seeds had been sown.

Wycliffe, discredited at court after the Revolt, was already anathema to the Church. He would not keep his counsel, however. In that fateful year he publicly denied transubstantiation. In 1382 the secular party in Oxford was compelled (though it tried to resist) to expel him and his followers. He withdrew to Lutterworth where, in 1384, he suffered a stroke during mass and died. After Wycliffe's death, his community of 'poor preachers' – who founded the Lollard sect – survived, eventually joining the Lutherans in the sixteenth century. Wycliffe's writings became one of the cornerstones of Puritanism.

The conflict of Faith and Reason, the hunger for a *reasonable faith,* or for a reasonable institution to transmit the unreasonable core of faith, was not new. Nor did Wycliffe invent the controversy. The England he was born into was already awake to religious argument: there was debate about Occam and Scotus with their inherent mysticism, the reaffirmation of St Augustine's laws of grace, and numerous other arguments, but generally these were conducted within the Church. Wycliffe's first controversies were confined to scholastic philosophy: he followed Plato not Aristotle, Augustine not Occam, Bradwardine and not free will. Always an intellectual and not an evangelist, he never became a proto-Protestant to the extent of believing in individual grace and revelation. Yet he took hard ideas into the pulpit and shared them with the laity. Those of a puritan disposition tuned in to him. His followers were men who believed that bad priests should not administer the sacraments, and were opposed to hierarchy. Debate about transubstantiation and consubstantiation was prevalent. More *individual* faith was developing. Wycliffe did not invent doubts; he merely organized them into a coherent body of criticism. His spirit touched English writers. It inspired John Purvey to complete the English Bible in 1388, and after Purvey, there appear to be no new Latin manuscript versions of the Bible. English was official. The Word was out.

Wycliffe's Promethean treachery in aspiring to give people direct access to the Word of God was punished beyond the grave. Over twenty years later, in 1409, the Pope ordered all books by him or attributed to him to be burned. A famous bonfire of his work was built and lit in 1411 at Carfax, Oxford. In Prague, the Wycliffite Jan Hus was excommunicated, but he continued to preach and defend Wycliffe. In 1415 at the Council of Constance Wycliffe's writings were unanimously condemned and Hus was ordered to recant his heresies, as if on the dead Wycliffe's behalf. He refused and was burned at the stake. Thirteen years later the Council of Constance ordered that Wycliffe's bones be dug up, burnt, and chucked into the River Swift.

Wycliffe was for everyone, not the trained few. He believed that everyone had a right to the Bible, because otherwise only an educated elite could know what the theologians and Church politicians were up to. He interrogated church government because it was closed and corrupt. He advocated disendowment, rejected much of the Pope's authority and much of established papal authority already weakened by rivalry between Urban VI and Clement VII. He attacked the privileges of Bishops and religious orders, the abuse of indulgences, pardons and sanctuaries, an issue that much engages Chaucer's Canterbury pilgrims, especially the Pardoner. Wycliffe's adoption of English rather than Latin is a radical but not a surprising step. As a scholar, he regarded Latin as proper for deep thought; but as a priest, he believed each soul should have access to the Word. A medieval world in which the educated were connected by Latin and the people divided by dialect was beginning to alter. Nations with distinct priorities, languages and literatures were emerging. Wycliffe used Latin as a scholar of the old order, but English as a prophet of the new. The use of English was *political*. It pointed in the direction of populism, not of nationalism. Wycliffe did not choose English because it was singularly beautiful or expressive (on the contrary), but because it was the language people used.

We can set aside images of ivory towers. Wycliffe's Oxford *was* democratic, including people from all places and all walks of life. Knowledge spilled out; the knowledgeable (like Rolle) spilled into each corner of the land. Latin came to seem a great spiritual and social barrier, to be cast down.

The North of England is more durably Wycliffe's country than the South ever was and not only because he was a Yorkshireman. The North is where Middle English poetry, in its early years, remained defiantly English. A native tradition dominated for two centuries. In French there was the vigorous *lang d'oc* which did not prevail against the courtly, smooth tones of the *lang d'oeil*; similarly the English court, and the city where it lived, in the end provided the orthography, the literary conventions, and to some extent the accent of an English suitable for a verse that aspired to travel beyond its region. The North's *scharp, slyttyng,* and *frotyng* energies remained a resource, and the language of 'myddel Engelond' occupied a middle ground.

The South imposed conformity and eventually decorum, so that Sir Philip Sidney shamefacedly declares in 1581, 'I must confess my own barbarousness, I never heard the old song of Percy and Douglas' – the 'Ballad of Chevy Chace' (**19**) – 'that I found not my heart moved more than with a trumpet; and yet it is sung out by some blind crowder, with no rougher voice than a rude style; which, being so evil apparelled in the dust and cobwebs of that uncivil age, what would it work trimmed in the gorgeous eloquence of Pindar?' The version of this trumpet-call of a poem retrieved in the indispensable *Percy Reliques* of 1765 may have been close to the one Sidney knew. It is certainly in a 'Northeron' language whose rusticity appealed to Sidney's taste even as it repelled his refined judgement, and is attributed to a blind fiddler:

> The Percy out of Northumberland,
>   And a vow to God made he,
> That he would hunt in the mountains
>   Of Cheviat within dayès three,
> In the mauger of° doughty Douglas,   *despite*
>   And all that ever with him be.

It's hard to see that a Pindar, or a Sidney, could improve on the sinewy idiom. It was the vulgar tongue, but it became a common poetic register.

   Polite society, north and south, from the end of the fourteenth century until well into the eighteenth, shunned once-popular ballads, as the Normans had shunned native English narrative. It was a snobbery, a distrust of the Borders and the Scots, an unease at the localizing vigour of dialect and a suspicion of violent feeling and passion. To begin with, taste-makers (in the monasteries and feudal houses) preferred (if they lacked both French and Latin) translations of French romances, domesticated in idiom and occasional in imagery, which remained alien to the native tradition. There should have been nothing wrong with local tradition: it had served well enough both barons and village folk who wanted music and entertainment. But such verse existed for a locality, and as England became knitted more tightly together in itself, and to other countries by trade, taxation and war, the privileged and entrepreneurial classes were exposed to 'superior' foreign customs. A gap grew between what the common people of a locality liked and what their masters affected. The masters' culture became a national culture. They were keen to belong to the wider world of Europe and to be accepted on the terms which that wider world proposed. Serious poets of every land wrote in French or Latin to be understood by the educated in every land.

So, in the fourteenth century, begins the redskin v. paleface conflict that pervades English poetry up to our own day and has less to do with education than with social attitudes. It is north v. south, folk v. court, Anglo-Saxon v. Norman or Latin, native legend v. classical myth, plain style v. Petrarchan or aureate style. The Bible is on the redskin side, not because it is crude but because its subtleties touch the common nerve, while the decorous courtesies of the classics belong to the paleface. Yet the scholarship and care that went into the Authorised Version are probably more austere than the scholarship of the classical humanists, solemnly disporting themselves among Greek and Latin texts.

The dual tension was there even as the language bunched itself into regional dialects and was subjected to rules made from the centre, in books, in debate and government. The English spoken in London, Southwark, Westminster, and by extension in Canterbury, Oxford and Cambridge, was prevalent. It was there that the scriptoria prospered and the first rules of writing and copying were agreed.

At the centre men were educated, and were then exported to the rest of the country as judges, priests and administrators, along with manuscripts and decrees. Local lords came to the London Court and took home London manners and affectations. The South triumphed, with its Norman and Latinate courtly tradition, its classical proprieties a condition for social success. The suppressed traditions simmered, rather as in the Highlands a Scots Gaelic tradition survived, and an Irish in Ireland, a Welsh in Wales. They survived despite repression and neglect. The manuscripts were not collected: hand-me-downs of oral tradition wore thin or were forgotten – but so slowly that in the eighteenth century versions of songs five or six hundred years old could still be harvested. The success of southern English was, on a small scale, a foretaste of the success of English in the Empire. It retarded and distorted, but did not destroy, native traditions.

'IN STORI STIF AND STRONGE...'

Clerk of Tranent eik he has tane,
That maid the anteris of Gawane.
Schir Gilbert Hay endit has he.
Timor mortis conturbat me.

from William Dunbar, *'Lament for the
Death of the Makaris'* (73)

We begin the classic period of Middle English poetry, the latter fourteenth century, with a poet whose name we do not know. We call him the *Gawain* poet after his most famous poem, *Sir Gawain and the Green Knight*. He is not the Clerk of Tranent whom Dunbar laments a century later, though he draws on the same stories and characters. He is believed to have written three other poems, most notably *Pearl*. We start with him because he is in some ways the most unaccommodating and old-fashioned of Middle English poets, retaining much from the alliterative tradition and northern diction; but also because his radical originality had no issue. However, centuries later, and with no knowledge of *Gawain* or *Pearl*, Christopher Smart wrote *A Psalm to David* and, in the latter half of the nineteenth century, Gerard Manley Hopkins composed *The Wreck of the Deutschland*. Both works are similar in kind – remote cousins.

The *Gawain* poet went his own way, and that way was towards English legend and French poetic antecedents. What English and poetry were doing in the South didn't detain him. He embarked upon what some critics call 'the alliterative revival' and produced in *Gawain* a work intensely English, *older* English in language and feeling than Chaucer's and Gower's and Langland's, yet so closely analogous in plot structure and verse form to the French Arthurian romances of the age that the poem has sometimes been thought a translation from a lost French original. Which is it to be: profoundly native, belonging (after the ascendancy of Yorkshire) uniquely to the North *West* (Cheshire and South Lancashire); or a remarkable translation or transposition? Could so accomplished a poem stand quite alone in English, without antecedent or heir, or has a whole tradition been almost lost, with only *Gawain* and *Pearl* by miracle surviving? Could a provincial English poet, with no distinctive sustaining culture, have achieved such work?

Who was this man? (No one has assumed the poet to have been a woman, despite the rich textures of fabric, the eye for detail and the curious perspectives on erotic and familial love.) He was born around 1330, probably in Lancashire or Cheshire. His father may have had aristocratic connections; the poet understands the large house and courtly arrangements and romanticizes the grand architecture of the day. He read in French *The Romance of the Rose* and other fashionable literature and may have been familiar with the medieval versions of the Latin classics with their moralizing embroideries. He knew scripture, too. He was learned, possibly a clerk, probably not a full member of the clergy. There is little else for us to suppose about him, except for occasional hints in the poems, and the overall authority and command of the poems themselves.

Gawain survives in one manuscript only. It is the last of four untitled poems (the first three being the luminous romance which editors have dubbed *Pearl*, followed by works they call *Purity* or *Cleanness* and *Patience*) in MS Cotton Nero A. x, preserved in the British Museum and dating from the late fourteenth century. It is a small vellum volume, about seven inches by five, and it was carelessly copied in the sense that some of the pages were folded on to one another before the ink was dry and sometimes, in order to interpret a letter or word, one must use a mirror and refer to the facing page. A dozen plain, caricaturish illustrations are scattered through the manuscript. One of the four which relate to *Gawain* shows the hero asleep on a bed, thoroughly cocooned in bedclothes like a swaddled figure on a medieval tomb; the Lady, in what looks like a dressing gown with wide sleeves and polka dots, with a long neck and her hair done up in what cannot be curlers, with her left hand, the middle finger, is just touching the end of his beard.[12]

The first edition appeared in 1839, a loving and accurate transcription. Twenty-five years later the indispensable Early English Texts Society produced an edition which was standard until Sir Israel Gollancz revised it in 1897 and again in 1912. The eloquence and brilliance of J.R.R. Tolkein's edition, produced with E.V. Gordon, forced *Gawain* onto a wider (largely undergraduate) readership, and though the poem has never been quite popular, given its lexical complexity, it has been several times translated and is now firmly restored to the Middle English canon; a brilliant, awkward text in the abundant fourteenth century. Its absence from the scene for almost half a millennium – between its writing down and the 1836 edition – is an

---

[12] 'The scene reminds me,' writes the Austrian poet Evelyn Schlag, 'of one of my favourites in Romanesque Burgundy – a stone relief called *The Sleep of the Three Magi* in Autun. It is in the Cathedral museum and shows the three kings with their heads on one large pillow, bodies wrapped in a large round blanket, crepe-wise. The heads stick out like asparaguses. An angel is standing behind them pointing at a star [the star that guided them home from Bethlehem] with one hand, and with the forefinger of the other hand he touches the king next to him. Just one finger. Incredibly soft even in stone, maybe because it is in stone.'

impoverishment: Chaucer, Spenser, Milton and others might have enjoyed and variously benefited from it; conceivably, the history of English prosody would have been different had it been available to contemporary and later poets.

The story draws on Arthurian legend and folklore, the usual mix of heroism, magic and daftness that characterizes the romances. The poet's tone and intention are hard to determine, but because of the richness of texture and the comedy of manner if not of manners, it is hard not to assume that the writer was sophisticated and good humoured and perhaps gently parodic in his intentions. *Gawain and the Green Knight* (**42**) was intended to be read on the page quite as much as listened to by an audience. The satisfactions of the form are not formulaic but more broadly traced, in ways to which the reading eye responds more acutely than the listening ear. Had Chaucer's Criseyde been reading this poem instead of a romance of surrender on the day that Pandarus advanced Troilus's interests upon her, she might have averted heartbreak, or if not that, at least her own infidelity. It is *edifying*, but that seems secondary to the fact that it is deeply amusing and, at crucial points, quite erotic. The eroticism does not always focus on Gawain and the Lady.

In form, the poem combines complex alliterative unrhymed lines with, at the end of each run (variable in length, but averaging eighteen lines) a little coda consisting of a short line (two to four syllables) and a rhymed quatrain. It is misleading to call these irregular components 'verse paragraphs' is closer to the form. In the original manuscript, the paragraphs are not numbered. Divisions within the poem are signalled by large blue initial letters, with red decorations.

Like many medieval romances, *Gawain* begins by establishing its legit-imacy as a history, tracing its narrative back to Troy. A two-paragraph preface reminds us of Troy's fall, and the legends of the diaspora of the heroes. Aeneas 'the athel' – the noble – and his 'highe kinde' became subjectors of new lands, and masters 'of all the wealth in the west isles'. Romulus builds Rome, Tirius colonizes Tuscany, Langaberde in Lombardy builds homes and 'far over the French flood Felix Brutus' on many a hillside has begun the adventure that is Britain.

Time passes, and eventually in Brutus' line come Arthur and his knights. The poem's action begins in the British King's court. It is New Year. There is dancing and mirth richly brought alive in a feast of descriptive language. The King calls for a high, heroic tale to be told before he will break bread. Suddenly, instead of a tale, a genuine adventure begins: into the party bursts a Green Knight on a green horse, lavishly described in the detail of his richly wrought costume and his features, including his flowing hair that fell to his shoulders, and his beard which 'as a bush over his breast hangs'. Here is a force of nature indeed, contained wonderfully in imagery of nurture: it is magic, the marriage of folklore and legend. The poet saves the crucial details for the fourth paragraph of his description: the Green Knight wears no helmet or halbard, no armour or shield, but bears a bunch ('bobbe') of holly in one hand and a huge, hideous (Danish) axe in the other. It is a full ell in length, and broad, made of green steel and gold, and the blade is razor sharp. 'Where,' he demands is, 'the governor of this ging?'

He challenges the knights: one of them must deal the first blow to him, on condition that, twelve months later, the knight who accepts the challenge will seek out the Green Knight for a return match, subjecting himself to a counter blow. Arthur's knights are understandably squeamish, so the elderly Arthur, out of a sense of honour, begins to accept the challenge. But Gawain, Arthur's nephew, the son of Loth, the youngest knight and a popular Arthurian hero, proposes himself. The Green Knight does not flinch: Gawain chops off his head which rolls away from the block. The Green Knight gets to his feet, collects his head, tucks it under his arm and rides off, reiterating the conditions of the challenge as he goes.

Gawain honours his pledge and sets out on his journey to the Green Knight's domain. Just as we have seen in detail the Green Knight's attire, we now see Gawain's, the poet lingering on his red shield with the pentangle motif, a symbol of truth, the knot that cannot be undone. Its five points affirm that Gawain is incorruptible in his five senses, and evoke the other fives: Christ's wounds, Mary's joys, and so on. Mary's image faces him within the shield. The poet also dresses Gringolet, Gawain's steed, in great detail, as if he was applying gilding and enamel to his images. We only see what Gringolet wears, not the creature himself: he is purely a clothes horse.

We trace Gawain's journey north through marvellous and ominous landscapes, through winter and through battles with odd, fierce creatures (**42a**). On Christmas Eve, Gawain, weary and depressed, prays for guidance from the Virgin and crosses himself three times. A moated castle appears out of nowhere, among the trees. The parkland is green; winter does not have this estate in its icy clutches. This is Bertilak de Hautdesert's castle, and Gawain is invited to stay for Christmas. He meets the host's beautiful young wife and the crone who is her chaperone.

The celebrations last for three days, after which Gawain plans to seek his foe, using Bertilak's castle as his *pied à terre*. He and Bertilak agree that, on each of the three days, while Bertilak goes hunting, Gawain will pursue his own interests at the castle. When Bertilak returns, he will give Gawain the day's catch, and in return Gawain will give him whatever he has managed to gather at home. Bertilak goes on a wonderful hunt. Gawain stays abed and is visited by the beautiful lady of the house, who tries to seduce him (**42b**). They exchange a kiss and compliments. In the evening Bertilak presents Gawain with deer, and Gawain gives Bertilak a kiss. They repeat the process the next day. Bertilak hunts for wild boar; Gawain gets two kisses and gives them to his host in the evening. On the third day Bertilak pursues the wily fox. Gawain is beset by the lady of the house. She kisses him thrice but his libidinal resolve holds. She at last persuades him at least to accept a token of her esteem, a green lace or garter, which will help protect him from the Green Knight's powers. That evening Gawain fails to keep his part of the bargain with Bertilak. He gives his host the three kisses but keeps the garter for himself.

The next morning he rides off to his rendezvous with magic in the wilderness of the Cheshire Wirral, to the Green Chapel, a kind of cave. The Green Knight materializes with his familiar blade. Gawain prepares to take his blow and kneels down, but as the blade falls he flinches and the Green Knight scorns his cowardice. A second time he is steadfast as a rock, but now it is the Green Knight who misses his mark. On the third attempt the Green Knight nicks him, but the wound is neither deep nor threatening. Gawain has had enough, he has honoured his part of the bargain with the Green Knight. Then the Knight reveals himself as Bertilak in fancy dress. He knows all that has occurred beneath his roof – he planned it all – and chides Gawain for withholding the lace or garter (his punishment was the little wound), but he praises him for having resisted the advances of the lady. In paraphrase: 'I sent her to assay you, and truly I think you the faultlessest fellow that ever walked upright; as pearls are than white peas of price much more, so is Gawain, in good faith, than other gay knights.' Morgan le Fay, Arthur's crafty half-sister, contrived the trial to test the hero's nerve. Gawain goes home wearing what he regards as the badge of his dishonour, the green girdle. He tells his story and the delighted court of the Round Table undertake to wear a green garter in honour of his adventure and success.

This is a story the poet found written in a book, probably originally in French, though it ties in with numerous Celtic and other folk tales and legends. Its source is less interesting than what the poet makes of it: a beautiful staging, bright, charming and cheerful-sinister; and his remarkable use of language to evoke places, textures and atmospheres. True, there is magic and symbolism and an inexhaustible pretext for scholarly research. The three literal hunts (timid deer, wild and angry boar, and wily fox) parallel the symbolic hunts (the Lady's attempts on Gawain's virtue) which parallel the three attempts with the axe. The landscape, the costumes and every other detail are grist to the scholar's and the interpretative critic's mills. But underlying the anthropology, numerology and folklore, there is a poem of major proportions, a great and unique work which holds its own with Chaucer's and Langland's and Gower's. Indeed, its originality of form is superior to Langland's and its language richer than Gower's. As the poet Basil Bunting says, the *Gawain* poet is writing an English poem while the followers of Chaucer and Gower were trying to write French poems in English. And he also makes a crucial point about the poem's specifically *poetic* qualities, given its didactic intentions: '. . . the poet never forces his allegory. The whole thing is allegorical from beginning to end, yet he never takes you by the neck and says "Get down to it, that's an allegory, you've got to interpret it", the way most allegorists do. The detail intertwines and repeats, and yet the richness of detail never obscures the balance, the beautiful balance and symmetry of the main design of that poem.'

The language of *Pearl* (41) is easier of access than that of *Gawain*. It is much closer in sound and texture (though insistently alliterative) to early Chaucer, but plainer and more assured in its faith and its allusions; more complex in prosody and form than anything in Gower, and more compelling in the feelings it evokes. Like *Gawain*, it is a unique and uniquely beautiful work, but while *Gawain* tends to epic and romance, *Pearl* is elegy and consoled lament.

The central image is of a man who has lost a priceless pearl in a garden. He falls asleep on the spot where it vanished into a mound of earth (41a). Within this allegorical figuration is another – *real* – story. A man grieves for a child, dead before her second year. Falling asleep, he has a vision of her, transformed into a queen of Heaven. From across a flowing river she teaches him the lessons of faith and patience, and she lets him glimpse the Holy City. She is one of many maidens and, eager to be with her, he throws himself into the stream to swim across – and wakes, recumbent on her grave (41b). 'My head upon that hill was laid . . .' It is a poem rooted at once in the Book of Revelation and in *The Romance of the Rose*, an allegory and a genuine lament. The fact that the beloved is a child rather than a woman removes the vexed element of courtly eroticism.

The clarity of purpose and the innocence of the voice are unprecedented in English poetry. The twelve four-stress lines that make the stanzas have between eight and eleven syllables. The stanzas themselves are tightly rhymed into a sonnet-seeming octave and quatrain: *abababab bcbc*. The reader is carried forward, once again, not by suspense and excitement of narrative but by the sustained beauty of the prosody, the rich mixture of Old English and Norman elements in the diction, and the brightness of the detailed imagery. There is a sense of true feeling, and in the unfolding theology a sense of deep and consoling belief. Here are the roots of a religious verse devoted to love and transcendence, unmarred by the devilments of the Church or the harsh realities of a social world. It is a poem which has no commerce with the city where Langland, Gower and Chaucer worked. The North West survives in its dialect and tones, and yet it is as European a work as anything that London published. Had Chester, not London, become the capital of English poetry a different language and literature would have emerged. Sir Israel Gollancz a little but not entirely implausibly likens the *Gawain* poet's sensibility to Wordsworth's. But *Pearl* is more ambitious and perfect than any work that Wordsworth produced. Its complexities, and *Gawain*'s, might suggest a closer affinity with Samuel Taylor Coleridge.

'IN ENGLISH FORTO MAKE A BOOK...'

'... who so ever prayeth for the soul of John Gower, he shall, so oft as he so doth, have a thousand five hundred days of pardon.'

From an indulgence table that once hung by Gower's tomb.

Sir John Gower, well into his fifties, the poet who had composed more than 32,000 lines of French verse and 11,000 lines of Latin elegiacs, began – in 'the Monthe of Maii' the poem says – in the year 1386(ish), in a high room beside the priory church of St Mary Overie, Southwark – to write his first poem in English.

He was a man of substance. He had his own scriptorium, which is to say that he was a fourteenth-century publisher, employing a team of scribes to copy books and documents for friends and clients. Having written 43,000 lines of verse, he could hardly have been expected to copy it all out a second time whenever a customer or a patron required.

He gives the impression, generally, of having been decorous and quiet. On that day in May his scribes must have felt his physical presence as if for the first time, a kind of sudden storm, though he'd been their master for years. His grey lips were pink under his moustache, pursing, shaping sounds. They saw *him*, his long, pinched face pleated with age, the acorn headpiece gathering a silky abundance of white hair that, where it escaped, curled upward like the hair of an ageing child. He might have been a cleric, a parched disciple of Wycliffe! His moustache and the slightly forked beard – like Chaucer's, except Chaucer was rounder of face – took on a life of their own; his hand wrote the sounds he did not voice aloud, the fingers danced as if counting beads or syllables. Were his scribes shocked? English was a vulgar tongue, the language men like Sir John used chiefly when speaking to peasants and servants. Better conversation and private thought was voiced in French. *The Lover's Confession* or, as he dignified it with a Latin title, the *Confessio Amantis*, was the poem Gower embarked on.

Strange matter, one might think, for such a religious old man. *Senex et cecus Iohannes Gower.* Old and almost blind, his eyes froze over completely a few years later. When Sir John regained his composure on that astounding day, he had memorialized the occasion in the verse itself. After writing so much in the language of the court (French), and of the church (Latin), he turned to English almost by chance. He had bumped into King Richard II, still 'the boy king' but nearing his majority, on the river Thames. The King invited his poet aboard the royal barge and asked him to write 'some newe thing' in English. Despite ill-health, the poet promised to oblige 'for king Richardes sake', to provide 'wisdome to the wise / And pley to hem that lust to pleye'. The King's was a momentous request. When a poet like Sir John cast aside the sanctioned instruments of his trade, the languages of secular and spiritual power, and took up native clay, the mess that was English, and breathed coherent life into it, the language began to glow.

English was not foreign to poetry. But it *was* foreign to the great *poetae docti*, and it is the learned poets whose works survived. All the early poets were learned, but few were talented. Gower was different: he wrote feverishly, under compulsion, and as the work grew in his mind to enormous proportions, he dictated to his scribes. For days they must have taken down his recitation, the words he'd thought out in the night or translated extempore from French or Latin books, or which he wrested from the air.

He had set up his copying house at St Mary's. The scribes – French, English, failed students from University, poor clerks earning a crust – were paid to copy his works and any that his noble or church patrons required. There were probably several scribes in 1380. Some prepared the parchments, pinning and lining them, readying the inks. The scribes themselves worked from a master copy or from the poet's dictation, in which case several copies could be made at the same time. There was an illuminator who decorated the parchments with colour and – if the final work was intended for a noble patron – gilt. The first and best copy was reserved for the King. Other copies were for lesser patrons who needed books to read aloud to provincial courts and convocations, or privately on long winter nights.

When there were errors, they went undetected until a scholar centuries later read over and collated surviving copies. At every point of difference the editor had to make a decision. The creative process continued: a scribe mishearing or inventing silently, a scholar discovering and making new emendations. The text of a great poem was always fluid at the edges, whether taken down by hand or later set in type. It was never a final, authoritative version.

That is a Renaissance notion: a *final version* of a poem. Before then, a poem was never *finished*. Like a church it grew; bits were added or removed to make new space. Even as the poet dictated, scribes might sketch in a bit, a fancy, a memory, a 'correction'; or, when they grew tired and dozed, miss whole passages. Hovering over them was an ideal poem which the poet almost knew. But even he could change his mind: the poem he made one year might be out of date the next. Gower wrote his *Confessio* for King Richard, but when Richard proved unworthy, he made it over, adding an allegorical record of royal errors. Poems can die – or be killed or neglected – unless the poet re-fashions and refreshes them. If he learns something new, he has to add it. The aim is to delight, but the purpose is to instruct. Delight without precept is pointless.

In the revised version, which he worked on in 1391, Gower mentions Henry of Lancaster, and the third version of 1393 is dedicated to the future king. Sir John was rewarded with an ornamental collar and when Henry was in due course crowned Henry IV, he allowed him two pipes of Gascony wine a year. Sir John was thus his laureate and praised him sincerely, not to get patronage – he was a man of means and didn't need charity or wages – but because he admired his strength. He deserted Richard, who was weak and impressionable. The truths a poet tells alter as the things he sees change. There are scratchings out, repentances. Andrew Marvell and John Dryden, William Wordsworth and W.H. Auden in their later centuries are no different. Hypocrites, their critics say; but no, they were just engaged writers, changing and growing up.

In 1390 – the year after Richard declared he had come of age and took the reins of power in his own hands – Gower completed his book in its first version. It *was* in the English that the King spoke, that Geoffrey Chaucer spoke, that the clerks used when at leisure. It was a language not deliberately poetical but precise, easier on the ear than French, Latin, or the harsher English of the North (which is the dialect of the *Gawain* poems) or the rugged idiom of the ballads. William Langland, we might think, wrote closer to the inflections of the common man.

Sir John's English was accessible rather than ambitious. It is not resonant or inventive like Chaucer's. The lines are for the most part tetrameter couplets, as in Chaucer's early poems. It was a well-worn French measure which Sir John made supple. He had learned to handle the form skilfully in French: it was polite, simple, courtly, with the unassertive firmness of conversation – a mark of the best French poems. French was his apprenticeship. He understood *extension*: how to play line against sentence and draw the sense out evenly. The novelty, as the weakness, of *Confessio Amantis* is its Frenchness. We speak of mid-Atlantic accents: in his case it is mid-Channel.

A tetrameter line in the *Confessio* generally has eight syllables, or four iambic feet, teTUM teTUM teTUM teTUM. Because of the rhyme, the eye and ear take the line, or two lines together – the couplet – as a basic unit. But the reading mind, what Wycliffe called the 'understanding', is looking for larger parcels of sense. The ear is satisfied when the metre is balanced and the rhyme struck, but the sentence is incomplete and the mind seeks its satisfaction in the resolution of the sense. Sense resolves, but not at the rhyme, so eye and ear move on to their next fulfilment. By the counterpoint – a kind of suspense – created between the arrangement of sounds and the construing of sense, a pace builds and a drama develops that has nothing to do with details of the story or its moral. One critic described it as 'leap-frog'. This drama *in* the language is the *poetry* of the poem. It can bring even the most exhausted tale alive. And that is the thing that never changes, from the time of Homer, or Gower, until today: poetry is *in* language: one can paraphrase the sense, but not the *poetry* of an achieved poem.

Confessio Amantis (**44**) should be read rather briskly, and in long runs. Imagine the speaker, a man not unlike Sir John at the time, getting on in years, unlucky in love, yet ironically called Amans: Lover. He has complained to Venus that he can't get anywhere with his beloved. The goddess sends him a Confessor called Genius to bring him to his senses: what is a man so long in the tooth up to, looking in the month of May for the love of a young lady? Such love belongs to youth and virtue. Genius interrogates the supplicant, describing one by one each of the seven deadly sins and their sub-categories, illustrating them with stories and challenging Amans to confess to one of them. Amans denies the sin of Sloth. He tells Genius of his devoted – if fruitless – attention to his beloved:

> I bow and proffer my service,
> Sometime in chamber, sometime in hall,
> Right as I see the timès fall.
> And when she goeth to hearè mass,
> That timè shall not overpass,
> That I n'approach her ladyhood,
> In aunter° if I may her lead   *chance*
> Unto the chapel and again.
> Then is not all my way in vain,
> Some deal I may the bettrè fare,
> When I, that may not feel her bare,
> May lead her clothèd in mine arm . . .

This is simple and sensual. It is about desire, which won't let his pulse stop hoping, and her cool indifference. It's hard for the old man; he can't get her body out of his mind:

> But afterward it doth me harm
> Of pure imagination;
> For thenè this collation
> I make unto myselven oft,
> And say, 'Ha lord, how she is soft,
> How she is round, how she is small!
> Now wouldè God I had her all

Withoutè danger at my will!'
And then I sigh and sittè still ...

She controls him; he follows with no will of his own. If she stands, he stands. If she sits, he kneels beside her. Erotic hope returns, the verse heats up, sentences grow breathless: And, And, And, And ... He turns his attention to her pets, her pages and chambermaids, anything that is hers upon which he can lavish attention, gain commendation and deflect passion:

But when she tak'eth her work in hand
Of weaving or embroidery,
Then can I not but muse and pry
Upon her fingrès long and small,
And now I thinke, and now I tell,
And now I sing, and now I sike,°   *sigh*
And thus my countenance I pike.°   *probe*
And if it fall, as for a time
Her liketh not abidè bime,
But busien her on other things,
Then make I other tarryings
To drech° forth the longè day,   *stretch*
For me is loath depart away.
And then I am so simple of port,
That forto feignè some desport
I playè with her little hound
Now on the bed, now on the ground,
Now with her briddès° in the cage;   *birds*
For there is non so little page,
Ne yet so simple a chamberere,
That I ne make hem allè chere,
All for they shouldè speakè well:
Thus may you see my busy wheel,
That goeth noght idly about.
And if her list to riden out
On pelrinage or other stede,°   *occasion*
I comè, though I be not bede,°   *bid*
And take her in mine arm aloft
And set her in her saddle soft,
And so forth lead her by the bridle,
For that I wouldè not be idle.
And if her list to ride in chair,
And then I may therof be ware,

Anon I shapè° me to ride   *prepare*
Right even by the chairès side;
And as I may, I speak among,
And otherwhile I sing a song
Which Ovid in his books made,
And saidè, 'O which sorrows glad,
O which woefull prosperity
Belongeth to the property
Of Love, who so will him serve!
And yet therefrom may noman swerve,
That he ne mot his law obey.'
And thus I ridè forth my way,
And am right busy overall
With heart and with my body all,
As I have said you here tofore.   *earlier*
My goodè father, tell therefore,
Of idleness if I have guilt.'

He plays back and forth between *nakid* and *clothed*, and it is sexy, candid. It feels like a true confession of desire heightened by a subtly disclosing discretion. The poetry keeps almost concluding, then starting again in a different key: memory, imagination, strategy, confession. This is remarkable writing 'in character' – a character speaks, acts out his obsession in the way he constructs and arranges the language. A knight is reduced by passion to mere temporizer. That is one of love's effects.

What did he feel like, this Englishman already 'for my dayes olde, ... feble and impotent', devoted to an England of which he wrote (in French), 'O gentile Engleterre a toi iescrits'? What did he feel, to be writing verse for the first time in his native tongue? It must have been like discovering a new world in his own mouth.

But just as he was not the first, his was not the only *way* of writing into the tongue. There were other resources – notably those of the *Gawain* poet – which the success of this kind of writing overshadowed. The old measures may have been driven to the edges of England, but the new rhymers at the centre of things, because they imitated French without understanding how to transpose its forms into English, or because they tried to revive old forms that had lost their power over a changed language, might occasionally take off, but they seldom stayed in the air for long. Such verse-writers weren't *all* flying at Kitty Hawk. But English even in Gower's time was a language that, shire by shire, borough by borough, was parcelled out into more or less mutually-obscure dialects.

English verse right up to the end of the fourteenth century was scattered through monasteries, castles and manor houses in manuscript books, each a chaos of orthography and diction, to be read out after a winter supper, or as an alternative to scriptural collations. Or it was recited by minstrels who bought verses from monks or dreamed them up for feast-days and market days. To speak of such material as a *literature* mis-states its purpose and its merit. Gower was actually a *poet*, not a scribe, a mere versifier or an entertainer.

His king sent him home to write a poem in English, and he eventually wrote 34,000 lines. There is no hesitation in his art. He knew the English poems – the poor crabbed ones that his scribes must sometimes have had to copy out for clients and patrons; he knew the sweet new style of Chaucer who, in 1385, dedicated to him *Troilus and Criseyde*. It was for '*Moral* Gower and philosophical Strode' – the very Strode with whom Wycliffe conducted friendly logical disputations at Oxford. Some say that Strode wrote *Pearl* and *Gawain*; but it is hard to imagine the logician as a poet: he put such stuff behind him in favour of more sober studies, though the almost mathematical precision of the poetic structures might lend support to his claims. Strode was eminent for his scholastic knowledge.

Sir John knew the limping verse histories and romances. But his verse, like Chaucer's, was fluent. The *Confessio* immediately inspires confidence: here is a man who knows how a voice shapes a sentence, and how, in verse, it can imitate the movement of thought and feeling. Still, it probably felt strange to write in his daily language. He kept coming back to his unease in the poem itself, now apologetically, now affirming his aims. Chaucer was there for him, making astonishing new poems even as Gower composed the *Confessio*. Sir John would not have considered Chaucer a *great* poet: he never wrote great works in Latin or French. And all of Chaucer's longer works, except for *Troilus and Criseyde*, are fragments.

Gower's claims do diminish when we set his work beside Chaucer's, Langland's and others'. If Chaucer did not write the interminable French lines of Sir John's *Speculum Meditantis* or the Latin hexameters of his *Vox Clamantis*, bravo Chaucer! Think of the sheep whose skins were spared the parchment treatment. Yet Gower's claims are large and genuine. The reader who understands him understands his century and gets a handle on the beginning of English poetry – what is our *real* poetry, in a way that verse in Old English, a foreign language, or the limping chronicles and romances that came after, never can be. Sir John had suggestive antecedents in English but his poetry was fathered by French and after he finished the *Confessio*, French gathered him back to its bosom. He only wrote one further poem in English, for Henry IV, around 1399. It was called 'In Praise of Peace'. But for seven years – writing and revising – he gave himself up to English, let his scribes' hands shape English words which English ears warmed to. He read in a firm Kentish voice.

His success was unprecedented in English. *Confessio Amantis* was the first English poem to be translated into the languages of the Continent. This is an ambiguous tribute: it was readily *translatable*. He used a French metre, the conventions of fashionable European verse, and much of his poem was adapted from the languages that welcomed it back. Long before Caxton printed it in English, Spanish and Portuguese versions existed. The *Confessio* is as much a part of the international literature of the 'clerks', with Latin and French affinities, as it is of English. Gower's great poetic risk is to choose English. Beyond that, he uses sanctioned forms, intent on conventional matter, the stories he tells, the lessons he teaches. He is not inventive but efficient, a virtue in a moral writer. But if his work illuminates the mind and temper of his age, it casts only a dim light on the social world that lent them substance: the world he lived in.

He is a European although his French and Latin poems are forgotten, along with almost all the French and Latin verse of the first six centuries of our poetry. Nowadays we read Milton's Latin and Italian verses in translation, for what they tell us about his father, his early attitudes and his friendships, but we seldom approach them as *poetry* in their own right. Yet well into the seventeenth century, for some writers – Francis Bacon among them – a book didn't exist until it existed in Latin and belonged to the culture of Europe on Europe's terms, that is, written in a purified, classical humanist spirit, much like the terms of medieval culture: Latin, though no longer the adaptable and expressive Latin of the medieval church. In the end it isn't Gower's timeless Latin or fashionable French but his English poem that lives. He did something for the pleasure of his king and the kingdom. A labour as much as a pleasure for him. When it was done he felt released back to his natural culture:

> And now to speak as in final,
> Touchendè that I undertook
> In English forto make a book
> Which stant between earnest and game,
> I have it made as thilkè same
> Which axe° forto ben excusid, *asks*
> And that my book be not refusid
> Of lerèd° men, whan they it see, *learned*
> For lack of curiosity:
> For thilkè° school of eloquence *the same*
> Belongeth not to my science,
> Upon the form of rhetoric
> My words forto paint and pike,
> As Tullius some timè wrote.
> But this I know and this I wot,

That I have do my trewè pain°   *endeavour*
With rudè wordis and with plain,
In all that evere I couthe and mighte,
This book to write as I behight,
So as sicknesse it soffrè would;
And also for my dayès old,
That I am feeble and impotent,
I wot not how the world is went . . .

SOUTHWARK

... In Southwark at the Tabard as I lay
Ready to wenden on my pilgrimage...

Chaucer, General Prologue, *The Canterbury Tales*,
ll. 20–21 (**48a**)

Looking today across the river to Southwark you see a reconstruction of Shakespeare's Globe Theatre, its pennants rattling in the breeze. Southwark Cathedral – bleached by restoration – takes you back two centuries further. Sir John Gower contributed to rebuilding it in its elegant form, a beautiful pattern of the lighter Gothic; at the same time he founded, at his tomb, a perpetual chantry. He might recognize his church even today.

Visitors shoulder in, past memorials to great men and great names: Launcelot Andrewes, the divine beloved of T.S. Eliot and, centuries before, of John Donne and the Metaphysical poets who attended to his sermons and learned ways of seeing and strategies of expression from him; Edmund Shakespeare, William's brother, partner in establishing the Globe in 1599, has a memorial here; as does John Harvard, less forgotten because he established a great university. The space Gower's scriptorium occupied is now built over a dozen times, but his tomb survives, gaudily restored. Under a stone canopy his effigy reclines, overlooked by three allegorical angel muses, his feet resting on a benign mastiff or lion, his head propped awkwardly on his three principal works: the French *Mirour de l'homme (Speculum Meditantis*, 1376–9), the Latin *Vox Clamantis* (c. 1381) and the *Confessio Amantis*. His hands press together in prayer. The tomb has altered substantially and the effigy does not resemble surviving portraits. It's taller than in life, more jauntily and tidily bearded, wearing a long red gown embroidered with gold foliage like a figure out of allegory, a monument fitting for a man of such imaginative and material substance. He came of a prominent family with estates in Yorkshire, Suffolk, Norfolk and Kent. Had he not written a word he would still have merited such a tomb, perhaps with more comfortable pillows.

He was born around 1330 with every advantage landed wealth affords: security, leisure, education 'liberal and uncircumscribed', as Thomas Warton, that patient historian of our early literature, puts it. Gower received training for legal and civil office. He grew learned. He was certainly more than the common or 'burel' clerk ('burel' was the coarse, perhaps brown wool cloth in which men following this modest vocation were clothed) that his Amans claims to be. Poor William Langland was the real burel clerk. Langland had none of Gower's advantages, though some claim he had twice his originality and genius.

Sir John bought and sold estates, dividing his time between rural and urban abodes until in 1377 he took up residence at what was then St Mary Overie (Over the River) Priory. If he had a first wife, she died before 1380. In 1398 and nearly blind, he married Agnes Groundolf in his own private oratory in the priory. He lived for another decade, then went to his sumptuous rest.

Gower wrote poems specifically for recitation, while Chaucer, the first bourgeois poet, wrote poems to be read silently, in the privacy of one's room, or between two or three people, preferably lovers. His best poems and fragments are too long and richly-textured for an audience of monks or courtiers or common folk on feast days. The step from Gower to Chaucer is the step from pulpit or lectern into unbuttoned private comfort.

Gower is complex, of course, and long. But his complexity is old-fashioned allegory. His length, as often as not, is long-windedness. The *Speculum Meditantis* is allegory and takes itself seriously. Warton says it illustrates the 'general nature of virtue and vice, enumerates the felicity of conjugal fidelity ... and describes the path which the reprobate ought to pursue for the recovery of divine grace'. A tidy summary. Gower provides a genealogy of sin, a catalogue of vices and virtues, illustrated with precept, homily and story. In this and other ways the poem foreshadows the *Confessio*. You might even call it, ungenerously, the French original, or first draft.

After writing it he confronted his fear and anger at the events of 1381. His Latin poem *Vox Clamantis* – he chose Latin as befitting a sombre occasion, or because he believed he had mastered the medium – is less deliberately conceived than *Speculum*. He had to speak out, about the Peasants' Revolt, and indirectly about how Wycliffe was in many respects right but in crucial respects misunderstood. *Vox* is a dream fable, a freer form than the *Speculum*, and less systematic in argument. The *Confessio*, properly speaking, is an allegorical dream fable, marrying the forms of the first two poems. The Latin elegiacs illustrate the ways in which irresponsible action at both the head and the foot of the body politic leads to the kingdom's undoing.

Gower is a descriptive moralist rather than an innovator (except in his puzzling leniency over incest). He seems to believe what the best (religious) minds had believed for centuries and the poem shapes around those beliefs. He sets out to define and deepen, not to change moral attitudes. Religious belief and a structured and stable society guarantee a common humanity.

When Church or state fumble, each of us is threatened. English people were once candid: 'Of mannes hertè the corage / Was showèd then in the visage.' In that happy time, words were close to what they named, not distorted by hyperbole and misuse. 'The word was like to the conceit / Withoutè semblant of deceit.'

In 1381 things turn topsy-turvy. Even the Church is at fault.

> In to the sword the churchè key
> Is turnèd, and the holy bede
> Into cursing.

A little radical, but not very. He speaks not with anger like Langland or sardonically like Chaucer, but with civic and spiritual sorrow.

> For if men look at holy church,
> Between the word and that they werch
> There is a full great difference

and

> For now aday is many one
> Which speakth of Peter and of John
> And thinketh Judas in his hearte.

He keeps distance from an age in which 'stant the crop under the root'.

The governing convention of the *Confessio* is courtly love – drawn from French and other Romances about devoted knights and the unattainable ladies they woo and serve. Behind this convention is something serious, concerned with civic love, order, natural hierarchy. The *Confessio* endorses a pure, old-fashioned feudal order. What alternative was there – Wat Tyler and his rabble? Besides, such stability is an ideal, not an actual possibility. It never truly existed in a sustained form over generations. In his tales the wheel of fortune turns. The mighty rise in pride and power, then fall under it; the poor and unfortunate reap rewards as in the Beatitudes. Man is responsible for his fallen state and needs institution and instruction to reclaim himself. It's a severe task:

> Who that lawe hath upon hand,
> And spareth for to do justice
> For mercy, doth not his office.

The *Confessio* is haunted by the poet's studious reading. The ghost of one writer in particular fascinates him, as it did King Alfred, Chaucer and

Queen Elizabeth I (all of whom translated him or caused him to be translated into English). That writer was Anicius Manlius Severinus Boethius, Chaucer's Boece, of the noted Praenestine family, the Anicii, born in Rome in 480, consul under Theodoric the Ostrogoth, father of consuls and notables. Boethius fell foul of Theodoric and got himself condemned to death. In prison in Pavia he was visited – his poem tells us – by Dame Philosophy to whom he made a confession. She consoled him. He wrote his consolatory poem only to be cruelly executed in 524. For more than a millennium most European poets would have named *The Consolation of Philosophy* as one of the great books of all time, for its matter and manner, a mixture of prose and verse. Philosophy does not save Boethius; it reconciles him to his fate. It's a dream, but a dream of truth. The *Consolation* stands behind everything Gower wrote. Behind Boethius, a little hazily, stand the works of Plato and Aristotle. He set out to translate both into Latin, then tried to harmonize their doctrines. The *Consolation* is *applied* philosophy.

Edward Gibbon, who knew the Romans better than they knew themselves, called *De Consolatione Philosophiae* 'a golden volume not unworthy of the leisure of Plato or of Tully'. It was so well-known in the Dark and Middle Ages that eight translations in French survive from before the end of the fifteenth century, one by Jean de Meung, author of Part II of the *Romance of the Rose*.

Gower also drew heavily on *that* poem, which Chaucer in part translated. The French poem conventionalized, sometimes tongue-in-cheek, the ceremonial of courtly love. A large, disorderly masterpiece, it was written by two men of contrasting temperaments. Not a good formal model, perhaps, but Gower, like others, followed it. He includes too much of it in the deliberately encyclopedic *Confessio*: everything he knows, and then some.

Gower's 'Prologue' in general terms passes state, Church and commons in review. From that turbulent, plaguey world we retreat to Book One. *Since I cannot put the world to rights, I speak of love.* As in most courtly love poems, the month is May, the world is young. Amans speaks of his condition. 'For I was further fro my love / Than Earth is fro the heaven above.' He falls asleep, and who can blame him? Many medieval poets fall asleep to evade the phenomenal world and have their vision of truth. It is as though the waking world is a veil which the poet can only penetrate by means of the symbol-structures of dream.

Amans meets Venus, odd for a decidedly Christian poet, but his Venus is a conventional figure rather than a buxom Roman goddess. She summons her priest to hear Amans' confession. No one found it sacrilegious that he made literary play of the sacrament of confession. The poem – paganizing in conceit – is clearly Christian in intent. The deadly sins provide a structure. There is one book for each, explored in its different variations. Finally Venus shows Amans his wizened face in a mirror and he gets the message, the melancholy at the poem's heart: Amans has been virtuous by default. It isn't 'Love cured by Age' or 'Passion at war with Time', as C.S. Lewis has it, but more the Virtues of Amorous Ineptitude: Amans knows *all* about love from reading, but his body is outside the equation. Love is in the pulse of the characters in the tales. But Venus and Passion and Genius are insubstantial figures. This is more a case of Will controlled by 'Resoun', or consoled by 'Resoun'. It is a *cool* poem, whereas Chaucer can be hot, releasing doubtful impulses in the reader. Gower's Amans accepts his fate. At the end of the poem, in the 'Epilogue', Amans is delivered back to the waking world of England and the 1390s. It is a mechanical construction, a moral grid. Chaucer outstrips Gower in terms of larger form.

But Gower never overreached himself. He finished all the big projects he started. He was ambitious but did not presume to know *more* than the huge disorderly amount he knew – about science or history or religion. Or about the people in his stories. This is part of his *English* charm: 'He thoughtè more than he said.' A long poem but always thrifty of language. He likes verbs of action. He is sparing with adjectives and adverbs. He focuses on observable fact, the essence of a moral art. He leaves imagery, decoration, the panoply of adjectives, to others – to Chaucer for example.

If we set Gower's 'Tale of Florent' (**44b**) beside Chaucer's 'The Wife of Bath's Tale' (**48c**) we might expect no contest. Yet if we look closely, we find that there is. The two poets, let loose on the same story, work at distinct paces to different ends. Gower wrote his tale first. Florent is set the task of discovering 'What alle women most desire'. Chaucer tells his version in 407 rhymed pentameter couplets as against Gower's 455 rhymed tetrameters. Chaucer narrates in a more complex way than Gower: his story attaches to its fictional narrator, the Wife of Bath, and reflects *her* character. She weaves Arthurian motifs into her story, giving it colour and *visual* substance, to painterly rather than dramatic effect. For her, Florent's sin against love is rape.

To set the stories justly side by side, we must unplug 'The Wife of Bath's Tale' from *The Canterbury Tales* (**48**). How different the moral Florent whom Gower portrays! He is not a sinner but an epitome of honour tried and tested. Gower spares detail; there is a minimum of gilding. The physical ugliness of the crone Florent must marry to learn the answer to his appointed question and save his honour and his neck Gower does stress, to emphasize Florent's integrity and pluck. His is a drama of motive, conscience and action. The Wife's version, by contrast, is entertainment, and hardly moral. Gower's tale is believable at the level of character, and it is *dramatic*. It reads better aloud than Chaucer's: it is spoken more than written for the reading eye. It is also less re-readable. But there are incomparable moments. When Gower's Florent reluctantly goes to bed with his hideous wife before her transformation, the poet renders his feelings in two lines which touched the Shakespeare of *Henry V.* ' "For now," she sayeth, "We be both one." / And he lay stille as any stone.' Where Chaucer makes individual characters, Gower personifies. His tale tends towards abstraction, which is crucial to the sometimes tediously universal themes the poem explores.

Had Chaucer finished *The Canterbury Tales*, we might have had occasion to call him mechanical and tediously universal, too – though I doubt it. Because his poem is unfinished he will always have an advantage over Gower, who completed what he began. Given the allegorical mode, structure *has* to be mechanical. Allegory has meanings that can't be arbitrary but must cohere at different levels. If 'the Crown' does something, it means the living person of the sovereign, the institution of sovereignty, and what it contains of the divine, within a human order. An image must inevitably contain several meanings. If you are going to write allegory you choose a mechanical structure because figures must connect at many levels. The form is a form of *belief*, unoriginal because belief in a revealed religion cannot be 'original'. So much – one might suppose – for the poetry being in the language. Beyond literal sense, the situation of the dreamer and the entertaining stories he hears, there's a constant didactic purpose with religious dimensions. What qualifies the mechanical feel is the wry melancholy of Amans' voice and the severity of his confessor. Amans has a tone, close to Sir John Gower's we might infer, composed of humility, wry self-deprecation, and charity.

Gower's poem might leave a common Londoner or an English country person cold. It contains little of the living England. It lacks *world*. We acquire instead a universal morality unfolded in tales familiar to readers of Romances and a sufficient, if primitive psychology. The poem entertains and instructs in two ways: teaching 'facts' (which time has turned to fable – tedious 'histories' of religion, royal instruction, astrology) and inculcating 'virtue'. In its themes, even in the play of metaphor, the explosive politics of the day – Richard's vices, his fate, the Peasants' Revolt, anarchism and barbarity – are hardly a murmur beyond the priory wall. This *kind* of poem is insulated against real weather. Gower's Latin poem was more topical, direct, troubled by contemporary issues. But it is in Latin and will never have an audience of readers.

Gower's excellence is evident in discrete parts. Academic critics make a case for the aesthetic wholeness of the *Confessio*. It's an academic, not a poetic case: a pattern can be drawn on the blackboard, but it does not emerge from our experience as we read. Anyone prepared to read the work right through comes away as from a vast anthology: one poet-editor assembled it, but out of such varied materials that the parts exceed the whole. If we focus on passages or stories – 'Deianira and Nessus', 'Constantine and Sylvester', 'Pygmalion', 'Demephon and Phyllis', 'Ceïx and

Alceone', 'Jason and Medea' or a score of others – and on the words of Amans, the link man, whose disappointment is the poem's ostensible occasion, we find the poet there. In the 'Prologue' and 'Epilogue', briefly, we come close to the world he inhabited.

He knew Chaucer well and he survived him. By 1378 their friendship was established. Chaucer left Gower power of attorney in his affairs when he travelled abroad. He may even have encouraged Gower to try his hand at English. As I said, Chaucer dedicated *Troilus and Criseyde* 'to moral Gower'. Gower returned the compliment by dedicating the first recension of the *Confessio* to Richard II and, obliquely, to Chaucer. Later recensions dropped the dedication to Richard and the encomium to Chaucer. Some say the poets fell out, that Gower identified passages in *The Tale of Sir Thopas* as Chaucer poking fun at some of Gower's beliefs.

For three centuries after his death, Gower had champions among poets and critics. Skelton said his 'matter was worth gold', praising the content, especially the moral content. He appears as the moralizing chorus in Shakespeare's *Pericles*, and Shakespeare used his tales in shaping plots. Ben Jonson in his *English Grammar* cites Gower more often than any other writer as a model of correctness. But his hold on readers weakened. Now confined to specialist students of Middle English, he deserves to be given back, not whole but in judicious bits, with modernized orthography, to a new audience. If we read aloud, difficulties of diction and prosody resolve themselves before our ears.

But Gower's poems didn't come to him as naturally – in Keats's phrase – as leaves to a tree. He approached the language tentatively, advancing with the responsible caution of a prose writer. C.S. Lewis calls him 'our first formidable master of the plain style', and unlike the Augustan poets, 'noble rather than urbane'. (Chaucer can be urbane and is only intermittently noble.) Taken in large doses he is – monotonous. 'It dulleth oft a mannes wit / To him that shall it allday read.' He is *easy* in a good sense, much easier to get on with than Spenser or Milton, even when the language is old, because his verse is unpresumingly efficient, his sense of pace well-gauged, his moral clear. The *Confessio* illuminates the temper of his social class and intellectual milieu, just as Langland's *Piers Plowman* illuminates the very world that Gower does not address and excludes the world that Gower's imagination inhabits. To hear and see the age at large, we have to turn to Chaucer. Remember what Venus tells Amans in the poem:

'And greet well Chaucer when ye meet,
As my disciple and my poet:
For in the flowers of his youth
In sundry wise, as he well couth,°   *understands*
Of ditties and of songès glad,

The which he for my sakè made,
The land fulfill'd is overall.'
Whereof to him in special
Above all other I am most hold.°   *beholden*
Forthi now, in his dayès old,
Thou shalt him tellè this message,
That he upon his latter age,
To set an end of all his werk,
As he which is mine ownè clerk,
Do make his testament of love,
As thou hast do thy shrift above,
So that my Court it may record.'

'AND AS I LAY AND LEANED AND LOOKED
IN THE WATERES'

Quoth Perkyn° the Plowman, 'By Saint Peter of Rome,	*Peter*
I have an half acre to erye° by the high way.'	*plough*

from *Piers Plowman*

If I postpone Chaucer a little longer it is because, when he appears, he pushes his contemporaries into the margins. Each deserves attention – Chaucer, a generous man, might have said as much himself. Each is different from him: he may have learned from them, reading them in manuscripts, or hearing their verse recited of an evening, at a feast or with a friend. Perhaps he heard these lines:

'By Christ,' quoth Conscience then, 'I will become a pilgrim,
And walken as wide as all the world lasteth,
To seek Piers the Plowman ...'

Piers Plowman (**43**) was one of the most popular poems of its time. It survives in over forty manuscripts from the fifteenth century.

When popular works with a religious or political edge are no longer topical they fall into neglect. *Piers Plowman* vanished from sight in the late sixteenth century and re-emerged only in the later eighteenth. Thomas Warton helped to restore it to the conscious tradition in the 1770s. It has not lacked readers since. In fact, for every reader of Gower, there are a score of Langland readers. Poetic value is not democratically established, but if a work survives with a readership after six centuries, it must have something to recommend it. And in this case it isn't the poet's life. William Langland – called Long Will because (we are told) he was so tall – is almost anonymous. His name may not even have been William. Warton calls him Robert Longlande, following Robert Crowley who first printed the poem in 1550. His name may not have been Langland. He may have been born about 1331, possibly out of wedlock, in Cleobury Mortimer, Shropshire, or in Shipton-under-Wychwood, Oxfordshire, or in Somerset, Dorset or Devon, where Langland connections exist. He seems to have been claimed by, and to have a claim upon, the whole country. E.K. Chambers constructs a plausible biography, diverging from the Reverend Walter W. Skeat's equally credible hypotheses. Warton makes him a secular priest, fellow of Oriel College, Oxford. But Long Will may have received a clerical education at Malvern Priory, where he was perhaps made a clerk or scholar. This accommodates the Malvern references in the poem. He was certainly a *poeta doctus*, learned if threadbare (of which there is little doubt), and his poem is littered with scholastic digressions and embellishments.

The first (A) text of the poem seems to date from 1362, a rather young man's poem. Shortly afterwards Langland settled in London, in Cornhill, with his wife Kitte and his daughter Calote. In 1376 the second (B) text was begun. It's generally held to be poetically the best. The third (C) text, over-long and over-embellished, was composed between 1392 and 1398. If all three texts are by the same man, the poem was the work of a lifetime. Warton speaks of other poems written in Langland's manner and quotes them; but the similarities are sparse. True, these other poems alliterate and don't rhyme, but they lack the dense particularity of *Piers Plowman* and are translations or retellings of legend. *Piers Plowman* doesn't do much of that. Its method is not adaptable to continuous historical narrative, partly because the line-by-line dynamic, compressed for social observation, dialogue and allegorical concision, won't 'flow' for straight story-telling. In 1399 he probably composed the angry poem, 'Richard the Redeles'. Then he vanishes.

In *Piers* we meet a poet – *the* poet? – *Lange Wille* (George Gascoigne, also tall, was dubbed 'Long George'). If he took minor orders, because he married he failed to ascend in the church hierarchy. He was poor, earning his keep by 'saying prayers for people richer than himself' and copying legal documents. The poem reveals his knowledge of courts, lawyers and legal procedures. A proud man, he is reluctant to defer to lords, ladies and other social superiors unless he feels they merit deference. His 'I' is strong and affirmative – one might say 'modern' in the way of Ezra Pound and Wyndham Lewis – as compared with Gower's and Chaucer's reticences.

In *Piers Plowman* – its full title is *The Vision of William about Piers the Plowman and the Vision of the Same about Do-Well, Do-Better, and Do-Best* – we must picture Long Will striding in threadbare garb through the streets of London (his principal setting), with eyes wide open, conscience stung and amazed by what he sees. Our first reformer poet, he is visionary but not revolutionary. Calmly, using allegory, he exposes corruptions in church, state and society. He wants people to understand the causes of their suffering and put things right, not to throw the hierarchies down. It was – and is now – fashionable to convert Langland into another sort of radical. But he was as troubled as most of his contemporaries were by the Wat Tyler *fracas*, even if he was more in touch with the grievances, having so many of his own. Still, he was a devout Catholic – the sort Wycliffe would have welcomed heartily, though the Archbishop of Canterbury would have refused to shake his hand. He believed in the kingdom – of Heaven, of this world – and that virtue and faith could make a highway between them. The secular king had duties and was not above judgement. People who shared this view – like the anonymous author of 'Piers Plowman's Crede' – were more decidedly Wycliffite than he was. His poem was used in ways he never intended. Such a fate can distort a poem: remember the misuse to which William Blake's 'Jerusalem' has been put.

Piers first appears, well into the poem, as a ploughman, representing the common laity, then metamorphosing into a priest, and finally into a Bishop with St Peter and his papal successors, 'Petrus, id est Christus', upon which rock ... He is exemplary; his developing model of morality inspires love and respect, and indicts those who fail to follow him.

Ford Madox Ford's impression of the poem is partial but illuminating. *Piers* has, he says, 'the air of having been written in a place of public assembly. As if, while [Langland] wrote, individuals came up and whispered into his hooded ear: "Don't forget the poor cooks," or: "Remember the hostelers," or: "Whatever you do, don't forget to expose the scandalous living of the lousy friars." ' No one is forgotten: 'Kokes and her knaves crieden, "hote pyes, hote! / Good goos and grys go we dyne, go we!" '

You can hear such demotic strains in the eighteenth century, in Jonathan Swift and John Gay, each vocation acknowledged in its own voice and idiom. Langland's public tone belongs in the sermon tradition, explaining the unfamiliar through the familiar. Chaucer has tales, Gower has legends, Langland has homilies. It is all a question of audience.

Verse form sets Langland apart from Chaucer and Gower. So does his direct teaching. He draws on the everyday world but writes of types, not characters. For him, more than for Chaucer, social conduct is spiritual. He uses the dream convention to cross into a 'real' world from the partial, semblant secular world; to go less into fantasy – a world of animals, dreams of an old lover, a 'house of fame' – more into truth. This is beautifully symbolized in the 'Prologue' (**43a**) where, by a stream, he first falls asleep:

And as I lay and leaned and looked in the waters,	
I slumbered in a sleeping, it sweyved° so merry,	*sounded*
Then gan° I to meten* a mervellous sweven,‡	*began; dream; dream*
That I was in a wilderness wist° I never where;	*knew*
As I beheld into the east an high to the sun,	
I saw a tower on a toft trielich y-maked;°	*hill excellently made*
A deep dale beneath, a dungeon therein,	
With deep ditches and dark and dreadful of sight	
A fair field full of folk found I there between,	

Of all manner of men, the mean and the rich,
Working and wandering as the world asketh

Allegory is second nature to Langland. Men in the fair field make their way either to the tower of truth or to the dungeon of falsehood. His vision includes social, moral and spiritual worlds. A pull of opposites coordinates his poem: between tower and dungeon, Christ and Anti-Christ, good shepherd and bad. Langland writes in an expansive, digressive tradition. This is the poem's virtue and its vice. It includes *longueurs* – especially in the later versions – as well as arresting detail.

They may not have understood even in a literal sense half the time, but how many of us understand poetry even half of the time? For them there wasn't a separate category called 'the poem', something to stand back from in order to receive an aesthetic *frisson*. *Piers Plowman* was part of their Christian world.

True allegory – Langland's is more true, more antique in feel, than Gower's or Chaucer's – requires intuitive and analytical comprehension from a reader. We don't possess that intuition any longer, and the process of allegorical analysis can be mechanical, its fruits arcane. Unless you are an archaic Roman Catholic, Dante's cosmology is a fiction; Shakespeare's political structures have a varnished, or bloodied, feel, as do Blake's angels with sandals on their heads, Wordsworth's burly pantheism and Yeats's funneling gyres. Allegory was at least a form universally practised and figuratively based, a dependable lens, in an age of strict orthodoxies, through which to read pre-Christian writers like Virgil without getting into trouble. Allegory, the quintessential medieval Christian form, rests on a belief that the Creator can be perceived in each level of his creation, that every created thing signifies in relation to the Creator. The poet witnesses – beyond the particulars of experiences – their significance in a wider scheme, 'rendering imaginable what was before only intelligible'. Gower's allegory works on two main levels, a 'parable sense' – transferring meaning to the present world; and a moral sense, which he will not let us forget. Chaucer's secular allegory works on three levels: a literal, even a *social* level; a 'parable-sense'; and a moral sense, more subtly delivered than in Gower. In Langland there is – as in classic allegory – a fourth level, the anagogical, which opens on a spiritual world of being. A consistent allegorical interpretation of the whole poem on four levels should be possible. For medieval listeners, allegory was a way of seeing. They didn't have to unpack a poem like customs officials. They marvelled at how it delivered multiple meanings. They *felt* them.

Taking the B Text as our poem, *Piers Plowman* has four parts. First we witness the world of human transactions and meet Piers. Debates and trials are enacted involving, among others, Holy Church and Lady Meed, supported by lesser allegorical figures, especially the Seven Deadly Sins. Avarice is especially horrible:

> He was beetlebrowed and babberlipped also,
> With two bleared eye-en as a blind hag;
> And as a leathern purse lolled his chekes,
> Well sydder° than his chin they chiveled for eld;*   *even lower; shivered with age*
> And as a bondman of his bacon his beard was bidraveled.°   *bedraggled*
> With a hood on his head, a lousy hat above,
> And in a tawny tabard of twelve winter age,
> All totorn and baudy° and full of lice creeping ...   *tattered and dirty*

When one says the lines aloud one finds the mouth forced by the consonants into all sorts of shapes, and spittle gathers on the lips. We see Avarice: we see and feel what the words mean. Visual and moral detail are transmitted simultaneously.

The first part of the poem ends with a general decision to make a pilgrimage to St Truth. Piers the Plowman offers to serve as guide, provided the pilgrims first help him to finish harrowing his field. After a few further complications, the poet wakes up. In the second part of the poem he reflects on his vision. Piers returns in the third part, and the poem builds beyond its theological to its spiritual climax, evoking God as man in the Incarnation, Crucifixion and descent into Hell. The final part tells of Christ's triumph over sin and death, and our triumph through Him and his authority vested in Peter (now Piers). The poem resolves not in triumph but in a determination to seek the exalted Piers, after Holy Church has been besieged by Anti-Christ. The *poem* is finished. It has set the reader, or the audience, on a path of truth. The unresolved dialectic can be solved only by individual conscience and effort.

Though he uses a rich vocabulary drawn from every current and archaic source, Langland does not avail himself of the 'improvements' of English. Rather than advance the language, he deliberately makes it *old*, using the unrhymed alliterative verse of a dying tradition – dying, in any event, in the South of England. Is this caprice in a learned man? Having chosen the constraint of strict alliteration, he keeps departing from natural word order. Yet he gives the impression of being often closer to the daily speech of the people and popular priests of his time than Gower is. And unlike Chaucer or Gower he does not write in the first person. Langland creates an every-man for the men and women who warmed to the Miracle and Mystery plays, pageantry and religious festivals. He pursues general moral truth, not psychology, certainly not the 'bourgeois individualism' that begins in Chaucer. He addresses a congregation of like-minded souls, not a single reader, certainly not an assembled court. His poetic constituency is the people at large.

That is why his manner strikes us as perplexing and perplexed, even obscure. Yet his vocabulary is just as riddled with Norman French and 'new words' as Chaucer's. This reveals how wide a currency that vocabulary had, how little Chaucer was the sole inventor of our language. Some suggest that Chaucer knew *Piers Plowman* and used it in the 'Summoner's Tale'. One thing is certain: if he read Langland, he appreciated his comedy. Langland may not display 'wit', but there is knockabout and lively jest, as in the street plays of the day.

Still, his form *is* constricting. Gower wrung a variety of paces and syntactical licences from his couplets. In the accentual alliterative line of Langland, with its varying number of syllables but constant number of stresses, a strong caesura is required around the middle of each line; there is seldom a run-on rhythm or cadence. It is *bunched* poetry, even when used with Langland's freedom: a line of knots, not a smooth thread. This has some advantages, for instance his ability to vary the register abruptly to excellent effect. The verse accommodates numerous voices, from snatches of the cries of street-vendors and exclamations of the poor to the honeyed words of Lady Meed and the eloquence of moral lawyers. He tightens the texture on repeated words, using internal assonance and rhyme to rhetorical effect. Despite its seeming rusticity, this most English of poems is in no sense crude. Like Gower, Langland is a moralist who asks us to attend to his matter, not his manner. He seeks to portray not only the world, but the truth: he is a man speaking not to students and professors but to men.

If we set Gower alongside Langland (Chaucer stands alone, as Shakespeare and Milton do) we can contrast two emerging styles which become the poles of English poetry in time to come: one rigorously formal, restrained, metrical and rhymed, the other answering a cadenced norm. Both imitate speech but sing it in different ways. One is classical, the other Biblical. One is more artificial and constructed, based, initially at least, on alien models; the other more 'native'.

'GO, LITEL BOK'

Roughly speaking, we may say that Chaucer, the first English writer of sustained imaginative pieces, was also the first English writer for the Press – a writer, that is to say, for the individual reader in his closet rather than a composer of lays, ballads, roundels, or even epics, for recitation.

Ford Madox Ford, *The English Novel*

The George Inn in Southwark is photogenic. The neighbourhood is pure history. At a pub in White Hart Yard Jack Cade had his headquarters for the revolt of 1450. It's where Mr Pickwick met Sam Weller a few centuries later. Chaucer's Tabard Inn was in Talbot Yard. All the coaches set off from here for places south and east. The George is how people imagine Chaucer's Tabard, though it arrived on the site four hundred years after the pilgrims set out on their adventure.

Critics attack Coleridge for not finishing major works (Wordsworth, Byron and others were as bad offenders – all those trunks that never develop legs and arms, or heads that stop short at the neck). They forget that of the great poets the most incomplete is Chaucer, author – as the literary historian George Saintsbury put it – of *torsi*. There is unfinished and unfinished, of course. *The House of Fame* is a fragment, but *The Canterbury Tales* is such a huge fragment that we imagine we can infer a whole. Chaucer did finish *Troilus and Criseyde* (**47**), just as Coleridge finished 'The Rime of the Ancient Mariner', not to mention *Biographia Literaria*.

Both men are steeped in literature. But Chaucer is at the start of something. Thus his *envoi* from *Troilus* (**47c**):

Go, little book, go, little mine tragedyè
There God° thy maker yet, ere that he die,   *May God*
So sendè might to make in° some comedyè!   *compose*
But little book, no making thou n'envie,°   *don't envy anyone else's creation*
But subject be to allè poesyè;
And kiss the steps, where as thou seèst pace
Virgil, Ovid, Homer, Lucan, and Stace.°   *Statius*

Modesty, first: 'little book' for the great English epyllion. A habit of self-deprecation, especially evident in *The House of Fame* and *The Canterbury Tales*. After reading even his lesser works we feel we know him. But who is he? Is Ford Madox Ford right to see him as *im*personal, as much so as the great French novelist Flaubert? In these lines Chaucer recognizes that he has produced a work different in genre from any he has written, and from any written before in English: a tragedy. The awful truth of the poem makes him long to write a comedy to follow. He prays for this, and that his book may find a humble place among authors he considers masters. It aspires at most to kiss the steps where they pass. Yet it is doubtful that he read Homer, and who now reads Lucan and Statius?

He prays too that his poem will be properly copied and properly recited.

> And for there is so great diversity
> In English and in writing of our tongue,
> So pray I God that none miswritè thee,
> Ne thee mismetre for default of tongue.

He knows English is an unstable medium, the copying scribes did – they might be young, some days lazy, occasionally careless – fill him with concern. He wrote a poem cautioning his copyist, Adam:

Adam scriveyn,° if ever it thee befall	*scribe*
Boece° or Troilus for to writen newè,	*Chaucer's version of Boethius*
Under thy long locks thou most have the scalle,°	*May you have a scaly scalp*
But° after my making thou write more truè;	*Unless*
So oft a-day I might thy work renewè,	
It to correct and eek° to rub and scrape;*	*also; rub and scrape to erase errors*
And all is through thy negligence and rape.	

Chaucer led an active life. Compared with Gower, who pottered about in his own way at his own pace, Chaucer belonged to the wider world. He was born around 1340 and survived for sixty years. He died as the century turned, in 1400. 'The English Tityrus', 'the well of English undefiled', Edmund Spenser called him; 'O reverend Chaucer, rose of rethoris [rhetoricians] all', was Dunbar's tribute; and Skeleton's:

> Chaucer, that famous clerk
> His termès were not dark,
> But pleasant, easy, and plain;
> No word he wrote in vain.

In one manuscript Thomas Hoccleve leaves a line portrait of him, 'to put other men in remembrance / Of his person'; and this is the basis for our physical image of Chaucer in his maturity: a fine two-pointed beard, wide thin-lipped mouth, long straight nose, eyes of a vivid, calm paleness under half-closed lids. His hair, covered in the picture, was covered in life, but where it showed it was pale brown. In his left hand he tells a string of beads, tasselled at the end: worry beads, perhaps, they are too large for a rosary. With his right hand he points in gentle emphasis. 'By this painturè,' says Hoccleve, we 'may again him find.'

In his poetry Chaucer draws a different figure of himself, a small man, hooded, a little beard, eyes used to gazing to the side – eyes that, says Robert Graves, see what, to right or left, you're up to, while, the face averted, you're unaware that he's observing ... Lydgate celebrates him in his *Life of the Virgin Mary* as one who used to 'ammend and correct the wrong traces of my rude pen'. Kind and generous to his younger contemporaries, he had foreign admirers, too. The historian Froisart praised him as a diplomat. Eustache Deschamps wrote a laudatory ballade to him as a translator. In the mid-sixteenth century Lilius Giraldus, the eminent Italian humanist, recognized his accomplishment.

But a hundred years later Abraham Cowley described Chaucer as 'a dry, old-fashioned wit, not worth reviving'. What is our opinion of Cowley? Dryden acknowledges that Chaucer 'must have been a man of a most wonderful comprehensive nature ... because he has taken into the compass of his *Canterbury Tales*, the various manners and humours of the whole English nation, in his age.' Dryden 'modernized' Chaucer and wrote one of the first great English essays in literary criticism largely about him. He calls him 'the father of English poetry', to be venerated as the Greeks did Homer. He remembers how 'Spenser more than once insinuates, that the soul of Chaucer was transfused into his body; and that he was begotten of him two hundred years after his decease. Milton has acknowledged to me, that Spenser was his original.' Wordsworth, too, 'modernized' Chaucer. Matthew Arnold may miss in him the highest poetic seriousness, but he recognizes the value of 'his large, free, simple, clear yet kindly view of human life', for he 'gained the power to survey the world from a central, a truly human point of view.' Few English poets before the First World War were entirely free of a debt to him, and it is to be hoped that the poets of this century may find their way back to him. His language is easy in its strangenesses, his prosody incomparably lucid and varied, and his world much fuller than our own.

He was born in London, maybe in Thames Street. His father, John Chaucer, was citizen and vintner in London, himself son of Robert le Chaucer who was collector of customs on wine. John Chaucer served Lionel, son of Edward II, later Duke of Clarence. Chaucer's mother, Agnes, outlived John and in 1367 married again. Well placed as the Chaucers were with regard to the court, they remained a merchant family. Despite patronage Geoffrey was never assimilated into courtly life, nor did he – as

Gower did – stand aloof from the world. He was a man of affairs first and a poet after.

Was he educated at St Paul's cathedral school? It is unlikely that he attended university, though he was a member of the Inns of Court. As a young man, some report, he was fined two shillings for beating a Franciscan friar in Fleet Street. In 1357 he received a suit of livery as a member of Lionel's household. In his late teens – it was 1359 – he entered military service, was sent to France and taken prisoner near Rennes or Reims. By March 1360 he was freed on payment of a ransom: the King subscribed £16 to it. Some believe that during his captivity he translated part of *The Romance of the Rose*.

Philippa Chaucer, his wife, was awarded an annuity of 10 marks for life in 1366. She was born Roet, daughter of Sir Payn Roet, a Hainault knight, and sister of the third wife of John of Gaunt. This helps explain, if virtue is not enough, Gaunt's long patronage of the poet and Chaucer's familiarity with Wycliffe whom Gaunt (fatefully) patronized as well.

The King gave Chaucer an annuity of 20 marks in 1367 as *dilectus valettus noster* [our beloved valet] and by the end of 1368 he was an esquire. Six years later he was granted a pitcher of wine per day (commuted to a money gift). He rejoined the army, and in 1370 went abroad on public duty of some kind. He must have been successful because other commissions followed. In 1372 he spent a year away, part of it in Genoa arranging the selection of an English port for the Genoese trade. He went to Florence and perhaps to Padua. Petrarch died in 1374, but it has been suggested that Chaucer was introduced to him in Italy, at the wedding of Violante, daughter of the Duke of Milan, with the Duke of Clarence, and that it is not impossible that Boccaccio was also of the party. It is a tempting but unlikely scenario. Certainly, though, he took their poetry, like Dante's, to heart. Indeed, Italian writing may have helped purge him of his French enthusiasms. In *The Canterbury Tales* the Clerk pays a tribute in his Prologue which, if taken literally, gives substance to the legend of a meeting. It generously records a debt:

I will you tell a talè which that I
Learnèd at Padua of a worthy clerk,
As provèd by his wordès and his work.
He is now dead and nailèd in his chestè,
I prey to God so give his soulè restè!
      Francis Petrarch, the laureat poetè,
Hightè° this clerk, whose rhetoricè sweetè   *was named*
Enlumined al Itail° of poetry...   *Illuminated all Italy*

Back home, Chaucer leased Aldgate gatehouse; he was prospering. Later in the year he was made controller of customs for wools, skins and hides in the Port of London, with an extra £10 pension from John of Gaunt. How did he conduct his duties and manage to write as well? In 1377 he was back on diplomatic business in Flanders and France. He was in France once more when Edward III died and Richard came to the throne in 1378, and then went to Italy, on a mission to Bernabo Visconti.

The controllership of petty customs was added to his duties in 1384, and two years later he sat in Parliament as a knight of the shire of Kent. He lived for a time in Kent where around 1386 he began planning *The Canterbury Tales*. Then the wheel of fortune began to turn: during Gaunt's absence in Spain the Duke of Gloucester rose, Gaunt was eclipsed and Chaucer lost his controllership. In 1387, Philippa died. The next year he assigned his pensions and property to someone else, a sign of financial distress. Then in 1389 the Duke of Gloucester fell, Gaunt was reinstated, and Chaucer became clerk of works to the King for two years. He was also a commissioner responsible for maintaining the banks of the Thames. He was rising again but it was hard. In 1390 he fell among the same thieves twice in a day and was robbed of public money, but excused from repaying it. In that year and the next he held the forestership of North Petherton Park, Somerset, and in 1394 his pension was refreshed: £20 a year from Richard II. But he remained needy. Richard gave him an additional tun of wine a year, and in Richard's wake his third royal patron, Henry IV, added forty marks to the pension Richard had restored. 'Envoy to Scogan' and 'Complaint to his Purse' suggest that Chaucer continued impecunious. Henry gave him a purple robe trimmed with fur, and he felt secure enough to lease a house in the garden of St Mary's, Westminster, close by the palace. He enjoyed it briefly. On 25 October 1400 he died and was buried in the Abbey, in the chapel of St Benedict. Poets' Corner came into being, with Chaucer as cornerstone and first tenant.

Tradition says he lived in Woodstock. Tradition says many things. He is not above re-telling stories of himself, and like all storytellers, he embroiders. His admirers want him to have more of a life than written evidence entitles him to. There is one mysterious incident: in 1380 Cecilia de Chaumpaigne gave him a release *de raptu meo*.[13] It's hard to think of Chaucer as a rapist. This may refer to a more commonplace matter, an attempt to kidnap a ward or minor and marry him or her to someone for money.

Did Chaucer have children? The *Astrolabe* is dedicated to 'little Lewis my son', aged ten when it was written. Philosophical Strode may have tutored 'little Lewis' at Oxford. Cancellor Gascoigne, a generation after Chaucer died, speaks of Thomas Chaucer, rich and well-placed, as Geoffrey's son. This Thomas took the coat of arms of Rouet – his mother's maiden name –

---

[13] Of my abduction or rape.

late in life. In 1381 Gaunt established an Elizabeth Chaucer as a nun at Barking. She may have been the poet's daughter.

Why dwell on such a scatter of fact and hearsay? To show at how many points and in how many ways Chaucer touched his age.

His work divides into three periods, conveniently labelled French, Italian and English, or mature. Before 1373 – he was a 'late starter' and may not have taken up his pen to write English verse until he was almost thirty – he composed the *ABC, The Book of the Duchess* (1369–70), early Ballades and Complaints, his translations of Boethius and about a third of *The Romance of the Rose*. This is the period of French influence, dominated by the octosyllabic couplet.

Young Chaucer was infatuated with the *Romance*, but abandoned the project of translation. Maybe Petrarch's emphatic rejection of it affected him. Petrarch, when Guy de Gonzago sent him a copy, received it as a cold, merely artificial and 'extravagant composition'. Chaucer's version, perhaps only partly by him, runs to 7,700 lines, compared with the more than 24,000 lines of Guillaume de Lorris's and Jean de Meung's composite original. It embodies the lore and literary conventions of courtly romance: dream, allegorical garden, cardboard personification. The latter part of the original includes satire on women, church and the established order. Such satire struck a chord with Chaucer.

The Book of the Duchess (45) shows him almost fully fledged. It is a consolatory romance for John of Gaunt on the death of his first wife, Blanche, and draws on the *Romance*. The octosyllabic couplets foreshadow Gower's fifteen years later; but Chaucer's poem keeps close to a single subject and illustrates a crucial difference between him and Gower. Gower is encyclopedic by design; Chaucer is inclusive by nature. His verse is integrated because the human and poetic context admits more. Allusion and illustration are means, not ends. The moral is implicit in the poem, not appended to it. *The Book of the Duchess* hints at what is to come: a dream frame, a garden, personification, confession, allegory, May morning and the hunt. There is also a debt to Ovid's *Metamorphoses*.

What makes it Chaucerian is the actual-seeming grief and sympathy, acknowledging the impotence of consolation. The sense of grief depends on the creation of two credible human figures, the poet and the mourner.

'She is dead!' 'Nay!' 'Yes, be my trouthè!'
'Is that yourè loss? By God, it ys routhè!'°   *sad, to be rued*

Chaucer alludes abundantly to Blanche, to Lancaster and Richmond (Yorkshire), John of Gaunt's seat. He marries Love Vision and the traditional elements of elegy. This might argue for a later date: such a deliberated and courtly composition would not answer the needs of immediate, unassimilated grief. But if we read the later love visions, it is clear that this must be the earliest, fresh and complete as few of the later poems are. Some readers are unbeguiled and consider it apprentice work. The weakness is allegory and Chaucer's discomfort within its constraints, against which his whole writing life was a struggle.

Did Keats get 'La Belle Dame sans Merci' from it? Lines 448–9 and what precedes and follows, the dense wood, the aloneness, the colour:

> 'Lord,' thought I, 'who may that be?
> What aileth him to sitten here?'

The poem is so well-judged and handled that it is fully expressive: the sleepless narrator, the tale of Ceix and Alcyone, how he at last falls asleep and dreams the hunt, the knight in the forest; his account of the chess game with Dame Fortune, the story of emotional reversals; after the conceits, the knight's confession of his youthful wandering eye, his eventual true love conveyed in physical terms which are a window on the beloved's moral beauty, his courtship, his loss. The interlocutor wakes up. The verse has some of the ruggedness of the accentual tradition but is 'correct' when properly voiced.

> 'But which a visage had she thereto!
> Allas! mine heart is wonder woo
> That I ne can describen it!
> Me lacketh both English and wit
> For to undo it at the fullè . . .'

Then comes the Italian phase, Dante and Boccaccio in the ascendant, when he uses the 'heroic' stanza of seven lines and begins to use heroic couplets. This is a wonderful early maturity. It begins (1372–80) with *The House of Fame*, *Saint Cecilia* (which in the Chaucerian ecology of recycling would become 'The Second Nun's Tale'), the tragedies used for the *Monk's Tale*; *Anelida* and some lyrics. The defining impact of Italian poetry is made clear and then assimilated in the work of the next six years (1380–86), *The Parliament of Fowls*, *Palamon* (later to become *The Knight's Tale*), *Troilus and Criseyde*, with *Boece* (his Boethius) probably a bit before; short poems, Boethian ballades, *The Legend of Good Women*, and some of *The Canterbury Tales*.

Maturity (1386–1400) includes major parts of *The Canterbury Tales*, the prologues, and work where he is 'purely and intensely English'. 'The figures are all British, and bear no suspicious signatures of Classical, Italian, or French imitation.' 'He made England what she was and, having made her, remains forever a part of his own creation.'

The *House of Fame* (**46**) is my favourite torso – unfinished, unfinishable: he bit off more of Dante than he could chew. Pope liked it enough to translate it into his century, but out of vigorous, quick octosyllabics and into stately heroic couplets. Warton didn't like Pope's version: he imitated Chaucer, with elegance of diction and harmonious versification, but he warped the story and changed the character of the poem. In correcting its extravagance he overlooked the fact that extravagance was crucial to this kind of work, that its beauties consisted in embellishments. 'An attempt to unite order and exactness of imagery with a subject formed on principles so professedly romantic and anomalous, is like giving Corinthian pillars to a Gothic palace.' Chaucer's amazing, amusing eagle vanishes altogether from Pope's version.

Chaucer controls the pace, with a new eloquence learned in part from Dante, chunks of whose *Divine Comedy* the poem swallows as it proceeds. A love-vision, it incorporates several love stories, French material, an abridgement of the *Aeneid*,

> I will now singen, if I can,
> The armès, and also the man
> That first came, through his destiny,
> Fugitive of Troy country,
> In Italy, with full much pain
> Unto the strandès of Lavyne.

The tone is comic. There's a hint of autobiography in his boredom with routine, his mundane job, and a vivid portrait of a bookish poet who goes home after work, ignores his neighbours and – as the eagle says –

> '... when thy labour done all is,
> And hast y–made thy reckonings,
> In stead of rest and newè things,
> Thou goest home to thy house anon;
> And, also dumb as any stone,
> Thou sittest at another book
> Till fully dazèd is thy look,
> And liv'st thus as an heremitè,
> Although thine abstinence is lightè.' (**46b**)

He had a big library for his time – perhaps forty books – which he pored over again and again. There is a Breton poem called *Sir Orfeo, Sir Launfal and Lay le Freine*. One of the *Orfeo* manuscripts may have belonged to him. Its dialect is Londonish. It is, with *The Wife of Bath's Tale* and *The Franklin's Tale*, among the most successful lyrical-narrative 'lays' in English. We do not have an inventory of his library, but he knew the Latin literature current in his century, especially Ovid. He had no scholastic instruction in English (though he had it in French, and in Italian perhaps). English was unknown in schools even for the modest purpose of construing, until the next century. He made his own path through the untamed – or uncodified – wilds of his native tongue.

Metrically *The House of Fame* is similar to *The Book of the Duchess* and uses a love vision (deployed again in *The Legend of Good Women*). A technical advance on *The Book of the Duchess*, it is more learned and has been brushed by the Italian wing – Dante, not Boccaccio. In a sense it is our first great comic poem. How *visualized* the fantasy is; as clear and astonishing as a painting by Hieronymous Bosch: the architecture, the 'science' that underpins it, the sense of heat and cold, and the narrator's fear, effort, exhaustion and exaltation. Love is the theme, but Chaucer turns to fame, the fame of lovers. His ostensible motive is to escape the routine of life and visit a place of extraordinary persons, stories and events. Allegorical readers try to attach it to his disappointment at lack of recognition by those patrons he had hoped to attract; others tie it to court events. Is it possibly just simple, lively entertainment?

Unlike the *Tales* it's drawn from books, not from life. The narrator, like Ganymede who was 'made the goddès' bottèler', is plucked up by an eagle and swept off in one of the earliest English dreams of non-spiritual and non-mechanized flight. But he isn't going to Olympus to mix martinis for Jove. This isn't transcendental or mystical in that way; and the eagle keeps 'articulating' as they fly. His first word is 'Awake'!' – a squawky word in 'the samè voice and stevenè / That useth one I couldè nevene' – perhaps Mrs Chaucer. The eagle reassures him, but when the poet opens his eyes he is scared out of his wits. Does Jove want to make him into a star? He is not Enoch or Elijah or Romulus or Ganymede. But Jupiter is rewarding him for his laborious, bookish research into love and for his writing. Jupiter knows his man, a customs officer, a solitary even in the social world. The eagle takes the crabbed functionary to the House of Fame for instruction and distraction. He calls his passenger 'Geffrey', becomes philosophical, explains the natural order, how sound works, and much else. As they ascend, the world dwindles below. Looking up, the poet sees enlarged the Milky Way and the stars.

The Invocation in Book One is to the god of sleep, in Book Two to 'every manner man / That English understondè can' (**46a**). Book Three invokes Apollo, and Chaucer lets the rhyme carry the reader from the Invocation into the dream. In the Invocation he wryly sets himself in the same relation to Apollo as Apollo is to Daphne. Reflecting on the vanity of Fame, he climbs a crystal hill: 'A rock of ice, and not of steel.' The ice image is developed: the words and names are so melted he cannot read them (as gravestones are in old churchyards). On the other side of the hill the names are unmelted: true fame, protected from heat by the shadow of the castle. He cannot describe the castle, it is too beautiful. But he can tell the 'substance' of what it contained, so big, seamless and precious: 'and full eke of windowès, / As flakes fall in greatè snowès.' He evokes the musicians he hears:

> And many flute and lilting horn,
> And pipès made of greenè corn,
> As have these little herdè-grooms,
> That keepèn beasties in the brooms.

This is the poetry that shaped Edmund Spenser's voice in the *Shepherdes Calendar.*

Finally he goes into the House of Fame, having seen more than he can tell, and there he sees still more. Abundance of vision makes it hard for him to finish his work. Inside he finds a huge lady, Fame, enthroned, her head touching the sky, her feet the earth. She is covered with eyes like Virgil's Rumour. He evokes the Apocalypse, but here a secular, or classicized, version: an interesting marriage of Roman and Biblical divinity.

In the poem he does not distinguish between historical, legendary and mythical figures. They are an equal resource for the poet; his audience will expect all three. Josephus, Statius, Virgil, Ovid, Lucan, Claudian, the chroniclers of Troy do the same, and disagree, some favouring Troy, some Greece:

> One said that Homer madè lies,
> Feigning in his poetries,
> And was to Greekès favourable;
> Therefore held he it but fable.

As in Dante, parties of the damned and of the blessed appear, petitioning Good Fame. The Lady is fickle and disappoints. Then comes Aeolus, god of wind, whom she gets to blow bad fame abroad. Images of coprology and farting hover near the surface. The poet witnesses the wronging of right reputation, the unjust whims of Fame, how it is louder the further away it gets from Aeolus's smelly trumpet. A third party of good petitioners arrives and she promises better fame than they deserve. Aeolus blows his golden horn. Again, the poet responds to smell more than sound. The black trumpet is all stink, the gold trumpet's mouth is balm in a basket of roses. Another group asks that their deeds remain unknown. A fifth group asks anonymity, but she refuses since their good deeds, known, will breed good deeds. A sixth group of semi-wastrels gets good fame. The lazy and covetous get the thumbs down. Then come traitors, 'shrews', men who have been utterly bad and courted fame for fame's sake.

Geoffrey gets into conversation. Why is he there – as petitioner? Certainly not, says the poet. He is led out to the Labyrinth, Dedalus's construction. The quaint house spins and is never still: the dizziness of Fame. Lightly built of twigs, with holes to let sound escape, it's an ever restless, sleepless place. The poet sees his eagle perched nearby, asks leave to visit the spinning labyrinth, and the eagle agrees, but points out that he needs a guide – otherwise he won't get in (or out again). The poem stops.

Though the figures are literary, the world imagined is concrete, particular, the voices 'real': it was a short step to put real characters into a world seen rather than visualized. At the end of the poem the rush of people eager to gain a view of the 'man of great authority' is especially clear: they 'troden fast on others' heelès, / And stampen, as men doon after eelès.'

In *The Parliament of Fowls* we meet the mature Chaucer. Another love-vision, it is also a bird and beast fable, pointing towards the 'Nun's Priest's Tale'. Again a gormless poet, who knows not love 'in deed' but only from books, is reading. He dozes, dreams: a supernatural guide conveys him through an allegorical vision. What is the poem's occasion? A Valentine entertainment? No better explanation has been offered. There is more social satire than Chaucer practised before, rising out of a conflict between the 'gentle' and the 'churls', or common birds. The opening lines are among his best-known. The craft he speaks of in the first line is not poetry, but love:

> The life so short, the craft so long to learnè,
> Th' assay so hard, so sharp the conquering,
> The dreadful joy, that always slid so yerne,°   *quickly*
> All this mean I by love

His professed ignorance of love-craft, his desire to learn from books and dreams rather than action in the field of love, add to the humour. The volume he reads before his dream is the apocryphally Ciceronian *Somnium Scipionis*, a classic of dream literature attributed to Scipio Africanus, neglected today but with an importance for medieval writers second only to Boethius's *Consolation*.

> For out of oldè fieldès, as men sayth,
> Com'th all this newè corn from year to yearè,
> And out of oldè bookès, in good faith,
> Com'th all this newè science that men lerè.°   *learn*

Night falls on his reading and 'Bereftè me my book for lack of light' so 'to my bed I gan me for to dressè', depressed because he has what he doesn't want and lacks what he wants. In sleep, Scipio Africanus calls on him. The dream is wish fulfilment: a hunter in dream revisits the wood, a barrister dreams successful cases. Scipio takes him to a garden, and the first inscription over the gate is a reversal of Dante's *Inferno* lettering (the second is bleak, for failed love):

> Through me men gon into that blissful place
> Of heartès hele° and deadly woundès cure;   *whole, healthy*
> Through me men gon unto the well of grace,
> There green and lusty May shall ever endure.
> This is the way to all good aventùre.
> Be glad, thou reader, and thy sorrow off-castè;
> All open am I – pass in, and speed thee fastè!

The poet stands affrighted until Scipio shoves him through, assuring him that as he has no taste for love he is in no peril: he can gather useful subject matter for his writing. He is led into a forest of immortal trees. An idyllic river flows, flowers bloom: the superb description again foreshadows Spenser and early Milton. Each tree and creature is assigned an attribute from a human world: 'The saying fir', 'the drunkè vine', 'the victor palm' and so forth.

Cupid and his daughter Will are sharpening arrows. All the courtly virtues are personified. 'I saw Beauty withouten any atire'. Venus. The Goddess Nature. And here is the hierarchy of birds for mate-choosing, and a quite wonderful catalogue of birds which prefigures Skelton's lists. Nature holds on her hand a loved female formel eagle, the catalyst for the courtship debate. Nature insists that the female has to consent to being chosen. A tersel eagle claims the formel and declares terms and conditions of perfect courtly servitude. Other tersels of lower condition interject and the debate commences.

In *The Parliament* Chaucer *visualizes*. He attributes this power to his reading and stresses the derivative nature of his work: he's a re-teller of tales. But he is no regurgitator. He assimilates and re-tells past knowledge in present terms. Selection and collation are preliminaries to creation. In *The Legend of Good Women* he makes the point the other way round: 'And if that oldè bookès weren awayè, / Yloren [lost] were of remembraunce the keyè.' Translation and creation go hand in hand. He chooses, participates in the text, adapts, prunes and patches it.

Troilus and Criseyde (47) his great *finished* poem, is the outstanding verse narrative in English, the more remarkable for standing so near the threshold of our poetry. Sidney marvelled at it: 'Chaucer, undoubtedly, did excellently in his *Troilus and Criseyde*; of whom, truly, I know not whether to marvel more, either that he in that misty time could see so clearly. Or that we in this clear age go so stumblingly after him. Yet had he great wants, fit to be forgiven in so reverent an antiquity.' It goes with 'The Knight's Tale', his second great narrative, and like it is rooted in Boccaccio. He claims to be translating and asks pardon for aught amiss: 'For as mine auctor saidè, so say I.' This is a way of borrowing authority, the authority of a classic text. But he is not translating: he is adapting. *The Knight's Tale* condenses a huge story, *Troilus* expands a small one in the *Filostrato*. The characters are different from Boccaccio's. Though the structure is allegorical, Chaucer's characters outgrow the figurative and take on dramatic life; he lets them, he makes them real. Warton conjectures from certain images in the poem that it may have been composed on Chaucer's travels: had he composed it at home other metaphors and images would have occurred to him. Or is it based on an Italian original more closely than we suppose?

Chaucer's telling of *Troilus* in five books improves on the plot and characters of Boccaccio and provides philosophical and dramatic coherence and a visualized setting. Saintsbury calls Chaucer a hermit crab, crawling into someone else's shell, this time Boccaccio's, and making it his own, a common medieval practice. The woodenness of Chaucer's allegorical figures softens here into a kind of realism we do not find again in our poetry before Christopher Marlowe (the poet of *Hero and Leander*, not the dramatist of *Tamburlaine* and *Doctor Faustus*). Characters may be representative; they are not stylized.

The poem begins with Calkas treacherously going over to the Greeks. He has read the oracles. He leaves his daughter Criseyde in Troy. Hector forgives her when she begs mercy for herself. It is April, a month fatal for lovers, who repair to the temple for their ceremonies.

> Among these other folk was Criseyda,
> In widow's habit black; but natheless,
> Right as our first letter is now an *A*,
> In beauty first so stood she, makeless.°   *matchless*

Chaucer alludes prettily here to Anne of Bohemia, Richard's queen. Troilus is cruising in the temple and teasing his friends for falling in love. Then he sees Criseyde. He resists but at last allows himself the full rein of love. He sings his love song, then burns for her volubly, but she is ignorant of his love and he takes her non-response for indifference or as an indication that she has another beau.

Pandarus arrives. He courts Troilus's confidence with banter and concern. The language moves into courtly-love gear. He offers to help – how the devil can you help me, says Troilus, you who never prospered in love yourself? (In this Pandarus recalls the narrators of *The House of Fame* and *The Parliament of Fowls*.) Keeping to courtly rules, Troilus resists naming his beloved. Pandarus tells him that if even the elected *she* does not know of his love, she will do nothing but despise him if he dies and she knows no cause; besides, he's making himself unlovable. 'Unknow, unkissed, and lost, that is unsought'. Pandarus evokes Boethius's wheel of fortune. At last Troilus confesses, repents to the God of Love for past cynicism, and Pandarus goes to work. Troilus has the fervent zeal of the convert. His indolence is turned to action, his vices to virtues, he returns to the field of battle and all are delighted to look into his face.

The second book shifts to Criseyde. 'Out of these blackè wavès for to sail, / O wind, O wind, the weather ginneth clearè . . .' (**47a**). April is gone. It is May, mother of happy months. Procne awakes Pandarus with her sad song and he hies to Criseyde's. He finds her listening to a maid reading from the tales of the siege of Thebes (this is one of Chaucer's unsettling anachronisms). Pandarus pricks her curiosity, and women – we know from Pandora – cannot resist temptation. He starts praising Troilus. Criseyde attends. At last she persuades him to come clean and he drops his bomb-shell; if she doesn't respond, Troilus will kill himself and so will he. He weeps. Criseyde hears him out but doesn't immediately respond. He gives advice. She accuses him of letting her down. He starts to kill himself; she slyly humours him. He lies about how he found out Troilus's love. He goes, she repairs to her closet 'And sat her down as still as any stone'. Then Troilus rides below her window, returning from battle.

> Criseyde gan all his cheer° aspien,   *face*
> And let it so soft in her heartè sinkè,
> That to herself she said, 'Who gave me drinkè?'   (**47b**)

Her love is not sudden: she talks herself into it. She is concerned first for her own *estaat* or situation, then for his *heele* or well-being. In sleep she dreams that a bone-white eagle removes her heart. As she sleeps, Chaucer takes us back to Troilus. Pandarus persuades him to write a letter, then convinces Criseyde to reply. They meet and declare fidelity.

It cannot last. Book Four invokes the furies, the end of the affair. The focus of the Proem is on Criseyde. After a day of battle, a truce for the exchange of prisoners is declared. Calkas asks that Criseyde be sent over in exchange for Antenor. Troilus, a courtly lover, cannot name his love. Hector says the Trojans do not sell women and she is no prisoner. The people resist, with perhaps an allusion to 1381 and Jack Straw:

> The noise of people up strite then at once,
> As breme° as blaze of straw yset on fire;   *fiercely*
> For infortune it wouldè, for the nonce,

They shouldèn hirè confùsion desire.
'Hector,' quod they, 'what ghost may you inspire,
This woman thus to shield, and don us lose°   *allow us to lose*
Don Antenor – a wrong way now you choose –'

The political irony is not lost on Chaucer: Antenor later turned traitor. The common will is not to be trusted.

At moments of special tension Chaucer resorts to heavy alliteration:

And as in winter leavès been bereft,
Each after other, till the tree be bare,
So that there n'is but bark and branch yleft,
Lieth Troilus, bereft of each welfare,
Ybounden in the blackè bark of care,
Disposèd wood out of his wit to breyde,°   *disposed to go mad (pun on 'wood')*
So sore him sat the changing° of Criseyde.   *exchanging*

Troilus laments hugely and long. Pandarus comes and bucks him up. First he argues that Troilus has had his love: let her go, seek out another. But Troilus, doggedly faithful, accuses Pandarus of playing racket, 'to and fro, / Nettle in, dock out, now this, now that.' Pandarus urges Troilus to ravish her (with her consent) before she goes. Criseyde meanwhile is raising her own moan, reading her will and testament to the air. Pandarus comes and talks her round.

Pandarus summons Troilus from the temple, lectures him in a Boethian spirit, then takes him to Criseyde. Their meeting is touching:

Sooth is, that when they gonnen first to meetè,
So gan the pain their heartès for to twistè,
That neither of them other mightè greetè
But them in armès took, and after kisstè.

Briefly they are too full of feeling for language. She puts her head on his breast and faints. He thinks her dead and designs to kill himself. He finds his voice and makes another speech, she comes around and cries his name, he is overjoyed and kisses her some more, to this effect: 'For which her ghost, that flickered aye aloftè, / Into her woeful heart again it wentè.' Seeing his drawn sword she chides him for considering suicide. She suggests they go to bed and discuss matters further since day is drawing nigh. And thus in Romeo-and-Juliet haste they make their way to consummation. In bed they plan secret meetings. She has a low opinion of her father and thinks to bribe and corrupt him. She unfolds her plot, and Chaucer comments, as if to absolve her from what comes later:

And truèly, as written well I findè,
That all this thing was said of good intentè;
And that her heartè truè was and kindè
Towards him, and spake right as she meantè,
And that she starf for woe nigh,° when she wentè,   *almost died for woe*
And was in purpose ever to be true . . .

Troilus comes round to her point of view, recovers, gets excited and 'Began for joy th'amorousè dance'. Speech has cleared their hearts as bird-song makes a morning. She swears and swears fidelity with huger and huger oaths. Note: she does not doubt his faith for an instant.

Like the fifth act of a Shakespearean tragedy, the Parcas or Fates wait at the threshold of the final book. Diomede comes to take Criseyde away. He senses Troilus's love. As he leads Criseyde among the Greeks he chats about the Greek world and how she will feel at home there. He takes her to Calkas's tent and declares his new love for her. Back in Troy, Pandarus tries to distract Troilus, but he wants to see his beloved. Criseyde's house is shut up. He remembers, then reverts to grief. 'Men might a book make of it, like a story.'

We return to Criseyde, busy being courted by Diomede and pushed by her father into his arms, until she falls. After a couple of months she has forgotten Troilus. Diomede is virile and eligible. Criseyde is beautiful with only one fault: her eyebrows join. Troilus is more a paragon than Diomede, but he is no longer there. Diomede pleads with Calkas and with her. She gives him hope, and having given him hope, she must in time give the rest. She does so with diminishing reluctance, calculating her need, forgetting her troth. She laments her infidelity, knowing what it is and deliberately turning – she laments, but does not repent. The author can't say how long it took her to turn. His sources are unclear. He suggests the time was brief, but gives her the benefit of the doubt.

Troilus and Pandarus are on the walls, straining their eyes for a sighting of Criseyde. They keep gazing, conversing and japing. Troilus imagines he sees her but it is a distant cart. Night falls. After some days, Troilus is overcome by jealousy. He weakens and everyone, from King Priam down, is concerned. One night he goes to bed and dreams of a wood with a large sleeping boar, in whose arms lies Criseyde, kissing it. Pandarus counsels him to write a letter, which he does eloquently. She replies, her reply not transcribed for us, promising to come in due course. Troilus asks Cassandra to interpret his boar dream which she does, relating it to Tideus who was Diomede's father. Her interpretation is long, its conclusion merciless: 'Weep if thou wilt, or lef! [desist] For, out of doubt, / This Diomede is in, and thou art out.' No one believes Cassandra; that is what she is famous for. Troilus is no exception. He keeps his hope a little longer.

When Hector is slain, Troilus becomes chief warrior. He sneaks out to try to glimpse Criseyde in the night, in vain. Then she writes again, this letter quoted in the poem (47c). At last Troilus understands. Deiphobus in battle has rent from Diomede Criseyde's brooch, which Troilus gave her. He still loves but knows he cannot have or trust her ever again. He refers to her as 'bright Criseyde', an epithet that recurs seventeen times in the poem. He goes to battle and triumphs over all but Diomede.

Chaucer begs pardon from his lady readers. They will find elsewhere, in other sources, that Criseyde proved false. It isn't his story, he is just the teller of an historical tragedy.

He must release Troilus's soul. Slain by Achilles, our hero ascends to heaven and looks down on the little spot of earth, embraced by the sea. Gazing at where he was slain, he despises earth's vanity. He laughs at those who lament his passing. Chaucer urges readers to set their young minds on higher things, to love God and Christ who died and rose. *He* will not betray. Finally Chaucer condemns the pagan world and its rites, its gods, its (and our) appetites. The classical gods are rascals. There is a final, gracious hand-washing in the dedication:

> O moral Gower, this book I direct
> To thee and to thee, philosophical Strode,
> To vauchènsafe, there need is, to correct,
> Of your benignities and zealès good.
> And to that soothfast Christ, that starf on rode,'   *died on the cross*
> With all mine heart of mercy ever I pray...   (47c)

And he prays, he prays with Dante of the *Paradiso*, in a register that changes the key of his whole poem. The prayer rounds up the tone from passion to a kind of transcendence, a change of key which is not so extended as to deflect the impact of the poem but which brings it from the treacherous brink of the erotic and subversive back into the realm of courtly and divine love.

In *Troilus and Criseyde* the plot holds no surprises. The poet tells us the outcome in the opening passages: 'The double sorrow of Troilus', 'From woe to well, and after out of joy', and as early as line 55 we are prepared for Criseyde's bad faith: 'the double sorrows here / Of Troilus in loving of Criseyde, / And how that she forsook him ere he diedè.' It is not the working of plot but the philosophical process of predestination and the motive and development of character we watch. In the fifth book the poet insistently intervenes, to hold our sympathy at bay so that we can judge characters fairly. They have grown too big for the moral clarity he seeks. Criseyde is too beguiling. Yet we do keep a certain distance. Chaucer insists, even as he makes Troy visible, that it is remote in time, a different world altogether.

Facts are foreknown and static. Narrative need not be linear. It can turn back on itself, allow gaps in sequence. Chaucer stops and starts action, accelerates and brakes, lingers when we would have him hurry and hurries when we would have him stay. It is a technique he uses in 'The Knight's Tale' too, leaving Palamon and Arcite 'ankle deep' in blood while he visits another part of the story. Our perspective becomes all-inclusive, as Troilus's does when his 'lightè ghost' escapes his body and ascends to the highest sphere.

There are two time schemes, historical and symbolic. It is April in the first book, May in the second and third; Book Four takes place three years later, in autumn; Book Five passes in a cold season. The strictly poetic chronology provides images and a satisfying cycle, an additional unity. With autumn the tone begins to change.

The philosophical theme is proven by facts in the narrative. Dreams never lie: Troilus's dream of the boar and Criseyde's of the eagle are symbolically true. Pandarus who, like Criseyde's turncoat father, is an astrologer, foresees what is to be and catalyses it. His foreknowledge is great. At one point the poet tells us, 'But God and Pandarus wist all what this meant.' Only the lovers cannot see ahead.

Criseyde, when she falls in love, is natural and passionate, her virtue pragmatic. We learn little of her past except that she has been widowed. Her father's teachery made her presence in Troy precarious. Pandarus advises her to love Troilus in part to protect herself. All these facts tend a little to exculpate her. If she is natural and active once aroused, Troilus the knight and warrior in matters of love proves phlegmatic and philosophical. Just when we expect his heart to break, he launches into Boethian lectures on predestination: 'For all that com'th, com'th by necessity, / Thus to been lorn, it is my destiny.' When he first falls in love his response is not virile and eager but passive and reflective. The word 'think' is associated with Criseyde. Talking (at length) is the prerogative of Troilus. Action characterizes Pandarus. These are, despite particular characterization, their modes of being. To this extent Chaucer's characters are thematic clauses in an argument.

It is the narrator (not 'Chaucer himself') who alters most during the course of the poem. An innocent servant of the servants of Venus – a sort of Pandarus himself – he is overcome by what he has to tell. He tries to draw a positive moral; it defeats him. He interrupts the story to pre-empt our objections. In the end, with tender pity, he lets Criseyde go. He condemns reluctantly – but absolutely: 'Men say'n, – I not, – that she gave him [Diomede] her heartè.' His effort to keep us at a moral distance from the story has snared him in it.

Chaucer makes emotional abstractions accessible to the senses through homely metaphors. When Troilus loves, his heart like a loaf of bread begins to 'spread and rise'. Epic simile behaves this way, likening great with familiar things. Bayard the horse remembers his horsiness after a moment's abandon to feeling; there is the snail, lyming of bird feathers, a snare; 'Now art thou hent, now gnaw thine owèn chain!'; a whetstone, or

> ... but also cold in love towards thee
> Thy lady is, as frost in winter moon,
> And thou foredone, as snow in fire is soon.

Criseyde's memory of Troy: a knotless thread drawn painlessly through her heart. The language is fully transitive. Characters fight, touch, kiss, embrace. Dialogue is credible, even dramatic. Pandarus reports to his niece from the battlefield: 'There n'was but Greekès blood, – and Troilus.' That pause sparks the best hyperbole in the poem.

Chaucer develops an architecture, balancing scene against scene, linking by echo and reiteration passages in different books. This patterning begins in the stanza form. Naturally the pivot of the stanza is in the fourth line, the centre. The language builds to it, then changes tone or direction into the final couplet. The pivot can be the line, a word, or a subject and verb carefully placed. In Book Two, we read Pandarus's subtle exhortation:

> Now, niecè mine, the kingès dearè son,
> The good, wisè, worthy, fresh, and free,
> Which alway for to do well is his wone,°   *custom*
> The noble Troilus, so loveth thee,
> That, but° ye help, it will his banè be.   *unless*
> Lo, here is all! What should I morè say?
> Do what your lest,° to make him live or die.   *you please*

There at the stanza's heart is 'Troilus, so loveth,' preceded by his virtues and followed by his desires.

There is also Chaucer's mastery of the enjambement. One example, Troilus's declaration:

> But from my soul shall Criseydès dart
> Out never mo ...

Is 'dart' a noun? 'Out' comes at the head of the line with the emphasis of a verb. It becomes a preposition only in retrospect. It is 'dart out', no talk of darts but of mingled souls; yet the dart hovers at the edge of metaphor.

Some critics claim *Troilus and Criseyde* as the first English novel. Since Ford sets the poet alongside Flaubert, we might dwell briefly on the *kind* of novelist we have in Chaucer. He 'renders the world as he sees it,' Ford says of Flaubert, 'falsifying no issues and carrying the subject – the Affair – he has selected for rendering, remorselessly out to its logical conclusion.' It is precisely this remorselessness, however sweetly voiced, however resisted, that makes the poem harrowing and true. Specificity of detail roots it in a world which, while not our own, becomes our own: an amalgam of a Troy filtered through Roman eyes, medieval London, and what our own imaginations bring to bear.

After *Troilus and Criseyde*, Chaucer's next production, *The Legend of Good Women* (c. 1385) is minor: a penance exacted by the God of Love for his defamation of woman in *Troilus and Criseyde*. He must write of 'Cupid's saints'. Another love vision (all the love visions have the word 'of' in the title, emblematizing possession), it is most original and interesting in the Prologue, where the daisy undergoes her memorable metamorphosis into that most faithful of Trojan women, Alceste. The poet worships the daisy on the first of May. The Prologue is a sort of Palinode, a poem of celebration. Here Chaucer uses for the first time the rhymed decasyllabic couplets which become heroic couplets. The poem has a secure place in the history of English prosody.

Apart from minor and miscellaneous works, his last great poem, largely from his mature period, is *The Canterbury Tales* (**48**). As Dryden comments in his Preface to *Fables Ancient and Modern*: 'Here is God's plenty!' Dryden 'modernized' some of *The Canterbury Tales*. 'All the pilgrims in *The Canterbury Tales*, their humours, their features, and the very dress, [I see] as distinctly as if I'd supped with them at the Tabard in Southwark.' The breadth of Chaucer's direct knowledge and observation is formidable. 'He is a perpetual fountain of good sense; learned in all sciences; and therefore speaks properly on all subjects. As he knew what to say, so he knows also when to leave off; a continence which is practised by few writers.' In particular, few medieval writers. The accuracy of detail impressed Dryden. 'Chaucer followed nature everywhere; but was never so bold to go beyond her.' In their scope the *Tales* reveal 'a most wonderful comprehensive nature', learning and social vision, despite what the Roman Catholic Dryden sees as Wycliffite blemishes in his thought – evident especially in 'The Parson's Tale', though certainly not stridently so.

The Canterbury Tales is an anthology of stories of many kinds set in the framework of a pilgrimage, the medieval equivalent of a vacation, with spiritual overtones. The tales are told by individuals, the first such *characters* in English literature, passing the time on their journey from Southwark to the tomb of St Thomas à Beckett at Canterbury. Our first interest is in the pilgrims, introduced one by one in the Prologue (**48a**), Chaucer's most original verse, evoking season, place and motive for the gathering, then the pilgrims themselves, in order of social eminence: a knight at the top, a ploughman at the bottom, and in between representatives of the Church in its various manifestations, also a shipman, a cook, a franklin, a widow, and so on. The host of the Tabard Inn becomes master of ceremonies and accompanies them on the journey.

The sequence of tales was to include four by each pilgrim, but exists only in extended fragments. Rivalries and friendships are suggested; surrounding the drama of each tale is the drama of the storytellers revealed in their prologues. A tale can provide a window on their enthusiasms and hostilities. Friar and Summoner expose one another in their true colours. By savagely criticizing the Church from the mouths of members of its corrupt and privileged classes, Chaucer 'made it true' and wryly distanced himself from controversy. 'The Knight's Tale' is obliquely answered by the Miller's coarse, delightful tale (**48b**), which in turn gives offence to the Reeve and provokes from him a further low tale.

'The Knight's Tale' introduces the dominant themes: love, marriage, justice, predestination, the wheel of fortune – a courtly, civic and philosophical opening of a pilgrimage that finishes – though since the *Tales* are incomplete does not *conclude* – with the tedious theological didacticism of 'The Parson's Tale'. Chaucer finally recants all but his moral works: the translation of Boethius, the legends of saints, homilies, moralities and devotions. Between Knight's and Parson's stretch the other tales, twenty-four in all, not all complete even in themselves.

Chaucer's women are among his best creations. Criseyde, his completest and most complex woman, is a triumph. In the *Tales* we meet others. The Prioress faints at the sight of blood, mothers her puppies and swoons if one dies (**48a**). She combines courtliness with an easy religious vocation: *amor vincit omnia* is her motto. She suffers a frustrated desire to be a mother. Hence her dogs and her tale about the murder of a child. Chaucer makes her physically and psychologically present. Her hypocrisies charm, but they remain hypocrisies.

'The Wife of Bath's Prologue' and her 'Tale' (**48c**) express rather than reflect her character. Her syntax, her face, her *couture*, her stars, her past, all particularize her. Her dress is out of fashion: it is the fashion of her youth, her better years. She introduces her five husbands. Her vitality makes us overlook her numerous peccadilloes. Opposite and hostile to her is the repugnant Pardoner; she, the insatiable, throbbing but sterile woman faces in him the bitterly impotent man.

Chaucer is the father of English poetry for two reasons. The first is technical: adapting continental forms he evolves a relaxed and distinctly English style; he enriches the poetic vocabulary; and he introduces through translation and adaptation the great Latin, French and Italian poets into English *poetry*. The second reason relates to the first. In his powerful and original style Chaucer provides a formal and a thematic model. He brings *England* into the new English poetry. Langland portrays London, but his is a moralized, allegorical metropolis, in the spirit of didactic documentary. Chaucer introduces the diversity of English character and language, of English society at large. He has themes, not polemics or moral programmes. His eyes are mild and unclouded. Gower writes from books. Chaucer started writing from books, but the world takes over his verse.

Of the poems doubtfully attributed to Chaucer, one, 'Merciless Beauty', a triple roundel, touched Ezra Pound to the quick:

> Your eyen two will slay me suddenly;
> I may the beauty of them not sustain,
> So woundeth it throughout my hearte keen. (49)

Doubtful attribution in the centuries after his death meant that almost any unattributed poem of merit (and some that were attributed) were put on Chaucer's account, as it were, and his œuvre grew and grew until Thomas Tyrwhitt (1730–86), Chaucer's first great editor in the eighteenth century, stripped the body of work down to what could decisively be identified, from internal evidence, as the poet's own work. In 1775 he published an edition of *The Canterbury Tales* with prefatory matter and a glossary. Not a theorist, just a learned scholar of classical and medieval literature who had enjoyed legal training and possessed an impeccable ear, Tyrwhitt first realised that Chaucer's metrics depended on the voicing of the 'feminine "e"'. This 'discovery' re-opened the ear to fourteenth- and fifteenth-century prosody. Indeed, it even affects how we can read Thomas Wyatt in the sixteenth. Tyrwhitt is one of those rare scholar-critics who merit an honoured place in Poets' Corner, along with all the great printers and publishers.

SING CUCCU!

And forth they goed together, twain and twain
That to behold, it was a worthy sight...

from *The Flower and the Leaf*, possibly written by
a Lady, in the manner of Geoffrey Chaucer

Anon is a poet without dates, parents or gender. Anon appears in the fourteenth and in the twentieth centuries, in Britain and Australia and Africa, always with a song in the heart. Often the song is sad, as though something important – perhaps the author's identity – has been lost. 'Reverdie' is Anon's, subtitled 'Rondel'. Two lines precede it:

Sing cuccu nu! Sing cuccu!
Sing cuccu! Sing cuccu nu!

'Rondel' means round in form, the poem circles back on itself with a refrain, like a cuckoo's woodland repetitions. The poem feels like a fragment of a longer piece:

Sumer is icumen in,
    Lhudè sing cuccu;
Groweth sed and bloweth med
    And springth the wodè nu.
        Sing cuccu!
Awè bleteth after lomb,
    Lhouth after calvè cu;
Bulluc sterteth, buckè verteth;
    Murie sing cuccu.
        Cuccu, cuccu,
    Wel singès thu, cuccu,
    Ne swik thu naver nu.

That is all there is, recorded in a Reading Abbey manuscript dating from around 1275, which includes musical notation so that it could be performed as a canon in four parts, with two voices. The language is not hard if you listen and imagine the voices alternating lines: Summer is coming in, the cuckoo sings loudly. The seed grows, the meed blows and the wood springs anew. Sing, cuckoo. The ewe bleats after the lamb, the cow lows after the calf, the bullock leaps, the buck – verteth? Has it something to do with green, the 'vert' that the French brought with them? Or is the 'v' pronounced 'f' as in German, and is the buck making another sort of sound? sing merrily cuckoo, cuckoo, cuckoo, you sing well cuckoo; then the sting of the poem, that word 'swik' which means cease or give up – *never stop singing.*

It celebrates, like the opening of *The Canterbury Tales*, a change for the better; knowing – a rondel – that spring gives way to summer, autumn to winter. It asks – it prays, with Franciscan candour – to the cuckoo, spirit of the wood, that this new beginning remain new, that the cuckoo never cease its song. Modernized, the poem evaporates, but the original, with strange accent and vocabulary, is necessary, full of feeling. It is small, whole (even if only a fragment) and complex. This ancient piece moves us in the way that a good song does. After the immense allegories of Gower and Langland and the hectic world of Chaucer, this strikes us with the freshness of nursery rhyme and goes straight into memory. It is artful, not artificial. It is not trying to be anything but itself. Who wrote it? Perhaps some scribe, or a monk, or a casual reader who jotted or copied it down in a margin, where it survives, as an annotation. Was Anon a man or woman? Our instinct is to call the medieval Anon 'him', but perhaps the name is forgotten because Anon was a woman, and the society of known poets was virtually all male at the time. If women sang their own songs, as they worked, as they watched over their children, they would have sung in English: we need only remember that Rolle wrote in English because the women he wrote for, even though they lived in a religious community, were not educated to speak Latin.

How many poems of the virtue of 'Sumer is icumen in' got lost because people did not value their own language? Welsh, Scots Gaelic and Irish, Cornish and Manx – all the little languages on which English played the colonial trick – no doubt possessed such verse. Some survives, though the language of power prevails. A surviving poem from Ireland, not written in Irish, is nevertheless in love with its land and its saints:

> Icam of Irlaunde,
> Ant of the holy londe
>   Of Irlande.
> Gode sire, pray ich the,
> For of saynte charitè,
> Come ant daunce wyt me
>   In Irlaunde.

Behind strange spellings, the English language is thinly veiled: I am of Ireland, and of the holy land of Ireland. Good sir, I pray you, for the sake of holy charity, come and dance with me, in Ireland. Said like that it flows away like sand through the fingers: what holds it, all that *can* hold it, is its original sounds, which are inseparable not from the sense but from the experience of that sense.

Here is another poem by Anon. What does it *do* to us, with four little lines?

> Western wind, when will thou blow,
>   The small rain down can rain?
> Christ, if my love were in my arms
>   And I in my bed again!

A copyist can standardize spelling, as I have done: the poem does not depend on quaintness. It strikes us as more 'modern', despite a folk feeling, than the poems that have come before. It is not about our experience. It is about open space, longing and love, with an oath that is at once a prayer.

Anon is the greatest of the neglected English poets (19–40). We know much of him or her by heart, in hymns, in bawdy songs, and in early poems, lullabies and carols such as 'Lullay, lullay', 'Adam lay ybunden', 'I sing of a maiden that is makeless', 'There n'is no rose of swych virtue', 'There was a friar of order gray'. More of Anon's lyrics will be found in years to come, each bringing us close, as any good lyric must do, to the unchanging heart of the matter.

ENTR'ACTE

Why does vernacular poetry falter in the fifteenth century? The Renaissance, which it ushers in, is soon mired in classical humanism. Petrarch, the embodiment of this new spirit, urges the use of Latin in preference to the coarse vernacular; languages just gathering confidence were rolled back before the universal claims of Latin. Even champions of vernacular reneged. They incorporated their experience into that of classic writers, remote from the street-cries, lullabies, ballads and working songs of the oral tradition, and remote too from the new literature of the previous century.

Absolute requisites of Renaissance humanism were authority and precedent, elements which resided in the almost sacred authoritative text. It was the heyday of the editorial scholar, not the editor. When vernacular literature crept out again, it found readers in the market for masters, canonical classics and those who imitated them so well that they sounded like them. Anon has no place at the high table; writers like Langland are beneath contempt. The classics are found among the Italians, or at home – apologetically – in Chaucer and Gower. Later they emerge proudly in Sidney, Spenser, and pre-eminently in Milton. Shakespeare is a bit too near the ground to be regarded as classical. He is too profuse and varied to be a fountainhead, and generally, too anarchic. He broke most of the rules of dramatic (and poetic) form. He extended syntax and muddied diction in preposterous ways, and the plays are suspect because he never saw them through the press. Few writers in the fifteenth century dared to ask: what is a natural language? Is it what we daily speak, what we write in and pray in, or is it an old-newfangled Roman idiom with cold purities and a marbly outline? We have learned to forget the English Latin poets, even the good ones. We forget most of the English poets who wrote in French – and the French forget them too.

An exception is Wace, born in Jersey in the twelfth century, His *Le Roman de Vrut* was a sort of translation of Geoffrey of Monmouth's Latin *History of the Kings of Britain*. Wace finished it in 1155 and presented to Eleanor of Acquitaine, Henry II's queen. Also in the twelfth century there's Thomas d'Angleterre, who must have been English – his *Tristram* survives in bits and pieces. But who reads Wace? Who reads d'Angleterre? We also forget (or *almost* do) the French poets who wrote in English. Charles of Orleans (1394–1464/5) (**50–54**) is usually left out of account. Aristocratic, with an easy directness, he deserves attention. He is like a Tudor poet born a century too early.

Few Frenchmen (indeed, few Englishmen) mastered English as well as he did in the shadows of an English court where he was held prisoner for years, just as earlier Chaucer (more briefly, and with a far modester ransom on his head) was imprisoned in France. Detention was an important part of education. A grandson of Charles V of France, Charles of Orleans fathered a son by his third wife Marie of Clèves who was to become King Louis XII. His cousin Isabel was married off to King Richard II of England at the age of seven and was kept in custody after the King was killed because his successors did not wish to repay her dowry. She married Charles when he was twelve, and was so distressed to lose the title of Queen of England that she wept throughout the ceremony. Charles's cousin Catherine became the wife of Henry V and a character in Shakespeare's play. Charles was himself a possible heir to the French crown.

His pedigree is full and complex and would have fascinated a man like Proust. Born in Paris in 1394, he was the eldest son of mad King Charles VI's only brother. At thirteen he became head of his house and faction, when his father was murdered with the collusion of the Duke of Burgundy. His earliest mission was to avenge his father. His first wife died in childbirth, leaving a daughter. He married Bonne d'Armagnac, who was twelve, and continued pursuing his family enemies. He signed a marriage contract between his daughter, then nine months old, and the six-year-old Duke of Alençon, who later fought beside Joan of Arc. Defeated, excommunicated for political reasons, he struggled back to grace and was restored in 1412 (he was eighteen), his father's reputation cleared, and the Duke of Burgundy discredited. Then, at Agincourt, the English found him under a heap of dead Frenchmen. They took him and held him for ransom. In Canterbury he was paraded through the streets and endured a Cathedral service of thanksgiving for his defeat. His brother was also a hostage. They were held in various prisons: the Tower, where James I of Scotland was also interned; Pontefract, where Richard II was murdered; Fotheringay; Ampthill; Windsor. The ransom was too much for his estates, which had been beggared by war. The Clarences and Somersets were greedy. Prisoners were chattels to be sold, milked and bequeathed in wills.

His brother had *The Canterbury Tales* copied out and the brothers read it to one another, getting to know the characters and the language. They read Boethius, a consolation in the circumstances, and composed prayers. Henry V recommended in his will that they should not be released until Henry VI – who inherited the thrones of England and France when he was nine months old – should come of age. Charles was eventually freed in 1440, at the age of forty-six. He married Marie of Clèves – then fourteen – and worked for peace between England, France and the factions, retiring to Blois after a few more bloody noses. There he gave himself up to the arts, including literary gatherings and the competitions between poets which he sponsored.

'Ther nys leef nor flowre that doth endewre / But a sesoun as sowne doth in a belle.' Sometimes he translated his own French poems, allegories and amorous pieces, but half his poems in English were composed in the language of his captors and a few of the French poems are translated from English originals. It is hard to tell whether a poem is English first or French. Writers in other centuries have done this – for example, James Joyce and Samuel Beckett in the twentieth.

Some said he could not have done the English poems: no Frenchman could have. But where versions of a poem exist in both French and English we see the differences, because in making English poems he was making *poems*, not committing translations: they survive in his own handwriting. His detractors ignore the quality of his versions, and of the originals which occasioned them: English is closed to foreigners, even foreign prisoners held for twenty-five years. This linguistic hubris reflects a common fear of the alien, though the English had no difficulty in believing that their poets could write in French (or Latin) according to their degrees of skill. Like Gower, Charles wrote religious poems in Latin as well as French and English. His manuscript book – he was a royal scribe, as it were, doing his own dirty work[14] – shows how, as he learned the language, he found his (metrical) feet. There is a rondel he composed, remembering – ('When I am hushed it marvel is to me / To hear my heart, how that he talketh soft') – a beloved.

> The smiling mouth and laughing eyen gray
> The brestès round and long small armes twain
> The handès smooth the sidès straight & plain
> Your feetès light what should I further say
> It is my craft when ye are far away
> To muse thereon in stinting of my pain
>   The smiling
>   The breastès
> So would I pray you if I durst or may
> The sight to see as I have seen

---

[14] The key manuscript of his poems is his private copy, now held in the Bibliothèque Nationale in Paris where it is called (as though it, too, is prisoner) MS. fr. 25458.

Forwhy that craft me is most fain°   *desirable*
And will been to the hour in which I die
    The smiling
    The breastès

We can take the repeated phrases as a reprise rather than a refrain. They linger, with sadness and desire. Thomas Wyatt a century later may conceivably have known his verse: he seems to remember him, as he manifestly remembers Gower and Chaucer.

A chief person in his poems is Heart, now clad in black, now in a dungeon, occasionally thrilled by the Lady's beauty, then cast down again by her *hauteur*. Heart has moods, Heart speaks, counts money and tears, counsels, despairs of counselling, complains, hopes, celebrates. He's part of the allegory of love and, in the end, of faith. *Charles* isn't Heart; the poems are not anecdotal confessions. The ladies, like Dame Philosophy in Boethius, are representative rather than specific figures. They are not one of his three wives, the Queen or any lady of the English court. The poems do not arise from a passing carnal passion. Charles wrote lyric poems of subtlety a century before the Tudor poets got going, in the tedious age of those interminable, yawning poems by Hoccleve and Lydgate.

What of Thomas Hoccleve? Was he so *very* bad? Warton says he is 'the first poet that occurs in the reign of Henry the Fifth'. His verdict is peremptory: 'Occleve is a feeble writer, considered as a poet ...' Considered as a man, he is little better. But he took into a new century and reign improvements of language that Chaucer and Gower effected. Hoccleve is the first – there is hardly another until Wyatt and then George Gascoigne – to speak in his poems not only *as* himself but *of* himself. His candour is excessive: he lays himself open without a sense of irony, the ur-Confessional. His version of Gower's Amans is not a papery fiction but a man in need of psychiatric attention. Even so, his poetry is deficient in 'world', in the coloured, scented, sounding particulars that confront and affront him.

Hoccleve was born around 1368 and vanishes from view around 1426. He may have come from Bedfordshire. For years he worked as a clerk in the office of the Lord Privy Seal but seems not to have distinguished himself. He had a modest pension, was always poor and sometimes loopy. If he indulged in dissipation, he did it in taverns and without much style. In 1409 his pension increased to £13.6s.8d a year. (All we know for sure about our early poets has to do with money: what they got paid. Even now, when poets get together, money is what they tend to talk about.) Around 1411 he married. Five years later he was quite mad. In 1424 he got a benefice (or a *corrody* or charge on a monastery).

Hoccleve is the first large-scale poet for whom we have several manuscripts in his own hand. They reveal the writerly habits of the day. He also left autobiographical lines which, Saintsbury says, 'make him (in a very weak and washed out way, it is true) a sort of English and crimeless Villon, to the actual picture of his times that we have in *London Lickpenny*.' Saintsbury refers to *Le Male Règle*, in which the poet petitions for his salary to be paid and unfolds a mildly vicious nature.

The state of his texts is unstable: many manuscripts remain unprinted. His most important piece is a version of Aegidius's *De Regimene Principium* which he calls the *Regement of Princes* (**58**) and addresses to Henry, Prince of Wales. It runs to 5,500 lines. Much is commonplace but the first 2000 lines, a dialogue between the poet and a beggar, are interesting, as are the sections of autobiography, and the address to Chaucer. In the Prologue (not printed at the time) he apostrophizes the patron of his muse:

> O master dear, and father reverent,
> My master Chaucer, flower of eloquence,
> Mirror of fructuous entendement,°   *fruitful understanding*
> O universal father in science,°   *knowledge*
> Alas that thou thine excellent prudence
> In thy bed mortal mightest not bequeathe ...

These lines, written just after Chaucer died, were worked back into the Prologue. His poems recycle material from different periods without embarrassment.

After the *Regement* in importance are the verse stories from *Gesta Romanorum*: 'The Emperor Jereslaus's Wife' and 'Jonathas', *La Male Règle* with its confessions, and the 'Complaint' and 'Dialogue' (largely autobiographical), 'and a really fine *Ars Sciendi Mori*' (**57**) says Saintsbury which one critic describes as (uncharacteristically) 'manly'. Somehow he attracted a great patron of the age, Duke Humphrey, who in about 1440 gave to the University of Oxford one of the finest libraries of the day – six hundred volumes. 'They were the most splendid and costly copies that could be procured,' says Warton, 'finely written on vellum, and elegantly embellished with miniatures and illuminations.' Most of the books were removed as 'popish' under Edward VI and destroyed or scattered. Duke Humphrey was also Lydgate's patron and a friend of European scholars and writers in the arts and sciences.

Hoccleve was an unpalatable man of the world. John Lydgate, being a myopic monk – he was among the first English poets to wear spectacles – had acres of time after prayers and was turned into a verse machine by his superiors, churning the stuff out by the yard. In 1800 Warton's redoubtable and rather mad foe, the literary antiquary Joseph Ritson, described him as a 'prosaick and driveling monk'. Thomas Gray and Samuel Taylor Coleridge valued him highly. The bulk of his work is huge, yet little is known of his life: not much of it is invested in the verse. There must be more than 140,000 lines. Longer than Wordsworth. Longer than Milton. Longer than Milton and Wordsworth put together. There is occasional humour. But Lydgate is not consistently funny as Chaucer can be. He has little control of tone and veers towards prosodic incompetence and prolixity. Saintsbury sees his vice as an over-emphatic caesura with discord at both ends of the line: 'even in rime royal, his lines wander from seven to fourteen syllables'.

Born around 1370, Lydgate died in 1450 or thereabouts. He reached his highest eminence under Henry VI, around 1430. He'd become a monk at the big Benedictine abbey of St Edmund's Bury in Suffolk at a young age, after being educated at Oxford and on the Continent, from where he returned a master of the languages and literatures of both France and Italy. So proficient was he that he opened a school in his monastery to teach sons of noble houses the elegancies of composition. This might stand as one of the earliest writing schools and, like later versions, was presided over by a copious lesser talent. Like Gower, Lydgate set himself apart: his acquisitions were those of study, not derived from the world of affairs. His *Miracles of St Edmund* and other huge devotional poems emerged from his cloister.

Robert Graves tells how he 'was forced (apparently against his will) to become a sort of scholarly *Versificator Regis*. The rules of his Order compelled every monk to unthinking obedience; so Henry V commissioned Lydgate, through his superior, to translate Giovanni delle Colonne's 30,000-line *Historia Trojana*, which took eight years; then the Earl of Warwick called him to Paris in 1426 to turn into English a French poetical pedigree proving Henry VI to be the rightful King of France. In the same year the Earl of Salisbury set him another translation task: the 20,000 line *Pélérinage de la Vie Humaine* – an allegory. Next, the Duke of Gloucester commanded him to translate Boccaccio's 36,000-line *De Casibus Illustrium Virorum* (*Fall of Princes*), an even more formidable commission.'

Graves quotes these lines:

> Thus my self remembering on this book
> It to translate how I had undertake,
> Full pale of cheer,° astonished in my look,   *face*
> Mine hand gan tremble, my pen I feltè quake.
>
> I stood checkmate for feare when I gan see
> In my way how little I had run.

His horror at the size of the task does not translate into self-pity, as Hoccleve's would have done. He chooses metaphor, expressing himself in the language of chess.

Lydgate is mired in his age, if not in the age before, yet he points forward.

His *Fall of Princes* (**63**), *Siege of Troy* and *Destruction of Troy* (**62**) can be read not entirely without pleasure. The *Fall* is a 'set of tragedies', a prototype for the *Mirrour for Magistrates* that so entertained and instructed the sixteenth century. Characters appear before the interlocutor Bochas and report on their downfalls. The best copy of the poem has a portrait of Lydgate. When Adam arrives he greets his interlocutor as 'Cosyn Bochas'.

Lydgate's *Story of Thebes* pretends to be an additional *Canterbury Tale*. The narrator arrives in Canterbury, chances on the Pilgrims, goes back to their inn, is welcomed by the Host who comments on his threadbare outfit, and the next day, on the return from Canterbury, Monk Lydgate is enjoined to tell his enormous tale, interrupted by a steep descent near Broughton.

Warton finds some delight in *The Life of Our Lady* (**60**), and Saintsbury says the best way in to this most copious poet is via *The Complaint of the Black Knight*, with its sub-Chaucerian opening, its dogged development and ultimately firm melody. Thomas Gray and Coleridge valued him, and he is worth a patient attempt. Shortly after his death William Dunbar pays tribute to Chaucer, Gower and Lydgate in 'The Golden Terge', as though they could justly inhabit a stanza together:

> Your angel mouthès most mellifluate
> Our rudè language has clear illuminate,
> And fair o'ergilt our speech, that imperfite°   *unperfected or imperfect*
> Stood, ere your golden pennès shaped° to write: *prepared*
> This isle before was bare and desolate
> Of rhetoric or lusty fresh endyte.°   *writing*

Lydgate is one of the first English writers 'whose style is clothed with that perspicuity, in which the English phraseology appears at this day to an English reader'. And what a range of forms, themes and tones he displays! It is his prolixity that makes him a problem for modern readers. Excerpted, he shines, and Warton finds lines of miraculous compression and originality. From *The Life of Our Lady* he singles out a passage in which Lydgate argues the virgin birth against unbelievers. His argument is clinched in metaphor:

> For he that doth the tender branches springè,
> And the fresh flow'res in the greatè meed,
> That were in winter dead and eke droopingè,
> Of balmè all y-void and lustyhood;
> May he not make his grain to grow and seed,
> Within her breast, that was both maid and wife,
> Whereof is made the soothfast bread of life?

The grain is transformed into bread *within the virgin*, a breathtaking consistency of metaphor that works allegorically at every level, emerging in incarnation and the transubstantiated Host. Conceit gathers force and finally bursts to the surface in a literal meaning.

Warton isolates other instances of Lydgate's talent for particularity, more lyrical and generally less metaphysical in character, such as: 'Like as the dew descendeth on the rose / With silver drops . . .' and

> When he of purple did his banner spread
> On Calvary abroad upon the rood,
> To save mankind . . .

Lydgate is easy to read, easier than Chaucer, but his language is less precise, less thrifty. He's easy but too smooth. He soon bores even the scholar. Moments of reward, which in Chaucer occur in almost every line, are not frequent here. Language is in excess of its occasion. He is a rhetorician in both the good and bad senses: he is absolute master of the figures of rhetoric, but he also spins ideas out too far, in a very thin thread, or in no thread at all. Like any writer with a sure control of the surface, his peril is that he can lose the underlying structure in mere abundance of words. His verse will accommodate anything, and the result is prosaic – in terms of both structure and movement. Yet he was popular for a couple of centuries. Henry VIII got Pynson to print *The History Siege and Destruction of Troye* in 1513. Another, more correct, edition was printed in 1555 by Thomas Marshe.

When Chaucer and Gower and Langland were about, it seemed that English poetry had a centre that would hold and grow stronger as the language cohered and poetic skills evolved. But in the powerful South the fifteenth century belonged to fat language and prolixity. The growth of pedantic humanism in Europe and in England, the hunger for authority and legitimacy which drove poets and scholars back on the classics, made English appear as unserviceable as it had when the Normans set out to suppress it. Hoccleve wasn't substantial enough to rebut the humanists by example, and Lydgate was the equivalent to a modern journalist, churning out matter for a market – in his case a court wanting history and verse delivered in assimilable form. And Henry V was not enthusiastic about panegyrics, or about English poetry. Patronage for him was more a custom than a choice; in the troubled times of his successors it was a custom often honoured in the breach.

At about this time, however, a new talent *almost* emerged, that of the first named English woman verse-writer, Juliana Berners, who was born around 1388. She contributed (it is believed) 'advice literature' to *The Book of St Albans* (1486). Her succinct and unabashed definitions of hunting terminology and her advice to hunters may have been translated from prose originals, but they have a new-minted feel. They are practical verses – no one would claim they are poetry – yet more pleasurable, instructive and *concise* than much that passed for poetry at the time. They point the way for Thomas Tusser, a century later.

'MERELY WRITTEN FOR THE PEOPLE'

... our ancient English bards and minstrels, an order of men who were once
greatly respected by our ancestors, and contributed to soften the roughness
of a martial and unlettered people by their songs and by their music.

Thomas Percy, from 'The Preface', *Percy's Reliques of Ancient English Poetry*

Shunned by the court and the universities, vernacular literature returned
where it had survived on the tongue during the suppression of English; in
ballads, street cries and street poems (**19–26**). It drifted from centres of
influence – London and Oxford – to the Marches, the Borders, into Scot-
land, where a different king reigned with another court. Indeed, James V
of Scotland composed 'The Gaberlunzie Man'. Three centuries later, Bishop
Percy puts it this way: 'as our southern metropolis must have been ever the
scene of novelty and refinement, the northern countries, as being most
distant, would preserve their ancient manners longest, and of course the
old poetry, in which those manners are so peculiarly described.'

True ballads are nobody's property. Invariably Anon's, they exist in
various versions depending on when and by whom they were written down.
Two versions, separated in time and space, can each have a distinct value
and authority. There is no 'definitive version'. The most wonderful of them,
'The Ballad of Sir Patrick Spence', has the name of Sir Patrick substituted
in some versions with the name of the famous Scottish admiral Sir Andrew
Wood. Where scansion allowed, ballads could be taken off the peg for quite
different occasions from those originally celebrated.

O long, long, may the ladies stand
   Wi' their gold combs in their hair,
Waiting for their own dear lords,
   For they'll see them now no more. (**21**)

Sung in a minor key, usually with 'tragic' or savage endings, the ballads'
chief concerns are battle, love and death. If careless singers or printers
struggling with unfamiliar dialect claimed the right to exploit and spoil
them (some printers and publishers lived off the back of ballads which were

for a long time hugely popular), who can deny us the right – Robert Graves asks – to guess how the originals went? More than any other form of literature, ballads emancipate the scholar and the poet: the text is not sacred, creative involvement can, in a sense *must*, take place. For William Empson, even the literary ballad, 'The Rime of the Ancient Mariner' by Coleridge, for example, was fair game for editorial intervention and 'creation'. In Graves's case too, invention goes too far, but as he accounts for his adjustments we learn about his techniques of composition, and about the ballad form itself.

Some English ballads survive by historical chance. Antwerp printers issued work for English readers, filling in gaps left by Caxton. Around 1503, Adraien van Berghen printed Richard Arnold's *Chronicle*, a miscellany which, between a list of the tolls of Antwerp and the differences between English and Flemish coinage, includes the ballad 'The Nut Brown Maid' (**26**). Some survived through plays, or were gathered with 'real' poems into books. But the ballad, when confined to the page after printing came in, usually travelled as a single or folded sheet and was sold for half a penny. In 1520, a man who bought two halfpenny ballads could have used the same money for two pounds of cheese or a pound of butter. For 2d. he could have bought a hen, and for 6d. a pair of shoes. Printed ballads were cheap to produce and popular even before publishers learned the art of titling and packaging. In 1595, title pages did not acknowledge an author or give his credentials unless he was already well-known. Early printed ballad titles were unwieldy and unmemorable. 'The Norfolk gent his will and testament and howe he committed the keeping of his Children to his owne brother who dealt moste wickedly with them and howe God plagued him for it' came to be known in later times as 'The Babes in the Wood'.

Ballads were especially hard for the authorities to control. They sprang up of their own accord and travelled from mouth to mouth without benefit of the censor. When they were printed, however, they might be monitored and controlled. In 1586, the Star Chamber decreed an end to provincial printing or 'imprinting of bookes, ballades, chartes, pourtraictures, or any other thing, or things whatsoever, but onlye in the cittie of London' – plus Oxford and Cambridge (one printer each). With the approach of the Civil War, vigilance was relaxed. Ballads needed to be controlled because they contained news, sometimes in biased or subversive form, and city people were hungry for information. With the ballad, journalism is born.

It was 1622 before news report publications, called *Corantos*, first appeared. They mainly reported foreign news and none of it was dangerously new. From 1632 to 1638 the *Corantos* were suspended by the Star Chamber after complaints from the Spanish ambassador. In 1641 home news was permitted in the first of the *Diurnalls*, followed by *Weekly*

Accounts, Mercuries, Intelligencers and accounts of the progress of the Civil War. The first publication that was recognizably an ancestor of our newspapers was the *London Gazette* (1665). But the inevitable result of censorship was that news was disseminated in the form of fiction. Ballads outnumbered all other forms of publication, though 'prognosticating almanacs' became for their publishers 'readier money than ale or cakes', as Thomas Nashe recalls. Many high-minded individuals (Puritans especially) were against the 'sundrie bookes, pamfletes, Poesies, ditties, songes, and other workes ... serving ... to let in a mayne Sea of wickednesse ... and to no small or sufferable waste of the treasure of this Realme which is thearby consumed and spent in paper, being of it selfe a forrein and chargeable comoditie' (William Lambarde). Already, in the seventeenth century, killjoys of the press were present, arguing against the importation of paper and other materials on the grounds that it was unpatriotic, and against information on the grounds that it provoked wickedness.

We cannot establish relative prices in the early period: nothing in manuscript is comparable to the halfpenny ballad sheet and there is no direct comparison between manuscripts and printed books. Clearly, printed texts were cheaper than scribal texts, and readership developed – a broad popular readership for ballads. The ballad sheets passed from eager hand to hand. After the Great Fire of London in 1666, book and ballad prices shot up because stocks were destroyed.

It may at first seem ironic that the eighteenth century with stiff manners, powdered wigs and slavish-seeming decorum was the great age for re-discovering and preserving ballads. The apparent rusticity and simplicity of the verse appealed to poets, scholars and readers so long gagged by proprieties that any coarseness, any deviation from good taste with the sanction of antiquity was tonic. The work of poets like Robert Burns and Sir Walter Scott, and the scholarly transcription and exposition of the Bishop of Dromore Thomas Percy (1729–1811), mean that we have a substantial morsel of oral literature, especially from the North, and a 'literary' ballad tradition that grows directly from 'folk' roots.

The Scot James Macpherson's forgeries of the ancient poems of the Gaelic poet Ossian (1760) and his later fabrications inspired many poets, including Thomas Gray. Apparent formal freedom (the translations are in highly charged, mannered prose), the 'primitive' music booming across the restraints and politenesses of a caustic Cambridge, hinted to Gray that poetry might one day breathe fresher air, as it had in earlier centuries. Johnson declared: 'Sir, a man might write such stuff for ever, if he would abandon his mind to it.' It was precisely that abandon that the poets impressed by Ossian desired, and they found it, too, in the more authoritatively-sanctioned verses that Bishop Percy put in the *Reliques*.

In Macpherson's forgery, Ossian's 'Songs of Selma' conclude: 'Such were the words of the bards in the days of song; when the king heard the music of harps, the tales of other times! The chiefs gathered from all their hills, and heard the lovely sound. They praised the voice of Cona! the first among a thousand bards! But age is now on my tongue, my soul has failed!' And so on. It is the Celtic twilight over a century before it officially fell, and the authentic voice of the old poems, which sounds English in the ballads, is here muffled under a pillow of inhibition. Hazlitt takes the Ossianic poems seriously (as indeed they should be taken despite Macpherson's subterfuge) because they touch a chord with his age. He says: 'As Homer is the first vigour and lustihead, Ossian is the decay and old age of poetry.' From that decay William Blake took some of his zanier bearings. Old age is often simulation, falsification, a groping into a past which is so forgotten that old age itself can become a sufficient authority. The unchecked, uncheckable recollections of the old should always be handled with care.

Macpherson was a catalyst for Bishop Percy, who, whatever he felt for the old poems, was keen to demonstrate his descent from the noble Percys of Northumberland and to celebrate his family (quite a few of the ballads bring his ancestors' deeds into focus). Macpherson based his forgeries – remotely, perhaps – on the Scots Gaelic oral traditions of his childhood, embroidering and extending them in English. He was compelled to forge the originals as well, when his deceit was suspected. In 1765 *Percy's Reliques of Ancient English Poetry*, with no hint of scandal and with exhaustive editorial probity, brought a refreshing blast of genuine popular poetry (and some literary imitation) into the neo-classical drawing-room. He was not above including work of known authorship – by Skelton, Marlowe, Raleigh, Shakespeare, Queen Elizabeth, Beaumont and Fletcher, Samuel Daniel James I, Lovelace, Suckling, Jonson and others. His purpose in combining literary and popular was to reveal a coherent strand in poetry, perhaps to show how anonymous ballads could hold their own in more refined company and thus acquire legitimacy. Some of the anonymous ballads, with their unstable texts, existing as they do in dozens of versions with different endings and emphases, began in literary texts but were taken over by the people and made malleable to their needs, like the Spanish ballads of Antonio Machado and Federico García Lorca which, in the 1930s, were adopted by the people and sung or recited in taverns in Spain, the authors unacknowledged and unknown.

Yet in the *Reliques* literary ballads and anonymous popular ballads prove different in kind. Percy's old friend Doctor Johnson was not impressed. He parodied the metre of 'The Hermit of Warkworth: a Northumberland Ballad' in memorable quatrains, including:

I put my hat upon my head
And walked into the Strand;

And there I met another man
Whose hat was in his hand.

He found distasteful the way many ballads parcelled out prose matter in tidy, risible quatrains – risible, that is, if you stand back from quaintness and archaic language and look meaning in the face, and if you are unable to imagine the music that the poems shed in passing into print.

Sir Walter Scott read *The Reliques* in 1782 and they determined the course of his literary life. His three volume *Minstrelsy of the Scottish Border* is, with F.J. Child's four volume *The English and Scottish Popular Ballads*, the place to look for great ballads. Percy, much earlier and with clouded motive, was a reasonable scholar: he discovered an old folio manuscript from the middle of the previous century which belonged to Humphrey Pitt of Shifnal, in his native Shropshire. It included ancient material and ballads from the seventeenth century. 'As most of them are of great simplicity, and seem to have been merely written for the people, he was long in doubt, whether, in the present state of improved literature, they could be deemed worthy the attention of the public.' Encouraged by Joseph Addison, Lord Dorset and others, he undertook the project with an unlikely colleague, the poet William Shenstone (1714–1763), famous for the artificiality and 'prettiness' of his work, and for his 'improvements' to his estate near Halesowen. He died before the *Reliques* was complete, but perhaps his influence opened the book out to poems which are ballads only by a wilful extension of the term.

Augustan gentlemen reading the *Reliques* may not always have reflected that popular ballads voice opposition, celebrate resistance and lament defeat. They are the voice of the *other*. There are poems from the age of Chaucer (who alludes to the old poems and knew them at first hand) to the Civil War, 'but not one that alludes to the Restoration'. Either by that time popular and oral traditions no longer functioned as previously, or the men from whom this literature emanated did not identify with the Restoration.

The word 'ballad' is from Norman French, spelled 'ballet', a song to which people danced. Dance and song are now as separate as ballet and ballad, but it is worth recalling that they shared a cradle. Ballads were originally a record and re-enactment of deeds; later, by a strange analepsis, the term came to refer to any kind of poem, homespun, old- or ill-fashioned. Early English dance-ballads are now often called 'folk songs'. The 'Song of Songs' was known as the 'Ballad of Ballads', suggesting a confluence between the ballad, the vernacular Bible (with the politics that it implied) and the hymn which often adapts ballad forms. The Puritans, hostile to lascivious balladry, purged and converted many of them into religious songs.

Old ballads are tied in with pre-Christian lore. Robert Graves stresses the pagan witchiness of surviving ballads. He classifies ballads under four heads:

1) Festival songs
2) Songs to lighten repetitive tasks: spinning, weaving, grinding corn, hoeing, etc; 'occupational ballads'
3) sea shanties
4) entertainments to pass an evening.

Another category of ballads exists to keep in memory historical events which, with the passage of time, are refined to legend. And there are savage and satirical ballads to avenge an ill or pillory a wrong-doer. Scurrilous poems and satirical ballads may have led to the first statute against libels in 1275, under the title: 'Against slanderous reports, or tales to cause discord betwixt king and people'. Later satirists and libellers managed to 'publish' their poems to advantage, 'although they did not enjoy the many conveniences which modern improvements have afforded for the circulation of public abuse'. One poem, in the time of Henry VI, was stuck on the palace gates while the King and his counsellors were sitting in Parliament. A few years earlier, when Henry V returned after Agincourt, ballads celebrating his deeds were pinned to the gates, but he discouraged this cult of personality.

Ballads were originally a minstrel's job, working to a lord ('minstrel' means 'a dependent'). In *Piers Plowman* one monk knows the ballads and rhymes better than his *pater noster*. Monasteries, for a fee, provided minstrels with fresh, or reheated songs and stories and themselves used them for holy days. Some abbeys and monasteries supported a resident minstrel. Welsh abbeys occasionally sustained a Welsh-language bard and were repositories for the poetry of the Britons. But as times grew harder minstrels were fired by employers, or grew bored with the court or monastery, or were set loose by military defeat (especially in Scotland and the North), and began to wander like mendicants, but singing rather than preaching the word of God or selling indulgences. The dissemination of printing dealt them a final blow: a printed ballad became common property: 'the many good Bookes and variety of Turnes of Affaires, have putt all the old Fables out of doors: and the divine art of Printing and gunpowder have frighted away Robin-good-fellow and the Fayries.' Strolling minstrels disappear in Elizabeth's reign, arrested as vagabonds or displaced by the circulation of 'town literature': the ballad seller on his rounds. For two centuries after Shakespeare's death, broadsheet ballads kept printers alive. Inn walls displayed them, they appeared in public places. Not until Dickens's time did they too begin to fade out. In *The Winter's Tale*, Clown announces a ballad seller and Mopsa says: 'Pray now, buy some! I love a ballad in print o' life, for then we are sure they are true.'

Their truth is of course not of an historical order. Detecting bits of the old religion is a fascinating activity with ballads, as is filling in the scene, imagining the full plot, when the history is fragmented or missing altogether. The point at which they are written down may have been a point beyond which their literal sense still resonated for the common balladhearer. For the first audiences, too, there may have been mysteries (we need not call them obscurities). Graves reminds us that a coven is a group of thirteen. ' "Robin" was a title often given to the male leader of a witch coven, the female leader being called the "Maid" – hence "Maid Marian".' Pagan and Christian marry, but another element is history, valuable to a poet less as fact than for the types and tales it throws up. Graves demonstrates the historical reality of Robin Hood through his employment (documented) by Edward II to train up good archers in the royal army.

The ballad-minstrel tradition thrived most and survived longest in Scotland and the Borders. Indeed it never quite died, Graves reminds us, in the 'chimney corners of English and Scottish farmhouses, as also in the hills of Virginia, Kentucky and Tennessee'. Wordsworth's 'Solitary Reaper' is doing nothing less than warbling a ballad when the poet beholds her single in the field. Because most minstrels and balladeers were from the North of England or Scotland, there is a 'prevalence of the northern dialect' in their work. Percy stresses that real minstrels did not write down their poems. By that token, the *Reliques* is the echo of an echo. Some of the fifteenth century can be heard in, or inferred from it.

'NOT AS I SULD, I WRAIT, BUT AS I COUTH'

They are not the prophets of a morning-time, and the soul that shines in their verse has the splendid weariness of full experience, not the hot enthusiasm of an epoch's youth.

from George Eyre-Todd's Preface, *Mediæval Scottish Poetry* (Abbotsford Series)

Scotland provided more than ballads in the fifteenth and early sixteenth centuries. It was there that the major poetry in English was composed by writers whose learning is as great as that of Chaucer and Gower, yet whose anonymity is almost as complete as that of the ballad makers.

Robert Henryson was born probably around 1425. His death is a guess too, though it may have been in 1508. It is alluded to in stanza twenty-one of William Dunbar's sonorous 'Lament for the Makaris' (**74**). Henryson is the first and greatest of the so-called 'Scottish Chaucerians', and the most obviously directly indebted to the English poet. His greatest poem makes no bones about it:

To cut the winter night and make it short,
I took a quair,° and left all other sport,* *book (quire of pages); pastime*
Written by worthy Chaucer glorious,
Of fair Cresseid, and worthy Troilus.

(**66**)

He is not first in line. The unknown author of the beautiful love-vision. *The Kingis Quair* (possibly James I, King of the Scots) holds that honour. If it was the King, he may have composed the poem around 1424, alluding to his time in prison in England twenty years earlier – his cell near Charles of Orleans' – and his love for Joan Beaufort. He returned to Scotland and brought with him the poems of Chaucer and of Petrarch. William Dunbar is also of the company and, less generously, Gavin Douglas. Douglas acknowledges debts to 'worthy Chaucer glorious' but is less enthusiastic than his fellow Scots.

The term 'Scottish Chaucerians' is now resented by critics as reductive, though it is not inaccurate. Chaucer's spirit moves in Scottish literature well into the sixteenth century. 'Chaucer was the "rose of rethoris all", the "horleige and regulier" for the future movements of poetry,' the Scottish poet Edwin Morgan reminds us. But 'their references to Chaucer's "sugarit lippis", "aureate termis", and "eloquence ornate" rather than to his pathos, his simplicity, or his narrative gift help to betray the background of their eulogies'. Chaucer is undeniably behind them, but not too close: a grand-father, not a father. He is a legitimate authority, an accessible classic.

These poets are truer to Chaucer's spirit than his immediate English heirs were. They are true, at the same time, to a Scottish tradition, alliterative and intensely formal, which includes narrative of sophistication and passion. If Scottish critics stress the Scottish sources of Henryson and Dunbar, English critics as often disregard them. Though their different languages admit elements of dialect, none of these poets adopts an historical, spoken Scottish idiom. Each employs 'an artificial, created, "literary" language, used, for almost a century, by writers of very different locality and degree, with an astonishing measure of uniformity'. Chaucer is crucial especially to Henryson: his most important poem is a postscript to *Troilus and Criseyde*. Only Douglas finds it necessary to call the language he uses 'Scots', to distinguish it from the tongue of the 'Inglis natioun'. Before his time, 'Scots' was used with reference to the Celtic language of the Highlands, the language Macpherson's Ossian would have sung in had he sung at all.

Henryson's fame rests, first, on his *Testament of Cresseid* (**66**). It 'completes' Chaucer's *Troilus and Criseyde* and is the great moral romance of the fifteenth century. Sir Francis Kinaston in 1640 gave a sour account of Henryson's purpose: 'he learnedly takes upon him in a fine poetical way to express the punishment and end due to a false inconstant whore'. The poem is more humane and moral than this suggests. Henryson was as fond of Criseyde as Chaucer had been, as troubled as he by her inconstancy and fate. Henryson wrote other poems, notably the *Morall Fabillis of Esope*, which set him among the few great fabulists in our literature.

Little is known of his life, less even than of Langland's. Kinaston calls him 'sometime chief schoolmaster in Dunfermling' (at the Benedictine abbey grammar school) and adds that he was 'a learned and witty man'. Already 'licentiate in arts and bachelor in decrees', he may have attended the University of Glasgow in 1462 (it was established in 1451). He may have studied in France. Of all the Scottish poets of his time, only he was not connected closely with the court; he was a humble schoolmaster with a divine gift. Kinaston records the only anecdote we have about the poet: 'being very old he died of a diarrhoea or flux', to which he appends a 'merry' if 'unsavoury' tale. When the physician despaired of his cure, an old witch came to the bedside and asked Henryson if he would be made better. She indicated a 'whikey tree' in his orchard and instructed him to walk about it three times, repeating the words: 'whikey tree whikey tree take away this flux from me.' Henryson, too weak to go so far, pointed to an oak table in his room and asked, 'gude dame I pray ye tell me, if it would not be as well if I repeated thrice theis words oken burd oken burd garre me shit a hard turd.' The hag departed in a rage and 'half a quarter of an hour' later, Henryson was dead.

H. Harvey Wood prepared the excellent 1933 edition of Henryson's *Poems and Fables*. He claims his poet to be the greatest of the Scottish *makars*, a judgement with which many non-Scottish readers concur. Henryson isn't so startling a technician as Dunbar, though he is every bit as expert within his range. He lacks Dunbar's eccentricity. He possesses a humanity well beyond Dunbar's, and a capacity for observing detail and human conduct equal to Chaucer's. Dunbar is 'A Poet', always anxious to prove it; Henryson is a moralist who writes poems. Dunbar is literary, with a following among poets. Henryson is an illustrator of common truths, a storyteller who uses verse as his medium, and appeals to the common reader. Dunbar is a poet of abrupt changes of tone. Henryson can manage such changes, but is capable of subtler modulations as well.

Modulations take various forms in his work. In the *Testament*, they are emotional: the progress of Cresseid, of her father Calchas, and of Troilus himself, correspond to changes in the moral argument which rhythm and diction underpin. A clearer example is to be found in the fable entitled 'The Preaching of the Swallow'. The seasonal stanzas move from a Spring of lush, latinate and aureate diction to a thoroughly native diction, bristling with consonants, as the year moves into Winter. Though Henryson uses Chaucerian techniques, he is closer to the old alliterative tradition than is sometimes acknowledged. In descriptions and in passages of action he will employ what Chaucer called the old alliterative *rim ram ruf* with gusto, normally adopting a vocabulary almost without Latinisms and largely monosyllabic. Chaucer was a crucial resource, but not an invariable model.

The tradition of allegory lived on in fifteenth-century Scotland. Henryson is a better moral allegorist than Gower because, though he appends a moral to his fables and other poems, the poetry substantiates and embodies the lesson drawn. Again and again you feel the informing presence of Dante in his verse. Sometimes the tone is so unmistakably Dantesque that you wish he had done for the *Divine Comedy* what Gavin Douglas does for the *Aeneid*. Take, as an example, the prologue to the fable of 'The Lion and the Mouse'. The poet in sleep is visited by his master Aesop. He is at once inquisitive and respectful:

> 'Displease you not, my good maister, thocht° I   *though*
> Demand your birth, your faculty, and name,
> Why ye come here, or where ye dwell at hame?'
> 'My son,' (said he), 'I am of gentil blood,
> My native land is Rome ...'

Nothing could be clearer: it is voices talking. And like Dante, Henryson selects his metaphors exactly, and his diction can be mimetic, as in 'The Harrowis hoppand in the saweris trace' ['The harrow's hopping in the sower's trace']. This is language in the spirit of William Barnes.

We can't but think of Dante in 'Orpheus and Eurydice'. Henryson sends Orpheus to an underworld not pagan but very like Hell. Orpheus allows himself (as we sometimes wish Dante would) certain merciful liberties with the damned. He plays his instrument so that the waters are still and Tantalus can drink; briefly Tityrus is relieved of agony. Though it is a Hell where all are dying 'and nevirmoir sall de' ['And nevermore shall die'], Orpheus performs acts of charity, similar to the benevolence which Henryson evinces in the *Testament* both for Cresseid and for Troilus.

The *Testament* grows out of Chaucer's poem, which is extraordinary considering that *Troilus and Criseyde* is so complete and so distinctively Chaucerian. Henryson's temper is different, but the gap is no greater than that between Christopher Marlowe's and George Chapman's passages in that great Elizabethan epyllion *Hero and Leander*. In the midst of winter Henryson, who presents himself as an old man, takes down Chaucer's poem to while away the night. Both the season and the narrator's age suit the theme. What happened to Cresseid, he wonders. He answers: Diomede cast her off, she went home to her father Calchas who received her with love as a returning prodigal. She visited Venus's temple to pray, but in her prayer she railed against Cupid and Venus. She fell asleep and dreamed that those gods summoned their peers to try her. Saturn, the judge, an old, repellent figure, found her guilty and Cynthia, the moon, struck her with a leprosy. Waking, Cresseid finds the dream to be true. She departs, disfigured and lamenting (in nine-line stanzas which contrast with the Chaucerian seven-line stanzas of the rest of the poem), drawing a partial moral:

> Nought is your fairness but a fading flower,
> Nought is your famous laud° and high honour *praise*
> But wind inflate° in other mennes earès.* *blown into; ears*
> Your roising reid° to rotting shall retour.* *rosy cheeks; shall return*

In the sequel she learns a fuller moral lesson. Urged by a leper lady to 'mak vertew of ane neid' (make virtue of necessity), 'To leir to clap thy clapper to and fro, / And leir efter the Law of Lipper Leid', she goes begging by the roadside. Troilus passes that way,

> And with a blenk° it come into his thocht, *glance*
> That he somtime her face before had seen
> But she was in such plight he knew her not.

He recalls but does not recognize her, but he feels a spark of love and empties his purse into her lap. Cresseid does not know him either, but another leper announces the knight's name. Cresseid swoons, recovers, and comes to a full recognition of her guilt. She writes her testament and dies. The ruby ring Troilus had given her is returned to him. Henryson hints that he may have built a marble monument for her and rounds off the poem with a moral for the women in his audience.

On the strength of this poem alone Henryson would have a place well above the tree-line on Parnassus. But there is more. The eclogue 'Robene and Makyne', and 'The Garmont of Gud Ladeis', 'The Bludy Serk', 'Orpheus and Eurydice', and especially the *Fables*, all contribute to our sense of his achievement, which includes allegorical satire: the animals in the fables represent classes and types of men and the fable form liberates them from a specific milieu into a general significance.

There are thirteen fables. Henryson pretends they are translations of Aesop, though the best – 'The Country Mouse and the Town Mouse' – is from Horace, and others belong to the profusion of fabliaux current at the time. With further modesty, he claims to be ignorant of rhetoric and promises to write 'In hamelie [homely] language and in termes rude'. Though the low style prevails, the rhetoric is impeccable. Unlike other fable writers, he does not tell and moralize at the same time but keeps the moral for the end of the poem.

The fable of the mice – 'The Tale of the Uponlandis Mouse, and the Burges Mouse' (**65**) – is the most achieved, vivid in visual detail corresponding closely to social types, and full of good humour and good sense. His narrative is dramatic as well. The town mouse sets out to seek her sister:

> Barefoot alone, with pikestaff in her hand,
> As pure pilgrim she passèd out of town,
> To seek her sister both o'er dale and down. (**65**)

Speech – mouse-speech married to common speech – is rendered. When, back in town, the mice are first surprised at their dinner by a servant, the country mouse falls and swoons. Her sister calls, 'How faire ye, sister? cry peip, where ever ye be.' The arrival of 'Gib hunter, our jolie Cat' (Gilbert – a common name for cats well into the sixteenth century), who catches the country mouse, is full of suspense:

> From foot to foot he cast her to and fro,
> Whiles° up, whiles down, as cant* as any kid;   *now; lively*
> Whiles would he let her run under the straw,

Whiles would he wink and play with her buk-heid.°	*play hide and seek with her*
Thus to the selie° Mouse great pain he did,	*innocent [cf. silly]*
While at the last, through fortune and good hap,°	*good luck*
Betwix ane burdè° and the wall she crap.*	*floorboard; crept*

As in the *Testament*, so in the *Fables* trial and confession motifs add to the Chaucerian tone. Patrick Crutwell, comparing Henryson and Chaucer, comments that Henryson's 'picturesque detail owes its effectiveness to the solidity and seriousness of what it grows from'. Picturesque and transparently allegorical: the frog is both frog and more than, or other than frog:

her fronsit° face,	*creased up*
Her runkillit° cheikis, and her lippis side,*	*wrinkled; wide*
Her hingand browis, and her voice so hace,°	*hoarse*
Her logerand° leggis, and her harsky* hide…	*dangling; rough*

There emerges from the *Fables* – by analogy – a more or less complete human world, to be appraised in moral terms.

Gavin Douglas (1475?–1522), despite his dates, belongs with Henryson and Dunbar rather than with the poets of the early sixteenth century. He acknowledges his debt to Henryson more generously than he does his debt to Chaucer. In reading his *Aeneados* (**68**), the translation of Virgil's *Aeneid*, we sense the nature of that debt in Douglas's control of his couplets and his skill at writing directly, especially in the original prologues that preface each book of translation. He knows the huge challenge he has set himself:

Beside Latin our language is imperfit,	
Which in some part is the cause and the wyte°	*reason*
Why that of Virgil's verse the ornate beauty	
Into our tongue may not observèd be.	(**68b**)

He is harsh on his own language: it lacks variety of tone, inflection and diction.

Between *genus, sexus* and *species*	
Diversity in our leid° to seek I cease.	*language*
For *objectum* or *subjectum* also	
He war expert couth° find me termes two,	*could*
Which are as rife amongès clerks in school	
As ever fowls plunged in lake or pool.	

But his language brings a kind of rough energy to Virgil that the Latin poet would hardly have recognized. Douglas is blisteringly harsh on Caxton's prose version of the *Aeneid* – as close to the original, he says, as the devil is to St Augustine: 'I read his work with harmys at my heart', he declares, that Caxton's book should even share a title with the divine Virgil's. His assault is, for its time, a brilliant essay on the art of translation and on Caxton's literary shortcomings.

Douglas was the third son of 'Bell-the-Cat', fifth Earl of Angus, and thus a nobleman without prospects. After a good education he was caught in the political struggles of the day on the 'other side' (the victorious side) in the Battle of Flodden and its aftermath. He entered St Andrews University in 1490, took his Master's degree in 1494, and in 1501 was Provost of St Giles, Edinburgh. He probably studied in Paris as well. He took orders and ultimately, after much controversy, became Bishop of Dunkeld (1515). He died, out of favour, of the Plague in London in 1522. His poetic labours had come to an end almost a decade earlier. When he completed the *Eneados* he wrote, 'Thus up my pen and instrumentis full yor / On Virgillis post I fix for evermore ...' He would wait 'solitar, as doth the bird in cage', his youth over. It took him some eighteen months to translate Virgil. The *Aeneados* is the first important complete translation into English of a major classical poem. His other works include the 'Palice of Honour', a substantially original dream allegory. Some of his poems and translations, notably his version of Ovid's *Art of Love*, have not survived.

Douglas's working text of Virgil was hardly perfect; a full commentary was appended to it. He translated keeping close to the original but interpolating matter from the commentary. He also included Mapheus Vegius's apocryphal thirteenth book (1428). His poem is almost twice as long as Virgil's, yet close to it in spirit. Renaissance humanists in their passion for pure Latinity divorced the poem from its wide audience by academicizing it. Douglas was on the common reader's side.

Ezra Pound declares, 'Gavin Douglas re-created us Virgil, or rather, we forget Virgil in reading Gavin's *Aeneids* and know only the tempest, Acheron, and the eternal elements that Virgil for most men glazes over.' This tribute to Douglas's directness reflects Pound's own sense – many readers share it – that the Virgil we read is filtered through centuries of scholarship and exegesis, so that we can hardly see his face. Douglas could see it, or a version of it, and in reading him we experience Aeneas' adventures afresh.

Reflecting on the work of Chaucer, Gower, Henryson and Douglas, we can understand what Dryden meant when he wrote of Chaucer, 'the genius of our countrymen in general' is 'rather to improve an invention, than to invent themselves; as is evident not only in our poetry, but in many of our manufactures'. Translation nourishes a native literature. 'Improvement' is too strong a word to apply to Douglas's Virgil; but his transposition of the poem into courtly idiom with a peculiarly Scottish flavour is characteristic of the writing of the age. Douglas achieved much with few decent models to work from. His modesty remains genuine: 'Not as I suld, I wrait, but as I couth.'

He uses roughly one couplet per Latin hexameter: twenty syllables for sixteen, with numerous poetic auxiliaries and doublets to plump out his measure, giving roughness to its rightness. He is naturally most himself in the originality of his prologues where he experiments in alliterative verse (Book Eight) and he states his mind. Warton praised particularly the Prologue to Book Twelve: the lines 'are effusions of a mind not overlaid by the descriptions of other poets but operating, by its own Force and bias, in the delineation of a vernal landscape, on such objects as really occurred.' Douglas loved to write (the excesses of 'The Palice of Honour' attest to this), and he was clear in his mind about style and genre. This he reveals in the Prologue of Book Nine, only lightly modernized here:

The ryall° style, clepyt heroicall,	*splendid*
Full of worship and nobillness our° all,	*above*
Suldbe compiled but thewhes or void word,°	*cliches or empty words*
Kepand honest wys sportis whar they bourd,°	*to the jests where they occur*
All lowus° langage and lychtnes lattand be,*	*loose; letting remain*
Observing beauty, sentens° and gravity.	*meaning*
The sayer eik should well consider this,	
His matter, and whomto it entitilit is:	
Aftir myne authors wordes, we aucht tak tent°	*remain attentive*
That both accord, and ben convenient,	
The man, the sentense, and the knychtlyke style,	
Sen we mon carp° of vassalage* a while.	*speak; courage*

He develops principles of poetic decorum functional and far less restricting than those that Renaissance humanists promoted. He is modest again when he says, 'If aught be well, thank Virgil and not me.' The faults are his, since he is unequal to his original's 'ornate fresh endyte'. If he has 'pervert' Virgil, he has also caught the movement and spirit of the *Aeneid*, and woven into the poem his prologues which we can read as northern eclogues.

Dunbar (**69–74**) is more famous than either Henryson or Douglas. His credit this century has risen thanks to Hugh MacDiarmid's attempt to 'recreate' a distinctively Scottish literature with the cry, 'Not Burns – Dunbar!' The masculinity of Dunbar's verse, its formal skill and verve, its effective malice, its variety, set him apart from his contemporaries, both English and Scottish. He wrote allegories like 'The Golden Targe' – where the poet puts in an appearance at the sumptuous court of Venus – and occasional poems which address a variety of subjects in many forms and cannot usefully be described as Chaucerian. They are his major achievement. Bumptious, overbearing, unbridled, he knows no taboos. A friar? Not in his verse, which abounds in everything but charity. 'Tidings from the Session' lays into the courts; 'Satire on Edinburgh' tells the truth about conditions in a then disgusting city. 'The Dance of the Sevin Deidlie Synnis' and the 'General Satire' say things which had not been said or sayable in English verse before, in tones not previously heard. He is a flayer, a Juvenalian satirist. Never gentle, he can be 'elfin'. 'At first it may seem absurd to try to recover at this time of day,' MacDiarmid says, 'the literary potentialities of a language which has long ago disintegrated into dialects. These dialects even at their richest afford only a very restricted literary medium, capable of little more than kailyard usages, but quite incapable of addressing the full range of literary purpose.'

MacDiarmid builds his polemic almost exclusively on Dunbar, his chosen ancestor, and only nods *en passant* at Douglas and Henryson, insisting that, 'Dunbar is in many ways the most modern, as he is the most varied, of Scottish poets . . .' Dunbar is vulnerable to MacDiarmid's nationalist argument, marrying a moribund but still viable alliterative inheritance to a French syllabic tradition. There is none of Henryson's transparency of language or Douglas's directness. The sound surface of Dunbar's poems calls attention to itself: we are required to admire the often astounding technique. He is the closest thing we have in English (though MacDiarmid might not like to hear it called English) to the candour, self exposure and excess of Villon. He may have been in France when Villon's poems were published posthumously in 1489. He is more like Villon than like Skelton, though he has been called 'the Scottish Skelton'. In 1500 he was back in Scotland, no longer a Franciscan friar of the strict Observantine but a court priest with a royal pension. In 1501 he received ten marks from Henry VII of England for his poem with the refrain, 'London thou art the Flower of Cities all' (**69**), and two years later he wrote his celebrated 'The Thistle and the Rose' (**71**) to mark the marriage of James IV of Scotland and Margaret Tudor. Thus he came to be admired on both sides of the border.

Dunbar (1460?–1520?) worked in the courtly tradition, friar and courtier in one, busy about other people's lives and secrets. James IV was his patron. He chafed under the restraints of his order and seems to have enjoyed wandering, perhaps as far as Picardy and other parts of France. His poems 'are fundamentally and exclusively Scottish'. However they are not intentionally nationalist, and it is an irony that the radical Nationalist and Communist Hugh MacDiarmid built so much on an apolitical poet enamoured of romance, engaged in the ephemeral scheming of courtly life, and very much a creature of the establishments of the day. He may have graduated from the University of St Andrews as a Bachelor of Arts in 1477. He survived and lamented the defeat of Flodden in 1513. His verse is part of the decisive, brief, flowering of aristocratic culture which finished with his work. James IV was a responsive patron, though less so than has been suggested. He was among the last great princes of chivalry, as his heroic death proved. Learned, a linguist in as many as eight tongues, he cultivated the arts and sciences in his court and in his country. Dunbar celebrates all this. He also shows a darker side.

His love of ceremony and pomp emerges in several poems, even in the organization of imagery (much of it in heraldic colours), and is most prominent in 'The Thistle and the Rose' and 'The Golden Terge'. The aureation he learned from Chaucer contributes to the surface of his verse, but he also deploys the coarse colloquial diction of his day. His style is an amalgam of literary English and the demotic, mingling registers and passing from sublime to grotesque in a single sentence. He is a master of parody, at times a scurrilous rogue, especially in the 'Flyting of Dunbar and Kennedie' – his rival Walter Kennedy, whom he later celebrates in the great 'Lament for the Makaris', where he first mourns Chaucer.

Rime Royal, short stanzas, couplets, alliterative forms: the technical range dazzles. And he is at home in many modes: allegory, dream vision, hymn, prayer, elegy, panegyric, lyric, comic narrative, satire and flyting. Edwin Morgan writes, 'His first mark is a certain effectual brilliance that may commend him more keenly to the practising poet than to the ordinary reader – an agility, a virtuosity in tempo and momentum, a command of rhythm.' Warton says, 'I am of opinion, that the imagination of Dunbar is not less suited to satirical than to sublime allegory: and that he is the first poet who has appeared with any degree of spirit in [that] way of writing since *Piers Plowman*.' Sadly, Warton did not have access to the work of Henryson. On Dunbar, he continues: 'The natural complexion of his genius is of the moral and didactic cast.' And yet he has not Langland's social scope or conscience, nor Chaucer's bemused humanity. Ungenerosity of spirit mars the verse; it vanishes only in the elegies and religious poems. He flays his foes; his greatest pleasure is in the flyting, the bawdy, the grotesque. His longest poem, and one of his best, 'The Treatise of the Two Married Women and the Widow', combines bawdy satire and moral censure in a single unrhymed alliterative parody of the romantic mode.

His is a poetry without intimacy and is in that respect like Langland's. Feelings, when they are apparent, attach more to the subject and the chosen form than to the poet's candid emotion. It is not that the poems are insincere: sincerity is beside the point. He invests emotion only in his elegies. His religious poems, C.S. Lewis writes, are 'public and liturgical' rather than devotional. He brings an equal lucidity and professional polish to flytings and elegies. One does not look for psychological depth or perceptual accuracy beneath the polish. For all his courtliness, his political and diplomatic activity, and the potency of his technical arsenal, he was a poet local to a time and place: James IV's court. There is no wider world, but the narrow scope compels.

In 'The Dregy of Dunbar' (72) he parodies liturgical form, presenting the King's stay in Stirling as purgatory and his return to Edinburgh as a return to heaven. 'Requiem Edinburgi dona eis, Domine,' he says. The interweaving of Latin among other language registers can be parodic or, in the sombre poems, add ritual emphasis. He appears to have been born a technician: there is an even excellence of composition and we cannot detect development or establish stylistic chronology among the poems. Throughout, comedy tends towards the grotesque, the nightmare. Primary colours, little shading, nothing overheard.

Edwin Morgan points to his 'startling indifference to theme in poetry'. He is a poet one cannot but admire, yet it is hard for the non-Scot to do more than admire. Sir Walter Scott regards him as 'unrivalled by any which Scotland ever produced', and it is tempting to think that MacDiarmid agreed with him, but MacDiarmid, so similar in spirit but so immensely copious, tends to use Dunbar as a weapon with which to beat poor Robert Burns and Burns's admirers over the head. Whatever we say in Dunbar's favour, he is limited to the courtly. He is brilliant and narrow, a medieval poet with more economy of expression than the English Chaucerians, greater formal resources, and a wry humour. He has been touched by the new French poetry. In his work the old elements are made serviceable one last time – vivid, real, fully expressive.

And what had England to show for itself at this time, on the cusp of the Tudor century? Stephen Hawes, the archetypal 'transitional figure' (75–77). His situation was especially hard in terms of the language he had to use. It is important to bear in mind with him as with the first Tudor poets that throughout the fifteenth and early sixteenth century difference in dialects made it hard for people from one shire to understand those from another. Literature of the past became incomprehensible to the ear: the voiced final '-e' was vanishing gradually and unevenly, area by area, word by word. Men in Henry VII's reign couldn't understand each other, much less the past. Henry VII made his laureate a French poet, the blind Bernard André of Toulouse, preferring the French to the chaotic native muse. Either Scottish poets were less diverse in dialect, or the language was evolving less briskly; they had a chance while the English ear was at sea.

Much of the readable early fifteenth century is to be found in the Chaucer apocrypha. Like a great magnet his œuvre attracted not only corruptions introduced by scribes but the verse of any genuinely competent poet. It's worth hunting down *The Flower and the Leaf, The Cuckoo and the Nightingale* and others. In fact, it is rather sad that Chaucer's act has been so scrupulously cleaned up by later scholar-editors since, in the end, the work they excluded has almost vanished.

Printing was finding a place and promised to bring eventual conformity to the language. The scribes 'retrained' – those who didn't became jobbing legal copyists, frightened of new technology. They turned into type designers, rubricators. They discussed patterns and rules, letter forms and how a poem might best be accommodated on the page. Medieval English poetry was more or less over. There was in every area an oral tradition of poetry in dialect, and the morality plays were still around. But for literary poetry, a settled prosody was unthinkable, unless one froze poetic language at a certain point and declared: this is it, these are poetic sounds. Stephen Hawes seems to have done something of the kind.

He stands at the door of a new age, but – still a medievalist in his digressive, allegorical approach and in the value-structure of his verse – he does not pass through. His chief innovation is 'ynkhorn' terms, the pedantic invention of new and compound words which smell of the lamp and, with his awkward word order, make him sound peculiar and even comic. He stands between Chaucer and Edmund Spenser. *The Passtyme of Pleasure, or History of Graunde Amoure and la Bel Pucel* (77) is a kind of poor uncle, though not a parent, of *The Faerie Queene*. W. Murison shows a number of parallels and perhaps analogues or direct debts. But Spenser's poem lives because for him *La Bel Pucel* of Hawes is embodied in the Queen of England: everything acquires a specific political as well as a chivalric meaning. Spenser writes from an actual, an attestable occasion, even when his allegory wanders off down baroque side streets.

Hawes (1475?–1523/1530?) saw himself as the last, lonely 'faithful votary of true poetry'. In the 5800 line rime royal *Passtyme* (Wynkyn de Worde says it was written in 1505–6), he laments his uniqueness, how he has been abandoned by a departed culture, and at the same time displays his considerable learning. He was educated at Oxford and visited several foreign universities. He entered Henry VII's household as a groom of the chamber. His life was an example of virtue. He was a great reciter of verse, especially Lydgate's. He did produce a few remarkable pieces, not least a shaped poem against swearing, in fact a passage in a much longer poem (75). Like his fifteenth-century predecessors, he is best in extract, but the good extracts are perhaps even fewer than are to be found in Hoccleve and Lydgate. All the same, there is something fine and firm in his simple, reactionary devotion to his art; he is not content to be a jobbing poet, a translator by the yard. 'Accordingly,' Warton says with benign condescension, 'his failure excites sympathy rather than contempt.'

THE WATERSHED

'... the Price of Writing of Manuscripts, before the use of Printing, was xxx shillings per quire ...'

Aubrey *Brief Lives*

Though William Caxton was a man of medieval taste and temperament, he introduced a sea change in our culture, in the dissemination of works of literature and ways of literacy. He contributed no theories to the intellectual world. His writings are largely forgotten. He invented nothing. But the impact of his entrepreneurial work has proven more radical than the ideas of Wycliffe, Latimer, Cromwell, or any other Englishman. He fathered what was to become an informed democracy. And that democracy would eventually spread through a decaying empire. It is thanks to him that I write, and you read, this book.

Humanism was well begun by the time Erasmus first visited England late in the fifteenth century. The Greek scholar William Grocyn had established principles of critical scholarship; John Colet was lecturing on the Pauline Epistles and setting them into an historical context. 'Pure' or classical Latin was being re-established at court 'for diplomacy and historiography'. Against this background Caxton's activity seems to propose a different programme, as though English printing would run in the teeth of the universities and their specialisms. The books Caxton printed between 1475 and 1491 answered to medieval tastes. The new elements in popular literature are books of fools or follies, *The Ship of Fools*. Just as 'cutting edge' writers were slow to rise to the challenge of electronic publishing in the twentieth century, so humanists and printers, even when they approached the classics, were differently impelled. Entrepreneurial and intellectual cultures never made comfortable bedfellows in Britain, though in other anglophone cultures the situation has fortunately been different.

It is almost an accident that Caxton occupies the place he does. Had it not been Caxton, another enterprising expatriate returning home from the Continent might have brought the technology he acquired, though another would have pursued different editorial ends.

The key to the invention of printing lay in movable type. Johannes

Gutenberg of Mainz, born at the end of the fourteenth century, is credited with the introduction of the craft. His Latin edition of the Bible, known as the Mazarin Bible (1450–55), was the first book to be printed in Europe and is still one of the most beautiful. Printing was perfected and it spread, as journeymen left masters and set up for themselves. Printed works appeared in Italy (1453), Basel (1466), France (1470), Hungary (1473), Spain (1473), Poland (1474), Bruges (1474), England (1476), Sweden (1483), and Mexico (1539). By the end of the fifteenth century, as many as 40,000 items had been issued. Books usually appeared as quartos bound between wooden boards and decorated copiously with woodcuts. Print runs were small, averaging fewer than 500, with a few notable exceptions. The vernacular gained ground, but most fifteenth-century productions were religious or legal works in Latin.

The earliest printed books are called *incunabula*, from the Latin for 'swaddling clothes': publications from the infancy of printing. An incunabulum, or incunable, is any printed book, booklet, or broadside from the fifteenth century. Incunables resemble the manuscripts they supersede. They do not sport a title page; instead, author, title, printer, place, and date of publication are provided in a final paragraph, a 'colophon'. Some printers devised a woodcut for identification, and the word 'colophon' gradually transferred to that emblem. During the Reformation and Counter-Reformation many incunables were destroyed; those that survive are prized, some more so than the laboured manuscripts of the scribes, who had created their predecessors.

Caxton was hard-working, an artist in his craft, a dedicated writer-printer (the term 'publisher' gained currency later, in the eighteenth century). Few men of the time possessed his taste or his range of interests, which were those of a cultured dilettante with only himself and his patrons to satisfy. He shows style in his judgement and his writing. About a third of the more than 100 books he printed were his own translations. When moved to be emphatic, he is 'almost as vigorous as Latimer himself. In this power of writing with a naive vivacity, while deliberately striving after a more ornate manner, Caxton belongs to his age. He provides, as it were, a choice of styles for his readers.' His most popular book is *The Golden Legend*.

Born in Kent around 1422, he lived almost to the age of seventy. The English of his childhood he describes as 'broad and rude', coloured with idioms and accents of the large Flemish community that lived in Kent. He received – we don't know where – a good education (though he never trusted his Latin) and began, as many of his class did, whether English or Flemish, as a cloth merchant. By 1463 he was governor of the merchant adventurers in the Low Countries. Six years later he gave this up and entered the service of the Duchess of Burgundy, turning to literary work. In 1471 he made a visit to Cologne, saw a printing press at work, and there the prosperous mercer settled down and learned how to print.

In 1474 he acquired two founts of type. They were cut in imitation of ordinary scribal hand. He founded a press in Bruges before returning to England. His first book was *Recuyell of the Histories of Troy*, dated 1475 – the first of his own translations that he printed. It had been popular and much in demand in manuscript. He tired of having it copied and went for print. His versions generally carry a prologue or epilogue – sometimes in verse – that reveals his sense of humour and due modesty.

In 1476 he returned to England and the next year his press 'in a house with the sign of the Red Pale' at Westminster produced *Dictes or Sayenges of the Phylosophers*, the first dated book printed in England. He printed pamphlets: Lydgate's *Temple of Glass*, Chaucer's *Anelida and Arcite* and others. His version of *The Canterbury Tales*, a massive undertaking, appeared at this time, as did *The Moral Proverbs of Christine de Pisan*, the first book by a woman printed in England. He went on to print more than ninety editions.

Only 370 books of all kinds were printed in Britain before 1500, and this includes different editions of the same work. Because English printing started late and impecuniously, it was largely a vernacular publishing culture. The classics had to be imported because the cost of acquiring founts was so high. And because the publishing culture was vernacular and Caxton was Caxton, the literary values were generally high.

What else did he print? In 1482, Higden's *Polychronicon*, with Caxton revising Trevisa's 1387 English version and updating it to 1467. This continuation is the one major original work by Caxton that we possess. In 1481: three of his own translations including *Reynard the Fox*. In 1483: more Lydgate, plus a new edition of *The Canterbury Tales*, with his prologue showing the esteem in which he held Chaucer. He placed a memorial tablet to his poet in Westminster Abbey. About this time he also published *Troilus and Criseyde*, *The House of Fame* and, in September 1483: Gower's *Confessio Amantis*. In 1485: Sir Thomas Malory's *Morte d'Arthur*. In 1489: *The Fayttes of Arms* generally attributed to Christine de Pisan. In 1490: *Eneydos*, not a translation but a romance based on *Aeneid* – the book that so irritated Gavin Douglas. Caxton in his Preface reflects on the speed of change in English: 'And certainly our language now used varyeth farre from that which was used and spoken when I was born.' He comments on variety of dialect and declares: 'And thus between plain, rude, and curious I stand abashed, but in my judgement the common terms that be daily used be lighter to be understood than the old and auncient english.' John Skelton helped revise the book for the press, so Douglas's blame should be spread between Caxton and the first great English poet of the sixteenth century.

In 1491 he died, having just completed translating St Jerome's *Lives of the*

Fathers which Wynkyn de Worde, his foreman who became his successor, published as an act of piety in 1495, declaring that the version was completed on the last day of Caxton's life.

Given his background and his independence of means, Caxton never printed for a market but consulted his own taste, leading rather than following his readers. His editions were small. He edited with care, a custom his immediate successors did not honour. Wynkyn de Worde and Richard Pynson were printers more than publishers. Pynson published a *Canterbury Tales* among the law books that were his speciality. Three years after Caxton died Pynson printed Lydgate's *Fall of Princes*, translated from Boccaccio. He also first published *Mandeville's Travels* and in 1509 Barclay's translation of *The Ship of Fools*. His most durable literary text appeared between 1523 and 1525: Froisart's *Chronicle*, translated by John Bourchier, Lord Berners. But he suffered from lack of type, especially Greek. Scholars sent their work abroad when English manufacturers were unequal to the typographical challenge.

When the manuscript of a printed text survives, often the printed version shortens or abridges the original – especially with Pynson (whose English was poor). Due to lack of type and the cost of composition in time and resources, such truncations were published and may have displaced original texts. Scribes had drowsed from time to time, or – unable to keep up – dropped a line here and there. But what Pynson did was more harmful. One scribe may err while another gets it right. But 500 copies, all identically corrupt, do damage. Technology replicates cheaply; it can also spread corruption. This was as true of the printing press as of the world wide web.

Wynkyn de Worde was more interested in poetry than Pynson. But his 1498 version of *The Canterbury Tales* shows his carelessness: the text was hardly edited at all. He did not always date his books but many of them were literary, including Skelton's *The Bowge of Court*. Wynkyn printed at least 640 books, 150 poems and romances. Robert Copland was his chief translator and could be a good editor. In 1518 he wrote the poor play *The Castell of Pleasure*, in which a sceptical exchange between author and printer occurs:

AUTHOR ... Emprint this book, Copland, at my request,
And put it forth to every maner state.

COPLAND At your instance I shall it gladly impresse,
But the utterance, I thinke, will be but small.
Books be not set by: their times is past, I guess;
The dice and cardes, in drinkynge wine and ale,
Tables, cayles, and balles, they be now sette a sale.
Men lete their children use all such harlotry,
That buyinge of bookes they utterly deny.

Like publishers down the generations, he laments the demise of the printed book as a force to be reckoned with, but his lament is issued before the art of printing in England has had even half a century's innings.

After 1521, new English books were fewer, but not for the reasons Copland adduced. The revival of learning meant a concentration on educational works and classical texts. Erasmus was not good for English-language publishing. The English printers were poor and growing poorer; continental printers, especially the Dutch, Belgians and French, targeted the English market. When, in 1525 at Worms, an edition of Tyndale's *New Testament* was issued, a change began: thereafter many foreign publications were controversial or subversive: works by exiles, refugees and 'unsettlers'. The Stationers' Company, incorporated 1557, was granted a national monopoly of printing. The issue was one of control, both of the industry and the contents of its product. The result stemmed the flood of foreign imports and limited the independence of native printers.

Proper gentlemen in England were contemptuous of books made by machine. So great was the prejudice that scribes sometimes copied from print for the 'authentic' reader, the medieval intellectual equivalent of the real-ale enthusiast. Early typecasters designed letters that imitated scribal practice. The new crept in under the guise of the old. If prejudice was pronounced in England, it existed on the Continent as well. The Abbot of Spanheim's letter *De laude scriptorum manualium* urges continuance of parchments and manuscripts as more durable and more appropriate than printed books. If the reproduction of texts became a secular activity, the Church would lose income and control – which it did. Some English and many German monasteries got presses, changing in order to stay the same.

Caxton's revolution was decisive but not dramatic. It took a long while for its effects to work their way through the literary system. The author might have been expected to derive some benefits; and he did, three hundred years later. Until the eighteenth century, there was close commerce, but not equal dealing, between authors and printer-publishers. Some relationships were exemplary. Erasmus lived at his printer-publisher Froben's house. Gabriel Harvey was maintained by his printer. Authors might be professional servants or employees of the publisher. They called regularly at their printer's works to correct proofs – part of the agreement. The printer considered himself absolved from all errors: the author was responsible. (Caxton was the exception: he had been a scrupulous proofreader. Wynkyn de Worde was content with a lower standard than his master. Proofreaders were costly professionals. Often, too costly.)

Printing took place near the markets where manuscripts were available for sale. Cathedral precincts were most popular: Paternoster Row at St Paul's, or the Red Pale near Westminster, Caxton's almonry, Oxford, Cambridge, Southwark, St Albans, York, Tavistock. They appeared wherever there were strong ecclesiastical interests or major civic institutions. A few bootleg printers emerged, servicing the outlawed religious groups – to begin with, the Puritans. One such dissident ended up publishing from Manchester.

Printing increased during the fifteenth century. When the sixteenth century dawned, though the old scribal arts survived and the taint of 'trade' made publishing distasteful to gentlemen, the multipally-produced text was a fact of life to which readers and writers were learning to adjust, just as today there is an adjustment between producers, readers and publishers to new technology in the form of electronic publishing. Caxton provided crucial texts and an even more crucial example. After his return from Bruges in 1476, things would change and keep on changing. The way a poet conceives and then visualizes a poem, the way a reader sees it disposed on the page, the alteration of feel to the fingers from vellum to paper, the loss of contact with readers, the emergence of middlemen between writer and audience, the greater authority of a multipally- or mass-produced text, the development of rules and consistencies of usage: all these considerations weighed with every person, writer or reader, for whom a poem was a creative space. The architecture of that space was adjusted to something more available and yet less flexible, as though language was under arrest and enduring the disciplines that would bring it to a seemingly classical 'stability' and perfection. The seeds of the eighteenth century are contained in the late fifteenth, though it took them a while to begin to grow.

Anthology

PREFACE

Medieval poetry, in two respects at least, is merciless to anthologists. First, so many of the poems they would like to represent are very long and not easily excerptable. Apart from the Scots, the lyric poets and the balladeers, the fifteenth century makes of length a prime virtue, and the language is often thinly spread. 'The Owl and the Nightingale' would like to be here but will not fit; Barbour's *Bruce* is similarly distended and does not respond to excerpting. It is painful to boil down great poets like Chaucer and Henryson in order to produce something like an essence of their work. The alchemy can never quite work.

Then there is the problem of making a text. To what extent is the orthography established by scholars 'authoritative', given that few of the manuscripts are in the poets' own hands, no two manuscripts are the same, and diverse scholars provide diverse texts? And, assuming a manuscript *has* some authority, to what extent is its authority phonetic? If it possesses phonetic authority, the related questions must arise, as they do in the recording of 'authentic' early music: can we say with any certainty what the language sounded like *then*, making allowance for dialect, and the transcription of texts from one dialect in another; and can we with our very different ears respond to the unascertainable sounds in the ways that contemporary listeners and readers did?

I have taken a controversial decision in compiling this anthology. Old English poetry is generally read in modern English translations, except by the dwindling crew of specialists in Anglo Saxon, a discipline which was compulsory in gaining an English degree in many British universities until quite recently. What turns some young readers away from Middle English is the strangeness of the orthography, and I have decided that accessibility is crucial in an introductory book. Chaucer is not difficult, and nor is Gower; the superficial difficulties are the look of the text. What is unfamiliar is actually the familiar masked behind archaic spellings which have no special authority beyond that of a manuscript, set down in an age before spelling was standardized. Some spellings hold the key of pronunciation or accent, but for new readers what matters is the flow of the verse, and that is what this anthology, without translation as such except in the Old English section, seeks to provide. If the transparency of the texts is here and there excessive, the hope is that a reader progressing from this version of Langland or Gower or Henryson to an edition of those poets' works, will have an ear predisposed to the sounds that are audible there. The perils of such a procedure are obvious, and primarily these: that in a modernized text many semantic nuances are blurred or lost, along with etymologies and the like; and some are anachronistically added by using the modern form of the word, because the modern form conveys the modern meaning. I can only hope that context will help qualify and contain this tendency.

The chief interpretative problem from my point of view has been prosodic, the famous or notorious 'voiced "e" ' and where it should properly *be* voiced. I have put an 'ĕ' when the letter is, to my hearing, either to be pronounced, or subliminally 'heard' as a slight inflection of voice where ellisions are intended. I err perhaps on the side of greater metrical regularity, wanting to hear in Chaucer's pentameters at least the five stresses in roughly the right places.

The anthology is intended to be used with the extended excerpts in the Introduction. There Gower's Amans and the anonymous lyric poets are given voice. I have tried not to duplicate matter too much but to make the anthology complementary to the Introduction, growing as it does out of the general argument. Poetically, the Wife of Bath's 'Prologue' is more compelling than her (nonetheless excellent) 'Tale', but I wanted the reader to be able to compare Chaucer's story directly with Gower's 'Tale of Florent'. Such a comparison clarifies the relative merits of both poets.

In compiling the modernized text, I have had recourse to various editions and these are listed in the Bibliography. No single source can be adduced for any particular extract or poem. In the ballads I have taken the liberties of old balladeers and of later editors including Bishop Percy, Robert Burns, Sir Walter Scott, Robert Graves and William Empson: where two or more versions exist I have tried to combine elements, and where there are longueurs I have omitted stanzas: there are no final authorities here.

I have also represented Hoccleve, Lydgate and Hawes at greater length than they are usually accorded. (Indeed, sometimes they are excluded altogether.) They help to make sense of Chaucer's and Gower's legacy, and also of the great poetry that begins to be written in the sixteenth century (some of the poems included here were written at the start of that century but belong to the imaginative world of the century before). The sixteenth century gets off to a wild and rumbustious start with Skelton who, breaking with the rigorous impoverishments of the new humanism in which he was trained, with the mechanical copiousness of Hawes and the legacy of Lydgate, brought English poetry back to the Englishness of Chaucer and the anonymous ballad and lyric writers. It is with Skelton that the second anthology properly begins.

OLD ENGLISH

1. The Dream of the Rood

Hwaet!
I'll tell you of the best of dreams,
this that I dreamt at deepest night,
when sleeps mankind, speech stilled.
It seemed I saw the rarest tree
borne aloft, light-clad,
of all beams brightest. All that beacon was
adorned with gold. Jewels stood
fair at its bounds, five of these in all,
and it spanned heavens. I saw there angel-hosts,
fair through eternity – no crook's gallows this,
while there looked on celestial spirits,
mankind on earth, and all creation's might.

Splendid the triumph-tree, and I sin-tainted,
crippled with guilt. I saw the tree of glory
wondrously clothed, shine merrily,
girt over with gold; jewels stood
skilfully set into the Ruler's tree.
Yet I through that gold could there discern
wrongdoings age-old; now it began to bleed,
first on its right-hand side. And there was I, all swayed by sorrows,
fearful at that fair sight; I saw the living Sign
shift shades and skins: now with blood bedewed,
soaked slick with gore, now with treasures gilded.

And I lay there a long while yet,
heart-sick I watched the Saviour's tree,
lay till I heard it utter word;
the best of boughs began to speak;
'It was long ago – well I recall it –
that I was felled at forest's edge,

stirred of my roots. Strong foes seized on me,
crafted me for a spectacle, a rack for wrongdoers;
bore me shoulder-high to the knoll prepared me,
there the host secured me. Now I saw the Lord of man
approach me eagerly, his will was to climb me.

'I did not shirk the Master's bidding,
nor bowed nor broke when trembling rent
the ground beneath. I could have felled them all,
have slain the sinners, yet I stood firm.
Then the young Saviour – this was God almighty –
disrobed, strong, steadfast, to ascend his gallows,
brave before many, for he would free mankind.
I shook at his embrace; yet did not budge,
nor fall to earth, but stood sure, as I must.
Rood was I reared up; I raised the mighty King,
the Lord of heaven; and I did not yield.

'Dark nails they drove through me; on me are left gashes,
open hate-wounds; still I did not harm them.
Together they reviled us; and his blood it soaked me,
sprung from that man's side after he sent forth his soul.
I on that hill had endured
cruel fates aplenty: I saw the Lord of hosts
starkly stretched. Darkness had come,
shrouded in night the Ruler's corpse;
over its radiance, shadows surged onwards
wan under the skies. All creation wept,
mourned the King's fall. Christ crucified.
Yet eager ones came from afar,
to the great Prince; and I saw all of this.
Sorely I was with sorrows driven, yet bowed down humbly,
eagerly to soldiers' hands. They seized almighty God,
lifted of that grim torture; there they left me
anguished in blood, crippled by nail-points.

'Limb-weary they laid him; standing at his body's head
they looked down on heaven's Lord; he was for now at rest,
spent from that struggle. Soldiers began a tomb,
hewn from bright stone before my sight, his slayer's;
there they set the King of victories. They made a sorrow-song
then journeyed home, wretched in the eventide,
weary at heart, left the great Leader. He rested there alone, scarce company.

We three stood yet, rued a good while
stuck at our stations; song had gone up
from the soldiers; corpse cooled,
fair life-house. Then men again
felled us to earth; bitter fate.
They dug for us a deep grave; yet men of the Lord,
friends, found out my place of rest,
decked me in gold and silver.

'Now you may acknowledge, beloved companion,
how I have endured sharp sorrows,
sin-dwellers' deeds. Now the time has come
that I am exalted hither and yon;
mankind on earth, and all creation's might,
pray to this Sign. On me the Son of God
suffered awhile; for that, I now wax great,
mighty under the heavens, and my power is to save
each and all who is in awe of me.
Then was I ordained the hardest torment,
loathed in all lands, ere I laid open
the path of life for all mankind to know.

'Behold, I am honoured by the Lord of glory
above all woods' trees, heaven's royal Ward;
just as he has his mother, Mary herself,
whom Almighty God, for all mankind,
exalted over all the race of women.

'Now I bid of you, beloved companion,
speak to men of this vision;
reveal in words this is the tree of glory
on which almighty God long ago suffered,
for the manifold sins of all mankind,
and for Adam's past transgression.
Death he there tasted; yet the Lord arose
with mighty strength, to save all men.
To heaven he ascended. Hither he'll return
to this middle-earth to seek mankind
on the day of doom, the Lord himself,
almighty God in his angels' midst,
when he will deem, he who has judgment,
each and all as they deserve,
as earlier earned in this fleeting life.

There can be no man unafraid
of that word which the Lord will utter:
he'll ask of many where the man is
who for the Ruler's name would wish to taste
of bitter death, as once he did upon that tree.
But they'll take fear, and few shall know
how they'll begin to answer Christ.
Yet no man need be fearful there
who's borne that blessed Sign within.
Every soul from this middle-earth
must through the Rood seek heaven's land
who'd think to dwell with the Almighty.'

Prayed I then to that tree blithe in spirit,
with heartfelt zeal, though I stood alone,
scarce company. My mind was fixed
with longing on my going-forth, keenest awaited
of longed-for times. It is my life's desire
that I should seek the triumph-tree
alone, more often than all other men,
give worthy worship. My will for this
swells in my heart, and my mind is set
fixed on the Rood. Few well-placed friends
have I on earth; they have gone before,
plucked from pleasures, sought the King of glory;
live now in heaven with the High Father,
dwelling in splendour; and I look fondly
to the day when the Lord's rood comes for me –
that tree which I saw once on earth –
when from this fleeting life it will fetch me,
bring me to that place where bliss is great,
joy in the heavens, there the Lord's folk
forever seated, there the endless bliss;
set me up there, there after death
may I dwell in glory, with the holy ones
have share of joys. Be God friend to me,
that God who suffered once upon this earth,
was hanged upon that tree for mankind's sins;
he set us free, to us granted life
and home in heaven. Hope was made new,
with blessing and with bliss, for those that suffered hell.
Steadfast was the Son, triumphant his journey,
strongly and surely shall he with many come,

bring ranks of the righteous to God's own kingdom,
to bliss with angels and all that's holy,
all that is in heaven, to dwell with him,
imperial Almighty; there the Ruler comes,
almighty God, there his fatherland.

2. The Seafarer

This verse is my voice, it is no fable,
I tell of my travelling, how in hardship
I have often suffered laborious days,
endured in my breast the bitterest cares,
explored on shipboard sorrow's abodes,
the welter and terror of the waves. There
the grim night-vigil has often found me
at the prow of the boat when gripped by the cold
it cuts and noses along the cliffs.
There my feet were fettered by frost,
with chains of zero, and the cares were whistling
keen about my heart, and hunger within me
had torn my sea-dazed mind apart.
The theme is strange to the happy man
whose life on earth exults and flourishes,
how I lived out a winter of wretchedness
wandering exiled on the ice-cold sea,
bereft of my friends, harnessed in frost,
when the hail flew in showers down.
There I heard only the ocean roar,
the cold foam, or the song of the swan.
The gannet's call was all my pleasure,
curlew's music for laughter of men,
cries of a seagull for relish of mead.
There tempests struck the cliffs of rock,
and the frozen-feathered tern called back,
and often the eagle with glistening wings
screamed through the spindrift: ah what prince
could shield or comfort the heart in its need!
For he who possesses the pleasures of life
and knows scant sorrow behind town-walls
with his pride and his wine will hardly believe
how I have often had to endure

heartbreak over the paths of the sea.
Black squalls louring: snow from the north:
world-crust rime-sealed: hail descending,
coldest of harvests –
                            Yet now the thoughts
of my heart are beating to urge me on
to the salt wave-swell and tides of the deep.
Again and again the mind's desire
summons me outward far from here
to visit the shores of nations unknown.
There is no man on earth so noble of mind,
so generous in his giving or so bound to his lord
that he will cease to know the sorrow of sea-going,
the voyages which the Lord has laid upon him.
He has no heart for the harp, or the gift of rings,
or the delight of women, or the joy of the world,
or for any other thing than the rolling of the waves:
he who goes on the sea longs after it for ever.

When groves bloom and castles are bright,
when meadows are smiling and the earth dances,
all these are voices for the eager mind,
telling such hearts to set out again
voyaging far over the ocean-stream.
With its sad call too the cuckoo beckons,
the guardian of summer singing of sorrow
sharp in the breast. Of this the prosperous
man knows nothing, what some must endure
on tracks of exile, travellers, far-rangers.
And now my own mind is restless within me,
my thought I send out through all the world
to the floods of ocean and the whale's kingdom,
until it comes back yearning to me
unfed, unquenched; the lone flier cries,
urges my desire to the whale's way
forward irresistibly on the breast of the sea.

And keener therefore when they strike my heart
are the joys of the Lord than this mortality
and loan of life; it is not my faith
that the riches of the earth will be everlasting.
One of three things to every man
must always loom over his appointed day:

sickness, old age, or enemy's sword
shall drive out life from the doomed man departing.
And then it is best that those who come after
and speak of the dead should be able to praise him,
that he in this world before his end
should help the people with deeds of courage
against the malice of foes and the devil,
so that afterwards the children of men
will exalt his name, and his praise with angels
will remain for ever, everliving glory,
bliss among the hosts. Great days have gone,
pomp and magnificence from the world's dominions.
Now there are neither kings nor emperors
nor gold-givers such as once there were
when in their realms they dealt with the utmost
honour, and lived in the nobility of fame.
Fallen is all this chivalry, their joys have departed.
And the world is wielded by shadows of men
ruling under affliction. Oh glory brought low,
splendour of this earth grown withered and old
like man himself now through all the world!
See age come up to him, and his face go pale,
a grey head in grief recalling friends gone,
the children of men given back to the earth.
Nor can body of flesh when life has fled
taste for him any sweetness or be sensible of sorrow,
nor will hand have touch, nor the mind its thought.
And though he should strew the grave with gold
where his own brother lies, with numberless treasures
in a double burial, none will go with him
on that voyage, nor can gold avail
for the soul with its sin before God's wrath
who hoards it here while he still has breath.

Dreadful is the terror of the Creator, when the world has turned through
   time.
He established the great abyss, the leagues of the earth and the sky.
The fool has no fear of the Lord: death falls on him unwarned.
The blessed man lives in humility: on him heaven's mercies descend:
he trusts the power of his Maker in the battlements of his mind.

3. The Wanderer

The solitary man lives still in hope
of his Maker's mercy, though with anxious mind
over the ocean-roads he has long to go,
rowing in his boat on the rime-cold sea,
voyaging out his exile while fate is fulfilled.

The words of the wanderer recalling hardships,
savage encounters, falling of kinsmen:
'In the doom of loneliness dawn after dawn
I lament my cares; there is none now alive
to whom I might dare reveal in their clearness
the thoughts of my heart. It is true I know
that the custom shows most excellent in a man
to lock and bind up all his mind,
his thought his treasure, let him think what he will.
Nor can the wearied work against fate,
nor painful remembrance have present aid;
those after glory must often hide
a dark thought deep in their mind.
So I in my grief gone from my homeland
far from my kinsmen have often to fetter
the images of the heart in iron chains,
for now it is long since the night of the earth
lay over my lord and I then forlorn
wintered with sorrow on freezing seas,
seeking in sadness some gold-giver's dwelling,
if only I could find whether far or near
one to show favour to me in the mead-hall,
one to give solace to me friendless,
to treat me with kindness. He who has felt it
knows how care is a cruel companion
to the man deprived of his dear protectors:
wandering is his, not winding gold,
a breast of grieving, not world's glory.
He remembers the retainers at the giving of treasures,
and how he in his youth was feasted and pleasured
by his friend and lord; that joy quite gone!
This is his suffering who has so long missed
the counselling voice of his cherished prince,
when sorrow and daydream often together
seize the unhappy man in his solitude:

it all comes back, he embraces and kisses
the lord he is loyal to, lays on his knee
hands and head as he did long ago
when he knew the triumphs and treasures of the throne.
Then the unfriended man wakens again,
watches in front of him waves of grey,
sea-birds swimming and flashing their wings,
snow falling, hoarfrost thickened with hail.
Then the heart's wounds are the more harrowing,
graver is his longing for that loved man.
Grief is revived when the vision of kinsmen
gathers in his mind and he greets them with joy
and eagerly searches the dear faces;
but fighters and retainers float off and dissolve,
and the mind receives from these seafarers
scant song of speech; care comes again
to him who must send his ceaseless heart
in its weariness over the frozen waves.

There is no cause indeed in all the world
why my thoughts here should not grow dark,
when I ruminate the life of noble men,
how they suddenly left the halls in death,
warriors in their pride. And so this earth
from day to day declines and decays,
nor is any man wise before his due
of worldly years. Wisdom is patience:
to be neither too temperless nor too sharp of tongue,
nor too feeble in fight nor too heart-heedless,
nor too deep in fear, in pride or in greed,
nor ever too boastful of things unknown.
A man should be wary in uttering his vows
till he stands proud in sure knowledge
of where thought and mind are ready to bend.
The wise man perceives how terrible is the time
when all the wealth of the world lies waste,
as now scattered throughout this earth
walls are standing where winds howl round
and hoarfrost hangs, in crumbling courts.
Wine-halls are sinking, kings are at rest
bereft of joy, all the flower of men
has fallen by those walls. War took some,
bore them from the world; one the winged ship

drove over the deep; one the grey wolf
gave to death; and one sad-faced
a man buried in a cave of the earth.
So the Maker of men laid waste this globe,
till those old cities, the labour of titans,
stood in their desolation silent after revelry.

He then who ponders wisely in his mind
and goes over this life in its darkness and its origins
with insight of heart recalls the carnage
of far-off myriads and speaks these words:
"Where has the horse gone? the rider? the treasure-giver?
the halls of feasting? Where are man's joys?
The dazzling goblets! The dazzling warriors!
The splendour of the prince! Ah, how that time
has gone, has darkened under the shadow of night
as if it had never been! Now in the place
of that beloved chivalry a wall is standing
marvellous in height, sculptured with serpents.
The men have been seized by the strength of spears,
by death-hungry weapons, illustrious destiny,
while tempests beat on this steep stone,
the blizzard falling binds the ground,
the terror of winter roaring in darkness
when the night-storm blackens and sends from the north
fierce hail-showers in malice to men.
All the kingdom of the world is in labour,
earth under heaven revolves through its cycle.
Here riches will pass, here friends will pass,
here man will pass, here woman will pass,
and the whole foundation come to dissolution." '

So spoke the wise man in his mind, sitting in meditation by himself.
Good is the man who holds faith: he must never too readily tell
the grief he has in his heart, unless he has solace before him
in the daring a man may win. Blessed is he who implores
his grace and comfort from heaven, where the dooms of us all are shored.

4. The Ruin

Wonder holds these walls. Under destiny destruction
splits castles apart. Gigantic battlements are crumbling,
roofs sunk in ruin, riven towers fallen,
gates and turrets lost, hoarfrost for mortar,
rain-bastions beaten, cleft, pierced, perished,
eaten away by time. Earth's fist and grasp
holds mason and man, all decayed, departed.
The soil grips hard. There a hundred generations
of the people have dwindled and gone. This wall bore well,
moss-grey and reddened, the revolutions of kingdoms,
stoutly withstood tempests. That great gate fell . . .
Magnificent rose the fortresses, the lavish swimming-halls,
the profuse and lofty glory of spires, the clangour of armies,
the drinking-halls crammed with every man's delight,
till that was overturned by steadfast fate.
The broad walls were sundered, the plague-days came,
the brave men were rapt away by the bereaver,
their war-ramparts razed to desolate foundations,
their city crumbled down. The restorers lie asleep,
armies of men in the earth. And so those halls are wastes,
the old purple stone and the tiles and wood are lying
scattered with the smashed roofs. Death crushed that place,
struck it flat to the hill, where once many a man
brilliant with gold and adazzle with costliest war-trappings,
happy, proud, and wine-flushed, glittered there in his battle-armour,
gazed over his treasures, on the silver and the curious stones,
on the rich goods and possessions, on the preciously cut jewels,
and on this splendid city of the far-spread kingdom.
The stone courts stood then, the hot stream broke
welling strongly through the stone, all was close and sweet
in the bright bosom of the walls, and where the baths lay
hot at the heart of the place, that was the best of all . . .

Seven Riddles

5.

A meal of words made by a moth
seemed to me when I heard the tale
curious and phenomenal:

that such a mite like a thief in the night
should swallow up the song of a poet,
the splendid discourse and its solid setting!
But the strange robber was none the wiser
for all those words and all that eating.

6.

My garment sweeps the world in silence,
whether indoors or troubling the waters.
Watch me taken over human houses
by my armour-trappings and by soaring airs:
see how the power of the clouds carries me
far and wide above men. My adornments
loudly and melodiously sound and resound,
sing bright and clear, when I rise from my rest,
a spirit moving over field and flood.

7.

Here is my head beaten with a hammer,
cut with sharp tools, carved by a file.
Often I swallow what stands before me,
when I thrust hard, clashing in my rings
against a hard object; pierced from behind
I have to push forward the thing that keeps
the delight of my master's mind at midnight.
Sometimes again I retract my nose,
guardian of treasure, when my master's aim
is to take the spoils of those he has had killed
by avenging force with wishes of blood.

8.

I am not loud; where I live's not silent.
The Lord laid down our course of life
inseparable. I am swifter than he is,
I am stronger sometimes, but he persists more steadily.
At times I rest; he runs on always.
I dwell in him every day I live.
Divide us and you doom me to death.

9.

Sometimes my master miserably binds me,
sends me under the vast swell
of the flourishing fields and forces me to be still,
drives down my strength supine into darkness,
furiously into a den where the earth presses
crouching on my back. From that monstrous place
no way of turning I know but to trouble
and stir the home of man: Heorots
rock, dwelling-houses, walls tremble
terrible above hall-counsellors. Tranquil they seem,
sky over landscape, sea in its silence
till I drive upward, rise from my prison,
in the hand of him who guides me, who gave me
in the beginning my bonds and fetters, bound me
never to bend but the way he beckons!

Sometimes from above I shake the waves,
wreathe the ocean-stream, throw to the shore
the flint-grey flood: foam's in the fight
of wave against sea-wall: mountainous above the main
it looms in darkness, and black on its track
its neighbour travels in the water-tumult
till they clash breaking at the brink of land,
at the soaring bluffs. There the ship seethes
through the sailors' clamour, the steep rock-falls
quietly stand for the sea's assailing,
for the crash in the stone-split when crested mass
crowds to crush cliffs. There over the boat
a hard strife hangs if the sea should seize it
with its freight of souls in fearful hour,
torn if it should be from course and command
riding foam-white with its life outfought
on the back of the waves. Unblest, awesome,
manifest to men, each terror I unwrap
adamant in my wayfaring, and for whom will it be still?

Sometimes I career through what clings to my back,
the black wave-pourers, press far apart
the sea-feeding cloud-brims and suddenly let them
slap again together: it is the king of sounds
bursting above cities, boldest of crashes

when cloud on cloud edge to edge
cracks dark and sharp. Creatures of blackness
scurrying in the sky shower down fire,
fire-pallor, fire-flare, with tremors roll on
dull, din-resonant above the distraught,
all battle forward, letting fall
rustling from their breast wet mist and gloom,
rain from their womb. The dreaded army
advances in its feud, fear arises,
a great anxiousness among mankind,
all places are appalled, when the quicksilver phantom
shoots in flashes with his sharpest weapons.
The fool fears nothing of those mortal spears,
but the fool lies dead if the living God
lets an arrow fly to him from the far whirlwind
right to his heart, through the falling rain
a falling bolt. Few remain
whom lightning pins at weapon's point.

I establish that strife in its origins
when I go out among the cloud-congress
forcing through its press with my vast host
on the bosom of the stream – the lofty war-throng
breaks into great sound. Then again I bow
low down to land in the hollow of the air
and load on my back what I have to bear,
admonished in the majesty of my own master.
So I act and battle, a servant but glorious,
now beneath the earth, now beneath the waves
sunk in humility, now over the main
rousing the ocean-streams, now risen up
flinging the sky-wrack far and wide
in my vigour and race. Say what is my name,
or who shall raise me when I cannot rest,
or who shall support me when I must be still.

10.

I caught sight of a wonderful creature,
an air-vessel, luminous, elegantly adorned,
bringing booty held in her horns,
bringing booty home from the foray.
She wanted a bower to be built in the fortress,

a snug retreat, if so it might be.
A wonderful creature topped the crag then,
a creature known to every country,
seized the booty and sent the wanderer
unwilling home – she slid back west
vowing vengeance, and soon vanished.
Dust rose skyward, dew fell on earth,
night took its way. No man afterwards
could guess the course of the creature's journey.

11.

A strange being slipped along the waves,
lovely on shipboard, shouted to land,
loud and resounding. Hair-crawling laughter
made earth shiver. Edges were sharp.
A cruel creature, grudging engagement
but grim in encounter, it savaged, ravaged
the stove-in ship, bound bad spells round it,
spoke with cunning on its own creation:
'My mother is of dearest maiden kin,
she is my daughter fully developed
and brought to greatness as all men believe,
all living folk, she will walk in delight
through fields of every earthly land.'

12. Beowulf

(a)

[1–193] *Introductory: history and praise of the Danes, and account of
Grendel's attacks on Heorot*

How that glory remains in remembrance,
Of the Danes and their kings in days gone,
The acts and valour of princes of their blood!
   Scyld Scefing: how often he thrust from their feast-halls
The troops of his enemies, tribe after tribe,
Terrifying their warriors: he who had been found
Long since as a waif and awaited his desert
While he grew up and throve in honour among men

Till all the nations neighbouring about him
Sent as his subjects over the whale-fields   10
Their gifts of tribute: king worth the name!
Then there was born a son to succeed him,
A boy for that house, given by God
As a comfort to the folk for all the wretchedness
He saw they had lived in, from year to year
Lacking an overlord; and the overlord of Life,
Of Glory, gave the man worldly excelling,
Till his fame spread far, the fame of Beowulf
The son of Scyld, on Scandinavian soil.
So should magnanimity be the young man's care,   20
Rich gifts and royal in his father's household,
That when he is old his ready companions
Will remain with him still, his people stand by him
When war returns; a man shall flourish
By acts of merit in every land.
   Then Scyld departed in the ripeness of time,
Old in deeds, to the Lord's keeping.
They carried him down to the restless sea,
His beloved retainers, as he himself had asked
While words served him, the lord of the Scyldings   30
And their dear king who had ruled them long.
There at the harbour stood the ring-prowed boat,
The prince's vessel, ice-cased, sea-keen;
Deep in the ship they laid him down,
Their beloved lord, the giver of rings,
The hero by the mast. Great treasures there,
Far-gathered trappings were taken and set:
No ship in fame more fittingly furnished
With weapons of war and battle-armour,
With mail-coat and sword; there lay to his hand   40
Precious things innumerable that would go at his side
Voyaging to the distant holds of the flood.
By no means poorer were their rich offerings,
The treasures they gave him, than those given
By the men who cast him at his life's beginning
A child out over the waves alone.
Lastly they put up high above his head
A gold-woven banner, and let the sea bear him,
Gave him to the main; their hearts grieved,
Mourning was in their minds. And whose were the   50
    shores –

Who can say with truth, whether counsellor in hall
Or warrior on earth – where this freight was washed?
   That country then saw Beowulf of the Scyldings
Renowned among the peoples, a beloved king
Ruling many years – his father and lord
Having gone from the world – until there was born to him
Noble Healfdene; war-grim, aged,
Lifelong guardian of the illustrious Scyldings.
By him four children reckoned in all
Were born into this world, princes of men,   60
Heorogar and Hrothgar and the good Halga
And she [. . .], who was Onela's queen,
The dear consort of the warlike Swede.
To Hrothgar in time came triumph in battle,
The glory of the sword, and his friendly kinsmen
Flocked to serve him till the band of them was great,
A host of eager retainers. And his mind
Stirred him to command a hall to be built,
A huger mead-house to be made and raised

(b)

       Gliding at midnight
Came the gloomy roamer. The soldiers were sleeping –
Those who were guarding the gabled building –
All except one. Men well knew
That that malefactor in the forbidding of the Creator
Was powerless to draw them down beneath the shades;
But he, wideawake with heart-pent fury
And anger for the ravager, awaited fight's fortune.
Now by the swirling bluffs from his wasteland   710
Grendel came stalking; he brought God's wrath.
His sin and violence thought to ensnare
One of our kind in that hall of halls.
He moved through the night till with perfect clearness
He could see the banquet-building, treasure-home of men
Gold-panelled and glittering. Not his first visit
Was this for attacking the house of Hrothgar;
In no day of his life before or after
Did he find hall-men or a hero more dangerous!
Up then to the building the man came prowling   720
Devoid of all delighting. The door, firm-iron-bound,

Flew at once ajar when he breached it with his fists;
The hall's mouth he tore wide open, enraged
And possessed by his evil. Quickly after this
The fiend stepped over the stone-patterned floor,
Moved with fury; there started from his eyes
Unlovely light in the very form of fire.
Many a soldier he saw in the hall,
The company of kinsmen all asleep together,
The young warrior-band; and his heart exulted,   730
He aimed to divide, before day came,
Monstrous in frightfulness, life from limb
In every man of them, now that he had hope
Of ravening to gluttonousness. But the fate was finished
That could keep him after that night carnivorous
On human kind. The kinsman of Hygelac
Watched in his strength to see how the killer
Would go about his work with those panic hand-grips.
Nor did the monster mean to be backward,
But flashed to seize at the first opportunity   740
A soldier from his sleep, tore him unopposed,
Gnashed flesh from bone, at veins drank blood,
Gulped down the feast of his wounds; in a trice
He had the last of the dead man devoured,
To the feet and the fingers. He stepped farther in,
Caught then with his hand the iron-purposed
Warrior in his bed, the fiend with his fist
Reached out to seize him; he quickly gripped
The spite-filled creature, and rose upon his arm.
As soon as evil's dalesman discovered   750
That never had he known a stronger hand-grasp
In any other man beneath the sun
Throughout earth's acres, his mind began
To fear for his flesh; by that he escaped
None the more readily! He strained to be off,
To strike den and dark, join the devil-covens;
His fate in that place was without a fellow
Among his days before. Then the good warrior,
The kinsman of Hygelac recalled what he had said
That evening, stood up, and grappled him close;   760
Joints cracked aloud; the giant moved off,
The man strode after him. The byword for malice
Was minded, if he could, to slip into the distance
To the shelter of the fens – saw his fingers' force

In the fierce man's fist holds. A bitter coming
The persecutor had of it when he made for Heorot!
The royal hall rang; to all the Danes,
To all the fortress-men, the brave, the warriors
Came panic horror. Both hosts-of-the-hall
Were in rage, in ferocity. The building reverberated.   770
It was more than a marvel that that wine-house
Stood up to the battle-darers, that the splendid walls
Didn't fall to the ground; but it had the solidity,
It was cleverly compacted both inside and out
With its bands of iron. Many were the mead-benches
Sumptuous with gold that were wrenched there from the floor,
Beside the antagonists in their epic fury.
– A thing undreamed of by Scylding wisdom
That any man could ever, in any manner,
Shatter it as it stood stately and horn-spanned,   780
By sleights disrupt it: till fire's embrace
Should become its furnace. A sound mounted up
Uncouth, unceasing: terror unparalleled
Fell upon the Danes, upon every soul of them
Who listened by the ramparts to the noise of crying,
To the God-hated howling a lay of horror,
Song of lost triumph, the hell-fettered man
In lament for pain. He held him fast
Who at that hour of this earthly life
Was master of manhood of all mankind.   790
    Nothing would make the protector of warriors
Let slaughter's emissary escape alive,
Nor would he reckon many days left to him
Of profit to any man. Then Beowulf's soldiers
Brandished here and there their ancient swords,
Anxious to defend the body of their lord,
Of the illustrious prince, as they might be able –
Ignorant of this, when they moved to fight,
Iron-minded men of arms,
Thinking to strike on every side,   800
To pierce to his spirit: that the lawless ravager
Was not to be reached by any war-blade,
Not by the choicest metal on earth,
For every sword-edge and weapon of victory
He had blunted by wizardry. – Wretched his future
Now at that hour of this earthly life
Cut off from breath: far had the uncanny

Soul to wander into fiends' dominions.
For then he discovered, who often before
Had in his transgressions tormented the mind   810
Of human kind, he God's antagonist,
That his own body would not obey him,
But the kinsman of Hygelac in undaunted encounter
Had him in his grasp; each was to the other
Abhorrent if alive. The appalling demon
Bore flesh-agony; on his shoulder became manifest
A monstrous wound, sinews quivering,
Tendons ripped open. To Beowulf was granted
Triumph in that fight; but to Grendel the flight
In distress to death by the looming marshlands,   820
To his joyless home; he had no more doubt
That the end of his life had arrived in sight,
The lease-date of his light. All the Danes' desire
Was met and fulfilled by bloodshed of that fight.

(c)

    The old king leapt up, gave thanks to God,
To the Lord in his power, for what the man had spoken.
Hrothgar's horse then was bitted and bridled,
The wavy-maned mount. The wise-minded prince   1400
Rode off in his armour; a troop of shieldsmen
Marched at his side. There lay the footmarks
Visible far and wide through the woodland paths,
The track across the plains, the way she had headed
Over the gloomy moor, carrying off lifeless
That best of retainers, the chief of those
Who kept with Hrothgar watch in the hall.
Then the children of men passed over
Precipitous rock-falls, narrow pathways,
Dangerous defiles, a road unmapped,   1410
Abrupt promontories riddled with kraken-caves;
He with a handful of wary-minded men
Rode on in front scanning the country,
Till he came suddenly upon the mountain-trees
Bending low over hoary rock,
A joyless forest; beneath lay the water
Labouring and blood-thickened. To the Scylding company,
To all the Danes came vexation of heart
Hard to be borne, to many a retainer,

To every man grief when they found   1420
On the cliffs of the lake, Aeschere's head.
Waves welled blood as the people looked,
Boiled with crimson. At intervals the horn
Sang its sharp troop-summons. Foot-soldiers sat then
And saw over the water serpentkind congregated,
Strange sea-dragons making trial of the tarn,
Krakens too, lying on the headland slopes,
Like those which often in morning forays
Gally the mariners' thoroughfare,
Reptiles, wild creatures. They backed away   1430
Irritated, angered; they recognized the blast,
The war-horn-song. A man of the Geats
With his bow cut one of them off from life,
From warring with the waves, a hard battle-arrow
Boring into its lifeblood; it was the slacker in swimming
Over the ocean after death seized it.
At once it was closely cornered in the waves
By keen-barbed boar-pikes, forcibly taken
And drawn up on the headland, an amazing denizen
Of wave and flood; the men gazed at it,   1440
Grisly thing and uncouth!
                              Beowulf put on
The garments of battle, of his own life heedless;
The broad war-corslet designed with art,
Close-hand-woven, must probe the water,
War-corslet expert to protect his body,
Lest battlehold of the enraged, lest malicious clutch
Might have power to attain his heart and his life;
And his head was guarded by that gleaming helmet
Which must trouble and stir the abysses of the lake,
Visit the mulling of streams, bejewelled,   1450
Chain-circled, princelike, just as long ago
The weapon-smith made it, marvellously forged it,
Set boar-figures round it, that never thereafter
Might sword or war-metal be able to shear it.
That too was not the meagrest of mainstays
Which Hrothgar's spokesman lent him at need:
Hrunting was the name of that hafted sword;
It was one famous among ancient treasures;
The blade was of iron, poison-twig-patterned,
Battle-blood-hardened; never did it fail   1460
Any man at war who grasped it in his hands,

Who dared adventure in exploits of danger,
In the homestead of fighters; not for the first time
Was it now to accomplish an act of valour.
The son of Ecglaf strong in power
Was indeed forgetful of what he said before
With wine in his words when he lent that weapon
To a finer swordsman; himself fearful
Of venturing his life under the waves' uproar,
To manifest his heroism: losing glory so,   1470
Fame of good acts. With the other how different
Once he had put on the garments of battle!
   Beowulf spoke, Ecgtheow's son:
'Recall now, illustrious heir of Healfdene,
Wise prince, now that I am ready to go,
Gold-friend of men, what we two have said,
That if I in your service should lose my life
You would stand always in the place of a father
To me after I had gone from the world.
Embrace in your protection my young retainers,   1480
My comrades-in-arms, if war should take me;
Also send Hygelac, Hrothgar my friend,
Those precious things you have made me a gift of,
And the lord of the Geats may in that gold perceive,
Hrethel's son see when he gazes on that treasure,
That I found a ring-giver noble in all kingly
Liberalities, and enjoyed them while I was able.
And let Unferth have the ancient heirloom,
Let the far-famed man have the hard-edged sumptuous
Wave-scrolled sword; I with Hrunting   1490
Shall win my glory, or death shall take me.'
   After these words the man of the Geats
Hastened off eagerly – by no means lingering
For any rejoinder; the surging water
Closed over the warrior. It was almost a day then
Before he could make out the form of the lake-floor.
She at once, guardian of the field of floods
For a century of seasons, savage-ravenous,
Grim and gluttonous, discovered some man
Was sounding there, down towards dominions of demon-kind.   1500
She grappled with him then, gripped the warrior
In frightful fistholds; hurting none the sooner
The firm flesh within – the casing chain-armour
Kept him round about, the war-dress unpierced,

The interlocked mail-coat by her fierce fingers.
When the wolfish water-fiend reached the bottom
She carried the ring-giver, the prince, to her hall,
So that he couldn't – whatever his bravery –
Make use of his weapons, and then through the water
Countless strange things harassed him, sea-beasts   1510
Of many kinds tried with their battle-tusks to slash
His chain-mail, monsters tormented him. Then the man
Saw he was in some hall of his enemy's,
Where not a drop of water would harm him,
Where a vaulted chamber kept the sudden
Flood-fall from touching him; and he saw firelight,
A gleam and a flashing brilliantly shining.
    The good fighter saw then the abyss's curse,
The great sea-demon-woman; a tremendous onslaught
He made with his war-sword, his hand drove its stroke,   1520
Till the ring-banded blade rang out on her head
Its hungry battle-song. Then the stranger found
That the glittering metal refused to bite,
Would not hurt life, but the edge failed
The prince in his need; it had borne brunt before
Of many an encounter, hacked many a helmet
And doomed man's war-dress; for the precious treasure
This was the first time its glory faltered.
    Resolute again was Hygelac's kinsman,
Not backward in bravery, mindful of all audacity.   1530
The warrior now infuriated threw down on the ground
The wave-marked sword steel-edged and stubborn
With its bands of rare handiwork; he put faith in strength,
In the hand-grip of power. So shall a man act
When in the midst of war he takes heart to win
Long-living praise: careless of his life.
The man of the Geats then seized by the shoulder –
No shrinking in that fight! – Grendel's mother,
And roused by rage to battle-relentlessness
Swung the desperate enemy till she fell to the floor.   1540
She in turn quickly gave him a requital
With her cruel clawholds and closely grappled him;
Then the foot-soldier, strongest of warriors,
Exhausted in spirit, slipped and fell,
And she bestrode her hall-guest, and drew her knife
Broadbladed, burnished; vengeance she wanted
For her child, her only son. On his shoulder lay

The chain-net of his war-mail protecting his flesh,
Forbidding the piercing of spear-point and sword-edge.
The son of Ecgtheow and champion of the Geats   1550
Would then have been lost under the vastness of the earth
If his coat of armour had not furnished him help,
His unyielding battle-mail – and God in holiness
Drawn the fight to triumph: in his wisdom the Lord
The Ruler of the heavens gave his simple
Decree for the right, when he rose once more.
Then he saw a sword, a victor among weapons,
A blade of old time, giant-forged, tough-edged,
An honour for its bearers; it was the best of arms,
Only greater in bulk than could ever be carried   1560
By any other man into press of battle,
Trustworthy, a splendour, the labour of titans.
The chained hilt he seized then, the Scyldings' champion
In fierceness and war-anger, brandished the ringed blade
Despairing of life, and in fury struck,
So that it bit hard into her neck
Till the backbone broke: the iron pierced through
A doomed shell of flesh; she dropped to the floor;
The sword was bloodstained, the man's work gladdened him.
    Radiance flashed out, the light sprang within,   1570
Twin to the candle of heaven as in clearness
It shines from the sky. Hygelac's retainer
Looked along the vault, turned by the wall,
Lifted up the weapon firmly by its hilt,
Angry and unrelenting – the warrior didn't count
That swordblade despicable, but was eager to be quick
In repaying Grendel for the multitude of attacks
He had made warring on the Danish nation
Oftener by far than on that one occasion
When he slaughtered Hrothgar's hearth-companions   1580
Lying at their rest, devoured fifteen
Folk of the Danes, slumbering men,
And went carrying off as many more again,
Plunderings of horror. For that he had rewarded him,
The fierce-minded fighter, so that now he could gaze on
Grendel lying moveless, war-drained of his force,
Lifeless, as the battle in hours gone
Had crushed him in Heorot. The corpse burst open,
When he suffered a blow even after death,
A keen sword-stroke; so he beheaded him.   1590

Immediately the wise-hearted men who were looking
With Hrothgar at the water saw that its waves
In their streaming tumult were all stirred turbid,
That the flood was blood-flecked. The grey-streaked heads,
The old men drew together speaking of the good warrior,
How they thought the prince would never return,
Come back in victory to visit again
The illustrious king; it was what many feared then,
That the wolfish sea-demon-woman had been his destruction.
Now it was the ninth hour of the day. The valiant   1600
Scyldings left the cliff; the gold-lord of men
Turned from there to his home. The strangers sat
Sick at heart and stared across the lake;
They desired and they despaired to look on the living flesh
Of their lord and friend. Then that sword, that war-blade
Bloodied by the fight began wasting away
In battle-icicles: it was a thing to marvel at
When it all melted down as if it was the ice
The Father unleashes from the chain of frost,
Water-bonds he slips whose power keeps   1610
All times and seasons; he in truth is God.
The man of the Geats took no more from that place
In the way of rich possessions (though he saw plenty there)
Than the head of Grendel and with it that hilt
Bristling with jewels; the sword had dissolved,
The scrolled blade fused: so hot that blood was,
So venomous the hell-fiend who dined in that hall.
Quickly he swam off; he had fought before to see
His enemies war-felled; he thrust up through the water.
Cleansed were the tumult and swirl of the waves,   1620
Pure the vast reaches, when the alien soul
Left living days and this lease of creation.
The protector of seafarers came then to land,
Swimming resolutely; he rejoiced in the sea-booty,
In the weighty burden he carried with him.
The splendid retinue went then to meet him,
They gave thanks to God, they were gladdened by the prince
Now that their eyes could see him unharmed.
Then the brave warrior's helmet and chain-mail
Were speedily loosened. The tarn lay still,   1630
The water with death's red stained under the sky.
They followed the footpaths forward from that place,
They were happy at heart, they marched across the earth,

On the well-known road; noble in valour
Men took the head from the lake-side cliff,
And every one of them, a soldier and distinguished,
Found the task hard; four of them were needed,
And trouble was needed, to bear on the spear-shaft
Grendel's head to the hall of gold,
Till presently the men, the fourteen Geats   1640
War-keen and daring came up to the house;
The lord of the retinue, soldierly among his throng,
Walked with them along the mead-hall's approaches.
And so the prince of warriors came in,
The man bold of act, the battle-brave hero
In glory revered, to greet Hrothgar.
Then Grendel's head was brought by the hair
Into the hall where the retinue were drinking,
A horror before the nobles and the woman with them,
A spectacle and a wonder; men's eyes were transfixed.   1650

MIDDLE ENGLISH

Richard Rolle

13. 'When Adam delved and Eve span'

When Adam delved and Eve span, spir,° if thou will speed,* *enquire; succeed*
Where was then the pride of man, that now mars his meed?° *reward*
Of earth and slime, as was Adam, makèd to noise and need,
Are we as he makèd to be, while we this life shall lead.
With I and E, born are we, as Solomon us hight,° *promised*
To travel here, while we are far, as fowlès to the flight.
In worldè were we cast for to care, til we be brought to wend° *go*
To wele° or woe, one of the two, to wone* withouten end. *joy; live*
Forthy° while thou may helpe thee now, amend thee and have *Therefore*
    mindè
When thou shall go, he be thy foe, that ere was here thy friendè. 10
With E and I, I read forthy, thou think upon these three:
What we are, and what we were, and what we shall be.
Were thou as wisè praised in price, as was Solomon,
Fairer food, of bone and blood, than was Absalon,
Strengthy and strong, to wreke° thy wrong, as ever was Sampson: *avenge*
Thou ne might a day, no more than they, did withstand alone.
With I and E, dead to thee shall come as I thee kenne,° *teach*
Thou ne wat,° in what estate, how, nor where, nor when. *do not know*
Of earthè aught that thee was wrought, thou shall not have, I hetè,° *promise*
But seven foot, therein to rot, and thy winding-sheetè. 20
Forthy give, while thou may live, or° all goes that thou getè, *before*
Thy ghost from god, thy goods olod,° thy flesh fouled under feete. *lost*
With I and E, secure thou be that thy secutours° *executors*
Of thee ne will rek, but skulk and skek° full boldly in thy bowers. *explore*
Of wealth and wit, this shall be it, in world that thou here wrought,° *made*
Reckon° thou man, and yield reason of thing that thou here *Consider*
    thought.

May no false help in thisè case,° ne counsel gets thou nought,   *situation*
Gift nor gracè none there goes, but broke as thou has brought.
With I and E, the book bids thee, man, beware of thy works:
Terme of the year has thou none here, thy mede° is there   *reward;*
    thy murks.*   *darkness 30*
What may this be that I here see, the forehead of thy facè?
Thy ble° so bright, thy mane, thy might, thy mouth that   *complexion;*
    merry mas?*   *sound*
All man as was to powder pass, to deathè when thou goes:
A grisly guest beèst then thy breast in armès to embracè;
With I and E, siker thou be, there is none, I thee hete,
Of all thy kith, would sleep thee with, a night under sheetè.

14. 'Unkind° man'   *unnatural*

Unkind man, give keep til me°   *attend to me*
And look what pain I suffer for thee.
Sinful man, on thee I cry,
Alonely° for thy love I die.   *solely*
Behold the blood from me down rins,°   *runs*
Not for my guilt, but for thy sins.
My hands, my feet, with nails are fast,
Sins° and vainès all to-brast.*   *sinews; burst*
The blood out of my heartè-rootè,
Look it falls down to my footè.   *10*
Of all the pain that I suffer sore,
Within my heart it grieves me more,
The unkindness that I find in thee,
That for thy love thus hanged on tree.
Alas, why lovès thou me not:
And I thy love so dear has bought?
But° thou me love, thou does me wrong,   *unless*
Since I have lovèd thee long.
Two and thirty year and more
I was for thee in travail° sore,   *labour (as of childbirth) 20*
With hunger, thirstè, heat and cold;
For thy love both bought and sold,
Painèd, nailed and done° on tree: *killed*
All, man, for the love of thee.

Love thou me, as thee well aw,°   *you ought for your wellbeing*
And from sinnès thou thee draw.
I give thee my body with woundès sorè.
And thereto shall I give thee morè:
Over allè this I-wiss,°   *indeed*
In earth my grace, in heaven my bliss.   30
        Jesus. Amen.

15. 'Memento Homo Quod Cinis Es'

Memento Homo Quod Cinis Es,°   *Remember man that thou art ash*
Et in Cenerem Reuerteris.°   *And will return to ash*

Limus°	Earth out of earthè: is wonderly wroghte,*	*Mud; made*
	Earth has getten° an earthè: a dignity of noughtè,	*begotten*
Homo primus°	Earth upon earthè: has set all his thoughte,	*First man*
	How that earth upon earthè: may be high brought.	
	Earth upon earthè: would be a kinge;	
Sordens°	But how that earth to earthè shall: thinks he nothing.	*Filth*
	When earth breeds earth: and his rentès° home bring,	*income*
Mutare Nequimus°	Then shall earth earthè: have full hard parting.	*We refuse to change*
	Earth upon earthè: wins castles and towers,	
	Then says earth un-to earthè: 'This is allè ours';	10
Vnde°	When earth upon earthè: has bigged up his bowris,*	*Whence; built his dwelling*
	Then shall earth upon earthè suffer sharp scowers.	
	Earth goes upon earthè: as gold upon goldè:	
Superbimus°	He that goes upon earthè: glittering as goldè,	*Too proud*

Like as earth never-more: go to earthè
  shoulde,

Terram° And yet shall earth unto earthè: yea *To the earth;*
  rather* than he wouldè. *sooner*

Terra° Now why that earth loves earthè: wonder *Earth*
  me thinkè,

Or why that earth for earthè: should
  others sweat or swinkè;° *work*

Redimus° For when that earthè upon earthè: is *We redeem*
  brought within brinkè,

Then shall earth of earthè: have a foul *20*
  stinkè.

16. 'Lo lemman° sweet, now may thou see'   *beloved*

Lo lemman sweet, now may thou see
That I have lost my life for thee:
What might I do thee more?
For this I pray thee specially
That thou forsake ill company
That woundès me so sore,
And take mine armès prively
And do them in thy treasury,
In what stedè° so thou dwellès.   *town*
And sweetè lemman, forget thou not   10
That I thy love so dear have bought,
And I ask thee nought else.

17. 'Three good brothers are ye'

Three good brothers are ye,
Godès gatès gangè° ye,   *go*
Holy thingès seekè ye.
He says, will you tell me?
He says, blessèd, lord, might you be,

It may never getten° be,   *profit*
Lordè, but° your willès be.   *unless*
Settis down upon your knee,
Greatly° athe* swear you me   *willingly; oath*
By Mary Mother milk so free;   10
There is no man that ever has need,
Ye shall him charme and ask no meed.°   *reward*
And here shall I lere° it thee.   *teach*
As the Jewès wounded me,
They went to wonde° me from the ground: *remove*
I healed myself both hale and sound.
Go to the crag of Olivette,°   *Mount of Olives*
Take oil of bays, that is so sweet,
And thrice about this worm ye strike.
This beèth the worm, that shoutten° not,   *cry out* 20
Nor canker not, nor fallow° not;   *reproduce*
And als° clear hale* from the groundè,   *thus; drawn up*
As Jesu did with his faire wounds.
The father and the son and the holy ghostè,
And Godès forbid, thou wicked wormè,
That ever thou make any resting or any sojournè,
But away must thou wendè
To the earth and the stonè.

18. 'My truest treasure so traitorly taken'

My truest treasure so traitorly taken,
So bitterly bonden with biting bands;°   *cruel bonds*
How soone of thy servants was thou forsaken,
And loathly for my love hurled with their hands.
My well of my wele° so wrongously wryed,*   *happiness; changed*
So pulled out of prison to Pilate at primè;
Their dulls° and their dyntès* full drerely‡ thou   *fooleries; blows; sorrowfully*
    dread,
When they shot in thy sight both slaver and slime.
My hope of my hele° so high to be hanged,   *salvation*
So charged with thy crossè and crownèd with thorn;   10
Full sore to thy heart thy steppès thee stungen,
Me think thy back burden broke, it bendès forborne.°   *refrained from*
My salve of my sore so sorrowful in sightè,

So naked and nailed, thy rig° on the rood*   *back; cross*
Full hideously hangèd; they heaved thee on high,
They left the stab in the stone, all stekked° that there stood.   *stared*
My dear-worthy darling so dolefully died,
So straightly upright strained on the rood:
For thy mickel° meekness, thy mercy, thy might,   *great*
Thou bete° all my bales* with botè‡ of thy blood. *atoned for; sins; remedy* 20
My fiends and my foes so fonden° in the field,   *tested you*
So lovely lighting° at the evensong-tide;   *shining*
Thy mother and her menyhe° unlaced thy scheld,*   *household; body*
All weeped that there were, thy wounds were so wide.
My peerless princè, als pure I thee pray:
The mind of this mirror° thou let me nought missè: *reflection*
But wind up my wille to won° with thee aye,*   *live; forever*
That thou be buried in my breast, and bring me to blissè. Amen.

Ballads

19. from *The Ancient Ballad of Chevy Chase*

19a. *The First Fit*

The Percy out of Northumberland,
    And a vow to God made he,
That he would hunt in the mountains
    Of Cheviat within dayès three,
In the mauger of° doughty Douglas,   *despite*
    And all that ever with him be.

The fattestè hartès in all Cheviat
    He said he would kill, and carry them away:
By my faith, said the doughty Douglas again,
    I will let° that hunting if that I may.   *stop* 10

Then the Percy out of Banborow came,
    With him a mighty many;
With fifteen hundred archerès bold;
    They were chosen out of shirès three

This began on a Monday at morn
   In Cheviat the hillès so he;°   *high*
The child may rue that is unborn,
   It was the more pity.

The drivers through the woodès went
   For to raise the deer;   20
Bow-men bickarte° upon the bent*   *deceived; plain*
   With their broad arrows clear.

Then the wild through the woodès went
   On every sidè sheer;
Greyhoundès through the grovès glent°   *rushed*
   For to kill their deer.

They began in Cheviat the hillès above
   Early on a Monday;
By that it drew to the hour of noon
   A hundreth fat hartès dead there lay.   30

They blew a mort° upon the bent,   *end of the hunt*
   They sembled° on sidès sheer;   *assembled*
To the quarry then the Percy went
   To see the brittling° of the deer.   *breaking up*

He said, 'It was the Douglas's promise
   This day to meet me here;
But I wistè he would fail verament.'°   *in truth*
   A great oath the Percy swear.

At the last a squire of Northumberland
   Looked at his hand full nigh,   40
He was ware of the doughty Douglas coming;
   With him a mighty many,

Both with spear, billè° and brand:*   *bill hook; sword*
   It was a mighty sight to see.
Hardier men both of heartè nor hand
   Were not in Christianity.

There were twenty hundred spearmen good
    Withouten any fail;
They were borne along by the water at Tweed,
    In the boundès of Tividale.   50

'Leave off the brittling of the deer,' he saidè,
    'And to your bowès take good heed;
For never since you were of your mothers borne
    Had ye never so mickle° need.'   *much*

The doughty Douglas on a steedè
    He rode his men beforn;
His armour glittered as did a glede;°   *red hot coal*
    A bolder bearn was never born.

'Tell me what men ye are,' he says,
    'Or whose men that ye be: 60
Who gave you leave to hunt in this
    Cheviat Chase in the spite of me?'

The first man that ever him an answèar made,
    It was the good lord Percy:
'We will not tell thee what men we are,' he says,
    'Nor whosè men that we be;
But we will hunt here in this chase
    In the spite of thine, and of thee.'

'The fattestè harts in all Cheviat
    We have killed, and cast to carry them away.'   70
'By my troth,' sayd the doughty Douglas again,
    'Therefore the tone° of us shall die this day.'   *one or the other*

Then said the doughty Douglas
    Unto the lord Percy:
'To kill all these guiltèless men,
    Alas! it were great pity.'

'But, Percy, thou art a lord of land,
    I am an earl called within my country;
Let all our men upon apart stand;
    And do the battle of thee and of me.'   80

'Now Christs curse on his crown,' said the lord Percy,
   'Whosoever thereto says nay.
By my troth, doughty Douglas,' he says,
   'Thou shalt never see that day;

Neither in England, Scotland, nor France,
   Nor for no man of a woman born,
But and° fortune be my chance,   *if*
   I dare meet him one man for one.'

Then bespake a squire of Northumberland,
   Richard Witherington was his name;   90
'It shall never be told in the South-England,' he says,
   'To King Henry the Fourth for shame.

I wot you been great lordès two,
   I am a poor squire of land;
I will never see my captain fight on a field,
   And stand myself, and look on,
But while I may my weapon wield
   I will not fail both heart and hand.'

That day, that day, that dreadfull day:
   The first fit° here I find.   *episode* 100
And you will hear any more of the hunting at the Cheviat
   Yet is there more behind.

19b. *The Second Fit*

The English men had their bows ybent,
   Their hearts were good enough;
The first of arrows that they shot off,
   Seven score spearmen they slough.°   *slew*

Yet bides the earl Douglas upon the bent,
   A captain good enoughè,
And that was seenè verament,
   For he wrought home both woe and wouche.°   *wounds*

The Douglas parted his host in three,
   Like a chief chieftan of pridè,   10
With surè spears off mighty tree
   They come in on every sidè.

Through our English archery
    Gave many a woundè full widè;
Many a doughty they gard° to die,   *caused*
    Which gainèd them no pridè.

The English men let their bowès be,
    And pulled out brandès that were bright;
It was a heavy sight to see
    Bright swords on basnetes° light.   *helmets* 20

Through richè mail, and mine-ye-ple°   *chainmail or armour*
    Many stern° they struck down straight: *warrior*
Many a freykè,° that was full free,   *knight*
    There under foot died lightè.

At last the Douglas and the Percy met,
    Like two captains of might and main;
They swapte together till the both sweat°   *struck*
    With swordès, that were of fine Milan.°   *Milan steel*

These worthy freykès for to fight
    Thereto they were full fainè,°   *eager* 30
Till the blood out of their basnets sprent,   *spurted*
    As ever did hail or rainè.

'Hold thee, Percy,' said the Douglas,
    'And i' faith I shall thee bring
Where thou shalt have an earl's wages
    Of James our Scottish king.

'Thou shalt have thy ransom free,°   *lavish*
    I hight° thee here this thing,   *promise*
For the manfullestè man yet art thou,
    That ever I conquered in field fighting.'   40

'Nay then,' said the lord Percy,
    'I told it the beforn,
That I would never yielded be
    To no man of a woman born.'

With that there came an arrow hastily
    Forth off a mighty onè,°   *one (archer)*
It hath stricken the earlè Douglas
    In at the breast bonè.

Through liver and lungs both
    The sharp arrow is gone,   50
That never after in all his life days
    He spokè more wordès but one,
That was, 'Fight ye, my merry men, whilst ye may,
    For my life days be gone.'

The Percy leanèd on his brand,
    And saw the Douglas die;
He took the dead man by the hand,
    And said, 'Woe is me for thee!

'To have savèd thy life I would have parted with
    My landès for yearès three,   60
For a better man of heart, nor of hand
    Was not in all the north country.'

Of all that see a Scottish knight,
    Was callèd Sir Hewe the Montgomery,
He saw the Douglas to the death was died;
    He spendyd° a spear a trusty tree: *bound*

He rode upon a coursiare°   *steed*
    Through a hundred archery;
He never stinted, nor never blane°   *stopped*
    Till he came to the good lord Percy.   70

He set upon the lord Percy
    A dynt,° that was full sore;   *blow*
With a sure spear of a mighty tree
    Clean through the body he the Percy bore,

At the other side, that a man might see,
    A large cloth yard and more:
Two better captains were not in Christianity,
    Than that day slain were there.

An archer of Northumberland
    Saw slain was the lord Percy,   80
He bore a bend-bow in his hand,
    Was made of trusty tree:

An arrow, that a cloth yarde was long,
   To th'hard steele hailèd he;
A dint, that was both sad and sore,
   He set on Sir Hewe the Montgomery.

The dynt it was both sad and sore,
   That he of Montgomery set;
The swan-feathers that his arrow bore
   With his heart blood they were wet.   90

There was never a freyke one foot wold flee,
   But still in stour° did stand,   *battle*
Hewing on each other, while they might dree,°   *endure*
   With many a baleful brand.

This battle began in Cheviat
   An hour before the noonè,
And when evensong bell was rung
   The battle was not half donè.

They tooke on° on either hand   *carried on*
   By the light of the moonè;   100
Many had no strength for to stand,
   In Cheviat the hills aboonè.°   *above*

Of fifteen hundred archers of Engelond
   Went away but fifty and three;
Of twenty hundreth spearmen of Scotland,
   But even five and fifty . . .

. . . So on the morrow they madè them biers   131
   Of birch, and hazel so grey;
Many widows with weeping tears,
   Came to fetch their mates away.

Tivydale may carp° of care,   *talk*
   Northumberland may make great moan,
For two such captains, as slain were there,
   On the march parti° shall never be none.   *March areas (borders)*

Word is comen to Edinburgh
    To Jamie the Scottish king,   140
That doughty Douglas, life-tenant of the Marches,
    He lay slain Cheviat within.

His handès did he weal° and wring,   *twist*
    He said, 'Alas, and woe is me!
Such another captain Scotland within,'
    He said, 'in faith should never be.'

Word is comen to lovely London
    To the fourth Harry our king,
That lord Percy, lieutenant of the Marches,
    He lay slainè Cheviat within.   150

'God have mercy on his soul,' said King Harry,
    'Good lord, if thy will it be!
I have a hundred captains in England,' he said,
    'As good as ever was he:
But Percy, and I brook° my life,   *stake*
    Thy death well quitè° shall be.' ...   *requited*

20. Sweet Willie and Lady Margery

Willie was a widow's son,
    And he wore a milkwhite weed,° O   *garment*
And well could Willie read and write,
    Far better ride on steed. O

Lady Margery was the first lady
    That drank to him the winè,
And aye as the healths gade° round and round,   *went*
    'Laddy, your love is minè.'

Lady Margery was the first lady
    That drank to him the beerè,   10
And aye as the healths gade round and round,
    'Laddy, you're welcome here.'

'You must come into my bower
    When the evening bells do ring,
And you must come into my bower
    When the evening mass doth sing.'

He's taken four and twenty broad arrows,
    And laced them in a whang,°   *fan*
And he's away to Lady Margery's bower,
    As fast as he can gang.°   *go* 20

He set one foot on the wall,
    And the other on a stone,
And he's killed all the king's lifeguards,
    And he's killed them every man.

'Oh open, open, Lady Margery,
    Open and let me in;
The wet wets all my yellow hair,
    And the dew drops on my chin.'

With her feet as white as sleet
    She strode her bower within,   30
And with her fingers long and small
    She's letten Sweet Willie in.

She's louten° down unto her foot   *stooped*
    To loose Sweet Willie's shoèn;
The buckles were so stiff they would not loose,
    The blood had frozen in.

'O Willie, Willie, I fear that thou
    Has bred me dole and sorrow;
The deed that thou hast done this night
    Will kyth° upon the morrow.'   *be known* 40

In then came her father dear,
    And a broad sword by his garè,°   *side*
And he's given Willie, the widow's son,
    A deep wound and a sarè.°   *sore*

'Lie yont,° lie yont, Willie,' she says,   *over there*
    'Your sweat wets on my sidè;
Lie yont, lie yont, Willie,' she says,
    'For your sweat I downa bidè.'

She turned her back unto the wa',°   *wall*
   Her face unto the room,   50
And there she saw her old father,
   Walking up and down.

'Woe be to you, father,' she said,
   'And an ill deed may you die!
For you've kill'd Willie, the widow's son
   And he would have married me.'

She turned her back unto the room,
   Her face unto the wa',
And with a deep and heavy sigh
   Her heart it broke in twa.°   *two* 60

21. Sir Patrick Spence

The king sits in Dumfermline town,
   Drinking the blood-red wine:
Says, 'Where will I get a fine skipper,
   Would sail this ship of mine?'

Out and spake an old rich knight,
   'And an ill death may he die!'
Says, 'Young Patrick is the best skipper
   That ever set sail on sea.'

The king did write a braid letter,°   *unsealed, patent letter*
   Signed it with his own hand,   10
And he sent it to Young Patrick,
   Was walking on the sand.

When Young Patrick read the letter long,
   The tear blinded his eye;
Says, 'Who is this, or who is that,
   That's told the king of me?
Altho he had been better than what he is,
   He might have asked leave of me.

'But busk,° O busk, my merry men a',*   *get dressed; all*
    O busk and make your bray,   20
For blow the wind what air it will,
    Our ship she must away.

'Drink, O drink, my merry men all,
    Drink of the beer and wine,
For gin Wednesday by twelve o'clock
    We'll a' be in our long home.

    'Make haste, make haste, my merry men all,
      Our good ship sails the morne.'
'O say not so, my master dear,
    For I fear a deadly storm.   30

    'Late, late yestreen° I saw the new moon   *yester-evening*
      Wi' the old moon in her arm;
And I fear, I fear, my dear master
    That we will come to harm.'

Out and spake a pretty little boy:
    'I fear a deadly storm;
I too saw the new moon late yestreen,
    And the old one in her arm,
And readily, master,' said he,
    'That's the sign of a deadly storm.'   40

Aye they sat, and aye they drank,
    They drank of the beer and wine,
And gin Wednesday gin ten o'clock,
    Their hair was wet abune.°   *above*

'Where would I get a pretty little boy,
    That wants to win hose and shoèn,
Would up to the top of my mainmast go,
    See if he could spy land?'

'O here am I, a pretty little boy,
    Wants to win hose and shoèn;   50
I'll up to the top of your mainmast go,
    Though I should never come down.'

'Come down, come down, my pretty little boy,
   I think thou tarries long;
For the jaw is coming in at my coat-neck,
   Going out at my right hand.'

But there came a shower out of the Northwest,
   Of dreadful hail and rain,
It made Young Patrick and his men
   A' flat with the sea foam.   60

O our Scots nobles were right loath
   To wet their cork-heeled shoon;°   *shoes*
But long after all the play was played,
   Their hats they swam aboon.

O long, long, may the ladies sit
   With their fans into their hands,
Or e'er they see young Patrick Spence
   Come sailing to the land.

O long, long, may the ladies stand
   Wi' their gold combs in their hair,   70
Waiting for their own dear lords,
   For they'll see them now no more.

Young Patrick's lady sits at home,
   She's sewing her silken seam;
And aye when she looks to the salt sea waves,
   'I fear he'll never return.'

Young Patrick's lady sits at home
   Rocking her oldest son;
And aye when she looks to the salt sea waves,
   'I'm feared he'll never come home.'   80

Have over, have over to Aberdoure,
   It's fifty fathom deep:
And there lies all our brave Scots lords,
   Young Patrick's at their feet.

22. The Wife of Usher's Well

There lived a wife at Usher's Well,
　And a wealthy wife was she;
She had three stout and stalwart sons,
　And sent them o'er the sea.

They had not been a week from her,
　A week but barely one,
When word came to the carlin° wife   *old*
　That her three sons were gone.

They had not been a week from her,
　A week but barely three,   10
Whan word came to the carlin wife
　That her sons she'd never see.

'I wish the wind may never cease,
　Nor fishes in the flood,
Till my three sons come home to me,
　In earthly flesh and blood.'

It fell about the Martinmass,°   *November*
　When nights are long and mirk,°   *dark*
The carlin wife's three sons came home,
　And their hats were of the birch.   20

It neither grew in syke° nor ditch,   *stream*
　Nor yet in any sheugh;°   *furrow*
But at the gates of Paradise,
　That birch grew fair enough.

'Blow up the fire, my maidens,
　Bring water from the well;
For all my house shall feast this night,
　Since my three sons are well.'

And she has made to them a bed,
　She's made it large and wide   30
And she's taken her mantle her about,
　Sat down at the bedside.

Up then crew the red, red cock,
   And up and crew the grey;
The eldest to the youngest said,
   'Tis time we were away.'

The cock he had not crowed but once,
   And clapp'd his wings at a',°   *all*
When the youngest to the eldest said,
   'Brother, we must away.

'The cock doth crow, the day doth dawn,
   The channerin° worm doth chide;   *complaining*
Gin° we be must out of our place,   *If*
   A sore pain we must bide.

'Fare ye well, my mother dear!
   Fareweel to barn and byre!°   *stable*
And fare ye well, the bonny lass
   That kindles my mother's fire!'

23. Kinmont Willie

O have ye not heard of the false Sakeldè?
   O have ye not heard of the keen Lord Scroop?
How they have taken bold Kinmont Willie,
   On Hairibee to hang him up?

Had Willie had but twenty men,
   But twenty men as stout as he,
False Sakelde had never the Kinmont taken,
   With eight score in his company.

They bound his legs beneath the steed,
   They tied his hands behind his back;   10
They guarded him, fivesome on each side,
   And they brought him over the Liddelrack.

They led him through the Liddelrack,
   And also through the Carlisle sands;

They brought him to Carlisle castle,
    To be at my Lord Scroope's commands.

'My hands are tied, but my tongue is free,
    And who will dare this deed avow?
Or answer by the border law?
    Or answer to the bold Buccleuch?'   20

'Now hold thy tongue, thou rank reiver!°   *scoundrel*
    There's never a Scot shall set ye free;
Before ye cross my castle gate,
    I trow ye shall take farewell of me.'

'Fear not ye that, my lord,' quoth Willie;
    'By the faith o my body, Lord Scroop,' he said,
'I never yet lodged in a hostelry
    But I paid my lawing° before I goed.'   *bill*

Now word is gone to the bold Keeper,
    In Branksome Hall where that he lay,   30
That Lord Scroop has taken the Kinmont Willie,
    Between the hours of night and day.

He has taken the table with his hand,
    He garred° the red wine spring on high;   *caused*
'Now Christ's curse on my head,' he said,
    'But avenged of Lord Scroop I'll be!

'O is my basnet° a widow's curch?*   *helmet; kerchief*
    Or my lance a wand of the willow tree?
Or my arm a lady's lily hand?
    That an English lord should lightly me?   40

'And have they taken him Kinmont Willie,
    Against the truce of Border tide,
And forgotten that the bold Bacleuch
    Is keeper here on the Scottish side?

'And have they een taken him Kinmont Willie,
    Withouten either dread or fear,
And forgotten that the bold Bacleuch
    Can back a steed, or shake a spear?

'O were there war between the lands,
    As well I wot° that there is none,   *know* 50
I would slight° Carlisle castle high,   *demolish*
    Though it were builded of marble stone.

'I would set that castle in a low,
    And sloken° it with English blood;   *slake*
There's never a man in Cumberland
    Should ken° where Carlisle castle stood.   *know*

'But since no war's between the lands,
    And there is peace, and peace should be,
I'll neither harm English lad or lass,
    And yet the Kinmont freed shall be!'...   60

He has called him forty marchmen bold,
    Were kinsmen to the bold Buccleuch,
With spur on heel, and splent on spauld,°   *armour on shoulder*
    And gloves of green, and feathers blue.

There were five and five before them all,
    With hunting horns and bugles bright;   70
And five and five came with Buccleuch,
    Like Warden's men, arrayed for fight.

And five and five like a mason gang,
    That carried the ladders long and high;
And five and five like broken men;
    And so they reached the Woodhouselee.

And as we crossed the Bateable Land,
    When to the English side we held,
The first of men that we met with,
    Who should it be but false Sakelde!   80

'Where be ye going, ye hunters keen?'
    Quoth false Sakelde; 'come tell to me!'
'We go to hunt an English stag,
    Has trespassed on the Scots country.'

'Where be ye going, ye marshalmen?'
    Quoth false Sakelde; 'come tell me true!'
'We go to catch a rank reiver,
    Has broken faith with the bold Buccleuch.'

'Where are ye going, ye masonlads,
    With all your ladders long and high?'
'We're going to herry° a corbie's* nest,   *drag; raven's* 90
    That wons° not far from Woodhouselee.' ...   *lives*

'Why trespass ye on the English side?
    Row-footed outlaws, stand!' quoth he;
Then never a word had Dickie to say,
    So he thrust the lance through his false body.   100

Then on we held for Carlisle town,
    And at Staneshawbank the Eden we crossed;
The water was great, and meikle° of spait,*   *great; spirit*
    But there never a horse nor man we lost.

And when we reached the Staneshawbank,
    The wind was rising loud and high;
And there the laird garrd° leave our steeds,   *made us*
    For fear that they should stamp and neigh.

And when we left the Staneshawbank,
    The wind began full loud to blow;   110
But 'twas wind and wet, and fire and sleet,
    When we came beneath the castle wall.

We crept on knees, and held our breath,
    Till we placed the ladders against the wall;
And so ready was Buccleuch himself
    To mount the first before us all.

He has taken the watchman by the throat,
    He flung him down upon the lead:°   *earth*
'Had there not been peace between our lands,
    Upon the other side thou hadst gaed.°   *gone* 120

'Now sound out, trumpets!' quoth Buccleuch;
    'Let's waken Lord Scroope right merrily!'
Then loud the Warden's trumpets blew,
    'O who dare meddle with me?'

Then speedily to work we goed,
    And raised the slogan one and all,
And cut a hole through a sheet of lead,
    And so we won to the castle hold.

They thought King James and all his men
    Had won the house with bow and spear;   130
It was but twenty Scots and ten
    That put a thousand in such a stir!

With coulters and with forehammers,
    We garrd the bars bang merrily,
Until we came to the inner prison,
    Where Willie of Kinmont he did lie.

And when we came to the lower prison,
    Where Willie of Kinmont he did lie,
'O sleep ye, wake ye, Kinmont Willie,
    Upon the morn that thou's to die?'   140

'O I sleep soft, and I wake oft,
    It's long since sleeping was fled from me;
Give my service back to my wife and bairns,
    And all good fellows that spear for me.'

Then Red Rowan has hente° him up,   *taken*
    The starkest° men in Teviotdale: *strongest*
'Abide, abide now, Red Rowan,
    Till of my Lord Scroope I take farewell.

'Farewell, farewell, my good Lord Scroope!
    My good Lord Scroope, farewell!' he cried;   150
'I'll pay you for my lodging-mail
    When first we meet on the borderside.'

Then shoulder high, with shout and cry,
    We bore him down the ladder long;
At every stride Red Rowan made,
    I wot the Kinmont's irons playèd clang.°   *clanged*

'O mony a time,' quoth Kinmont Willie,
    'I have ridden horse both wild and wood;°   *crazy*
But a rougher beast than Red Rowan
    I ween° my legs have never bestrode.   *believe* 160

'And many a time,' quoth Kinmont Willie,
    'I've pricked a horse out over the furze;

But since the day I backed a steed
    I never wore such cumbrous spurs.'

We scarce had won the Staneshawbank,
    When a' the Carlisle bells were rung,
And a thousand men, on horse and foot,
    Came with the keen Lord Scroope along.

Buccleuch has turned to Eden Water,
    Even where it flowd from bank to brim,   170
And he has plunged in with all his band,
    And safely swam them thro the stream.

He turned him on the other side,
    And at Lord Scroope his glove flung he:
'If ye like not my visit in merry England,
    In fair Scotland come visit me!'

All sore astonished stood Lord Scroope,
    He stood as still as rock of stone;
He scarcely dared to trew° his eyes   *believe*
    When thro the water they had gone.   180

'He is either himself a devil from hell,
    Or else his mother a witch must be;
I would not have ridden that wan° water   *pale*
    For all the good in Christianity.'

24. Riddles Wisely Expounded

'O what is higher than the trees?
    Gar° lay the bent to the bonny broom   *cause*
And what is deeper than the seas?
    And you may beguile a fair maid soon

'O what is whiter than the milk?
Or what is softer than the silk?

'O what is sharper than the thorn?
O what is louder than the horn?

'O what is longer than the way?
And what is colder than the clay?   10

'O what is greener than the grass?
And what is worse than woman was?'

'O heaven's higher than the trees,
And hell is deeper than the seas.

'And snow is whiter than the milk,
And love is softer than the silk.

'O hunger's sharper than the thorn,
And thunder's louder than the horn.

'O wind is longer than the way,
And death is colder than the clay.

'O poison's greener than the grass,
And the Devil's worse than e'er woman was.'

25. Robin, the Kitchie-Boy°   *kitchen-boy*

It was a king, and a verray° great king,   *truly*
   And a king of muckle° fame,   *much*
And he had a lovely daughter fair,
   And Dysie was her name.

She fell in love with the kitchie-boy,
   And a verray bonnie boy was he,
And word has gone to her father dear,
   And an angry man was he.

'Is it the laird? or is it the lord?
   Or a man of high degree?   10
Or is it to Robin, the kitchie-boy?
   O Dysie make no lie.'

'It's not the laird, nor is it the lord,
　　Nor a man of high degree,
But it's to Robin, the kitchie-boy;
　　What occasion have I to lie?'

'If it be to Robin, the kitchie-boy,
　　As I trust well it be,
The morn, afore ye eat meal or drink,
　　You'll see him hangèd high.'　　　　　　　　　　20

They have taken Robin out,
　　His hair was like threads of gold;
That verray day afore it was night,
　　Death made young Dysie cold.

26. The Nut Brown Maid

Be it right or wrong, these men among, on women do complainè;
Affirming this, how that it is a labour spent in vainè
To love them well; for never a deal they love a man againè;
For let a man do what he can, their favour to attainè
Yet if a new to them pursue, their first true lover then
Laboureth for nought; and from her thought he is a banished man.

I say not nay, but that all day it is both writ and said
That woman's faith, is as who sayeth, all utterly decayed;
But nevertheless, right good witness in this case might be laid
That they love true and continue; recorde the Nutbrown Maid,　　10
Whichè from her love, when, her to prove, he came to make his moan,
Would not depart, for in her hearte she lovèd but him alonè.

Than between us let us discuss, what was all the manner
Between them two; we will also tell all the paine in-ferè°　　　*together*
That she was in; now I begin, so that ye me answerè.
Wherfore all ye, that present be, I pray you give an earè:-
I am the knight, I come by night, as secret as I can,
Saying; – 'alas, thus stondeth the case, I am a banished man.'

And I, your will for to fulfill, in this will not refuse,
Trusting to show, in wordès few, that men have an ill use　　　20

To their own shame, women to blame, and causeless them accuse;
Therefore to you, I answerè now, all women to excuse:-
'Mine own heart dear, with you what cheer? I pray you tell anon,
For in my mind, of all mankind, I lovè but you alone.'

'It standeth so, a deed is do,° wherof much harm shall growè   *done*
My destiny is for to die a shameful death, I trowè,
Or else to flee; the tonne° must be, none other way I knowè   *one or the other*
But to withdraw, as an outlaw, and take me to my bowè
Wherfore adieu, my own heart true, none other rede I can,   *advice*
For I mustè to the greenè woode go, alone, a banished man.'   30

'O Lord, what is this worldès bliss, that changeth as the monè!
My summers day, in lusty May, is darked before the noonè;
I hear you say, "Farewell"; nay, nay, we depart not so soonè;
Why say ye so, whither will you go, alas! what have ye donè;
All my welfare to sorrow and care should changè, if ye were gonè;
For, in my mind, of all mankind, I love but you alonè.'

'I can believe, it shall you grieve, and somewhat you distrain;°   *distress*
But afterward, your painès hard within a day or twain
Shall soon aslake,° and ye shall take comfort to you againè.   *diminish*
Why should ye not? for to take thought your labour were in vainè,   40
And thus I do, and pray you, lo! as heartily as I can;
For I mustè to the grene wood go, alone, a banished man.'

'Now sith that ye have showed to me the secret of your mindè,
I shall be plain to you again, like as ye shall me findè;
Since it is so, that ye will go, I will not leave° behindè,   *stay*
Shall never be said, the Nutbrown Maid was to her love unkindè;
Make you ready, for so am I, although it were anon,
For, in my mind, of all mankind, I love but you alone.'

'Yet I you rede° to take good heed, what men will think and say;   *advise*
Of young and old it shall be told, that ye be gone away,   50
Your wanton will for to fulfillè, in green wood you to play,
And that ye might from your delight no longer make delay.
Rather than ye shuld thus for me be called an evil woman,
Yet would I to the green wood go, alone, a banished man.'

'Though it be sung of old and young, that I should be to blame,
Theirs be the charge, that speak so large in hurting of my name;
For I will prove that faithful love, it is devoid of shame,

In your distress and heaviness, to part with you the same;
And sure all those, that do not so, true lovers are they none;
But in my mind, of all mankind, I love but you alone.'   60

'I counsel you, remember how it is no maidens lorè°   *teaching*
Nothing to doubt, but to run out to wood with an outlawè:
For you must there in your hand bear, a bow ready to drawè,
And as a thief thus must you live, ever in dread and awè,
By which to you great harm might grow, yet had I lever° than   *rather*
That I had to the green wood go,° alone, a banished man.'   *gone*

'I think not nay, but as ye saye, it is no maidens lorè;
But love may make me, for your sake, as ye have said beforè,
To come on foot, to hunt and shoot to get us meat and storè;
For so that I your company may have, I askè no morè;   70
From which to part, it maketh my heart as cold as any stone,
For in my mind, of all mankind, I love but you alone.'

'For an outlaw this is the law, that men him take and bindè
Without pity, hangèd to be, and waver with the windè.
If I had need, as God forbid, what rescue could ye findè?
For sothe I trow, you and your bowe shall draw for far behindè;
And no marvel, for little avail were in your counsel then;
Wherfore I too the woode will go, alone, a banished man.'

'Full well know ye, that women be full feeble for to fight,
No womanhood is it indeed, to be boldè as a knight;   80
Yet in such feare if that ye were, among enemies day and night,
I would withstand, with bow in hand, to grieve them as I might,
And you to save, as women have, from death men many one;
For in my mind, of all mankind, I love but you alone.'

'Yet take good heed, for ever I dread, that ye could not sustain
The thorny ways, the deep valley, the snow, the frost, the rain,
The cold, the heat; for dry or wet, we must lodge on the plain;
And, us above, none other roof, but a brake,° a bush or twain;   *windbreak*
Which sun should grieve you, I believe, and ye would gladly then,
That I had to the green wood go, alone, a banished man.'   90

'Sith I have here been partner with you of Joy and bliss,
I must also part of your woe endure, as reason is;
Yet am I sure of one pleasure, and shortly it is this,
That where you be, me seemeth, pardè, I could not fare amiss.
Without more speech, I you beseech, that we were soon agone;
For in my mind, of all mankind, I love but you alone.'

If ye go thither, you must consider, when you have lust to dine,
There shall no meat be for to getè, nor drinkè, beer, ale, ne wine,
No sheetès clean to lie between, made of thread and twine;
None other house but leaves and boughs, to cover your head and
    mine: 100
Lo! mine heartè sweet, this ill diet should make you pale and wan,
Wherefore I to the wood will go, alone, a banished man.'

'Among the wild deer such an archèr as men say that ye be
Ne may not fail of good vittail,° where is so great plenty;   *victuals*
And water clear, of the river, shall be full sweet to me,
With which in health I shall right well endure, as you shall see;
And ere we go, a bed or two I can provide anon,
For in my mind, of all mankind, I love but you alone.'

'Lo yet, before, ye must do more, if you will go with me,
As cut your hair up by your ear, your kirtle° by the knee,   *gown* 110
With bow in hand, for to withstand your enemiès, if need be:
And this same night, before daylight, to woodward will I flee;
And if ye will all this fulfill, do it shortèly as ye can,
Else will I to the green wood go, alone, a banished man.'

'I shall as now do more for you than long'th to womanhood,
To short my hair, a bow to bear, to shoot in time of need.
O my sweet mother, before all other for you have I most dread;
But now adieu; I must ensue where fortune doth me lead:
All this make ye; now let us flee, the day com'th fast upon;
For in my mind, of all mankind, I love but you alone.'   120

'Nay, nay, not so, you shall not go, and I shall tell you why;
Your appetite is to be light of love, I well aspy;
For right as you have said to me, in like ways hardèly
You would answer, whosoever it were, in ways of company.
It is said of old, soon hot, soon cold, and so is a woman;
Wherefore I to the woodè will go, alone, a banished man.'

'If you take heed, yet is no need such wordès to say by me,
For oft you prayed, and long assayed, ere I loved, pardee;
And though that I, of ancestry, a baron's daughter be,
Yet have you proved° how I you loved, a squire of low degree,   *tested* 130
And ever shall, what so befell, to die therefore anon;
For in my mind, of all mankind, I love but you alone.'

'A baron's child to be beguiled, it were a cursed deed;
To be fellow with an outlawè, almighty God forbid!
Yet better were the poorè squire alone to forest yede,°   *went*
Than you shall say, another day, that be my wicked deed
Ye were betrayed; wherefore, good maid, the best rede that I can,
Is, that I to the green wood go, alone, a banished man.'

'Whatsoever befall, I never shall of this thing you upbraid,
But if ye go and leave me so, then have ye me betrayed;   140
Remember you well how that you deal, for if you, as you said,
Be so unkind, to leave behind your love, the Nutbrown Maid,
Trust me truly that I shall die, soone after you be gone,
For in my mind, of all mankind, I love but you alone.'

'If that ye went, ye should repent, for in the forest now
I have purveyed me of a maid, whom I love more than you.
Another fairer than ever ye were, I dare it well avow;
And of you both, each should be wroth with other, as I trow:
It were mine ease to live in peace; so will I, if I can;
Wherefore I to the wood will go, alone, a banished man.'   150

'Though in the wood I understood you had a paramour,
All this may not remove my thought, but that I will be your;
And she shall find me soft and kind, and courteous every hour,
Glad to fulfill all that she will command me, to my power;
For had ye, lo! an hundred more, yet would I be that one;
For in my mind, of all mankind, I love but you alone.'

'Mine own dear love, I see the proof that you be kind and true;
Of maidè and wife, in all my life, the best that ever I knew.
Be merry and glad, be no more sad, the case is changèd new;
For it were ruth, that for your troth you should have cause to rue.   160
Be not dismayed; whatsoever I said to you, when I began,
I will not to the green wood go, I am no banished man.'

'These tidings be more glad to me, than to be made a queen,
If I were sure they should endure; but it is often seen,
When men will break promise, they speak the wordès on the spleen.
You shape some wile, me to beguile, and steal from me, I wen;
Then were the case worse than it was, and I more woebegone;
For in my mind, of all mankind, I love but you alone.'

'You shall not need further to dread, I will not disparage
You, God defendè, since you descendè of so great a lineage: 170
Now understand, to Westmoreland, which is my heritage,
I will you bring, and with a ring, by way of marriage
I will you take, and lady make, as shortly as I can;
Thus have you won an earl's son, and not a banished man!'–

Here may you see that women be in love meek, kind, and stable,
Let never man reprove them then, or call them variable;
But rather pray God that we may to them be comfortable,
Which sometime proveth° such as he loveth, if they be charitable: *tests*
For sith men wouldè that women shouldè be meek to them each one,
Much more ought they to God obey, and serve but him alonè.

Lyrics, Poems of Celebration and of Faith

27. 'Green Groweth the Holly'

Green groweth the holly so doth the ivy.
Though winter blastes blow never so high
Green groweth the holly.

As the holly groweth green.
And never changeth hue
So I am ever hath been
Unto my lady true
   Green groweth &c.

As the holly groweth green:
With ivy all alone   10
When flowers cannot be seen
And green wood leaves be gone
   Green groweth &c.

Now unto my lady
Promise to her I make

From all other only
To her I me be take
   Green groweth &c.

Adieu mine own lady.
Adieu my special.   20
Who hath my heart truly
He sure & ever shall
   Green groweth &c.

28. 'Blow, northern wind'

  Blow, northern wind,
Send thou me my sweeting!
  Blow, northern wind,
   Blow, blow! blow!
Ichot° a burdè* in bowerè bright   *I know; lady*
That sully seemly° is on sight,   *so attractive*
Menskful° maiden of might,   *noble*
  Fair and free to fondè.
In all this wurhlichè wonè°   *world*
A burdè of blood and of bone   10
Never yet I nustè° none   *have not known*
  Lussomore° in landè.   *More lovely*
  Blow, &c.
  With lockès lovely and long,
With front and facè fair to findè,
With mirthès many must she mongè,°   *among*
That bride so bremè° in bower,   *glorious*
  With lissom eyè great and goodè,
With browen blissful under hood.
He that restè him on the rood°   *cross* 20
That leflich life honourè!
  Blow, &c.
Herè lure° lumès* light   *cheek; glows*
As a lantern at night,
Her bleo° blinketh* so bright,   *face; shines*
  So fair she is and fine.

A sweetly swire° she hath to holdè,   *neck*
With armès, shoulder as man wouldè°   *would like*
And fingers fairè for to foldè.°   *embrace*
   God woldè she were minè!   30
Middle she hath menskful° small;   *extraordinarily*
Her lovely chere as crystal,
Thighès, leggès, feet, and all
   Y-wrought° was of the bestè.   *made*
A lissom lady lastèless
That sweeting is and ever was;
A better burdè never nes°   *was*
   Y-heryed° with the hestè.*   *praised; commandment*
She is dearworth in day,
Gracious, stout, and gay,   40
Genteel, joly so the jay,
   Workliche when she waketh.
Maiden murgest° of mouth;   *prettiest*
By east, by west, by north and south,
There nis viol nor crouth°   *violin*
   That such mirthès maketh.
She is coral of goodnessè,
She is ruby of rightfulnessè,
She is crystal of cleanness,
   And banner of beauty;   50
She is lily of largessè,°   *generosity*
She is periwinkle of prowessè,
She is solsecle° of sweetnessè,   *marigold*
   And lady of loyalty.
To Love, that lovely is in landè,
I tolde him, as ich understandè,
How this hendè° hath hent* in handè   *fair creature; taken*
   One heartè that mine was,
And her knightès me have so sought,
Sighing, Sorrowing, and thought,   60
Those three me have in balè° brought   *sorrow*
   Against the poor of Peace.
To Love I puttè plaintès mo,°   *more*
How Sighing me hath sued° so,   *pursued*
And eke thought me thereat to slo°   *slay*
   With mastery, if he mightè,
And Sorrowè sore in baleful bendè°   *bondage*
That he woldè for this hendè
Me leadè to my livès endè

Unlawfullich in lightè.   70
Here love me listned each word
And bent him to me over bord,°   *table*
And bad me hentè that hoard
     Of mine heartè helè,°   *whole*
'And beseecheth that sweetè and swotè,°   *lovely one*
Ere then thou fallè as fen of footè,
That she with thee wolle of botè°   *remedy*
     Dereworthliche° dealè.'   *lovingly*
For her love I carke° and carè,   *fret*
For her love I droopnè and darè,   80
For her love my blissè is barè,
     And all I waxè wan;
For her love in sleep I slakè,°   *grow weak*
For her love all night I wakè,
For her love mourning I make
     More than any man.

29. 'You and I and Amyas'

You and I and Amyas
Amyas and you and I
To the green wood must we go Alas
You and I my love and Amyas.

The knight knocked at the castle gate
The lady marvelled who was there at
     You and I & Amyas (reprise)...

To call the porter he would not blin°   *stop*
The lady said he should not come in
     You & I & Amyas...   10

The portress was a lady bright
Strangènes that lady hight°   *was called*
     You & I & Amyas...

She asked him what was his name
He said: Desire your man, madame
     You & I & Amyas...

She said: desire what doth he here?
He said: madame as your prisoner!
   You & I & Amyas...

He was counsellèd to breffe° a bill   *compose* 20
And show my lady his ownè will
   You & I & Amyas...

Kindness, said she, would it bear.
And pity, said she, would be there.
   You & I & Amyas...

Thus how they did we can not say
We left them there & went our way
   You & I & Amyas...

30. 'Herefore, and therefore'

Herefore, and therefore, and therefore I came,
And for to praise this pretty woman.
There were three wily, yet wily there were;
A fox, a friar, and a woman.
There were three angry, three angry there were:
A wasp, a weasel, and a woman.
There were three chattering, three chattering there were:
A pie,° a jay, and a woman.   *magpie*
There were three would be betin,° three would be betin   *ornamented*
   there were:
A mill, a stoke fish, and a woman.   10

31. 'Bring us home good ale, sir'

Bring us home good ale, sir, bring us home good ale,
And for our dearè Lady love, bring us home good ale.

Bring us home no beef, sir, for that is full of bones,
But bring home good ale e-nough, for I love wellè that.
   But, Bring...

Bring us home no brownè bread, for that is full of bran,
Neither no ryè bread, for that is of that same.
    But, etc.

Bring us home no porkè, sir, for that is very fat,
Neither no barly bread, for neither loves I that.
    But, etc.   10

Bring us home no mutton, sir, for that is tough and lean,
Neither no tripès, for they be seldom clean.
    But, etc.

Bring us home no veal, sir, for that will not dure,°   *endure*
But bring us home good ale e-nough to drinkè by the fire.
    But, etc.

Bring us home no beefè, for there is many bones,
But bring us in good ale, for that goeth down at once;
    But, etc.   20

Bring us home no eggès, for there are many shells,
But bring us in good ale, and give us nothing else;
    But, etc.

Bring us in no butter, for therein are many hairs;
Nor bring us in no piggès flesh, for that will make us bores;
    But, etc.

Bring us in no puddingès, for therein is all Gods good;
Nor bring us in no venison, for that is not for our blood;
    But, etc.

Bring us home no cider, nor no paldè wine,   30
For and thou do thou shalt have Christ's curse and mine.
    But, etc.

32. 'Lenten is come with love to town'

Lenten is come with love to town,
With blossomen and with briddes roune,°   *birdsong*
    That all this blissè bringeth.
Daisies in these dales,
Notes sweet of nightingales,
    Each fowl song singeth.
The threstelcock° him threteth* oo;‡   *song thrush; wrangles; often*
Away is their winter woe
    When wooderuff springeth.
These fowlès singeth ferly° felè,*   *wonderfully; many* 10
And wliteth° on their wynnè welè,*   *warble; great joy*
    That all the woodè ringeth.
The rose raileth° herè rodè,*   *puts on; red face*
The leaves on the lightè° wood   *bright*
    Waxen° all with willè.   *grow*
The moonè mandeth° herè bleo,*   *sends forth; radiance*
The lily is lissom to seo,°   *see*
    The fennel and the fillè.°   *wild thyme*
Wowès° these wildè drakes;   *make love*
Miles° murgeth* their mates,   *animals; encourage* 20
    As a stream that striketh° stillè.   *flows*
Modi meneth,° so doth mo;*   *spirited men complain; more*
Ichot° I am one of tho,*   *I know; those*
    For love that likès illè.

The moon mandeth her light;
So doth the seemly sunnè bright,
    When briddes singeth bremè°   *strongly*
Dewès donketh° the downs;   *make wet*
Deorès° with their dernè* rounès,   *animals; secret*
    Domès° for to demè;*   *Stories; tell* 30
Wormès woweth under clodè,
Women waxeth wonder° proudè,   *wondrously*
    So well it will them seemè.°   *suit them*
If me shall wontè will of one°   *(i.e. acquiescence)*
This wunnè weol° I will forgon*   *joy; forgo*
    And wiht° in woodè be flemè.*   *live; fugitive*

33. 'All night'

All night by the rose, rose –
   All night by the rose I lay;
Durst I not the rosè steal
And yet I bare the flower away.

34. 'There is no rose'

There is no rose of such virtue
As is the rose that bare Jesu.
   Alleluia.
For in this rose contained was
Heaven and earth in little space;
   Res miranda.
By that rose we may well see
That he is God in persons three,
   Pari forma.
The angels sungen the shepherds to: 10
Gloria in excelsis Deo:
   Gaudeamus.
Leave we all this worldly mirth,
And follow we this joyful birth;
   Transeamus.

35. A Boar's Head

Caput apri differo°	*A boar's head in hand bring I*
Reddens laudens Domino°	*Sounding praises to the On High*
The boar's head in hand bring I	
With garlands gay and rosemary	
I pray you all sing merrily	
Qui estis in convivio.°	*who are at this banquet*

The boar's head I understand	
Is the chief service in this land	
Look where ever it be find.	
Servite cum cantico.°	*Serve it with a song* 10

Be gladè lords both more and lessè
For this hath ordained our stewardè
To cheer you all this Chistmassè
The boars headè with mustardè.

36. 'This endris° night'   *latter*

This endris night
I saw a sight,
   A star as bright as day;
And ever among
A maiden sung
   Lullay, by by, lullay.

This lovely lady sat and sang, and to her childè sayè,
'My son, my brother, my father dear, why liest thou thus in hayè.
  My sweetè bird,
    Thus it is betide,   10
     Though thou be king verray°;   *truly*
  But nevertheless
  I will not cease
    To sing, by by, lullay.'

The child then spake in his talking, and to his mother said,
'I bekythe am king in cribbè there I be laid.
  For angelès bright
  Done to me light,
    Thou knowest it is no nay;
  And of that sight   20
  Thou mayest be light
    To sing, by by, lullay.'

'Now, sweetè son, since thou art king, why art thou laid in stall?
Why ne thou ordend° thy bedding in some great kingès   *fittingly place*
    hall?
  Me thinketh it is right,
  That king or knight

Should lie in good array;
And then among
It were no wrong
  To sing, by by, lullay.'   30

'Mary mother, I am thy child, though I be laid in stall,
Lords and dukes shall worship me and so shall kingès all.
  Ye shall well see
  That kingès three
    Shall come the twelfthè day,
  For this behest°   *promise*
  Give me thy breast,
    And sing, by by, lullay.'

'Now tell me, sweet son, I thee pray, thou art my love and dear,
How should I keepè thee to thy pay° and make thee glad of *satisfaction*
    cheer.   40
  For all thy will
  I would fullfill,
    Thou wittest full well in fay,°   *in faith*
  And for all this,
  I will thee kiss,
    And sing, by by, lullay.'

'My dear mother, when time it be, thou take me up on loft,° *high*
And set me upon thy knee, and handle me full soft.
  And in thy armè
  Thou will me warmè,   50
    And keepè° night and day;   *protect*
  If I weepè,
  And may not sleepè,
    Thou sing, by by, lullay.'

'Now, sweet son, since it is so, that all thing is at thy will,
I prayè thee grant me a boon, if it be both right and skill.° *reasonable*
  That child or man
  That will or can
    Be merry upon my day,
  To bliss them bring,   60
  And I shall sing,
    Lullay, by by, lullay.'

37. 'Lullay, my child, and weep no more'

Lullay, my child, and weep no more,
    Sleep and be now still;
The king of bliss thy father is,
    As it was his will.

This endris° night I saw a sight,   *latter*
    A maid a cradle keep,°   *watched over*
And ever she sung and said among,
    Lullay, my child, and sleep.

'I may not sleep, but I may weep,
    I am so woe begone;   10
Sleep I wold, but I am cold,
    And clothès have I none.'

Me thought I heard, the child answered,
    And to his mother he said,
My mother dear, what do I hear,
    In crib why am I laid.

I was born and laid beforn°   *before*
    Beastès, both ox and ass.
My mother mild, I am thy child,
    But he my father was.   20

Adam's guilt this man had spillt,
    That since grievèd me sore;
Man, for thee here shall I be
    Thirty winter and more.

Dole° it is to see, here shall I be   *Sad*
    Hung upon the rood,°   *Cross*
With baleis° to-bete,* my woundès to-wet,   *torture; beaten*
    And give my flesh to botè.°   *to boot, or in addition*

Here shall I be hanged on a tree,
    And die as it is skill;°   *just* 30
That I have bought lose will I not,
    It is my father's will.

A spear so sharp shall pierce my heart,
   For deedès that I have done.
Father of grace, where thou has
   Forgotten thy little son.

Withouten pity they shall abide,
   And make my flesh all blo.°   *bruised*
Adam i-wys,° this death it is   *indeed*
   For thee and many mo.°   *more* **40**

38. Regina celi letare°   *Rejoice in the Queen of Heaven*

Gabriel, that angel bright,
Brighter than the sun is light,
From heaven to earth he took his flight.
   Letare.°   *Rejoice*
In Nazareth that great city,
Before a maiden he kneeled on knee,
And said, Mary, God is with thee.
   Letare.
Hail, Mary, full of grace,
God is with thee and ever was;   **10**
He hath in thee chosen a place.
   Letare.
Mary was afraid of that sight,
That came to her with so great light.
Then said the angel that was so bright,
   Letare.
Be not aghast of least nor most,
In thee is conceived the holy ghost,
To save the souls that were forlost.
   Letare.   **20**

39. Mother white as lily flower

As I up rose in a morning,
My thought was on a maid ying,°   *young*
That sung asleep with her lulling

Her sweet son, our Saviour.
As she him heldè in her lap,
He took her lovely by the pap,°   *breast*
And thereof sweetly he took an appe,°   *nipple*
 And sucked his fill of the liquor.
To his mother gan he sayè,
'For this milkè me must dyè,   10
It is my kind° therewith to playè,   *nature*
 My sweet mother par amour.'°   *for love*
The maiden freely gan to sing,
And in her song she made mourning,
How he that is our heaven king
 Should shed his blood with great dolour.
Mother, thy weeping grieveth me sore,
But° I would die, thou hadst been lore;*   *unless; lost*
So away, mother, and weep no more;
 Thy lulling lesseth my langour.'°   *sickness* 20
Such mourning as the maiden made,
I can not tell it in this hour;
Therefore be merry and glad
 And make us merry for our Saviour.

40. Timor mortis conturbat me°   *Fear of death unsettles me*

As I went in a merry morning,
I heard a bird both weep and sing;
This was the tenor of her talking,
 Timor, etc.
I asked that bird what she meant.
'I am a musket both fair and gent,°   *noble*
For dread of death I am all schent;°   *panicked*
 Timor, etc.
When I shall die I know no day,
What country or place I can not say;   10
Wherefore this song sing I may,
 Timor, etc.
Jesu Christ, when he should die,
To his father he gan° say,   *began to*
'Father,' he said, 'in trinity,
 Timor, etc.
All Christian people behold and see,

This world is but a vanity,
And replete with necessity;
   Timor, etc.   20
Wake I or sleep, eat or drink,
When I on my last end do think,
For greatè fear my soul do shrink;
   Timor, etc.
God grant us grace him for to serve,
And be at our end when we sterve,°   *die*
And from the fiend he us preserve;
   Timor, etc.

The *Gawain* Poet

41. from **Pearl**

41a. I.

Pearl, pleasant to princes pay,°	*to please a prince*
To clanly close° in gold so clear,	*radiantly set*
Out of orient I hardèly° say,	*boldly*
Ne proved° I never her precious peer,	*found*
So round, so reken° in each array,	*fresh*
So small, so smooth her sidès were.	
Wheresoe'er I judgèd gemmès gay,	
I set her singèly in singlurè;°	*as unique*
Alas! I lost her in an erberè,°	*grassy place*
Through grass to ground it from me yot;°	*fell* 10
I dewyne° fordolked* of love dangerè,	*pine; grievously wounded*
Of that privy° pearl withouten spot.	*my own*

Sythen° in that spot it from me sprangè°,	*Since*
Oft have I waited, wishing that wealè,°	*grace*
That wont was while° devoid* my wrangè,‡	*used to; dispel; sorrow*
And helèn° my hap* and all my healè,‡	*bless; happiness; health*
That dost but thrich° my heartè thrangè,*	*afflict; oppressively*
My breast in bale° but bolne and belè.*	*sorrow; swells and burns*
Yet thought me never so sweet a songè,	

As stillè stoundè° let to me stealè,   *time* 20
For soth° there fleeten to me felè,*   *truly; many*
To think her colour so clad in clods;
O mould° you mar a myry* jewel.   *grave soil; fair*
My privy pearl withouten spot,

That spot of spices might needè spreadè,
There° such riches to rot is run;   *Where*
Blossoms black and blue and redè,
There shines full schyr° again the sun.   *bright*
Flower and fruite may not be fadedè,
There it down drof° in moldes dun,* *was buried; brown earth* 30
For each grasse must grow of grainès deadè,
No wheat were else to wones wonnè;° *brought to dwellings*
Of good each good is aye begunnè.
So seemly° a seed might failè not,   *lovely*
That springand spices up ne sponnè,°   *sprung*
Of that precious pearle withouten spot.

To that spot that I in speech expound
I entred in that erber greenè,
In August in a high season,
When corn is carven with crookès° keenè.   *sickles* 40
On huile° there pearl it trendeled* down, *mound; rolled*
Shadowed this wortes° full schyr and schenè *plants*
Gillyflower, ginger and gromilioun,°   *gromwell*
And peonies powdered aye betweenè.
If it was seemly on to seenè,
A faire reflayr° yet from it float,   *fragrance*
There wonys° that worthily I wot and weenè,* *dwells; know and believe*
My precious pearl, withouten spot.

Before that spot my hand I spenned,°   *clasped*
For care full cold° that to me caste;   *grievous* 50
A denely dele° in my heart denned,* *forlorn grief; crept*
Though reason set myselven sayte.°   *reconciled*
I plained° my pearl that there was spenned* *pined; imprisoned*
With fiercè skilles° that fastè foughtè,   *logic*
The kind° of Christ me comfort kenned,* *nature; taught*
My wretched will in woe aye wraitè.°   *was distressed*
I fell upon that flowery flaitè,°   *earth*
Such odour to my hernès° shot;   *brain*
I slode° upon a sleeping-slaytè,* *slid; into a sudden sleep*
On that precious pearl withouten spot.   60

II.

From spot my spirit there sprang in spacè,° — *after a time*
My body on balk° there bade in sweven,* — *mound (ie grave); a dream*
My ghost is gone in Godly gracè,
In adventurè where marvels meven;° — *exist*
I ne wist in this worldè where that it was,
But I knew me kestè° where cliffs cleaven; — *I was set down*
Towards a forest I bear the face,
Where rich rockès were to descrien;
The light of them might no man leven,° — *believe*
The gleaming glory that off them glent;° — *glinted 70*
For were never webbey° that wights weaven, — *fabrics*
Of half so dear adubbement.° — *splendour*

Dubbed° were all those downès sedès* — *adorned; hill sides*
With crystal cliffs so clear as day,
Holtwoods bright about them bides;
Of bolley° as blue as ble of Inde,* — *tree-trunks; hue of Indigo*
As burnished silver the leaf on slidès,° — *unfolded*
That thickly con trill on each a tindè,° — *quivered on each branch*
When gleam of glodes° against them glideth, — *unclouded patches of sky*
With shimmering shine full schrill° they shined. — *dazzling 80*
The gravel that on ground can grindè
Were precious pearlès of oriente;
The sunnès beams but blo° and blindè, — *dim*
In respect of that adubbement.

The adubbementè of those downès dearè
Garten° my ghost all grief forget — *causes*
So fresh flavours of fruitès were,
As food it can me fair refete.° — *refresh*
Fowls there flewen in fryth° in fere,* — *wood; together*
Of flaumband° hues, both small and greatè, — *glowing 90*
Both sytole-string° and gyternerè,* — *citole; cithern*
Here recken° mirth* might not repeatè, — *cheerful; music*
For when those birds their wings beatè
They sung with a sweet assent;
So gracious glee could no man getè
As here and see their adubbement.

So all was dubbet° on dear asyse;* *adorned; fashion*
That fryth there fortune forth me feres;° *transports*
The derth° thereof for to devisè* *splendour; describe*
Nis no wys° worth that tongue berey.* *man; possess* 100
I walk aye forth in wely wisè,° *blissful manner*
No bank so big that did me delay,
The further in the fryth the fairer con risè,
The plain, the plantès, the spice, the pearès
And rawey° and randes* and rich riverès, *hedgerows; banks*
As fildor° fine her bankès brent.* *golden thread; steep*
I went to a water by shore that scherès,° *twists (meanders)*
Lord! deare was this adubbement!

The dubbemente of those dear worth deepè° *depths*
Were bankes bene° of beryl bright; *fair* 110
Swingendè sweet the water con sweptè
With a rownande rourdè° raykand* aright; *whispering murmur; flowing*
In the founce° there standen stony steppè, *bottom*
As gleams the glass that glowed and glint,
A streamand stars when strothèmen° sleepè, *men of the earth*
Stars in welkyn° in winter night; *heavens*
For each a pebble in poolè there pight° *fixed*
Was emerald, sapphire, other gems gent,° *noble*
That all the loyè° gleamèd of light, *pool*
So dearè was its adubbèment. 120

III.

The dubbement dear of down and dales;
Of wood and water and wlonkè° plainè, *noble*
Built in me bliss, abated my bales,
Fordidden° my distress, destroyed my painè. *removed*
Down after a stream that dryly hales,° *continually flows*
I bowed in bliss, brimful my brains;
The farre° I followed those floty* valley, *further; well irrigated*
The more strength of joy mine heartè straineth,
As fortune fares° there as she fraynes,* *behaves; makes trial*
Whether solace she sends other else sore, 130
The wight, to whom her wille she waynes,° *shows*
Hyttes° to have aye more and more. *attains*

More of weale was in that wayè
Than I coude tell if I time hadè,

For earthely hurte might not suffice
To the tenth dole° of that gladness gladè; *part*
For-thy I thought that paradise
Was there other gayn° those bankè bradè; *opposite*
I hoped the water were a division
Between mirthès by merès° made, *pools* 140
Beyond the brook by slantè° or by slade,* *slope; valley*
I hoped that motè° markèd* were. *walled city; situated*
But the water was deep I durst not wade
And ever me longed a more and more.

More and more, and yet well more,
Me list to see the brook beyondè,
For if it was fair there I con fare,° *where I was going*
Well lovelier was the farrè land.
About me con I stood and stare
To find a ford, fast° con I fondè,* *diligently; tried* 150
But wothès° more i-wisse there were, *perils*
The farre I stalkèd by the strondè,
And ever me thought I schould not wondè° *shrink*
For woe, there welès so winnè° were. *delight so precious*
Then new note° me came on handè *matters*
That moved my mind aye more and more,

More mervails com my dom° adaunt;* *reason; astonish*
I saw beyond that merrie mere,
A crystal cliff full relusant,° *gleaming*
Many royal ray con from it reare; 160
At the foot thereof there sat a fant,° *child*
A maiden of menske,° full debonair; *courtesy*
Blisnandè° white was her bleaunt,* *Gleaming; mantle*
(I knew her well, I had seen her ere)
As glissand gold that man con sheerè,° *cut*
So shone that schen° an under shore;* *fair maiden; at the foot of the shore*
On length° I lookèd to her there, *For a long time*
The longer I knew her more and more

The more I frayst° her fairè face. *examined*
Her figure fine, when I had found, 170
Such gladdening glory con to me glacè,° *glide*
As little before thereto was wont;

To call her list con me enchacè,° *Call her I wished to, I urged myself on*
But baisment° gave mine heart a brunt,* *confusion; blow*
I saw her in so strange a placè,
Such a burre° might make mine heartè blunt.* *blow; stunned*
Then veres° she up her fairè front,* *raises; brow*
Her visage white as plain ivore,° *ivory*
That stung my heart full stray astount,° *in bewilderment*
And ever the longer, the more and more. 180

. . .

41b. XXI.

Delight me drove° in eye and earè, *entered*
My manès mind to madding meltè;° *gave way to madness*
When I saw my fairly° I would be there, *fair one*
Beyond the water, where she was set,
I thought that nothing might me derè° *harm*
To fetch me bur° and take me haltè;* *To fetch me a blow (to hinder me); stop*
And to start° in the stream should none me stere,* *rush; restrain*
To swim the remnant, though I there swaltè,° *died* 1160
But of that munt° I was bi-talt;* *resolve; moved*
When I should start in the stream astray,
Out of that caste° I was by-calt;* *intention; called back*
It was not at my Prince's pay,° *pleasure*

It pained him not that I so flung,
Over marvellous mere so mad arayd.° *madly*
Of rush though I were rash and ronk,° *impetuous*
Yet rapely° therein I was restored; *quickly*
For right as I sparred unto the bank,
That brathe° out of my dream me braidè;* *impetuousness; pulled* 1170
Then wakened I in that erber wlonk,° *lovely*
My head upon that hill was laid,
There as my pearl to groundè strayed;
I raxled° and fell in great affray,* *stretched; dismay*
And sighing to myself I said:
'Now all be to that Prince's pay.'

Me painèd full ill to be out-flemè,° *driven out*
So suddenly of that fair region,
From all those sightès so quick and quemè.° *lively and lovely*
A longing heavy me struck in swoonè, 1180
And ruefully then I con to remè;° *lament*
'O pearl,' quoth I, 'of rich renown,

So was it me dear that thou con deemè,
In this verray° avision; *true*
If it be verray and soth sermoun,° *true account*
That thou so stikes° in garlandès gay, *are set*
So well is me in this dole-dungeon,
That thou art to that Princè pay.'

To that Prince's pay had I aye bentè,° *submitted*
And yearned no more then was me given, 1190
And holden me there in true intent,
As the pearl me prayèd that was so thriven,° *blessed*
As heldè° drawn to Goddès presence, *likely*
To more of his mysteries I had been driven.° *brought*
But aye would man of happ° more hentè* *happiness; take*
Than might be right upon him clyven;° *belong to him*
Therefore my joy was soon to-riven,° *torn away*
And I castè of kithey° that lasteth aye. *kingdom*
Lord! mad they are that against thee strivè,
Or to profer thee aught against thee pay.° *rather than pay you* 1200

To pay the Prince or to setè sayte° *propitiate*
It is full easy to the good Christian;
For I have found him bothè day and night,
A god, a lord, a friend full fine.
Over this hill this lotè I lastè,° *fortune I received*
For pity of my pearl encline,° *lay down*
And since to God I it by-tastè,° *committed*
In Christs dear blessingè and mine,
That in the form of bread and wine,
The priest us showèth each a day; 1210
He gave us to be his homely hynè,° *humble servants*
And precious Pearls unto his pay.

42. from **Gawain and the Green Knight**

42a. VII

First he was founden° faultless in his five wittes,* *found; senses* 640
And after failed never the freke° in his five fingers, *knight*
And all his afiaunce° upon fold* was in the five wounds *trust; earth*
That Christ caught on the cross, as the Creed tells;

And wheresoever this man in melly° was stad,* *battle; placed*
His thorough thought was in that, thury° all other thinges, *over*
That all his forceness° he fong* at the five joys *tenacity; took*
That the hendé° heaven queen had of her child; *gracious*
At this cause the knight comelyly had *courteously*
In the inner-more half of his shield her image depainted,
That when he blushed° thereto, his beld* never *looked; courage;*
 paired.‡ *failed* 650
The fifth five that I find that the freke used,
Was fraunchyse° and fellowship for-be* all thing; *generosity; before*
His cleanness and his courtesy croked° were never, *failed*
And pity, that passes all points, – these pure five
Were harder happed° on that hathel* than on any other. *firmly fastened; hero*
Now all these five sythes,° forsooth, were fetled* on this knight, *cases; fixed*
And echone° halched* in other, that no end had, *each one; joined*
And fixed upon five points, that failèd never,
Ne samned° never in no side, ne sundred* neither, *came together; came apart*
Withouten end at any nook I wis nowhere find, 660
Wherever the gomen° began or glod* to an end. *process; came*
Therefore on his shene° shield schapen* was the knot *bright; fashioned*
Royally with red gold upon red gowlez, *gules*
That is the pure pentangle which the people called with lore.° *learning*
 Now graithed° is Gawain gay,* *arrayed; gaily*
 And layt° his lance right there, *took*
 And gave them all good day,
 He wende° for ever more. *believed*

VIII

He spurred the steed with the spurs, and sprang on his way 670
So stif° that the stone-fire* struck out there-after;‡ *boldly; sparks; behind him*
All that saw that seemly sighed in heart,
And said soothly° all same segges* til other,‡ *truly; people; to the other*
Carande° for that comely: by Christ, it is scathe* *Grieving; a shame*
That thou, leude,° shall be lost, that art of life noble! *knight*
To find his fere° upon folde,* in faith, is not ethe;‡ *equal; earth; easy*
Warloker° to have wrought* had more wit‡ *more warily; behaved; sensible*
 bene,
And have dight° yonder dere* a duke to have *appointed; nobleman;*
 worthed;‡ *been made*
A lowand° leader of ledes* in land him well seemeth, *brilliant; men*
And so had better have been then britned° to nought, *destroyed* 680

Headed° with an elfish man, for angardey* pryde.   *Beheaded; excessive*
Who knew ever any king such counsel to take,
As knights in cavilation° on Christmass games?   *petty disputes*
Well much was the warm water that watered of eyèn
When that seemly sir set from the wones°   *dwellings*
        that day;
  He made non abode,°   *delay*
  But wightily° went his way,   *quickly*
  Many wilsum° ways he rode,   *confusing*
  The book as I heard say.   690

IX

Now rides this renk° through the realm of Logres,*   *knight; England*
Sir Gawain, on Gode's halve,° though him no gomen* thought;   *behalf; game*
Oft leudles° alone he lengs* on nights,   *companionless; stays*
There he found not him before the fare° that he liked, –   *food*
Had he no fere° but his foal by friths* and downs,‡   *companion; woods; hills*
Ne no gome° but God by gate* with to karp,‡   *man; on the way; speak*
Til that he neared full nigh in to the North Wales;
All the isles of Anglesey on left half° he holds,*   *side; beholds*
And fares over the fords by the forelands,   *headlands*
Over at the Holy Head, till he had eft° bank   *again* 700
In the wilderness of Wirral; woned° there but light*   *lived; few*
That either God other gome with good heart loved.
And aye° he frained,* as he ferde,‡ at frekes that he met,   *always; asked; went*
If they had heard any karp° of a knight green,   *talk*
In any ground° there-about, of the green chapel;   *region*
And all nikked° him with nay, that never in their life   *said no*
They saw never no segge° that was of such hues   *man*
    Of green.
  The knight took gatès° straunge*   *roads; unmapped*
  In many a bank unbene,°   *dreary* 710
  His cheer full oft con change,   *mood*
  That chapel ere he might seen.

X

Many cliffs he over-clamb in countries strange;
Far floten° fro his friends fremedly* he rides;   *wandering; as a stranger*
At each warthe° other* water there the way passed,   *ford; or*
He found a foe him before, but ferly° it were,   *unusual*
And that so foul and so fell° that fight him behoved.   *fierce*
So many marvels by mount° there the man finds,   *among the hills*
It were too tore° for to tell of the tenth dole.*   *hard; part*

Somewhile with worms° he wars, and with wolves also,   *dragons* 720
Somewhile with wodwos,° that woned* in the   *forest trolls; lived;*
   knarrey,‡   *crags*
Both with bulls and bears and boars other-while,
And etayns° that him anelede,* of the high felle;   *giants; chased*
Nade° he ben doughty and dryye,* and Dryhten‡   *Had he not; enduring; God*
   had served,
Doubtless he had ben dead and dreped° full oft.   *slain*
For war wrathed° him not so much, that* winter was worse,   *afflicted; but*
When the cold clear water fro the clouds shed,
And froze ere it fall might to the falle° earth;   *fallow*
Near° slain with the sleet he slept in his irons*   *Nearly; armour*
More nights then enough in naked rokkey,°   *crags* 730
There as clattering from the crest° the cold burn runs,*   *cliff-tops; flowed*
And hanged high over his head in hard icicles.
Thus in peril and pain and plights full hard
By country carries° this knight till Christmas even,   *rides*
   alone;
   The knight well that tide°   *time*
   To Mary made his moan,°   *plaint*
   That she him red° to ride,   *direct*
   And wisse° him to some wone.*   *guide; dwelling*

XI

By a mount° on the morn merrily he rides   *mountain* 740
Into a forest full deep, that ferly° was wild,   *wonderfully*
High hills on each a half, and holt-woods under
Of hore° oaks full huge a hundred together;   *ancient*
The hazel and the hawthorn were harled° all samen,*   *tangled; together*
With rough ragged moss railed* ay-where,   *arranged*
With many birds unblithe° upon bare twigs,   *mournful*
That piteously there piped for pain of the cold.
The gome upon Gringolet glidès them under
Through many misy° and mire, man all him one,*   *bog; alone*
Carand° for his costs,* lest he ne kever‡   *grieving; hardships; manage*
   should   750
To see the service of that sire,° that on that self* night   *(Christ); same*
Of a burde° was born, our baret* to quell;   *virgin; sorrows*
And therefore sighing he said, 'I beseech thee, Lord,
And Mary, that is mildest mother so dear,
Of some herber° where holy I might hear mass,   *lodging*
And thy matins tomorn, meekly I ask,

And thereto prestly° I pray my *Pater** and *Ave*‡   *promptly; Our Father; Hail Mary*
    and *Creed*.'
  He rode in his prayer
  And cried for his misdeed,°   *sins* 760
  He signed him in sythes sere°   *made the sign of the cross several times*
  And said 'Cross-Christ° me speed!'   *Christ's cross*

XII

Nad° he signed himself, seggè, but three,   *Hardly*
Ere he was war° in the wood of a won* in a moat,   *aware; dwelling*
Above a laund,° on a lawe,* locken under boughs   *field; knoll*
Of many borelich° bole,* about by the ditches,   *strong; tree-trunks*
A castle the comeliest that ever knight ayte,°   *owned*
Pitched° on a prayer,* a park all about,   *Erected; meadow (pun on 'prayer')*
With a piked palace,° pinned* full thick,   *spiked palisade; enclosed*
That umbete° many tree mo than two mile.   *surround* 770
That hold° on that one side the hathel* avysed,‡   *stronghold; knight; beheld*
As it shimmered and shone through the sheer° oaks;   *shining*
Then hats° he hendly* off his helmet, and highly‡   *takes; reverently; devoutly*
  he thank
Jesus and Saint Julian, that gentle are both,
That courteously had him kidde° and his cry harkened.*   *shown; heard*
'Now bone hostel,° quoth the burne,* 'I beseeche you   *good lodging; knight*
  grant!'
Then girds° he to Gryngolet with the gilt heles,*   *spurred on; spurs*
And he full chauncely has chosen to the chief gate   *by chance*
That brought bremly° the burne to the bridge end   780
          in haste;
    The bridge was breme° up-braid*   *stoutly; drawn*
    The gates were stoken° fast,   *shut*
    The walls were well arrayed,°   *built*
    It doubt° no windès blast . . .   *feared*

42b. xiv

She commes to the curtain and at the knight totes,°   *peeps*
Sir Gawain her welcomed worthy° on first,*   *noble lady; immediately*
And she him yelds again° full yerne* of her words,   *replies; eager*
Settes her softly by his side, and swithely° she laughs,   *briskly*
And with a lovely look she laide him° these words: *uttered* 1480
'Sir, if ye be Gawain, wonder me thinks,

Wight that is so well wrast° always to good,   *disposed*
And connes° not of company the costes*   *knows; disposition;*
   undertake,‡   *perceive*
And if man kennes° you them to know, ye cast them of your mind;   *teaches*
Thou hast forgotten yederly° that yesterday I taught   *quickly*
By alder-truest° token of talk that I couth.'*   *the truest (ie the clearest); knew*
'What is that?' quoth the wight,° 'I-wiss I wot   *knight;*
   never;*   *Indeed I never knew*
If it be soothe that ye breve,° the blame is mine owen.'   *declare*
'Yet I kend° you of kissing,' quoth the cleare* then,   *taught; fair lady*
'Where-so countenance° is couthe,* quickly to claim;   *reward; given* 1490
That becomes each a knight that courtesy uses.'
'Do way,'° quoth that derf* man, 'my dear, that speeche,   *cease; brave*
For that durst I not do, lest I devayed° were,   *denied*
If I were werned,° I were wrong, i-wiss, if I proffered.'   *refused*
'Ma fay,'° quoth the merè* wife, 'ye may not be werned,   *My word; merry*
Ye are stiff° enough to constrain with strength, if you likes,   *strong*
If any were so villainous that you devaye° would.'   *refuse*
'Yes, by God,' quoth Gawayn, 'good is your speech,
But threat is un-thrivande° in thede* there I lend,‡   *unworthy; land; live*
And each gift that is given not with good will;   1500
I am at your commandèment, to kiss when you like,
Ye may lach° when you list,* and leve‡ when you   *start; like; stop soon after*
   thinkes,
       in space.'
   The lady louts° a-down   *bends*
   And comlyly° kisses his face,   *prettily*
   Much speech they there expoun°   *exchange*
   Of druries° greme* and grace.   *love's; grief*

XV

'I woled wit at you,° wise,' that worthy there said,   *wanted to learn from you*
'And you wrathed not° therewith, what were the skill*   *were not angry; reason*
That so young and so yepe° as ye at this time,   *brave* 1510
So courteous, so knightly, as ye are known out,
And of all chivalry to chose, the chief thing a-losed°   *praised*
Is the loyal layk° of love, the lettrure* of armes;‡   *sport; code; knightliness*
For to tell of these teveling° of this true knightes,   *deeds*
It is the titelet° token and text of their werkkes,*   *inscribed; deeds*
How ledes° for their loyal love their lives have auntered,*   *people; risked*
Endured for their drury° doleful stounds,*   *love; hours*
And after venged with their valour and voided their care°   *suffering*
And brought bliss into bower° with bounties their own.   *her rooms*

And ye are knight comeliest kid° of your eld,*   *reputed; generation* 1520
Your word and your worship walks ay-where,
And I have seten° by yourself here sere* twice,   *sat; occasions*
Yet heard I never of your hed° helde* no words   *mouth; come*
That ever longed° to love, lesse ne more;   *belonged*
And you, that are so courteous and coint° of your hetes,*   *gracious; vows*
Ought to a younge° think gern* to show   *young person; readily*
And teach some tokens of truelove crafts.
Why! are you lewed,° that all the laus* weldes‡   *ignorant; renown; possess*
Other else you deem me too dull your dalliance° to   *courtly conversation*
              hearken?
    For shame!   1530
  I come hither single and sitte
  To learn at you some game,
  Dos,° teach me of your witte,   *Come*
  While my lord is from hame.°   *home*

XVI

'In good faith,' quoth Gawain, 'God you foryelde!°   *reward*
Great is the good glee,° and gomen to me huge,   *joy*
That so worthy as ye would winne° hithere   *come*
And paine you° with so poor a man, as play with your
    knight   *take pains with*
With anyskinnes° countenaunce,* it kevers‡ me   *any kind of; favour; gives*
    ease;
But to take the toruail° to my-self to true love expound   *challenge* 1540
And touch the themes of text and tales of arms
To you that, I wot well, wields more sliyt°   *skill*
Of that art, by the half, or° a hundredth of suche   *than*
As I am other° ever shall, in earth there I leve,*   *or; believe*
It were a folly felefold,° my fre,* by my troth.   *manifold; noble lady*
I wolde your willing° work at my might,*   *will; if I can*

As I am highly beholden, and ever-more will
Be servaunt to yourselfen, so save me Drighten!'°   *God*
Thus him frayned° that fre* and fondet‡ him oft,   *tested; noble lady; tempted*
Forto have wonnen him to woo, whatso she thought else,   1550
But he defended him so fair that no fault seemed,
Ne non evil on neither half° neither they wisten,*   *side; knew*
      but bliss;
  They laughed and laiked° longe,   *frolicked*
  At the last she con° him kisse,   *did*

Her leave faire con she fonge,°   *took*
And went her way iwysse.°   *indeed*

XVII

Then ruthes° him the renk* and rises to the Mass,   *bestirs; knight*
And sithen° their dinner was dight* and derely‡   *after; prepared; splendidly*
   served.
The lede° with the ladies laiked* all day,   *knight; frolicked* 1560
But the lord over the lands launced° full oft,   *was dashing*
Swey° his uncely* swine, that swinges‡ by the bankes   *Chasing; savage; rushes*
And bit the best of his braches° the backes in sunder,*   *hounds; asunder*
There he bode in his bay,° till bowmen it breaken,   *stood at bay*
And made him, maw-gref° his head, forto move outer,   *despite*
So fell flones° there flete* when the folk gathered;   *arrows; sped*
But yet the stiffest° to start* by stounds‡ he made,   *bravest; flinch; at times*
Till at the last he was so mat,° he might no more runne,   *tired*
But in the haste that he might, he to a hol winnes°   *reaches*
Of a rasse,° by a rocke, where runs the burne;   *ledge* 1570
He got the bank at his back, beginnes to scrape,°   *dig*
The froth foamed at his mouth unfair° by the wikes,*   *ugly; corners*
Whets his white tusks; with him then irked°   *were tired*
All the burns° so bold that him by stooden,   *knights*
To annoy him onfarum,° but near him non durst   *from a distance*
    for wothe;°   *danger*
   He had hurt so many beforn
   That all thought thenne full loathe
   Be more with his tusks torne,
   That breme° was and brain-wod* both.   *fierce; brain-mad (frenzied)* 1580

XVIII

Till the knight come him-self, kachand° his blonk,*   *spurring on; steed*
Saw him bide at the bay, his burnes beside;
He lights luflich° adown, leaves his corsour,*   *graciously; horse*
Braides° out a bright bront* and bigly forth strides,   *Pulls; sword*
Founds° fast through the ford where the fell* bides.   *Hurries; wild beast*
The wild was ware of the wight with weapon in hand,
Hef° highly the hair, so hetterly* he fnast,‡   *bristled; suddenly; snorted*
That fele° feared for the freke,* lest fell him the warre;‡   *many; knight; worst*
The swine settes him out on the segge° even,   *man*
That the burne and the boar were both upon heapes   1590
In the wightest° of the water, the werre* had that   *fiercest; worst;*
   other;‡   *(the beast)*
For the man marks him well, as they mette first,

Set sadly° the scharp in the slot* even,   *firmly; base of the throat*
It him up to the hilt, that the heart sundered,
And he yarrande° him yield, and yedown* the water   *snarling; was swept into*
   full tight;°   *quickly*
  A hundred hounds him hent,°   *took*
  That bremely° con him bite,   *fiercely*
  Burnes° him brought to bent*   *Knights; the bank*
  And dogges to death endite.°   *killed* 1600

XIX

There was blowing of pris° in many breme*   *(announcing capture); splendid*
   horne,
High hallowing on high with hatheless that might;
Brachetes° bayed that beast, as bidden the masteres,   *Hounds*
Of that chargaunt° chase that were chief huntes.   *toilsome*
Thenne a wise that was wise upon wood-craftes
To unlace° this boar lufly* beginnes;   *cut up; skilfully*
First he hews off his head and on high settes,
And sithen rendes him all roughe° by the rigge* after,   *roughly; back*
Braides° out the boweles, brennes* them on   *Pulls; boils;*
   glede,‡   *red-hot charcoal*
With bread blent° therewith his braches rewardes;   *mixed* 1610
Sithen he britnes° out the brawen* in bright brode sheldes‡ *slices; flesh; slabs*
And has out the hastlettes,° as highly be-seemly;   *entrails*
And yet them halches° all whole the halves* together,   *fasten; sides*
And sithen on a stiff stange° stoutly them hanges.   *pole*
Now with this ilk swine they swengen° to home;   *rushed*
The bores head was borne before the burnes° selven   *knight's*
That him forferde° in the forth* through force of his hande   *killed; stream*
   so strong;
  Till he saw Sir Gawaine
  In hall him thought full long;°   *a long time*
  He called, and he came°   *promptly*
  His fees° therefor to fong.*   *payment; receive*

William Langland

43. from *The Vision of William concerning Piers the Plowman* [B text]

43a. from *Prologue*

In a summer season · when soft was the sun,
I shope° me in shrouds · as I a shepe* were,   *prepared (i.e. dressed); shepherd*
In habit as an heremit · unholy of workes,°   *deeds*
Went wide in this world · wonders to heare.
Ac° on a May morning · on Malverne Hills   *But*
Me befell a ferly° · of fairy me thoughte;   *marvel*
I was weary forwandred° · and went me to reste   *from walking*
Under a broad banke · by a bornes° side,   *brook's*
And as I lay and leaned · and looked in the waters,
I slumbered in a sleeping · it sweyved° so merry.   *sounded* 10
    Then gan° I to meten* · a merveillous sweven,‡   *began; dream; dream*
That I was in a wilderness · wist° I never where,   *knew*
As I beheld into the east · on high to the sun,
I saw a tower on a toft · trieliche y-maked;°   *hill excellently made*
A deep dale beneath · a dungeon therein,
With deep ditches and darke · and dreadful of sight.
A fair field full of folke · found I there between,
Of all manner of men · the mean and the rich,
Working and wandering · as the world asketh.
Some putten them to plowe · played full selde,°   *seldom* 20
In setting and in sowing · swonken° full harde,   *laboured*
And wonnen° what wastours* · by gluttonye destroyeth.   *homes; wasters*
    And some putten them to pride · apparaled them there-after,
In countenaunce° of clothing · comen disguised.   *display*
    In prayers and in penance · putten them manye,
All for love of our lorde · liveden full straighte,
In hope for to have · heaveneriche° blisse;   *heavenly*
As ancres° and heremites · that holden them in their celles,   *anchorites*
And coveten not in country · to kairen aboute,°   *go up and down*
For no likerous liflode° · they likam to please.   *gluttonous diet* 30
    And some chosen chaffare° · they achieven* the better,   *trade; thrive*
As it seemeth to our sight · that such men thriveth;
And some mirthes to make · as minstreles canneth,
And geten gold with their glee° · guiltless, I lieve.*   *music; believe*

Ac japers° and janglers* · Judas childeren,   *tricksters; gossips*
Feignen them fantasies · and fooles° them maketh,*   *pretend to be fools*
And han their witte at wille° · to work yif they shoulde.   *keep their wits at will*
That Paul preacheth of them · I nel not prove° it here;   *put it to the test*
Qui turpiloquium loquitur · is Luciferes hyne[1].

   Bidders° and beggares · fast aboute yede,*   *tramps; wandered* 40
With their belly and their bagges · of bread full y-crammed;
Fayteden° for their foode · foughten at ale;*   *begged with lies; ale house*
In gluttonye, God it wote · gone they to bedde,
And risen with ribaudye° · those roberdes* knaves;   *debauchery; thieving*
Sleepe and sorry sloth · sueth° them ever.   *pursues*

   Pilgrims and palmers · pliyted° them together   *gathered*
To seeke Saint James · and saintes in Rome.
They went forth on their waye · with many wise tales,
And hadden leave to lie° · all their life after.   *could lie about it*
I saw some that saiden · they had y-sought saintes;   50
To eache a tale that they told · their tongue was tempered to lie,
More than to say soth° · it seemed by their speeche.   *truth*

   Heremits on an heap° · with hookede staves,*   *a host of; staffs*
Wenten to Walsingham · and their wenches after;
Great lobbyes° and longe* · that loath were to swinke,‡   *lubbers; tall; toil*
Clotheden them in copes · to be knownen from othere;
And shopen them heremites · their ease to have.

   I founde there Friars · alle the four orders,
Preached the people · for profit of themselven,
Glossed° the gospel · as them good liked,   *Explained* 60
For covetise° of copes · construed it as they woulde.   *greed*
Many of these master° Friars · may clothen them at liking,   *learned*
For their money and merchandise · marchen° togideres.   *increase*
For since charity hath been chapman° · and chief to shrive*   *pedlar; confess*
   lordes,
Many ferlis° han fallen · in a fewe yeares.   *marvels*
But° holy church and they* · hold better togideres,   *Unless; (the friars)*
The most mischief° on molde* · is mounting well faste.   *evil; earth*

   There preached a Pardonere · as he a priest were,
Brought forth a bulle° · with bishopes seales,   *religious document*
And said that himself · might absolven them alle   70
Of falsehood of fasting° · of vowes y-broken.   *broken fasts*

   Lewed men loved him well · and liked his wordes,   *Uneducated*
Comen up kneeling · to kissen his bulles;

---

[1] '*He who speaks filth* is Lucifer's servant.'

He bonched° them with his breuet* · and bleared   *struck; letter of pardon*
   their eyes,
And rauyte° with his ragman* · ringes and brooches.   *seized; parchment*
Thus they given here golde · gluttones to keepe,°   *to support gluttons*
And lieveth° such loseles* · that lechery haunten.   *believe; scoundrels*
Were the bishop y-blessed · and worth bothe his eares,
His seal should not be sent · to deceive the people.
Ac it is not by° the bishop · that the boy preacheth,   *by permission of* 80
For the parish priest and the pardoner · parten° the silver,   *divide*
That the poraille° of the parish · should have if they nere.*   *poor; weren't by*
   Parsones and parish priestes · plained° them to the bishop,   *complained*
That their parishes were poore · sith the pestilence° time,   *plague*
To have a licence and a leave° · at London to dwelle,   *leave of absence*
And singen there for simony · for silver is sweete.
   Bishops and bachelors both · masters and doctors,
That han cure under Christe · and crowning in tokne°   *tonsure as a proof*
And sign that they shoulden shriven° · their parishioners,   *hear confession of*
Preachen and pray for them · and the poor feede,   90
Liggen° in London · in Lenten, an else.*   *Living; even*
Somme serven the king · and his silvere tellen,°   *count*
In checker° and in chancery · challengen* his debtes   *exchequer; claim*
Of° wardes and of wardmotes,* · waifes and strayes.   *From; wardship-hearings*
   And some serven as servants · lordes and ladies,
And instead of stewards · sitten and demen.°   *judge*
Their masse and their matins · and many of their hours
Are done undevoutly; · dread is at the laste
Lest Christ in consistorie° · accurse full many.   *ecclesiastical court*
I perceived of° the power · that Peter had to kepe,   *observed* 100
To bind and to unbinde · as the book telleth,
How he it left with love · as our lord hight,°   *commanded*
Amonges four virtues · the best of all virtues,
That cardinals been called · and closing gates,
There Christ is in kingdom · to close and to shutte,
And to open it to them · and heavene bliss showe.
Ac of the cardinals atte Court · that caut of° that name,   *were called by*
And power presumed in them · a Pope to make,
To han that power that Peter had · impugnen I nelle;°   *do not want to*
For in love and letterure° · the election belongeth,   *learning* 110
Forthy I can and can nought · of court speake more.
   Then come there a king · knighthode° him ledde,   *knights*
Might of the comunes° · made him to reigne,   *common people*
And then came kinde° wit · and clerkes he made,   *common sense*
For to counselle the king · and the comune sawe.

The king and the knighthode · and clergy bothe
Casten° that the comune · shoulde themself finde.*   *Propose; provide for them*
   The comune contrived · of kinde witt craftes,°   *trades*
And for profit of alle the people · plowmen ordained,
To toil and travaile° · as true life asketh.   *labour* 120
The king and the comune · and kinde witte the thirde
Shaped lawe and loyalty · eache man to know his owne.
   Then looked up° a lunatick · a leane thing with-alle,   *appeared*
And kneeling to the king · clerkly he saide;
Christ kepe thee, sir king · and thy kingriche,°   *kingdom*
And leave thee leade thy lande° · so loyalty thee love,   *rule thy land*
And for thy rightful ruling · be rewarded in heavene!
   And sithen° in the air an high · an angel of heaven   *afterwards*
Lowed to speak in Latin · for lewed men ne coulde   *stooped*
Jangle nor judge · that justify them shoulde,   130
But sufferen and serven – · forthy° said the angel,   *therefore*
Sum Rex, sum Princeps · neutrum fortasse deinceps; –
O qui iura regis · Christi specialia regis,
Hoc quod agas melius · iustus es, esto pius!
Nudum ius a te · vestiri vult pietate;
Qualia vis metere · talia grana sere.
Si ius nudatur · nudo de iure metatur.
Si seritur pietas · de pietate metas![2]
      Then grieved him° a Goliardes* · a glutton   *irritated him; buffoon*
         of wordes,
And to the angel on high · answered after,   140
Dum rex a regere dicatur · nomen habere,
Nomen habet sine re · nisi studet iura tenere.[3]
   And thene gan all the commune · cry in verse of Latin,
To the kinges counsele · construe how-so wolde –
Precepta Regis · sunt nobis vincula legis.[4]
   With that ran there a route° · of ratones* at once,   *crowd; rats*
And smalle mice with them · more than thousande,
And comen to a counselle° · for their common profit;   *meeting*
For a cat of the courte · came when him liked,
And overleapt them lightly · and lauyt° them at his wille,   *caught* 150
And played with them perilously · and possed° them about.   *pushed*

---

[2] You say *I am king, I'm a Prince*, but in time you may be neither. O you the laws of Christ must especially uphold. To do this better be as pious! Robe naked justice with mercy, and sow as you would reap. If you sow justice you will be judged by justice alone; if you sow mercy, you will reap mercy.

[3] As a king is only entitled to be called a king by governing, he is a king in name only if he fails to uphold the laws.

[4] The king's orders bind us as much as the law does.

'For doubt° of diverse dreades · we dare not well looke;   *fear*
And if we grucche° of his games · he will grieve us alle,   *complain*
Scratch us, or clutch us · and in his clutches holde,
That us loatheth the life · or° he lete us passe.   *unless*
Might we with any witte · his wille withstande,
We mighte be lordes aloft · and liven at our ease.'
 A raton of renown · most renable° of tongue,   *eloquent*
Said for a sovereign° · help to him-selve; –   *excellent*
'I have y-seen segges,'° quoth he · 'in the city of London   *men* 160
Bearen biyes° full bright · abouten their neckes,   *neck rings*
And some collars of crafty work; · uncoupled° they wenden   *unrestrained*
Both in warrene and in waste° · where them leve liketh;   *wasteland*
And otherwhile they aren elsewhere · as I heare telle.
Were there a belle on their biy° · by Jesu, as me thinketh,   *neck*
Men mighte wite where they went · and awaye runne!
And right so,' quoth that ratoun, · 'reason me showeth,
To bugge° a bell of brass · or of bright silver,   *buy*
And knitten on a collar · for our comune profit,
And hangen it upon the cates hals° · then heare we mowen*   *neck; may* 170
Where° he ritte* or reste · or runneth to playe.   *Whether; rises*
And if him list for to laike° · then looke we mowen,   *play*
And peren° in his presence · there while him play liketh,   *appear*
And if him wratheth,° be y-war* · and his waye shunne.   *gets angry; wary*
 All this route of ratones · to this reason they assented.
As though the bell was y-bought · and on the biy hanged,
There ne was ratoun in alle the route · for all the realm of France,
That durst have y-bounden the bell · about the cat's necke,
Ne hangen it about the cat's hals · all Engeland to winne;
And helden them unhardy° · and their counsel feeble,   *timid* 180
And leten their labour as lost · and all their long study.
 A mouse that muche good · couth, as me thoughte,
Stroke° forth sternly · and stood before them alle,   *Strode*
And to the route of ratones · rehearsed these wordes:
'Though we culled° the cat · yet should there come another,   *killed*
To scratch us and all our kinde · though we crept under benches.
Forthy I counsel alle the comune · to let the cat worthe,°   *be*
And be we never so bolde · the bell him to showe;
For I heard my sire sayen · is seven year y-passed,
There the cat is a kitten · the court is full elyng;°   *wretched* 190
That witnesseth holy writ · who-so will it reade,
 Ve terrae ubi puer rex est, etc.[5]

---

[5] 'Woe to the land where the child is king.'

For may no renk° there rest have · for the ratones by nighte;　　*creature*
The while° he catcheth conneys · he coveteth not our　　*So long as;*
　　caroyne,*　　*flesh*
But fête him all with venison · defame we him never.
For better is a little loss · than a long sorrowe,
The mase° among us all · though we misse a schrewe.**confusion; depraved one*
For many mannes malt · we mice would destroye,
And also you route of ratones · rend manes clothes,
Never that cat of that courte · that can you overleap;　　200
For had ye rattes your wille · ye could not rule your-selve.
I say for me,' quoth the mouse, · 'I see so mickle° after,　　*much*
Shall never the cat nor kitten · by my counsel be grieved,
Ne carping° of this collar · that costed me never.　　*discussion*
And though it had coste me catel° · beknowen* it I nolde,　　*capital; admit*
But suffer as himself would · to do as him liketh,
Coupled° and uncoupled · to catch what they mowe.　　*leashed*
Forthy each a wise wighte° I warn · wite* well his own.' –　　*creature; knows*
　　What this meteles° bemeaneth · ye men that be merry,　　*vision*
Divine ye, for I ne dare · by dear God in heavene!　　210
　　Yet hoved° there an hundredth · in hoves of silke,　　*hovered*
Servants it seemed · that serveden° at barre,　　*served*
Pleaden for pennies · and poundes the lawe,
And not for love of our lorde · unless° their lippes onis.*　　*loosen; once*
Thou mightest better mete° the miste · on Malvern hilles,　　*measure*
Than get a momm° of their mouthe · but* money were　　*mumble; unless*
　　showed.
　　Barons and burghers · and bonde-men als°　　*also*
I saw in this assembly · as ye shall hear after.
Baxsteres° and brewesteres* · and butchers many,　　*bakers; brewers*
Woolewebsteres° · and weavers of linen,　　*wool weavers* 220
Tailors and tinkers · and tolleres° in markets,　　*toll-collectors*
Masons and miners · and many other craftes.
Of alkin° libbyng* laboreres · lopen‡ forth some,　　*all kinds; living; appeared*
As dikers° and delvers · that doth their deedes ille,　　*ditchers*
And driven forth the longe day · with *Dieu vous save, Dame Emme!* [6]
Cooks and their knaves° · crieden, 'Hote pies, hote!　　*lads*
Good gris° and geese · go dine, go!'　　*piglets*
　　Taverners° until them · told the same,　　*Tavern-keepers*
'White wine of Oseye° · and red wine of Gascoigne,　　*Alsace*
Of the Rhine and of the Rochel · the roaste to defie.'° –　　*digest* 230
All this saw I sleeping, · and seven sythes° more.　　*times*

---

[6] 'God save you, Dame Emma!'

43b. *Passus* VII

Truthe heard tell hereof · and to Peres° he sente,   *Piers*
To taken his team · and tillen the earthe,
And purchased him a pardon · *a pena and a*
 culpa°   *from penance and punishment*
For him, and for his heires · for evermore after.
And bade him holde him at home · and eryen° his   *plough;*
 leyes,*   *fallow lands*
And alle that help hym to erye, · to set or to sowe,
Or any other mister · that mighte Peres availle,°   *help*
Pardon with Peres Plowman · Truth hath y-granted.
 Kings and knyytes · that kepen° holychurche,   *protect*
And rightfully in realmes · rulen the people,   10
Han° pardon through purgatory · to passe full lightly, *Have*
With patriarchs and prophets · in paradise to be fellowes.
 Bishopes y-blessed · if they be as they shoulden,
Legistres of bothe° the lawes · the lewed* therewith *secular and religious; lay*
 to preache,
And in as much as they may · amende alle sinful,
Are peers with the apostles · this pardon Piers showeth,
And at the day of dome° · atte high daise to sitte.   *judgment*
 Merchants in the margin · hadden many yeares,
Ac none *a pena et a culpa* · the Pope nolde° them grante, *did not want to*
For they holde nought her holidays · as holychurch teacheth, 20
And for they sweare by her soul · and 'so god must them helpe,'
Against cleane conscience · their catel° to selle.   *chattels*
 Ac under his secret seal · truth sent them a letter,
That they shoulde buy boldely · that° them best liked, *whatever*
And sithenes° selle it again · and save the winninge,* *afterwards; profit*
And amend mesondieux° therewith · and miseis* folke *hospitals; troubled*
 helpe,
And wicked ways° · wightly* them amende;   *roads; speedily*
And do bote° to bridges · that to-broke* were, *rebuild; broken*
Marrien maidens · or maken them nunnes;
Poor people and prisoners · finden them here foode,   30
And set scholars to school · or to some other craftes;
Relieve Religion · and renten them bettere;° *provide them better income*
And I shall send you myselfe · Saint Michael mine archangel,
That no devil shall you dere° · ne fear you in your dying, *harm*
And witen° you from wanhope · if ye will thus worke, *guard; despair*
And sende your soules in safety · to my saints in joye.
 Then were Merchants merry, · many wepten for joye,

And praiseden Peres the Plowman · that purchased this bulle.
    Men of lawe least pardon had · that pleaden for Mede,°   *reward*
For the psalter saveth them not · such as taketh giftes,°   *bribes* 40
And namely° of innocents · that none evil ne kunneth;*   *especially; suspect*
    Super innocentem munera non accipies.[7]
Pleaderes should peynen° them · to pleade for such, and
    helpe,   *take pains for*
Princes and prelates · should paye for their travaille;   *troubles*
    A regibus et principibus erit merces eorum.[8]
    Ac many a justice and juror · would for John do more,
Than *pro dei pietate*° · leve* thou none other!   *for the love of God; believe*
Ac he that spendeth his speeche · and speaketh for the poore
That is Innocent and needy · and no man appeireth,°   *injures*
Comforteth him in that case · without covetise° of giftes,   *desire* 50
And showeth law for our lordes love · as he it hath learned,
Shall no devil at his death-day · deren° him a mighte,   *harm*
That he ne worth° safe and his soule · the psalter beareth witnesse; *become*
    Domine, quis habitabit in tabernaculo tuo, etc.[9]
    Ac to buye water, nor winde, · nor witte,° nor fire the fourthe, *intelligence*
These foure the father of heaven · made to this folde° in common;   *earth*
These be truthes treasures · true folke to helpe,
That never shall wax nor wane · with-out God himselfe.
    When they drawen on to die · and Indulgences would have,
Their pardon is full petit° · at their parting hence,   *small* 60
That any mede° of meane* men · for her mooting‡ *recompense; poor; counsel*
    taketh.
You legislators and lawyers · holdeth this for truthe,
That, if that I lye · Matthew is to blame,
For he bad me make° you this · and this proverb me tolde,   *tell*
    Quodcumque vultis ut faciant vobis homines, facite eis.[10]
    Alle living laboreres · that liven with their handes,
That trewlich° taken · and trewlich winnen,*   *honestly; profit*
And liven in love and in law · for their lowe heartes,
Haveth the same absolution · that sent was to Peres.
    Beggares ne bidderes° · ne beeth not in the bulle,   *tramps* 70
But if the suggestion be sooth · that shapeth° them to begge.   *conditions*
For he beggeth or bid · but if° he have neede,   *unless*
He is false with the fiend · and defraudeth the needy,
And also he beguileth the giver · against his wille.

---

[7] 'Take no bribes from the innocent.'
[8] 'They shall receive their wages from kings and rulers.'
[9] 'Lord who shall live in your tabernacle.'
[10] 'Do unto others as you would have others do unto you.'

For if he wist he were not needy · he would give that another,
That were more needy than he · so the neediest should be helped.
Cato kenneth° men thus · and the clerk of the stories,   *teaches*
Cui des, videto° · is Cato's teaching,   *'be careful to whom you give alms'*
And in the stories he teacheth · to bestowe thine almes;
    Sit elemosina tua in manu tua, donec studes cui des.[11]   80
    Ac° Gregory was a goode man · and bade us given alle   *But*
That asketh, for his love · that us all lendeth: –
    Non eligas cui miserearis, ne forte pretereas illum qui meretur
      accipere. Quia incertum est pro quo Deo magis placeas.[12]
    For wite° you never who is worthy · ac God wote* who hath   *know; knew*
    neede,
In him that taketh is the treachery · if any treason were;
For he that giveth, yieldeth · and yarketh° hym to reste,   *prepares*
And he that biddeth,° borroweth · and bringeth himself in debte.   *begs*
For beggars borrowen evermore · and their borghe° is God   *collateral*
    Almighty,
To yelden° them that giveth them · and yet usure*   *repay; give better terms*
    more: 90
    Quare non dedisti peccuniam meam ad mensam, ut ego
      veniens cum usuris exegissem illam?[13]
Forthy biddeth not, ye beggares · but if ye have great neede;
For whoso hath to buyen him bread · the booke beareth witness,
He hath enough that hath bread enough · though he have nought else:
    Satis dives est, qui non indiget pane.[14]
Let usage be youre solace · of saintes lives readinge,
The booke banneth beggary · and blameth them in this mannere:
    Iunior fui, etenim senui; et non vidi iustum derelictum,
      nec semen eius quaerens panem.[15]
    For your lives in no love · nor no lawe
    holde;°   *aren't governed by any love or law* 100
Many of you ne wedde not · the women that ye with dealen,
But as wild bestis with wehe° · worthen uppe* and   *heehaw; mount;*
    worken,‡   *rut*
And bringeth forth bairns · that bastards men call.
Or the back or some bone · he breaketh in his youth,

[11] 'Keep your alms in your own hand until you have studied to whom you give.'
[12] 'Do not select whom you pity nor overlook accidentally one who deserve alms. For it is unclear by which giving you will most please God.'
[13] 'Why did you not put my money in the bank so that when I came again I should have received the principal with interest?'
[14] 'He is sufficiently rich if he does not lack bread.'
[15] 'I have been young, and now am not too old, and I have never seen the righteous forsaken, nor his offspring begging for bread.'

And sitthe° gon faiten* with your infants · for   *afterwards; beg deceitfully*
   euermore after.
There is more misshapen people · amonge these beggeres,
Than of all manner men · that on this molde° walketh;   *earth*
And they that live thus their life · may loathe the time,
That ever he was man wrought · when he shall hence fare.°   *die*
   Ac olde men and hore° · that helpless be of strengthe,   *hoary* 110
And women with childe · that worke ne more,
Blinde and bedered° · and broken theire membres,*   *bedridden; limbs*
That taketh this mischief meekly · as meseles° and othere,   *lepers*
Have as plain pardon · as the plowman himself;
For love of their lowe hertis · oure Lorde hath them granted
Their penaunce and their purgatory · here on this earthe.
   Peres, quoth a priest tho° · thy pardon must I reade,   *then*
For I will construe eache clause · and kenne° it thee on Englishe.   *explain*
   And Peres at his prayere° · the pardon unfoldeth,   *entreaty*
And I behinde them both · behelde all the bulle.   120
All in two lines it lay · and not a leafe more,
And was written right thus · in witnesse of truthe:
   Et qui bona egerunt, ibunt in vitam eternam;
   Qui vero mala, in ignem eternum.[16]
   Peter! quoth the priest · there I can no pardon finde
But do well and have well · and God shall have thy soule,
And do evil, and have evil · hope thou none other
But after thy death-day · the devil shall have thy soule!
   And Peres for pure tene° · pulled it atweyne,* and said   *rage; tore it in two*
   Si ambulavero in medio umbre mortis, non timebo mala:
     quoniam tu mecum es.[17]   130
I shall ceasen of my sowing, quoth Piers · and swynke° not so harde,   *work*
Ne about my belly joye° · so busy be no more!   *stomach's pleasure*
Of prayers and of penance · my plough shall be here-after,
And weepen when I shoulde sleepe · though wheate bread me fail.
   The prophet his pene° eat · in penance and in sorwe,   *bread*
By that the psalter sayeth · so dide other many;
That loveth God loyally · his liflode° is full easy: *livelihood*
   Fuerunt mihi lacrimae meae panes die ac nocte.[18]
   And, but if Luke lie · he lereth° us by fowles,   *teaches*
We shoulde not be too busy · about the worlde's blisse;   140
Ne solliciti sitis° · he sayeth in the gospel,   *be not solicitious*

---

[16] 'Those who have done good will enter eternal life; those who have done bad go to everlasting fire.'
[17] 'Though I walked through the valley of the shadow of death, I should fear no evil; for you are with me.'
[18] 'My tears were my bread day and night.'

And showeth us by examples · us selve to wisse.°   *ourselves to know*
The fowles in the field · who finds them meat at winter?
Have they° no granaries to go to · but God finds them alle.   *They have*
   What! quoth the priest to Perkin, · Peter! as me thinketh,
Thow art lettred° a little · who learned* thee on book?   *able to read; taught*
Abstinence the abbesse, quoth Peres · mine a, b, c, me taughte,
And Conscience come afterward · and kenned° me much more.   *taught*
   Were thou a priest, Peres, quoth he, · thou mightst preach
     where thou shouldest,
As divinour in divinity · with *dixit insipiens*° to thy   *'the fool spoke';*
    teme.*   *text* 150
   Lewed lorel!° quoth Peres · little looks thou on the Bible,   *Ignorant lout*
On Solomones sawes° · seldom thou beholdest,   *proverbs*
   Eice derisores et iurgia cum eis, ne crescant, etc[19]
   The priest and Perkin · opposed either other,
And I through their wordes a-woke · and waited aboute,
And saw the sunne in the south · sitte that time,
Meatless and moneyless · on Malverne hilles,
Musing on this meteles;° · and my waye ich yede.*   *dream; went*
   Many times this meteles · hath maked me to study
Of that I saw sleepinge · if it so be mighte,   160
And also for Peres the plowman · full pensive in hearte,
And which° a pardon Peres hadde · alle the people to comforte, *what kind of*
And how the priest impugned° it · with two proper*   *found fault with; fine*
    wordes.
Ac I have no savoure in songewarie° · for I see it ofte   *taste for dream lore*
    faille;
Cato and canonistres° · counselleth us to leve*   *practisers of canon law; desist*
To sette sadness° in songewarie · for, *sompnia ne cures.**   *trust; ignore dreams*
   Ac for the booke Bible · beareth witnesse,
How Daniel divined · the dreames of a kinge,
That was Nebuchadnezzar · nempned° of clerkis.*   *called; scholars*
Daniel saide: Sire Kinge · thy dreameles° betokeneth,   *dream* 170
That uncouth° knights shall come · thy kingdom to cleue;* *unknown; split up*
Amonges lowere lordes · thy land shall be departed.*   *more humble; divided*
And as Daniel divined · indeed it felle after,
The kinge lost his lordshippe · and lower men it hadde.
   And Joseph mette° merveillously · how the moone and the sonne, *dreamed*
And the elevene starres · hailed° him alle.   *saluted*
Then Jacob judged° · Josephes swevene: *interpreted*
Beau filtz,° quoth his father · for defaute* we shallen, *Beautiful son; helplessness*

---

[19] 'Eject the scorners and refute them with words, lest they increase.'

I myself and my sones · seeke thee for neede°.   *when we need help*
It befell as his father saide · in Pharaoh's time,   180
That Joseph was Justice · Egypte to loken,°   *in charge of*
It befell as his father tolde · his friendes there him soughte.
And all this maketh me · on this meteles to thinke;
    And how the priest proved · no pardon to Do-well,
And deemed that Do-well · indulgences passed,°   *surpassed*
Bienniales and trienniales° · and bishopes letters, *commemorations of the dead*
And how Do-well at the day of doom · is dignely°   *worthily;*
    vnder-fongen,*   *received*
And passeth all the pardon · of Sainte Peters churche.
    Now hath the Pope powere · pardon to grante the people
Withouten any penance · to passen into heaven;   190
This is oure belief · as lettered men us teacheth,
    Quodcumque ligaveris super terram, erit ligatum et in celis, etc.[20]
And so I lieve° loyally · (lordes forbide ellis!)   *believe*
That pardon and penance · and prayeres do save
Souls that have sinned · sevene sithes° deadly.   *times*
Ac to trust to these triennales · truely me thinketh,
Is not so syker° for the soule · certis, as is Do-well.   *certain*
    Forthy I rede° you, renkes* that rich ben on this earthe,   *advise; men*
Upon trust of youre treasoure · triennales to have,*   *trusting your wealth; buy*
Be you nevere the bolder to break the ten hestes;°   *commandments* 200
And namely,° you masters · mayores, and judges,   *particularly*
That han the wealthe of this world · and for wise men ben holden,
To purchase you pardon · and the Pope's bulles.
At the dreadeful doome · when deade shallen rise,
And comen alle before Christ · acountes to yielde,
How thou leadest thy life here · and his lawes keptest,
And how thou didest day by day · the doome will rehearse;
A poke° full of pardon there · ne provinciales letters,   *bag*
Though ye be founde in the fraternity · of alle the four orders,
And have indulgences double-folde · but if Do-well you helpe,   210
I set your patentes° and your pardones · at one pies hele![21]   *letters of privilege*
    Forthy I counsell alle Christiane · to crye° God mercy,   *ask of*
And Marie his mother · be oure mean° betweene,   *middle (i.e. mediator)*
That God give us grace · ere° are we gone hennes,   *before*
Such workes to work · while we been here,
That after oure death-day · Do-well reherce,

---

[20] 'Whatever you bind on earth, will be bound in Heaven …' (and whatever you release on earth shall be released in Heaven).

[21] *one magpie's health* (i.e., nothing at all)

At the daye of doom · we dide as he highte.°   *commanded*
  Explicit visio Willelmi de Petro Plowman.[22]

John Gower

44. from *Confessio Amantis*

44a. from *Prologue* (1392)

Of them that written us tofore°	*before*
The bookès dwell,° and we therefore	*survive*
Been taught of that was writè tho:°	*then*
Forthy° good is that we also	*therefore*
In ourè time among us here	
Do write of newè some matter,	
Exampled of these oldè ways	
So that it might in such a wise,	
When we be dead and elèswhere,	
Beleavè° to the worldès ear	*bequeathed* 10
In time commendè° after this.	*to come*
But for men sayen, and sooth it is,	
That who that all of wisdom writ	
It dulleth oft a mannès wit	
To him that shall it all day read,	
For thilkè° cause, if that you read,	*same*
I wouldè go the middle way	
And write a book between the twey,°	*two*
Somewhat of lust°, somewhat of lorè,*	*pleasure; teaching*
That of the lessè or of the morè	20
Some man may like of that I write:	
And for that° fewè men endite*	*because; compose verse*
In ourè English, I thinkè make°	*intend to*
A book for Engèlandes sake,	
The year sixteenth of King Richard.	

---

[22] 'Here ends the vision of Peter Plowman.'

What shall befall here afterward
God wot, for now upon this tide
Men see the world on every side
In sundry wayès so diversed,
That it well nigh stand all reversed,   30
As forto speak of time ago.
The causè why it changeth so
It needeth not to specify,
The thing so open is at eye
That every man it may behold:
And ne'er the less be dayès old,
When that the bookès weren leverè,°   *more loved*
Writing was beloved everè
Of them that weren virtuous;
For here in earth amongès us,   40
If no man write how that it stood,
The prize of them that weren good
Should, as who sayeth, a greatè part
Be lost: so for to magnify
The worthy princes that then were,
The bookès showen here and there,
Wherof the world exampled is;
And then that deaden then amiss
Through tyranny and cruelty,
Right as they stooden in degree,°   *rank* 50
So was the writing of their work.
Thus I, which am a burel° clerk,   *common*
Proposè forto write a book
After the world that whilom took°   *once occurred*
Long time in oldè dayès passed:
But for men see it is now lassed,°   *diminished*
In worsè plight than it was tho,
I thinkè forto touch also
The world which neweth° every day,   *renews itself*
So as I can, so as I may.   60
Though I sickness have upon handè
And long have had, yet will I fondè°   *try*
To write and do my businessè,
That in some part, so as I guessè,
The wisè man may be avised.°   *forewarned*
For this prologue is so assised°   *contrived*
That it to wisdom all belongeth:
What wise man that it underfongeth,°   *undertakes*

He shall draw into remembrance
The fortune of this worldès chance,   70
The which no man in his person
May knowè, but the God all one.
When the prologue is so dispended,
This book shall afterward be ended
Of love, which doth many a wonder
And many a wise man hath put under.
And in this wise I thinkè tretè
Towardès them that now be greatè,
Between the virtue and the vice
Which longeth unto this office.   80
But for my wittès be too smallè
To tellen every man his talè,
This book, upon amendèment
To stand at his commandèment,
With whom mine heart is of accord,
I send unto mine ownè lord,
Which of Lancaster is Henry named:
The highè God him hath proclaimed
Full of knighthood and allè gracè.
So will I now this work embracè   90
With whole trust and with whole believe;
God grant I might it well achieve ...

44b. *Tale of Florent*

There was whilom be dayès oldè
A worthy knight, and as men toldè
He was nephew to th'emperor
And of his Court a Courtier: 1410
Wifeless he was, Florent he hightè,°   *was called*
He was a man that muchel mightè,°   *might achieve great things*
Of armès he was desirous,
Chivalèrous and amorous,
And for the fame of worldès speechè,
Strange adventurès forto seechè,°   *seek*
He rode the Marches° all about.   *border lands*
And fell a time, as he was out,
Fortune, which may every thread
To break and knit of mannès spedè,°   *success* 1420
Schop,° as this knight rode in a pace,   *Intended*
That he by strengthè takè was,

And to a Castle they him led,
Where that he few friendès had:
For so it fell that ilkè stoundè°   *hour*
That he hath with a deadly woundè
Feihtende° his own handès slain   *Fighting*
Branchus, which to the Captain
Was Son and Heir, wherof been wrothè°   *angry*
The father and the mother bothè.   1430
That knight Branchus was of his hand°   *for his part*
The worthiest of all his land,
And fain they wolden do vengeance
Upon Florent, but remembrance
That they took of his worthinessè
Of knighthood and of gentilessè,°   *chivalry*
And how he stood of cousinage
To themperor, made them assuage,°   *hesitate*
And dursten not slay him for fearè:
In great disputàtion they werè   1440
Among themself, what was the bestè.
There was a lady, the slyestè°   *most skilled*
Of allè that men knewè tho,
So old she might unethès° go,   *scarcely*
And was grandame unto the deadè:°   *victim*
And she with that began to readè,
And said how she will bring him innè,
That she shall him to deathè winnè
All only of his ownè grant,°   *consent*
Through strength of verray covenant°   *true promise* 1450
Withoutè blame of any wight.°   *person*
Anon she sendè for this knight,
And of her Sonè she alleidè°   *alleged*
The death, and thus to him she saidè:
'Florent, how so thou be to wite°   *blame*
Of Branchus death, men shall respite°   *delay*
As now to takè vengementè,
Be so thou stand in judgementè
Upon certain condition,
That thou unto a question   1460
Which I shall ask shalt answerè;
And over this thou shalt eke° swearè,   *also*
That if thou of the sothè° failè,   *correct answer*
There shall none other thing availè,
That thou ne shalt thy death receive.

And for men shall thee not deceive,
That thou thereof might be advised,
Thou shalt have day and time assised°   *appointed*
And leavè safely forto wendè,°   *go*
Be so that at thy dayès endè   1470
Thou come again with thine avis.'°   *judgment*
 This knight, which worthy was and wise,
This lady prayeth that he may witè,°   *know*
And have it under Sealès writè,
What question it shouldè be
For which he shall in that degree
Stand of his life in jeopardy.
With that she feigneth company,°   *fellowship*
And sayeth: 'Florent, on love it hangeth
All that to mine asking longeth: 1480
What allè women most desire
This will I ask, and in th'empire
Where as thou hast most knowledgingè
Take counsel upon this askingè.'
 Florent this thing hath undertakè,
The day was set, the timè takè,
Under his seal he wrote his oath,
In such a way and forth he goeth
Home to his Emès° court again;   *uncle's*
To whom his adventurè plain   1490
He told, of that him is befallè.
And upon that they weren allè
The wisest of the land a-sent,°   *summoned*
But ne'er the less of one assent
They mightè not acordè plat,°   *agree*
One saidè this, another that.
After the disposition
Of natural complexion
To some woman it is pleasancè,
That to another is grievancè;   1500
But such a thing in special,
Which to them all in general
Is most pleasant, and most desired
Above all other and most conspired,°   *agreed about*
Such a thing can they noghtè findè
By Constellationè° ne kindè:*   *astrology; natural signs*
And thus Florent withoutè curè
Must stand upon his aventurè,°   *take his chance*

And is all shape° unto the lerè,*
As in default of his answerè.
This knight hath lever° for to die
Than break his troth, and for to lie
In placè there as he was sworè,
And shapeth° him gone again thereforè.
When timè came he took his leavè,
That longer would he not belevè,°
And prayeth his Em he be not wroth,
For that is a point of his oath,
He sayeth, that no man shall him wrekè,°
Though afterward men hearè speakè
That he par aventurè° die.
And thus he wentè forth his way
Alone as knight adventurous,
And in his thought was curious
To witè what was best to do:
And as he rode alonè so,
And came nigh there he woldè be,
In a forest under a tree
He saw where sat a creature,
A lothly° wommanish figure,
That forto speak of flesh and bone
So foul yet saw he neverè none.
This knight beheld her redèly,°
And as he would have passèd by,
She clepèd° him and bade abidè;
And he his horse heavèd asidè
Then turneth, and to her he rodè,
And there he hoveth° and abodè,
To witè° what she wouldè meanè.
And she began him to bemoan,
And said: 'Florentè be thy name,
Thou hast in handè such a game,
That but thou be the better advised,
Thy death is shapen and devised,
That all the world ne may thee save,
But if that thou my counsel have.'
  Florent, when he this talè heardè,
Unto this oldè wight answerdè
And of her counsel he her prayed.
And she again to him thus said:
'Florent, if I for thee so shapè,

prepared; for the loss
1510
would rather

prepares

tarry

avenge
1520
chance

ugly 1530

briefly

addressed

halted
know
1540

1550

That thou through me thy death escapè
And take worship of thy deedè,
What shall I havè to my medè?'°   reward
'What thing,' quoth he, 'that thou wilt ax,'°   ask
'I biddè° never a better tax,'*   asked for; recompense
Quoth she, 'but first, ere thou be sped,°   gone
Thou shalt me levè° such a wedd,*   allow; pledge
That I will have thy troth in handè
That thou shalt be mine husèbandè.'   1560
'Nay,' sayeth Florent, 'that may not be.'
'Ride thenè forth thy way,' quoth she,
'And if thou go withoutè red,°   advice
Thou shalt be sikerlichè° dead.'   certainly
Florent behiht° her good ynowh*   promised; a great deal
Of land, of rent, of park, of plough,
But all that compteth° she at noght.   accounted
Then fell this knight in muchel thought,
Now goeth he forth, now cometh again,
He wot not what is best to sayen,   1570
And thought, as he rode to and fro,
That choose he must one of the two,
Or° forto take her to his wife   Either
Or elsè forto lose his life.
And then he cast his advantagè,
That she was of so great an agè,
That she may livè but a while,
And thought to put her in an isle,
Where that no man her shouldè knowè,
Til she with death were overthrow.   5180
And thus this youngè lusty° knight   vigorous
Unto this oldè lothly° wight   ugly
Then said: 'If that no other chance
May make my deliverance,
But only thilkè samè speechè
Which, as thou sayst, thou shalt me teach,
Have here mine hand, I shall thee weddè.'
And thus his troth he layeth to weddè.
With that she frounceth° up the browè: wrinkled
'This covenant I will allowè,'   1590
She sayeth: 'if any other thing
But that thou hast of my teaching
From death thy body may respite,
I will thee of thy troth acquite,

And elsè be none other way.
Now hearken me what I shall say.
When thou art come into the place,
Where now they maken great menace
And upon thy coming abide,°   *wait*
They will anon the samè tide°   *hour* 1600
Opposè thee of thine answerè.
I wot thou wilt nothing forebearè
Of that thou wenest° be thy best,   *believe*
And if thou might so findè rest,
Well is, for then is there no more.
And elsè this shall be my lore,
That thou shalt say, upon this Mold°   *earth*
That allè women lievest wolde°   *most desire*
Be sovereign of mannès love:
For what woman is so above,   1610
She hath, as who sayeth, all her willè;
And else may she not fulfillè
What thing her were lievest have.
With this answerè thou shalt save
Thyself, and other wisè not.
And when thou hast thine endè wroght,
Come here again, thou shalt me findè,
And let nothing out of thy mindè.'
He goeth him forth with heavy cheerè,
As he that not° in what mannerè   *knows not* 1620
He may this worldès joy attain:
For if he die, he hath a pain,°   *punishment*
And if he live, he must him bindè
To such one which of allè kindè
Of women is th'unseemliestè:
Thus wot° he not what is the bestè: *knew*
But be him lief° or be him loath,   *willing*
Unto the Castle forth he goeth
His full answerè for to givè,
Or for to die or for to livè.   1630
Forth with his counsel came the lord,
The thingès stooden of record,
He send up for the lady soonè,
And forth she came, that oldè monè.°   *Shrew*
　In presence of the remènant
The strength of all the covenant
Then was rehearsed openly,

And to Florent she bade forthi°   *forthwith*
That he shall tellen his avis,°   *opinion*
As he that woot what is the price.   1640
Florent sayeth all that ever he couthè,°   *knew*
But such word came there none to mouthè,
That he for gift or for behest
Might any ways his death arrest.°   *stop*
And thus he tarryeth long and latè,
Till that this lady bade algatè°   *eventually*
That he shall for the dom° final   *judgment*
Give his answer in special
Of that she had him first opposed:°   *asked*
And then he hath truely supposed   1650
That he him may of nothing yelpè,°   *boast*
But if so be those wordès helpè,
Which as the woman hath him taughtè;
Whereof he hath an hopè caughtè
That he shall be excusèd so,
And told out plain his willè tho.
And when that this Matronè heardè
The manner how this knight answerdè,
She said: 'Ha treason, woe thee be,
That hast thus told the privitè,   1660
Which allè women most desire!
I wolde that thou were afire.'
But neer the less in such a plight
Florent of his answerè is quite:
And then began his sorrow newè,
For he must go, or be untruè,
To her which his trothè haddè.
But he, which allè shamè dreaddè,
Goeth forth instead of his penance,
And taketh the fortune of his chance,   1670
As he that was with troth affaited.°   *ruled*
 This oldè wight him hath awaited
In placè where as he her leftè:
Florent his woeful head upliftè
And saw this veckè° where she sat,   *hag*
Which was the lothliestè what
That ever man cast on his eyè:
Her nosè bas,° her browès high,   *flat*
Her eyen small and deepè set,
Her cheekès ben with tearès wet,   1680

And rivelen° as an empty skin   *shrivelled*
Hangend down unto the chin,
Her Lippès shrunkèn been for age,
There was no grace in the visage,°   *face*
Her front° was narrow, her lockès hore,*   *brow; hoary*
She looketh forth as doth a Moor,
Her Neck is short, her shoulders curved,
That might a mannès lust disturb,
Her body great and nothing small,
And shortly to describe her all,   1690
She hath no lith° without a lack;   *limb*
But like unto the woolèsack
She profferth her unto this knight,
And bad him, as he hath behiht,°   *vowed*
So as she hath been his warrant,
That he her holdè covenant,
And by the bridel she him seizeth.
But God wot how that she him pleaseth
Of suchè wordès as she speaketh:
Him thinks well nigh his heartè breaketh   1700
For sorrow that he may not flee,
But if° he would untruè be.   *unless*
Look, how a sick man for his helè°   *health*
Taketh baldemoin° with canelè,*   *gentian; cinnamon*
And with the myrrh taketh the sucrè,°   *sugar*
Right upon such a manner lucrè°   *profit*
Stands Florent, as in this dietè:
He drinketh the bitter with the sweetè,
He medleth° sorrow with liking,   *mixes*
And liveth, as who sayeth, dying;   1710
His youth shall be cast away
Upon such on which as the whey
Is old and lothly overall.
But need he must that needè shall:
He would algate° his trothè holdè,   *above all*
As every knight therto is holdè,
What hap so ever him is befallè:
Though she be the foulest of allè,
Yet to th'honour of womanhoodè
Him thought he shouldè taken heed;   1720
So that for purè gentilèssè,
As he her couthè best addressè,
In raggès, as she was totorè,°   *tattered*

He set her on his horse toforè
And forth he taketh his way softè;
No wonder though he sigheth oftè.
But as an owl flieth by nightè
Out of all other briddès° sightè,   *bird (pun on bridde: sweetheart)*
Right so this knight on dayès broad°   *in broad daylight*
In close him held, and schop° his road   *prepared* 1730
On nightès timè, til the tidè
That he came there he wold abidè;
And privèly withoutè noise
He bringeth this foul greatè Coisè°   *rump*
To his Castle in such a wise
That no man might her shape avise,°   *observe*
Til she into the chamber came:
Where he his privy counsel nam°   *took*
Of suchè men as he most trustè,
And told them that he needès mustè   1740
This beastè weddè to his wife,
For elsè had he lost his life.
The privy women were a-sent,   *trusted*
That shoulden been of his assent:°   *that he could trust*
Her raggès they anon off drawè,
And, as it was that timè lawè,
She haddè bath, she haddè restè,
And was arrayed to the bestè.
But with no craft of combès broad
They might her hoarè lockès schod,°   *disentangle* 1750
And she ne woldè not be schorè°   *she would not be shorn*
For no counsel, and they therefore,
With such attire as then was used,
Ordainen that it was excused,
And hid so craftily aboutè,
That no man mightè see them outè.
But when she was fully arrayed
And her attire was all assayed,°   *assessed*
Then was she fouler on to see:
But yet it may none other be,   1760
They were wedded in the night;
So woebegone was neverè knight
As he was then of marriage.
And she began to plain and rage,
As who sayeth, I am well enough;
But he therof nothing ne lowh,°   *laughed*

For she took thennè chiere on hondè°   *began to be cheerful*
And clepeth him her husèbandè,
And sayeth, 'My lord, go we to bed,
For I to that intentè wed,   1770
That thou shalt be my worldès blissè:'
And proffreth him with that to kissè,
As she a lusty Lady were.
His body mightè well be there,
But as of thought and of memory
His heartè was in purgatory.
But yet for strength of matrimoine
He mightè makè non essoine,°   *excuse*
That he ne might algatès plie°   *nonetheless comply*
To go to bed of companyè: 1780
And when they were a-beddè nakèd,
Withoutè sleep he was awakèd;
He turneth on that other side,
For that he would his eyèn hide
From looking on that foulè wight.
The chamber was all full of light,
The curtains were of cendal° thinnè,   *silk*
This newè bride which lay withinnè,
Though it be not with his accord,
In armès she beclipt° her lord,   *embraced* 1790
And prayed, as he was turnèd fro,
He would him turn againward° tho;   *towards her*
'For now,' she sayeth, 'we be both one.'
And he lay still as any stone,
But ever anon she spoke and prayedè,
And bade him think on that he saidè,
When that he took her by the hand.
He heard and understood the bond,
How he was set to his penancè,
And as it were a man in trancè   1800
He turneth him all suddenly,
And saw a lady lay him by
Of eighèteenè winters agè,
Which was the fairest of visagè
That ever in all this world he saw:
And as he would have take her nigh,°   *near*
She put her hand and by his leave
Besought him that he wouldè leave,°   *desist*
And sayeth that for to win or lose

He mustè one of two things choose,   1810
Where° he will have her such on night,   *whether*
Or elsè upon dayès light,
For he shall not have bothè two.
And he began to sorrowè tho,
In many a ways and cast his thought,
But for all that yet could he not
Devise himself which was the bestè.
And she, that would his heartès restè,
Prayeth that he should choose algate,
Til at lastè long and late   1820
He said: 'O ye, my lifès helè,
Say what you list° in my querelè,*   *like; situation*
I not° what answer I shall give: *know not*
But ever while that I may live,
I will that ye be my mistressè,
For I can not myselfè guessè
Which is the best unto my choice.
Thus grant I you mine wholè voice,
Choose for us bothen, I you pray;
And what as ever that you say,   1830
Right as ye willè so will I.'
   'My lord,' she saidè, 'grant mercy,
For of this word that ye now say,
That ye have made me sovereign,
My destiny is overpassed,
That never hereafter shall be lassed°   *reduced*
My beauty, which that I now have,
Til I be takè into my gravè;
But night and day as I am now
I shall alway be such to you.   1840
The Kingès daughter of Cizile°   *Sicily*
I am, and fell but siththe awhile,°   *recently*
As I was with my father late,°   *lately*
That my Stepmother for an hate,
Which toward me she hath begun,
Forshop° me, til I hadè won   *Transformed*
The love and sovereignètè
Of what knight that in his greè
All other passeth of good name:
And, as men sayen, ye be the same,   1850
The deedè proveth it is so;
Thus am I yourès evermoe.'

Then was pleasance and joy enough,
Each one with other played and lowh;°   *laughed*
They livèd long and well they fared,
And clerkès that this chancè heard
They written it in evidence,
To teach how that obedience
May well fortune a man to love
And set him in his lust above,   1860
As it befell unto this knight.

44c. *Deianira and Nessus*

Of Falsesemblant° which is believed   *Twoface*
Full many a worthy wight is grieved,
And was long time ere we were bore.°   *born*
To thee, my Son, I will therefore
A talè tell of Falsesemblant,
Which falseth many a covenant,°   *agreement* 2150
And many a fraud of false counsel
There been hangend upon his Seal:
And that aboghten° guilteless   *suffered*
Both Deianyre and Hercules,
The which in great diseasè° fellè   *trouble*
Through Falsesemblant, as I shall tellè.
When Hercules within a throwè
All only hath his hertè throwè
Upon this fairè Deianira,
It fell him on a day desirè,   2160
Upon a River as he stood,
That pass he would over the flood
Withoutè bot,° and with him lead   *help*
His lovè, but he was in dreadè
For tendresse of that sweetè wight,
For he knew not the ford aright.
There was a Giant thennè nigh,
Which Nessus hihtè,° and when he saw   *was called*
This Hercules and Deianyre,
Within his heart he gan° conspire,   *began to* 2170
As he which through his treachery
Hath Hercules in great envy,
Which he bore in his hertè lockè,
And then he thoughte it shall be wrokè.°   *wreaked*
But he ne durstè neer the less

Against this worthy Hercules
Fall in debat as for to fightè;
But feigneth Semblant all by slightè°   *outward appearance*
Of friendship and of allè goodè,
And cometh where as they both stoodè,   2180
And maketh them all the cheer he can,
And sayeth that as their ownè man
He is all ready for to do
What thing he may; and it fell so
That they upon his Semblant tristè,°   *trusted*
And asken him if that he wistè°   *knew*
What thing them were best to done,
So that they mighten safe and sound
The water passè, he and she.
And when Nessus the privete°   *secret* 2190
Knew of their heartè what it meant,
As he that was of double intent,
He made them right a glad visage;
And when he heard of the passage
Of him and her, he thoughtè guile,°   *deception*
And feigneth Semblant for a while
To do them pleasance and service,
But he thought all an other wise.
This Nessus with his wordès sly
Gave such counsel tofore° their eye   *before* 2200
Which seemeth outward profitable
And was withinnè deceivable.
He bade them of the Streamès deep°   *river's depth*
That they beware and takè keep,
So as they knowè not the pas;°   *pace*
But for to help in such a cas,°   *situation*
He sayeth himself that for their ease
He wouldè, if that it might them please,
The passage of the water take,
And for this lady undertake   2210
To beare unto that other strondè°   *shore*
And safe to set her upon londe,
And Hercules may then also
The wayè know how he shall go:
And hereto they acorden° allè.   *agreed*
But what as after shall befallè,
Well paid° was Hercules of this,   *pleased*
And this Giant also glad is,

And took this lady up aloft
And set her on his shoulders soft,   2220
And in the flood began to wade,
As he which no groucchingè° made,   *complaints*
And bore her over safe and soundè.
But when he stood on dryè groundè
And Hercules was far behindè,
He set his troth all out of mindè,
Who so there of be lief° or loath,   *glad*
With Deianyre and forth he goeth,
As he that thoughtè to dissever
The company of them for ever.   2230
When Hercules thereof took heedè,
As fast as ever he might him speedè
He hieth after in a throwe;°   *immediately*
And happneth that he had a bow,
The which in allè haste he bent,
As he that would an Arrow send,
Which he tofore° had envenomed.   *earlier*
He hath so well his shotè timed,
That he him through the body smotè,
And thus the falsè wight he lettè.°   *delayed* 2240
    But list° now such a felony: *hear*
When Nessus wist he shouldè die,
He took to Deinayre his shirtè,
Which with the blood was of his heartè
Throughout destained° over all,   *darkened*
And toldè how she it keep shall
All prively° to this intent,   *secretly*
That if her lord his heartè went
To love in any other place,
The shirt, he sayeth, hath such a grace,   2250
That if she may so muchel make
That he the shirt upon him take,
He shall all otherè lete° in vain   *leave*
And turn unto her love again.
Who was then glad but Deianyre?
Her thought her heartè was afire
Til it was in her cofferè lockè,
So that no word therof was spokè.
    The days go on, the yearès pass,
The heartès waxen lass and lass   2250
Of them that be to love untruè:

This Hercules with heartè newè
His love hath set on Eolen,
And therof speaken allè men.
This Eolen, this fairè maid,
Was, as men thilkè time said,
The kingès daughter of Eurice;
And she made Hercules so nice°   *foolish*
Upon her Love and so assotè,°   *besotted*
That he him clotheth in her coatè,   2270
And she in his was clothèd oft;
And thus feebless is set aloft,
And strength was puttè under foot,
There can no man thereof do bote.°   *remedy*
Whan Deianyre hath heard this speechè,
There was no sorrow forto seekè:
Of other helpè wot she none,
But goeth unto her coffer anon;
With weepend eye and woeful heartè
She took out thilk unhappy shirtè,   2280
As she that wendè° well to do,   *intended*
And brought her work aboutè so
That Hercules this shirt on dede,
To such intent as she was bid
Of° Nessus, so as I said erè.*   *By; earlier*
But therof was she not the nerè,
As no fortune may be weyved;°   *avoided*
With Falsesemblant she was deceived,
That when she wendè best have wonnè,
She lost all that she hath begun.   2290
For thilke shirt unto the bone
His body set afire anon,
And cleaveth so, it may not twinnè,°   *be removed*
For the venom that was thereinnè.
And he then as a wildè man
Unto the highè wood he ran,
And as the Clerkè Ovid telleth,
The greatè trees to ground he felleth
With strength all of his ownè might,
And made an hugè fire upright,   2300
And leapt himself there-in at once
And brende° him both flesh and bones.   *burned*
Which thing came all through Falsesemblant,
That falsè Nessus the Giant

Made unto him and to his wife;
Whereof that he hath lost his life,
And she sorry for everemore . . .

44d. *Pyramus and Thisbe*

I read a tale, and telleth this:
The City which Semiramis°   *Queen of Assyria*
Enclosèd hath with wall about,
Of worthy folk with many a rout°   *crowd*
Was inhabited here and there;
Among the whichè two there were
Above all other noble and greatè,
Dwellendè then within a Streetè
So nigh together, as it was seenè,
That there was nothing them betweenè,   1340
But wow° to wow and wall to wall.   *partition*
This one lord had in special
A son, a lusty° bachelor,   *vigorous*
In all the town was none his peer:
That other had a daughter ekè,°   *also*
In all the land that for to seekè
Men wisten° none so faire as she.   *knew of*
And fell° so, as it shouldè be,   *befell*
This fairè daughter nigh this Son
As they together thennè wone,°   *lived* 1350
Cupid hath so the thingès shapè,
That they ne might his hand escapè,
That he his fire on them ne castè:
Wherof her heart he overcastè
To follow thilkè lore° and suiè*   *teaching; obey*
Which never man yet might eschew;
And that was love, as it is happed,
Which hath their heartès so betrapped,
That they be allè wayès seekè
How that they mighten win a speechè,   1360
Their woeful painè for to lissè.°   *lessen*
     Who loveth well, it may not missè,°   *fail*
And namèly when there be two
Of one accord, how so it go,
But if that they some wayè findè;
For love is ever of such a kindè
And hath his folk so well affaitèd,°   *trained*

That howso that it be awaitèd,
There may no man the purpose lettè:°   *escape*
And thus between them two they settè
An hole upon a wall to make,
Through which they have their counsel take
At allè timès, when they mightè.
This fairè maiden Thisbe hightè,
And he whom that she loveth hotè°   *passionately*
Was Pyramus by namè hotè.°   *called*
So longè their lecoun° they recorden,   *conversation*
Til at lastè they accorden°   *agreed*
By nightès timè forto wendè
Alone out from the townès endè,   1380
Where was a well under a Tree;
And who came first, or° she or he,   *either*
He shouldè stillè there abide.
   So it befell the nightès tide
This maiden, which disguisèd was,
All prively° the softè pace   *secretly*
Goeth through the largè town unknowè,
Til that she came within a throwè
Where that she liketh for to dwellè,
At thilk unhappy° freshè wellè,   *ill-fated* 1390
Which was also the Forest nigh.
Where she comend° a Lion saw   *coming*
Into the field to take his preyè,
In haste and she then fled awayè,
So as fortunè shouldè fallè,
For fear and let her wimple fallè
Nigh to the well upon th'erbage.°   *the grass*
This Lion in his wildè rage
A beastè, which that he found outè,
Hath slain, and with his bloody snoutè,   1400
When he hath eaten what he woldè,
To drink of thilkè streamès coldè
Came to the wellè, where he found
The wimpel, which out of her hand
Was fall, and he it hath todrawè,°   *torn to pieces*
Bebled° about and all forgnawè;*   *stained; gnawed*
And then he strawhte° him forto drinkè   *went*
Upon the freshè wellès brinkè,
And after that out of the plain
He turneth to the wood again.   1410

And Thisbe durstè not remue,°   *stir*
But as a bird which were in mew°   *bird-pen*
Withinnè a bush she kept her close
So stillè that she noght arose;
Unto herself and plaineth° aye.   *laments*
    And fell, while that she therè lay,
This Pyramus came after soonè
Unto the well, and by the Moonè
He found her wimple bloody there.
Came never yet to mannès earè   1420
Tidingè, ne to mannès sightè
Merveilè, which so sore aflihtè°   *afflicted*
A mannès heart, as it then deadè
To him, which in the same stedè°   *place*
With many a woeful complainingè
Began his handès forto wringè,
As he which demeth sikerly°   *certainly*
That she be dead: and suddenly
His sword all naked out he breid°   *drew*
In his fool haste, and thus he said: 1430
'I am cause of this felony,
So it is reason that I die,
As she is dead because of me.'
And with that word upon his knee
He fell, and to the goddès allè
Up to the heaven he gan to callè,
And prayed, sithen° it was so   *since*
That he may not his love as tho
Have in this world, that of their gracè
He might her have in other placè,   1440
For herè wold he not abidè,
He sayeth: but as it shall betidè,
The pommel of his sword to groundè
He set, and through his hearte a woundè
He made up to the bare hiltè:
And in this wise himself he spiltè
With his fool haste and death he nam;°   *took*
For she within a whilè cam,
Where he lay dead upon his knife.
So woeful yet was never life   1450
As Thisbe was, when she him saw:
She mightè not one word on high
Speak out, for her heartè schettè,°   *shut*

That of her life no price she settè,
But dead swoonendè down she fell.
Till after, when it so befell
That she out of her trance awoke,
With many a woefull piteous look
Her eyè alwey° among she castè   *continually*
Upon her love, and attè lastè   1460
She caughtè breath and saidè thus:
'O thou which clepèd art Venùs,
Goddess of love, and thou, Cupidè,
Which lovès cause hast forto guidè,
I wot now well that ye be blindè,
Of thilk unhapp which I now findè
Only between my love and me.
This Pyramus, which here I see
Bleedendè, what hath he deserved?
For he your hest° hath kept and served,   *commands* 1470
And was young and I both also:
Alas, why do ye with us so?
Ye set our heartè both afirè,
And maden us such thing desirè
Wherof that we no skillè couth;°   *reasons knew*
But thus our fresshè lusty youth
Withoutè joy is all dispended,
Which thing may never been amended:
For as of me this will I sayè,
That me is leverè° for to diè   *preferable* 1480
Than live after this sorghful° day.'   *sorrowful*
And with this word, where as he lay,
Her love in armès she embraceth,
Her ownè death and so purchaseth
That now she wept and now she kissed,
Till attè last, er she it wistè,
So great a sorrow is to her fall,
Which overgoeth her wittès all.
As she which might it not astertè,°   *prevent*
The swordès point against her heartè   1490
She settè, and fell down thereupon,
Wherof that she was dead anon:
And thus both on one sword bledendè
They weren foundè dead liggendè.°   *lying*

44e. *Pygmalion*

I find how whilom° there was one,   *once*
Whose namè was Pygmalion,
Which was a lusty° man of youthè: *vigorous*
The workès of entail° he couthè*   *sculpture; knew*
Above all other men as tho;
And through fortune it fell him so,
As he whom lovè shall travailè,°   *trouble*
He made an image of entailè
Like to a woman in semblancè
Of feature and of countenancè,   380
So fair yet never was figurè.
Right as a livès creaturè
She seemeth, for of ivor° white   *ivory*
He hath her wroght of such delight,
That she was ruddy on the cheek
And red on both her lippès eke;°   *also*
Wherof that he himself beguileth.°   *fooled*
For with a goodly look she smileth,
So that through pure impression
Of his imagination   390
With all the heart of his coragè°   *spirit*
His love upon this fair imagè
He set, and her of lovè prayed;
But she no word againward said.
The longè day, what thing he didè,
This image in the samè stedè°   *place*
Was ever by, that atè meatè°   *at dinner*
He would her serve and prayed her eatè,
And put unto her mouth the cuppè;
And when the board was taken uppè,   400
He hath her into chamber nome,°   *taken*
And after, when the night was come,
He laid her in his bed all naked.
He was forwept,° he was forwakid,*   *wept out; exhausted*
He kissed her coldè lippès oft,
And wisheth that they weren soft,
And oft he rouneth° in her Earè,   *whispered*
And oft his arm now here now there
He laid, as he her would embrace,
And ever among he asketh grace,   410
As though she wistè what he meantè:

And thus himself he gan tormentè
With such disease of lovès pain,
That no man mightè him more pain.
But how it were, of his penance
He madè such continuance
Fro day to night, and prayeth so longè,
That his prayer is underfongè,°   *received*
Which Venus of her gracè heard;
By night and when that he worstè feerde,°   *feared* 420
And it lay in his naked armè,
The cold image he feeleth warmè
Of flesh and bone and full of life.
   Lo, thus he won a lusty° wife,   *lively*
Which obeissant° was at his willè;   *obedient*
And if he would have hold him stillè
And nothing spoke, he should have failed:
But for he hath his word travailèd°   *belaboured*
And durstè speak, his love he sped,
And had all that he wold a-bed.   430
For ere they wentè then a-two,
A knavè° child between them two   *male*
They getè, which was after hote°   *called*
Paphus, of whom yet hath the note
A certain isle, which Paphos
Men clepe,° and of his name it rose.   *call*

44f. *Ceïx and Alceone*

This find I writ in Poesie:
Ceïx the King of Trocinie°   *Trachis*
Had Alceonè to his wife,
Which as her ownè heartès life   2930
Him loveth; and he had also
A brother, which was cleped° tho   *called*
Dedalion, and he per cas°   *by chance*
From kind of man forschapè° was *transformed*
Into a goshawk of likenessè;
Wherof the king great heavinessè
Hath take, and thought in his corage°   *heart*
To go upon a pilgrimage
Into a strangè region,
Where he hath his devotion   2940
To do his sacrifice and prayè,

If that he might in any wayè
Toward the goddès findè grace
His brother helè° to purchase,   *health*
So that he mightè be reformed
Of that he haddè be transformed.
To this purpose and to this endè
This king is ready for to wendè,
As he which woldè go by shipè;   *wanted to*
And for to do him fellowshipè   2950
His wife unto the sea him broughtè,
With all her heart and him besoghtè,
That he the time her woldè sayen,
When that he thoughtè come again:
'Within,' he sayeth, 'two monthè day.'
And thus in all the haste he may
He took his leave, and forth he saileth
Weepend, and she herself bewaileth,
And turneth home, there she came fro.
But when the monthès were ago,   2960
The which he set of his comingè,
And that she heardè no tidingè,
There was no carè for to seekè:
Whereof the goddès to beseechè
Then she began in many ways,
And to Juno her sacrifice
Above all other most she didè,
And for her lord she hath so bedè°   *prayed*
To wit and know how that he fared,
That Juno the goddess her heard,   2970
Anon° and upon this matterè   *Soon*
She bade Iris her Messagerè
To Sleepès house that she shall wendè,
And bid him that he make an endè
By swevene° and showen all the cas*   *dreams; situation*
Unto this lady, how it was.
    This Iris, fro the highè stage°   *high place (Olympus)*
Which undertake hath the Message,
Her rainy copè° did upon,   *cloak*
The which was wonderly begon   2980
With colours of diversè huè,
An hundred more than men it knewè;
The heaven° like unto a bow   *skies*
She bend, and so she came down low,

The god of Sleep where that she foundè.
And that was in a strangè landè,
Which marcheth° upon Chimery:* *borders; Cimmeria (perpetual darkness)*
For there, as sayeth the Poesie,
The god of Sleep hath made his house,
Which of entail° is marvellous.   *construction* 2990
Under an hill there is a Cave,
Which of the Sunnè may nought have,
So that no man may know aright
The point between the day and nightè:
There is no fire, there is no sparkè,
There is no doorè, which may charkè,°   *creak*
Wherof an eyè should unshuttè,
So that inward there is no lightè.
And forto speak of that withoutè,
There stands no great Tree nigh aboutè   3000
Whereon there mightè crow or pie°   *magpie*
Alightè, forto clepe° or crie: *call*
There is no cock to crowè day,
Ne beastè none which noisè may
The hill, but all aboutè round
There is growend upon the ground
Poppy, which beareth the seed of sleep,
With other herbès such an heap.°   *number*
A stillè water for the nones°   *by the way*
Runnend upon the smallè stones,   3010
Which hight of Lethes the riverè,° *was called Lethe (Oblivion)*
Under that hill in such mannerè
There is, which giveth great appetitè
To sleep. And thus full of delightè
Sleep hath his house; and of his couchè
Within his chamber if I shall touchè,
Of hebenus° that sleepy Tree   *ebony*
The bordès all aboutè be,
And for he should sleepè soft,
Upon a featherbed aloft   3020
He lieth with many a pillow of down:
The chamber is strewèd up and down
With swevenes° many thousandfold.   *dreams*
Thus came Iris into this hold,
And to the bed, which is all black,
She goeth, and there with Sleep she spak,
And in the wise as she was bid

The Message of Juno she did.
Full oft her wordès she rehearseth,
Ere she his sleepy earès pierceth;   3030
With muchel woè but at lastè
His slumbrende eyen he upcastè
And said her that it shall be do.
Whereof among a thousand tho,
Within his house that sleepy were,
In special he chose out there
Three, which shoulden do this deedè:
The first of them, so as I readè,
Was Morpheüs, the whose nature
Is forto takè the figurè   3040
Of what personè that him liketh,
Wherof that he full oft entriketh°   *deceives*
The life which sleepè shall be nightè;
And Ithecus that other hightè,
Which hath the voice of every soun,°   *sound*
The chiere° and the condition   *face*
Of every life, what so it is:
The thirde suivende° after this   *following*
Is Panthasas, which may transformè
Of every thing the rightè formè,   3050
And change it in an other kindè.
Upon them three, so as I findè,
Of swevenes stant all th'appearence,   *stands*
Which otherwhile is evidence
And otherwhilè but a japè.
But ne'er the less it is so shapè,°   *destined*
That Morpheüs by night alone
Appeareth until Alceone
In likenessè of her husbandè
All naked dead upon the strondè,°   *sea-shore* 3060
And how he dreyntè° in special   *drowned*
These other two it showen all.
The tempest of the blackè cloudè,
The wode° Sea, the windès loudè,   *furious*
All this she mettè,° and saw him dyen;   *dreamed*
Whereof that she began to cryen,
Sleepend abeddè there she lay,
And with that noise of her affray
Her women sterten° up aboutè,   *sprang*
Which of their lady were in doubtè,   3070

And asken her how that she ferdè;°   *fared*
And she, right as she saw and heardè,
Her sweven hath told them everydel.°   *every bit*
And they it halsen° allè well   *interpreted*
And seen it is a token of good;
But til she wist° how that it stood,   *knows*
She hath no comfort in hire heartè,
Upon the morrow and up she stertè,
And to the Sea, where that she mettè°   *dreamed*
The body lay, withoute lettè°   *delay* 3080
She drew and when that she came nigh,
Stark dead, his armès spread, she saw
Her lord floatend upon the wave.
Wherof her wittès been withdraw,
And she, which took of death no keep,°   *notice*
Anon forth leapt into the deep
And would have caught him in her armè.
This infortune of double harmè
The goddès fro the heaven above
Beheld, and for the truth of love,   3090
Which in this worthy lady stood,
They have upon the saltè flood
Her dreinte lord and her also
From death to livè turnèd so,
That they been shapen into briddès°   *birds*
Swimmend upon the wave amiddès.
And when she saw her lord livendè
In likenesse of a bridd swimmendè,
And she was of the samè sort,
So as she might do desport,   3100
Upon the joyè which she haddè
Her wingès both abroad she spraddè,°   *spread*
And him, so as she may suffisè,°   *was able*
Beclipte° and kissed in such a wisè,   *embraced*
As she was whilom° wont to do: *long ago*
Her wingès for her armès two
She took, and for her lippès soft
Her hardè bill, and so full oft
She fondeth in her briddes form,
If that she might herself conform   3110
To do the pleasance° of a wife,   *the pleasant duty*
As she did in that other life:
For though she had hir poorè lore,°   *learning*

Her will° stood as it was tofore,   *desire*
And serveth him so as she may.
Wherof into this ilkè day
Together upon the Sea they wonè,
Where many a daughter and a sonè
They bringen forth of briddès kind;
And for men shoulden take in mind   3120
This Alceoun the truè queenè,
Her briddes yet, as it is seenè,
Of Alceoun the namè bearè…

44g. *The Supplication* (from Book Eight)

The woeful pain of lovès malady,
Again° the which may no physic avail,   *against*
Mine heartè hath so bewhaped° with sotie,*   *confused; foolishness*
That where so that I rest or I travailè,°   *labour* 2220
I find it ever ready to assailè
My reason, which that can him not defend:
Thus seek I help, wherof I might amend.

First to Nature if that I me complain,
There find I how that every creàturè
Some time a year hath love in his demeine,°   *possession*
So that the little wren in his measurè
Hath yet of kind° a love under his curè;   *by nature*
And I but one desire, of which I missè:
And thus, but° I, hath every kind his blissè.   *except* 2230

The reason of my wit it overpasseth,
Of that Naturè teacheth me the wayè
To love, and yet no certain she compasseth°   *plots*
How I shall speed, and thus betwen the tweiè°   *two*
I stand, and not° if I shall live or dyè.   *know not*
For though reason against my will debatè,
I may not flee, that I ne love algatè.°   *in any event*

Upon myself is th'ilke talè come,
How whilom° Pan, which is the god of kindè,   *once*
With love wrestledè and was overcome: 2240
For ever I wrastle and ever I am behindè,
That I no strength in all mine heartè findè,

Wherof that I may standen any throwè;°　　　　　　　　*length of time*
So far my wit with love is overthrowè.

Whom needeth help, he must his helpè cravè,°　　　　　　　*beg*
Or helpèless he shall his needè spillè:
Plainly throughsought my wittès all I have,
But none of them can help after my willè;
And as so well I mightè sittè stillè,
As pray unto my lady any helpè:　　　　　　　　　　　2250
Thus wot° I not whereof myself to helpe.　　　　　　　　　*know*

Unto the greatè Jove and if I biddè,
To do me grace of th'ilke sweetè tunnè,°　　　　　　　*tun (of wine)*
Which under keyè in his celler amid
Lith couchèd, that fortune is overrunnè,
But of the bitter cup I have begunnè,
I not° how oft, and thus find I no game;*　　　　　*know not; pleasure*
For ever I ask and ever it is the same.

I see the world standè ever upon eschange,°　　　　　　　　*flux*
Now windès loud, and now the weather softè;　　　　　　2260
I may see eke the greatè moonè change,
And thing which now is low is eft° aloft;　　　　　　　　　*next*
The dreadful warrès into peace full oft
They turn; and ever is Danger in one place,
Which will not change his will to do me grace.

But upon this the greatè clerk Ovidè,
Of lovè whan he makth his remembrancè,
He sayeth there is the blindè god Cupidè,
The which hath love under his governancè,
And in his hand with many a fiery lancè　　　　　　　　2270
He woundeth oft, there he will not healè;
And that somdiel° is cause of my querelè.*　　　*in part; complaint*

Ovid eke sayeth that lovè to parfornè°　　　　　　　　　　*enact*
Stands in the hand of Venus the goddessè,
But when she takth her conseil with Saturnè,
There is no grace, and in that time, I guessè,
Began my love, of which mine heavynessè

Is now and ever shall, but° if I spedè: *unless*
So wot I not myself what is to redè.°   *be advised*

Forthy° to you, Cupid and Venus bothè,   *Therefore* 2280
With all mine heartès obeissance I prayè,
If ye were atè firstè timè wrothè,
When I began to love, as I you sayè,
Now stint, and do th'ilk infortune awayè,
So that Danger, which stands of retenue
With my lady, his placè may remuè.°   *remove*

O thou Cupidè, god of lovès lawè,
That with thy Dart brennend° hast set afire   *burning*
Mine heartè, do that woundè be withdrawè,
Or give me salve such as I desirè: 2290
For service in thy Court withouten hirè
To me, which everè yet have kept thine hestè,°   *command*
May never be to lovès law honestè.

O thou, gentle Venus, lovès queenè,
Withoutè guilt thou dost on me thy wreche;°   *vengeance*
Thou wost° my pain is ever alichè grenè*   *know; always vulnerable*
For love, and yet I may it not arechè:°   *achieve*
This would I for my lastè word beseechè,
That thou my love acquit as I deservè,
Or else do me plainly for to stervè.°   *die* 2300

Geoffrey Chaucer

45. from *The Book of the Duchess*

45a. *The Dream*

Me thoughtè thus: – that it was May,
And in the dawning there I lay,
Me mette° thus, in my bed all naked: –   *dreamed*

I lookèd forth, for I was wakèd
With smallè fowls a greatè heap,
That had affrayed° me out of sleep   *frightened*
Through noise and sweetness of their song;
And, as me mette, they sat among,
Upon my chamber-roof without,
Upon the tilés, all about,   300
And sungen, ever each in his wisè,°   *in his way*
The mostè solemnè servicè
By note,° that ever man, I trow,   *in harmony*
Had heard; for some of them sang low,
Some high, and all of one accord.
To tellè shortly, at one word,
Was never y-heard so sweet a steven,°   *voice*
But it had been a thing of heaven; –
So merry a sound, so sweet entunès,
That certès, for the town of Tunis,   310
I noldè° but I had heard them sing,   *would not want*
For al my chamber gan to ring
Through singing of their harmony.
For instrument nor melody
Was nowhere heard yet half so sweet,
Nor of accordè half so mete;°   *appropriate*
For there was none of them that feigned
To singe, for each of them him pained°   *took pains*
To find out merry crafty° notes;   *artful*
They ne sparèd not their throats.   320
And, sooth to say'n, my chamber was
Full well depainted, and with glass
Were all the windows well y-glazed,
Full clear, and not an hole y-crased,°   *cracked*
That to behold it was great joyè,
For wholly all the stories of Troyè
Was in the glazing y-wroght thus,
Of Hector and King Priamus,
Of Achilles and Lamedon,
Of Medea and of Jason,   330
Of Paris, Helen, and Lavine.°   *figures of classical legend (esp. Trojan)*
And all the wall with colours fine
Were painted, bothè text and gloss,
Of all the Romance of the Rose.
My windows werèn shut each one,
And through the glass the sunnè shone

Upon my bed with brightè beams,
With many gladès golden streams;
And eek the welkin° was so fair,   *sky*
Blue, bright, clearè was the air,   340
And full attempre, for sothe,° it was;   *truly*
For neither cold nor hot it n'as,
Nor in all the welkin was no° cloud.   *any*
   And as I lay thus, wonder loud
Me thought I heard an huntè blowè
T'assay his horn, and for to knowè
Whether it were clear or hoarse of sound.
I heardè going, up and down,
Men, horses, hounds, and other thing;
And all men speakèn of hunting,   350
How they would slay the hart with strength,
And how the hart had, upon length,
So much embosed,° I not* now what.   *exhausted; I know not*
   Anon right, when I heardè that,
How that they would on hunting gone,
I was right glad, and up anon;
I took my horse, and forth I went
Out of my chamber; I never stent°   *stopped*
Till I came to the field without:
There overtook I a great rout   360
Of hunts and eek° of foresters,   *also*
With many relays° and lymeres,*   *packs of hunting dogs; bloodhounds*
And hied them to the forest fast,
And I with them; – so at the last
I asked one, leading a lymere: –
'Say, fellow, who shall hunten here?'
Quoth I; and he answered again,
'Sir, th'Emperor Octavien,'
Quoth he, 'and is here fastè by.'
'A God's halfe,° in good time,' quoth I,   *behalf* 370
'Go we fast!' and gan to ride.
When we came to the forest-side,
Every man did, right anon,
As to hunting fell to doon°.   *do*
The master-hunt anon, foot-hot,
With a great horn blew three moot°   *notes*
At the uncoupling of his houndès.
Within a while the hart y-found is,
Y-halooed, and rechasèd fastè

Longè time; and at the lastè,   380
This hart rused° and stole away   *looped back*
From all the hounds a privy way.
The hounds had overshot them allè,
And were on a defaut y-fallè;
Therewith the huntè wonder° fastè   *wonderfully*
Blew a forloin° at the lastè.   *signal that the hart was lost*
    I was go walkèd° from my tree,   *had walked*
And as I went, there came by me
A whelp, that fawned me as I stood,
That had y-followed, and coude no good.°   *did not know where to go* 390
It came and crept to me as lowè,
Right as it haddè me y-knowè,
Held down his head and joined his earès,
And laid all smoothè down his hairès.
I would have caught it, and anon
It fledè, and was from me gone;
And I him followed, and it forth wentè
Down by a flowery greenè wentè°   *path*
Full thick of grass, full soft and sweet,
With flowers fele,° fair under feet,   *many* 400
And little used, it seemèd thus;
For both Flora and Zephirus,°   *west wind*
They two that make flowers grow,
Had made their dwelling there, I trow;
For it was, on to beholdè,
As though the earthè envy wouldè
To be gayer than the heaven,
To have more flowers, suchè seven°   *seven times as many*
As in the welkin starrès be.
It had forgot the poverty   410
That winter, through his coldè morrows,
Had made it suffer, and his sorrows;
All was forgotten, and that was seen.
For all the wood was waxen green,
Sweetness of dewè had made it wax.
    Hit is no need eek for to axe
Where there were many greenè greves,°   *branches*
Or thick of trees, so full of leaves;
And every tree stood by himself
From other well ten foot or twelve.   420
So greatè trees, so huge of strengthè,
Of forty or fifty fathom lengthè,

Clean withoutè bough or stikke,°   *twig*
With croppès° broad, and eek as thicke –   *crowns*
They were not an inch asunder –
That it was shadow overall under;
And many a hart and many an hindè
Was both before me and behindè.
Of fawns, sourès,° buckès, does   *young bucks*
Was full the wood, and many roes,   430
And many squirellès that set
Full high upon the trees, and ate,
And in their manner madè feastès.
Shortly, it was so ful of beastès,
That though Algus,° the noble counter,   *inventor of Arabic numbers*
Set to reckon in his counter,°   *abacus*
And reckoned with his figures ten –
For by those figures may all ken,
If they be crafty, reckon and number,
And tell of every thing the number –   440
Yet should he fail to reckon even°   *accurately*
The wonders, me met in my swevèn . . .

45b. *Lament and Consolation*

'Alas! and I will tell thee why;
My song is turnèd to plaining,°   *complaining*
And all my laughter to weeping,   600
My gladè thoughts to heavinessè,
In travail is mine idlenessè
And eek my rest; my wele° is woe.   *happiness*
My good is harm, and evermoe°   *evermore*
In wrath is turnèd my playing,
And my delight into sorrowing.
Mine hele° is turned into sicknessè,   *health*
In dread is all my sikernesse.°   *certainty*
To dark is turnèd all my light,
My wit is folly, my day is night,   610
My love is hate, my sleep waking,
My mirth and mealès is fasting,
My countenance° is nicete,*   *manner; bashfulness*
And all abaved° whereso I be,   *confused*
My peace, in pleading and in warrè;
Allas! how might I farè warrè?°   *get worse*
My boldness is turnèd to shame,

For false Fortune hath played a game
At chess with me, alas the while!
The traitress false and full of guile,   620
That all behoteth° and nothing halt,*   *promises; delivers*
She goeth upright and yet she halt,°   *limps*
That baggeth° foul and looketh fair,   *squints*
The dispiteous debonair,
That scorneth many a creature!
An idol of false portraiture
Is she, for she will soonè wrien;°   *betray*
She is the monster's head ywryen,°   *concealed*
As filth over-ystrawed with flowers;
Her mostè worship and her flower is   630
To lyen, for that is her nature;
Withoute faith, law, or measure
She is false; and ever laughingè
With one eye, and that other weepingè.
That is brought up, she set all down.
I liken her to the scorpion,
That is a false flattering beast;
For with his head he maketh feast,
But all amid his flatteringè
With his tailè he will stingè,   640
And envenom; and so will she.
She is the envious charity
That is aye° false, and seemeth well,   *ever*
So turneth she her falsè wheel
About, for it is nothing stable,
Now by the firè, now at table;
For many one hath she thus yblent.°   *blinded*
She is play of enchantèment,
That seemeth one and is not so,
The falsè thief! What hath she do,   650
Trowest thou? By our lord, I will thee say.
At chess with me she gan to play;
With her falsè draughts diverse°   *antagonistic moves*
She stole on me, and took my fers.°   *queen*
And when I saw my fers away,
Alas! I could no longer play,
But saidè, 'Farewell, sweet, ywis,°   *indeed*
And farewell all that ever there is!'
Therewith Fortunè said, 'check here!'
And 'mate!' in mid point of the checker°   *board* 660

With a pawn errant, alas!
Full craftier to play she was
Than Attalus, that made the game
First of the chess: so was his name.
But God would I had once or twice
Ycould and know° the jeopardies   *studied and learned*
That couth° the Greek Pythagoras!   *knew*
I should have played the bet° at chess,   *better*
And kept my fers the bet thereby;
And though wherto?° for truely,   *why* 670
I hold that wish not worth a stree!°   *straw*
It had be never the bet for me.
For Fortune can so many a wile,
There be but few can hir beguile,
And eek she is the less to blame;
Myself I would have done the same,
Before God, had I been as she;
She ought the more excusèd be.
For this I say yet more thereto,
Had I be God and might have do°   *done* 680
My willè, when she my fers caughtè,
I would have draw the samè draughtè.°   *made the same moves*
For, also wise God give me restè,
I dare well swear she took the bestè!
But through that draughtè I have lorn
My bliss; alas! that I was born!
For evermore, I trowè truely,
For all° my willè, my lust* wholly   *despite; pleasure*
Is turned; but yet what to doone°?   *do*
By our Lord, it is to die soonè;   690
For nothing I leave it not,
But live and die right in this thought;
There nis° planet in firmamentè,   *there is no*
Nor in air, nor in earth, none elementè,
That they ne give me a gift each one
Of weeping, when I am alone.
For whan that I advise me well,
And bethinke me every deal,
How that there lieth in reckoning,
In my sorrow, for nothing;   700
And how there leaveth no gladnessè
May gladdè me of my distressè,
And how I have lost suffisancè,

And therto I have no pleasancè,
Then may I say I have right nought.
And when all this falleth in my thought
Alas! then am I overcome!
For that is done is not to come.
I have more sorrow than Tantale.'° ...   *Tantalus*

46. from *The House of Fame*

46a. from *Book II: Proem*

Now hearkeneth, every manner man
That English understandè can,   510
And listeneth of my dream to lear;°   *learn*
For now at erstè° shall ye hear   *for the first time*
So sely° an avisioun,*   *holy; visionary dream*
That Isayè, °nor Scipion,   *Isaiah*
Nor King Nabugodonosor,°   *Nabuchadnezzar*
Pharoh, Turnus, nor Elcanor,
Ne mettè° such a dream as this!   *Never dreamed*
Now fairè blissful, O Cypris,°   *Venus*
So be my favour at this time!
And ye, me to endite° and rhymè   *write down* 520
Helpeth, that on Parnassus dwell
By Helicon the clearè well.
O Thought, that wrote all that I mettè,
And in the treasury it shette°   *locked*
Of my brain! now shall men see
If any virtue in thee be,
To tellen all my dream aright;
Now kythè° thine engyn* and might!   *display; ingenuity*

46b. *The Dream*

This eagle, of which I have you told,
That shone with feathers as of gold,   530
Which that so highè gan to soar,
I gan beholdè more and more,
To see the beauty and the wonder;
But never was there dint of thunder,
Nor that thing that men callè foudre,°   *thunderbolt*
That smote sometime a tower to powder,

And in his swiftè coming brendè,°   burned
That so swithè° gan descendè,   swiftly
As this fowl, when it beheld
That I aroam° was in the feld;*   wandering; field 540
And with his grimmè pawès strongè,
Within his sharpè nailès longè,
Me, fleeing, in a swoop he hentè,°   grabbed
And with his soars again up wentè,
Me carrying in his clawès stark°   strong
As lightly as I were a lark,
How high, I can not tellè you,
For I came up, I niste° how.   knew not
For so astonished and aswevèd°   dazed
Was every virtue in my heved,°   head 550
What with his soars and with my dreadè,
That all my feeling gan to deadè;°   die
Forwhy it was too great affray.
    Thus I long in his clawès lay,
Till at the last he to me spake
In mannès voice, and said, 'Awake!
And be not aghast so, for shame!'
And callèd me then by my name,
And, for I should the bet° abraidè,*   better; wake up
Me mette, 'Awake,' to me he saidè,   560
Right in the samè voice and stevene°   tone
That useth one I couldè nevene;°   name
And with that voice, sooth for to sayen,
My mindè came to me again;
For it was goodly said to me,
So was it never wont to be.
    And herewithal I gan to stirrè,
And he me in his feet to bearè,
Till that he felt that I had heat,
And felt eek° then mine heartè beat.   also 570
And tho gan he me to disport,
And with wordès to comfort,
And saidè twice, 'Saint Marie!
Thou art noyous° for to carry,   nuisance
And nothing needeth it, pardee!°   by God
For also wise God helpè me
As thou none harm shalt have of this;
And this case,° that betid thee is,   situation
Is for thy lore and for thy prow;° –   benefit

Let see! darest thou yet look now? 580
Be full assurèd, boldèly,
I am thy friend.' And therewith I
Gan for to wonderen in my mind.
'O God,' thought I, 'that madest kind,°   *nature*
Shall I no other wayès die?
Where° Jovès will me stellifye,*   *Whether; turn into a star*
Or what thing may this signify?
I neither am Enoch, nor Elye,°   *Elijah*
Nor Romulus, nor Ganymede
That was y-borè up, as men read, 590
To heaven with dan° Jupiter,   *lord*
And made the goddès bottèler.'°   *bottle-bearer or butler*
Lo, this was then my fantasy!
But he that bare me gan espy
That I so thought, and saidè this: –
'Thou deemest of thyself amiss;
For Jovès is not therabout –°   *is not about*
I dare well put thee out of doubt –
To make of thee as yet a starè.
But ere I bear thee muchè ferrè,°   *further* 600
I will thee tellè what I am,
And whither thou shalt, and why I cam°   *came*
To do this, so that thou takè
Good heart, and not for feare quakè.'
'Gladly,' quoth I. 'Now well,' quoth he: –
'First I, that in my feet have thee,
Of which thou hast a fear and wonder,
Am dwelling with the god of thunder,
Which that men callèn Jupiter,
That doth° me fly full oftè far   *makes* 610
To do all his commandèment.
And for this cause he hath me sent
To thee: now hearketh, by thy trothè!
Certain, he hath of thee routhè,°   *pity*
That thou so longè truèly
Hast servèd so attentively
His blindè nephew Cupido,
And fair Venus goddess also,
Withoutè guerdon° ever yit,*   *reward; yet*
And nevertheless hast set thy wit –   690
Although that in thy head full lightè is –
To makè bookès, songès, ditties,

In rhyme, or elsè in cadence,
As thou best canst, in reverence
Of Love, and of his servants eek,
That have his service sought, and seek;
And painest thee to praise his art,
Although thou haddest never part;
Wherfore also, God me blessè,
Jovès halt° it great humblessè,   *considers* 630
And virtue eek, that thou wilt makè
Anight full oft thine head to achè,
In thy study, so thou writest,
And evermore of love enditest,
In honour of him and in praisingès,
And in his folkès furtheringès,°   *endorsements*
And in their matter all devisest,
And nought him nor his folk despisest,
Although thou mayst go in the dance°   *(of love)*
Of them that him list not advance.   640
     'Wherefore, as I said, y-wis,
Jupiter considereth this,
And also, beau sir, other thingès;
That is, that thou hast no tidingès
Of Lovès folk, if they be glad,
Nor of nought else that Goddè made;
And nought only from far country
That there no tiding cometh to thee,
But of thy very neighèbourès,
That dwellen almost at thy doorès,   650
Thou hearest neither that nor this;
For when thy labour done all is,
And hast y-made thy reckonings,
Instead of rest and newè things,
Thou goest home to thy house anon;
And, also dumb as any stone,
Thou sittest at another book,
Till fully dazèd is thy look,
And liv'est thus as an hermitè,
Although thine abstinence is lightè.   660
     'And therefore Jovès, through his grace,
Will that I bear thee to a place,
Which that hight the House of Fame,
To do thee some disport and game,
In some recompensation

Of labour and devotion
That thou hast had, lo! causeless,
To Cupido, the reckèless!
And thus this God, through his meritè,
Will with some manner thing thee quitè,°   requite 670
So that thou wilt be of good cheer.
For trustè well that thou shalt hear,
When we be comen there I say,
More wonder thingès, dare I lay,
Of Lovès folkè more tidings,
Both sothè sawès and lesings;°   true reports and lies
And more loves newè begunnè,
And long y-servèd lovès wonnè,
And more lovès casually°   fortuitously
That been betide, no man wot why,   680
But as a blind man starts a hare;
And more jolity and fare,
While that they findè love of stellè,
As thinketh them, and overall wellè;
More discords, and more jealousies,
More murmurs,° and more novelris,*   rumours; novelties
And more dissimulations,
And feignèd reparations;
And more berdis° in two hours   ruses
Withoutè razour or scissors   690
Y-made, then graines be of sands;
And eek more holding in hands,
And also more renovelauncès°   renewals
Of old forgotten acquaintancès;
More lovè-dayès and accords
Then on instruments be cords;
And eek of lovès more exchanges
Than ever cornès were in grangs;°   granaries
Unethe° mayest thow trowen* this?' –   hardly; believe
Quoth he. 'No, help me God so wise!' –   700
Quoth I. 'No? why?' quoth he. 'For it
Were impossible, to my wit,
Though that Fame had all the pies°   trouble
In all a realm, and all the spies,
How that yet she should hear all this,
Or they espie it.' 'O yes, yes!'
Quoth he to me, 'that can I prove
Be reason, worthy for to leave,

So that thou give thine advertencè°   *heed*
To understandè my sentencè . . .'°   *meaning* 710

47. Troilus and Criseyde

47a. from *Book II, Proeme*

Out of these blackè wavès for to sail,
O wind, O wind, the weather ginneth clearè;
For in this sea the boat hath such travail,
Of my cunning that unnethe° I it steerè: *scarcely*
This sea clepe° I the tempestous mattere   *call*
Of despair that Troilus was in:
But now of hope the calendès° begin.   *first day*

O lady mine, that callèd art Clio,
Thou be my speed from this forth, and my musè,
To rhymè well this book, til I have do;°   *done* 10
Me needeth here none other art to usè.
Forwhy to every lover I me excusè,
That of no sentiment° I this enditè,*   *personal knowledge; write*
But out of Latin in my tonguè it writè.

Wherefore I will have neither thank nor blame
Of all this work, but pray you meekèly,
Disblameth me, if any word be lame,
For as mine author saidè, so say I.
Eek though I speake of love unfeelingly,
No wonder is, for it nothing of new is;
A blind man cannot judgen well in hues.

Ye know eek,° that in form of speeche is change   *also*
Within a thousand year, and wordès then
That hadden price, now wonder nice° and strange   *absurd*
Us thinketh them; and yet they spake them so,
And sped° as well in love as men now do;   *succeeded*
Eek for to winnè love in sundry ages,
In sundry landès, sundry been usàges.°   *customs*

And forthy if it hap in any wise,
That here be any lover in this place 30
That hearkeneth, as the story will devise,
How Troilus came to his lady grace,
And thinketh, so nolde I° not love purchase, *would not I*
Or wondreth on his speech and his doing,
I noot;° but it is me no wondering; *don't know*

For every wight which that to Romè went,
Halt° not one path, or always one manner; *kept*
Eek in some land were all the gamen shent,° *fun spoiled*
If that they fared in love as men do here,
As thus, in open doing or in cheer,° *appearance* 40
In visiting, in form,° or said their saws;* *formally; sayings*
Forthy men sayen, each country hath its laws.

Eek scarcely been there in this placè three
That have in love said like, and done, in all;
For to thy purpose this may liken thee,
And thee right nought, yet all is said or shall;
Eek some men grave° in tree, some in stone wall, *carve*
As it betide; but since I have begun,
Mine author shall I follow, if I can.

47b. from *Book Two: Criseyde reflects*

But as she sat alone and thoughtè thus, 610
Th' outcry arose of skirmish all without,
And men cried in the street, 'See, Troilus
Hath right now put to flight the Greekès rout!'
With that gan all her meyne° for to shout, *household*
'Ah! Go we see, cast up the lattice wide;
For through this street he must to palace ride;

'For other way is from the gatè none
Of Dardanus, there open is the chain.'
With that came he and all his folk anon
An easy pace riding, in routès twain, 620
Right as his happy day was, sooth to sayn,
For which, men say, may nought disturbèd be
That shall betiden of necessity.

This Troilus sat on his bayè steed,
All armèd, save his head, full richèly,
And wounded was his horse, and gan to bleed,
On which he rode a pace, full softèly;
But such a knightly sightè, truèly,
As was on him, was nought, withouten failè,
To look on Mars, that god is of battailè.   630

So like a man of armès and a knight
He was to seen,° full filled of high prowessè;   *appeared*
For both he had a body and a mightè
To do that thing, as well as hardinessè;
And eek to seen him in his gear him dressè,
So fresh, so young, so weldy° seemèd he,   *lively*
It was an heaven upon him for to see.

His helm tohewèn° was in twenty places,   *hacked*
That by a tissue hung, his back behindè,
His shield todasshèd was with swords and maces,   640
In which men mightè many an arrow findè
That thirled° haddè horn and nerf and rinde;*   *pierced; outer coating of shield*
And aye° the people cried, 'Here cometh our joye,   *ever*
And, next his brother, holder up of Troye!'

For which he waxed a little red for shame,
When he the people upon him heardè cryen,
That to beholde it was a noble game,
How soberly he castè doun his eyen.
Criseydè gan all his cheer aspien,
And let it so soft in her heartè sinkè,   650
That to herself she said, 'Who gave me drinkè?'

For of her ownè thought she wex all red,
Remembering her right thus, 'Lo, this is he
Which that mine uncle sweareth he must be dead,
But° I on him have mercy and pity;'   *Unless*
And with that thought, for pure ashamèd, she
Gan in her head to pull, and that as fastè,
While he and all the people forby passedè,

And gan to cast and rollen up and down
Within her thought his excellent prowess,   660
And his estate, and also his renown,

His wit, his shape, and eek his gentilless;
But most her favour was, for his distress
Was all for her, and thought it was a ruth°   *pity*
To slay such one, if that he meantè truth.

Now mightè some envìous jangle° thus,   *complain*
'This was a sudden love, how might it be
That she so lightly lovèd Troilus
Right for the firstè sightè; yes, pardee?'
Now whoso sayeth so, may he never thrive!   670
For everything, a ginning hath it need
Ere all be wrought, withouten any dread.

For I say not that she so suddenly
Gave him her love, but that she gan incline
To like him first, and I have told you why;
And after that, his manhood and his pain
Made love within her hertè for to mine,
For which, by process and by good service,
He got her love, and in no sudden wise.

47c. from *Book Five: Criseyde's letter and the rest*

'Cupidès son, example of goodlyhedè,°   *excellence* 1590
O, sword of knighthood, source of gentiless!
How might a wight in torment and in dreadè
And helèless,° you send as yet gladness?   *in poor health*
I heartèless, I sigh, I in distress;
Since you with me, nor I with you may dealè,
You neither send I heartè may nor helè.°   *health*

'Your letters full, the paper all ypleynted,°   *wept over*
Conceivèd hath mine heartès pìetyè;
I have eek seen with tearès all depainted
Your letter, and how that you requirèn me   1600
To come again, which yet ne may not be.
But why, lest that this letter foundèn were,
No mention ne make I now, for fear.

'Grievous to me, God woot, is your unreste,
Your haste, and that, the goddès ordenance,
It seemeth not you take it for the beste.
Nor other thing is in your remembrance,

As thinketh me, but only your pleasancè.
But be not wroth, and that I you beseech;
For that I tarry, is all for wicked speech. 1610

'For I have heard well morè than I wendè,° *anticipated*
Touching us two, how thingès han° y-standen; *have*
Which I shall with dissembling amendè.
And be not wroth, I have eek understondè,
How ye ne do but holden me in honde.° *deceive me*
But now no force,° I can not in you guessè *But that does not matter*
But allè truth and allè genteelessè.

'Come I will, but yet in such disjointè° *difficulty*
I stand as now, that what year or what day
That this shall be, that can I not appointè. 1420
But in effect, I pray you, as I may,
Of your good word and of your friendship ay.
For truèly, while that my life may dure,° *last*
As for a friend you may in me assure.

'Yet pray I you on evil° you ne take, *miss*
That it is short which that I to you writè;
I dare not, there I am, well letters make,
Ne never yet ne could I well endite.
Eek great effect men write in placè litè.° *little*
Th'intent is all, and not the letters' spacè; 1630
And fareth now well, God have you in his gracè!
                    La vostre C.'° *Your very own Criseyde*

This Troilus this letter thought all strangè,
When he it saw, and sorrowfully he sighed;
Him thought it like a kalendès° of changè; *first day*
But finally, he full ne trowen mightè
That she ne would him holden that she hightè;° *hold to what she swore*
For with full evil will° list him to leave *very reluctantly*
That loveth well, in such cas, though him grieve.

But natheless, men sayen that, at the last,
For° any thing, men shall the soothè* see; *Despite; truth* 1640
And such a case betid, and that as fast,
That Troilus well understood that she
Nas not so kind as that her oughtè be.

And finally, he woot now, out of doubt,
That all is lost that he hath been about.

Stood on a day in his melancholy
This Troilus, and in suspicioun
Of her for whom he wendè for to die.
And so befell, that throughout Troyè town,   1650
As was the guise, y-bore was up and down
A manner coat-armour, as sayeth the story,
Before Deiphebe, in sign of his victory,

The whichè coat, as telleth Lollius,
Deiphebe it had rent° from Diomedè   *torn from*
The samè day; and when this Troilus
It saw, he gan to taken of it heedè,
Avising of° the length and of the breadè,*   *taking in; breadth*
And all the work; but as he gan behold,
Full suddenly his heartè gan to cold,

As he that on the collar found within   1660
A brooch, that he Criseyd gave that morrow
That she from Troyè mustè needès twin,°   *depart*
In remembrance of him and of his sorrow;
And she him laid again her faith to borrow°   *she promised him*
To keep it aye; but now, full well he wistè,
His lady nas no longer one to tristè°.   *trust*

He goeth him home, and gan full soonè send
For Pandarus; and all this newè chauncè,°   *happening*
And of this brooch, he told him word and end,
Complaining of her heartès variancè,   1670
His longè love, his troth, and his penancè;
And after death, withouten wordes more,
Full fast he cried, his rest° him to restore.   *peace*

Then spake he thus: 'O lady mine Criseydè,
Where is your faith, and where is your behestè?
Where is your love, where is your troth,' he saidè;
'Of Diomede have you now all this feastè!
Alas, I would have trowèd at the leastè,
That, since you nold° in trothè to me stand,   *would not*
That you thus nold han holden me in hand!°   *deceive me* 1680

'Who shall now trow on any oathès more?
Alas, I never would have wend,° ere this,   *believed*
That ye, Criseydè, could have changèd so;
Ne, but I had aguilt and done amiss,
So cruel wend I not your heart, y-wis,
To slay me thus; alas, your name of truth
Is now fordone, and that is all my ruth.

'Was there no other brooch you listè letè°   *give up*
To feffè° with your newè love,' quoth he,   *bond*
'But thilke brooch that I, with tearès wetè,   1690
You gave, as for a remembrance of me?
No other cause, alas, ne hadè ye
But for despite, and eek for that you meantè
All utterly to showen your intentè!

'Through which I see that clean out of your mind
You have me cast, and I ne can nor may,
For all this world, within mine heartè find
To unlove you a quarter of a day!
In cursed time I born was, wellaway!
That you, that do me all this woe
    endure,°   *that make me endure all this woe* 1700
Yet love I best of any creature.

'Now God,' quoth he, 'me sendè yet the grace
That I may meeten with this Diomede!
And truèly, if I have might and space,
Yet shall I make, I hope, his sidès bleed.
O God,' quoth he, 'that oughtest taken heed
To furtherèn troth, and wrongès to punyce,°   *punish*
Why nil thou do a vengeance on this vice?

'O Pandarus, that in dreams for to trust
Me blamèd hast, and wont art oft upbraid,   1710
Now mayst thou see thyself, if that thee list,
How true is now thy niecè, bright Criseyde!
In sundry formès, God it wot,' he said,
'The goddès shewen bothè joy and tenè°   *distress*
In sleep, and by my dream it is now seenè.

'And certainly, withouten morè speechè,
From henceforth, as far forth as I may,

Mine own death in armès° will I seekè;   *battle*
I reckè° not how soonè be the day!   *care*
But truèly, Criseydè, sweetè may,   1720
Whom I have aye with all my might y-servèd,
That you thus do, I have it not deservèd.'

This Pandarus, that all these thingès heardè,
And wistè well he said a sooth of this,°   *spoke truly*
He not a word again to him answerdè;
For sorry of his friend's sorrow he is,
And shamèd, for his niece hath done amiss;
And stands, astonished of these causes tweyè,
As still as stone; a word ne could he sayè.

But at the lastè thus he spake, and said,   1730
'My brother dear, I may thee do no more.
What should I say? I hate, y-wis, Criseyde!
And God wot, I will hate her evermore!
And that thou me besoughtest did of yore,
Having unto mine honour ne my rest
Right no reward, I did all that thou lest.

'If I did ought that mightè liken thee,
It is me leef;° and of this treason now,   *pleasure*
God woot, that it a sorrow is unto me!
And dreadèless, for heartès ease of you,°   *to ease your heart* 1740
Right fain would I amend it, wist I how.
And from this world, almighty God, I pray,
Deliver her soon; I can no morè say.'

Great was the sorrow and plaint of Troilus;
But forth her course Fortune aye gan to holdè.
Criseydè loveth the son of Tydeus,
And Troilus must weep in carès coldè.
Such is this world; whoso it can beholdè,
In each estate is little heartès rest;
God leave us for to take it for the best!   1750

In many cruel battles, out of dread,
Of Troilus, this ilkè noble knight,
As men may in these oldè bookès read,
Was seen his knighthood and his greatè might.
And dreadèless, his irè, day and night,

Full cruelly the Greekès aye abought;°   *suffered*
And always most this Diomede he sought.

And oftè times, I findè that they met
With bloody strokès and with wordès greatè,
Assaying how their spearès weren whet;   1760
And God it woot, with many a cruel hetè°   *oath*
Gan Troilus upon his helm to beatè.
But natheless, Fortune it nought ne woldè,
Of other's hand that either dièn shouldè.

And if I had y-taken for to write
The armès of this ilkè worthy man,
Then would I of his battlès endite.
But for that I to writè first began
Of his love, I have said as that I can.
His worthy deedès, whoso list them hear,   1770
Read Dares, he can tell them alle y-fere.° –   *together*

Beseeching every lady bright of hue,
And every gentle woman, what she be,
That all be° that Criseydè was untrue,   *although*
That for that guilt she be not wroth with me.
You may her guilt in other bookès see;
And gladlier I will writen, if yow lestè,
Penelopèès troth and good Alcestè.

Nor say I not this all only for these men,
But most for women that betrayèd be   1780
Through falsè folk; God give them sorrow, amen!
That with her greatè wit and subtlty
Betray you! and this commoveth° me   *moves*
To speak, and in effect you all I pray,
Beware of men, and hearkeneth what I say! –

Go, little book, go little mine tragedyè,
There God° thy maker yet, ere that he die,   *May God*
So sendè might to make in° some comedyè!   *compose*
But little book, no making thou n'envie,°   *don't envy anyone else's creation*
But subject be to allè poesiè;
And kiss the steps, whereas thou seèst pace
Virgil, Ovid, Homer, Lucan, and Stace.

And for there is so great diversity
In English and in writing of our tongue,
So pray I God that none miswritè thee,
Ne thee mismetre for default of tongue.
And read whereso thou be, or elsè sung,
That thou be understood I God beseech!
But yet to purpose of my rather° speech. –   *earlier*

The wrath, as I began you for to say,   1800
Of Troilus, the Greekès boughten dear;
For thousandès his handès maden die,
As he that was withouten any peer,
Save Hector, in his time, as I can hear.
But wellaway, save only Godès will,
Dispiteously him slew the fierce Achill.

And when that he was slain in this mannerè,
His lightè ghost full blissfully is went
Up to the hollowness of the seventh spherè,
In converse letting° every elementè;   *leaving behind* 1810
And there he saw, with full avisèment,°   *view*
The erratic starrès,° harkening harmony   *planets*
With soundès full of heavenish melody.

And down from thence fast he gan avyse
This little spot of earth, that with the sea
Embracèd is, and fully gan despise
This wretched world, and held all vanity
To respect of the pleyn° felicity   *perfect*
That is in heaven above; and at the last,
There he was slain, his looking down he cast;   1820

And in himself he laughed right at the woe
Of them that wepten for his death so fast;
And damnèd all our work that followeth so
The blindè lust, the which that may not last,
And shoulden all our heart on heaven cast.
And forth he wentè, shortly for to tell,
There as Mercury sorted him to dwell. –

Such fin° hath, lo, this Troilus for love,   *end*
Such fin hath all his greatè worthiness;

Such fin hath his estatè real above,   1830
Such fin his lust, such fin hath his nobless;
Such fin hath falsè worldès brittleness.
And thus began his loving of Criseydè,
As I have told, and in this wise he diedè.

O youngè, freshè folkès, he or she,
In which that love up groweth with your age,
Repaireth home from worldly vanity,
And of your heart upcastè the visage
To thilke God that after his image
Yow made, and thinketh all nis but a fairè   1840
This world, that passeth soon as flowers fairè.

And loveth him, the which that right for love
Upon a cross, our soulès for to buyè,
First starf,° and rose, and sits in heaven above;   *died*
For he nill falsen° no wight, dare I sayè,   *will not betray*
That will his heart all wholly on him layè.
And since he best to love is, and most meek,
What needeth feignèd lovès for to seek?

Lo here, of pagans cursèd oldè rites,
Lo here, what all their goddès may avail;   1850
Lo here, these wretched worldès appetites;
Lo here, the fin and guerdon° for travail   *reward*
Of Jove, Apollo, of Mars, of such rascail!°   *rascals*
Lo here, the form of oldè clerkès speech
In poetry, if you their bookès seek. –

O moral Gower, this book I direct
To thee, and to thee philosophical Strode,
To vauchènsafe, there need is, to correct,
Of your benignities and zealès good.
And to that soothfast Christ, that starf on rode,°   *died on the cross* 1860
With all mine heart of mercy ever I pray;
And to the Lord right thus I speak and say:

Thou one, and two, and three, eterne on-livè,
That reignest aye in three and two and one,
Uncircumscript, and all mayst circumscrivè,°   *embrace*
Us from visible and invisible foèn°   *foes*
Defend; and to thy mercy, every each one,

So make us, Jesus, for thy gracè dignè,°   *worthy*
For love of maid and mother thine benignè!
        Amen.

48. from *The Canterbury Tales*

48a. *General Prologue*

When that Aprillè with his showrès sootè°   *sweet*
The drought of March hath piercèd to the rootè,
And bathèd every vein in such liquour,
Of which virtue engendred is the flower;
When Zephirus° eek* with his sweetè breath   *Spring wind; also*
Inspired hath in every holt° and heath   *wood*
The tendrè croppès, and the youngè sunnè
Hath in the Ram his halfè course y-runè,°   *(it is mid-April)*
And smallè fowlès maken melodyè,
That sleepen al the night with open eyè,   10
(So pricketh° them natùre in their coràges*):   *incites; hearts*
Then longen folk to go on pilgrimàges
(And palmers° for to seeken strangè strands)   *pilgrims*
To fernè hallows,° couth* in sundry lands   *shrines; known*
And specially, from every shirès end
Of Engèland, to Canterbury they wend,
The holy blissful martyr for to seekè,
That them hath helpen, when that they were sickè.
   Befell that, in that season on a day,
In Southwark at the Tabard as I lay,   20
Ready to wenden on my pilgrimage
To Canterbury with full devout corage,
At night was come into that hostelry
Well nine-and-twenty in a company,
Of sundry folk, by aventure y-fallè°   *by chance fallen*
In fellowship, and pilgrims were they allè,
That tòward Canterbury woulden ride.
The chambers and the stables weren wide,
And well we weren easèd attè bestè.
And shortly, when the sunnè was to restè,   30
So had I spoken with them every one

That I was of their fellowship anon,°   *soon*
And madè forward° early for to rise,   *arrangement*
To take our way, there as I you devise.°   *tell*
    But natheless, while I have time and space,
Ere that I further in this talè pace,°   *proceed*
Me thinketh it accordant to reasòn,
To tellè you all the condition°   *circumstances*
Of each of them, so as it seemèd me,
And which they weren, and of what degree;°   *social class* 40
And eek in what array that they were in;
And at a knight then willl I first begin.
    A Knight there was, and that a worthy man,
That from the timè that he first began
To riden out, he lovèd chivalryè,
Troth and honour, freedom° and courtesyè.   *generosity*
Full worthy was he in his lordes warrè,
And thereto had he riden, (no man ferrè°)   *further*
As well in Christendom as heathenessè,°   *heathen countries*
And ever honoured for his worthinessè.
At Alexandria he was, when it was wonnè;   50
Full oftè times he had the board bigonnè°   *taken the place of honour at table*
Abovè allè nations in Prussia
In Lettow° had he reysèd* and in Russia   *Lithuania; campaigned*
No Christian man so oft of his degree.
In Gernade° at the siege eek had he be   *Granada*
Of Algezir,° and riden in Belmarye.*   *Algeciras; Morocco*
At Lyeys° was he, and at Satalye,*   *Ayah; Antalia (Turkey)*
When they were won; and in the Greatè Sea
At many a noble army° had he be.   *expedition* 60
At mortal battles had he been fifteen,
And foughten for our faith at Tramissen°   *Tlemcen (North Africa)*
In listes° thrice, and ayè slain his foe.   *duels*
This ilke worthy knight had been also
Sometime with the lord of Palatye,°   *Bala (Turkey)*
Against another heathen in Turkey:
And evermore he had a sovereign prize
And though that he were worthy, he was wise,
And of his port° as meek as is a maid.   *demeanour*
He never yet no villainy ne said   70
In all his life, unto no manner wight.°   *person*
He was a verray° perfect genteel knight.   *truly*
But for to tellen you of his array,
His horse were goodè, but he was not gay.

Of fustian° he wearèd a gipoun*   coarse cloth; tunic
All bismattered° with his habergeon;*   stained; chain mail
For he was late y-come from his voyagè,
And wentè for to do his pilgrimagè.
    With him there was his sonnè, a young Squire,
A lover, and a lusty° bachelor,   spirited 80
With lockès curled, as they were laid in pressè.
Of twenty year of age he was, I guessè.
Of his stature he was of even lengthè,°   average height
And wonderly deliver,° and great of strengthè.   nimble
And he had been some time in chivachie,°   cavalry crusade
In Flaunders, in Artois, and Picardy,
And borne him well, as of so little space,°   time
In hope to standen in his lady's gracè.
Embroidered was he, as it were a mede°   meadow
All full of freshè flowers, white and red.   90
Singing he was, or fluting, all the day;
He was as fresh as is the month of May.
Short was his gown, with sleevès long and wide.
Well couth° he sit on horse, and fairè ride.   knew how to
He coudè songès make and well endite,°   compose
Joust and eek dance, and well portray and write.
So hot he lovèd, that by nightertalè°   night-time
He slept no more than doth a nightingale.
Courteous he was, lowly, and servisable,°   eager to serve
And carved before his father at the table.   100
    A Yeoman had he, and servants no mo°   more
At that time, for him listè° ridè so;   liked to
And he was clad in coat and hood of green;
A sheaf of peacock-arrows bright and keen
Under his belt he bore ful thriftily;°   properly
(Well could he dress his tackle yeomanly:
His arrows droppèd not with feathers low)
And in his hand he bore a mighty bow.
A not-head° had he, with a brown visàge,   close-shaven head
Of wood-craft well couth he all the usàge.   110
Upon his arm he bore a gay bracer,°   arm guard (for archery)
And by his side a sword and a buckler,°   shield
And on that other side a gay dagger,
Harnessed well, and sharp as point of spear;
A Cristopher on his breast of silver sheen.
A horn he bore, the baldrick° was of green;   belt
A for'ster was he, soothly, as I guessè.

There was also a Nun, a Prioressè,
That of her smiling was full simple and coy;
Her greatest oath was but, 'By Saintè Loy;'°   *Saint Eligius* 120
And she was clèped° Madame Eglantine.   *called*
Full well she sung the servicè divine,
Entunèd in her nose full seemely;°   *properly*
And French she spoke full fair and fetisly,°   *in a cultivated manner*
After the school of Stratford-attè-Bow,
For French of Paris was to her unknow.°   *unknown*
At meatè well y-taught was she withalle;
She let no morsel from her lippès fallè,
Ne wet her fingers in her saucè deep.
Well coude she carry a morsel, and well keep,   130
That no drop ne fell upon her breast.
In courtesy was set full much her lest.°   *pleasure*
Her over-lippè wipèd she so cleanè,
That in her cup there was no farthing seenè
Of greasè, when she drunken had hir draughtè.
Full semèly after her meat she raughtè,°   *stretched*
And sikerly° she was of great disport,*   *to be sure; deportment*
And full plesànt, and amiable of port,
And painèd her° to counterfitè cheerè*   *she took pains; manner*
Of court, and been estately of mannerè,   140
And to ben holden dignè° of reverence.   *worthy*
But, for to speaken of hir conscience,
She was so charitable and so piteous,
She wouldè weepe, if that she saw a mouse
Caught in a trap, if it were dead or bleddè.
Of smallè houndès had she, that she feddè
With roasted flesh, or milk and wastel-bread.°   *expensive bread*
But sore weep she if one of them were dead,
Or if men smote it with a yerdè° smert;*   *stick; smartly*
And all was conscience and tender heart.   150
Full seemèly her wimpel pinchèd was;
Her nose tretis°; her eyè grey as glass: *graceful*
Her mouth full small, and thereto° soft and red;   *also*
But sikerly she had a fair forehead;
It was almost a spannè° broad, I trow;   *(about nine inches)*
For, heartily, she was not undergrowè.
Full fetis° was her cloak, as I was warè.*   *well made; as I perceived*
Of small coral about her arm she barè
A pair of beadès, gauded all with green;
And thereon hung a brooch of gold full sheen,   160

On which there was first writ a crownèd A,
And after, *Amor vincit omnia.*°   *Love conquers all*
   Another Nunnè with her haddè she,
That was her chapèlain, and Priestès three.
   A Monk there was, a fair for the maistrie,°   *surpassing all others*
An outrider, that lovèd venery;°   *hunting*
A manly man, to be an abbot able.
Full many a dainty horse had he in stable:
And, when he rode, men might his bridle hear
Jingling in a whistling wind as clear,   170
And eek as loud as doth the chapel bell.
There as this lord was keeper of the cell
The rule of Saint Maurè or of Seint Beneit°   *Benedict*
Because that it was old and somewhat strait,
This ilke monk let oldè thinges pacè,°   *pass*
And held after the newè world the spacè.
He gave not of that text a pulled hen,
That sayeth, that hunters been not holy men;
Nor that a monk, when he is cloisterless,
Is likened to a fish that is waterless;   180
This is to sayen, a monk out of his cloister.
But thilke text held he not worth an oyster;
And I said, his opinion was good.
What should he study, and make himselven wood,°   *mad*
Upon a book in cloister alway to pore,
Or swinken° with his handès, and labour,   *work*
As Austin° bid? How shall the world be served?   *St Augustine*
Let Austin have his swink to him reserved.
Therefore he was a pricasour° aright;   *hunter on horseback*
Greyhounds he had, as swift as fowl in flight;   190
Of pricking° and of hunting for the hare   *galloping*
Was all his lust, for no cost would he spare.
I saw his sleeves purfilèd° at the hand   *fur-lined*
With grys,° and that the finest of a land;   *squirrel-fur*
And, for to fasten his hood under his chin,
He had of gold y-wrought a curious pin:
A loveknot in the greater end there was.
His head was bald, that shone as any glass,
And eek his face, as he had been anoint.
He was a lord full fat and in good point;°   *condition* 200
His eyès steep,° and rolling in his head,   *bright*
That steamèd as a furnace of a leed;°   *cauldron*
His bootès supple, his horse in great estate.

Now certainly he was a fair prelate;
He was not pale as a forpined° ghost.   *tortured*
A fat swan loved he best of any roast.
His palfrey was as brown as is a berry.
    A Friar there was, a wanton and a merry,
A limitour,° a full solemnè man.   *begging friar*
In all the orders four° is none that can*   *religious orders; knows* 210
So much of dalliance and fair languàgè.
He haddè made full many a marriàgè
Of youngè women, at his ownè cost.
Unto his order he was a noble post.
Full well beloved and familiar was he
With franklins overall in his country,
And eek with worthy women of the town;
For he had power of confession,
As saidè himself, more than a curate,
For of his order he was licenciat.°   *licensed* 220
Full sweetly heardè he confession,
And pleasant was his absolution;
He was an easy man to give penance
Thereas he wist° to have a good pittance;   *knew*
For unto a poor order for to give
Is signè that a man is well y-shrive.°   *forgiven his confessed sins*
For if he gave, he darèd make avaunt,°   *declaration*
He wistè that a man was repentant.
For many a man so hard is of his heart,
He may not weep although him sorè smart.   230
Therefore, instead of weepingè and prayers,
Men must give silver to the poorè freres.°   *friars*
His tippet° was aye farsed full* of knives   *hood; crammed full*
And pinnès, for to given fairè wives.
And certainly he had a merry note;
Well coude he sing and playen on a rote.°   *a stringed instrument*
Of yeddings,° he bore utterly the prize.   *ballad-singing*
His neckè white was as the fleur-de-lys;°   *lily*
Thereto he strong was as a champion.
He knew the taverns well in every town,   240
And every hostiler and tappester°   *barmaid*
Better than a lazar° or a beggar;   *lepper*
For unto such a worthy man as he
Accorded not, as by his faculty,
To havè with such lazars acquaintance.
It is not honest, it may not advaunce

For to dealen with no such poraille,°   *paupers*
But all with rich and sellers of vitaille.°   *victuals*
And overal, there as profit should arise,
Courteous he was, and lowly of service.   250
There was no man nowhere so virtuous.
He was the bestè beggar in his house;
For though a widow haddè not a shoe,
So pleasant was his *In principio,*°   'In the beginning'
Yet would he have a farthing, ere he wentè.
His purchase was well better than his rentè.
And rage° he could, as it were right a whelp.*   *flirt; puppy*
In lovè-days there coudè he much help.
For there he was not like a cloisterer,
With a threadbare cope, as is a poor scholar,   260
But he was like a master or a pope.
Of double worsted was his semicope,
That rounded as a bell out of the press.
Somewhat he lispèd, for his wantonnessè,
To make his English sweet upon his tongue;
And in his harping, when that he had sung,
His eyen twinkled in his head aright,
As do the starrès in the frosty night.
This worthy limitour was clepèd Huberd.

    A Merchant was there with a forkèd beard,   270
In motèley, and high on horse he sat,
Upon his head a Flandrish° beaver hat;   *Flemish*
His bootès claspèd fair and fetisly.
His reasons° he spoke full solempnely,*   *opinions; solemnly*
Sounding alway the increase of his winning.°   *profit*
He would the sea were kept° for any thing   *defended*
Bitwixtè Middelburgh° and Orewell.*   *Dutch port; Orwell, near Harwich*
Well coude he in exchangè sheeldès° sell.   *borrowed money*
This worthy man full well his wit beset;°   *busied*
There wistè no wight that he was in dettè,   280
So estatly° was he of his governance,*   *serene; behaviour*
With his bargains, and with his chevisaunce.°   *borrowings*
For sooth he was a worthy man withallè,
But sooth to say, I noot° how men him callè.   *know not*

    A Clerk° there was of Oxenford also,   *scholar*
That unto logic haddè long y-go.°   *dedicated himself*
As leanè was his horse as is a rake,
And he was not right fat, I undertake;
But lookèd hollow and thereto soberly.°   *serious*

Full threadbare was his overest courtepy;°   *overcoat* 290
For he had geten him yet no benefice,°   *church employment*
Ne was so worldly for to have office.°   *secular employment*
For him was lever° have at his beddès head   *preferable*
Twenty bokès, clad in black or red,
Of Aristotle and his philosophy,
Than robès rich, or fiddle, or gay sautrie.°   *harplike instrument*
But all be that° he was a philosòpher,   *although*
Yet haddè he but little gold in coffer;
But all that he might of his friendès hentè,°   *seize*
On bookès and on learning he it spentè,   300
And busily gan for the soulès prayè
Of them that gave him wherewith to scholayè.°   *attend university*
Of study took he most care and most heedè.
Not one word spoke he morè than was needè,
And that was said in form and reverence,°   *respect*
And short and quick, and full of high sentence.
Souning in° moral virtue was his speech,   *tending to*
And gladly would he learn, and gladly teach.
    A Sergeant of the Law,° wary and wise,   *senior lawyer*
That often haddè been at the Parvys,°   *porch of St Paul's Cathedral* 310
There was also, full rich of excellence.
Discreet he was, and of great reverence:
He seemèd such, his wordès were so wise.
Justice° he was full often in assize*,   *judge; assize court*
By patent, and by plain commission;
For his science, and for his high renown
Of fees and robès° had he many one.   *clients' gifts*
So great a purchaser° was nowhere none.   *buyer (of land)*
All was fee simple° to him in effect,   *unrestricted possession*
His purchasing might not be infect.°   *revoked* 320
Nowhere so busy a man as he there nas,
And yet he seemed busier than he was.
In termès° had he cas and domès* allè,   *accurately; legal precedents*
That from the time of King William were fallè.
Therto he could endite, and make a thing,°   *compose a deed*
There coudè no wight pinch at° his writing;   *fault*
And every statute coud he plain° by rote.   *recite*
He rode but homely in a medlee° coatè   *parti-coloured*
Girt with a ceint° of silk, with barrès* smallè;   *belt; stripes*
Of his array tell I no longer talè.   330
    A Frankèlin was in his company;
White was his beard, as is the daièsie.°   *daisy*

Of his complexion he was sanguìne.
Well loved he by the morrow° a sop* in wine.   *morning; piece of bread*
To liven in delight was ever his wone,°   *custom*
For he was Epicurus' ownè son,
That held opinion that plain delight
Was verrily felicity parfit.°   *perfect*
An householder, and that a great, was he;
Saint Julian he was in his country.   340
His bread, his ale, was alway after one;°   *uniformly good*
A better envined° man was nowhere none.   *wine-stocked*
Withoutè bakèd meat was never his house,
Of fish and flesh, and that so plenteous,
It snowèd in his house of meat and drink,
Of allè dainties that men coudè think.
After the sundry seasons of the year,
So changèd he his meat and his supper.
Full many a fat partrìdge had he in mew,°   *pen*
And many a bream and many a luce° in stew.*   *pike; fishpond* 350
Woe° was his cook, but if his saucè were   *woebegone*
Poignant° and sharp, and ready all his gear.*   *spicy; cutlery*
His table dormant in his hallè alway
Stood ready covered all the longè day.
At sessions,° there was he lord and sire;   *court*
Ful oftè time he was knight of the shire.°   *local representative in Parliament*
An anlas° and a gipser* all of silk   *dagger; purse*
Hung at his girdle, white as morning milk.
A sheriff had he been, and a countour;°   *auditor*
Was nowhere such a worthy vavasour.°   *land owner* 360
    A Haberdasher and a Carpenter,
A Webbe,° a Dyer, and a Tapicer,*   *weaver; tapestry maker*
Were with us eek, clothed in one livery,
Of a solemn and great fraternity.°   *guild*
Full fresh and new their gear apikèd° was;   *decorated*
Their knivès were y-chapèd° not with brass,   *capped*
But all with silver, wroght full clean and well,
Their girdles and their pouches° every-deal.   *purses*
Well seemèd each of them a fair burgess,
To sitten in a guildhall on a dais.   370
Every, for the wisdom that he can,
Was shapely for to been° an alderman.   *have been*
For chattels haddè they enough and rentè,
And eek their wivès would it well assentè;
And elès certain werè they to blame.

It is full fair to be y-clept° *ma dame*,   *addressed as*
And go to vigiliès all bifore,°   *lead the way to feasts*
And have a mantel royally y-bore.
   A Cook they haddè with them for the nones,°   *occasion*
To boil the chickens with the marrow bones,   380
And poudre-marchant° tart, and galingale.*   *spice; sweetener*
Well coude he know a draught of London ale.
He coudè roast, and seethe,° and boil, and fry,   *simmer*
Maken mortreux,° and well bake a pie.   *stews*
But great harm was it, as it thoughtè me,
That on his shin a mormal° haddè he.   *ulcer*
For blankmanger,° that made he with the bestè.   *creamed fowl, sweet-stewed*
   A Shipman was there, woning° far by westè: *living*
For aught I woot,° he was of Dartèmouth.   *know*
He rode upon a rouncy,° as he couth,   *cart-horse* 390
In a gown of falding° to the knee.   *rough cloth*
A dagger hanging on a lass° had he   *string*
About his neck under his arm adown.
The hot summer had made his hue all brown;
And, certainly, he was a good fellowè.
Full many a draught of wine had he y-drawè
From Bordeaux-ward, while that the chapman° sleep.   *merchant*
Of nicè conscience tookè he no keep.°   *notice*
If that he fought, and had the higher hand,
By water he sent them home to every land.   400
But of his craft° to recken well his tides,   *skill*
His streamès° and his daungers* him besides,   *currents; dangers*
His harbours and his moon, his lodemenage,°   *pilotage*
There nas noon such from Hullè to Carthage.
Hardy he was, and wise to undertake;°   *in what he undertook*
With many a tempest had his beard been shake.
He knew all the havens, as they were,
From Gottland to the cape of Finistere,
And every creek in Britain and in Spain;
His barge y-clepèd was the Madelaine.   410
   With us there was a Doctor of Physic,°   *medical doctor*
In all this world ne was there noon him like,
To speak of physic and of surgery;
For he was grounded in astronomy.
He kept° his patient a full great deal   *cared for*
In hours by his magic natural.°   *natural magic*
Well couth° he fortunen the ascendent*   *knew; calculate the ascendant*
Of his images for his patient.

He knew the cause of every malady,
Were it of hot or cold, or moist, or dry,   420
And where engendred and of what humour;
He was a verray parfit practicer.
The cause y-know,° and of his harm* the rootè,   *once known; illness*
Anon he gave the sickè man his botè.°   *remedy*
Full ready had he his apothecaries,
To send him drugès and his letuaries,°   *medicines*
For each of them made other for to winnè° –   *each profited the other*
Their friendship nas not newè to beginnè.
Well knew he the old Esculapius,
And Deiscorides, and eek Rufus,   430
Old Hipocras, Halley, and Galien;
Serapion, Razis, and Avicen;
Averroës, Damascien, and Constantine;
Bernard and Gatèsden, and Gilbertine.°   *medical authorities*
Of his dietè measurable was he,
For it was of no superfluity,
But of great nourishing and digestible.
His study was but little on the Bible.
In sanguine° and in pers* he clad was all,   *blood red; Persian blue*
Linèd with taffata and with sendal;°   *silks* 440
And yet he was but easy of dispence;°   *a cautious spender*
He kept that he won° in pestilence.*   *earned; Plague*
For gold in physic is a cordial,°   *medicine*
Therefore he lovèd goldè in special.
    A good Wife was there of besidè Bath,
But she was somedeal deaf, and that was scath.°   *a shame*
Of cloth-making she haddè such an haunt,°   *skill*
She passèd° them of Ypres and of Gaunt.*   *surpassed; Ghent*
In all the parish wife ne was there none
That to the offring° before her should gone;*   *giving in church; go* 450
And if there did, certain, so wroth was she,
That she was out of allè charity.
Her coverchiefs° full finè were of ground;*   *head-coverings; texture*
I durstè swear they weighèden ten pound
That on a Sunday were upon her head.
Her hosen° were of finè scarlet red,   *stockings*
Full straight y-tied and shoes full moist and newè.
Bold was her face, and fair, and red of hue.
She was a worthy woman all her life:
Husbands at churchè-door she haddè five,   460
Withouten° other company in youth;   *excluding*

But thereof needeth not to speak as nouth.°   *just now*
And thrice had she been at Jerusalem;
She haddè passèd many a strange stream;°   *a foreign sea*
At Rome she haddè been, and at Boulogne,
In Galice at Saint James, and at Cologne.°   *pilgrim destinations*
She coudè much of wandring by the way;
Gat-toothèd° was she, soothly for to say.   *gap-toothed*
Upon an ambler° easily she sat,   *steady horse*
Y-wimpled well, and on her head an hat   470
As broad as is a buckler or a targe;°   *shield*
A foot-mantel° about her hippès large,   *skirt*
And on her feet a pair of spurès sharp.
In fellowship well could she laugh and carp.°   *gossip*
Of remedies of love she knew perchauncè,
For she couth of that art the oldè dance.
   A good man was there of religion,
And was a povrè° Parson of a town;   *poor*
But rich he was of holy thought and work.
He was also a learnèd man, a clerk,   480
That Christès gospel truèly would preach;
His parishens° devoutly would he teach.   *parishioners*
Benign he was, and wonder diligent,
And in adversity full patient;
And such he was i-provèd ofte sithes.°   *many times*
Full loth were him to cursen° for his tithes,   *damn*
But rather would he given, out of doubt,
Un-to his povrè parishens about
Of his offring, and eek out of his substance.°   *income*
He couth in little thing han suffisance.°   *he could make do* 490
Wide was his parish, and houses far asunder,
But he ne laftè not,° for rain ne thunder,   *did not neglect*
In sickness nor in mischief, to visitè
The farthest in his parish, much and littè,°   *great or small*
Upon his feet, and in his hand a staff.
This noble example to his sheep he gaff,°   *gave*
That first he wrought,° and afterward he taught;   *did (gave example)*
Out of the gospel he the wordès caught;
And this figure° he added eek thereto,   *maxim*
That if gold rustè, what shall iron do?   500
For if a priest be foul, in whom we trust,
No wonder is a lewed° man to rust.   *common*
And shame it is, if a priest take keep,
A shiten° shepherd and a cleanè sheep.   *impure*

Well ought a priest example for to give,
By his cleaness, how that his sheep should live.
He settè not his benefice to hire
And leet° his sheep encombred* in the mire,   *left; stranded*
And ran to London, unto Saintè Pauls,
To seeken him a chantèry for souls,°   *the job of a chanter* 510
Or with a brotherhood° to been withholdè;*   *guild; chaplain*
But dwelt at home, and keptè well his foldè,°   *flock*
So that the wolf ne made it not miscarry;
He was a shepherd and not a mercenary.
And though he holy were, and virtuous,
He was to sinful man not despitous,°   *unpitying*
Ne of his speechè daungerous° ne dignè,*   *overbearing; arrogant*
But in his teaching discreet and benignè.
To drawen folk to heaven by fairness
By good ensample, was his business: 520
But it were any person obstinate,
What-so he were, of high or low estate,
Him would he snibben° sharply for the nones.   *scold*
A better priest I trow that nowhere none is.
He waited after no pomp and reverence,
Nor maked him a spiced° conscience,   *over-refined*
But Christès law, and his apostles twelvè,
He taught, and first he followed it him-selvè.
  With him there was a Ploughman, was his brother,
That had y-lad° of dung ful many a fother,*   *hauled; cartload* 530
A truè swinker° and a good was he,   *labourer*
Living in peace and perfect charity.
God loved he best with all his wholè heart
At allè times, though him gamed° or smert,*   *benefited; hurt*
And then his neighbour rightè as him-selvè.
He wouldè thresh, and there-to dyke° and delvè,*   *ditch; dig*
For Christès sake, for every poorè wight,
Withouten hire,° if it lay in his might.   *payment*
His tithes paidè he full fair and well,
Both of his proper swink° and his catel.*   *labour; possessions* 540
In a tabard° he rode upon a mare.   *tunic*
  There was also a Reeve and a Miller,
A Sommoner and a Pardoner also,
A Manciple,° and my-self; there were no mo.   *Manager*
  The Miller was a stout carl,° for the nones,   *chap*
Full big he was of brawn, and eek of bones;
That provèd well, for overall there he camè,

At wrestling he would have alway the ramè.°   *always win*
He was short-shouldred, broad, and thickè knarrè,°   *thick-set knave*
There nas no door that he nold° have off harrè,*   *wouldn't; hinge* 550
Or break it, at a running, with his head.
His beard as any sow or fox was red,
And thereto broad, as though it were a spade.
Upon the cop° right of his nose he had   *top*
A wart, and thereon stood a tuft of hairs,
Red as the bristles of a sowès ears;
His nosèthirlès° blackè were and widè.   *nostrils*
A sword and bokeler bore he by his sidè.
His mouth as great was as a great furnace.
He was a janglere and a goliardeys,°   *crude story-teller and jester* 560
And that was most of sin and harlotries.°   *obscenities*
Well couth he stealen corn, and tollen thrice;°   *take money for it three times*
And yet he had a thomb of gold,° pardee.   *(to weight the scales)*
A white coat and a blue hood wearèd he.
A baggèpipe well couth he blow and sown,°   *play*
And there-with-al he brought us out of town.
   A genteel Manciple was there of a temple,
Of which achateurs° mightè take example   *caterers*
For to be wise in buying of vitaillè.°   *victuals*
For whether that he paid, or took by taillè°,   *on credit* 570
Algate he waited so in his achat°,   *purchase*
That he was aye before and in good staat.°   *creditworthiness*
Now is nat that of God a full fair grace,
That such a lewèd mannès wit shall pass°   *surpass*
The wisdom of a heap of learned men?
Of maistres had he more than thricè ten,
That were of law expert and curious;
Of which there were a dozen in that house,
Worthy to been stewards of rent and land
Of any lord that is in Engèlond,   580
To make him livè by his propre° good,   *own*
In honour debtèless, but° he were wood,*   *unless; mad*
Or live as scarcely as him list desire;
And able for to helpen all a shire
In any case that might fall or hap;°   *chance*
And yet this manciple set hir aller cap.°   *tricked them all*
   The Reeve° was a slender coleric man,   *estate overseer*
His beard was shaved as nigh as ever he can.
His hair was by his ears full round y-shorn;
His top was dockèd like a priest biforn.   590

Full longè were his leggès, and full lean,
Y-like a staff, there was no calf y-seen.
Well couth he keep a gerner and a binnè;°   *granary and a meal bin*
There was no auditor couth on him winnè.°   *outwit*
Well wist he, by the droughth, and by the rain,
The yielding of his seed, and of his grain.
His lordès sheep, his neet,° his dayeryè,*   *cattle; dairy*
His swine, his horse, his stoor,° and his poultryè,   *stock*
Was wholly in this reevès governing,
And by his covenant gave the reckoning,°   *account* 600
Since that his lord was twenty years of age,
There couth no man bring him in arrerage.°   *arrears*
There nas bailif, ne herd,° ne other hynè,*   *shepherd; labourer*
That he ne knew his sleight° and his covynè;*   *duplicity and deceitfulness*
They were adrad° of him, as of the death.   *afraid*
His woning° was full fair upon an heath: *dwelling*
With greenè trees y-shadowed was his place.
He couthè better than his lord purchase.
Full rich he was astorèd privele,°   *privately*
His lord well couth he pleasen subtlely,°   *craftily* 610
To give and lend him of his ownè good,
And have a thank, and yet a coat and hood.°   *(bailiff's perks)*
In youth he learnèd had a good mister;°   *skill*
He was a well good wright, a carpenter.
This reeve sat upon a full good stot,°   *steed*
That was all pomely° grey, and hightè* Scot.   *dappled; named*
A long sur-coat° of pers upon he had,   *over-coat*
And by his side he bore a rusty blade.
Of Norfolk was this reeve of which I tell,
Beside a town men clepèn Baldeswell.   620
Tucked he was, as is a friar, about,°   *he wore his coat tucked up, like a friar*
And ever he rode the hindrest° of our rout.*   *last; company*
    A Summoner° was there with us in that place,   *(from the ecclesiastical court)*
That had a fire-red cherubimès face,
For sawcefleem° he was, with eyen narrow.   *covered with spots*
As hot he was and lecherous as a sparrow;
With scalèd° browès black, and pilèd* beard;   *scaly; moulting*
Of his visagè chldren were a-feared.
There nas quick-silver, litarge, ne brimstone,
Boras, ceruce, ne oil of tartar none,°   *(medicinal cures)* 630
Ne ointèment that wouldè cleanse and bite,°   *disinfect*
That him might helpen of his whelkès° white,   *pimples*
Nor of the knobbès sitting on his cheeks.

Well loved he garlic, onions, and eek leeks,
And for to drinken strong wine, red as blood.
Then would he speak, and cry as he were wood.
And when that he well drunken had the wine,
Than would he speakè no word but Latin.
A fewè termès had he, two or three,
That he had learnèd out of some decree;°   *Latin text* 640
No wonder is, he heard it all the day;
And eek you knowen well, how that a jay
Can clepen 'Watte'° as well as can the pope.   *can say 'Walter'*
But whoso couth in other thing him grope,°   *examine*
Then had he spent all his philosophy;°   *learning*
Aye '*Questio quid juris*'° would he cry.   *'Which point of law?'*
He was a gentle harlot° and a kindè;*   *clown; natural fool*
A better fellow shouldè men not findè.
He wouldè suffer, for a quart of wine,
A good fellow to have his concubine   650
A twelve-month, and excuse him attè full:
Full privèly a finch eek coud he pull.°   *deceive*
And if he found o-where° a good fellow,   *anywhere*
He wouldè teachen him to have none awe,°   *fear*
In such case, of the archèdeacon's curse,
But if a mannès soul were in his purse;
For in his purse he should y-punished be.
'Purse is the archèdeacon's hell,' said he.
But well I woot° he lièd right in deed;   *know*
Of cursing° ought each guilty man him dread, *excommunication* 660
For curse will slay, right as absolving saveth,
And also war him of a *Significavit*.°   *sentence to prison*
In daunger had he at his ownè gise° *he had under his control, as he wished*
The youngè girlès° of the diocese,*   *boys and girls; parish*
And knew their counsel,° and was all their reed.* *secrets; counsellor*
A garland had he set upon his head
As great as it were for an alè-stake;°   *sign denoting a pub*
A buckler had he made him of a cake.°   *loaf of bread*
  With him there rode a genteel Pardoner°   *indulgence-seller*
Of Rounceval, his friend and his compeer,   670
That straight was comen from the court of Rome.
Full loud he sang, 'Com hither, lovè, to me.'
This Summoner bare to him a stiff burdoun,°   *ground melody*
Was never trump of half so great a soun.°   *sound*
This pardoner had hair as yellow as wax,
But smooth it hung, as doth a strike° of flax;   *string*

By ounces° hung his lockès that he haddè,   *strands*
And therewith he his shoulders overspraddè;°   *covered*
But thin it lay, by colpons° one and one;   *strands*
But hood, for jolity,° ne weared he none,   *attractiveness* 680
For it was trussèd up in his wallèt.°   *bag*
Him thought, he rode all of the newè jet;°   *current fashion*
Dishevellè,° save his cap, he rode all bare.   *with uncovered hair*
Such glaring eyen had he as a hare.
A vernicle° had he sewed upon his cap.   *emblem of St Veronica*
His wallet lay biforn him in his lap,
Bretful of° pardon, come from Rome all hot.   *crammed full of*
A voice he had as small as hath a goat.
No beard had he, ne never shouldè have,
As smooth it was as it were late y-shave;   690
I trowe he were a gelding or a mare.
But of his craft, from Berwick unto Ware,
Ne was there such another pardoner.
For in his male° he had a pillow-bear,*   *bag; pillow-case*
Which that, he said, was Ourè Lady° veil: *the Virgin Mary's*
He said, he had a gobet° of the sail   *portion*
That Saintè Peter had, when that he wentè
Upon the sea, till Jesu Christ him hentè.°   *summoned*
He had a cross of latoun° full of stones,   *gold-plate*
And in a glass he haddè piggès bones.   700
But with these relickès, when that he found
A poorè parson dwelling upon lond,°   *in the countryside*
Upon a day, he got him more money
Than that the parson got in monthès twey.°   *two*
And thus, with feignèd flattery and japes,
He made the parson and the people his apes.
But truèly to tellen, attè last,
He was in churchè a noble ecclesiast.
Well couth he read a lesson or a story,
But alderbest° he sang an offertory;   *best of all* 710
For well he wist, when that song was sungè,
He mustè preach, and well affile his tonguè°   *refine his language*
To winnè silver, as he full well coudè;
Therefore he song the merrierly and loudè.

    Now have I told you shortly, in a clause,
Th'estate, th'array, the number, and eek the cause
Why that assembled was this company
In Southwark, at this gentle hostelry,
That hight the Tabard, fastè by the Bell.

But now is timè to you for to tell | 720
How that we baren us that ilke night,
When we were in that hostelry alight.° | *arrived*
And after will I tell of our voyagè,
And all the remnant of our pilgrimagè.
But first I pray you, of your courtesy,
That you n'arette it not° my villainy, | *consider it*
Though that I plainly speak in this matterè,
To tellè you their wordès and their cherè;° | *behaviour*
Ne though I speak their wordès properly.
For this you knowen also well as I, | 730
Whoso shall tell a tale after° a man, | *imitating*
He must rehearse, as nigh as ever he can,
Every each a word, if it be in his charge,
All° speak he never so rudèly and large; | *Even if*
Or elsè he must tell his tale untrue,
Or feignè thing, or findè wordès new.
He may not spare, although he were his brother;
He might as well saye one word as another.
Christ spake himself full broad in holy writ,
And well you woot, no villainy is it. | 740
Eek Plato sayeth, whoso that can him read,
The wordès must be cousin to the deed.
Also I prey you to forgive it me,
All have I not set folk in their degree° | *social order*
Here in this tale, as that they shouldè stand;
My wit is short, ye may well understand.
    Great cheerè made our host us every one,
And to the supper set he us anon;
And served us with victuals at the best.
Strong was the wine, and well to drink us lest.° | *enjoyed* 750
A seemly man our Hostè was withallè
For to han been a marshall in an hallè;
A largè man he was with eyèn steepè,° | *bright*
A fairer burgess is there none in Cheapè:° | *Cheapside (London)*
Bold of his speech, and wise, and well y-taught,
And of manhood him lackèdè right naught.
Eek thereto he was right a merry man,
And after supper playen he began,
And spake of mirth amongès other things,
When that we haddè made our reckonings; | 760
And saidè thus: 'Now, lordings, truèly,
Ye been to me right welcome heartily:

For by my troth, if that I shall not lie,
I saw not this year so merry a company
At once in this herberwè° as is now.   *accommodation*
Fain would I doon you mirthè, wist I how.
And of a mirth I am right now bethought,
To doon you ease, and it shall costè nought.
   'Ye goon to Canterbury; God you speedè,
The blissful martyr quitè° you your medè.*   *requite; reward* 770
And well I woot, as you goon by the way,
Ye shapen° you to tellen and to play;*   *prepare; entertain*
For truely, comfort ne mirth is none
To ridè by the way dumb as a stone;
And therefore will I maken you disport,°   *enjoy*
As I said erst, and do you some comfort.
And if you liketh all by one assent
Now for to standen at my judgèment,
And for to worken as I shall you say,
To-morrow, when you ridèn by the way,   780
Now, by my father soulè that is dead,
But you be merry, I will give you my head!
Hold up your hands, withouten morè speech.'
   Our counsel was not longè for to seche;°   *seek*
Us thought it was nought worth to make it wise,°   *resist*
And granted him withouten more avise,
And bade him say his verdict, as him lestè.
'Lordings,' quoth he, 'now hearkneth for the bestè;
But take it not, I pray you, in disdain;
This is the point, to speaken short and plain,   790
That each of you, to shorten with our way,
In this voyage, shall tellè talès twey,
To Canterbury-ward, I mean it so,
And homeward he shall tellen other two,
Of adventures that whilom° han befall.   *once upon a time*
And which of you that beareth him best of all,
That is to say, that telleth in this case
Tales of best sentencè° and most solace,   *meaning*
Shall have a supper at our aller° cost   *of all of us*
Here in this place, sitting by this post,   800
When that we come again from Canterbury.
And for to makè you the morè merry,
I will my-selven gladly with you ride,
Right at mine ownè cost, and be your guide.
And whoso will my Judgement withsay

Shall pay all that we spenden by the way.
And if you vouchèsafe that it be so,
Tell me anon, with-outen wordès mo,°   *more*
And I will early shapè me therefor.'
   This thing was granted, and our oathès swore   810
With full glad heart, and prayden him also
That he would vouchèsaf for to do so,
And that he wouldè been our governor,
And of our talès judge and reporter,
And set a supper at a certain price;
And we would rulèd been at his device,°   *wish*
In high and low; and thus, by one assent,
We been accordèd to his Judgèment.
And thereupon the wine was fetched anon;
We drunken, and to restè went each one,   820
Withouten any longer tarrying.
   A-morrow, when that day began to spring,
Up rose our host, and was our aller cock,
And gathered us together, all in a flock,
And forth we riden, a little more than pas,°   *slightly faster than a slow walk*
Unto the watering° of Seint Thomas.   *horse trough*
And there our host began his horse arrest,
And said; 'Lordinges, herkneth, if you lest°   *wish*
You woot your forward, and I it you recordè.°   *you recall, and I remind you*
If evensong and morrowsong accordè,°   *agree* 830
Let see now who shall tell the firstè tale.
As ever might I drinkè wine or ale,
Whoso be rebel to my Judgèment
Shall pay for all that by the way is spent.
Now draweth cut,° ere that we further twinnè;*   *draw lots; go*
He whih that hath the shortest shall beginnè.
Sir Knight,' quoth he, 'my master and my lord,
Now draweth cut, for that is mine accord.
Cometh near,' quoth he, 'my lady Prioressè;
And you, Sir Clerk, let be your shamefacednessè,   840
Ne studieth nought; lay hand to, every man.'
Anon to drawèn every wight began,
And shortly for to tellen as it was,
Were it by aventure, or sort, or cas,°   *chance*
The sooth is this, the cut fell to the Knight,
Of which full blithe and glad was every wight;
And tell he must his tale, as was reason,
By forward and by composition,°   *rank and agreement*

As you have heard; what needeth wordès more?
And when this good man saw it was so, 850
As he that wise was and obedient
To keep his forward by his free assent,
He saidè: 'Since I shall begin the game,
What, welcome be the cut, in Goddès name!
Now let us ride, and hearkneth what I say.'
And with that word we riden forth our way
And he began with right a merry cheerè
His tale anon, and said as ye may hearè.

48b. *The Miller's Tale*

Whilom° there was dwelling at Oxenford   *Once upon a time*
A richè knave, that guestès held to board,
And of his craft he was a Carpenter.
With him there was dwelling a poor scholar,   3190
Had learnèd art, but all his fantasy
Was turnèd for to learn astrology,
And couth° a certain of conclusiouns*   *understood; astrological lore*
To demen by interrogations,
If that men askèd him in certain hours,
When that men should have drought or elsè showers,
Or if men askèd him what should befallè
Of every thing, I may not reckon hem allè.
   This clerk was clepèd° hendè* Nicholas;   *called; gracious*
Of dernè° love he couth and of solace;   *secret* 3200
And thereto he was sly and full priveè,°   *secretive*
And like a maiden meekè for to see.
A chamber had he in that hostelry
Alone, withouten any company,
Full fetishly° y-dight* with herbès sweetè;   *elegantly; adorned*
And he himself as sweet as is the rootè
Of licorice, or any cetewalè.°   *gingery-plant*
His Almagest° and bookès great and smallè,   *Ptolemy's treatise on astrology*
His astrolabie, longing for his art,
His augrim-stonès° layen fair apart   *algorithm stones* 3210
On shelves couchèd at his beddès head:
His press y-covered with a falding° red.   *coarse wool cloth*
And all above there lay a gay psaltry,
On which he made a nightès melody
So sweetly, that all the chamber rang;
And *Angelus ad virginem* he sang;

And after that he sang the Kingès Note;
Full often blessèd was his merry throat.
And thus this sweetè clerk his timè spent
After his friendès finding° and his rent.*   *donations; income* 3220
   This Carpenter had wedded new a wife
Which that he lovèd morè than his life;
Of eightè-teenè years she was of agè.
Jealous he was, and held her narrow in cagè,
For she was wild and young, and he was old,
And deemed himself been like a cokewold.°   *cuckold*
He knew not Catoun,° for his wit was   *basic school text (i.e. he was uneducated)*
   rude,
That bad man should wed his similitude.
Men shouldè wedden after their estate,
For youth and eld° is often at debate.   *age* 3230
But since that he was fallen in the snare,
He must endure, as other folk, his care.
   Fair was this youngè wife, and therewithall
As any weasle her body gent° and smal.   *slender*
A ceint° she wearèd barrèd* al of silk,   *belt; striped*
A barmcloth° eek* as white as mornè milk   *apron; also*
Upon her loins, full of many a gore.°   *flounce*
White was her smock, and broidered all before
And eek behind, on her collar aboutè,
Of coal-black silk, within and eek withoutè.   3240
The tapès of her whitè voluper°   *night cap*
Were of the samè suit of her collar;
Her filet° broad of silk, and set full high: *headband*
And sikerly° she had a likerous* eye.   *certainly; lecherous*
Full small y-pullèd were her browès two,
And they were bent and black as any sloe.
She was full more blisfull on to see
Than is the newè pearè-jonette° tree;   *early-fruiting pear*
And softer than the wool is of a wether.°   *sheep*
And by her girdel hung a purse of leather   3250
Tasselled with silk, and pearlèd with latoun.°   *gilding*
In all this world, to seeken up and down,
There is no man so wisè, that could thench°   *imagine*
So gay a popelote° or such a wench.   *doll*
Full brighter was the shining of her hue°
Than in the Tower° the noble* y-forged new.   *mint; coin*
But of her song, it was as loud and yernè°   *yearning*
As any swallow sitting on a barnè.

Thereto she couthè skip and makè gamè,
As any kid or calf following his damè.   3260
Her mouth was sweet as bragot° or the meeth,*   *honey-drink; meed*
Or hoard of apples laid in hay or heath.
Winsing° she was, as is a jolly colt,   *Fickle*
Long as a mast, and upright as a bolt.
A brooch she bare upon her lowè collar,
As broad as is the boss of a buckeler.°   *shield*
Her shoes were lacèd on her leggès high;
She was a primerole,° a piggesnye,*   *primrose; (name of flower)*
For any lord to layen in his bed,
Or yet for any good yeoman to wed.   3270
     Now, sir, and eft,° sire, so befell the case,   *again*
That on a day this hendè Nicholas
Fell with this youngè wife to rage° and playè,   *frolic*
While that her husband was at Osèneyè,
As clerkès been full subtle and full quaint;°   *clever*
And privily he caught her by the queynt°   *exquisite thing (also, pun)*
And said, 'I-wis,° but if* I have my will,   *indeed; unless*
For dernè° love of thee, lemman,* I spill.'‡   *secret; belovèd; die (also, pun)*
And held her hardè by the haunchè-bones,
And saidè, 'Lemman, love me all at once,   3280
Or I will dyen,° also God me save!'   *die*
And she sprang as a colt doth in the
     trave,°   *wooden frame used during shodding*
And with her head she writhèd fast away,
And said, 'I will not kiss thee, by my fey,
Why, let be,' quoth she, 'Let be, Nicholas,
Or I will cry out "harrow"° and "alas."   *help*
Do wey° your handès for your courtesy!'   *take away*
     This Nicholas gan mercy for to cry,
And spoke so fair, and proffered him so fast,
That she her love him granted attè last,   3290
And swore her oath, by Saint Thomas of Kent,
That she would be at his commandèment,
When that she may her leisure well espy.
'My husband is so full of jealousy,
That but you waitè well and been priveè,
I woot° right well I am but dead,' quoth she.   *know*
'You must been full dernè, as in this case.'
     'Nay thereof care thee nought,' quoth Nicholas,
'A clerk had litherly° beset his while,*   *vainly; spent his time*
But-if° he coude a Carpenter biguile.'   *unless* 3300

And thus they been accorded and y-sworn
To wait a time, as I have told beforn.
　　When Nicholas had done thus every deal,
And thakked° her about the loinès well,　　　　　　　　　　*fondled*
He kissed her sweet, and taketh his sautry,°　　　　　　　*psaltery*
And playeth fast, and maketh melody.
　　Then fell it thus, that to the parish-churchè,
Christès ownè workès for to workè,
This goodè wife went on a holiday;
Her forehead shone as bright as any day,　　　　　　　　3310
So was it washen when she left her work.
Now was there of that church a parish-clerk,
The which that was y-cleped° Absalon.　　　　　　　　　*called*
Curled was his hair, and as the gold it shone,
And strouted° as a fannè large and broad;　　　　　　　*spread out*
Full straight and even lay his jolly shode.°　　　　　　　*parting*
His rode° was red, his eyen grey as goose;　　　　　　　*complexion*
With Paulès window carven on his shoes,
In hoses° red he wentè fetishly.*　　　　　　　*stockings; elegantly*
Y-clad he was full small and properly,　　　　　　　　　3320
All in a kirtel° of a light watchet;*　　　　　　　　　*tunic; blue*
Full fair and thickè been the pointès° set.　　　　　　　*laces*
And thereupon he had a gay surplice
As white as is the blossom upon the rys.°　　　　　　　*spray*
A merry child he was, so God me save,
Well couth he letten blood and clip and shave,
And make a charter of land or a quittance.
In twenty manner couth he trip and dance
After the school of Oxenfordè then,
And with his leggès casten to and fro,　　　　　　　　3330
And playen songès on a small rubiblè;°　　　　　　　*rebeck*
There-to he sang some-time a loud quiniblè;°　　　　　　*treble*
And as well couth he play on his giterné.°　　　　　　　*cither*
In all the town nas brewhouse ne taverné
That he ne visited with his solas,°　　　　　　　*entertainment*
There any gaylard° tappester* was.　　　　　　　*jolly; bar-maid*
But sooth to say, he was some deal squaymous°　　*somewhat squeamish*
Of farting, and of speechè daungerous.°　　　　　　　*fastidious*
　　This Absalon, that jolly was and gay,
Goeth with a censer on the holy-day,　　　　　　　　3340
Censing the wivès of the parish fastè;°　　　　　　　*nearby*
And many a lovely look on them he castè,
And namely on this carpenterès wife.

To look on her him thought a merry life,
She was so proprè° and sweet and likerous.   *shapely*
I dare well say, if she had been a mouse,
And he a cat, he would her hent° anon.   *caught*
This parish-clerk, this jolly Absalon,
Hath in his heartè such a love-longing,
That of no wife ne took he none offering;°   *alms* 3350
For courtesy, he said, he woldè none.
    The moon, when it was night, full brightè shone,
And Absalon his gitern hath y-takè,
For paramours° he thoughtè for to wakè.   *with romantic devotion*
And forth he goeth, jolly and amorous,
Till he came to the carpenterès house
A little after cockès had y-crowè;
And dressèd him up by a shot-windowè°   *hinged window*
That was upon the carpenterès wall.
He singeth in his voice gentle and small,   3360
'Now, dearè lady, if thy willè be,
I prayè you that you will rue° on me,'   *have pity*
Full well accordant to his giterning.°   *strumming*
This carpenter awoke, and heard him sing,
And spoke unto his wife, and said anon,
'What! Alison! hearest thou not Absalon
That chanteth thus under our bower's wall?'
And she answered her husband therewithal,
'Yes, God wot, John, I hear it everydeal.'
    This passeth forth; what will you bet than
        well?°   *what more could you want?* 3370
From day to day this jolly Absalon
So wooeth her, that him is woebegone.
He waketh all the night and all the day;
He kembeth° his lockès broad, and made him gay;   *combed*
He wooeth her by meenés° and brocagé,*   *messengers; subterfuge*
And swore he wouldè be her ownè pagè;
He singeth, broking° as a nightingale;   *chirping*
He sends her piment,° mead, and spicèd ale,   *sweet wine*
And wafers,° piping hot out of the gledè;*   *cake; oven*
And for she was of town, he proffered meedè.°   *money* 3380
For some folk will be won for richnessè,
And some for strokes, and some for gentilnessè.
    Sometime, to show his lightness and maistry,°   *savoir-faire*
He playeth Herod on a scaffold° high.   *stage*
But what availeth him as in this case?

She loveth so this hendé Nicholas,
That Absalon may blow the buckés horn;
He ne had for his labour but a scorn;
And thus she maketh Absalon her ape,
And all his earnest turneth to a jape.   3390
Full sooth is this proverb, it is no lie,
Men sayen right thus, 'always the nigh sly
Maketh the farrè lovè to be loathed.'
For though that Absalon be wood° or wroth,   *mad*
Becausè that he far was from her sight,
This nearè Nicholas stood in his light.
    Now bear thee well, thou hendé Nicholas!
For Absalon may wail and sing 'allas'.
And so befell it on a Saturday,
This carpenter was gone to Oseney;   3400
And hende Nicholas and Alison
Accorded been to this conclusion,
That Nicholas shall shapen° him a while   *prepare*
This silly jealous husband to beguile;
And if so be the gamè went aright,
She shouldè sleepen in his arms all night,
For this was his desire and hers also.
And right anon, withouten wordès moe,°   *more*
This Nicholas no longer wouldè tarry,
But doth full softly unto his chamber carry   3410
Both meat and drinkè for a day or twey,°   *two*
And to her husband bade her for to say,
If that he askèd after Nicholas,
She shouldè say she nisté° where he was,   *did not know*
Of all that day she saw him not with eye;
She trowèd that he was in malady,
For for no cry her maidé coud him callè;
He nolde answer for thing that mightè fallè.
    This passeth forth all thilke° Saturday,   *the same*
That Nicholas still in his chamber lay,   3420
And eat and sleep, or didè what him lest,
Till Sunday, that the sunnè goeth to rest.
This silly carpenter hath greet marvel
Of Nicholas, or what thing might him ail,
And said, 'I am afraid, by Saint Thomas,
It standeth not aright with Nicholas.
God shieldè that he diedè suddenly!
This world is now full tikel,° sikerly;   *precarious*

I saw today a corpse y-born to churchè
That now, on Monday last, I saw him workè.   3430
　'Go up,' quoth he unto his knave anon,
'Clap at his door, or knockè with a stoon,
Look how it is, and tell me boldèly.'
　This knave goeth him up full sturdily,
And at the chamber door, while that he stood,
He cried and knockéd as that he were wood:–
'What! how! what do you, Master Nicholay?
How may you sleepen all the longè day?'
　But all for nought, he heardè not a word;
A hole he found, full low upon a board,   3440
There as the cat was wont in for to creepè;
And at that hole he lookèd in full deepè,
And at the last he had of him a sight.
This Nicholas sat gaping ever upright,
As he had kikéd° on the newè moon.   *gazed*
Adown he goeth, and told his master soon
In what array he saw this ilke man.
　This carpenter to blessen him began,
And saidè, 'Help us, Saintè Frideswidè!
A man woot little what him shall betide.   3450
This man is fallè, with his astromy,
In some woodness or in some agony;
I thought ay well how that it shouldè be!
Men should not know of Goddès privitee.
Yes, blessèd be always a lewèd° man,   *unlearned*
That nought but only his believè can!
So ferde another clerk with astronomy;
He walkèd in the fieldès for to prye°   *peer*
Upon the starrès, what there should befall,
Till he was in a marlèpit y-fall;   3460
He saw not that. But yet, by Saint Thomas,
Me rueth sore of hendè Nicholas.
He shall be rated° of his studying,   *berated*
If that I may, by Jesus, heaven's king!
Get me a staff, that I may underspore,°   *see from below*
While that thou, Robin, heavest up the door.
He shall out of his studying, as I guessè' –
And to the chamber door he gan him dressè.
His knave was a strong carl° for the nones,*   *chap; by the way*
And by the hasp he heaved it up at once;   3470
Into the floor the doorè fell anon.

This Nicholas sat ay as still as stone,
And ever gaped upward into the air.
The carpenter wend° he were in despair,   *believed*
And hente° him by the shoulders mightily,   *seized*
And shook him hard, and crièd spitously,°   *plaintively*
'What! Nicholay! what, how! what, look adown!
Awake, and think on Christès passion;
I crouche° thee from elvès and from wightès!*'   *mark with the cross; creatures*
Therewith the nightspell said he anon-rightès   3480
On four halvès° of the house about,   *sides*
And on the threshold of the door without: –
'Jesus Christ, and Saintè Benedite,°   *Benedict*
Bless this house from every wicked wight,   *true*
For nightès verey,° the white *pater-noster*!
Where wentès° thow, Saint Peter's soster?'*   *go; sister*
    And attè last this hendè Nicholas
Gan for to sigh sore, and saidè, 'Alas!
Shall all the world be lost eftsoonès now?'°   *immediately*
    This carpenter answerede, 'What says thou?   3490
What! think on God, as we do, men that swink.°   *labour*
    This Nicholas answeredè, 'Fetch me drink;
And after will I speak in privetee
Of certain thing that toucheth me and thee;
I will tell it none other man, certain.'
    This carpenter goeth down, and com'th again,
And brought of mighty ale a largè quart;
And when that each of them had drunk his part,
This Nicholas his door fastè shuttè,
And down the carpenter by him he settè.   3500
    He saidè, 'John, mine hostè lief and dear,
Thou shalt upon thy trothè swear me here,
That to no wight thou shalt this counsel wreyè;°   *betray*
For it is Christès consel that I sayè,
And if thou tell it man, thou art forlore;°   *doomed*
For this vengeancè thou shalt han therefore,
That if thou wreyè me, thou shalt be wood!'
'Nay, Christ forbade it, for his holy blood!'
Quoth then this silly man, 'I nam no blabber,
No though I say, I nam nat lief to gab.   3510
Say what thou wolt, I shall it never tellè
To child nor wife, by him that harrowed hellè!'
    'Now John,' quoth Nicholas, 'I will not lie;
I have y-found in my astrology,

As I have lookèd in the moonè brightè,
That now, a Monday next, at quarter-nightè,
Shall fall a rain and that so wild and wood,
That half so great was never Noah's flood.
This world,' he said, 'in less than in an hour
Shall all be drowned, so hideous is the shower;   3520
Thus shall mankindè drench and lose their life.'
This carpenter answered, 'alas, my wife!
And shall she drench? alas! my Alison!'
For sorrow of this he fell almost a down,
And said, 'is there no remedy in this case?'
    'Why, yes, for God,' quoth hendè Nicholas,
'If thou wilt worken after lore and reed;°   *learning and advice*
Thou may not worken after thine own head.
For thus sayeth Solomon, that was full truè,
'Work all by counsel, and thou shalt nat ruè.'   3530
And if thou worken wilt by good counsel,
I undertake, withouten mast and sail,
Yet shall I saven her and thee and me.
Has thou not heard how savèd was Noah,
When that our Lord had warnèd him before
That all the world with water should be lorn?'°   *lost*
'Yes,' quoth this carpenter, 'full years ago.'
'Has thou not heard,' quoth Nicholas, 'also
The sorrow of Noah with his fellowshipè,
Ere that he mightè get his wife to shipè?   3540
Him had be lever, I dare well undertake,
At thilkè tyme, than all his wetherès° black,   *sheep*
That she had had a ship herself alone.
And therefore, wost thou what is best to done?
This asketh haste, and of an hasty thing
Men may not preach or maken tarrying.
Anon go get us fast into this inn
A kneading-trough, or else a kimelin,°   *bin for brewing beer*
For each of us, but look that they be large,
In which we might swim as in a barge,   3550
And han thereinn victuals sufficient
But for a day; fye on the remenant!
The water shall aslake° and go away   *abate*
Aboutè prime° upon the nextè day.   *nine in the morning*
But Robin may not wite of this, thy knave,
Ne eek thy maidè Gill I may not save;
Ask not why, for though thou askè me,

I will not tellen Goddès privetee.
Sufficeth thee, but if° thy wittès mad,   *unless*
To han as great a grace as Noe had.   3560
Thy wife shall I well saven, out of doubt,
Go now thy way, and speed thee here-about.
    But when thou hast, for her and thee and me,
Y-geten us these kneading-tubbès three,
Then shalt thou hang them in the roof full high,
That no man of our purveyancè spy.
And when thou thus hast done as I have said,
And hast our victuals fair in them y-laid,
And eek an axe, to smite the cord a two
When that the water cometh, that we may go,   3570
And break an hole on high, upon the gable,
Unto the garden-ward, over the stable,
That we may freely passen forth our way
When that the greatè shower is gone away –
Than shalt thou swim as merry, I undertake,
As doth the whitè duck after her drake.
Then will I clepe, 'How! Alison! how! John!
Be merry, for the flood will pass anon.'
And thou wilt say, 'Hail, master Nicholay!
Good morrow, I see thee well, for it is day.'   3580
And then shall we be lordès all our life
Of all the world, as Noè and his wife
    But of one thing I warnè thee full right:
Be well advised, on that ilke night
That we be entered into shippès board,
That none of us ne speakè not a word,
Nor clap, nor cry, but be in his prayerè;
For it is Goddès ownè hestè° dearè.   *order*
    Thy wife and thou must hangè far a-twin,°   *apart*
For that betwixtè you shall be no sin,   3590
No more in looking than there shall in deed;
This ordinance is said, go, God thee speed!
Tomorrow at night, when men be all asleep,
Into our kneading-tubbès will we creep
And sitten there, abiding Goddès gracè.
Go now thy way, I have no longer spacè
To make of this no longer sermoning.
Men sayeth thus, 'send thee wise, and say no thing;'
Thou art so wise, it needeth thee not teach;
Go, save our life, and that I thee beseech.'   3600

This silly carpenter goeth forth his way.
Full oft he said 'alas' and 'wellaway,'
And to his wife he told his privetee;
And she was war, and knew it bet° than he,   *better*
What all this quaintè° cast was for to say.   *ingenious*
But natheless she feared as she would die,
And said, 'Alas! go forth thy way anon,
Help us to scape, or we be dead each one;
I am thy truè, verray° wedded wife;   *lawfully*
Go, dearè spouse, and help to save our life.'   3610
    Lo! which a great thing is affection!
Men may dien of imagination,
So deepè may impressioun be take.
This silly carpenter beginneth quake;
Him thinketh verrily that he may see
Noès flood come wallowing as the sea
To drenchen Alison, his honey dear.
He weepeth, waileth, maketh sorry cheer,
He sigheth with full many a sorry swogh.°   *groan*
He goeth and getteth him a kneading-trough,   3620
And after that a tub and a kimelin,
And privily he sent them to his inn,
And hung them in the roof in privetee.
His ownè hand he madè ladders three,
To climben by the rungès and the stalks°   *uprights*
Unto the tubbès hanging in the balks,°   *beams*
And them victualèd, both trough and tub,
With bread and cheese, and good ale in a jub,°   *jug*
Sufficing right enough as for a day.
But ere that he had made all this array,   3630
He sent his knave, and eek his wench also,
Upon his need to London for to go.
And on the Monday, when it drew to night,
He shut his door with-outè candle-light,
And dressèd allè thing as it should be.
And shortly, up they climben allè three;
They sitten stillè well a furlong-way.°   *a brief period of time*
    'Now, *Pater-noster*, clom!'° said Nicholay,   *Pray and then be silent*
And 'Clom,' quoth John, and 'Clom,' said Alison.
This carpenter said his devotion,   3640
And still he sit, and biddeth his prayerè,
Awaiting on the rain, if he it hearè.
    The deadè sleep, for weary businessè,

Fell on this carpenter right, as I guessè,
Aboutè curfew-time, or little more;
For travail of his ghost° he groaneth sore,   *spirit*
And eft he routeth,° for his head mislay.   *snores*
Down of the ladder stalketh Nicholay,
And Alison, full soft adown she speddè;
Withouten wordès more, they go to beddè   3650
Thereas the carpenter is wont to lie.
There was the revel and the melody;
And thus lieth Alison and Nicholas,
In business of mirth and of solace,
Till that the bell of laudès° gan to ring,   *early church service*
And friars in the chancel gannè sing.
   This parish-clerk, this amorous Absalon,
That is for love always so woebegone,
Upon the Monday was at Oseney
With company, him to disport and play,   3660
And asked upon case° a cloisterer   *by chance*
Ful prively after John the carpenter;
And he drew him apart out of the churchè,
And said, 'I noot,° I saw him here not workè   *don't know*
Since Saturday; I trow that he be went
For timber, there our abbot hath him sent;
For he is wont for timber for to go,
And dwellen at the grange° a day or two;   *farm*
Or elsè he is at his house, certain;
Where that he be, I can not soothly sayn.'   3670
   This Absalon full jolly was and light,
And thoughtè, 'now is time to wake all night;
For sikirly° I saw him not stirringè   *certainly*
About his door since day began to springè.
   So might I thrive, I shall, at cockès crow,
Full prively knocken at his window
That stands full low upon his bowers wall.
To Alison now will I tellen all
My love-longing, for yet I shall not missè
That at the leastè way I shall her kissè.   3680
Some manner comfort shall I have, parfay,
My mouth hath itchèd all this longè day;
That is a sign of kissing attè leastè.
All night me mette° eke, I was at a feastè.   *dreamed*
Therefore I will go sleep an hour or twey,
And all the night then will I wake and play.'

When that the first cock hath crowed, anon
Up rose this joly lover Absalon,
And him arrayeth gay, at point-devise.°   *in every way*
But first he cheweth grain and licoris,   3690
To smellen sweet, ere he had combed his hair.
Under his tongue a trewè-love° he bear,   *spice*
For thereby wend° he to be gracious.   *intended*
He rometh to the carpenterès house,
And still he stood under the shot-window;
Unto his breast it reached, it was so low;
And soft he cougheth with a semy° sound –   *small*
'What do ye, honeycomb, sweet Alison?
My fairè bride, my sweetè cinamon,
Awaketh, lemman mine, and speaketh to me!   3700
Well little thinken ye upon my woe,
That for your love I swelté there° I go.   *faint wherever*
No wonder is though that I swelt and sweatè;
I mourn as doth a lamb after the teatè.
Y-wis, lemman, I have such love-longing,
That like a turtle° true is my mourning;   *dove*
I may nat eat no morè than a maid.'
    'Go from the window, Jackè fool,' she said,
'As help me God, it will not be *come by me*,°   *come kiss me*
I love another, and else I were to blame,
Well bet° than thee, by Jesu, Absalon!   3710
          better
Go forth thy way, or I will cast a ston,
And let me sleep, a twenty devil way!'
    'Alas,' quoth Absalon, 'and wellaway!
That true love was ever so evil beset!
Then kissè me, since it may be no bet,
For Jesus love and for the love of me.'
    'Wilt thou then go thy way therewith?' quoth she.
    'Yes, certès, lemman,' quoth this Absalon.
    'Then make thee ready,' quoth she, 'I come anon;'   3720
And unto Nicholas she saidè still,
    'Now hush, and thou shalt laughen all thy fill.'
    This Absalon down set him on his knees,
And said, 'I am a lord at all degrees;
For after this I hope there cometh more!
Lemman, thy grace, and sweetè bride, thine ore!'°   *favour*
    The window she undoth, and that in haste,
'Have do,' quoth she, 'come off, and speed thee fast,
Lest that ourè neighbours thee espie.'

This Absalon gan wipe his mouth ful dry;　　　　　　　　3730
Dark was the night as pitch, or as the coal,
And at the window out she put her hole,
And Absalon, him fell no bet ne worse,
But with his mouth he kissed her naked arse
Full savourly, ere he was ware of this.
Aback he stirt,° and thought it was amiss,　　　　　　　*started*
For well he wist a woman hath no beard;
He felt a thing all rough and long y-haired,
And saidè, 'Fie! alas! what have I do?'
　　'Tee hee!' quoth she, and clapped the window to;　　3740
And Absalon goeth forth° a sorry pace.　　　　　　　*steps back*
　　'A beard, a beard!' quoth hendè Nicholas,
'By goddès corpus, this goeth fair and well!'
　　This silly Absalon heard every deal,
And on his lip he gan for anger bite;
And to himself he said, 'I shal thee quite!'°　　　　　*requite*
　　Who rubbeth now, who froteth now his lippès
With dust, with sand, with straw, with cloth, with
　　　　chippès,
But Absalon, that sayeth full oft, 'alas!
My soul betake I unto Satanas,°　　　　　　　　*Satan* 3750
But me were lever than all this town,' quoth he,
'Of this despite awroken° for to be!　　　　　　　*avenged*
Alas!' quoth he, 'alas! I ne haddè y-bleynt!'°　　*turned back*
His hottè love was cold and all y-quent;°　　　　*quenched*
For from that time that he had kissed her arse,
Of paramours he settè not a cress,°　　*symbol of worthlessness*
For he was healèd of his malady;
Full oftè paramours he gan defy,
And weep as doth a child that is y-beatè.
A softè pace he went over the streetè　　　　　　　　3760
Until a smith men clepèd daun Gervais,
That in his forgè smithèd plough-harness;
He sharpens shar and culter° busily.　　　　　　*plough blades*
This Absalon knocketh all easily,
And saidè, 'Undo, Gervais, and that anon.'
　　'What, who art thou?' 'It am I, Absalon.'
'What, Absalon! for Christès sweetè tree,
Why rise ye so rathe,° hey, *benedicite*!　　　　　　　*early*
What aileth you? some gay girl, God it woot,
Hath brought you thus upon the viritoot;°　　*swift movement* 3770
By Saint Note, you woot well what I meanè.'

This Absalon ne roughtè° not a beanè   *cared*
Of all his play, no word again he gave;
He had morè tow on his distaf°   *things to attend to*
Than Gervais knew, and saidè, 'friend so dear,
That hottè coulter° in the chimney here,   *of a plough*
As lend it me, I have therewith to doon,
And I will bring it thee again ful soon.'
    Gervais answered, 'Certès, were it gold,
Or in a pokè° nobles all untold,   *bag* 3780
Thou shouldèst have, as I am truè smith;
Aye, Christès foe! what will you do therewith?'
    'Thereof,' quoth Absalon, 'be as be may,
I shall well tell it thee tomorrow day' –
And caught the culter by the coldè steel.
Full softly out at the door he gan to steal,
And went unto the carpenterès wall.
He cougheth first, and knocketh therewithall
Upon the window, right as he did ere.
    This Alison answerdè, 'Who is there   3790
That knocketh so? I warrant it a thief.'
    'Why, nay,' quoth he, 'God woot, my sweetè lief,°   *dear*
I am thine Absalon, my darèling!
Of gold,' quoth he, 'I have thee brought a ring;
My mother gave it me, so God me save,
Full fine it is, and there to well y-grave;
This will I givè thee, if thou me kissè!'
    This Nicholas was risen for to pissè,
And thought he would amenden° all the japè,   *improve upon*
He should kisse his arse ere that he scapè.   3800
And up the window did he hastily,
And out his arse he putteth prively
Over the buttock, to the haunchè-bone;
And therewith spake this clerk, this Absalon,
'Speak, sweetè bride, I know not where thou art.'
    This Nicholas anon let flee a fart,
As great as it had been a thunder-dent,
That with the stroke he was almost y-blent;°   *blinded*
And he was ready with his iron hot,
And Nicholas amid the arse he smote.   3810
    Off goeth the skin a handè-breadth about,
The hotè coulter burnèd so his tout,°   *buttocks*
And for the smart he wendè for to die.
As he were wood, for woe he gan to cry –

'Help! water! water! help, for Godès heartè!'
This carpenter out of his slumber startè,
And heard one cryen 'water' as he were wood,
And thought, 'Alas! now com'th Nowelis flood!'
He sat him up withouten wordès mo,
And with his axe he smote the cord a-two,   3820
And down goeth all; he found neither to sell,
No bread nor ale, till he came to the sill
Upon the floor; and there aswoon he lay.
   Up start her Alison, and Nicholay,
And crieden 'out' and 'harrow' in the street.
The neighbourès, bothè small and great,
In runnen, for to gazen on this man,
That yet aswoon he lay, both pale and wan;
For with the fall he busten had his arm;
But stand he most unto his ownè harm.   3830
For when he spoke, he was anon borne down
With hendè Nicholas and Alison.
They tolden every man that he was wood,
He was aghast° so of Nowelis flood   *frightened*
Through fantasy, that of his vanity
He had y-bought him kneading-tubbès three,
And had them hangèd in the roof above;
And that he prayèd them, for Goddès love,
To sitten in the roof, *par company*.
   The folk gan laughen at his fantasy;   3840
Into the roof they kiken° and they gape,   *gaze*
And turnèd all his harm unto a jape.
For what so that this carpenter answered,
It was for nought, no man his reason heard.
With oathès great he was so sworn adown,
That he was holden wood in all the town;
For every clerk anonright held with other.
They said, 'the man is wood, my leve brother;'
And every wight gan laughen of this strife.
Thus swivèd° was the carpenterès wife,   *seduced* 3850
For all his keeping and his jealousy;
And Absalon hath kissed her nether eye;
And Nicholas is scalded in the toutè.
This tale is doon, and God save all the routè!°   *company*

48c. *The Wife of Bath's Tale*

In th'oldè dayès of the King Arthour,
Of which that Britons speaken great honour,
All was this land full filled of faièriè.
The elf-queen, with her joly companyè,   *860*
Dancèd full oft in many a green meed;
This was the old opinion, as I read.
I speak of many hundred years ago;
But now can no man see no elvès mo.°   *any more*
For now the greatè charity and prayers
Of limitours° and other holy friars,   *begging friars*
That serchen° every land and every stream,   *frequent*
As thick as motès in the sunnè-beam,
Blessing hallès, chambers, kitchens, bowers,
Cities, boroughs, castles, highè towers,   *870*
Thorpès,° barnès, shipnès,* dayeriès,‡   *Hamlets; stables; dairies*
This maketh that there been no faièriès.
For where as wont° to walken was an elf,   *accustomed*
There walketh now the limitour himself
In undermelès° and in morweningès,*   *before noon; mornings*
And saith his matins and his holy thingès
As he goeth in his limitàciòun.
Women may go now safely up and down,
In every bush, or under every tree;
There is noon other incubus° but he,   *corrupt spirit* 880
And he ne will do them but dishonour.
   And so befell it, that this King Arthour
Had in his house a lusty bachelor,
That on a day came riding from river;
And happened that, alone as he was born,
He saw a maidè walking him biforn,
Of which maid anon, maugree° her heedè,*   *despite; will*
By very force he rafte° her maidenheadè;   *took*
For which oppression° was such clamour   *wrongdoing*
And such pursuit unto the King Arthour,   *890*
That damnèd was this knight for to be dead
By course of law, and should have lost his head –
Paraventure,° such was the statute tho* –   *Perhaps; then*
But that the queen and other ladies mo'°   *more*
So longè preyèden the king of grace,
Till he his life him granted in the place,
And gave him to the queen all at her will,

To choose, whether she would him save or spill.°   *kill*
  The queen thanketh the king with all her might,
And after this thus spake she to the knight,   900
When that she saw her time, upon a day:
'Thou standest yet,' quoth she, 'in such array,
That of thy life yet hast thou no suretee.°   *security*
I grant thee life, if thou canst tellen me
What thing is it that women most desiren?
Beware, and keep thy neckè-bone from iron.
And if thou canst not tellen it anon,
Yet will I give thee leavè for to gone°   *go*
A twelve-month and a day, to seek and lerè°   *discover*
An answer sufficient in this matterè.   910
And suretee will I have, ere that thou pace,
Thy body for to yielden in this place.'
  Woe was this knight and sorrowfully he siketh;°   *sighs*
But what! he may not do all as him liketh.
And at the last, he chose him for to wendè,°   *go*
And come again, right at the yearès endè,
With such answer as God would him purvey;
And tak'th his leave, and wendeth forth his way.
He seeketh every house and every place,
Whereas he hopeth for to findè grace,   920
To learn, what thing women loven most;
But he ne could arriven in no coast
Where as he mightè find in this matterè
Two creatures accordingè in-ferè.°   *who would agree*
Some saidè women loven best richessè,
Some saidè honour, some said jolinessè;
Some rich array, some saidè, lust a-bed,
And oftètime to be widow and wed.
Some saidè that our heartès been most eased
When that we been y-flattered and y-pleased.   930
He goeth full nigh the soth,° I will not lie;   *truth*
A man shall win us best with flattery;
And with attendance and with buisinessè
Been we y-lymèd,° bothè more and lessè.   *caught (limed)*
  And somè seyen that we loven best
For to be free, and do right as us lest,°   *wish*
And that no man reprove us of our vice,
But say that we be wise, and no thing nice.
For truly, there is no one of us allè,
If any wight° will claw us on the gallè,*   *person; irritate us* 940

That we nell° kickè, for he seith us sooth;   *will not*
Assay, and he shall find it that so dooth.
For, be we never so vicious withinnè,
We will be holden° wise, and clean of sinnè.   *considered*
 And somè say, that great delight have we
For to be helden stable and eek° secreè,*   *also; discrete*
And in one purpose steadfastly to dwell,
And not bewrayè° thing that men us tell.   *disclose*
But that tale is not worth a rakè-stelè;° *rake handle (no value)*
Pardee, we women cannè no thing helè;°   *keep quiet* 950
Witness on Myda; will you hear the talè?
 Ovid, amongès other thingès smallè,
Seid, Myda had, under his longè hairs,
Growing upon his head two asses' ears,
The whichè vice he hid, as he best might,
Ful subtilly from every mannès sight,
That, save his wife, there wist° of it no mo.   *knew*
He loved her most, and trusted her also;
He prayèd her, that to no creàture
She shouldè tellen of his disfigure.
 She swore him, 'Nay,' for all this world to win,
She noldè do that villainy or sin,
To make her husband have so foul a name;
She would not tell it for her ownè shame.
But na the less, her thoughtè that she diedè,
That she so longè should a counsel hidè;
Her thought it swelled so sore about her heartè,
That needely some word her must assertè;
And sith she durstè tell it to no man,
Down to a mareys° fastè by she ran;   *marsh* 970
Till she came there, her heartè was a-firè,
And, as a bittern bombleth in the myrè,° *bumbles in the mire*
She laid her mouth unto the water down:
'Betray me not, thou water, with thy sound,'
Quoth she, 'to thee I tell it, and no more;
Mine husband hath long assès erès two!
Now is mine heart all hool, now is it outè;
I might no longer keep it, out of doubtè.'
Here may you see, though we a time abide,
Yet out it must, we can no consel hide;   980
The remnant of the tale if you will hearè,
Read Ovid, and there you may it learè.°   *learn*
 This knight, of which my tale is specially,

When that he saw he might not come thereby,
This is to say, what women lovè most,
Within his breast full sorrowful was the ghost;°   *spirit*
But home he goeth, he might not sojournè.°   *linger*
The day was come, that homeward must he turnè,
And in his way it happened him to ride,
In all this care, under a forest-side,   990
Whereas he saw upon a dancè go
Of ladies four-and-twenty, and yet mo;
Toward the whichè dance he drew full yernè,°   *eagerly*
In hopè that some wisdom should he learnè.
But certainly, ere he came fully there,
Vanished was this dance, he niste° where.   *knew not*
No creàturè saw he that bore life,
Save on the green he saw sitting a wife;°   *woman*
A fouler wight there may no man devise.
Again° the knight this oldè wife gan rise,   *Towards* 1000
And said, 'Sir knight, hereforth ne lieth no way.
Tell me, what that you seeken, by your fey?°   *if you please*
Paraventure it may the better be;
These oldè folk ken muckle° thing,' quoth she.   *many*
   'My leve° mother,' quoth this knight, 'certain,   *dear*
I am but dead, but if that I can sayen
What thing it is that women most desirè;
Could you me wise,° I would well quite your hirè.'* *enlighten; reward you*
   'Plight° me thy troth, here in mine hand,' quoth she, *Pledge*
'The nextè thing that I requirè thee,   1010
Thou shalt it do, if it lie in thy might;
And I will tell it you ere it be night.'
   'Have here my trothè,' quoth the knight, 'I grantè.'
   'Then,' quoth she, 'I dare me well avantè,°   *brag*
Thy life is safe, for I will stand thereby,
Upon my life, the queen will say as I.
Let see which is the proudest of them allè,
That weareth on a coverchief or a callè,°   *caul*
That dare say nay, of that I shall thee teachè;
Let us go forth withouten longer speechè.'   1020
Then rounèd° she a pistel* in his earè,   *whispered; message*
And bade him to be glad, and have no fearè.
   When they be comen to the court, this knight
Said he had hold° his day, as he had hight,*   *kept to; promised*
And ready was his answer, as he said.
Full many a noble wife, and many a maid,

And many a widow, for that they been wisè,
The queen herself sitting as a Justicè,
Assembled been, his answer for to hear;
And afterward this knight was bade appear.   1030
To every wight commanded was silencè,
And that the knight should tell in audiencè
What thing that worldly women loven best.
This knight ne stood not still as doth a beast,
But to his question anon answerdè
With manly voice, that all the court it heardè:
    'My leige lady, generally,' quoth he,
'Women desiren to have sovereignty
As well over their husband as their love,
And for to be in mastery° him above;   control 1040
This is your most desire, though you me kill,
Do as you list,° I am here at your will.'   wish
    In all the court ne was there wife nor maid,
Ne widow, that contraried that he said,
But saiden he was worthy have his life.
And with that word up stirte° the oldè wife,   leapt
Which that the knight saw sitting in the greenè:
'Mercy,' quoth she, 'my sovereign lady queenè!
Ere that your court departè, do me right.
I taught this answerè unto the knight;   1050
For which he plighted me his trothè there,
The first thing that I would of him require,
He would it do, if it lay in his might.
Before the court then pray I thee, Sir knight,'
Quoth she, 'that thou me take unto thy wife;
For well thou wost° that I have kept thy life.   you know
If I say false, say nay, upon thy fey!'
    This knight answerd, 'Alas! and wellaway!
I woot right well that such was my behestè.
For Goddès love, as choose a new requestè;   1060
Take all my good, and let my body go.'
    'Now then,' quoth she, 'I shrew° us bothè two!   curse
For though that I be foul, and old, and poorè,
I noldè for all the metal, nor for orè,
That under earth is grave, or lieth above,
But if thy wife I were, and eek thy love.'
    'My love?' quoth he; 'nay, my damnation!
Alas! that any of my nation
Should everè so foul disparaged be!'

But all for nought, the end is this, that he   1070
Constrainèd was, he needès must her weddè;
And taketh his old wife, and go to beddè.
   Now woulden° some men say, paraventure,   *would*
That, for my negligence, I do no cure
To tellen you the joy and all th' array
That at the feastè was that ilkè day.
To which thing shortly answerè I shall;
I say, there nas no Joy nor feast at all,
There nas but heaviness and muchè sorrow;
For prively° he wedded her on the morrow,   *secretly* 1080
And all day after hid him as an owl;
So woe was him, his wife lookèd so foul.
Great was the woe the knight had in his thoughts,
When he was with his wife a-bed y-brought;
He waileth, and he turneth to and fro.
His oldè wife lay smiling evermo',
And said, 'O dear husband, *benedicite*!
Fareth every knight thus with his wife as ye?
Is this the law of King Arthurès house?
Is every knight of his so dangerous?°   *disdainful* 1090
I am your ownè love and eek your wife;
I am she, who savèd hath your life;
And certes, yet ne did I you never unright;
Why fare you thus with me this firstè night?
You faren° like a man had lost his wit;   *behave*
What is my guilt? For Gods love, tell me it,
And it shall be amended, if I may.'
   'Amended?' quoth this knight, 'alas! nay, nay!
It will not be amended never more!
Thou art so loathly,° and so old also,   *hideous* 1100
And thereto comen of so low a kindè,
That little wonder is, though I wail and windè.°   *writhe*
So wouldè God mine heartè wouldè burstè!'
   'Is this,' quoth she, 'the cause of your unrestè?'
   'Yes, certainly,' quoth he, 'no wonder is.'
   'Now, sir,' quoth she, 'I could amend all this,
If that me list, ere it were dayès three,
So well you mightè bear you unto me.
   'But, for you speaken of such gentillessè°   *nobility*
As is descended out of old richessè,   1110
That therefore shoulden ye be gentlemen,
Such arrogancè is not worth an hen.°   *anything*

Look who that is most virtuous always,
Privee and apart, and most intendeth ay
To do the gentle deedès that he can;
Take him for the greatest gentleman.
Christ wol,° we claim of him our gentilessè,   *commanded*
Not of our elders for their old richessè.
For though they gave us all their heritagè,
For which we claim to be of high paragè,°   *parentage* 1120
Yet may they not bequeathè, for no thing,
To none of us their virtuous living,
That made them gentlemen y-callèd be;
And bade us followen them in such degree.
   'Well can the wise poetè of Florence,
That hightè Dante, speak in this sentence;°   *meaning*
Lo, in such manner rhyme is Dante's talè:
'Ful seld° upriseth by his branches smalè   *seldom*
Prowess of man, for God, of his goodnessè,
Wol that of Him we claim our gentillessè;'   1130
For of our elders may we no thing claim
But temporal thing, that man may hurt and maim.
   'Eek every wight wot this as well as I,
If gentilless were planted naturally
Unto a certain lineage down the linè,
Privy and apart, than would they never finè°   *cease*
To do of gentilless the faire officè;
They mightè do no villainy or vicè.
   'Take fire, and bear it in the darkest house
Betwixt this and the mount of Caucasus,   1140
And let men shut the doorès and go then;°   *thence*
Yet will the fire as fair lie and bren,°   *burn*
As twenty thousand men might it beholdè;
His office natural ay will it holdè,
Up° peril of my life, till that it die.   *Upon*
   'Here may you see well how that genterye°   *gentility*
Is not annexèd to possession,
Since folk ne doon their operation
Always, as doth the fire, lo, in his kind.°   *nature*
For, God it woot, men may well often find   1150
A lordès son do shame and villainyè;
And he that will have prize of his gentryè
For he was borèn of a genteel house,
And had his elders noble and virtuous,
And nill° him-selven do no gentle deedès,   *will not*

Nor follow his genteel ancestors that dead is
He nis not genteel, be he duke or earl;
For villains' sinful deedès make a churl.
For gentillessè nis but renomee°   *renown*
Of thine ancestors, for their high bounty,   1160
Which is a strangè thing to thy person;
Thy gentillesse cometh from God alone;
Thence cometh our verray gentillesse of grace,
It was no thing bequeathed us with our place.
    'Thinketh how noble, as sayeth Valerius,
Was the ilke° Tullius Hostilius,   *same*
That out of poverty rose to high nobless.
Readeth Senec,° and readeth eek Boèce,*   *Seneca; Boethius*
There shall you seen express that it no dread is,
That he is genteel that doth genteel deedès;   1170
And therefore, leve° husband, I thus conclude,   *beloved*
All were it that° mine ancestors were rude,   *although*
Yet may the highè God, and so hope I,
Grant me grace to liven virtuously.
Then am I genteel, when that I beginnè
To liven virtuously and waivè sinnè.
    'And thereas you of poverty me reprovè,
The highè God, in whom that we believè,
In wilful poverty chose to live his life.
And certes every man, maiden, or wife,   1180
May understand that Jesus, heaven's King,
Ne would not choose a vicious living.
Glad poverty is an honest thing, certain;
This will Senec and other clerkès seyen.
Whoso that holds him paid of his povertyè,
I hold him rich, al° had he not a shirtè.   *even if*
He that coveteth is a povrè° wight,   *poor*
For he would han° that is not in his might.   *have*
But he that nought hath, ne coveteth to have,
Is rich, although you hold him but a knave.   1190
Verray° poverty, it singeth properly;   *True*
Juvenal sayeth of poverty merrily:
"The povre man, when he goeth by the wayè,
Before the thieves he may sing and pleyè."
Poverty is hateful good and, as I guessè,
A full great bringer out of businessè;
A great ammender eek of sapience°   *wisdom*
To him that taketh it in patience.

Poverty is this, although it seem alenge:°   *wretched*
Possession, that no wight will challenge.°   *claim* 1200
Poverty full oft, when a man is low,
Maketh his God and eek himself to know.
Poverty a spectacle is, as thinketh me,
Through which he may his verray friendes see.
And therefore, sire, since that I nought you grieve,
Of my poverty no more you me reprove.
Now, sire, of elde° you reprovè me;   *old age*
And certès, sir, though none authority
Were in no book, you genteels of honour
Say that men should an old wight do favour,   1210
And clepe° him father, for your gentillessè;   *call*
And authors shall I finden, as I guessè.
 'Now there you say that I am foul and old,
Then dread you not to be a cokèwold;°   *cuckold*
For filth and eldè, also moot I thee,°   *in truth*
Been greatè wardens upon chastity.
But nathe less, since I knowè your delight,
I shall fulfill your worldly appetite.
 'Choose now,' quoth she, 'one of these thingès tweyè:
To have me foul and old till that I diè,   1220
And be to you a truè humble wife,
And never you displease in all my life,
Or elsè you will have me young and fair,
And take your aventure° of the repair*   *chance; visitor*
That shall be to your house, because of me,
Or in some other placè, may well be.
Now choose yourselven, whether° that you liketh.' *whichever*
 This knight adviseth him° and sore siketh,* *considers; sighs*
But attè last he said in this mannerè,
'My lady and my love, and wife so dearè,   1230
I put me in your wisè governance;
Chooseth yourself, which may be most pleasance,
And most honour to you and me also.
I do no fors° the whether of the two;   *care*
For as you liketh, it sufficeth me.'
 'Then have I got of you mastery,' quoth she,
'Since I may choose, and govern as me lest?'
 'Yes, certes, wife,' quoth he, 'I hold it best.'
 'Kiss me,' quoth she, 'we be no longer wrothè;° *angry*
For, by my troth, I will be to you bothè,   1240
This is to say, yea, both fair and good.

I prey to God that I might sterven wood,°   *die crazy*
But I to you be also good and true
As ever was wife, since that the world was new.
And, but I be tomorn° as fair to seen   *tomorrow*
As any lady, emperess, or queen,
That is betwixt the east and eke the west,
Do with my life and death right as you lest.
Cast up the curtain, look how that it is.'
   And when the knight saw verrily all this,   1250
That she so fair was, and so young thereto,
For joy he hent her in his armès two,
His heartè bathed in a bath of blissè;
A thousand time a-rewe° he gan her kissè.   *in a row*
And she obeyèd him in every thing
That might do him pleasance or liking.
   And thus they live, unto their livè's endè,
In perfect joy; and Jesus Christ us sendè
Husbands meek, young, and fressh a-bed,
And grace t'overbide° them that we wed.   *outlive* 1260
And eek I prayè Jesu short their lives
That will not be governèd by their wives;
And old and angry nigards of dispence,
God send them soonè verray pestilence.

48d. *The Nun's Priest's Tale, of the Cock and Hen, Chauntecleer and Pertelote.*

A poorè widow, somdel° steep in agè,   *somewhat*
Was whilom° dwelling in a narwe* cottagè,   *once upon a time; narrow*
Beside a grovè, standing in a dale.
This widow, of which I tellè you my tale,
Since th'ilkè° day that she was last a wife,   *the very*
In patience led a fullè simple life,
For little was her catel° and her rentè;*   *property; income*
By husbandry,° of such as God her sentè,   *careful management*
She found herself, and eek° her daught'ren two.   *also*
Three largè sowès had she, and no mo',   4020
Three kine,° and eek a sheep that hightè* Mallè.   *cattle; named*
Full sooty° was her bower, and eek her hallè,   *sweet*
In which she ate full many a slender meal.
Of poignant° sauce her needed never a deal.   *spiced*
No dainty morsel passèd through hir throat;
Her diet was accordant to her coat.

Repletion° ne made her never sick; *Overeating*
A tempered diet was all her physic,° *medicine*
And exercise, and heartès suffisancè.
The gout lette° her nothing for to dancè, *stopped* 4030
N'apoplexy shentè° not her head; *harmed*
No wine ne drank she, neither white nor red;
Her board° was servèd most with white and black, *table*
Milk and brown bread, in which she found no lack,
Seynd° bacon, and sometimes an eye* or tweyè, *smoked; egg*
For she was, as it were, a manner deyè.° *a kind of dairywoman*
    A yard she had, enclosèd all about
With stickès, and a dryè ditch without,
In which she had a cock, hight Chauntecleer,
In all the land, of crowing nas° his peer. *there was not* 4040
His voice was merrier than the merry organ
On massè-days that in the churchè gone;
Well sikerer° was his crowing in his loggè,* *more accurate; lodging*
Than is a clocke, or an abbey orloggè.
By nature knew he each ascencion
Of the equinoxial in th'ilke town;
For when degrees fifteen weren ascended,
Then crew he, that it might not be amended.
His comb was redder than the fine coral,
And battailed,° as it were a castle-wall. *crenelated* 4050
His bill was black, and as the jet it shone;
Like azure were his leggès, and his toon;° *toes*
His nailès whiter than the lily flower,
And like the burnèd gold was his colour.
This genteel cock had in his governance
Seven hens, for to do all his pleasance,
Which were his sisters and his paramours,
And wonder like to him, as of colours.
Of which the fairest hueèd° on her throat
Was cleped° fair damosel* Pertelote. *named; miss* 4060
Courteous she was, discreet, and debonaire,
And compainable,° and bore herself so fair, *companionable*
Sin thilke day that she was seven night old,
That truèly she hath the heart in hold
Of Chauntecleer, locken in every limb;
He loved her so that well was him therewith.
But such a joy was it to hear them sing,
Whan that the brightè sunnè gan to spring,
In sweet accord, 'My lief is faren in londè.'° *my love is gone to the country*

For th'ilkè time,° as I have understoodè,   *at that time* 4070
Beastès and birdès couthè speak and sing.
   And so befell, that in a dawèning,
As Chauntecleer among his wivès allè
Sat on his perchè, that was in the hallè,
And next him sat this fairè Pertelotè,
This Chauntecleer gan groanen in his throatè,
As man that in his dream is drecched° sore.   *troubled*
And when that Pertelote thus heard him roar,
She was aghast, and said, 'O heartè dearè,
What aileth you, to groan in this mannerè?   4080
You be a verray sleeper, fie for shame!'
   And he answered and saidè thus, 'Madame,
I pray you, that you take it not a-grief:
By God, me mette° I was in such mischief   *dreamed*
Right now, that yet mine heart is sore afright.
Now God,' quoth he, 'my sweven° reck* aright,   *dream; interpret*
And keep my body out of foul prison!
Me mette, how that I roamèd up and down
Within our yard, whereas I saw a beastè,
Was like a hound, and would han° made arrestè   *have* 4090
Upon my body, and would han had me dead.
His colour was betwixtè yellow and red;
And tippèd was his tail, and both his ears,
With black, unlike the remnant of his hairs;
His snoutè small, with glowing eyèn tweyè.
Yet of his look for feare almost I diè;
This causèd me my groaning, doubtèless.'
   'Avoy!'° quoth she, 'fie on you, heartèless!   *Shame!*
Alas!' quoth she, 'for, by that God above,
Now han you lost mine heart and all my love;   4100
I can not love a coward, by my faith.
For certes,° what so any woman sayeth,   *certainly*
We all desiren, if it mightè be,
To han husbandès hardy,° wise, and free,*   *brave; generous*
And secreè,° and no niggard, nor no fool,   *judicious*
Nor him that is aghast of every tool,°   *weapon*
Nor none avauntour,° by that God abovè!   *braggart*
How durst you sayen, for shame, unto your lovè,
That any thing might makè you afeard?
Have ye no manès heart, and han a beard?   4110
Alas! and can you be aghast of swevenès?
Nothing, God wot,° but vanity, in sweven is.   *knows*

Swevenès engendrèn° of repletions,   *are produced by*
And oft of fumè, and of complexions,°   *mixture of humours*
When humours been too abundant in a wight.
Certes this dream, which you have met tonight,
Cometh of the great superfluity
Of yourè redè *colera*,° pardee,   *choler*
Which causeth folk to dreaden in their dreamès
Of arrows, and of fire with redè lemès,°   *flames* 4120
Of greatè beastès, that they will them bite,
Of conflict, and of whelpès great and lite;°   *small*
Right as the humour of melancholiè
Causeth full many a man, in sleep, to cryè,
For feare of blackè bears, or bullès black,
Or elsè, blackè devils will them take.
Of other humours could I tell also,
That worken many a man in sleep full woe;
But I will pass as lightly as I can.
    'Lo Cato, which that was so wise a man,   4130
Said he not thus, ne do no fors of° dreams?   *attach no power to*
Now, sir,' quoth she, 'when we fly from the beams,
For Goddès love, as take some laxitifè;
Up° peril of my soul, and of my lifè,   *upon*
I counsel you the best, I will not lie,
That both of choler and of melancholy
You purge you; and for you shall not tarry,
Though in this town is no apothecary,
I shall myself to herbès teachèn you,
That shall be for your health, and for your prow;°   *benefit* 4140
And in our yerd those herbès shall I findè,
The which han of their property, by kindè,
To purgen you beneath, and eek above.
Forget not this, for Goddès ownè love!
You been full choleric of complexion.
Warè° the sun in his ascencion   *Ware*
Ne findè you not replete of humours hotè;
And if it do, I dare well laye a grotè,°   *small coin*
That you shall have a fever tercianè,°   *every third day*
Or an ague, that may be yourè banè.   4150
A day or two you shall have digestives
Of wormès, ere you take your laxatives,
Of lauriol, centaur, and fumetere,
Or else of hellebore, that groweth there,
Of catapuce, or of gaitrès berries,

Of herb ivy,° growing in our yard, there merry* is;   *(various herbs); gay*
Peck them up right as they grow, and eat them in.
Be merry, husband, for your fathers kin!
Dreadeth no dream; I can say you no-more.'
    'Madame,' quoth he, 'grant mercy of your lore.   4160
But ne'er the less, as touching daun Catoun,°   *lord Cato*
That hath of wisdom such a great renown,
Though that he bade no dreamès for to dradè,
By God, men may in oldè bookès readè
Of many a man, more of authority
Than ever Cato was, so moot I thee,°   *so may I prosper*
That all the reverse sayen of this sentence,°   *meaning*
And han well founden by experience,
That dreamès be significations,
As well of joy as tribulations   4170
That folk enduren in this life present.
There needeth make of this no argument;
The very proofè showeth it in deedè.
    'One of the greatest authors that men readè
Sayeth thus, that whilom two fellowès wentè
On pilgrimage, in a full good intentè;
And happèd so, they come into a town,
Whereas there was such congregation
Of people, and eek so streit of herbergage,°   *short of places to stay*
That they ne found as much as one cottage,   4180
In which they bothè might y-lodgèd be.
Wherfore they musten, of necessity,
As for that night, departen company;
And each of them goeth to his hostelry,
And took his lodging as it wouldè fallè.
That one of them was lodgèd in a stallè,
Far in a yard, with oxen of the plough;
That other man was lodgèd well enow,°   *enough*
As was his aventure,° or his fortune,   *fate*
That us governeth all as in commune.   4190
And so befell, that, long ere it were day,
This man mette° in his bed, thereas he lay,   *dreamed*
How that his fellow gan upon him call,
And said, "Alas! for in an oxès stall
This night I shall be murdred where I liè.
Now help me, dearè brother, ere I diè;
In allè hastè come to me," he saidè.
This man out of his sleep for fear abraydè;°   *woke up*

But when that he was waknèd of his sleepè,
He turnèd him, and took of this no keepè;°   *no notice* 4200
Him thought his dream nas° but a vanity.   *was nothing*
Thus twicè in his sleeping dreamèd he.
And attè thirdè time yet his fellow
Came, as him thought, and saide, "I am now slain;
Behold my bloody woundès, deep and wide!
Arise up early in the morrow-tide,
And at the west gate of the town," quoth he,
"A cartè full of dung there shall you see,
In which my body is hid full privèly;
Do thilkè cartè arresten boldèly.   4210
My gold causèd my murder, sooth to sayn;"
And told him every point how he was slain,
With a full piteous facè, pale of hue.
And trustè well, his dream he found full true;
For on the morrow, as soon as it was day,
To his fellow's inn he took the way;
And when that he came to this oxès stallè,
After his fellow he began to callè.
    'The hosteler answerèd him anon,
And saidè, "Sire, your fellow is agone,   4220
As soone as day he went out of the town."
    'This man gan fallen in suspicion,
Remembering on his dreamès that he mettè,
And forth he goeth, no longer would he lettè,
Unto the west gate of the town, and found
A dung-cart, went as it were to dung land,
That was arrayèd in the samè wise
As you have heard the deadè man devise;
And with an hardy heart he gan to cry
Vengeaunce and justice of this felony: –   4230
"My fellow murdered is this samè night,
And in this cart he lieth gaping upright.
I cry out on the ministers," quoth he,
"That shouldèn keep and rulen this city;
Harrow!° allas! here lieth my fellow slain!"   *Help!*
What should I more unto this talè sayen?
The people out stert and cast the cart to ground,
And in the middle of the dung they found
The deadè man, that murdered was all newè.
    'O blissful God, that art so just and truè!   4240
Lo, how that thou bewrayest° murder always!   *betray*

Murder will out, that see we day by day.
Murder is so wlatsom° and abominable   *foul*
To God, that is so just and reasonable,
That he ne will not suffer it helèd° be;   *hidden*
Though it abide a year, or two, or three,
Murder will out, this my conclusion.
And right anon, ministers of that town
Han hent° the carter, and so sore him pained,   *apprehended*
And eek the hostiler so sore engyned,°   *tortured* 4250
That they biknewe° their wickedness anon,   *uncovered*
And were an-hanged by the neckè bone.
    'Here may men see that dreamès been to dread.
And certes, in the samè book I read,
Right in the nextè chapter after this,
(I gabbè° not, so have I joy or bliss,)   *lie*
Two men that would have passèd over sea,
For certain cause, into a far country,
If that the wind ne had been contrary,
That made them in a city for to tarry,   4260
That stood full merry upon an haven sidè.°   *port side*
But on a day, again the eventidè,
The wind gan change, and blew right as them lestè.
Jolly and glad they went unto their restè,
And casten them full early for to sail;
But to that one man fell a great marvel.
That one of them, in sleeping as he lay,
Him mette a wonder dream, again the day.
Him thought a man stood by his beddès side,
And him commanded, that he should abide,   4270
And saidè him thus, "If thou to-morrow wendè,
Thou shalt be dreynt;° my tale is at an endè."   *drowned*
He woke, and told his fellow what he mettè,
And prayèd him his voyage for to lettè;°   *abandon*
As for that day, he prayed him to abide.
His fellow, that lay by his beddès side,
Gan for to laugh, and scorned him fullè fastè.
"No dream," quoth he, "may so mine heart aghastè,
That I will lettè for to do my things.
I settè not a straw by thy dreamings,   4280
For swevens be but vanities and japes.
Men dream all-day of owlès or of apes,
And eke of many a mazè therewithal;
Men dream of thing that never was ne shall.

But since I see that thou wilt here abide,
And thus forslothen° willfully thy tide,   *wasted*
God wot it ruèth me; and have good day."
And thus he took his leave, and went his way.
But ere that he had half his course y-sailed,
Noot I not why, nor what mischance it ailed,   4290
But casually° the shippès bottom rent,   *by fate*
And ship and man under the water went
In sight of other shippès it beside,
That with them sailèd at the samè tide.
And therefore, fairè Pertelote so dear,
By such examples oldè mayest thou lere,°   *learn*
That no man shouldè be too reckèless
Of dreamès, for I say thee, doubtèless,
That many a dream full sore is for to dread.
    'Lo, in the life of Saint Kenelm, I read,   4300
That was Kenulphus son, the noble king
Of Mercenrike,° how Kenelm mette a thing;   *Mercia*
A lit ere° he was murdèred, on a day,   *little before*
His murder in his avision° he saw.   *dream*
His norice° him expounded* every deal   *nurse; explained*
His sweven, and bade him for to keep him well
For treason; but he was but seven years old,
And therefore little talè hath he told°   *he took little notice*
Of any dream, so holy was his heartè.
By God, I haddè lever° than my shirtè   *rather* 4310
That you had read his legend, as have I.
    'Dame Pertelote, I say you truèly,
Macrobius, that writ the avision
In Africa of the worthy Scipion,
Affirmeth dreams, and sayeth that they been
Warning of thingès that men after seen.
And furthermore, I pray you, looketh well
In the Oldè Testament, of Daniel,
If he held dreamès any vanity.
Read eek of Joseph, and there shall you see   4320
Where dreamès be sometime (I say nat allè°)   *always*
Warning of thingès that shall after fallè.
Look of Egypt the King, daun Pharao,
His baker and his buttèler also,
Where° they ne feltè none effect* in dreamès.   *Whether; significance*
Whoso will seeken acts of sundry reamès,°   *realms*
May read of dreams many a wonder thing.

Lo Croesus, which that was of Lydia king,
Mettè he not that he sat upon a tree,
Which signified he should anhangèd be?   4330
Lo here Andromachè, Hectorès wife,
That day that Hector shouldè lose his life,
She dreamèd on the samè night beforn,
How that the life of Hector should be lorn,
If thilke day he went into bataille;°   *battle*
She warnèd him, but it might not avail;
He wentè for to fightè ne'er the less,
But he was slain anon of° Achilles.   *by*
But th'ilke talke is all too long to tell,
And eek it is nigh day, I may not dwell.   4340
Shortly I say, as for conclusion,
That I shall have of this avision
Adversity; and I say furthermore,
That I ne tell of laxitives no store,°   *use*
For they been venomous, I woot it well;
I them defy, I love them never a deal.
   'Now let us speak of mirth, and stint° all this;   *stop*
Madame Pertelote, so have I bliss,
Of one thing God hath sent me largè grace;
For when I see the beauty of your face,   4350
You be so scarlet-red about your eyèn,
It maketh all my dreadè for to dièn;
For, also siker as *In pricipio*,
Mulier est hominis confusio;°   *'From the first, woman is man's undoing'*
Madame, the sentence of this Latin is –
Woman is mannès Joye and all his bliss.
For whan I feel a-night on your softè sidè,
Albeit that I may not on you ridè,
For that our perch is made so narrow, alas!
I am so full of joy and of solace   4360
That I defyè both sweven and dream.'
   And with that word he flew down from the beam,
For it was day, and eek his hennès allè;
And with a cluck he gan them for to callè,
For he had found a corn, lay in the yard.
Royal he was, he was no more afeard;
He feathered° Pertelotè twenty time,   *enfolded her in his wings*
And trad° her eek as oft, ere it was prime.   *stepped (mated)*
He looketh as it were a grim leoun;°   *lion*
And on his toes he roameth up and down;   4370

Him deignèd not to set his foot to ground.
He clucketh, when he hat a corn y-found,
And to him runnen then his wivès allè.
Thus royal, as a prince is in his hallè,
Leave I this Chauntecleer in his pasture;
And after will I tell his adventure.
  When that the month in which the world began,
That hightè March, when God first maked man,
Was complete, and y-passèd were also,
Since March began, thirty days and two,°   *(i.e., April 1)* 4380
Befell that Chauntecleer, in all his pride,
His seven wivès walking by his side,
Cast up his eyen to the brightè sunnè,
That in the sign of Taurus had y-runnè
Twenty degrees and one, and somewhat more;
And knew by kind, and by none other lore,
That it was prime, and crew with blissful steven.°   *voice*
'The sun,' he said, 'is climben up on heaven
Forty degrees and one, and more, y-wis.°   *indeed*
Madame Pertelote, my worldès bliss,   4390
Harkneth these blissful birdès how they singè,
And see the freshè flowers how they springè;
Full is mine heart of revel and solace.'
But suddenly him fell a sorrowful cas;°   *situation*
For ever the latter end of joy is woe.
God woot that worldly joy is soon ago;
And if a rhetor° coudè fair endite,   *public speaker*
He in a cronique° safely might it wrete,   *chronicle*
As for a sovereign notability.°   *significant fact*
Now every wise man, let him herknè° me;   *listen to* 4400
This story is also true, I undertake,
As is the book of Lancelot de Lake,
That women hold in full great reverence.
Now will I turn again to my sentence.
  A col-fox,° full of sly iniquity,   *fox with black tips*
That in the grove had wonèd° yearès three,   *lived*
By high imaginatiòn forecast,
The samè night throughout the hedges burst
Into the yard, where Chauntecleer the fair
Was wont, and eek his wivès, to repair;   4410
And in a bed of wortes° still he lay,   *cabbages*
Till it was passed undern° of the day,   *dawning*
Waiting his time on Chauntecleer to fallè,

As gladly done these homicidès allè,
That in await lyèn to murder men.
O falsè murderer, lurking in thy den!
O new Iscariot, newè Ganelon!
Falsè dissimilour,° O Greek Synon,   *deceiver*
That broughtest Troy all utterly to sorrow!
O Chauntecleer, accursed be that morrow,   4420
That thou into that yard flewè from the beams!
Thou were full well y-warned by thy dreams,
That thilke day was perilous to thee.
But what that God forewoot° must needè be,   *foreknew*
After the opinion of certain clerkis.
Witness on him that any parfit clerk is,
That in school is great altercation
In this matter, and great disputision,°   *debate*
And hath been of an hundred thousand men.
But I ne can not bolte it to the bren,°   *separate true from false* 4430
As can the holy doctor Augustine,
Or Boece,° or the bishop Bradwardyne,   *Boethius*
Whether that Goddès worthy forwitting
Straineth me needly for to doon a thing,
'Needely' clepe I simple necessity;
Or elles,° if free choice be granted me   *else*
To do that samè thing, or do it nought,
Though God forwoot it, ere that it was wroght;°   *done*
Or if his witting° straineth never a deal   *foreknowledge*
But by necessity conditional.   4440
I will not han to do of such materè;
My tale is of a cock, as you may hearè,
That took his counsel of his wife, with sorrow,
To walken in the yard upon that morrow
That he had met the dream, that I you toldè.
Womenès counsels been full oftè coldè;
Womenès counsel brought us first to woe,
And made Adam from Paradise to go,
Thereas he was full merry, and well at ease.
But for I noot, to whom it might displease,   4450
If I counsel of women wouldè blame,
Pass over, for I said it in my game.
Read authors, where they treat of such materè,
And what they say of women you may hearè.
This be the cockès wordès, and not mine;
I can noon harm of no woman divine.

Fair in the sand, to bathe her merrily,
Lieth Pertelote, and all her sisters by,
Against the sun; and Chauntecleer so free
Sang merrier than the mermaid in the sea;   4460
For Phisiologus sayeth sikerly,
How that they singen well and merrily.
And so befell that, as he cast his eyè,
Among the wortès, on a butterflyè,
He was ware of this fox that lay full low.
Nothing ne listè him then for to crow,
But cried anon, 'cock, cock,' and up he startè,
As man that was affraid in his heartè.
For naturally a beast desireth flee
From his contrary,° if he may it see,   *opposite* 4470
Though he ne'er erst had seen it with his eyè.
    This Chauntecleer, when he gan him espyè,
He would have fled, but that the fox anon
Said, 'Genteel sire, alas! where will ye go?
Be you afraid of me that am your friend?
Now certes, I were worsè than a fiend
If I to you would harm or villainyè.
I am not come your counsel for to spyè;
But truèly, the cause of my comingè
Was only for to herkne how that you singè.   4480
For truèly you have as merry a stevene°   *voice*
As any angel hath, that is in heaven;
Therewith you han in music more feelingè
Than had Boece, or any that can singè.
My lord your father (God his soulè bless!)
And eek your mother, of her gentleness,
Have in mine house y-been, to my great easè;
And certès, sire, full fain would I you pleasè.
But, for men speak of singing, I will say
So might I broukè° well mine eyèn twey,   *enjoy* 4490
Save you, I heardè never man so singè,
As did your father in the morèningè;
Certes, it was of heartè, all that he sangè.
And for to make his voicè the more strongè,
He would so pain him, that with both his eyèn
He mustè wink,° so loud he wouldè cryèn,   *blink*
And standen on his tiptoes therewithall,
And stretchè forth his neckè long and small.
And eek he was of such discretion,

That there nas no man in no region 4500
That him in song or wisdom mightè passè.
I have well read in "Daun Burnel the Assè",
Among his verse, how that there was a cockè,
For that a priestès son gave him a knockè
Upon his leg, while he was young and nice,
He made him for to lose his benefice.
But certain, there nis no comparison
Bitwixt the wisdom and discretion
Of yourè father, and of his subtlety.
Now singeth, sire, for Seintè Charity, 4510
Let see, can you your fader counterfeit?'
    This Chauntecleer his wingès gan to beat,
As man that couth his treason not espyè,
So was he ravished with his flatteryè.
    Alas! you lordès, many a false flatter
Is in your courts, and many a losengeour,° *sycophant*
That pleasen you well morè, by my faith,
Than he that soothfastness unto you sayeth.
Readeth Ecclesiast of flatteryè;
Beware, you lordès, of their treacheryè. 4520
    This Chauntecleer stood high up on his toes,
Stretching his neck, and held his eyèn close,
And gan to crowè loudè for the nones;
And daun Russell the fox start up at once,
And by the gargat° hentè Chauntecleer, *throat*
And on his back toward the wood him bore,
For yet ne was there no man that him sawed.
    O destiny, that mayst not been eschewed!
Alas, that Chauntecleer flew from the beamès!
Alas, his wife ne roghtè not of dreamès!
And on a Friday fell all this mischance.
O Venus, that art goddess of pleasance,
Sin that they servant was this Chauntecleer,
And in thy service did all his power,
More for delight, than world to multiplyè,
Why wouldst thou suffer° him on thy day to diè? *permit*
O Gaufred, dearè master sovereign,
That, whan thy worthy King Richard was slain
With shot, complainedest his death so sore,
Why ne had I now thy sentence and thy lore, 4540
The Friday for to chide, as diden you?
(For on a Friday soothly slain was he.)

Than would I show you how that I coude plainè
For Chauncteclerès dread, and for his painè
   Certes, such cry ne lamentation
Was never of ladies made, whan Illium
Was won, and Pyhrrus with his straightè sword,
When he had hent° King Priam by the beard,   *caught*
And slain him (as sayeth us *Eneiados*°),   Virgil's *Aeneid*
As maden all the hennès in the clos,°   *yard* 4550
When they had seen of Chauntecleer the sightè.
But sovereignly dame Pertelotè shrightè,°   *screamed*
Full louder than did Hasdrubalès wifè,
When that her husèband had lost his lifè,
And that the Romans haddè brend° Carthage;   *burned*
She was so full of torment and of rage,
That wilfully into the fire she startè,
And brend her-selven with a steadfast heartè.
O woeful hennès, right so cryden ye,
As, when that Nero brendè the city   4560
Of Rome, cryden senatourès wivès,
For that their husbands losten all their lyvès;
Withouten guilt this Nero hath them slain.
Now will I turnè to my tale again: –
   This silly° widow, and eek her daughters two   *simple*
Hearden these hennès cry and makèn woe,
And out at doorès starten they anon,
And seèn the fox toward the grove gone,
And bore upon his back the cock away;
And cryden, 'Out! harrow!° and wellaway!   *help!* 4570
Ha, ha, the fox!' and after him they ran,
And eek with staves many another man;
Ran Coll our dog, and Talbot, and Gerland,
And Malkin, with a distaff in her hand;
Ran cow and calf, and eek the very hoggès
So were they feared for barking of the doggès
And shouting of the men and women ekè,
They rannè so, them thought their heartè breakè.
They yowleden as fiendès do in hellè;
The duckès cryden as men would them quellè;   4580
The geese for fear flewen over the trees;
Out of the hivè came the swarm of bees;
So hideous was the noise, a! *benedicitè*!
Certès, he Jack Straw, and his manyè,°   *crowd*
Ne made never shoutès half so shrillè,

When that they woulden any Fleming killè,
As thilkè day was made upon the fox.
Of brass they broughten beamès,° and of box,*   *trumpets; wood*
Of horn, of bone, in which they blew and pouped,°   *puffed*
And therewithal they shriekèd and they whooped;   4590
It seemèd as that heaven shouldè fallè.
Now, goodè men, I pray you hearkneth allè!
Lo, how Fortuna turneth suddenly
The hope and pride eek of her enemy!
This cock, that lay upon the foxes back,
In all his dread, unto the fox he spake,
And saidè, 'Sire, if that I were as you,
Yet should I sayn (as wise God helpè me),
Turneth again, you proudè churlès allè!
A verray pestilence upon you fallè!   4600
Now am I come unto this woodès sidè,
Maugree your heed,° the cock shall here abidè;   *despite all you could do*
I will him eatè in faith, and that anon.' –
    The fox answered, 'In faith, it shall be done,' –
And as he spake that word, all suddenly
This cock broke from his mouth delivery,°   *agilely*
And high upon a tree he flew anon.
And whan the fox saw that he was y-gone,
'Alas!' quoth he, 'O Chauntecleer, alas!
I have to you,' quoth he, 'y-done trespass,   4610
Inasmuch as I makèd you afraid,
When I you hentè,° and broght out of the yard;   *seized*
But, sir, I did it in no wicked intentè;
Come down, and I shall tell you what I meantè.
I shall saye sooth to you, God help me so.'
    'Nay then,' quoth he, 'I shrew° us bothè two,   *curse*
And first I shrew myself, both blood and bones,
If thou beguile me oftener than once.
Thou shalt no morè, through thy flatteryè,
Do me to sing and winkè with mine eyè.   4620
For he that winketh, when he shouldè see,
All wilfully, God let him never thee!'
'No,' quoth the fox, 'but God give him mischancè,
That is so undiscreet of governauncè,
That jangleth when he shouldè hold his peace.'
Lo, such it is for to be reckèless,
And negligent, and trust on flattery.
But you that holden this tale a folly,

As of a fox, or of a cock and hen,
Taketh the morality, good men.   4630
For Saint Paul sayth, that all that written is,
To our doctrine it is y-write, y-wis.
Taketh the fruit, and let the chaff be still.
Now, goodè God, if that it be thy will,
As sayeth my lord, so make us allè good men;
And bring us to his higher bliss.
                      Amen.

49. Merciless Beauty: A Triple Rondel

I. CAPTIVITY

Your eyèn two will slay me suddenly,
I may the beauty of them not sustain,
So woundeth it throughout my hertè keen.

And but your word will healen hastily
My heartes woundè, while that it is green,
Your eyèn two will slay me suddenly,
I may the beauty of them not sustain.

Upon my troth I say you faithfully,
That you be of my life and death the queen;
For with my death the truthè shall be seen.   10
Your eyèn two will slay me suddenly,
I may the beauty of them not sustain,
So woundeth it throughout my hertè keen.

II.   REJECTION

So hath your beauty from your hearte chaced
Pity, that me ne availeth not to pleyn;°   *lament*
For Danger° holds your mercy in his chain.   *Scorn*

Guiltless my death thus han° ye me purchased;   *have*
I say you sooth,° me needeth not to feign;   *speak the truth to*
So hath your beauty from your heartè chased
Pity, that me ne availeth not to pleyn.   20

Alas! that nature hath in you compassed°   *drawn with compasses*
So great beauty, that no man may attain
To mercy, though he stervè° for the pain.   *die*
So hath your beauty from your heartè chased
Pity, that me ne availeth not to pleyn;
For Daunger halt your mercy in his chain.

III. ESCAPE

Since I from Love escapèd am so fat,
I never think to be in his prison lean;
Since I am free, I count him not a bean.

He may answer, and sayè this or that;   30
I do no fors,° I speak right as I mean.   *don't mislead*
Since I from Love escapèd am so fat,
I never think to be in his prison lean.

Love hath my name y-strike out of his slate,
And he is stricken out of my bookès clean
For ever-more; there is none other mean.°   *option*
Since I from Love escapèd am so fat,
I never think to be in his prison lean;
Since I am free, I count him not a bean.

Charles of Orleans

50. 'My ghostly father I me confess'

My ghostly father I me confess
First to god and then to you
That at a window wot° you how   *know*
I stole a kiss of great sweetness
Which done was out avisiness°   *without considering*
But it is done not undone now

My ghostly
First to
But you restore it shall doubtless
Again if so be that I mow°   *may* 10
And that God I make a vow
And else I ask forgivèness
   My ghostly
   First to

51. Ballade, 'When I am laid to sleep as for a stound'°   *time*

When I am laid to sleep as for a stound
To have my rest I can in no mannerè
For all the night mine heart a-readeth round
As in the romance of pleasant pancer°   *thought*
Me praying so as him to hark and hear
And I ne dare his love disobey
In doubting° so to do him displeasurè   *fearing*
This is my sleep y-fallè into decay

In this book which he read is writ & bound
As allè deedes of my lady dearè   10
Which doth mine heart in laughter oft abound
When he it read or telleth the matterè
Which greatly is to praise withoutè wear
For I myself delight it hear mafay°   *truly*
Which if they heard so wouldè each strangerè
Thus is my sleep y-fallè into decay

As with mine eyèn a respite to be found
As for an houre I ask not for a yearè
For which dispite well nigh he doth confound
That they ne can fulfillè my desirè   20
For which to rage and sigh as in a gere°   *erratic mood*
He fareth so that even as well I may
As make him stint° like out a coal of fire   *stop*
Thus is my sleep y-fallè into decay

Thus may I look more sooner win my bere°   *tomb*
Then make my froward heart to me obey

For with mine hurt he doth him self achere
Thus is my sleep y-falle as in decay

52. Ballade, 'But late ago went I my heart to see'

But late ago went I my heart to see
As of his fare to have some knowledging
I found him set with hope in company
That to him said these wordès comforting
O heart be glad for I good tiding bringè
So now let see pluck up thy lustyhead
For which I make the faithfull true promise
That I thee keep right surely out of dread
The whole treasure of lovès great riches

For this as truth to wite as do I thee   10
That the most fairest bornè or is living
She loveth thee of faithful fantasy
And with good will will do thy liking
In all to do that is to her sitting°   *suitable*
And these wordès sent thee of goodlihed
That spite of daunger° or his great rewdenes*   *power; harshness*
She will depart thee large maugrè° their head   *despite*
The whole treasure of loves great riches

For which my heart to say the truthe pardee
For joy hath fett a thousand sighed sicking   20
And thou to wearen black were usèd he
Yet was it then y-put in forgetting
And all his woe his pain and tormenting
In trust to finde it now or° he be dead   *before*
Both pleasarè comfort and gladness
And only in his governance to lead
The whole treasure of lovès great riches

My sabille heart with hope now blusheth red
And for comfort of you my fairè mistress
Which have me promised of your womanhood   30
The whole treasure of lovès great riches.

53. Ballade, 'In the forest of noyous° heaviness' *hurtful*

In the forest of noyous heaviness
As I went wandring in the monèth of May
I met of love the mighty great goddess
Which asked me whether I was away
I her answèrid as fortune doth convey
As one exiled from joy all be me loath
That passing well all folk me clepen° may *call*
The man forlost that wot° not where he goeth *knows*

Half in a smile again of her humblessè
She said my friend if so I wist° my faith *know* 10
Wherefore that thou art brought in such distressè
To shape thine ease I would my self assay
For heretofore I set thine heart in way
Of great pleasurè I not° who made thee wroth *do not know*
It grieveth me to thee see in such array
The man forlost that wot not where he goeth

Alas I said most sovereign good princessè
You know my case what needeth to you say
It is through death that showeth to all rudessè
Hath from me taken that I most love aye° *for ever* 20
In whom that all mine hope and comfort lay
So passing friendship was between us both
That I was not till false death did her die° *made her die*
The man for-lost that wot not where he goeth

Thus am I blind alas and weilaway
All far miswent with my staff grasping° way *groping*
That no thing ask but me a grave to clothe
For pity is that I live thus a day
The man for-lost that wot not where he goeth

54. Ballade, 'I have the obit° of my lady dearè' *funeral*

I have the obit of my lady dearè
Made in the church of love full solemnly
And for her soul the service and prayerè

In thought wailing have sung it heavily
The torches set of sighès pitously
Which was with sorrow set a-flame
The tomb is made als° to the same   *also*
Of careful cry depainted° all with tears   *decorated*
The which richèly is write about
That here lo lieth withouten doubt   10
The whole treasure of all worldly bliss

Of gold on her there lieth an image clearè
With sapphire blue y-set so inrichely
For it is writ and said how the sapphire
Doth token truth and gold to be happy
The which that well besettith° her hardily   *is fitting for*
Forwhy it was an ewrous° true madame   *fortunate*
And of goodness aye flowering may her name
For God the which that made her lo y-wys°   *indeed*
To make such one me thinkè I might be proud   20
For lo she was as right well be she mowt.°   *might*
The whole treasure of all worldly bliss

O peace no more mine heart astoneth° here   *is staggered*
To hear me praise her virtue so truely
Of her that had no fault withouten were
As all the world it sayeth as well as I
The which that knew her deedès inthoroughly
God hath her taken I trow for her good fame
His heaven the more to joy with sport and game
The more to please and comfort his saints   30
For certès well may she comfort a rowt°   *great number*
Now is she saint she was here so devout
The whole treasure of all worldly bliss

Not availith now though I complainè this
All must we die thereto so let us lowt°   *bow to*
For ay to keep there is no wight° so stout   *person*
The whole treasure of all worldly bliss

Thomas Hoccleve

55. Two Rondels

55a. *To Money*

Well may I pleyn on° you, Lady moneyè,   *complain of*
    That in the prison of your sharp scantnessè
    Suffren me° both in woe and heavynessè,   *Make me endure*
    And deignen not of succour me purveyè.°   *help*

When that I bore of your prison the keyè,
    Kept I you straitè?° nay, God to witnessè!   *confined*
Well may I pleyn on you, Lady moneyè,
    That in the prison of your sharp scantnessè
    Suffren me both in woe and heavynesse
And deignen not of succour me purveyè.   10

I let you out o, now, of your noblessè,
    Seeth° unto me, in your deffautè* I diè.   *Look; lack*
Well may I pleyne on you, Lady moneyè,
    That in the prison of your sharp scantnessè
    Suffren me both in woe and heavynessè,
    And deignen not of succour me purveyè.

Ye sailen all too far, return, I preyè!
    Comforteth me again this Christèmassè!
    Else I moot° in right a faint gladnessè   *must*
Sing of you thus and you accuse, and sayè: 20
    Well may I pleyn on you, Lady moneyè,
    That in the prison of your sharp scantnessè
    Suffren me both in woe and heavinessè,
    And deignen not of succour me purveyè.

55b. *Money's Reply*

Hoccleve I would it to thee knowen be,
    I, lady money, of the world goddessè,
    That have all thing under my buxomnessè,°   *command*
Not settè by thy plaintè rushes three.

Mine high might haddest thou in no charitee,°   *mercy*
 While I was in thy slipper° sikirnessè.*   *insecure; security*
Hoccleve I would it to thee knowen be,
 I, lady money, of the world goddessè,
 That have all thing under my buxomnessè,
Not settè by thy pleyntè rushes three.   10

At instance of° thine excessive largessè,   *owing to*
 Became I of my body delavèe.°   *destroyed*
Hoccleve, I wole it to thee knowen be,
 I, lady money, of the world goddessè,
 That have all thing under my buxomnessè,
Not settè by thy pleyntè rushes three.

And since that lordès great obeyen me,
 Should I me dreadè of thy poor simplessè?
 My golden head asketh for thy lewdnessè.° *ignorance*
Go, poorè wretch, who setteth aught by thee?   20
 Hoccleve I wole it to thee knowen be,
  I, lady money of the world goddessè,
  That have all thing under my buxomnessè,
 Not settè by thy pleyntè rushes three.

56. from *Thomas Hoccleve's Complaint*

PROLOGUE

After that harvest innèd° had his sheavès,   *lodged*
And that the brownè season of Michaelmas
Was come, and gan the trees rob of their leavès
That green had been and in lusty freshnessè,
And them into colourè of yellownessè
Had dyen° and down thrown under footè,   *dyed*
That changè sank into mine heartè rootè.

For freshly brought it to my remembrancè,
That stableness in this world is there nonè;
There is no thing but change and variancè;   10
How° wealthy a man be or well begonè,* *however; provided (for)*
Endure it shall not he shall it forgonè.°   *lose*
Death under footè shall him thrust adownè:
That is every witès° conclusionè.   *person's*

Whichè for to waive° is in no mannès might,   *avoid*
Howè rich he be, strong, lusty, fresh, and gay.
And in the end of November, upon a night,
Sighing sore as I in my bed lay,
For this and other thoughts which many a day
Before I tookè sleep came none in mine eyè,   20
So vexèd me the thoughtful maladyè.°   *worry*

I saw well, sythen° I with sickness last   *since*
Was scourgèd, cloudy hath been the favour
That shone on me full bright in timès past;
The sun abated and the darkè shower
Hilded° downè right on me and in langour   *poured*
He made me swimmè so that my witè
To livè no lust° had, nor no delightè.   *desire*

The grief about my heart so sorè swal°   *swelled*
And bolnèd° ever to and to so sore,   *tumesced* 30
That needès out I mustè therewithall;
I thought I nolde° it keepè close no more,   *did not want to*
Ne let it in me for to oldè° and hore;*   *grow old; grey*
And for to prove I camè of a woman,
I burst out on the morrowè and thus began.

THE COMPLAINT

Almighty God as liketh° his goodnessè,   *it pleases*
Visiteth folks alday° as men may see,   *continually*
   With loss of good and bodily sicknessè,
And amongè others he forgot not me;
Witness upon the wild infirmity   40
Which that I had as many a man well knew,
And which me out of my selfè cast and threw.

It was so knowen to the people and kouth,°   *understood*
That consel was it none ne known be mightè
How it with me stood was in every man's mouth,
And that full sore my friendès affrightè;
They for mine healthè pilgrimages hightè,°   *promised*
And sought them, some on horse and some on footè, –
God yield° it them – to geten me my botè.*   *gave; cure*

But although the substance of my memòry   50
Wentè to play as for a certain spacè,
Yet the lord of virtue, the king of glory,
Of his high might and his benignè gracè,
Made it to return into the placè
Whence it came whichè at All Hallowmasse,°   *November*
Was fivè yearè neither more nor lessè.

And ever sythen° – thanked be God our lord,   *since*
Of his goodè reconciliation, –
My wit and I have been of such accord
As we were ere the alteration   60
Of it was but by my salvation,
Since that time have I be sore set on fire,
And livèd in great torment and martyr;

For though that my wit were home come again,
Men would it not so understand or takè;
With me to deal hadden they disdain;
A riotous° person I was and forsakè;*   *dissolute; abandoned*
Mine oldè friendship was all overshakè;°   *disappeared*
No wight with me list makè daliancè;°   *conversation*
The world me made a strangè continuancè,°   *countenance* 70

Which that mine heartè sorè gan tormentè;
For oft when I in Westminster hallè,
And eke° in London among the pressè* wentè,   *also; crowd*
I saw the chere° abaten* and apallè‡   *faces; grow silent; grow pale*
Of them that weren wont me for to callè
To company, their head they cast awryè,°   *away*
When I them mettè as they not me syè.°   *saw*

As said is in the Psalter might I say,
They that me saw fledden away from me;
Forgetten I was all out of mind away,   80
As he that died was from heart's charitè;°   *friendship*
To a lost vessel likenèd might I be;
For many a wight about me dwellingè,
Heard I me blame and put in dispraisingè.

Thus spake many one and saidè by me:
'Althoughè from him his sicknessè savage
Withdrawn and passèd as for a time be,

Resort° it willè namely in such age   *return*
As he is of,' and thennè my visage°   *face*
Began to glowè for the woe and fearè;   90
Those wordès, them unwar° came to mine earè.   *unknown*

'When passing heat is,' quoth they, 'trusteth this,
Assail him will again that malady.'
And yet pardè° they tooken them amiss;   *by God*
None effect at all took their prophecy;
Many summers be past sithen remedy
Of that, God of his gracè me purveyed:
Thankèd be God it shopè° not as they said.   *happened*

What fallè° shall what men so deem or guessè,   *befall*
To him that wot° well every man's secrè,*   *knows; secrets* 100
Reservèd is. It is a lewednessè,°   *folly*
Men wiser them pretendè than they be;
And no wight knoweth be it he or she,
Whom, how nor when God willè him visit;
It happeth oftè when men wene° it lite.*   *expect; least*

Some time I wendè° as lite as any man,   *expected*
For to have fall unto that wildènessè
But God, when that him list may, willè and can,
Healthè withdraw and send a wight sicknessè;
Though man be well this day no sickernessè°   *guarantee* 110
To him behight° is that it shall endure;   *promised*
God hurtè now can and now heal and cure.

He suffreth° long but at the laste he smit;   *tolerates*
Whenè that a man is in prosperity,
To dread a fall commingè it is a wit;°   *shrewd*
Who so that taketh heedè° oft may see
This worldès change and mutability
In sundry wise how needeth not expressè:
To my matter straight willè I me dressè.

Men sayden, I lookèd as a wildè steer,°   *bullock* 120
And so my look about I gan to throwè;
Mine head too high another said I berè,°   *bore*
'Full bookish is his brain well may I trowè';°   *believe*
And said the thirdè, 'and apt is in the rowè°   *written line*

To citè of them that all reasonless reed
Can give no sadnessè is in his heed.'°   *head*

Changèd had I my pace some sayden ekè,
For here and there forth stirtè° I as a roe,   *frolicked*
None abode none arrest, but all brain-sickè.
Another spake and of me said also,   130
My feetè weren aye° weaving to and fro   *always*
When that I stondè° should and with men talkè,   *stand*
And that mine eyen soughten every halkè.°   *corner*

I laid an ear aye to as I by wentè,
And heardè all and thus in mine heart I castè:
Of long abiding here I may repentè;
Lestè, of hastiness I at the lastè
Answer amissè best is hence hye° fastè;   *hurry*
For if I in this press amiss me gyè,°   *behave*
To harmè will it me turn and to follyè.   140

And this I demèd well and knew well eke,
Whatsòever I should answerè or say,
They woulden not have hold it worth a leek;
For why as I had lost my tonguès key,
Kept I me close and trussèd° me my way,   *took*
Drooping and heavy and all woe bystad;°   *beset*
Small cause had I, me thoughtè, to be glad.

My spiritès laboured ever busily
To paintè countenancè chere and look,
For that men spoke of me so wonderingly,   150
And for the very shame and fear I quoke;°   *quaked*
Though mine heart had be dippèd in the broke,°   *brook*
It wet and moist enough was of my swot,°   *sweat*
Which was now frosty cold, now fiery hot.

And in my chamber at homè when I was
My self alone I in this wysè wroughtè:°   *made*
I straight unto my mirror and my glass,
To lookè how that me of my chere thoughtè,
If any other were it than it oughtè;
For fainè would I if it had not be right,   160
Amended it to my cunning and might.

Many assault made I to this mirror,
Thinking, if that I look in this manner
Amongè folk as I now do, none error
Of suspect look may in my face appear,
This countenance, I am sure, and this chere,
If I forth use is no thing reprovable
To them that have conceitès reasonable.

And therewithal I thoughtè thus anon:
Men in their ownè case° be blind alday,   *situation* 170
As I have heard say many a day agon,°   *before*
And in that samè plight I stondè may;
How shall I do which is the bestè way,
My troubled spirit for to bringè at rest?
If I wist how fain wouldè I do the best.

Sythen° I recovered was have I full oftè   *Since*
Causè had of anger and impatiencè,
Where I borne have it easily and softè,
Suffering wrong be done to me, and offencè,
And nought answered against but kept silencè,   180
Lest that men of me demè would, and sayen,
'See how this man is fallen in againè.'°   *relapsed*

As that I oncè fro Westminster cam,
Vexed full grievously with thoughtful heatè,
Thus thought I a great foolè I am,
This pavèment all dayès thus to beatè,
And in and out labourè° fast and sweatè,   *work*
Wondering and heaviness to purchasè,
Sythen I stand out of all favour and gracè.

And then thought I on that other sidè: 190
If that I not be seen among the press,
Men demè will that I mine headè hidè,
And am worse than I am it is no less.
O lordè, so my spirit was restèless,
I soughtè restè and I not it found,
But aye was trouble ready at mine hand.

I may not let° a man to imagine   *stop*
Far above the moonè if that him list;

Thereby the soothè° he may not determine,   *truth*
But by the proof be thingès known and wist;   200
Many a dome is wrappèd in the mist;   *fate*
Man by his deedès and not by his looks,
Shall knownè be as it is written in books.

By taste of fruit men may well wete° and knowè   *understand*
What that it is other proofè is there none;
Every man wot well that as that I trowè,°   *believe*
Right so they that demen my wittè is gone,
As yet this day there deemeth many a one
I am not well may, as I by them go,
Test and assay if it be so or no.   210

Upon a look is hardè, men them to growndè°   *form an opinion*
What a man is thereby the soothe is hid;
Whether his wittès sickè been or soundè,
By countenance it is not wist ne kyd;
Though a man hardè have once been bitid,
God should it should on him continue alway;°   *always*
By communingè° is the best assay.   *talking*

I meanè to commune of thingès meanè,°   *trivial*
For I am but right lewdè° doubteless,   *unlearned*
And ignorant my cunning is full leanè,   220
Yet homely reason know I nevertheless;
Not hope I founden be so reasonless
As men deemen. Mary, Christ forbidè!
I can no more. Provè may the deedè.

If a man oncè fall in drunkenessè,
Shall he continue therein ever mo?°   *more*
Nay, though a man do in drinking excessè
So ferforthe° that not speak he ne can, nor go,   *much so*
And his wittès well nigh been reftè° him fro,   *torn*
And buried in the Cuppè he afterward   230
Cometh to himself again else were it hard;

Right so though my wit were a pilgrimè,
And wentè far fro home he came again;
God me voided of this grievous venomè
That had infected and wildèd my brain.

See how the courteous leechè° mostè sovereign   *doctor*
Unto the sickè gaveth medicine
In need and them relieveth of their pain.

Now let this passè God wott, many a man
Seemeth full wise by countenance and cherè,   240
Which, and he tested werè what he can,
Men mighten liken him to a foolès peerè;°   *equal*
And some man looketh in fooltyshe° mannerè   *foolish*
As to the outward doom and judgement,
That at the price descreetè is and prudent.

But algates,° how so be my countenancè,   *all the same*
Debate is now none bytwixt me and my wit,
Although there were a disserverauncè
As for a timè betwixt me and it;
The greater harm is mine, that never yet   250
Was I well lettered, prudent and discretè,
There never stood yet wise man on my feetè.

The sooth is this, such conceit as I had,
And understanding all were it but small,
Beforè that my wittès weren unsad,
(Thankèd be our Lord Jesu Christ of all!)
Such have I now but blow is nigh over all
The reversè wherethrough much is the mornyngè
Whichè causeth me thus sigh in complainingè.

Sythen my good fortune hath changed his cherè,   260
High time is me to creep into my gravè,
To live Joyèless what do I herè?
I in minè heartè can no gladness havè;
I may but small say but if men deme° I ravè,   *without men judging that*
Sythen other thing than woe may I not gripè,
Unto my sepulturè° am I now ripè.   *tomb*

My welè,° adieu farewell, my good fortunè!   *joy*
Out of your tables° me playnèd* have ye;   *writing tablets; erased*
Sithen well nigh any wight for to communè
With me loathè is, farewell prosperity!   270
I am no longer of your livery;
Ye have me put out of your remembrancè;
Adieu, my good aventure and good chancè!°   *luck*

And as swithe after thus bethought I me:
If that I in this ways me despairè,
It is purchase of more adversityè;
What needeth it my feeble wit appearè;
Sith God hath made mine healthè home repairè
Blessèd be he and what men deme or speakè,
Suffer it, thinkè I and me not on me wrek.°   *avenge* 280

But somedeal° had I rejoicing amongè,   *sometimes*
And gladness also in my spiritè,
That though the people took them miss° and wrongè,   *amiss*
Me deeming of my sicknessè not quitè,
Yet for they complained the heavy plightè
That they had seen me in with tendernessè
Of heart's charity my grief was the lessè.

In them put I no default but one;
That I was whole they not ne demè could,
And day by day they see me by them gone   290
In heat and cold and neither still nor loud
Knew they me do suspectly. A darke cloud
Their sight obscurèd within and withoutè,
And for all that were they in such a doubtè.

Askèd have they full oftè syth, and freinèd°   *inquired*
Of my fellowès of the privè sealè,
And prayed them to tell them with heart unfeignèd,
How it stoodè with me whether ill or well.
And they the sothe told them every dell,
But they held[en] their wordès not but lies;   300
They mighten as well have holden their peace.

This trouble life hath all too long endurèd,
Not have I wist how in my skyn to turnè;
But now my self to my selfè have ensurèd,
For no such wondring after this to mourn;
As long as my life shall in me sojourn,
Of such imagining I not ne rechè;°   *think*
Let them deem as them list and speak and drechè.°   *imagine*

This other day a lamentation
Of a woeful man in a bookè I sye,   310
To whom wordès of consolation
Reason gave speaking effectually;
And well easèd mine heartè was thereby;
For when I had a while in the bookè read,
With the speechè of Reason was I well fed.

The heavy° man woeful and angwysshiows,*   sad; anguished
Complainèd in this wysè and thus said he:
My lifè is unto me full encumberous;
For whither or unto what place I fly,
My wickednesses ever followè me,   320
As men may see the shadow a body swe,°   follow
And in no manner I may them eschwe.°   escape

Vexation of spiritè and torment
Like I right not, I have of them plenty;
Wonderly° bitter is my taste and scent;   wonderfully
Woe be the timè of my nativity,
Unhappy man that ever should it be!
O death, thy stroke a salve is of sweetness
To them that liven in such wretchedness.

Greater plesaunce° were it me to die,   pleasure 330
By many fold° than for to livè so;   times
Sorrows so many in me multiply,
That my lifè is to me a weary foe;
Comforted may I not be of my woe;
Of my distressè see none end I can,
No force how° soon I stinte* to be a man.   it doesn't matter how; stop

Then spokè Reason, 'What meaneth all this farè?
Though wealthè be not friendly to thee, yet
Out of thine heartè voidè woe and carè!
By what skill how and by what rede° and wit,   advice 340
Saidè this woeful man might I done it?
Wrestlè,' quoth Reason, 'against heavynesses
Of the world troubles, suffring and duresses.°   difficulties

Behold how many a man suffreth decease
As great as thou and all a wayè greater;

And though it them pinchè sharply and sese,°   *seize*
Yet patiently they it suffer and bearè:
Think hereon and the lesse it shall thee dearè:°   *hurt*
Such sufferance is of man's guilt cleansing,
And them enableth to joy everlasting.   350

Woe, heaviness and tribulation
Common are to men all and profitable.
Though grevious be mannès temptation,
It slayeth man not to them that be sufferable,
And to whom goddes stroke is acceptable,
Purveyèd Joy is, for God woundèth tho
That he ordained hath to bliss to go.

Gold purgèd is thou seèst, in the furnace,
For the finer and cleaner it shall be;
Of thy disease the weightè and the peis° *heaviness* 360
Bear lightly for God, to provè thee,
Scurgèd thee hath with sharp adversity;
Not grouch° and sayè why sustain I this?   *complain*
For if thou do thou thee takest amiss;

But thus thou shouldest thinkè in thine heart,
And say, to thee, Lord God I have a guilt
So sore: I moot° for mine offences smart   *must*
As I am worthy. O lordè, I am spilt,°   *killed*
But° thou to me thy mercy grantè wilt.   *unless*
I am full sure thou mayest it not deny;   370
Lord, I me repent and I thee mercy cry.

Longer I thoughtè read have in this bookè,
But so it shopè that I ne mightè not;
He that it ought° again it to him tookè,   *owned*
Me of his haste unaware yet have I caught
Some of the doctrinè by reason taught
To the man as above have I sayèd,
Whereof I holdè me full well apayèd.°   *satisfied*

For ever sythen set have I the lessè
By the people's imagination,   380
Talking this and that of my sicknessè,
Which came of Goddès visitation;
Might I have be found in probation,

Not grouchingè° but have take it in suffrance,   *complaining*
Wholesome and wisè had be° my governaunce.   *been*

Farewell my sorrow I caste it to the cock.
With patience I henceforthè think unpikè
Of such thoughtful disease and woe the lock,
And let them out that have me made to sikè;°   *sigh*
Hereafter our lord God may, if him likè,   390
Make all mine old affection resortè;
And in hope of that will I me comfortè.

Through Godès just dome and his judgèment,
And for my bestè now I take and demè,
Gave that good lordè me my punishment:
In wealth I took of him none heed or yemè,°   *care*
Him for to please and him honour and quem,°   *delight*
And he me gave a bone on for to gnaw,
Me to correct and of him to have awe.

He gave me wit and he took it away   400
When that he see that I it miss despent,
And gave again when it was to his pay,°   *pleasure*
He grauntèd me my guiltès to repent,
And henceforward to sett mine intentè,
Unto his deity to do plesauncè,
And to amend my sinful governancè.

Laudè and honour and thank unto thee be,
Lord God that salve art to all heaviness!
Thank of my wealth and mine adversity,
Thank of mine eld and of my sickèness;   410
And thank be to thine infinitè goodness
For thy giftès and benefices° allè,   *largesses*
And unto thy mercy and grace I callè.

57. from *Ars Sciendi Mori*°   *The Art of Understanding Death*

57a.
... To learnè for to die is to han° aye*   *have; always* 50
Both heart and soul ready hence to go,

That when death cometh for to catch her prey,
Man ripè be the life to twynnè fro,°   *separate from*
And here to takè and receive also
As he that the coming of his fellowè
Desireth and is thereof glad and fawè.°   *eager*

But more harm is full many one shalt thou findè,
That against death maken no purveancè;°   *preparation*
Them loathen death for to have in their mindè;
That thought they holden thought of encumbrancè;   60
Worldly sweetnessè slayeth such remembrancè;
And sin to diè not learnèd han they,
Fro the world twynnè they would in no way.

They muchil° of their timè han dispended   *much*
In sin and forthy° when, unwarly,* death   *therefore; accidentally*
Upon them falleth and they not amended,
And shall from them bereavè wind and breath,
For she unready finds them when she slayeth
To hellè goen their souls miserable,
There to dwell in painè perdurable.°   *permanent* 70

Death would have oft a bridle put on thee,
And thee with her led away she wouldè,
Nadde° the hand of goddès mercy be.   *Has not*
Thou art full muchil unto that Lord holdè;°   *beholden*
That, for thou wrappèd were in sinnès oldè,
He spared thee thy sinnès now forsakè,
And unto my doctrinè thou thee takè!

More to thee profitè shall my lorè°   *teaching*
Than chosen gold or the bookès each one
Of Philosophrès and for that the morè   80
Fervently should it stir thy person
Under sensible ensemplè thee to one
To God, and thee the better for to thewè,°   *instruct*
The mystery of my lore I shall thee shewè.

Beholdè now the likeness and figurè
Of a man dying and talking with thee.
The disciple, of that speech took good curè,°   *notice*
And in his conceit busily soughtè he,
And therewithal consider he gan, and see

In himself put the figure and likenessè   90
Of a young man of excellent fairnessè,

Whom death so nigh ransackèd had, and soght,
That he within a whilè shouldè die.
And for his soules healthè had he right noght
Disposèd all unready hence to hie
Was he and therefor he began to cry
With lamentable voice in this mannerè,
That sorrow and pity great was it to hearè:

'Environd° han me, death's waymentyngès,*   *Circled; lamentations*
Sorrows of hellè han compassèd me;   100
Alas, eternal God! O King of Kingès,
Whereto was I born in this world to be;
O alas why in my nativity
Naddè I perishèd? O, the beginningè
Of my life was with sorrowè and with weepingè,

And now mine endè cometh hence must I go
With sorrow wailing and great heavinessè.
O, death, thy mind is full of bitter woe;
Unto an heartè wont° unto gladnessè,   *accustomed*
And nourishèd in delicate sweetnessè,   110
Horrible is thy presence and full grievable
To him that young is, strong and prosperable.

Little wend° I so soonè to han died: *expected*
O cruel death thy coming is sudden;
Ful unaware was I of thy thiefly breid;°   *lifting*
Thou hast as in await° upon me lain;   *ambush*
Thy coming unto me was uncertain;
Thou hast upon me stolen and me boundè;
Escape I may not now my mortal woundè.

Thou me with thee drawèst in iron chainès,   120
As a man damnèd wont is to be draw
To his torment. Outrageous been my painès.
Ah, now for sorrow and fear of thee and awe,
With handès clight° I cry and wouldè faw   *clenched*
Witè the place whither for to flee;
But such one findè can I none ne° see.   *nor*

I look on every sidè busily,
But help is none, help and comfort be deadè;
A voice horrible of death sownyng° hearè I,   *sounding*
That sayeth me thus which increaseth my dreadè: 130
"Thou die shalt reason none ne kindredè,
Friendshipè gold ne none other richessè
May thee deliverè out of deathès duressè.

Thine endè is comen, comen is thine endè,
It is decreed there is no resistancè."
Lord God shall I now die and hennès° wendè?*   *hence; go*
Whether not changèd may be this sentencè;
O Lord, may it not put been in suspensè?
Shall I out of this world so soonè go?
Alas will it none other be than so?   140

O death, o death, great is thy cruelty!
Thine office all too suddenly doest thou.
Is there no grace? lackest thou pity?
Spare my youth. Of agè ripe enow°   *enough*
To die am I not yet, sparè me now!
How cruel that thou art on me not kythè!°   *showing*
Take me not out of this world so swithè!° ...   *quickly*

... Though men full blindè been, and bestial.
Of that shal followè after this life present,
Forsight suchè folk han none at all.
I not bewaillè deathès judgèment;   180
But this is all the cause of my torment;
The harm of undisposèd death I weepè;
I am not ready in the ground to creepè,

I kepè° not that I shall hennès* twinè‡,   *care; hence; depart*
But of my dayès I the harm bewail,
Fruitless past, save with bitter fruit of sinnè;
I wroghtè in them nothing that might avail
To soulès health I didè no travail
To livè well but leanèd to the staff
Of worldly lustès to them I me gaf.   190

The way of truthè I leftè and drew to wrongè;
On me not shone the light of righteousnessè;
The sunnè of intellect not in me sprungè;

I am weary of my wroght wickednessè;
I walkèd have, wayès of hardnessè
And of perdition not kowdè° I knowè   *understood*
The way of God wicked seed have I sowè.

Allas, what hath pride profitted me,
Or what am I bet for richè richess heapingè?
All they as a shadow passèd be,   200
And as a messenger fastè runningè,
And also as a ship that is sailingè
In the waves and floodès of the Sea,
Whose kerfe° not founden is when passed is she.   *wake*

Or as a bird which in the air that fleeth,
No proof found is of the course of his flight;
No man espiè can it ne it see,
Save with his wingès the wind soft and light
He beateth and cutteth there by the might
Of suchè stirring and forth he fleeth his way;   210
And tooken after that no man see there may.

Or as an arrow shot out of a bow,
Twinneth° the air which that continually   *divides*
Again is closèd that man may not know
Where that it passed no wight the way see:
Right so sin that I born was farè have I
Continually I stynted for to be,
And token of virtue showèd none in me.

My dayes I dispent in vanity;
No heed I took of them but let them passè,   220
Nothing considering their preciousitee,°   *preciousness*
But held my self free born as a wildè assè.
Of thafterclap insightè had no man lassè;°   *less*
I over blind was I not saw ne dreadè,
With what woe death would hastè me to beddè.

And now as fishes been with hookes caught,
And as that birdès been take in a snare,
Death hath me hent, escapè may I not;
This unaware woeful hour me maketh bare
Of my customed joyè and my welfare;   230
The timè is past the time is gone for ay;
No man revoke or call again it may.

So short was not the timè that is gone,
But I, of ghostly lucres° and winnyngès,   *ill-gotten gains*
Aught have in it purchasèd many oon,°   *one*
Exceeding in value all earthly thingès
Incomparably but to his wingès
The time hath take him and no purveance
Therein made I my soule to avance.

Alas, I, caitif° for anguish and sorwè,   *captive*
My tearès tricklen by my cheekès down;
No salt water me needeth begg or borwè;
Mine eyen flowen now in great foysoun;°   *abundance*
Alas this is a sharp conclusion,
Though I the timè past complainè and mournè;
For all my carè will it not returnè...

57b.

... Lifte up thine eyèn, look about and see
Diligently how many folkès blind   870
In their conceites now a dayès be;
They close and shut the eyèn of their mind;
They nought keep, in their conceit search and find
Unto what end needès they shouldèn draw,
And all for lack of dread of God, and awe.

They stop their earès for they not° ne keep*   *do not wish; observe*
Here how converted be and receive healthè;
Correction is noon they let it sleep;
They been so drunken of this worldès wealthè,
That death, ere they be ware right in a stealthè 880
Falleth upon them which condition
Them causè shall hasty perdition.

The people now let seen innumerable
That for death undisposèd lost han be°   *have been*
Consider and if thy wit be thereto able
Number of their multitude the plenty
Eke° of them that in thy time with thee   *also*
Dwellt han look how that they been take away:
Thou seest well they from hence been past for aye;

And as they here han do so shall they have. 890
What multitude in yearès few ago,
That yet lying han laid been in their grave!
What brethren Cousins fellowès and mo° *more*
Of thy knowledge beholdè allè tho!° *then*
Thine eke, with them their old sin gone is;
Touch unto them speak and ask them of this,

And they with weeping and with lamentingè
Shall to thee say and thus again answer:
Blessed is he that can see the endingè,
And sincè that the soul hurtè and dear, 900
Eshew can and them fleè and forbear;
And that in my counsel hath good savour,
Disposing him alway unto that hour.

And therefore allè vicious thingès left,
Well thee dispose and ready makè thee
To diè lest the timè be thee reft
Or that thou be ware for no certainty
Hast thou thereof thou art no thing prive° *secret*
Thereto death is not far right attè° gate *at the*
She is be ready for to die algate!° *at any rate* 910

Right as a Merchant standing in a port,
His ship that chargèd is with merchandise
To go to far partiès for comfort
Of himself looketh that it in safè wyse° *ways*
Pass out right so, if thou work as the wise,
See to thy soulè so ere thou hence wendè,° *will go*
That it may han the life that hath no endè. *Amen!*

58. from *The Regement of Princes*

58a. *Hoccleve meets and talks with an old beggar*

Pass over when this stormy night was gone,
And day gan° at my windowè in to pry, *began*
I rose me up, for boot° found I none *benefit*
In mine unresty bed longer to lie;
Into the field I dressèd me in high,

And in my woe, I heartè-deep gan wade,
As he that was barren of thoughtès glad.

By that° I walkèd had a certainè time,   *after* 120
Were it an houre, I not° or more or lessè,   *know not*
A poor old horè° man cam walking by me,   *white haired*
And saidè, 'Good day, sire, and God you blessè!'
But I no word; for my sickly distressè
Forbade mine earès usen° their office,   *using*
For which this old man held me lewd° and nice,⋆   *ignorant; foolish*

Till he took heedè to my dreary chere,°   *face*
And to my deadly colour pale and wan;
Then thought he thus: – this man that I see here,
All wrong is wrestèd,° by ought that I see can: *controlled* 130
He startè° up to me, and saidè, 'Sleeps thou, man?   *came*
Awake!' and gan me shakè wonder° fastè,   *wonderfully*
And with a sigh I answerdè attè lastè.

'Ah! who is there?' 'I,' quoth this oldè greyè,
'Am here,' and he me toldè the mannerè
How he spake to me, as you heard me sayè;
'O man,' quoth I, 'for Christès lovè dearè,
If that thou wolt° ought donè at my prayerè,⋆   *would like; as I would like*
As go thy way, talkè to me no more,
Thy wordès all annoyèn me full sore;°   *grievously* 140

Void fro° me; me list⋆ no companyè;   *Go away; want*
Increasè not my grief; I have enow.'°   *enough*
'My son, hast thou good lust° thy sorrow dryè,   *wish to*
And mayst relieved be? what man art thou?
Work after me! it shall be for thy prow;°   *advantage*
Thou nart° but young, and hast but little seen,   *are only*
And full seld° is, that young folk wisè been.   *seldom*

'If that thee likè to be easèd well,
As suffer me with thee to talkè a while.
Art thou ought lettred?'° 'Yes,' quoth I, 'some deal.'   *educated* 150
'Blessèd be God! than hope I, by Saint Gyle,
That God to thee thy wit shall reconcile,
Which that me thinketh is far fro thee went,
Through the assent of thy grevious torment.

Lettered folk han greater discretion,
And bet° conceivè can a mannès saw,*   *better; discourse*
And rather will appliè to reason
And from follyè sooner them withdraw,
Than he that neither reason can,° nor law,   *knows*
Nor learned hath no manner of lettrurè:°   *learning* 160
Pluckè up thine heartè! I hope I shall thee cure.'

'Curè, good man? yea, thou art a fairè lechè!°   *doctor*
Curè thy self, that tremblest as thou goest,
For all thine art will enden in thy speechè;
It lieth not in thy power, poorè gost,°   *spirit*
To healè me; thou art as sick almost
As I; first on thy self kythè° thine art;   *demonstrate*
And if ought levè,° let me thennè havè part.   *survive*

Go forth thy way, I thee prayè, or be still;
Thou dost me more annoy than that thou wenest;°   *expects* 170
Thou art as full of clap° as is a mill;   *chatter*
Thou dost nought hear, but grievest me and tenest.°   *vexes*
Good man, thou wostè° but little what thou meanest;   *know*
In thee, lithè° not redressè* my nuisance,   *soothe; set right*
And yet thou mayest be well willèd perchance.

It mustè be a greater man of might
Than that thou art, that shouldè me relieve.'
'What, sonè mine! thou feelest not aright!
To hearkenè me, what shall it harm or grieve?'
'Peter! good man, though we talk here till eve,   180
All is in vainè; thy might may not attainè
To helè me, such is my woeful painè.'

'What that I may or can, ne wost° thou noght;   *know*
Hardily, sonè, tellè on how it is!'
'Man, at a word, it is encumbrous thought
That causeth me this sorrowè and farè° amiss.'   *goes*
'Now, sonè, and if there no thing be but this,
Do as I shall thee sayè, and thine estate
Amendè I shall, but° thou be obstinate,   *unless*

And wilfully rebellè and disobey,   190
And listè° not to my lorè* thee conformè;   *want; teaching*
For in such cas,° what shouldè I speakè or say,   *a situation*
Or in my bestè ways thee informè?

If thou it waive, and take an other formè
After thy childish misrulèd conceit,
Thou dost unto thyself harm and deceit.

O° thing say I, if thou go fearless   *One*
All solitary, and counsel lackè and rede,°   *advice*
As me thinketh, thy guise is doubtèless,
Thou likely art to bear a dotyd° head.   *feeble-minded* 200
While thou art solè, thought is wasting seed,
Such in thee, and that in greatè foyson,°   *abundance*
And thou redèless,° not canst voidè his poison. *without counsel*

The book sayeth thus, – I read it yore agon, –° *a long time ago*
Woe be to him that list to be alone!
For if he fallè, help ne hath he none
To rise; this say I by thy person;
I found the soul, and thy wittès each one
Far from thee fled, and disparpled° full widè;   *dispersed*
Wherefore it seemeth, thee needeth a guidè...'   210

58b. *Envoy*

O little book, who gave thee hardiness   5440
Thy wordès to pronounce in the presence
Of kingès Imp,° and princes worthiness,   *Imperial*
Since thou all naked art of eloquence?
And why approachest thou his excellence
Unclothèd, save thy kirtel° bare alone?   *cloak*
I am right sure his humble patience
The youthè hardinessè so to done.

But o thing wote I wellè: go where thou go,
I am so privy unto thy sentencè,°   *meaning*
Thou hast, and art, and will be evermo°   *evermore* 5450
To his highness, of such benevolence,
Though thou not do to him due reverence
In words, thy cheertè° not is the less.   *charity*
And if lust° be, to his magnificence,   *desire*
Do by thy rede:° his wealth it shall witness!   *advice*

Beseech him, of his gracious noblessè,
The hold excusèd of thine innocence

Of endityng;° and with hearts meeknessè,   *composition*
If any thing thee pass of negligence,
Beseech him of mercy and indulgence,   5460
And that, for thy good heart, he be not fo°   *against*
To thee that all seest of loves fervencè!°   *fervour*
That knoweth he, that no thing is hid fro.°   *from*

John Lydgate

59. London Lickpenny

To London once my steps I bent,
   Where truth in no wise° should be faint,*   *way; weak*
To Westminsterward I forthwith went,
   To a man of law to make complaint.
   I said, 'For Mary's love, that holy saint,
     Pity the poor that would proceedè.'
     But, for lack of money, I could not spedè.°   *succeed*

And as I thrust the press° amongè,   *crowd*
   By froward° chance my hood was gone,   *adverse*
Yet for all that I stayed not longè,   10
   Till at the King's bench I was come.
   Before the Judge I kneeled anon,
     And prayed him for God's sake to take heedè.
     But, for lack of money, I might not spedè.

Beneath them sat clerkès a great rout,°   *crowd*
   Which fast did write by one assent;
There stood up one and cried about,
   'Richard, Robert, and John of Kent!'
   I wist° not well what this man meant,   *knew*
     He cried so thickè there indeedè.   20
     But he that lacked money might not spedè.

Unto the common place I yodè° tho,*   *went; then*
 Where sat one with a silken hoodè;
I did hym reverence for I ought to do so,
 And told my case as well as I couldè,
  How my goodès were defrauded me by falsehoodè.
   I got not a mum° of his mouth for my meedè!* *mumble; reward*
   And, for lack of money, I might not spedè.

Unto the Rolls I got me from thence,
 Before the Clerkès of the Chauncerye,   30
Where many I found earning of pence,
 But none at all once regarded me.
 I gave them my plaint upon my knee,
  They liked it well, when they had it read;
  But, lacking money, I could not be sped.

In Westminster hall I found out one,
 Which went in a long gown of rayè;°   *striped cloth*
I crouched and kneelèd before him anon,
 For Mary's love, of help I him prayè.
 'I wot not what thou mean'st,' gan he say;   40
  To get me thence he did me bedè,°   *command*
  For lack of money I could not spedè.

Within this hall, neither rich nor yet poor
 Would do for me ought, although I should die.
Which seeing, I got me out of the door,
 Where fleminges° began on me for to cry: *poor traders*
 'Master, what will you copen° or buy?   *barter*
  Finè felt hattès, or spectacles to readè?
  Lay down your silver, and here you may spedè.'

Then to Westminster Gate I presently went,   50
 When the sun was at highè prime,
Cookès to me they took good intent,
 And proffered me bread with ale and wine,
 Ribs of beefè, both fat and full fine.
  A fairè cloth they gan for to spreadè,
  But, wanting money, I might not spedè.

Then unto London I did me hie,°   *hasten*
 Of all the land it beareth the prize:

'Hot pescodès,'° one began to cry;   *pea-pods*
   'Strawberry ripe, and cherrys in the rise!'   60
  One bade me come nearè and buy some spice;
    Pepper and saffron they gan me biddè.
    But, for lack of money, I might not spedè.

Then to the Chepè° I gan me drawè,   *Cheapside*
   Where much people I saw for to stand;
One offered me velvet, silk, and lawnè;°   *fine cloth*
   Another he taketh me by the hand,
   'Here is Paris thread, the finest in the land.'
    I never was used to such thingès in deedè,
    And, wanting money, I might not spedè.   70

Then went I forth by London stone,
   Throughout all Canwickè streetè;
Drapers much cloth me offered anon;
   Then comes me one, cried, 'Hot sheepès feetè.'
   One criedè, 'Mackerel; rishes° greenè,' another gan greetè.   *rushes*
    One bade me buy a hood to cover my head;
    But, for want of money, I might not be sped.

Then I hièd me into Eastchepe.°   *East Cheapside*
   One criès, 'Ribs of beefè, and many a pie!
Pewter pottès they clatterèd on a heapè;   80
   There was harpè, pipe, and minstrelsie.
   'Yea, buy cock! nay, buy cock!' some began cry;
    Some sung of Jenken and Julian for their medè.
    But, for lack of money, I might not spedè.

Then into Cornhill anon I yodè,
   Where was much stolen gerè° amongè;   *equipment*
I saw where hung mine ownè hoode,
   That I had lost among the throngè.
   To buy my own hood I thought it wrongè –
    I knew it well as I did my Creedè;   90
    But, for lack of money, I could not spedè.

The Taverner took me by the sleevè,
   'Sir,' sayeth he, 'will you our wine assay?'°   *try*
I answered, 'That can not much me grievè;
   A penny can do no more then it may.'
   I drank a pint, and for it did payè;

Yet sore a-hungered from thence I yedè,
And, wanting money, I could not spedè.

Then hied I me to Billingsgate,
    And one cried, 'Ho! goè we hence!'   100
I prayed a barge-man, for god's sake,
    That he would spare me my expense.
        'Thou scapst not here,' quoth he, 'under two pence';
            I list° not yet bestow my Almes-deedè.   *want to*
            Thus, lacking money, I could not spedè.

Then I conveyèd me into Kent,
    For of the law would I meddle no more,
Because no man to me tookè intent,
    I dight° me to do as I did before.   *prepared*
    Now Jesus that in Bethlem was bore,   110
        Save London, and send true lawyers their medè!
        For whoso wants money, with them shall not spedè.

60. from *Life of Our Lady: Book I, The Prologue*

O thoughtful heartè, plunged in distress
With slumber of slothè, this long winter's night
Out of the sleepè, of mortal heaviness
Awake anon, and lookè upon the light
Of thilke° star that with their beamès bright   *the same*
And with the shining, of her streamès° merryè   *rays of light*
Is wont to gladdè, all our Emisperyè°   *Hemisphere*

And to oppress the darkeness and the dolè°   *sadness*
Of heavy hearts that sorrowen and sighen oftè
I mean the starrè, of the brightè poolè   10
That with her beamès when she is aloftè
May all the trouble asuagèn and asoftè
Of worldly waves, which in this mortal sea
Have us beset, with great adversity

The Rage of which is so tempestuous
That when the calmè is most blandishing°   *soothing*
Then is the stream of death most perilous

If that we want, the light of her shining
And but the sight, alas, of her looking
From deathès brinkè, make us to escapè   20
The haven of life, of us may not be takè.

This star in beauty passeth Pleiades
Both of° shining and of streams clearè   *in its*
Botetes° Arthur and also Jades   *Surpasses*
And Hesperus when it doth appearè
For this is Spica with her brightè spherè
That towardè even at midènight and at morrowè
Down from the heaven adaweth° all our sorrowè   *arises*

Whose bright beamès shining from so farrè
That cloudès blacke may the light not findè   30
For this of Jacob, is the fairest starrè
That under wavès never doth declinè
Whose course is not under the cliptik° linè   *ecliptic*
But everylike of beauty may be seenè
Amiddè the ark of our meridynè°   *meridian*

And drieth up, the bitter tearès wetè
Of Aurora, after the mourwen° grey   *morning*
That she in weeping doth on flowerès fletè°   *float*
In lusty° April and in freshè May   *joyful*
And causeth Phoebus the bright summer's day   40
With his goldè wayn,° bourned* bright and fairè   *cart; burning*
Tenchase° the mistè of our cloudy airè   *To scatter*

For this is the starrè, that bore the bright sunnè
Which hold'th the sceptre of Juda in his handè
Whose streamès been, outè of Jesse runnè
To shed her lightè both, on sea and landè
Whose gladde beamès without eclipsing standè
Eastward to us in the orient full shenè°   *bright*
With light of grace, to voiden° all our tenè*   *remove; harm*

Now fairè star, O, star of starrès all   50
Whose light to see, angelès delight
So let the goldè dew of thy grace fall
Into my breast, like scalès, faire and white
Me to inspire of that I woulde endyte°   *compose*
With thilke beame, sent down by miracle
When the holy ghost, thee made his habitacle°   *dwelling*

And the liquor of thy gracè shed
Into my pennè,° to luminè this ditie*   *pen; poem*
Through thy supportè that I may proceed
Somewhat to say in laudè and praise of thee   60
And first I thinkè at the nativity
So that thine helpè, fro me nat ne twynnè,*   *leave*
Benignè lady, anon for to beginnè.

A flower of virtue full longè kept in closè
Full many ver° with wholesome leavès swotè*   *Springs; sweet*
Only by grace upon the stalke arose
Out of Jessè, springing fro the Rotè°   *root*
Of God ordainèd to be a resort and botè°   *remedy*
Unto mankindè our trouble to determine°   *end*
Full long afforn by prescencè divine   *before 70*

The whichè Flower, preserveth man from death
Unto the virtue, who so lust° take heede   *wants to*
That in a garden, amidès° of Nazareth   *in the middle*
So faire some timè gan to spring and spread
That through the worldè both in length and bred°   *breadth*
The freshè odour, and also the sweetnessè
Heartès comforteth, of all their heavinessè.

O Nazareth, with Beddelem° thee besidè   *Bethlehem*
This Flower, you maketh, of name more Ryall°   *splendid*
Than either Rome, elate and full of pridè   80
Or mighty Troyè, with the sturdy wall
Whose renown halteth, to be paragall°   *descended*
In Honour prize, Fame and Reverencè
Unto your passing,° worthy excellencè   *surpassing*

If for the fruit commendè be the tree
Thou hast more laudè, and commendation
For thilkè fruitè, that sprang out of thee
Than hath Aufryke° of worthy Scipion*   *Africa; Scipio*
Or Rome of Ceasar, or of Fabian
Though her name were some time grave° in goldè   *engraved 90*
Her Idle fame, to thine may not be toldè

Wherfore rejoicè, and be right glad and light,
O Nazareth of name, most flowering,

For out of thee, a flower most fair of sight
Most full of gracè, some time diddè spring
Of the whichè fully remembring
So long ago spoke holy Isaye°   *Isaiah*
When that he saidè in his prophecy

That on this flower plainly shouldè rest
The holy ghostè, for his chosen place   100
As for the fairest, and also for the best
That ever was and, most full of grace
Whose passing beauty, no stormè may deface
But ever like continueth freshè of hue
With outè fading, the colour is so true

For this is the flower, that God himself beheld,
The white lilly of the chosen vale
The sweetè Rosè, of the fairè field
Which of colour waxeth never pale
The violet, our langour to avail   110
Purple huèd, through mercy and pity
To succour allè, that in mischiefè be

And from the stalk,° of Joachim and Annè   *lineage*
This holy flower haddè her original
To them afforn,° by sting I shewed whennè   *before*
The Angel toldè them plainèly that there shall
Of them be bornè, a maid in special,
Chosen of goddè most chiefè of her alye°   *alive*
For her meeknessè and hattè° shall Mary   *be called*

And when the Angel, at the gate of goldè,   120
Had of this maid her birthè prophesied
And all the manner to bothè them toldè
In bookès oldè, as it is specified
Home to their houses anon they have them hied°   *hurried*
And she conceived, this faithful truè wife
By Joachim, the holy fruitè of life

Outè of the which gan growè all our grace,
Our oldè sorrows, fully for to fine°   *end*
The bitter gall, plainèly to enchace
Of the venom, callèd serpentine   130
For when that Annè, haddè monthès nine

Bornè this fruit so holy and entere°   *entire*
Through grace of God, anon it did appeare

The orient° to gladdè with all man kindè   *dawn*
With deadly error oppressedè of the night
With cloudès blackè, and with skyey blindè
Till they were cleared, with fairnessè of the light
Of whichè the Angel, some time had a sight
With Jacob wrestling, from him as he breyd°   *changed*
So longè aforn to him whennè he said,   140

'Let me depart, with outèn more affray
Ainè me, and make no resistance
The night is passèd, lo the morowen° grey   *morning*
The fresshè Aurora, so fairè in appearance
Her light dawneth, to voidè all offence
Of winter nightès full long and tediousè
With newè appearing, so glad and graciousè.'

This is to sayè, the holy dawning
Of this maid, at her Nativity
The night gan voidè, of our oldè morning   150
As the Angelè, in figurè did see
With such a touchè, madè Jacob be
Seer° in his sinews, like as it is foundè   *Dry*
In that membre,° where lust* doth most aboundè   *limb; pleasure*

61. The Fifteen Tokens Before the Doom

As the doctor Sanctus Jeronimus,°   *Saint Jerome*
    Which that knew by inspiratioun
Fifteenè tokens, the scripture telleth thus,
    And therof maketh a declaration,
    Afore the Jugement; and for conclusion

I

The first day, the sea shall rise on height
    Above all hillès, to their inspection,
Forty cubits in every mannès sight.

II

The secondè day, the sea shall eek° descendè   *also*
   That unnethè° it shall not well be seen.   *scarcely* 10
Wildè beastès upon the flood roarendè,

III

The thriddè° day herd on mount and plain,   *third*
   Fowl, beast and fish, shall tremble in certain,
Complaining in their hideous moan
   Up the skyès; this noise not made in vain,
For what they meanè, God shall know alone.

IV

The fourthè day, the water and the sea
   Shall brennè° as only flawmè* light.   *burn; flaming*

V

The fifthè day, herbè, fowl and tree
   Shall be bloody dewèd to the sight;   20
   And allè fowls for fear shall take their flight,
As they were each one of assent°   *in agreement*
   Neither eat nor drink, but losè strength and might,
Only for fear of Christès Judgement.

VI

The sixthè day, houses one and allè,
   Great castels, towers made of lime and stone
Plane with the Earth to groundè shall down fallè.
   Fiery floodès, and waters everyone,
   Brennyng° as coals with flamès over gone.   *Burning*
Sparing no thing, till all be waste and spent   30
   This fiery flood shall overspread anon,
And reach in heightè facè of the firmament.

VII

The seventh day, stonès one and allè
   All they together shall meetè suddenly
On fourè parties shall assunder fallè,
   And in their hurtling noisè dreadfully.

And no man shall knowè Openly
What all thing meaneth, they hid previte,°   *secretly*
   Nor enpownè° the tokenès* secretly,   *interpret; meanings*
But God alone, in his high majesty.   40

VIII

The eighth tokenè in Orderè ye shall havè,
   Following in sooth° as ye shall understandè,   *truth*
There shall be so great an earthèquavè°   *earthquake*
   That man nor beastè on their feet shall standè.

IX

   The ninthè day, plainly as is the strondè,°   *sea-shore*
Shall high mountainès turn into powder small,
   As men shall seen, bothè free and bondè,°   *enslaved*
Both hill and dale of measure so egal.°   *equal*

X

The tenthè day, from caverns and their cavès
   Men shall come out, like folk that can° no good,   *know* 50
And runnè abroad like drunkè men that ravès,°   *ravish*
   Or as they werè frantik, other° wood,*   *or; mad*
   Deadly palè, and devoidè of blood;
Not speakè a word one unto another,
   As witless people of reason and of meood,°   *mood*
No quaintance made, brother unto brother.

XI

The eleventh signè, plainly to devise,°   *describe*
   As it is remembered in scripture,
Dead bonès that dayè shall arise,
   And grisly standè on their sepulture,°   *tomb* 60
   And showèn outward a dreadful foul figure;
So to stand all day, with bones black and dunnè;
   Of doom abide° the dreadful aventure,*   *wait; event*
Till going downè of the bloody sunnè.

XII

The twelfth day, more dreadful than is werrè,°   *war*
   Against which shall be no resistancè,
Down from heaven shall fallen every starrè,

With firey leven° and fearful violencè,   *lightning*
And beastès allè shall comèn in presencè
Within a fieldè, and of verray dreadè   70
   Neither eat nor drinkè for non indigencè,
But cry, and howlè, and dare themself not feedè.

XIII

The thirteenth day, men that ben alive
   Shall dyè each one, this is well certain,
And after that they shall arisè blith,
   With other bodies to come to live again,

XIV

   The fourteenth day, there shall also be sayen
Heavenè and earth, verrayly° indeedè,   *truly*
   Withoutè refute or any manner geyn,°   *given*
Consumè and all into ashes deadè.   80

XV

The lastè day, accounted full fifteenè,
   As Saint Jerome plainly doth devise,
Heaven and earth all newè shall be seenè,
   And allè bodies shall that day arise;
As this doctor setteth the emprise°   *undertaking*
   Of this matter, God grantè, as I wissè,°   *know*
Afore this day that all men been so wise
   Through Christès passion, that they may come to bliss.

62. from *The Troy Book*

THE ENVOY

Go, little book, and put thee in the grace
Of him that is most of excellence;°   *King Henry*
And be not hardy to appearen in no place   *brave*
Withoutè support of his magnificence:
And whosoeverè in thee find offence,
Be not too bold for no presumption –
Thy self enarmè ay° in patience,   *always*
And thee submit to her correction.

And for thou art enlumined° with no flowers   *illuminated*
Of rhethoric, but with white and black,   10
Therefore thou must abide all showers
Of them that list set on thee a lack;
And when thou art most likely go to wrak,°   *destruction*
Against them thine error not defendè,
But humbly withdrawè and go aback,
Requiring them all that is miss° to amendè.   *wrong*

63. from *The Fall of Princes*

63a. *The Dance Macabre: Prologue*

O ye folks hard-hearted as a stone,
Whichè to this world give all your advertance,
Like as it should ever lasten in one, –
Where is your wit, where is your providence
To seen aforne° the sudden violence   *before*
Of cruel death, that be so wise and sage,
Which slayeth, alas, by stroke or pestilence°   *Plague*
Both young and old of low and high parage?°   *lineage*

Death spareth not low ne high degree,
Popes, kingès, nor worthy Emperors;   10
When they shine most in felicity,
He can abate° the freshness of their flowers,   *destroy*
Their brightè sun clipsen° with his showers,   *eclipse*
Make them plunge fro° their seas lowè; –   *from*
Mauger° the might of all these conquerours,   *despite*
Fortune hath them from her wheel y-throwè.°   *thrown down*

Considereth this, ye folkès that been wisè,
And it imprinteth in your memorial,°   *memory*
Like thensample° which that at Parisè   *the example*
I found depict once upon a wall   20
Full notably, as I rehearsè shall.   *relate*
Of a French clerk taking acquaintance,
I tookè on me to translaten all
Out of the Frenchè Macabreès dance

By whose advice and counsel at the lest,°   *least*
Through her steering and her motion,
I obèyed unto her request,
Thereof to make a plain translation
In English tongue, of intention
That proudè folks that beenè stout and bold,   30
As in a mirror toforne° in her reason   *before*
Her ugly fin° there clearly may behold.   *end*

By this example, that they in their intentès°   *resolves*
Amend their life in every manner age.
The whichè dancè at Saint Innocentès
Portrayèd is, with all the surplusage,°   *abundance*
Given unto us our livès to correct
And to declare the fin of our passage, –
Right anon my style I will direct
To showè this world is but a pilgrimage.   40

63b. The Words of the Translator

O creatures ye that be reasonable,
The life desiring which is eternal,
Ye may see here doctrine full notable
Your life to leadè, which that is mortal,
Thereby to learnè in especial,
How ye shall trace the dance of Macabree,
To man and woman alike natural;
For death ne spareth high ne low degree.

In this mirror every wight° may findè,   *man*
What him behooveth to go upon this dancè.   10
Who goeth toforn° or who shall go behindè,   *in front*
All dependeth in Goddès ordinancè.
Wherfore each man lowly take his chancè;
Death spareth neither poor nor blood royal:
Each man therefore have this in remembrancè,
Of one matter God hath y-forgèd° all.   *made*

James I, King of Scotland

64. from *The Kingis Quair*

Since thou virtue increaseth dignity,
And virtue flower and root is of noblay,°   *splendour*
Of any weal or what estate thou be,
His steppès sue,° and dread thee none affray: *follow*
Exile all vice, and follow truth alway:
Love mayest thy God, that first thy life began,
And for ilk° inch he will thee quite* a span.   *each; give*

Be not e'er proud in thy prosperity,
For as it comes, so will it pass away;
Thy time to count is short, thou may well see,   10
For of green grass soon comès wallowed° hay.   *rolled*
Labour in truth, while light is of the day.
Trust mayest in God, for he best guide thee can,
And for ilk inch he will thee quite a span.

Said word is thrall,° and thought is only free,   *captive*
Thou dant° thy tongue, that power has and may;   *silence*
Thou stake° thine eyen from worldly vanity;   *avert*
Refrain thy lust, and hearken what I say;
Grip or thou slide, and creep forth on the way;
Keep thy behest° unto thy God and man,   *promise* 20
And for ilk inch he will thee quite a span.

Robert Henryson

65. The Tale of the Uponlandis° Mouse, and the Burges* Mouse

country;
town

Aesop, mine Author, makès mention
Of two mice, and they were Sisters dear,
Of whom the eldest dwelt in a Borous° town,   *burgh*
The other wynnit° uponland* well near;   *lived; in the country*
Solitar, while° under busk,* while under briar,   *now; bush*
Whiles in the corn, in° other mennès skaith,*   *to; harm*
As outlaws do, and livès on their waith.°   *plunder*

This rural mouse into the winter tide°   *time*
Had hunger, cold, and tholit° great distress;   *endured*
The other mouse, that in the burgh° can bide,   *town* 10
Was Guild brother and made a free burgess;°   *citizen*
Toll-free° als,* but custom‡ more or less,   *tax-free; also; without duty*
And freedom had to go where ever she list,
Among the cheese in ark,° and meill* in kist.‡   *bin; flour; chest*

One time when she was full and unfutesore,°   *not footsore*
She took in mind her sister uponland,
And longèd for to hear of her welfare,
To see what life she had under the wand.°   *in the greenwood*
Barefoot, alone, with pikestaff in her hand,
As pure pilgrim she passèd out of town,   20
To seek her sister both o'er dale and down.

Forth many wilsum° wayès can she walk,   *wild*
Through moss and moor, through bankès, bush and briar,
From fur° to fur, crying from balk* to balk: *furrow; ridge*
'Come forth to me, my owèn Sister dear,
Cry peep anis!'° With that the Mouse could hear,   *just once*
And knew her voice as kinnèsmen will do,
By verray° kind;* and forth she com her to.   *true; nature*

The heartly joy, God! if ye had seenè,
Be kithit° when that thir* Sisterès meet;   *shown; these* 30
And great kindness was showen them betweenè,

For whiles they laugh,° and whiles for joy they greet,   *laughed*
Whiles kissèt sweet, whiles in armès plet;°   *enfolded*
And thus they fure° while* soberit‡ was their moodè, *acted; until; sobered*
Sine° foot for foot* unto the chamber yudè.‡ *Then; keeping pace; went*

As I heard say, it was a sober wane,°   *dwelling*
Of fog° and fernè full feeble was made,   *winter grass*
A sillie° scheill* under a steadfast stone,   *humble; hovel*
Of which the entres° was not high nor broad.   *entrance*
And in the same they went but° more abaid,* *without; delay* 40
Withoutè fire or candle birning bright,
For commonly sic° pikeris* love not light.   *such; pilferers*

When they were lugit° thus, the sely* Mice, *lodged; guileless*
The youngest sister into her buttery° glide,   *larder*
And brought forth nuts, and peas instead of spice;
If this was good fare, I do it on them beside.°   *leave*
The burgess mouse prompit forth° in pride,   *burst forth*
And said, 'Sister, is this your daily food?'
'Why not,' quoth she, 'is not this meat° right good?'   *food*

'No, by my soul, I think it but a scorn.'   50
'Madame,' quoth she, 'ye be the more to blame;
My mother said, sister, when we were born,
That I and ye lay both within one womb.
I keep the rate° and custom of my dame,*   *manner; mother*
And of my sire,° living in poverty,   *father*
For landès have we none in property.'

'My fair sister,' quoth she, 'have me excused.
This rude diet and I can not accord.
To tender meat my stomach is aye used,
For why° I fare as well as any Lord.   *because* 60
These withered peas, and nuts, ere they be bord,°   *broken*
Will break my teeth, and make my wame° full slender, *stomach*
Which was before usèd° to meatès tender.'   *accustomed*

'Well, well, sister,' quoth the rural Mouse,
'If it please you, sic° thing as ye see here,   *such*
Both meat and drink, harberie° and house,   *shelter*
Shall be your own, will ye remain all year.

Ye shall it have with blithe and merry cheer,°   *face*
And that should make the maissis° that are rude,   *dishes*
Among friends, right tender and wonder good.   70

'What pleasure is in the feastès delicate,
The which are given with a glowmand° brow?   *frowning*
A gentle heart is better recreate°   *revived*
With blithe courage, than seith to° him a cow.   *cook for*
A modicum° is more for to allow,*   *small portion; advisable*
Swa that° gude will be carver at the dais,*   *So long as; table*
Than thrawin° vult* and many spicèd maize.'   *bad-tempered; face*

For all her merry exhortation,
This burgess mouse had little will to sing.
But heavily she cast her browès down,   80
For all the dainties that she could her bring.
Yet at the last she said, half in hething,°   *derision*
'Sister, this victual and your royal feast,
May well suffice unto a rural beast.

'Let be° this hole and come into my place;   *Leave behind*
I shall to you show by experience
My Good Friday is better nor° your Pace;*   *than; Easter*
My dish lickings is worth your whole expense.
I have housès anew° of great defence;*   *aplenty; security*
Of Cat, nor fall,° nor trap, I have no dread.'   *box trap* 90
'I grant,' quoth she; and on together they yeid.°   *went*

In skugry° aye, through rankest grass and corne,   *secrecy*
And under bushès privily couth° they creep,   *could*
The eldest was the guide and went before,
The younger to her wayès took good keep.°   *notice*
On° night they ran, and on the day can sleep,   *At*
While in the morning, ere the Laverok° sang,   *skylark*
They found the town, and in blithly couth gang.°   *go*

Not far from thine° unto a worthy wane,*   *there; dwelling*
This burgess brought them soon where they should be.   100
Without 'God speid'° their herberie* was tane,‡   *God's blessing; lodging; taken*
In to a spence° with vittell* great plenty;   *larder; victuals*
Both cheese and butter upon their shelfès high,
And flesh° and fish enough, both freshè and salt,   *meat*
And sackes full of meal and eke of malt.

After when they disposed were to dine,
Withouten grace they wash and went to meat,
With all coursès that cookès could devine,°   *devise*
Mutton and beef, strikin° in tailyeis* great.   *cut; portions*
A lordès fare thus could they counterfeit,°   *imitate* 110
Except one thing, they drank the water cleir°   *pure*
Instead of wine, but yet they made good cheer.

With blithe upcast and merry countenance,
The eldest Sister sperit° at her guest   *asked*
If that she by reason found difference
Betwixt that chamber and her sorry nest.
'Yea, dame,' quoth she, 'but how long will this last?'
'For evermore, I wait,° and longer too.'   *know*
'If it be so, ye are at ease,' quoth she.

To eke° their cheer a subcharge* forth she brought, *increase; extra course* 120
A plate off grottis,° and a dish full of meal;   *groats*
Thraf cakes° as I trow* she sparèd nought,   *oatcakes; believe*
Abundantly about her for to deal.
And mane° full fine she brought in stead of jell,*   *white bread; jelly*
And a white candle out of a coffer° stole,   *chest*
Instead of spicè to gust their mouth° withall.   *please their mouths*

Thus made they merry while° they might no more   *until*
And 'Hail, yule, hail!' cryèd upon high;
Yet after joy ofttimes comès care,°   *sorrow*
And trouble after great prosperity.   130
Thus as they sat in all their jolity,
The spenser° come with keyès in his hand,   *steward*
Openèd the door, and them at dinner fand.°   *found*

They taryit° not to wash, as I suppose,   *delayed*
But on to go where that might formest win.   *fastest*
The burgess had one hole, and in she goes,
Her sister had no hole to hide her in:
To see that selie° Mouse it was great sin,   *innocent*
So desolate and will of° one good reid,*   *at a loss for; plan*
For verray dread she fell in swoon near dead.   140

But as God wald,° it fell an happy case,*   *wished; situation*
The spenser had no leisure for to byde,°   *stay*
Neither to seek, nor serch, to scare nor chase,

But on he went, and left the door up° widè.   *open*
The bold burgess his passing well has spied,
Out of her hole she come, and cried on high,
'How fare ye, sister? cry peep, where e'er ye be.'

This rural mous lay flatling on the ground,
And for the death she was full sore dredand,°   *dreading*
For to her heart struck many woefull stound,°   *pangs* 150
As in a fever she trembled foot and hand.
And when her sister in such ply° her fand,   *plight*
For verray pity she began to greit,°   *weep*
Syne comfort her with wordès honey sweet.

'Why lie ye thus? rise up, my sister dear,
Come to your meat, this peril is overpast.'
The other answered her with heavy cheer,
'I may not eat, so sore I am aghast;
I had lever° thir* forty dayès fast,   *rather; suffer*
With water cail,° and to gnaw beans or peas,   *weak soup* 160
Than all your feast in this dread and disease.'°   *distress*

With fair trety° yet she gart* her uprise,   *entreaty; caused*
And to the board they went and together sat,
And scantly° had thay drunken once or twice,   *scarcely*
When in come Gib Hunter, our jolly cat,
And bade 'God speed'. The burgess up with that,
And to her hole she went as fire° off flint;   *spark*
Bawdronis° the other by the back has hint.*   *(the cat); seized*

From foot to foot he cast her to and fro,
Whiles° up, whiles down, as cant* as any kid;‡ *now; lively; little goat* 170
Whiles would he let her run under the straw,
Whiles would he wink, and play with her buk-heid.°   *blind man's buff*
Thus to the selie° Mouse great pain he did,   *innocent [cf silly]*
While at the last, through fortune and good hap,°   *chance*
Betwixt ane burdè° and the wall she crap.*   *floorboard; crept*

And up in haste behind a parraling°   *wall-hanging*
She climbed so high, that Gilbert might not get her,
Sine° by the cluke* there craftily gan‡ hang   *Afterwards; claws; did*
Till he was gone; her cheer was all the better.
Sine down she lap° when there was none to let* her, *leapt; prevent* 180
And to the burgess mouse loud gan she cry,
'Farewell, sister, thy feast here I defy!'°   *reject*

'Thy mangerie° is mingit* all with care,   *feast; mixed*
Thy goose is good, thy gansel° sour as gall.   *sauce*
The subcharge° of thy service is but sore,*   *hidden charge; sorrow*
So shall thou find here afterward may fall.°   *happen*
I thank yon curtain and yon perpall wall*   *yonder; partition*
Of my defence now from yon cruel beast.
Almighty God, keep me from such a feast!

'Were I into° the kith* that I come fra,‡   *in; land; from* 190
For weil° nor woe should I never come again.'   *joy*
With that she took her leave and forth gan go,
Whiles through the corn, and whilès through the plain;
When she was forth and free she was full fane,°   *glad*
And merrily markèt° unto the moor.   *found her way*
I can not tell how well therafter she furè.°   *fared*

But I heard say she passèd to her den,
As warm as wool, suppose it° was not great,*   *even if; grand*
Full beinly° stuffit,* both but‡ and ben,   *well; filled; larder*
Of beans, and nuttès, peas, rye, and wheat.   200
Whenever she list, she had enough to eat,
In quiet and ease, withouten any dread;
But to her sister's feast no more she yeid.°   *went*

MORALITAS

Friendès, ye may find, and ye will take heed,
Into this fable a good morality.
As fitchis° myngit* are with noble seed,   *vetches (weeds); mingled*
Such intermingling is adversity
With earthly joy, so that no estate° is free,   *social class*
Without trouble and some vexation:
And namely they which climbès up most high,   210
That are not content with small possession.

Blessed be simple life withouten dread;
Blessed be sober feast in quiety;°   *peace*
Who has enough, of no more has he need,
Though it be little into quantity.
Great abundance and blind prosperity
Oft times makes an evil conclusion:
The sweetest life therefore, in this country,
Is sickerness° with small possession.   *security*

O wanton man! that uses° for to feed   *is accustomed* 220
Thy womb,° and makès it a God to be,   *stomach*
Look to thyself; I warn thee well but dread,
The Cat comès, and to the mouse has eye.
What vailès° then thy feast and royalty,*   *avails; splendour*
With dreadfull heart, and tribulation?
Best thing in earth, therefore, I say, for me,
Is blitheness in heart, with small possession.

Thy own fire, my friend, so it be but a gleid,°   *ember*
It warmès well, and is worth Gold to thee.
And Solomon says, if that thou will read,   230
'Under the heaven there can not better be,
Than aye° be blithe and live in honesty.'   *always*
Wherefore I may conclude by this reason:
Of earthly joy it bearès most degree,°   *is most important*
Blitheness in heart, with small possession.

66. *The Testament of Cresseid*

A doolie° season to one care-full* dyte‡   *doleful; sorrowful; style*
Should correspond, and be equivalent.
Right so it was when I began to write
This tragedy, the weather right fervent°   *severe*
When Aries, in the middès° of the Lent,   *midst*
Showers of hail gan from the north descend,
That scantily from the cold I might defend.

Yet nevertheless within mine oratur°   *oratory*
I study, when Titan had his beamès bright
Withdrawèn down and sylit° under cure*   *concealed; cover* 10
And fair Venus, the beauty of the night,
Uprose, and set unto the west full right
Her golden face, in opposition
Of god Pheobus, direct descending down.

Through out the glass her beamès brast° so fair   *pierced*
That I might see on every side me by
The northern wind had purified the air
And shed the misty cloudès from the sky;

The frost freezèd, the blastès bitterly
From Pole Arctic come whistling loud and shrill,   20
And caused me remove° against my will.   *leave*

For I trusted that Venus, lovès queenè,
To whom some time I hecht° obedience,   *vowed*
My faded heart of love she would make greenè,
And thereupon with humble reverence
I thought to pray her high magnificence;
But for° great cold as than I lattit* was,   *because of; stopped*
And in my chalmer° to the fire can pass.*   *chamber; went*

Though love be hot, yet in a man of age
It kindles not so soon as in youth-hood,   30
Of whom the blood is flowing in a rage,
And in the old the courage° doif* and dead,   *desire; dull*
Of which the fire outward is best remeid;°   *remedy*
To help by physic° where that nature failit*   *medicine; fails*
I am expert, for both I have assailit.°   *tried*

I mend the fire and beikit° me about,   *warmed*
Than took a drink my spirits to comfort,
And armed me well from the cold there out.
To cut the winter night and make it short,
I took a quair,° and left all other sport,*   *book (quire of pages); pastime* 40
Written by worthy Chaucer glorious,
Of fair Creisseid, and worthy Troilus.

And there I found, after that Diomeid
Received had that Lady bright of hue,
How Troilus near out of wit abraid,°   *went*
And weepèd sore with visage° pale of hue;   *face*
For which wanhope° his tearès can renew   *despair*
While Esperous° rejoicèd him again,   *the evening star (hope)*
Thus while° in joy he livèd, while in pain.   *now*

Of her behest° he had great comforting,   *promise* 50
Trusting to Troy that she should make retour,°   *return*
Which he desirèd most of earthly thing
For why° she was his only Paramour;   *because*
But when he saw passèd both day and hour
Of her gaincome,° then sorrow gan oppress   *return*
His woeful heart in care and heaviness.

Of his distress me needès nought rehearse,°   *relate*
For worthy Chaucer in the samè book
In goodly termès and in jolly verse
Compilèd has his carès, who will look.   60
To break my sleep another quair I took,
In which I found the fatal destiny
Of fair Cresseid, that ended wretchedly.

Who wait° if all that Chaucer wrote was true?   *knows*
Nor I wait not if this narration
Be authorised, or feignèd of the new
By some poet, through his invention,
Made to report the lamentation
And woeful end of this lusty° Cresseid,   *lively*
And what distress she thoillit,° and what deid.*   *suffered; death* 70

When Diomede had all his appetite,
And more, fulfilled of this fair Lady,
Upon another he set his whole delight
And sent to her a libel of repudie,°   *writ of rejection (divorce)*
And her excluded from her company.
Then desolate she walkèd up and down,
And some men says, unto the court common.°   *was promiscuous*

O fair Creisseid, the flower and A per se°   *paragon*
Of Troy and Greece, how was thou fortunate°   *predestined*
To change in filth all thy Feminity,   80
And be with fleshly lust so maculate,°   *stained*
And go among the Greekès ere° and late   *early*
So giglotlike,° taking thy foul plesance!   *whore-like*
I have pity thou should fall such mischance.

Yet nevertheless what ever men deme° or say   *judge*
In scornful language of thy brukkilness,°   *frailty*
I shall excuse, as far forth as I may,
Thy womanhood, thy wisdom and fairness:
The which Fortune has put to such distress
As her pleasèd, and nothing through the guilt   90
Of thee, through wicked language to be split.

This fair Lady, in this wise destitute
Of all comfort and consolation

Right privelie,° but* fellowship, on foot *secretly; without*
Disguised passèd far out of the town
A mile or two, unto a mansion
Builded full gay, where her father Calchas
Who then among the Greekès dwelling was.

When he her saw, the cause he gan inquire
Of her coming; she said, sighing full sore: 100
'From° Diomeid had gotten his desire *When*
He wax° weary, and would of me no more.' *grew*
Quoth Calchas, 'Daughter, weep thou not therefore;
Peraventure° all comès for the best; *Perhaps*
Welcome to me, thou art full dear a guest.'

This oldè Calchas, after° the law was tho,* *in accordance with; then*
Was keeper of the temple as a priest,
In which Venus and her son Cupido
Were honourèd, and his chalmer was them neist,° *nearest*
To which Cresseid with bail° enough in breast *sadness* 110
Usèd to pace, her prayrès for to say.
While at the last, upon a solemnè day,

As custom was, the people far and near
Before the noon, unto the Temple went,
With sacrifice, devout in their manner:
But still Cresseid, heavy in her intent,° *mind*
Into the kirk° would not her self present, *church*
For giving of the people any deming° *suspicion*
Of her expulse° from Diomeid the King; *expulsion*

But pased into a secret orature° *oratory* 120
Where she might weep her woefull destiny,
Behind her back she closed fast the door
And on her kneès bare fell down in hie.° *haste*
Upon Venus and Cupid angrily
She cryèd out, and said on this same wise,
'Alas that ever I made you sacrifice!

'Ye gave me once a divine responsail° *promise*
That I should be the flower of love in Troy;

Now am I made an unworthy outwail,°   *outcast*
And all in° care translated is my joy,   *into* 130
Who shall me guide? who shall me now convoy°   *accompany*
Since I from Diomeid and noble Troilus
Am clean excluded, as abject odious?

'O false Cupid, is none to wite° but thou,   *blame*
And thy mother, of love the blind goddess!
Ye caused me always understand and trow°   *trust*
The seed of love was sowen in my face,
And aye grew green through your supply and grace.
But now alas that seed with frost is slain,
And I fra° lovers left and all forlane.'*   *by; abandoned* 140

When this was said, down in an ecstasy,
Ravished in sprite,° into a dream she fell,   *spirit*
And by appearance° heard, where she did lie,   *apparently*
Cupid the king ringing a silver bell,
Which men might hear from heaven unto hell;
At whose sound before Cupid appears
The seven planets descending from their spheres,

Which has power of all thing generabil°   *created*
To rule and steer by their great influence,
Weather and wind, and coursès variable.°   *(of fortune)* 150
And first of all Saturn gave his sentence,
Which gave to Cupid little reverence,
But, as a busteous° churl* in his manner,   *rude; peasant*
Came crabbily with austere look and cheer.°   *manner*

His facè fronsit,° his lyre* was like the lead,   *wrinkled; complexion*
His teeth chattered, and shivered with the chin,
His eyèn° droopèd, how sunken in his head,   *eyes*
Out of his nose the meldrop fast can run,   *snot*
With lippès blue and cheekès lean and thin;
The icicles that from his hair down hang   160
Was wonder great, and as a spear as long.

Atovir° his belt his lyart* lockès lay   *Over; grizzled*
Felterit° unfair, o'erfret* with frostès hoar,   *matted; covered with*
His garments and his gyte° full gay of grey,   *cloak*
His widderit weid° from him the wind out woir;*   *tattered clothes; fluttered*
A busteous° bow within his hand he bore,   *large*
Under his girdle a flashe of fellon flanès,°   *sheaf of deadly arrows*
Featherèd with ice, and headed° with hailstonès.   *tipped*

Then Jupiter, right fair and amiable
God of the starnis° in the firmament,   *stars* 170
And nureis° to all thing generabil,   *nurse*
From his father Saturn far different,
With burly° face, and browès bright and brent,*   *handsome; lofty*
Upon his head a garland, wonder gay,
Of flowers fair, as it had been in May.

His voice was clear, as crystal were his eyèn,
As golden wire so glittering was his hair;
His garment and his guise full gay of greenè,
With golden listis° gilt on every gair;*   *hems; seam*
A burelie brand° about his middle bare;*   *strong sword; carried* 180
In his right hand he had a groundin° spear,   *sharpened*
Of his father the wrath from us to weir.°   *ward off*

Next after him come Mars, the god of Ire,
Of strife, debate, and all dissension,
To chide and fight, as fierce as any fire;
In hard harness,° hewmound* and habergeon,‡   *armour; helmet; mailcoat*
And on his hanchè° a rusty fell falchion;*   *hip; cruel scimitar*
And in his hand he had a rusty sword;
Writhing his face with many angry word,

Shaking his sword, before Cupid he came   190
With red visage, and grisly glowering eyèn;   *bubble*
And at his mouth a bullar° stoodè of foam
Like to a boar whetting his tuskès keen,
Right tuitlyeourlyke,° but* temperance in tenè;‡   *bully-like; without; rage*
A horn he blew, with many bosteous brag,°   *grating blasts*
Which all this world with war has made to wag.°   *tremble*

Then fair Phoebus, lanternè and lamp of light
Of man and beast, both fruit and flourishing,°   *blossom*
Tender nureis,° and banisher of night,   *nurse*
And of the world causing, by his moving   200
And influence, life in all earthly thing,
Without comfort of whom, of force° to nought*   *of necessity; nothing*
Must all go die that in this world is wrought.°   *made*

As king royal he rode upon his chair
The which Phaeton guided some time° unright;*   *once; off course*
The brightness of his face when it was bare
None might behold for piercing of his sight.
This golden cart with fiery beamès bright
Four yokèd steeds full different of hue,
But° bait* or tiring, through the spherès drew.   *Without; halting* 210

The first was soyr,° with mane as red as rose,   *sorrel*
Callèd Eyore into the Orient;
The second steed to name hight° Ethios,   *was called*
Whitely and pale, and some deal ascendent;°   *rearing*
The third Peros, right hot and right fervent;°   *passionate*
The fourth was black, callèd Philologie
Which rollès° Phoebus down into the sea.   *drives*

Venus was there present, that goddess gay,
Her sonès quarrel for to defend and make
Her own complaint, clad in a nice° array: *extravagant* 220
The one half greenè, the other half sable black;
White hair as gold combed and sched° aback;   *parted*
But in her face seemèd great variance,
Whilès perfyte truth, and whilès inconstance.

Under smiling she was dissimulait,°   *dissembling*
Provocative, with blenkès° amorous,   *glances*
And suddenely changed and alterait,
Angry as any serpent venomous,
Right pungitive,° with wordès odious.   *stinging*
Thus variant she was, who list take keep,°   *notice* 230
With one eye laugh, and with the other weep.

In taikning° that all fleshy paramour*   *Betokening; sexual love*
Which Venus has in rule and governance
Is some time sweet, some time bitter and sour,
Right unstable, and full of variance,
Mingit° with carefull joy and false plesance,*   *Mingled; pleasantry*
Now hot, now cold, now blithe,° now full of woe,   *happy*
Now green as leaf, now withered and ago.°   *over*

With book in hand then come Mercurius,
Right eloquent, and full of rethorie,°   *rhetoric* 240
With polite termès and delicious,

With pen and ink to report all ready,
Setting° songs and singing merriliy: *Composing*
His hood was red, heklit° atouir* his crown,   *fringed; over*
Likè to a poet of the old fashion.

Boxes he bore with fine electuairis,°   *elixirs*
And suggared syrups for digestion,
Spices belonging to the pothecaries,°   *chemists*
With many wholesome sweet confection,
Doctor in physic clad in a Scarlet gown,   250
And furrit° well, as such one ought to be,   *fur-clad*
Honest and good, and not one word could lie.

Next after him come Lady Cynthia,
The last of all, and swiftest in her sphere,
Of colour black, busked° with hornès two,   *arrayed*
As in the night she listes° best appear.   *likes*
Haw° as the lead, of colour nothing clear;   *Dull-coloured*
For all her light she borrowès at her brother
Titan, for of herself she has none other.

Her gyte° was grey, and full of spottès black,   *costume* 260
And on her breast a churlè° painted full even,*   *peasant; very accurately*
Bearing a bunch of thornès on his back,
Which for his theft might climb no near° the heaven.   *nearer*
Thus when they gathered were,° the goddès seven,   *clad*
Mercurius° they chosè with one assent   *Mercury*
To be fore-speaker° in the Parliament.   *first speaker*

Who had been there, and liken for to hear
His facound° tongue, and termès exquisite,   *eloquent*
Of rhetoric the prettick° he might leir,*   *practice; learn*
In brief sermon a pregnant sentence write: 270
Before Cupidè veiling° his Cap a lite,*   *raising; a little*
Speiris° the cause of that vocation,*   *Asks; calling together*
And he anon showed his intention.

'Lo!' quoth Cupidè, 'who will blaspheme the name
Of his own god, either in word or deed,
To all gods he does both lack° and shame,   *censure*
And should have bitter painès to his meed.°   *reward*

I say this by yon wretched Cresseid,
The which through me was some time flower of love,
Me and my Mother starkly can reprove,   280

'Saying of her great infelicity
I was the cause, and my mother Venus.
A blind goddess her called,° that might not see,   *she (Cresseid) called her*
With slander and defame injurious;
Thus her living unclean and lecherous
She would return° on me and my Mother,   *blame*
To whom I shew my grace above all other.

'And since ye are all seven deificat,°   *divine*
Participant of divinè sapience,°   *wisdom*
This great injury done to our high estate   290
Me think with pain we should make recompense;
Was never to goddès done such violence.
As well for you as for myself I say;
Therefore go help to revengè, I you pray.'

Mercurius to Cupidè gave answer
And said: 'Sir King my counsel is that ye
Refer you to the highest planet here,
And take to him the lowest of degree,
The pain° of Cresseid for to modify;*   *punishment; determine*
As god Saturnè, with him take Cynthia.'   300
'I am content,' quoth he, 'to take they twa.'°   *two*

Then thus proceeded Saturn and the Moonè,
When they the matter ripely had digest,°   *considered*
For the dispite° to Cupid she had done,   *contempt*
And to Venus open and manifest,°   *blatant*
In all her life with pain to be oppressed,
And torment sore, with sickness incurable,
And to all lovers be abominable.

This doleful sentence Saturn took on hand,
And passèd down where care-full Cresseid lay,   310

And on her head he laid a frosty wand;
Then lawfully° in this wise can he say: *in accordance with legal procedure*
'Thy great fairness and all thy beauty gay,
Thy wanton blood, and eik thy golden hair,
Here I exclude from thee for evermore.

'I change thy mirth into melancholy,
Which is the mother of all pensiveness;
Thy moisture and thy heat in cold and dry;
Thine insolence, thy play and wantonness
To great disease; thy pomp and thy riches   *320*
In mortal need; and great penuritie°   *poverty*
Thou suffer shall, and as a beggar die.'

O cruell Saturne! fraward° and angry,   *adverse*
Hard is thy doom,° and too malicious;   *judgement*
On fair Cresseid why has thou no mercy,
Which was so sweet, gentle and amorous?
Withdraw thy sentence and be gracious
As thou was never; so showès thou thy deed,
A wraikfull° sentence given on fair Cresseid.   *cruel*

Then Cynthia, when Saturn passed away,   *330*
Out of her seat descended down belyve,°   *briskly*
And read a bill° on Cresseid where she lay,   *formal statement*
Containing this sentence definitive:
'Fra heat of body I thee now deprive,
And to thy sickness shall be no recure,°   *recovery*
But in dolour thy dayès to endure.

'Thy crystal eyèn minglit with blood° I make,   *bloodshot*
Thy voice so clear, unpleasant, hoir° and hace,*   *rough; hoarse*
Thy lusty lyre° o'erspread with spottès black,   *complexion*
And lumpès haw° appearing in thy face.   *lead-hued 340*
Where thou comes, ilk° man shall flee the place.   *each*
Thus shall thou go begging from house to house
With cup and clapper like a lazarus.'°   *leper*

This doolie° dream, this ugly vision   *dismal*
Brought to an end, Cresseid from it awoke,
And all that court and convocation
Vanished away; than rose she up and took

A polished glass, and her shadow could look:
And when she saw her face so deformat° *deformed*
If she in heart was woe° enough God wat.* *sorrowful; knows* 350

Weeping full sore, 'Lo what it is,' quoth she,
'With fraward° language for to mufe* and steir‡ *ill-tempered; irritate; provoke*
Our crabby gods, and so is seen on me!
My blaspheming now have I bought full dear.
All earthly joy and mirth I set arear.° *in the past*
Alas this day, alas this woeful tide,° *time*
When I began with my goddès for to chide.'

Be° this was said a child come from the hall *When*
To warnè Cresseid the supper was ready,
First knockèd at the door and syne° could call: *after* 360
'Madame your Father biddès you come in hie.° *haste*
He has marvel so long on grouf° ye lie, *prostrate*
And says your beedès° been too long somedell; *prayers; somewhat*
The goddès wait° all your intent full well.' *know*

Quoth she: 'Fair child, go to my father dear,
And pray him come to speak with me anon.'° *soon*
And so he did, and said: 'Daughter, what cheer?'
'Alas,' quoth she, 'Father, my mirth is gone.'
'How so?' quoth he; and she gan all expone° *explain*
As I have told, the vengeance and the wraik° *punishment* 370
For her trespass Cupide on her could take.

He lookèd on her ugly leper face,
The which before was white as lily flower,
Wringing his hands oft times he said 'Alas'
That he had lived to see that woeful hour,
For he knew well that there was no succour° *help*
To her sickness, and that doubled his pain.
Thus was there care enough betwixt them twain.

When they together mourned had full long,
Quoth Cresseid: 'Father, I would not be kenned.° *found out* 380
Therefore in secret wise ye let me gang° *go*
Into yon hospital at the town's end.

And thither some meat for charity me send
To live upon, for all mirth in this eird°   *earth*
Is from me gone, such is my wicked weird.'°   *fate*

Then in a mantle and a beaver° hat,   *beaver-fur*
With cup and clapper, wonder° prively,   *very*
He openned a secret gate, and out thereat
Conveyèd her, that no man should espy,
Into a village half a mile thereby,°   *away* 390
Deliverèd her in at the spitail° house,   *[hos]pital*
And daily sent her part of his almous.°   *alms*

Some knew her well, and some had no knowledge
Of her because she was so deformait,°   *deformed*
With boilès black o'erspread in her visage,
And her fair colour faded and alterait.°   *altered*
Yet they presumèd for her high regret°   *extreme distress*
And still° mourning, she was of noble kin: *silent*
With better will therefore they took her in.

The day passed, and Phebus went to rest,   400
The cloudès black o'erheled° all the sky.   *overshadowed*
God wait° if Cresseid was a sorrowfull Guest,   *knows*
Seeing that uncouth fare° and harbery:*   *food; lodging*
But° meat or drink she dressit her* to lie   *Without; resigned herself*
In a dark corner of the house alone,
And on this wise, weeping, she made her moan:

THE COMPLAINT OF CRESSEID

'O sop of sorrow, sunken into care:
O caitive° Creisseid, for now and ever more   *wretched*
Gone is thy joy and all thy mirth on eird,°   *earth*
Of all blitheness now art thou blaiknit bare.°   *made destitute* 410
There is no salve may save° thee of thy sore,   *cure*
Fell is thy fortune, wicked is thy weird:°   *fate*
Thy bliss is banished, and thy bail° on breird,*   *sadness; increases*
Under the earth, God gif° I gravin* were: *grant; buried*
Where none of Greece nor yet of Troy might heard.

'Where is thy chalmer wantonly besene?° — *luxuriously set out*
With burely° bed and bankouris broiderit — *goodly;*
   bene,* — *well-embroidered covers*
Spices and wine to thy collation,° — *evening meal*
The cuppès all of gold and silver shine:
The sweetè Meats, servèd in platès cleanè, — 420
With saffron sals° of a good season: — *sauce*
Thy gay garmentès with many goodely gown,
Thy pleasant lawn pinned with golden prenè:° — *pins*
All is areir,° thy great royal* renown. — *lost; splendid*

'Where is thy garden with the greissis° gay? — *plants*
And freshè flowerès, which the queenè Floray° — *Flora*
Had painted plesantly in every panè,° — *bed*
Where thou was wont full merrily in May
To walk and take the dew be° it was day — *as soon as*
And hear the merle° and mavis* many one, — *blackbird; thrush* 430
With ladies fair in carroling to ganè,° — *go*
And see the royal rinks° in their array, — *men*
In garments gay garnished on every granè.° — *detail*

'Thy great triumphant fame and high honour,
Where thou was callèd of earthly wightès° flower, — *creatures*
All is decayed, thy weird° is weltered* so. — *fate; reversed*
Thy high estate is turned in darkness dour.
This leper lodge take for thy burelie bower.° — *fine chamber*
And for thy bed take now a bunch of stro,° — *straw*
For° waillit* wine, and meatès thou had tho,‡ — *In place of; choice; then* 440
Take mowlit° bread, peirrie* and cider sour: — *mouldy; perry*
But° cup and clapper, now is all ago. — *Except*

'My clear voice, and courtly carrolling,
Where I was wont with Ladies for to sing,
Is rawk° as rook, full hideous hoir and hace, — *rough*
My pleasant port° all otherès precelling:* — *bearing; excelling*
Of lustiness° I was held most conding.* — *liveliness; excellent*
Now is deformèd the figure of my face,
To look on it, na leid° now liking has: — *man*
Sowpit in syte,° I say with sore sighing, — *Drowned in sorrow* 450
Lodgèd among the leper leid° alas. — *folk*

'O Ladies fair of Troy and Greece, attend
My misery, which none may comprehend.

My frivoll° fortune, my infelicity: *frivolous*
My great mischief, which no man can amend.
Beware in time, approchès near the end;
And in your mind a mirror make of me:
As I am now, peradventure that ye
For all your might may come to that same end,
Or ellès war,° if any war may be. *worse* 460

'Nought is your fairness but a fading flower,
Nought is your famous laud° and high honour *praise*
But wind inflate° in other mennès earès. *blown into*
Your roising reid° to rotting shall retour.* *rosy complexion; return*
Example make of me in your memour,° *memory*
Which of such things woeful witness bearès,
All wealth in earth, away as wind it weiris.° *passes*
Be ware therefore, approachès near the hour:
Fortune is fickle, when she begins and stirs.'

Thus chiding with her dreary destiny, 470
Weeping, she woke the night from end to end.
But all in vain; her dole, her care-full cry
Might not remede,° nor yet her mourning mend. *remedy*
A leper lady rose and to hir wend,° *went*
And said: 'Why spurnès° thou against the wall, *kickest*
To slay thy self, and mend nothing at all?

'Since thy weeping doubles but thy woe,
I counsel thee make virtue of a need.
Go leir° to clap thy clapper to and fro, *learn*
And live after the law of lipper leid.' 480
There was no buit,° but forth with them she yeid,* *remedy; went*
From place to place, while cold and hunger sore
Compellèd her to be a rank beggar.

That samèn time of Troy the garrison,
Which had to° chieftan worthy Troilus, *as*
Through jeopardy of war had stricken down
Knightès of Greece in number marvellous,
With great triumph and laud victorious

Again to Troy right Royally they raid°   *rode*
The way where Cresseid with the lipper baid.°   *stayed* 490

Seeing that company they come all with one steven,°   *voice*
They gave one cry and shook cuppès goodè speed.
Said, 'Worthy Lords for goddès love of heaven,
To us lipper part of your Almous deid.'°   *give*
Then to their cry noble Troilus took heed,
Having piety, near by the place gan pass
Where Cresseid sat, not witting° what she was.   *knowing*

Then upon him she cast up both her Eyèn,
And with a blenk° it come into his thought,   *glance*
That he sometime her face before had seen.   500
But she was in such plight he knew her not,
Yet then her look into his mind it brought
The sweet visage and amorous blenking
Of fair Cresseid sometime his owèn darling.

Na wonder was, suppose° in mind that he   *even if*
Took her figure so soon, and lo now why?
The idolè of one thing, in case° may be   *a situation*
So deep imprinted in the fantasy
That it deludes the wittès outwardly,
And so appears in form and like estait,   510
Within the mind as it was figurait.°   *formed*

A spark of love then to his heart could spring
And kindled all his body in a fire.
With hot fever and sweat and trembling
Him took, while he was ready to expire.
To bear his shield, his breast began to tire;
Within one while° he changèd many hue,   *moment*
And nevertheless not one one other knew.

For knightly piety and memorial
Of fair Cresseid, one girdle° gan he take,   *belt* 520
A purse of gold, and many gay jewel,
And in the skirt of Cresseid down gan swak;°   *tossed*
Then rode away, and not one word he spak,
Pensive in heart, while he come to the town,
And for great care oft sighès almost fell down.

The leper folk to Cresseid then gan draw,
To see the equal distribution
Of the Almous,° but when the gold they saw, — *Alms*
Ilk° one to other privily gan roun,* — *each; whisper*
And said: 'Yon Lord has more affection, — 530
How ever it be, unto yon lazarous
Than to us all, we know by his Almous.'

'What Lord is yon,' quoth she, 'have ye no feill,° — *idea*
Has done to us so great humanity?'
'Yes,' quoth a leper man, 'I know him well,
Sir Troilus it is, gentle and fre.'° — *generous*
When Cresseid understood that it was he,
Stiffer than steel, there start a bitter stound° — *pang*
Throughout her heart, and fell down to the ground.

When she o'ercame, with sighing sore and sad, — 540
With many care-full cry and cold ochane:° — *alas*
'Now is my breast with stormy stoundès stad,° — *beset*
Wrappèd in woe, one wretch full will of wane.'° — *empty of hope*
Then swooned she oft or° she could refrain, — *before*
And ever in her swooning cryed she thus:
'O false Cresseid and true knight Troilus.

'Thy love, thy lawtie° and thy gentilness, — *loyalty*
I counted small in my prosperity,
So elevait° I was in wantoness, — *high*
And clam° upon the fickle wheel so high: — *climbed* 550
All faith and love I promisèd to thee,
Was in itself fickle and frivolous:
O false Cresseid, and true knight Troilus.

'For love of me thou kept good continence,° — *self-restraint*
Honest and chaste in conversation.
Of all women protector and defence
Thou was, and helpèd their opinion.° — *reputation*
My mind in fleshly foul affection
Was inclinèd to lustès lecherous:
Fie false Cresseid, O true knight Troilus. — 560

'Lovers beware and take good heed about
Whom that ye love, for whomè ye suffer pain.

I let you wit,° there is right few thereout*   *know; out in the world*
Whom ye may trust to have true love again.°   *in return*
Prove° when ye will, your labour is in vain.   *try*
Therefore, I reid,° ye take them as ye find,   *advise*
For they are sad° as weathercock in wind,   *constant*

'Because I know the great unstableness,
Brukkill° as glass, unto my self I say,   *brittle*
Trusting° in other as great unfaithfulness,   *Expecting* 570
As inconstant, and as untrue of fay.°   *faith*
Though some be true, I wit° right few are they,   *know*
Who findès truth, let him his lady ruse:°   *praise*
None but my self as now I will accuse.'

When this was said, with paper she sat down,
And in this manner made her testament.
'Here I beteiche° my corpse and carioun*   *bequeath; dead body*
With wormès and with toadès to be rent.°   *torn*
My cup and clapper and mine ornament,
And all my gold the leper folk shall have,   580
When I am dead, to bury me in grave.

'This royal ring, set with this ruby red,
Which Troilus in drowrie° to me send,   *as a sign of his love*
To him again I leave it when I am dead,
To make my care-full deed unto him kend:°   *known*
Thus I conclude shortly, and make an end,
My Spreit° I leave to Diane where she dwells,   *spirit*
To walk with her in waste woodès and wells.°   *streams*

'O Diomeid, thou has both brooch and belt,
Which Troilus gave me in takning°   *tokening* 590
Of his true love!' And with that word she swelt.°   *died*
And soon a Leper man took off the ring,
Syne° buried her withouten tarrying.   *Then*
To Troilus forthwith the ring he bare,
And of Cresseid the death he gan declare.

When he had heard her great infirmity,
Her Legacy and Lamentation,

And how she endèd in sic° poverty,   *such*
He swelt° for woe, and fell down in a swoon,   *fainted*
For great sorrow his heart to burst was boun:°   *about to* 600
Sighing full sadly, said: 'I can no more,
She was untrue, and woe is me therefore.'

Some said he made a tomb of marble grey,
And wrote her name and superscription,
And laid it on her grave where that she lay,
In golden letters, containing this ressoun:°   *inscription*
'Lo, fair ladies, Cresseid, of Troyès town,
Some time counted the flower of womanhood,
Under this stone, late° leper, lyès dead.'   *ugly*

Now, worthy women, in this ballet short,   *poem* 610
Made for your worship° and instruction,   *honour*
Of Charity, I monish° and exhort,   *admonish*
Ming° not your love with false deception.   *Mingle*
Bear in your mind this short conclusion
Of fair Cresseid, as I have said before.
Sen° she is dead, I speak of her no more.   *Since*

67. A Prayer for the Pest°   *Plague*

O eternè god, of power infinite,
To whose high knowledge no thing is obscure,
That is, or was, or ever shall be, perfyt,°   *perfect*
In to thy sight, while that this world endure;
Have mercy of us, indigent and poor;
Thou does no wrong to punish° our offence: *in punishing*
O Lord, that is to mankind haill° succure,*   *wholly; perfect*
Preserve us from this perilous pestilence.

We thee beseech, O Lord of lordès all,
Thy ears incline and hear our great regret;   10
We ask remeid° of thee in general,   *cure*
That is of help and comfort desolate;
But° thou with rewth* our heartès recreate,‡ *Unless; pity; revive*
We are but dead but only thy clemence:
We thee exhort, on knees low postrate,
Preserve us from this perilous pestilence.

We are right glad thou punish our trespass
By any kind of other tribulation.
Were it thy will, O Lord of heaven, alas,
That we should thus be hastily put down,   20
And die as beasts without confession,
That none dare make with other residence?
O blessed Jesu, that wore the thorny crown,
Preserve us from this perilous pestilence.

Use derth, O Lord, or sickness and hunger sore,
And slake thy plague that is so penetrive.°   *cruel*
Thy people are perished: who may remeid° therefore,   *assuage*
But thou, O Lord, that for them lost thy life?
Suppose our sin be to thee pungitive,°   *annoying*
Our death may nothing our sinnes recompense.   30
Have mercy, Lord, we may not with thee strive:
Preserve us from this perilous pestilence.

Have mercy, Lord, have mercy, heaven's king!
Have mercy of thy people penitent;
Have mercy of our piteous punishing;
Retreit° the sentence of thy just judgment   *Withdraw*
Against us sinners, that serves° to be schent:*   *deserve; punished*
Without mercy, we may make no defence.
Through that, but rewth,° upon the rood was rent,*   *pity; torn*
Preserve us from this perilous pestilence.   40

Remember, Lord how dear thou has us bought,
That for us sinners shed thy precious blood,
Now to redeem that thou has made of nought,
That is of virtue barren and denude;°   *naked*
Have rewth, Lord, of thine own similitude;°   *likeness*
Punish with pity and not with violence.
We know it is for our ingratitude
That we are punished with this pestilence.

Thou grant us grace for to amend our miss,°   *misdeeds*
And to evade this cruel sudden deid;°   *death* 50
We know our sin is all the cause of this,
For open° sin there is set no remeid.*   *blatant; remedy*
The justice of God mon° punish than but dread,*   *must; without fail*
For by the law he will with none dispense:

Where justice lacks there is eternal feid,°   *wrath*
Of God that should preserve from pestilence.

But would° the headsmen* that should keep the law   *should; leaders*
Punish the people for their transgression,
There would no deid° the people than o'erthrow;   *death*
But they are given so plainly to opression,   60
That God will not hear their intercession;
But all are punished for thair innobedience°   *disobedience*
By sword or deid withouttèn remission,
And has just cause to send us pestilence.

Superne Lucerne° govern* this pestilence,   *Supreme light; control*
Preserve and serve that we not sterve° therein.   *die*
Decline that pain be thy divinè prudence.   *Diminish*
O truth have rewth let not our sloth us twin.°   *divide*
Our syt° full tyt* were we contrite would blin.‡   *suffering; quickly; stop*
Dissever° did never who ever thee besought.   *Abandon* 70
Send grace with space and us embrace from sin.
Let not be tynt° that thou so dear has bought.   *lost*

O prince preclair° this care cotidiane,*   *renowned; daily*
We thee exhort distort° it in exile.   *turn it aside*
But° thou remeid,* this death is but a trane,‡   *Unless; remedy; snare*
For to deceive the laif° and themè beguile.   *others*
But thou so wisè devise to mend this byle°   *outbreak*
Of this mischief who might relieve us ought;
For wrang us win° but thou our sin oursill?*   *profit; hide*
Let not be tynt that thou so dear has bought.   80

Since for our Vice that Justice mon° correct,   *must*
O King most high now pacify thy feid:°   *wrath*
Our sin is huge, refuge we not suspect;°   *expect*
As thou art judge, deluge° us of this dread.   *remove*
In time assent or we be schent with deid;
We us repent and time mispent forthoht:°   *misused*
Therefore evermore be glory to thy Godhead
Let nought be tint that thou so dear has bought.

Gavin Douglas

68. from *Aeneados*

68a. *To Know the Translator*

The **GA**w° unbroken midled* with the **WYN**è,   *gallbladder; mingled*
The **DOW** joined with the **GLASS** rich in a linè:
Who knowès not the translatorès name,
Seek no further, for lo, with little pain
Spy leill° this verse: men clepys* him so at haym.‡ *carefully; call; home*

68b. *General Prologue*

Laud, honour, praisings, thankès infinite
To thee and thy dulcè° ornate fresh endyte,*   *sweet; composed*
Most reverend Virgil, of Latin poets prince,
Gem of engyne° and flood of eloquence,   *ingenuity*
Thou peerless pearl, patron of poetry,
Rose, regester,° palm, lawrer* and glory,   *regulator; laurel*
Chosen carbunkle,° chief flower and cedar tree,   *gem*
Lantern, lode star, mirror and A per se,°   *paragon*
Master of masters, sweet source and springing well
Wide where o'er all rung is thine heavenly bell –   10
I mean thy crafty workès curious
So quick,° lusty and most sententious,*   *lively; full of wisdom*
Pleasant, perfect and feelable° in all degree,   *producing emotion*
As who the matter beheld tofor° their eye,   *before*
In every volume which thee list do writè   *enjoy*
Surmounting far all other maner° enditè,*   *men's; writing*
Like as the rose in June with her sweet smell
The marigold or daisy doth excell.
Why should I then with dull forehead and vain,
With rude engyne and barren empty brain,   20
With bad, harsh speech and lewd° barbour* tongue *unlearned; barbarous*
Presume to write where thy sweet bell is rung
Or conterfeitè so precious wordès dear?
Na,° na, not swa,* but kneel when I them hear.   *no; so*
For what compare betwix° midday and night?   *between*
Or what compare betwix mirkness° and light?   *darkness*

Or what compare is betwix black and white?
Far greater difference betwix my blunt endite
And thy sharp sugured° song Virgilian,   *sweet*
So wisly wrought° with never a word in vain.   *made* 30
My wavering° wit, my cunning feeble at all,   *rambling*
My mind misty, there may not miss a fall –
Stra° for this ignorant blabbering imperfectè   *A straw*
Beside thy polished termès redymytè.°   *beautiful*
And ne'ertheless with support and correction,
For natural love and friendèly affection
Which I bear to thy workès and endytè –
Although God wait therein I know full lytè –
And that thy facund° sentence* might be sung *eloquent; meaning*
In our language as well as Latin tongue –   40
As well? Na, na, impossibile were, per de° –   *by God*
Yet with thy leave, Virgil, to follow thee
I would into my rural vulgar gross
Write some savouring of thine Eneados.°   *Aeneid*
But sure I dread forto disteyn° thee quitè   *spoil*
Through my corrupèt cadence imperfectè –
Disteyn thee? Nay, forsooth, that may I noght;°   *not*
Well may I show my burrel° bustious* thought *homespun; rough*
But thy work shall endure in laud and glory
But° spot or fault condine* etern‡ memory. *Without; suitable for; eternal* 50
Though I offend, onwemmed° is thy fame;   *unblemished*
Thine is the thank and mine shall be the shame.
Who may thy verses follow in all degree
In beauty, sentence and in gravity?
None is, nor was, ne yet shall be, trow° I,   *believe*
Had, has or shall have such craft in poetry.
Of Helicon so drank thou dry the flood
That of thy copious fouth° or plenitude   *abundance*
All must purchase drink at thy sugared tun;°   *barrel*
So lamp of day thou art and shining sun   60
All others on force must their light beg or borrow;
Thou art Vesper and the day star at morrow,° *in the morning*
Thou Phoebus lightner of the planets all –
I not° what duelly* I thee clepè‡ shall, *know not; properly; name*
For thou art all and some, what needès more,
Of Latin poetès that since was, or before.
Of thee writès Macrobius sans° fail   *without*
In his great volume clepit Saturnaill.
Thy sawès° in such eloquence doth fleit,* *sayings; frighten away*

So inventive of rhetoric flowers sweet   70
Thou art, and has so high profound sentence
Thereto, perfect but° onè indigens,*   *except for; failing*
That no lovingès° may do increase thy fame,   *praises*
Nor no reproach diminish thy good name.
But since I am compelled thee to translate,
And not only of my courage, God wat,°   *knows*
Durst enterprise° such outrageous folly,   *undertake*
Where I offend the less reproof serve° I;   *deserve*
And that ye know at whose instance° I took   *suggestion*
Forto translate this most excellent book,   80
I mean Virgillès volume most excellent,
Set this my work full feeble be of rent,°   *value*
At the request of a lord of renown
Of ancestry noble and illustir° baron,   *illustrious*
Father of bookès, protector to science and lair,°   *law*
My special good Lord Henry, Lord Saint Clair,
Who with great instance diverse timès seir°   *separate*
Prayed me translate Virgil or Homer,
Whose pleasure suthly° as I understoodè   *truly*
As near conjunct to his lordship in bloodè   90
So that me thought his request a command,
Half dispared° this work I tookè on hand   *despairing*
Not fully granting nor once saying yea,
But only to assay° how it might be.   *try*
Who might gainsay a lord so gentle and kind
That ever had any courtesy in their mind,
Which beside his innative° policy   *innate*
Humanity, courage, freedom° and chivalry,   *generosity*
Bookès to recollect, to read and see,
Has great delight as ever had Ptolome?   100
Wherefore to his nobility and estate,
What so it be, this book I dedicate,
Written in the language of Scottish nation,
And thus I make my protestation.
First I protest, beau sirs,° by your leave,   *good sirs*
Be well avised° my work or I thee repreif,*   *carefully; reprove*
Consider it warily, read ofter° than anys;*   *more often; once*
Well at a blenk° sle* poetry not tayn‡ is,   *glance; skilful; taken*
And yet forsooth I set my busy pain°   *exertion*
As that I couth° to make it braid* and plain,   *could; clear* 110
Keeping na sudron° but our own language,   *Southern language*
And speakès as I learnt when I was page.°   *a boy*

Nor yet so clean all sudron I refuse,
But some word I pronounce as neighbours does:
Like as in Latin been Grew° termès some,   *Greek*
So me behoved whilum° or then be dumb   *sometimes*
Some bastard Latin, French or English oyss°   *use*
Where scant was Scottish – I had none other choice.
Nocht for our tongue is in the selven° scant   *in itself*
But for that I the fowth° of language want   *abundance* 120
Where as the colour of his property
To keepè the sentens° thereto constrainèd me,   *meaning*
Or than to make my song short some time,
More compendious, or too likely° my rhyme.   *predictable*
Therefore, good friendès, for a gymp° or a bourd,*   *quibble; joke*
I pray you note° me not at every word.   *judge*
The worthy clerk heit° Lawrence of the Vale,   *called*
Among Latinès a great patron sans° fail,   *without*
Grants when twelve years he had been diligent
To study Virgil, scant knew what he meant   130
Than thou or I, my friend, when we best ween°   *believe*
To have Virgilè read, understand° and seen,   *understood*
The right sentence perchance is far to seek.
This work twelve yearès first was in making eke°   *also*
And not correct when the poet gan decess;°   *stopped*
Thus for small faults, my wise friend, hold thy peace.
    Adhering to my protestation,
Though William Caxton, of English nation,
In press has prent° one book of English gross,*   *printed; ugly*
Cleping° it Virgil in Eneados,   *Calling* 140
While that he says of° French he did translate,   *from*
It has no thing ado° therewith, God wat,   *to do*
Ne na more like than the devil and Saint Austin.°   *Augustine*
Have he no thank therefore, but lose° his pyne,*   *waste; effort*
So shamefully that story did pervert.
I read his work with harmès° at my heart,   *suffering*
That such a book but° sentence or engine*   *without; conception*
Should be intitillit after the poet divine;   *dedicated*
His ornate golden versès more than gilt.°   *gilding*
I spitted° for dispite to see so spoilt   *spat* 150
With such a wight,° who truely by mine intent*   *person; I reckon*
Knew never three words at all what Virgil meant –
So far he chowpis° I am constrained to flyte.*   *mumbles; attack*
The three first bookès he has ourhipped° quite   *skipped*
Salving° a little touching Polidorus   *Except for*

And the tempest forth sent by Eolus,
And that full simply on his owèn guise;
Virgil them wrote all in another wise,
For Caxton puttès in his bookè out of tune
The storm forth sent by Eolus and Neptune,   160
But whoso readès Virgil soothfastly°   *truthfully*
Shall find Neptune salf° Eneas navy.   *saved*
Me list° not show how the story of Dydo   *want*
By this Caxtoun is hail° pervertèd so   *wholly*
That beside where he feigns to follow Bocass,
He runs so far from Virgil in many place,
In so prolix and tedious fashion,
So that the third book of Eneadon,
Touching the life and death of Dido queen,
The two part° of his volume doth contain   *half* 170
That in the text of Virgil, trustis° me,   *believe*
The twelfth part scarce containès, as ye may see.
The fifth booke of the feastis funeral,°   *funeral feast*
The lusty° games and playès palustrall,*   *vigorous; athletic*
That is ourhipped quite and left behind –
No thing thereof ye shall in Caxton find.
The sixth book eke,° he grantès, that wantès hail,*   *also; completeness*
And, for thereof he understoodè nocht the tale,
He calls it feigned and not for to believe;
So is all Virgil perchance, for by his leave   180
Juno nor Venus goddessès ne'er were,
Mercur, Neptunè, Mars nor Jupiter;
Of Fortune eke nor her necessity,
Such thingès not authentic are, wait we,
Nor yet admittès that quaint philosophy
Holds° soulès hoppès from body to body,   *That contends that*
And many thingès which Virgil did rehearse,°   *relate*
Though I them write forthfollowing his verse.
Nor Caxton shrinks nocht cyclic° things to tell   *such*
As not were fabill but the passage to hell,   190
But trusts weill, who that ilk° sixth bookè knew,   *same*
Virgil therein a high philosopher him shew,°   *proved*
And under the cloudes of dark poesy
Hid° lies there many notable history –   *Hidden*
For so the poets be the crafty curys°   *covers*
In similitudes and under quaint figurès
The soothfast matters to hide and to constrain;
All is not false, trust weill, in case they fain.

Their art is so to make their workès fair,
As in the end of Virgil I shall declare.   200
Was it not eke as possible Eneas
As Hercules or Theseus to hell to pass,
Which is no gabbing° soothly nor no lie,   *deceit*
As Iohane Bocas in the Genealogy
Of Gods declarès, and like as ye may read
In the Recolles of Troy who list take heed.
Who wait if he in vision thither went
By art magicè, sorcery or enchantment,
And with his father's soul did speak and meet,
Or in the likeness with some other spreit,°   *spirit* 210
Like as the spreit of Samuel, I guess,
Raised to King Saul was by the Phitones?
I will not say all Virgil be all true
But that such thingès are possible this I show,
As in the days were ma° illusionès   *more*
By devilish workès and conjurations
Than now there be, so doth clerkès determ,°   *surmise*
For blessed be God, the faith is now more firm.
Enough thereof; now will I no more sayen
But onto Caxton thus I turn again.   220
The names of people or cities be so bad
Put by this Caxton that, but° he had been mad,   *unless*
The flood° of Tour for Tiber he had nocht writ: *river*
All men may know there he forvayt° quite.   *erred*
Palente the city of Evander king,
As Virgil plainly makès rehearsing,
Stood where in Rome now stands the chief palace;
This same book eke in more heaped° malice   *heaped up*
On the self river of Tour says plainly
Eneas did his city edify.   230
Thus aye° for Tiber Tour puttès he,   *always*
Which many hundred milès sundry° be,   *apart*
For sykerly,° less than wise authorès lyne,*   *truly; lie*
Ene° saw never Tour with his eyen,   *Anaeas*
For Tour dividès Greece from Hungary
And Tiber is chief flood of Italy,
Tour is kend° a grain* of that river   *known as; tributary*
In Latin hight Danubium or Hyster –
Or if it be Tanais he clepis° so,   *calls*
That flood dividès Europe from Asia.   240
In like ways eik this Caxton all in vain

Crispina clepis Sibilla Cumanè,°   *Cumaean Sibyl*
That in the text of Virgil, trustès us,
Hight Deiphebe daughter of Glaucus,
Which was Eneas conveyor° to hell.   *guide*
What should I longer on his errors dwell?
They be so plain and eke so manifold
The hundredth part thereof I leave untold.
The last six bookès of Virgil all inferis,°   *together*
Which containès strang° battles and wars,   *fierce* 250
This ilk Caxton so blaitly° lettis* o'erslip.‡   *dully; allows; escape*
I hold my tongue for shame, biting my lip.
The great affairs of either host and array,
The armour of Eneas, fresh and gay,
The quaint and curious casts poetical,°   *rhetorical figures*
Perfect similitudes and examples all
Wherein Virgil bearès the palm of laud,°   *praise*
Caxton, for dread they should his lippès scald,
Durst never touch. Thus shortly for the nonce.°   *present*
A twenty devil way fall his work at once,   260
Which is no more like Virgil, dare I lay,°   *wager*
Than the night owl resembles the popinjay.°   *parrot*
Wherefore, you gentle readers, I beseech
Trust on no ways as this my work be such,
Which did my best, as the wit might attain,
Virgilès versès to follow and nothing feign.
Ye worthy noblès, read my work forthy°   *therefore*
And cast this other book on side far by,°   *far off*
Which under colour of some strange French wight°   *creature*
So Frenchly lies, uneth° two wordès gets right.   *barely* 270
I nold° thee trust* I said this for dispite,‡   *would not want; believe; contempt*
For me list° with none* English bookès   *I do not wish; any;*
    flyte,‡   *slanging match*
Nor with no bogill° nor browny* to debate,   *will'o'wisp; pedant*
Neither old ghosts nor spirits dead of late,
Nor no man will I lacken° nor despise   *sell short*
My workès till° authorès be sik* wise,   *to; so*
But touching Virgils honour and reverence,
Who ever contrary,° I must stand at defence;   *argues*
And but° my bookè be founden worth sik three*   *unless; three such*
When it is read, do warp° it in the sea,   *throw* 280
Throw it in the fire or rent° it every crumb.   *tear*
Touching that part, lo, here is all and some.
    Since I defend and forbiddès every wight

That can not spell their Pater Noster right
For to correct or yet amend Virgil,
Or the translator blame in his vulgar style;
I know what pain was to follow him foot hot°   *immediately*
Albeit thou think my saying intricate.
Trust well, to follow a fixed sentence° or matter   *meaning*
Is more practick,° dificil* and far straighter,   *demanding; harder* 290
Though thine engine° been elevatè and high,   *vehicle*
Than forto write all ways at liberty.
If I had not been to a bounds° constrained,   *limits*
Of my bad wit perchance I could have feigned
In rhyme a ragment° twice as curious,   *gibberish*
But not be twenty part° so sententious.*   *a twentieth; full of matter*
Who is attached unto a stake, we see,
May go no further but wreil° about that tree: *twist*
Right so am I to Virgil's text ybound,°   *tethered*
I may not flee less than° my fault be found,   *lest* 300
For though I would transcend and go beside,
His work remains, my shame I may not hide.
And thus I am constrained as near I may
To hold his verse and go none other way,
Lest some history, subtle word or the rhyme°   *rhythm*
Causeth me make digression some time.
So though in my translation eloquence scant is,
No lusty cast of oratory Virgill wantès;°   *requires*
My studious brain to comprehend his sentence°   *meaning*
Let° me never taste his flood of eloquence.   *Allows* 310
And thus forsooth because I was not free,
My work is more obscure and gross per de,°   *by God*
Whereof, God wot,° Virgil has no wytè* –   *knows; trace*
Though mine be blunt, his text is most perfytè.°   *perfect*
And yet perceive I well, by my conceit°   *in my view*
The king of poetès ganys° not for rural estate   *befits*
Nor his fresh memor° for bowbardis;* he or she   *remembrance; rustics*
Who takès me not, go where they have ado° –   *done*
The sunnès light is never the worse, trust me,
All though thee back his bright beamès doth flee.°   *drive* 320
Green gentle ingynys° and breastès courageous,   *genius*
Such are the people that gainès best for us;
Our work desirès no lewd° ribaldail,*   *unlearned; vulgar people*
Full of nobility is the story all haill.°   *whole*
For every virtue belonging° a noble man   *belonging to*
This ornate poet better than any can

Paynting discribe in person of Eneas –
Not for to say such one Eneas was
Yet that by him perfectly blasons° he   *praises*
All worship, manhood and nobility,   330
With every bounty° belonging a gentle wight,   *gift*
A prince, a conquerour or a valiant knight.
In lovès cure° enough here shall ye find,   *theme*
And shortly Virgil left no thing behind
That might his volume illummin° or crafty* make.   *vivid; skilful*
Read who° him knowès, I dare this undertake,*   *whoever; affirm*
As oft as ye him read, full well I wait,°   *know*
Ye find each time some merry new conceit.°   *idea*
    Though venerable Chaucer, principal poet but° peer,   *without*
Heavenly trumpet, orlege° and regulier,*   *paragon; regulator* 340
In eloquence balmy, cundit° and dial,*   *well spring; measure*
Milky fountain, clear strand° and rose royal,   *thread*
Of fresh enditè,° through Albion island broad,   *composition*
In his legend of notable ladies said
That he could follow word by word Virgil,
Wiser than I may fail in lacker° style.   *worse*
Some time the text mon° have an exposition,   *must*
Some time the colour will cause a little addition,
And some time of a word I mon make three,
In witness of this term *oppetere*.   350
Eke well I wait° sundry expositors seir*   *know; different*
Makès of one text sentence° diverse to hear,   *meanings*
As them appearès, according their intent,
And for their part shows reasons evident.°   *manifest*
All this is ganand,° I will well it so be,*   *suitable; accept that it is so*
But one sentence° to follow may suffice me.   *meaning*
Some time I follow the text as near I may,
Some time I am constrained an other way.
Beside Latin our language is imperfit
Which in some part is the cause and the wyte°   *reason* 360
Why that of Virgil's verse the ornate beauty
Into our tongue may not observèd be,
For there be Latin wordès many one
That in our lewd ganand° translation has none   *fit*
Less than° we minish* their sentence and gravity   *unless; diminish*
And yet scant well expound. Who trews° not me,   *trusts*
Let them interpret *animal* and *homo*
With many hundred other termès mo°   *more*
Which in our language soothly as I ween°   *believe*

Few men can tell me clearly what they mean. 370
Between *genus, sexus* and *species*
Diversity in our leid° to seek I cease. language
For *objectum* or *subjectum* also
He were expert could find me termès two,
Which are as rife amongès clerks in school
As ever fowls plunged in lake or pool.
Logicians knowès° here in mine intent, understand
Under whose boundès lurks many strange went° path
Whereof the process as° now we mon* let be. as for; must
But yet touching our tongue's penurity,° poverty 380
I mean unto compare° of fair Latin in comparison with
That knowen is mostè perfect language fine,
I might also percase° cum lithir speed* perhaps; make slow progress
For *arbor* and *lignum* into our leid° language
To find different proper termès twain° two
And thereto put circumlocution nane.° none
Right so by aboutspech° often times periphrasis
And semabill° wordès we compile our rhymes. similar
God wat° in Virgil are termès many a hundir* knows; hundred
Forto expound made me a fellon° blunder. culpable 390
To follow alanerly° Virgilès words, I ween, alone
There should few understand me what they mean.
The beauty of his ornate eloquence
May not all time be kept with the sentence.° meaning
Saint Gregor° eke forbids us to translate Gregory
Word after word but sentence follow algait:° always
'Who halds,' quoth he, 'of wordès the properties
Full oft the verity of the sentence flees.'
And to the samèn purpose we may apply
Horatius° in his Art of Poetry: Horace 400
'Press nocht,' says he, 'thou traste° interpreter, faithful
Word after word to translate thy matter.'
Lo, he reproves and holdès misseeming° patent error
Ay word by word to reducè any thing.
I say not this of Chaucer for offence,
But to excuse my lewd insùfficiènce,
For as he stands beneath Virgil in gree,° degree
Under him as far I grant my self to be.
And ne'ertheless into some place, who kend° it, knew
My master Chaucer greatly Virgil offendèt. 410
Although I be too bold him to repreif,° reprove
He was far bolder, certès,° by his leif,* certainly; leave

Saying he followed Virgil's lantern toforn,°   *before*
Who Eneas to Dido was forsworn.
Was he forsworn? Then Eneas was false –
That he admittès and calls him traitor als.°   *as well*
Thus, weening° alone Ene to have reproved,   *thinking*
He has greatly the prince of poets grieved,
For, as said is, Virgil did diligence°   *tried hard*
But° spot of crime, reproach or ony offence   *Without* 420
Eneas for to loif° and magnify,   *praise*
And if he grants him mainsworn° foulèly,   *perjured*
Then all his care and crafty engine° goes quite,   *function*
His twelve years laubours were nocht worth a mite.
Certès Virgil shows Ene did nothing
From Dydo of Carthage at his departing
But what the gods commanded him beforn,
And if that their command made him mainsworn,
That were reproof to their divinity
And no reproach unto the said Eneè.   430
As in the first, where Ilioneus
Speaks to the queen Dido, says he not thus,
That cursed by fate was set till° Italy?   *bound to*
Thus might she not pretend no just cause why
Though Trojans after departès of° Carthage,   *from*
Since they before declarèd they their voyage.
Read the third book where Queen Dido is wroth,°   *angry*
There shall ye find Ene made never oath,
Promèt° nor bond with her forto abide: *promise*
Thus him to be maynsworn may never betide,   440
Nor none unkindness shew for to depart
At the bidding of Jove with rueful heart,
Since the command of God obey should all
And under his charge no wrongwise° deed may fall.   *evil*
   But sikkerly° one reason me behoofs*   *certainly; behoves*
Excuse Chaucer from all manner reproofs
In loving of the ladies lilly white
He set on Virgil and Eneas this wite,°   *wit*
For he was ever (God wat) all women's friend.
I say no more, but, gentle readers hend,°   *courteous* 450
Let all my faultès with this offence pass by.
Thou prince of poets, I thee mercy cry,
I mean thou King of Kingès, Lord Etern,
Thou be my muse, my guider and lode stern,°   *star*
Remitting my trespass and every miss

Through prayer of thy Mother, Queen of Bliss.
Onefold° godhead, aye lasting but discrepance,   *Unitary*
In persons three, equal, of one substance,
On thee I call, and Mary Virgin mild –
Calliope nor pagan goddès wild   460
May do to me no thing but harm, I ween:°   *know*
In Christ is all my trustè, and heaven's queen.
Thou, Virgin Mother and Maiden, be my muse,
That never yet no sinfull list° refuse   *wished to*
Who thee besought devoutly for supply.°   *help*
Albeit my song to thy high majesty
Accordès not, yet condescend to my write,
For the sweet licqour of thy pappès° white   *breasts*
Fostered that Prince, that heavenly Orpheus,
Ground of all good, our Saviour Jesus.   470
But furthermore, and lower to descend,
Forgive me, Virgil, if I thee offend.
Pardon thy scholar, suffer° him to rhyme   *permit*
Sin° thou was but a mortal man some time.*   *since; once*
In case I fail, have me not at disdain,°   *don't despise me*
Though I be lewd, my loyal heart cannot feign,
I shall thee follow; should I therefore have blame,
Who can do better, sa° forth in Goddès name.   *come*
I shrink not once corrected for to be
With any wight gruunded in charity,   480
And gladly would I both inquire and leir°   *learn*
And to each cunning wight lay to mine ear.°   *listen*
But loath me were but° other offence or crime   *without*
A brimell° body should intertrike* my rhyme.   *cruel; disarrange*
Though some would swear that I the text have varied,
Or that I have this volume quite miscarried,
Or threp° plainly that I come never near hand it,   *complain*
Or that the work is worse than ever I found it,
Or yet argue Virgil stoodè well before,
As now were time to shift the worst our score;°   *state the case* 490
Else have I said there may be no compare
Betwixt his versès and my style vulgar.
Although he stands in Latin most perfyte,°   *perfect*
Yet stood he never well in our tongue endyte°   *written*
Less than° it be by me now at this time.   *Unless*
If I have failed, boldly reprove my rhyme.
But first, I pray you, grape° the matter clean,   *examine*
Reproach me not while the work be o'erseen.°   *examined*

Be not o'er studious to spy a moat° in mine eye,   *speck*
That in your own a ferry boat can not see,   500
And do to me as ye would be done to.
Now hark, sirs, there is no more ado;
Who list attend, givès° audience and draw near,   *give us*
Me thought Virgil begouth° on this manner . . .   *began*

68c. from *Prologue: Book Seven*

As bright Phoebus, shein° sovereign heavennès e,*   *bright; eye*
The opposite held of his chymmis° high,   *astrological house*
Clear schining beamès, and golden summer's hue,
In laton° colour altering hail* anew,   *brass; whole*
Kithing° no sign of heat by his visage,   *Suggesting*
So near approchèd he his winter stage;
Ready he was to enter the third morn
In cloudy skiès under Capricorn;
Although he be the heart and lamp of heaven,
Forfeeble waxed his leaming° gilded levyn,*   *gleaming; light* 10
Through the declining of his large round sphere.
The frosty region ringès° of the year,   *cycles*
The time and season bitter, cold and pale,
The short days that clerkès clepe° brumaill,*   *call; wintry*
When brim° blastès of the northern art*   *fierce; direction*
Ourwhelmèd had Neptunus in his cart,
And all to shake the leavès off the trees,
The rage and storm o'erweltring° welly* seas.   *overriding; swelling*
Rivers ran red in spate with water brown,
And burnès° hurlès all their bankès down,   *brooks* 20
And landbrist° rumling* rudely with such beir,‡   *surf; roaring; voice*
So loud ne rumèst° wild lion or bear;   *roared*
Floods monstrous, such as mereswine° or whalès,   *dolphins*
From the tempest low in the deep devalis.°   *descends*
Mars occident,° retrograde in his sphere,   *Westward*
Provoking strife, reigned as lord that year;
Rainy Orion with his stormy face
Bewavèd° oft the shipman by his race;*   *blew off course; journey*
Forward Saturn, chill of complexion,
Through whose aspect dearth and infection   30
Been causèd oft, and mortal pestilence,
Went progressive the greis° of his ascens;*   *degree; ascent*
And lusty Hebè, Juno's daughter gay,

Stood spoiled° of her office and array. *despoiled*
The soil ysopped° into water wak,* *soaked; wet*
The firmament o'ercast with rokès° black, *clouds*
The ground fadèd, and faugh° waxed all the fields, *pale brown*
Mountain toppès sleeked with snow o'erheildès;° *are covered*
On rugged rockès of hard harsh whinstone° *hard, dark stone*
With frozen fronts cold clinty° clewis* shone. *stony; valleys* 40
Beauty was lost, and barren show the lands,
With frostès hair o'erfret° the fieldès stands. *covered*
Seer bitter bubbis° and the showers snell* *squalls; harsh*
Seemed on the sward° a similitude of hell, *turf*
Reducing to our mind, in every sted,° *place*
Gusty shaddows of eld° and grisly dead.* *old age; death*
Thick drumly° skuggis* darkened so the heaven, *cloudy; shadows*
Dim skies oft forth warped° fearfull levyn,* *wrapped by; lightning*
Flaggès° of fire, and many fellon* flow,‡ *flashes; savage; winds*
Sharpè soppès° of sleet and of the sniping* snow. *little clouds; biting* 50
The dolly° ditchès were all donk* and wait,‡ *sad; damp; wet*
The low valley floodered all with spait,° *spate*
The plane° streets and every highway *open*
Full of floschis,° dubbis,* mire and clay. *puddles; muddy water*
Laggered° leyès* wallowed‡ fernès show, *Bemired; fallows; withered*
Brown moors kythed° their wizened mossy hue, *displayed*
Brank, bray and bottom blanched° waxed and bare. *bleached*
For gurl° weather growed beastès hair. *stormy*
The wind made wave the red weed on the dyke,
Bedowen° in donkis* deep was every sike.‡ *Soaked; marshes; stream* 60
O'er craggès and the front of rockès seir° *several*
Hang great icicles long as any spear.
The ground stood barren, withered, dusk or gray,
Herbs, flowers and grasses wallowed° away. *shrivelled*
Woods, forrests, with naked boughès blowt,° *blown*
Stood strippèd of their weed° in every howt.* *garments; holt*
So busteously° Boreas his bugle blew, *violently*
The deer full dern° down in the dalès drew; *secret*
Small birdès, flocking through thick ronès° thrang,* *brambles; crowded*
In chirming° and with cheeping changed their song, *chirping* 70
Seeking hidlès° and hernès* them to hidè *hiding places; recesses*
From fearful thuddès of the tempestuous tide;
The waterlinnès° rowtis,* and every lynd‡ *waterfalls; roars; tree*
Whistled and brayèd° of the soughing* wind. *roars; whistling*
Poor labourers and busy husband° men *farming*
Went wet and weary dragled° in the fen. *bedraggled*

The silly° sheep and their little herd grooms*   *innocent; shepherds*
Lurkès under lee of bankès, woods and brooms;
And other danted° greater bestiall,*   *domesticated; animals*
Within their stablès sesed° into stall,   *placed* 80
Such as mulès, horses, oxen and ky,°   *cows*
Fed tuskèd boarès and fat swinè in sty,
Sustained were by mannès governance
On harvest and on summerès purveyance.
Wide whar° with force so Eolus schowtès chill   *far and wide*
In this congealed season sharp and chill,
The callour° air, penetrative and pure,   *fresh*
Dazing the blood in every creature,
Made seek warm stovès and bein° fyrès hot,   *comfortable*
In double garment clad and wily coat,   90
With mighty drink and meatès comfortivè,
Again° the stern winter for to strivè.   *Against*
Repaterred° well, and by the chimney bekit,*   *Fed; familiar*
At even betime down a-bed I me strekit,°   *stretched*
Wrappèd my head, cast on clothès three-fold,
For to expel the perilous piercing cold;
I crossed me, sinè bownyt° for to sleep,   *getting ready*
Where, leaming° through the glass, I did take keep*   *gleaming; notice*
Latonia,° the long irksome night,   *The moon*
Her subtle blenkis° shed and watery light,   *glances* 100
Full high up whirlèd in her region,
Till Phoebus right in opposition,
Into the Crab her proper mansion draw,
Holding the height although the sun went low.
Horned Hebowl, which we clepe the night owl,
Within her cavern heard I shout and yowl,
Loathly° of form, with crooked camsho* beak,   *Ugly; bent*
Ugsome° to her was her wild elrich* shriek;   *ugly; weird*
The wild geese clacking eke° by nightès tidè   *also*
Atour° the city flying heard I glidè.   *Beyond* 110
In slumber I slid full sad, and sleepèd sound
While the orient° upward gan rebound.   *dawn*
Phoebus' crownèd bird, the night's orlager,°   *timekeeper*
Clapping his wingès thrice had crawen° clear;   *crowed*
Approaching near the greking° of the day,   *dawning*
Within my bed I wakened where I lay;
So fast declinès Cynthia the moon,
And kays° cacklès on the roof aboon;*   *jackdaws; above*
Palamedès' birds grouping in the sky,

Flying on randon,° shapen like a Y, *headlong* 120
And as a trumpet rang their voices soun,° *sound*
Whose criès been prognosticatioun
Of wind blastès and ventosities;° *gales of wind*
Fast by my chamber, in high wizened trees,
The sore° glade whistlès loud with many a pew:* *sad; sound of birds*
Whereby the day was dawnèd well I knew,
Bade° build the fire and the candle alight, *Ordered*
Sine° blessèd me, and in my weedès* dight,‡ *Then; clothes; dressed*
A shot window unshut a little on char,° *ajar*
Perceived the morning blue, wan and har,° *hoary* 130
With cloudy gum° and rak* o'erwhelmèd the air, *mist; fog*
The sulie° stithly,* hasart,‡ rough and hair, *soil; anvil hard; grey*
Branchès brattling,° and blackened* show the brays‡ *rattling; pallid; hills*
With hirstis° harsh of wagging windill strays,* *hillsides; dry grass*
The dew dropès congealed on stubble and rynd,° *frozen mist*
And sharp hailstonès mortfunded° of kind* *cold-benumbed; by nature*
Hopping on the thatch and on the causway by.
The shot° I closèd, and drew inward in high, *shot-window*
Shivering for cold, the season was so snell,° *bitter*
Shupe° with hot flame° to fleym* the freezing fell. *Undertaking; expel* 140
And, as I bowned° me to the fire me by, *hurried*
Both up and down the house I did espy,° *look*
And seeing Virgil on a lectern stand,
To write anon I hynt° a pen in hand, *took*
For to perform the poet grave and sad,
When so far forth ere then begun I had,
And waxed° annoyed somedeal* in my heart *became; somewhat*
There rested uncompleted so great a part.
And to my self I said: 'In good effect
Thou mon° draw forth, the yoke lies on thy neck.' *must* 150
Within my mind compassing° thought I so, *considering*
No thing is done while aught remains to do;
For business, which occurrèd in case,
O'ervolved,° I this volume, lay a space; *laid aside*
And, though I weary was, me list° not tire, *would*
Full loath to leave our work so in the mire,
Or yet to stint for bitter storm or rain.
Here I assayed to yoke our plough again,
And, as I could, with afald° diligence, *single-minded*
This next book following of profound sentence 160
Had thus begun in the chill winter cold,
When frostès doth o'erfret° both firth and fold. *cover*

William Dunbar

69. 'London, thou art the Flower of Cities all'

London, thou art of townes A per se.°   *paragon*
 Sovereign of cities, seemeliest in sight,
Of high renown, riches and royalty;
 Of lordès, barons, and many goodly knight;
 Of most delectable lusty ladies bright;
Of famous prelates, in habites clerical;
 Of merchantès full of substance and mightè:
London, thou art the flower of Cities all.

Gladdeth anon thou lusty° Troynovaunt,   *lively*
 City that some time clepèd° was New Troy,   *called* 10
In all the earth, imperial as thou stant,°   *stand*
 Princess of towns, of pleasure and of joy,
 A richer restith° under no Christian roy;*   *exists; king*
For manly power, with craftès natural,
 Formeth none fairer sith° the flood of Noy:*   *since; Noah*
London, thou art the flower of Cities all.

Gem of all joy, jasper of jocundity,
 Most mighty carbuncle of virtue and valour;
Strong Troy in vigour and in strenuitie;°   *exertion*
 Of royal cities rose and geraflower;°   *gillyflower* 20
 Empress of townès, exalt° in honour;   *exalted*
In beauty bearing the crown imperial;
 Sweet paradisè precelling° in pleasure: *excelling*
London, thou art the flower of Cities all.

Above all rivers thy River hath renounè,
 Whose beryall° streamès, pleasant and preclarè,* *beryl; utterly clear*
Under thy lusty wallès runneth downè,
 Where many a swan doth swim with wingès fair;
 Where many a barge doth sail, and row with arè,° *grace*
Where many a ship doth rest with toppè-royal.   30
 O! towne of townès, patron and nought comparè:° *non pareil*
London, thou art the flower of Cities all.

Upon thy lusty Bridge of pillars whitè
  Been merchantès full royal to beholdè;
Upon thy streetès goeth many a seemely knightè
  All clad in velvet gowns and chains of goldè.
  By Julius Caesar thy Tower founded of oldè
May be the house of Mars victoriall,
  Whose artillery with tongue may not be toldè:
London, thou art the flower of Cities all.   40

Strong be thy walls that about thee standès;
  Wise be the people that within thee dwellès;
Fresh is thy river with his lusty strandès;°   *banks*
  Blithe be thy churches, wele° sounding be thy bellès;   *joyous*
  Rich be thy merchants in substaunce° that excellès;   *wealth*
Fair be their wives, right lovesome, white and small;
  Cleare° be thy virgins, lusty under kellis:*   *fair (implies pure); head-gear*
London, thou art the flower of Cities all.

Thy famous Mayor, by princely governancè,
  With sword of justice, thee ruleth prudently.   50
No Lord of Paris, Venice, or Florencè
  In dignity or honourè goeth to him niè.°   *compares with him*
  He is examplar, lode-star, and guyè;°   *guide*
Principal patronè and rose originall,
  Above all Mayors as master most worthy:
London, thou art the flower of Cities all.

70. from **The Two Married Women and the Widow**

Upon the Midsummer even, merriest of nightès,
I movèd forth alonè, near as midnight was past,
Beside one goodly green garth,° full of gay flowers.   *enclosure*
Hedged, of one huge height, with hawthorne treès;
Whereon one bird, on one branch, so burst out her notès
That never one blithefuller bird was on the bough heardè:
What through the sugurat° sound of her song gladè,   *sweet*
And through the savour sanative° of the sweet flowers,   *healing*

I drew in derne° to the dyk* to dirkin‡ after   *secretly; wall; clandestinely enjoy*
    mirthès;
The dew donkit° the dale, and dynarit* the fowlès.   *moistened; sang loudly* 10

I heard, under a holyn° heavenly green hewed,   *holly tree*
One high speechè,° at my hand, with hautand*   *loud conversation; haughty*
    wordès;
With that in haste to the hedge so hard I inthrang   *pushed in*
That I was heildit° with hawthorn, and with heind   *hidden;*
    leavès:*   *pleasant leaves*
Throw pykis° of the plet* thornè I presently lookit,   *spaces; hedged*
If any person would approachè within that pleasant garding.   *garden*
    I saw three gay ladies sit in a grene arbour,
All grathit° in to garlandès of freshè goodly flowers;   *adorned*
So glittering as the gold were their glorious gilt tresses,
While all the grasses did gleam of the glaid° huès;   *cheerful* 20
Kemmit° was their clear hair, and curiously sched*   *combed; carefully parted*
Attour° their shoulderès down schyre,* shining full bright;   *over; straight*
With curches,° cassen* them abone, of kirsp‡   *headscarves; thrown; gauze*
    clear and thin:
Their mantlès green were as the grass that grow in May season,
Fetrit° with their white fingerès about their fair sidès: *fastened*
Of ferliful° fine favour were their faces meek,   *wonderful*
All full of flourished° fairhood, as flowers in June;   *flourishing*
White, seemly,° and soft, as the sweetè lilies;   *pretty*
New upspred upon spray, as new spynist° rose,   *newly-opened*
Arrayed royally about with many rich verdour,°   *greenery* 30
That nature, full nobly, ennamalit° fine with flowers   *enamelled*
Of alkin° huès under heavin, that only hind* knew;   *every; noble person*
Fragrant, all full of freshè odour finest of smell,
One marbre° table covered was before the three ladies,   *marble*
With royal cowpis° upon rows full of rich winès: *goblets*
And of those fair wlonkes,° with tua* that wedded were with   *ladies; two*
    lordès,
One was a widow, I wist,° wanton of laitis.*   *know; habit*
And, as they talkit at the table of many tale sundry,
They watchit at° the witè* wine, and waris out‡   *quaffed; strong; spouted*
    wordès;
And syne they spoke more speedily, and sparèd no matterès.°   *subjects* 40
    'Beware,' said the Widow, 'ye wedded women ying,°   *young*
What mirth ye find in marraige, sen° ye were mennès wivès;   *since*

Reveal if ye rewit° that reckless conditioun?   *regret*
Or if that ever ye loved laid upon life° morè   *any living creature*
Nor° them that ye your faith has fastenèd for ever?   *Than*
Or if ye think, had ye choice that ye would choose better?
Think ye it not one blessed band that bindès so fast,
That none undo° it a deil* may say but the deathè   *loosen; even a bit*
   alone?' . . .

71. The Thistle and the Rose

When Marchè was with variant windès past
And April had, with her silver showers,
Tane leif at° nature with one orient* blast;   *Taken leave of; western*
And lusty May, that mother is of flowerès,
Had made the birdès to begin their hourès
Among the tender odouris° red and white,   *scented flowers*
Whose harmony to hear it was delight;

In bed at morrow,° sleeping as I lay,   *morning*
Me thought Aurora, with her crystal eynè,°   *eyes*
In at the window lookèd by the day,   10
And halsit° me, with visage pale and greenè;*   *greeted; fresh*
On whose hand a larkè sang from the spleenè,°   *from the heart*
'Awake, loverès, out of your slumbering,
See how the lusty° morrow does up spring.'   *vigorous*

Me thought freshè May before my bed upstoodè,
In weeds° depaint* of many diverse hue,   *garments; dyed*
Sober, benign, and full of mansuetude,°   *mildness*
In bright attire of flowerès forgit° new,   *made*
Heavenly of colour, white, red, brown and blue,
Balmit° in dew, and gilt with Phebus beamès,   *bathed* 20
While all the house illumined of her leamès.°   *rays*

'Sluggard,' she said, 'awake anon for shamè,
And in my honour some thing thou go write;
The lark has done the merry day proclaimè,
To raise up loverès with comfort and delight,
Yet nought increasses thy courage to indite,°   *compose*
Whose heart some time has glad and blissful been,
Songès to make under the leavès greene.'

'Whereto,' quoth I, 'shall I uprise at morrow,
For in this May few birdès heard I sing?   30
They have more cause to weep and plain° their sorrow,   *lament*
Thy air it is not wholesome nor benign;
Lord Eolus° does in thy seasonè reign;   *god of the winds*
So busteous° are the blastès of his horne,   *rough*
Among thy boughès to walk I have forborne.'

With that this lady soberly did smile,
And said, 'Uprise, and do thy observance;
Thou did promise, in Mayès lusty while,
For to describe the Rose of most pleasance.
Go see the birdès how they sing and dance,   40
Illumined o'er with orient° skyès bright,   *eastern*
Enamellèd richly with new azure light.'

When this was said, departed she, this queenè,
And entered in a lusty gairding° gent;*   *garden; lovely*
And then, me thought, full hastily beseenè,°   *clothed*
In serk° and mantle after her I went   *shirt*
In to this garth,° most dulce* and redolent   *garden; sweet*
Of herb and flower, and tender plantès sweet,
And greenè leavès doing of dew down fleit.°   *flowing*

The purpour° sunnè, with tender beamès red,   *crimson* 50
In orient bright as angel did appear,
Through golden skyès putting up his head,
Whose gilt tresses shonè so wonder° clear,   *wonderfully*
That all the world tookè comfort, far and near,
To look upon his fresh and blissful face,
Doing all sable° from the heavenès chase.   *darkness*

And as the blissful sound of cherarchy,°   *heavenly host*
The fowlès song through comfort of the light;
The birdès did with open voices cry,
'O, loverès foe, away thou dully night,   60
And welcome day that comforts every wicht;°   *person*
Hail May, hail Flora, hail Aurora schenè,°   *bright*
Hail princess Nature, hail Venus lovès queenè.'

Dame Nature gave an inhibition° there   *prohibition*
To fierce Neptunus, and Eolus the bold,

Not to perturb° the water nor the air, *put into confusion*
And that no showerès, nor blastès cold,
Affray° should flowerès nor fowlès on the fold;* *frighten; field*
She bade eke Juno, goddess of the sky, *also*
That she the heaven should keep amene° and dry. *pleasant* 70

She ordand° eke that every bird and beast *ordered*
Before her Highness should anon compeir,° *present themselves*
And every flower of virtue, most and least,
And every herb be° fieldè far and near, *from*
As they had wont° in May, from year to year, *were used to doing*
To her their maker to make obeisence,
Full low inclinand° with all due reverence. *bowing*

With that anon she sent the swift roe
To bring in beastès of all condition;
The restless swallow commanded she also 80
To fetch all fowl of small and great renown;
And to gar° flowerès compeir of all fassoun,* *oblige; species*
Full craftily conjurit° she the yarrow,* *implored; milfoil*
Whilk° did forth swirk* as swift as any arrow. *Which; spring quickly*

All present were in twinkling of an eye,
Both beast, and bird and flower, before the queenè,
And first the Lion, greatest of degree,
Was callèd there, and he, most fair to seenè,
With a full hardy countenance and keenè,
Before Dame Nature come, and did inclinè, 90
With visage bold, and courage leonine.

This awful beast full terrible was of cheir,° *countenance*
Piercing of lookè, and stout of countenance,
Right strong of corpès,° of fassoun* fair, but feir,‡ *body; build; without peer*
Lusty of shape, light of deliverance,° *motion*
Red of his colour, as is the ruby glancè;° *gleam*
On field of gold he stood full mightily,
With flower delicious circulit° lustely. *encircled*

This lady lifted up his cluvis° clear, *claws*
And let him listly° lean upon her knee, *graciously* 100
And crowned him with diadem full dear,
Of radious° stonès, most ryall* for to see; *radiant; splendid*
Saying, 'The King of Beastès make I thee,

And the chief protector in woodès and schawis;°   *groves*
Onto thy legès° go forth, and keepè the lawès.   *legs*

Exert justice with mercy and conscience,
And let no small beast suffer skaith,° nor scornès   *harm*
Of great beastès that be of more puisence;°   *power*
Do law alike to apes and unicornès,
And let no bowgle,° with his busteous* hornès,   *wild ox; rough* 110
The meek plough ox oppress, for all his pride,
But in the yoke go peaceable him beside.'

When this was said, with noise and sound of joy,
All kind of beastès in to their degree,
At oncè cryit loud, 'Vive le Roy!'°   *Long live the King*
And to his feet fell with humilityè,
And all they made him homage and fewtè;°   *fealty*
And he did themè receive with princely laitis,°   *manners*
Whose noble ire is *parcere prostaratis.*°   *protect the lowly*

Syne° crownd she the Eagle King of Fowlès,   *Afterwards* 120
And as steel dartès scherpit° she his pennis,*   *sharpened; feathers*
And bade him be as just to awppis° and owlès,   *finches*
As unto peacockès, papingais,° or crennis,*   *parrots; cranes*
And make a law for wycht° fowlès and for wrennès;   *strong*
And let no fowl of ravine° do afray,*   *bird of prey; cause terror*
Nor devour birdès but° his owèn prey.   *except*

Then callèd she all flowers that grew on field,
Discerning all their fashionès° and effeiris;*   *habits; behaviour*
Uponè the awful Thistle she beheld,
And saw him keepit° with a bushè of spears;*   *guarded; spears* 130
Considering him so able for the warès,
A radious crown of rubies she him gaif,°   *gave*
And said, 'In field go forth, and fend° the laif;*   *defend; rest*

And, sen° thou art a king, thou be discreet;   *since*
Herb without virtue held nought of sic° price   *such*
As herb of virtue and of odour sweet;
And let no nettle vile, and full of vice,
Her fellow to the goodly fleur delyce;°   *heraldic lily*
Nor let no wild weed, full of churlisheness,
Compare her to the lily's nobleness.   140

Nor hold non other flower in sic denty°   *favour*
As the freshè Rose, of colour red and white;
For if thou does, hurt is thine honesty,
Considering that no flower is so perfyt,°   *perfect*
So full of virtue, pleasance and delight,
So full of blissful angelic beauty,
Imperial birth, honour and dignity.'

Then to the Rose she turned her visage,
And said, 'O lusty daughter most benign,
Above the lily, illustarè° of lineage,   *famous* 150
Fro the stock royal rising freshè and ying,°   *young*
But° any spot or macull* doing spring;‡   *without; stain; arisen*
Come bloome of joy with gemès to be crownd,
For over the laif° thy beauty is renownd.   *rest*

A costly crown, with clarified stonès bright,
This comely queenè did on her head incloiss,°   *encircle*
While all the land illumined of the light;
Wherefore me thought all flowerès did rejoice,
Crying at oncè, 'Hail, be thou richest Rose!
Hail, herbès empress, hail, freshest queen of flowers,   160
To thee be glory and honour at all hourès.'

Then all the birdès sang with voicè on height,
Whose mirthful sound was mavellous to hear;
The mavis° song, 'Hail, Rose most richè and right,   *thrush*
That does up flourish under Pheobus° sphere;   *the sun's*
Hail, plant of youth, hail, prince's daughter dear,
Hail, blossom breaking out of the blood royal,
Whose precious virtue is imperial.'

The merle° she sang, 'Hail, Rose of most delight,   *blackbird*
Hail, of all flowers queenè and sovereign;'   170
The lark she sang, 'Hail, Rose, both red and white,
Most pleasant flower, of mighty coloures twain;'
The nightingale sung, 'Hail, naturès suffragene,°   *subordinate*
In beauty, nurture and every nobleness,
In richè array, renown and gentleness.'

The common voice uprose of birdès small,
Upon this way, 'O blessed be the hour
That thou was chosen to be our principal;

Welcome to be our princess of honour,
Our pearlè, our plesans° and our paramour, *pleasure* 180
Our peace, our play, our plain felicity,
Christ thee conserve from all adversity.'

Then all the birdès sang with sic a shout,
That I anonè awoke where that I lay,
And with a braid° I turnèd me about *start*
To see this court; but all were went away:
Then up I leant, halflingis° in affray,* *half; a fright*
And thus I wrote, as ye have heard to forrow,° *before*
Of lusty May upon the ninthè morrow.

72. The Dregy° of Dunbar made to King James the Fifth being in Stirling *dirge*

We that are here in heavenès glory,
To you that are in purgatory,
Commendès us° on our heartly wise;* *greet you; hearty way*
I meanè we folk in paradise,
In Edinburgh with all merriness,
To you at Strivilling° in distress, *Stirling*
Where neither pleasance nor delight is,
For pity° this epistle writis. *compassion; is written*
O! ye heremitès and hankersaidilis,° *anchorites*
That takès your penance at your tables, 10
And eatès not meat restorative,
Nor drinkès no wine comfortative,° *comforting*
Nor ale and what is thin° and small: *weak*
With few courses in your hall,
But company of lords and knightès,
Or any other goodly wightès,° *people*
Solitar walking your alone,
Seeing no thing but stock and stone;
Out of your painfull purgatory,
To ring you to the bliss and glory 20
Of Edinburgh the merry town

We shall begin a carefull soun;°   *sound*
A dirige° devot and meek,   *dirge*
The Lord of bliss doing beseik°   *beseeching*
You to deliver out of your noy,°   *trouble*
And bring you soonè to Edinburgh joy,
For to be merry among us;
And so the dirige beginnès thus.

LECTIO PRIMA°   *First lesson*

The Father, the Sonè and Holy Ghost,
The mirthful Mary virginè chaste,   30
Of angelès all the orderès nine,
And all the heavenly court divine,
Soonè bring you from the painè and woe
Of Stirling, every court-man's foe,
Again to Edinburghès joy and bliss,
Where worship, wealth and welfare is,
Play, plesance° and eke* honesty: *pleasure; also*
Say ye amen, for charity. *Tu autem Domine°*   '*Do thou, O Lord, have mercy…*'

RESPONSIO°   *Response*

Take consolation in your pain,
In tribulation take consolation,   40
Out of vexation come home again,
Take consolation in your pain.
Jube Domine benedicere°   *the blessing*
Outè of distress of Stirling town
To Edinburgh bliss, God make you boun.°   *ready to go*

LECTIO SECUNDA°   *Second lesson*

Patriarchès, prophetès and apostlès dear,
Confessorès, virginès and martyrès clear,
And all the saint celestial,
Devoutly we upon them call,
That soonè out of your painès fell,   50
Ye may in heaven here with us dwell,
To eat swan, crane, pertrik° and plover,   *partridge*
And every fishè that swimmès in river;
To drink with us the new fresche wine,
That grew upon the river of Rhine,
Freschè fragrant clarettès out of France,

Of Angers° and of Orleans, *Anjou*
With many a course of great dyntie:° *delicacy*
Say ye amen, for charity.
   Tu autem Domine 60

RESPONSORIUM

God and Saint Giles here you convoy° *bring*
Both soonè and well, God and Saint Gile
To sonce° and seill,* solace and joy, *plenty; happiness*
God and Saint Giles here you convoy.
   Iube, domine etc
Out of Stirling painès fell,° *foul*
In Edinburgh joy soonè must ye dwell.

LECTIO TERTIA° *Third lesson*

We pray to all the Saintès of heaven,
That are above the starrès seven,
You to deliver out of your penance, 70
That ye may soonè play, sing and dance
Here in to Edinburgh and make goodè cheer,
Where wealth and welfare is, but weir;° *certainly*
And I that does your painès describe
Thinkès° for to vissy* you belyve;‡ *intend; visit; shortly*
Not in desert with you to dwell,
But as the angel Saint Gabriel
Does go betweenè from heavenès glory
To themè that are in purgatory,
And in their tribulation 80
To give them consolation,
And show them, when their painès are past,
They shall to Heaven come at last;
And how none servès° to have sweetness *deserves*
That never tasted bitterness,
And therefore how ye should consider
Of Edinburgh bliss, when ye come hither,
But if ye tasted had before
Of Stirling town the painès sore? 90
And therefore take in patience
Your penance and your abstinence,
And ye shall come, ere Yule begin,
Into the bliss that we are in;
Which grant thee glorious Trinity!
Say ye amen, for charity.

RESPONSORIUM

Come home and dwell no more in Stirling;
From hideous hell come home and dwell,
Where fisch to sell is non but spirling;°   *smelts*
Come home and dwell no more in Stirling.   100

Et ne nos inducas in temptationem de
   Striuilling:°   *And lead us not into temptation of Stirling*
Sed libera nos a malo illius.°   *But deliver us from its evil*
Requiem Edinburgi dona eius, Domine,°   *Rest Edinburgh grant them, Lord*
And lux ipsius luceat eijs.°   *And may its light shine upon them.*
A porta tristitie de Striuilling,   *From Stirling's sad gate*
Erue, Domine, animas et corpora eorum.°   *Lead, Lord, their souls and bodies*
Credo gustare statim vinum Edinburgi,°   *I believe I shall taste Edinburgh wine*
In villa viuentium.°   *While still among the living.*
Requiescant Edinburgi. Amen.°   *May they rest in Edinburgh. Amen*

Domine, exaudi orationem meam°   *O Lord, hear my prayer* 110
et clamor meus ad te veniat.°   *And let my cry come unto thee . . .*

73. Done is a Battle on the Dragon Black

Done is a battle on the dragon black,
Our champion Christ confounded has his force;
The gates of hell are broken with a crack,
The sign triumphal raised is of the cross,
The devils trymmillis° with hideous voice,   *tremble*
The soulès are borrowit° and to the bliss* can go,   *redeemed; salvation*
Christ with his blood our ransoms does indoce:°   *endorse*
   Surrexit Dominus de sepulchro.°   *The Lord is risen from the grave.*

Dungin° is the deadly dragon Lucifer,   *Overcome*
The cruel serpent with the mortal sting;   10
The old keen tiger, with his teeth on char,°   *bared*
Which in a wait has lain for us so long,
Thinking to grip us in his clawès strong;
The merciful Lord would not that it were so,
He made him for to failè of° that fang:*   *fail of; prey*
   Surrexit Dominus de sepulchro.

He for our sake that suffered to be slainè,
And like a lamb in sacrifice was dight,°   *prepared*
Is like a lion risen up againè,
And as giant raxit him° on height;*   *rose up; on high* 20
Sprungèn is Aurora radiant and bright,
On loft° is gone the glorious Apollo,   *On high*
The blissful day departed from the night:
  Surrexit Dominus de sepulchro.

The great victor again is risen on height,
That for our quarrel to the death was wounded;
The sun° that wax* all pale now shinès bright, *sun/son; grew*
And, darkness cleared, our faith is now refounded;
The knell of mercy from the heaven is sounded,
The Christians are deliverèd of their woe,   30
The Jewès and their error are confounded:
  Surrexit Dominus de sepulchro.

The foe is chased, the battle is done cease,
The prison broken, the jailors fleit° and flemit;* *terrified; put to flight*
The war is gone, confirmèd is the peace,
The fetters loosès and the dungeon temit,°   *emptied*
The ransom made, the prisoners reedemit;° *redeemed*
The field is won, o'ercomèn° is the foe,   *overcome*
Dispoilt of the treasure that he yemit:°   *hoarded*
  Surrexit Dominus de sepulchro.   40

74. Lament for the Makaris,° when he was sick *poet*

I that in health was and gladness,
Am troubled now with great sickness,
And feeblit° with infirmity;   *made feeble*
  Timor Mortis conturbat me.° *Fear of death unsettles me.*

Our pleasance° here is all vain glory,   *pleasure*
This false world is but transitory,
The flesch is brukle,° the Fiend is sly;   *feeble*
  Timor Mortis conturbat me.

The state of man does change and vary,
Now sound, now sick, now blithe, now sary,°   *sorry* 10
Now dancing merry, now like to die;
    Timor Mortis conturbat me.

No state in earth here standès sickir;°   *secure*
As with the wind wavès the wicker,°   *willow*
So wavès this worldès vanity;
    Timor Mortis conturbat me.

On to the death goes all Estatès,
Princes, prelates, and potestatis,°   *potentates*
Both rich and poor of all degree;
    Timor Mortis conturbat me.   20

He takès the knightès in to field,°   *on the battle field*
Anarmit° under helm and shield;   *armed*
Victor he is at all mellè;°   *contest*
    Timor Mortis conturbat me.

That strong unmerciful tyrand°   *tyrant*
Takès on° the mother's breast suckand*   *from; sucking*
The babe, full of benignity;
    Timor Mortis conturbat me.

He takès the champion in the stour,°   *conflict*
The capitane° closit* in the tower,   *captain; locked* 30
The lady in bower full of beauty;
    Timor Mortis conturbat me.

He sparès no lord for his puisance,°   *power*
No clerk° for his intelligence;   *scholar*
His awful stroke may no man flee;
    Timor Mortis conturbat me.

Art magicinès, and astrologgès,
Rethoris,° logicians, and theologgès,*   *rhetoricians; theologians*
Them helpès no conclusionès sle;°   *clever arguments*
    Timor Mortis conturbat me.   40

In medicine the most practicianès,
Leechis, surigeonès, and physicianès,°   *Leeches, surgeons and physicians*
Them self from death may not supple;°   *save*
 Timor Mortis conturbat me.

I see that makaris° among the laif*   *poets; rest*
Plays here their pageant, syne° goes to grief;   *then*
Sparèd is not their faculty;°   *profession*
 Timor Mortis conturbat me.

He has done piteously devour
The noble of Chaucer, of makarès flower,   50
The Monk of Bury,° and Gower, all three;   *Lydgate*
 Timor Mortis conturbat me.

The good Sir Hugh of Eglinton,
And eke,° Heriot, and Winton,   *also*
He has tane° out of this country;   *taken*
 Timor Mortis conturbat me.

That scorpion foul has done infek°   *infected*
Master John Clerk, and James Affleck,
From ballad making and tragedy;
 Timor Mortis conturbat me.   60

Holland and Barbour he has bereavèd;°   *carried off*
Alas! that he nought with us leavèd°   *left*
Sir Mungo Lockhart of the Lee;
 Timor Mortis conturbat me.

Clerk of Tranent eke he has tane,
That made the anteris° of Gawain;   *adventures*
Sir Gilbert Hay ended has he;
 Timor Mortis conturbat me.

He has Blind Harry, and Sandy Traill
Slain with his shower of mortal hail,   70
Which Patrick Johnston might not flee;
 Timor Mortis conturbat me.

He has reft° Merseir his enditè,*   *torn; composition*
That did in love so lively writè,
So short,° so quick, of sentence high;*   *succinct; elevated thought*
 Timor Mortis conturbat me.

He has tane Roull of Aberdeen,
And gentle Roull of Corstorphine;
Two better fellowès did no man see;
 Timor Mortis conturbat me.   *80*

In Dunfermelyne he has done rounè°   *conversed*
With Master Robert Henryson;
Sìr John the Ross embracèd has he;
 Timor Mortis conturbat me.

And he has now tane, last of aw,°   *all*
Good gentle Stobo and Quentin Shaw,
Of which all wichtis° has pity: *people*
 Timor Mortis conturbat me.

Good Master Walter Kennedy,
In point of death° lies veraly,* *on the point of death; truly* 90
Great ruth° it were that so should be;   *pity*
 Timor Mortis conturbat me.

Since he has all my brothers tane,
He will not let me live alone,
On force° I man* his next pray be;   *of necessity; must*
 Timor Mortis conturbat me.

Since for the death remedy is none,
Best is that we for death dispone,°   *get ready*
After our death that life may we;
 Timor Mortis conturbat me.   *100*

Stephen Hawes

75. from *The Coercion of Swearers*

... Right mighty princes of every Christian region
I sendè you greeting much heartly and grace
Right well to govern upright your dominion
And all your lords I greet in like case°   *situations* 60
By this my letter your heartès to embrace
Beseeching you to print it in your myndè
How for your sake I took on me mankindè

And as a lambè most meekly did incline
To suffer the death for your redemption
And you my kingès which do now domine°   *reign*
Over my commons in terrestrial mansion
By princely preeminence and juridition°   *jurisdiction*
In your regal courtès do suffer me be rentè°   *torn*
And my tender body with blood all be spentè   70

Without my grace you may nothing prevail
Though you be kings for to maintain your see
To be a king it may nothing avail
But if my grace preserve his dignity
Behold your servants how they do tear me
By cruel oathès now upon every side
About the world lancing my woundès wide

All the graces which I have you showèd
Revolve in mind right oftè ententyfly°   *attentively*
Behold my body with bloody proppès endewèd   80
Within your realms now torn so piteously
Tossèd and tuggèd with oaths cruelly
Some my head some mine armès and face
Some my heartè do all to rant and race

They new again do hang me on the roodè°   *cross*
They tear my sides and are nothing dismayed

My wounds they open and devour my bloodè
I God and man most woefully arrayed
To you complain it may not be denied
You now to tug me you tear me at the rootè   90
Yet I to you am chief refuge and bootè°   *remedy*

Wherefore you kingès reigning in renownè
Reform your servants in your court abused
To good example of every manner townè
So that their oathès which they long have used
On pain and punishment be wholly refused
Meek as a Lamb I suffer their great wrongè
I may take vengeance though I tarry longè

I do forbear I would have you amend
And grant you mercy and° you will it take   *if* 100
O my sweet brethren why do you offend
Again to tear me which dièd for your sake
Lose my kindness and from sin awake
I did redeem you from the devil's chain
And spite of me you will to him again   *in spite*

Made I not heaven the most glorious mansion
In which I would be glad to have you in
Now come sweet brethren to mine habitation
Alas good brethren with your mortal sinnè
Why flee you from me to turn again beginnè   110
I wrought° you I bought you you can it not deny   *made*
You to the devil you go now willingly

See
Me
Be
Kind

Again
My pain
Retain
In mind   120

My sweet blood
On the rood
Did thee good
My brother

My face right red
Mine armès spread
My woundès bled
Think none other

Behold thou my side
Wounded so right wide   130
Bleeding sore that tidè°   time
All for thine own sake

Thus for thee I smarted
Why art you hard hearted
Be by me converted
And thy swearing aslake°   stopped

Tear me now no more
My woundès are sore
Leave swearing therefore
And come to my grace   140

I am ready
To grant mercy
To thee truely
For thy trespass

Come now near
My friend dear
And appear
Before me

I so
In woe   150
Did go
See see

I
Cry
Hie°   *Hurry*
Thee

Unto me dear brother my love and my heart
Torment me no more with thine oathès great
Come unto my joy and again revert
From the devillès snare and his subtle net   160
Beware of the world all about thee set
Thy flesh is ready by concupiscencè°   *desire*
To burn thy heart with cursed violencè

Though these three enemies do sore thee assailè
Upon every side with dangerous iniquity
But if thou list they may nothing prevailè
Nor yet subdue thee with all their extremity
To do good or ill all is at thy liberty
I do grant thee grace thine enemies to subdue
Sweet brother accept it their power to extue°   *avoid* 170

And you kings and princes of high nobleness
With dukes and lords of every dignity
Imdued with manhoodè wisdom and riches
Over the commons having the sovereignty
Correctè them whichè so do tear me
By cruel oathès without repentancè
Ammendè by time lest I take vengeancè . . .

. . . My wordès my prelates unto you do preachè
For to convert you from your wretchedness
But little availeth you now for to teachè
The world hath cast you in suchè blindness   230
Like unto stonès your heartès hath hardness
That my sweet wordès may not reconcile
Your heartès hard with mortal sin so vile

Woe worthè° your heartès so planted in pride   *betide*
Woe worthè your wrath and mortal envyè
Woe worthè sloth that doth with you abide
Woe worthè also immeasurable gluttony
Woe worthè your tedious sin of lechery
Woe worthè you whom I gave free will
Woe worthè covetise that doth your souls spill°   *kill* 240

Woe worthè short Joy cause of pain eternal
Woe worthè you that be so perverted
Woe worthè your pleasures in the sinnès mortal
Woe worthè you for whom I sore smarted
Woe worthè you ever but° you be converted   *unless*
Woe worthè you whose making I repentè
Woe worthè your horrible sin so violentè

Woe worthè you which do me forsakè
Woe worthè you which willingly offendè
Woe worthè your swearing which doth not aslakè   250
Woe worthè you which will nothing ammendè
Woe worthè vice that doth on you attendè
Woe worthè your greatè unkindness to me
Woe worthè your heartès withouten pityè

Woe worthè your falsehood and your doublenessè
Woe worthè also your corruptè Judgment
Woe worthè delight in worldly richessè
Woe worthè debate without extinguishment
Woe worthè your words so much impatient
Woe worthè you unto whom I did botè°   *remedy* 260
Woe worthè you that tear me at the rootè

Blessèd be you that love humilityè
Blessèd be you that love truth and patiencè
Blessèd be you following works of equityè
Blessèd be you that love well abstinencè
Blessèd be you virgins of excellencè
Blessèd be you which love well virtue
Blessèd be you which do the world eschew°   *avoid*

Blessèd be you that heavenly Joy do love
Blessèd be you in virtuous governance   270
Blessèd be you which do pleasures reprove
Blessèd be you that consider my grievance
Blessèd be you which do take repentance
Blessèd be you remembering my passion
Blessèd be you making petition°   *prayer*

Blessèd be you following my trace°   *tracks*
Blessèd be you loving tribulation
Blessèd be you not willing to trespass

Blessèd be you of my castigation
Blessèd be you of good operation   280
Blessèd be you unto me right kindè
Blessèd be you which have me in your mindè

Blessèd be you leaving ill company
Blessèd be you haunting the virtuous
Blessèd be you that my name magnify
Blessèd be you teaching the vicious
Blessèd be you good and religious
Blessèd be you in the life temporal
Which apply you yourselfè to Joy celestial

76. from *The Example of Virtue*

FIRST CHAPTER

In September in falling of the leafè
When Phoebus made his declination
And all the wheat gadred° was in the sheafè   *gathered*
By radiant heat and operation
When the virgin had full domination
And Diane entered was one degree
Into the sign of Gemini

When the golden starrès clear were splendent°   *shining*
In the firmament purified clear as crystal
By imperial course without encumberment   10
As Jupiter and Mars that be celestial
With Saturne and Mercury that were supernal
Mixèd with Venus that was not retrograde
That causèd me to be well fortunate

In a slumbering sleep with sloth oppressed
As I in my naked beddè was laid
Thinking all night to take my rest
Morpheus to me then made abreyd°   *appearance*
And in my dream me thought he said

'Come walk with me in a meadow amorous   20
Depeynted° with flowers that be delicious'   *Decorated*

I walkèd with him into a placè
Where that there grew many a fair flower
With Joyès replete and full of solacè
And the trees distilling redolent licquor
More sweeter far than the April shower
And tarry I did there by longè spacè
Till that I saw before my facè

A right fair lady of middle stature
And also endewèd with great virtue   30
Her apparel was set with pearlès pure
Whose beauty alwayès diddè renew
To me she said 'And you will extue°   *avoid*
All wildness I will be your guidè
That you to frailtyè shall not slidè'

Unto her I answerdè 'O lady glorious
I pray you tell me what is your name
For you seem to be right precious
And I am young and sore to blame
Of vices full and in virtue lame   40
But I will be rulèd now by your pleasurè
So that your order be made by measurè'

'Yclepyd° I am' she said 'Discretion   *Called*
And if you will be rulèd by me
You shall have Joy without reprehension
And never fall in to fragility
Youth lackingè me it is greatè pity
For in what place I am exiled
They be with sinnè right oft defiled

'It longeth ever unto my property
Youth to give couragè for to learnè
I will not meddle with no duplicity
But faithfulnessè I will discernè
And bring thy soul to blessè eternè
By wise example and moral doctrine
For youth having to me is a good sign

'Forsake also all evil company
And be foundè truè in wordè and deed
Remember that this worldè is transitory
After thy desert shall be thy mede°   *reward* 60
Love God always and ekè him dread
And for no mannès pleasure be thine ownè foe
Givè them fairè wordès and letè them go

'Be to thy kingè ever truè subject
As thou sholdest be by rightè and reason
Letè thy heartè lowèly on him be set
Without any spot of evilè treason
And be obedient at every season
Unto his grace without rebellion
That thou with truth may be companion   70

'Love neuer unlovèd for that is painè
While that thou liuest of that beware
Love as thou seest thee lovèd againè
Or elsè it will turnè thee to care
Be never taken in that fastè snare
Prove ere thou lovè that is most surè
And then thou in doubtè shalt not endurè

'Bewarè believè no flattering tonguè
For flatterers be most deceivable
Though that they company with thee longè   80
Yet at the endè they will be variable
For the by reason are not favourable
But evermorè false and double
And with their tonguès cause of great trouble

'This brittle worldè aye° full of bitterness   *always*
Always turningè like to a ball
No man in it can have no sikernes°   *certainty*
For when he climbeth he hath a fall
O wavering shadowè bitter as gall
O fatal wealth full soonè at endè   90
Though thou right high do oft ascendè'

When she to me had made relation
Of all these proverbès by good conclusion
She gavè to me an information

For to deprivè all ill abusion°   *abuse*
And to considerè the greatè derision
Whichè is in youth that may not see
No thingè appropred° to his prosperity   *appropriate*

Forth then we wentè to an haven sidè°   *port*
Where was a ship lyingè at rodè°   *prepared* 100
Tarring° after the windè and tidè   *tarrying*
And with muchè spices right wellè loadè
Upon it looking we longè abodè°   *waited*
Till colus with blastès began to roar
Then we her aboarded with painè right sore

This water yclepyd was vainèglory
Ever with jeopardy and tempestuous
And the ship callèd was right truly
The Vessel of the Passage Dangerous
The waves were high and greatly troublous   110
The captain callèd was Good Comfort
And the steerèsman Fairè Passport

SECOND CHAPTER

Long were we driven with wind and weather
Till we arrived in a fair Islandè
Where was a boat tièd with a tether
Of marvellous wood as I understandè
Precious stonès lay upon the sandè
And pointed diamands grew on the rockès
And coral also by right highè stockès

Amazèd I was for to beholdè
The precious stonès under my feetè
And the earth glistering of gold   10
With flowers fair of odour sweetè
Dame Discretion I did then greetè
Praying her to me to make relation
Who of this land hath domination

She said 'Four ladies in virtue excellentè
Of whichè the eldest is Dame Naturè
That daily formeth after her entent
Every beast and living creature

Both foul and fair and also pure
All that depending in her ordinancè
Where that she favoureth there is great pleasauncè

'The second is callèd Dame Fortune
Against whom can be no resistancè
For she doth sette the stringès in tunè
Of every person by her magnificencè
When they sound best by good experiencè
She will them loose and let them slip
Causing them fallè by her turning trip

'The thirdè called is Dame Hardiness
That often ruleth by her chivalry
She is right stout and of great prowess   *30*
And the captain of a lusty company
And ruleth them ever full hardèly
And to great honour and worldèly treasure
She putteth her oft in aventurè°   *luck*

'The fourth is Wisèdom a lady bright
Which is my sister as you shallè see
Whom I do love with all my might
For she inclineth ever to benignity
And medleth not with fraudè nor subtly   *40*
But maketh many noble clerkès
And ruleth them in all their workès

'They dwell all in a fairè castlè
Beside a river muchè deep and clear
And be expert in featès manual
That unto them can be no peer°   *equal*
Of earthèly personè that liveth here
For they be so fair and wounderous
That them to see it is solacious

'Long have they traverst° greatly in the lawè   *competed* 50
Whiche of them should have the pre-eminencè
And none of them their casè will withdrawè
Till of dame Justice they know the sentencè
They argue often and make defencè
Each unto other withouten remedyè
I will no longer of them specifyè'

from THIRD CHAPTER

Come on fairè youth and go with me
Unto that place that is delectable
Builded with towers of curiosity
And you though that you be lamentable
When thou art there you wilt be confortable
To see the mervellès that there be wrought°   *made*
No man can print it in his thought

A path we foundè right greatly used
Wherein we went till at the last
A castle I saw wherof I mused   10
Not fully from me a stonès cast
To see the towerès I was aghast
Set in a valley so strongly fortified
So gentle compassed and well edified

The towerès were high of adamond° stones   *adamant*
With fanès waveringè in the windè
Of right fine gold made for the nonès
And roebucks ran under the lindè
And hunters came them far behindè
A joy it was suchè saw I never   20
'Abidè' quoth she 'You shall see a better' . . .

from FOURTH CHAPTER

My good angel by his greatè virtue
Showèd me all this in a shortè space
And after him I did then pursue
With my wife unto the fairè place
That we came from full of all solace
Where was my father in the companyè
Of many saintès that did there tarryè

My wifè and me them for to bring
To the place of eternal glory
With heavenly tunès sweetly singing   10
That them to hear it was great melody
More than any tongue can specify
This was their song so sweet and glorious
That they did sing with voice so virtuous

'O celestial king one two and three
All people praise thee God and lordè
Which art in heaven o noble trinity
Whose royal power and misericordè°   *mercy*
Confirmed is by thine higher accordè
On us with truth for to endurè
Withouten endè as we are surè   20

'Glory be to the father almighty
And to the son and to the holy ghost
Three persons and one god truely
Whose power never can be lost
For he is lord of mightès most
And so hath been without beginning
And ever shall be without ending'

When we were in the air of azure
There did us meet the noble Hierarchy   30
As Cherubin and Seraphim so pure
With other angels in their company
That did proclaim and sing on high
With voice insaciat° most melodious   *unceasing*
To God above 'Sanctus sanctus sanctus'

There did I see the planets seven
Move in order by alteration
Too marvellè for me to neven°   *name*
For they ceased not their operation
Some ascended some made declination   40
Entering their houses of the twelve signès
Some indirectly and some by direct linès

To heaven we spièd a place most glorious
Where that we did behold the deity
With insatiable contenance most desirous
And truely then the more that we
Did look upon his sovereign beauty
The more our desire did increase
This is a Joy that shall not cease

This is a region most full of sweetness   50
This is a realm of delectation
This is a land of infinite gladness
Without any stormy tribulation

This place is of etern salvation
Where angels and saintès for their solace
Evermore do look on Goddès face...

... O heavenly king o eternal emperor
O three persons and one god èqual
I pray thee to kepè from all dolour*   *protect; sadness*
This mother with her son in special
With all their noble buddès in general   110
And laudè be to thee that did enhance
Him to his right and proper heritance°   *inheritance*

The white rose that with tempests troublous
Availèd was and eke° blowen aside   *also*
The red rose fortified and made delicious
It pleasèd God for him so to provide
That his redolent buddès shall not slide
But ever increase and be victorious
Of fatal brerès° which be contrarious   *briars*

Thus God by grace did well combine   120
The red rose and the white in marriage
Being oned° right clear doth shine   *united*
In all cleanness and virtuous courage
Of whose right and royal lineage
Prince Henry is sprung our king to be
After his father by right good equity

O noble Prince Henry our second treasure
Surmounting in virtue and mirror of beauty
O gem of gentleness and lantern of pleasure
O rubicound blossom and star of humility   130
O famous bud full of benignity
I pray to God well for to increase
Your high estate in rest and peace

O thoughful heart for lack of cunning°   *knowledge*
Now laid to sleep this long winter's night
Rise up again look on the shiningè
Of fair Lucina° clear and bright   *the moon*
Behold eke Mercury with his fair light
Casting adown his streamès merry
It may well glad thine emispery.°   *hemisphere* 140

77. from **The Pastime of Pleasure**

77a. *A Commendation of Gower, Chaucer and Lydgate*

O pensive heart in the stormy pery°	sphere 1310
Mercury northwest thou mayest see appear	
After tempest to glad thine emyspery°	hemisphere
Hoist up thy sail for thou must draw near	
Toward the end of thy purpose so clear	
Remember thee of the trace° and dancè	paths
Of poets old with all thy purveyancè	
As moral Gower whose sententious° dew	morally uplifting
Adown reflaireth with fair golden beamès	
And after Chaucer's all abroad doth show	
Our vices to cleanse his depared streamès	1320
Kindling our hearts with the fiery leamès°	rays of light
Of moral virtue as is probable	
In all his books so sweet and profitable	
The Book of Fame which is sententious	
He drew himselfè on his own invention	
And then the tragedè so piteous	
Of the nineteen ladies was his translation	
And upon his imagination	
He made also the Tales of Canterbury	
Some virtuous and some glad and merry	1330
And of Troilus and the piteous dolour°	sadness
For his lady Criseyd full of doubleness	
He did bewail full well the langour°	sad case
Of all his love and great unhappiness	
And many other bookès doubtèless	
He did compile whose goodly name	
In printed bookès doth remain in fame	
And after him my master Lydgate	
The Monk of Bury did him well apply	
Both to contrive and eke to translate	1340
And of virtue ever in especially	
For he did compile than full nially	
Of our Blessed Lady the conversation°	dealings of
Saint Edmundès life martyred with treason	

Of the Fall of Princes so right woefully
He did endite in all piteous wysè°   *ways*
Following his author Bocas ruefully
A right great book he did truely comprisè
A good ensample° for us to despisè   *model*
This world so full of mutability   1350
In which no man can have a certainty

And three reasons right greatly profitable
Under colour he cloakèd craftily
And of the churl he made the fable
That shut the bird in a cage so closely
The pamphlet showeth it expressèly
He feigned also the court of sapience°
And translated with all his diligencè

The great book of the last destruction
Of the city of Troy whilom° so famous   *once* 1360
How for woman was the confusion
And between virtue and the life vicious°   *immoral*
Of gods and goddesses a book solacious°   *pleasurable*
He did compile and the time to passè
Of love he made the bright Temple of Glassè

Were not these three greatly to commend
Which them applied such bookès to contrivè
Whose famous draughts° no man can ammend   *Moves (as in chess)*
The sin of sloth they did from them drivè
After their death for to abide alivè   1370
In worthy fame by many a nation
There books their acts do make relation

O Master Lydgate the most dulcet° springè   *sweetest*
Of famous rhetoric with ballad ryall
The chief original of my learningè
What vaileth° it on you for to call   *avails*
Me for to aid now in especial
Sythen° your body is now wrapt in chestè*   *Since; coffin*
I pray God to give your soul good restè

77b. from *Chapter Twenty One: How Grand Amour
        went to geometry and what geometry is*

So forth I went upon a craggy rockè
Unto the tower most wonderfully wrought°   *made* 2550
Of geometry and as I did approachè
The altitude all in my mind I sought
Six hundred foot as I by number thoughtè
Quadrant it was and did heave° and settè*   *heave; tip*
At every stormè when the wind was greatè

Thus at the last I came into an hallè
Hanged with arras rich and precious
And every window glazèd with crystallè
Like a place of pleasure much solacious
With knots six-angled gay and glorious   2560
The rose did hang right high and pleasantly
By geometry made right well and craftily

In this marvellous hall replete with richessè
At the high end she sat full worthily
I came anon unto her great noblesse
And kneeled adown before her meekèly
'Madame' I said 'you work full royally
I beseech you with all my diligence
To instruct me in your wonderful sciencè'

'My science' said she 'it is most profitable   2570
Unto astronomy for I do it measure
In every thing as it is probable
For I myself can right well discurè°   *discover*
Of every starrè which is seen in urè°   *fate*
The marvellous greatness by my measuringè
For God made all at the beginningè

'By good measuring both the height and deepness
Of every thingè as I understandè
The length and breadth with all the greatness
Of the firmament so compassing the landè   2580
And who my cunning list° to take in handè   *wishes*
In his emyspery° of high or low degree   *hemisphere*
Nothing there is but it may measure be

'Though that it be from us high and farrè
If any thing fall we may it truly see
As the sunnè or moon or ony other starrè
We may therof know well the quantity
Who of this science doth know the certainty
All mastryous° mightè measure perfectly   *powerful*
For geometry doth show it openly   2590

'Where that is measurè° there is no lackingè   *moderation*
Where that is measurè whole is the body
Where that is measurè good is the livingè
Where that is measurè wisdom is truely
Where that is measurè workè is directly
Where that is measurè naturès workingè
Nature increaseth by right good knowledginge°   *knowledge*

'Where lacketh measurè there is no plenty
Where lacketh measurè sickè is the courage
Where lacketh measurè there is iniquity   2600
Where lacketh measurè there is great outrage
Where lacketh measurè is none advauntage
Where lacketh measurè there is great gluttony
Where lacketh measurè is most unhappy

'For there is no highè nor greatè estatè
Without measurè can keep his dignity
It doth preserve him both early and latè
Keeping him from the pit of poverty
Measurè is moderate to all bounty
Greatly needful for to take the charge   2610
Man for to rule that he go not at large

Who loveth measurè can not do amiss
So perfectly is the high operation
Among all things so wonderful it is
That it is full of all delectation
And to virtue hath inclination
Measurè also doth well exemplify
The hasty doom° to suage* and modify   *judgment; assuage*

Without measurè woe worth° the Judgement   *betide*
Without measurè woe worth the tempèrance   2620
Without measurè woe worth the punishment

Without measurè woe worth the purveyance
Without measurè woe worth the sustenance
Without measurè woe worth the sadnessè
And without measurè woe worth the gladnessè

Measurè measuring mesuratly° taketh   *moderately*
Measurè measuring mesuratly doeth all
Measurè measuring mesuratly maketh
Measurè measuring mesuratly guide shall
Measurè measuring mesuratly doeth call   2630
Measurè measuring to right high pre-eminence
For always measurè is ground of excellence

Measurè measureth measure in effectè
Measurè measureth every quantity
Measurè measureth all way the aspectè
Measurè measureth all in certainty
Measurè measureth in the stabililt
Measurè measureth in every doubtful case
And measure is the lodestar° of all grace   *guiding star*

ACKNOWLEDGEMENTS

I am indebted to many individuals for forbearance, and for their help with *The Story of Poetry*. Rebecca Wilson is the best of editors; Sarah Rigby assisted with assembling and preparing the text and with much else; Charles Schmidt is responsible for the inclusion of Old English poetry, though not for any errors or omissions in my account; Evelyn Schlag commented on much of the *Informal History* as it was written or adapted from *Lives of the Poets*; colleagues at Carcanet – Pamela Heaton, Joyce Nield and Chris Gribble – encouraged me; colleagues at Manchester Metropolitan University, in particular Professor Janet Beer, were cheerfully supportive; at the John Rylands University Library the impeccable archivist Stella Halkyard was always available for consultation; and my friend Angel García-Gómez endured the hectic seasons of gestation, composition, correction, etc. with patience.

Always present in my mind are the defining voices of C.H. Sisson and Donald Davie; and also of Edgell Rickword, Idris Parry, I.A. Richards, Octavio Paz, Laura (Riding) Jackson, Elizabeth Daryush, David Wright, Elizabeth Bishop, John Ashbery, W.S. Graham, John Needham, David Arkell and others who down the years have meant and mean a great deal to me through their writings, example and friendship.

Some passages in this book draw on material included in my *50 British Poets 1300–1900* (1980) and on essays and reviews I have written over the last thirty years.

OUTLINE BIBLIOGRAPHY

A full bibliography for a book of this nature would be as long as the book itself. This is a summary list of editions of poetry I have consulted. Other editions exist. The dates I give are of editions I have used. I provide a merely preliminary list of anthologies and secondary works – critical and contextual. I omit most monographs. In the cases of some poets, critical volumes are in print while no edition of the work is currently available. Much of the critical text is developed from the opening of my *Lives of the Poets* (1998).

EDITIONS AND SELECTIONS (VERSE AND PROSE)

Old English

Beowulf and the Fight at Finnsburg ed. Fr Klaeber (third edition, London, 1950)
Battle of Maldon, The ed. Donald Scragg (Manchester, 1981)
Dream of the Rood, The ed. M. Swanton (Manchester, 1970)
Krapp, G.P. and E. Van Kirk Dobbie *The Anglo-Saxon Poetic Records* (London, 1931–53)
Old English Riddles of the Exeter Book ed. Craig Williamson (Chapel Hill, 1977)
The Vercelli Book ed. C. Sisam (Copenhagen, 1967)

Middle English

Barbour, John *The Bruce* (Edinburgh, 1997)
Barclay, Alexander *The Eclogues* (Early English Text Society Original Series 175, Oxford, 1998)
Caxton, William *The Prologues and Epilogues* (Early English Text Society Original Series 176, Oxford, 1999)
— *Eneydos* (Early English Text Society Extra Series 57, Oxford, 1963)
Chaucer, Geoffrey *Works* (ed. Robinson, Cambridge, Mass. 1974)
— *Complete Poetry and Prose* (ed. Fisher, London, 1977)
— *The Riverside Chaucer* (ed. Benson, Boston, 1987)
Douglas, Gavin *Selections from Gavin Douglas* (Oxford, 1964)
— *The Shorter Poems* (Edinburgh, 1967)
— *The Palis of Honour* (East Lansing, 1992)
Dunbar, William *Poems* (Oxford, 1970)
— *Selected Poems* (Manchester, 1997)

Gawain Poet *Sir Gawain and the Green Knight* (ed. Tolkien, Gordon and Davis, Oxford, 1967)

— *Pearl, Cleanness, Patience, Sir Gawain and the Green Knight* (London, 1976)

Gawain Poet *Sir Orfeo* (Oxford, 1966)

— *Pearl* (Oxford, 1953)

Gower, John *Confessio Amantis* (Oxford, New York, 1968)

— *The English Works* volume one *Confessio Amantis* Prologue Book V (Early English Text Society Extra Series 81, Oxford, 1963)

— *The English Works* volume two *Confessio Amantis* Books V–VIII, *In Praise of Peace* (Early English Text Society Extra series 82, Oxford, 1963)

Hawes, Stephen *The Pastime of Pleasure* Early English Text Society Original Series 173, Oxford, 2000)

— *The Minor Poems* (Early English Text Society Original Series 271, Oxford, 1974)

— in *English Verse between Chaucer and Surrey* (ed. Hammond, Oxford, 1927)

Henryson, Robert *Poems and Fables* (London, 1958)

— *The Poems* (Oxford, 1987)

Hoccleve, Thomas *Selected Poems* (Manchester, 1982)

— *The Minor Poems* volumes one and two (Early English Text Society Extra Series 61, Oxford, 1970)

— *The Regement of Princes and fourteen minor poems* (Early English Text Society Extra Series 72, Oxford, 1997)

Langland, William *The Vision of William Concerning Piers the Plowman, in Three Parallel Texts* (2 volumes, London, 1886)

— *Piers Plowman: 'B' version* (ed. Kane and Donaldson, London, 1975)

— *Piers Plowman: The A Version* (ed. Kane, London, 1960)

— *The Vision of Piers Plowman: A Critical Edition of the B-Text* (ed. Schmidt, London, 1995)

Layamon *Brut* volume one, lines 1–8020 (Early English Text Society Original Series 250, Oxford, 1963)

— *Brut* volume two, lines 8021—end (Oxford, 1978)

Lydgate, John *Poems* (London, 1966)

— *The Assembly of Gods* (Early English Text Society Extra Series 69, Oxford, 1976)

— *The Minor Poems* volume one *Religious Poems* (Early English Text Society Original Series 107, Oxford, 1963)

— *The Minor Poems* volume two *Secular Poems* (Early English Text Society Original Series 192, Oxford, 1997)

— *Fall of Princes* volume one (Early English Text Society Extra Series 121, Oxford, 1967)

— *Fall of Princes* volume two (Early English Text Society Extra Series 122, Oxford, 1967)

— *Fall of Princes* volume three (Early English Text Society Extra Series 123, Oxford, 1967)

— *Fall of Princes* volume four (Early English Text Society Extra Series 124, Oxford, 1967)

— *Siege of Thebes* volume one (Early English Text Society Extra Series 108, Oxford, 1996)

Lydgate, John *Siege of Thebes* volume two (Early English Text Society Extra Series 125, Oxford, 1998)
— *Temple of Glas* (Early English Text Society Extra Series 60, Oxford, 1997)
— *Troy Book* volumes one to three (Early English Text Society Extra Series 97, 103, 106, Oxford, 1996)
— *Troy Book* volume four (Early English Text Society Extra Series 126, Oxford, 2000)
MacPherson, James *Mark Akenside, James MacPherson and Edward Young: selected poems* (Manchester, 1994)
Orleans, Charles of *English Poems* (Oxford, 1941)
— *The English Poems* volumes one and two (Early English Text society Original Series 215, Oxford, 1970)
Percy, Thomas *Reliques of Ancient English Poetry* (London, 1765)
Rolle of Hampole, Richard, *The Life and Lyrics of Richard Rolle* (ed. Comper, London, 1928)
— *English Writings* (ed. Allen, Oxford, 1931)
— *The Fire of Love and the Mending of Life* (Early English Text Society Original Series 106, Oxford, 1996)
— *Prose and Verse from MS. Longleat 29 and related manuscripts* (Early English Text Society Original Series 293, Oxford, 1988)
Skelton, John *Poems* (Oxford, 1969)
Wyclif, John *English Works* (Early English Text Society Original Series 74, Oxford, 1998)

ANTHOLOGIES

Fifteen Poets from Gower to Arnold (Oxford, 1940)
Allison, A.W. et al. *The Norton Anthology of Poetry* (New York, 1983)
Bennett, J.A.W. and G.V. Smithers *Early Middle English Verse and Prose* (Oxford, 1968)
Bradley, S.A.J. *Anglo-Saxon Poetry* (Everyman, 1982)
Brown, Carleton *Religious Lyrics of the Fifteenth Century* (Oxford, 1939)
Burrow, J.A. and Thorlac Turville-Petre *A Book of Middle English* second edition (Oxford, 1996)
Chambers, E.K. and F. Sidgwick, *Early English Lyrics* (London, 1921)
Chambers, E.K. *The Oxford Book of Sixteenth Century Verse* (Oxford, 1966)
Davies, R.T. *Medieval English Lyrics: a critical anthology* (London, 1963)
Dobbie, E. Van K. *The Anglo-Saxon Minor Poems* (Oxford, 1942)
Graves, Robert *English and Scottish Ballads* (London, 1957)
Greene, R.L. *The Early English Carols* (Oxford, 1977)
Hall, Joseph *Selections from Early Middle English 1130–1250* (Oxford, 1920)
Hamer, Richard *A Choice of Anglo-Saxon Verse* (London, 1970)
Hill, Joyce *Old English Minor Heroic Poems* (Durham, 1983)
Klinck, Anne L. *Old English Elegies: a critical edition and genre study* (Montreal, 1992)

Mitchell, Bruce and Fred C. Robinson *A Guide to Old English* (fifth edition, Oxford, 1992)

Morris, Richard *Early English Alliterative Poems in the West-Midland Dialect of the Fourteenth Century* (EET, Oxford, 1865/1965)

Sands, Donald B. *Middle English Verse Romances* (Exeter, 1986)

Scott, Tom *The Penguin Book of Scottish Verse and Prose* (Oxford, 1922)

Sisam, C. and K. *The Oxford Book of Medieval English Verse* (Oxford, 1970)

Sweet's Anglo-Saxon Reader (see Whitelock, Dorothy)

Tottel, Richard *Songes and Sonettes* ('Tottel's Miscellany', Cambridge, Mass., 1924–37)

— *The Paradyse of Daynty Devises* (Cambridge, Mass., 1924–37)

Whitelock, Dorothy *Sweet's Anglo-Saxon Reader* (Oxford, 1967)

Williams, John *English Renaissance Poetry: a collection of shorter poems from Skelton to Jonson* (Fayetteville, Arkansas, 1990)

Woudhuysen, H.R. *The Penguin Book of Renaissance Verse* (Harmondsworth, 1993)

HISTORY AND SECONDARY

The Anglo-Saxon Chronicle (M.J. Swanton, London, 1996)

Aers, David *Community, Gender, and Individual Identity: English Writing 1360–1430* (London, 1988)

Baugh, A.C. (ed.) *A Literary History of England* (New York, 1967)

Baugh, A.C. and Kemp Malone *The Middle Ages* (New York, 1967)

Bede, *Ecclesiastical History of the English People* (J. McClure and R. Collins, Oxford, 1994)

Bennett, J.A.W. *Middle English Literature* (Oxford, 1986)

Bessinger, J.B. and S.J. Kahrl *Essential Articles for the Study of Old English Poetry* (Hamden, 1968)

Billings, A.H., *A Guide to the Middle English Metrical Verse Romances* (London, 1901)

Blair, P.H. *An Introduction to Anglo-Saxon England* (second edition, Cambridge, 1977)

Bolton, W.F. (ed.) *The Middle Ages* (London, 1986)

Bradford, Richard *A Linguistic History of English Poetry* (London, 1993)

Brewer, Derek (ed.) *Writers and their Background* (London, 1974)

Brogan, T.V.F. (ed.) *The New Princeton Handbook of Poetic Terms* (Princeton, 1994)

Burrow, J.A. *Ricardian Poetry: Chaucer, Gower, Langland and the 'Gawain' Poet* (London, 1971)

— *Medieval Writers and their Work: Middle English literature and its background 1100–1500* (Oxford, 1982)

— *Essays in Medieval Literature* (Oxford, 1984)

Cambridge History of English Literature (ed. Sir A.W. Ward and A.R. Waller, fifteen volumes, 1907)

Craig, Cairns ed. *History of Scottish Literature* (four volumes, Aberdeen, 1987–89)

Curtius, E.R. *European Literature and the Latin Middle Ages* (London, 1953)

Daiches, David ed. *A Critical History of English Literature* (four volumes, London, 1969)

Donaldson, E. Talbot *Speaking of Chaucer* (New York, 1970)

Elliott, R.W.V. *Chaucer's English* (London, 1974)

Fell, Christine *Women in Anglo-Saxon England* (London, 1984)

Ford, Boris (editor) *Medieval Literature: Chaucer and the Alliterative Tradition* (New Pelican Guide to English Literature Volume I, Harmondsworth, 1988)

Fowler, Alistair *A History of English Literature: forms and kinds from the Middle Ages to the present* (Oxford, 1987)

Greenfield, S.B. and D.G. Calder, *A New Critical History of Old English Literature* (London, 1986)

Hammond, E.P. *English Verse between Chaucer and Surrey* (Durham, North Carolina, 1927)

Hill, D. *An Atlas of Anglo-Saxon England 700–1066* (Oxford, 1981)

Kean, P.M. *Chaucer and the Making of English Poetry* (London, 1972)

Ker, W.P. *Medieval English Literature* (Oxford, 1912)

M. Lapidge and M. Godden (eds), *The Cambridge Companion to Old English Literature* (Cambridge, 1991)

Lewis, Clive Staples *The Allegory of Love: a study in mediaeval tradition* (Oxford, 1936)

— *English Literature in the Sixteenth Century* (Oxford, 1953)

— *The Discarded Image: an introduction to Mediaeval and Renaissance Literature* (Cambridge, 1964)

Lord, Albert B., *The Singer of Tales* (second edition, Cambridge, Massachusetts, 2000)

Meale, Carol M. (ed.) *Women and Literature in Britain 1150–1500* (Cambridge, 1993)

Patterson, Lee *Negotiating the Past: The Historical Understanding of Medieval Literature* (Madison, 1987)

Pearsall, Derek *Old English and Middle English Poetry* (London, 1977)

— *The Life of Geoffrey Chaucer* (Oxford, 1992)

Plant, Marjorie *The English Book Trade: an economic history of the making and sale of books* (London, 1939)

Preminger, Alex and T.V.F. Brogan eds *The New Princeton Encyclopaedia of Poetry and Poetics* (Princeton, 1993)

Renwick, W.L. and Harold Orton *The Beginnings of English Literature to Skelton 1509* (London, 1952)

Ricks, Christopher *The Force of Poetry* (Oxford, 1984)

Robinson, Fred C. *Old English Literature: a select bibliography* (Toronto, 1970)

Salter, Elizabeth *Fourteenth-Century English Poetry: Contexts and Readings* (Cambridge, 1988)

Southern, R.W. *The Making of the Middle Ages* (London, 1953)

Spearing, A.C. *Criticism and Medieval Poetry* (London, 1972)

— *Medieval Dream-Poetry* (Cambridge, 1976)

— *Readings in Medieval Poetry* (Cambridge, 1987)

Speirs, John *Medieval English Poetry: the non-Chaucerian Tradition* (London, 1957)

Spingarn, J.E. *A History of Literary Criticism in the Renaissance* (New York, 1908)

Stanley, E.G. *Continuations and Beginnings* (London, 1966)

Tolkien, J.R.R. *Beowulf: The Monsters and the Critics* (London, British Academy Lecture, 1936)

Waddell, Helen *The Wandering Scholars* (London, 1927)

Warton, Thomas *The History of English Poetry: from the close of the eleventh to the commencement of the eighteenth century* (four volumes, 1924)

Webb. J.F. and D.H Farmer *The Age of Bede* (Harmondsworth, 1983)

Wormald, Jenny *Court, Kirk and Community: Scotland 1470–1625* (Edinburgh, 1991)

GENERAL INDEX

Addison, Joseph 123
Aegidius 114
Ælfwine 24
Alcuin 13–14, 26–7
Alexander, Michael 38
Alfred (King) 25, 27, 73
André, Bernard 136
Andrewes, Launcelot 71
Anglo Saxon Chronicle 25
Aristotle 5, 52, 74
Arnold, Matthew 23, 87
Arnold, Richard 120
Arundel (Archbishop of Canterbury) 49
Aubrey, John 47, 138
Auden, W.H. 16, 23, 32, 64
Augustine (St) 27, 30, 52, 132

Bacon, Francis 69
Ball, John 51
Ballads 19, 22, 23, 41, 47, 53–4, 64, 110, 119–25, 126, **180–205**; *Ancient Ballad of Chevy Chase* (*The*), 53–4, **180–7**; 'Sweet Willie and Lady Margery', **187–9**; 'Sir Patrick Spence', 119, **189–91**; 'Wife of Usher's Well' (The), **192–3**; 'Kinmont Willie', **193–8**; 'Riddles Wisely Expounded', 198–9; 'Robin, the Kitchie-Boy', 199–200; 'Nut Brown Maid' (The), 200–5
Barbour, John 47–8
Barnes, William 129
Beaufort, Joan 126
Beaumont, Francis 122
Beckett, Samuel 112
Bede 7–8, 9, 10, 26, 27, 31; *Historia Ecclesiastica Gentis Anglorum*, 7
Benedict (Biscop) 26

Beowulf 10, 14, 16, 24, 25, 26, 32–8, **163–73**
Berghen, Adraien van 120
Berners, Juliana 117–18
Bishop Paulinus 7
Blake, William 81, 82, 122
Blanche of Gaunt 90
Boccaccio 88, 91, 93, 97, 115, 141
Boethius 18, 74, 86, 90, 91, 95, 98, 105, 111, 113
Bourchier, John 141
Bradwardine 52
Brookes, Stopford 26
Bunting, Basil 60
Burns, Robert 121, 133, 136
Burrow, J.A. 39
Byron, George Gordon (Lord) 85

Cædmon 7–14, 15, 18, 22, 25, 26, 30, 31
Causley, Charles 19
Caxton, William 69, 120, 131–2, 138–143
Chambers, E.K. 79–80
Charlemagne 13
Charles of Orleans 17, 111–13, 126; 'My ghostly father I me confess', **358–9**; 'When I am laid to sleep as for a stound', **359–60**; 'But late ago went I my heart to see', 360; 'In the forest of noyous heaviness', 361; 'I have the obit of my lady dearè', **361–2**
Charles V (King of France) 111
Charles VI (King) 111
Chaucer, Agnes 87
Chaucer, Elizabeth 90
Chaucer, Geoffrey 13, 16, 17, 18, 19, 22, 23, 31, 39, 41, 45, 47, 49, 51, 53, 56, 58, 60, 61, 62, 64, 68, 71, 72, 73, 74, 75, 76, 77, 79, 80, 81, 82, 83, 84, 85–106, 107, 108, 110, 111, 113, 114, 115, 116, 117, 123,

Chaucer, Geoffrey – *contd*
126, 127, 128, 129, 131, 132, 133, 135, 136,
137, 140, **274–358**; *Book of the Duchess*
(*The*), 90–1, 93, **274–81**; *House of
Fame* (*The*), 85, 86, 91, 92–5, 97, 140,
281–6; *Troilus and Criseyde*, 19, 58, 68,
77, 85–6, 91, 96–106, 127, 129, 140, **286–
97**; *Canterbury Tales* (*The*), 71, 75, 76,
85, 86, 87, 88, 89, 91, 104–106, 108, 111,
140, 141, **297–357** (*General Prologue*,
71, 104–5, **297–317**; *Miller's Tale* (*The*),
105, **317–32**; *Wife of Bath's Tale* (*The*),
75, 92, 105, **333–42**; *Nun's Priest's Tale*
(*The*), 95, **342–57**); Merciless Beauty,
106, **357–8**
Chaucer, John 87
Chaucer, Lewis 89
Chaucer, Philippa 88, 89
Chaucer, Thomas 89–90
Child, F.J. 123
Clement VII (Pope) 53
Coleridge, Samuel Taylor 61, 85, 114, 116,
120
Colet, John 138
Colonne, Giovanni delle 115
Comenius, John Amos 3
Copland, Robert 141–2
Cornwall, John 45
Cowley, Abraham 87
Cromwell, Oliver 138
Crowley, Robert 79
Crutwell, Patrick 131
Cynewulf 4, 5, 31; *Juliana*, 4; *Elene*, 4, 31;
Christ II, 4; *Fates of the Apostles*, 4

d'Angleterre, Thomas 110–11
Dalton, John 43
Daniel, Samuel 122
Dante 18, 82, 88, 91, 92, 93, 94, 96, 101,
128, 129
David (King) 44, 49, 56
'Deor' 24, 28
Deschamps, Eustache 87
Donne, John 23, 71

Douglas, Gavin 18, 126, 127, 128, 131–3,
134, 140, **425–40**; *Aeneados*, 128, 131–3,
425–40
'Dream of the Rood' (The) 25, 30–1, 32,
34, **149–53**
Dryden, John 64, 87, 104, 132
Dunbar, William 18, 19, 56, 86, 116, 126,
127, 128, 131, 133–6, **441–56**; 'London
thou art the flower of Cities all', 134,
441–2; Two Married Women and the
Widow (The), 135, **442–4**; Thistle and
the Rose (The), 134, 135, **444–9**; Dregy
of Dunbar (The), 136, **449–52**; 'Done
is a Battle on a Dragon Black', **452–3**;
Lament for the Makaris, 56, 126, 135,
453–6

Edward II (King) 87, 125
Edward III (King) 41, 45, 46, 47, 89
Edwin (King) 7
Egbert of York 26
Eleanor of Acquitaine 110
Eliot, T.S. 71
Elizabeth I (Queen) 74, 122, 124
Empson, William 120
Eormenric 24, 27
Erasmus 138, 142
Exeter Book 4, 25, 26, 28, 29, 32
Eyre-Todd, George 126

FitzRalph, Richard 50
Flaubert, Gustave 86, 103–4
Fletcher, John 122
Ford, Ford Madox 81, 85, 86, 103–4
Froben 142
Froisart 87, 141

Gascoigne, Cancellor 89
Gascoigne, George 80, 113
Gawain poet 10, 19, 22, 23, 39, 41, 56–61,
64, 67, **218–32**; *Pearl*, 47, 56, 57, 61, 68,
218–24; *Gawain and the Green Knight*,
47, 56, 57–61, 64, 68, **224–32**
Gay, John 81

Geoffrey of Monmouth 110
Gibbon, Edward 74
Giraldus, Lilius 87
Gollancz, Israel (Sir) 57, 61
Gonzago, Guy de 90
Gordon, E.V. 57
Gower, John 17, 18, 19, 22, 23, 30, 39, 41,
    45, 47, 49, 56, 60, 61, 62–70, 71–8, 79,
    80, 81, 82, 83, 84, 86, 88, 90, 101, 106,
    108, 110, 112, 113, 115, 116, 117, 126, 128,
    132, 140, 245–74; Confessio Amantis,
    30–1, 62, 63–70, 71–8, 140, 245–74
    (Prologue, 74–5, 77, 245–7; Tale of
    Florent, 75–6, 247–58; Deianira and
    Nessus, 76, 258–62; Pyramus and
    Thisbe, 262–5; Pygmalion, 76, 266–7;
    Ceïx and Alceone, 76, 267–72; Sup-
    plication, 272–4
Graves, Robert 19, 22, 87, 115, 120, 124,
    125
Gray, Thomas 114, 116, 121
Greenfield, Stanley 23
Gregory XI (Pope) 50
Grocyn, William 138
Groundolf, Agnes 72
Gutenberg, Johannes of Mainz 138–9

Hadrian, (Abbot) 26
Harvard, John 71
Harvey Wood, H. 128
Harvey, Gabriel 142
Hawes, Stephen 17, 19, 136–7, 457–74;
    Coercion of Swearers, (The) 457–62;
    Example of Virtue (The), 462–9;
    Pastime of Pleasure (The), 137, 470–4
Hazlitt, William 122
Heaney, Seamus 16, 33, 37–8
Helena (St) 31
Henry II (King) 110
Henry IV (King) 64, 68, 89
Henry V (King) 111, 115, 117, 124
Henry VI (King) 111–12, 115, 124
Henry VIII (King) 14, 117
Henryson, Robert 17, 18, 19, 126–31, 132,
    133, 134, 135, 399–424; Tale of the

Uponlandis Mouse, and the Burges
    Mouse (The), 130–1, 399–405; Testa-
    ment of Cresseid (The) 19, 127, 128–
    30, 131, 405–22; A Prayer for the Pest,
    422–4
Hesiod 5
Higden, Ranulf 45–6, 140
Hild (Abbess) 7, 8, 12, 30
Hoccleve, Thomas 17, 86–7, 113–14, 115,
    117, 137, 363–85; Two Rondels, 363–4;
    Thomas Hoccleve's Complaint, 364–
    75; Ars Sciendi Mori, 114, 375–81; Rege-
    ment of Princes (The), 114, 381–85
Homer 11, 12, 65, 85, 86, 87, 94, 122
Hopkins, Gerard Manley 23, 56
Hughes, Ted 19
Hus, Jan 49, 52
Hygebald (Bishop of Lindisfarne) 13–14

Isaiah 44
Isidore 27

James I (King of Scotland) 111, 122, 126,
    398; Kingis Quair (The), 126, 398
John of Gaunt 50, 88–9, 90
Johnson, Samuel 121, 122–3
Jonson, Ben 37, 77, 122
Joyce, James 112
Judith 17, 25
Junius, Franciscus (François Dujon) 8

Keats, John 77, 91
Kennedy, Walter 135
Kinaston, Francis (Sir) 127
Kirby, Margaret 43
Klaeber, Fr 33, 34, 36

Lambarde, William 121
Langland, William 10, 16, 17, 18, 19, 22,
    23, 30, 39, 41, 45, 49, 51, 56, 60, 61, 64,
    68, 72, 73, 77, 79–84, 105–6, 108, 110,
    117, 127, 135, 233–45; Piers Plowman,
    10, 30, 49, 51, 77, 79–84, 124, 135, 233–
    45
Latimer, Hugh 138, 139

Leofric 25
Lewis, C.S. 75, 77, 135
Lewis, Wyndham 80
Lorca, Federico Garcìa 122
Lorris, Guillaume de 90
Louis XII (King of France) 111
Lovelace, Richard 122
Lucan 86, 94
Lydgate, John 13, 17, 87, 113, 114, 115–17, 137, 140, 141, **385–97**; London Lickpenny, 114, **385–8**; *Life of Our Lady*, 116, **388–92**; Fifteen Tokens Before the Doom (The), **392–5**; *Troy Book* (*The*), 116, **395–6**; *Fall of Princes* (*The*), 115–16, **396–7**
Lyrics 47, 109, **205–18**; 'Green Groweth the Holly', **205–6**; 'Blow, northern wind', **206–8**; 'You and I and Amayas', **208–9**; 'Herefore, and therefore', **209**; 'Bring us home good ale, sir', **209–10**; 'Lenten is come with love to town', **211**; 'All night', **212**; 'There is no rose', **212**; A Boar's Head, **212–13**; 'This endris night', **213–14**; 'Lullay, my child, and weep no more', **215–16**; 'Regina celi leatre', **216**; 'Mother white as lily flower', **216–17**; Timor mortis conturbat me, **217–18**

MacDiarmid, Hugh 19, 133, 134, 136
Machado, Antonio 122
Macpherson, James 121–2, 127
Mandeville 15, 141
Marie of Clèves 111, 112
Marlowe, Christopher 97, 122, 129
Marshe, Thomas 117
Marvell, Andrew 64
Marx, Karl 49
Mercator 16
Meung, Jean de 74, 90
Milton, John 23, 41, 49, 58, 69, 77, 84, 87, 96, 110, 115
Morgan, Edwin 38, 127, 135, 136
Moses 44

Nashe, Thomas 121
Nassyngton, William 43
Nicholas of Guildford 31

Occam 52
Oswald (King) 30
Ovid 67, 85, 90, 93, 94, 132

Percy, Thomas 54, 119, 121, 122–3, 125
Petrarch 88, 90, 110, 126
Pindar 53–4
Pitt, Humphrey 123
Plato 52, 74
Pope, Alexander 92
Pound, Ezra 16, 23, 28, 32, 80, 106, 132
Proust, Marcel 111
Purvey, John 52
Pynson, Richard 117, 141

Raleigh, Walter (Sir) 122
Richard II (King) 45, 46, 49, 51, 63–4, 76, 77, 89, 111
Richard Rolle of Hampole 23, 30, 42–4, 46, 49, 108; *Pricke of Conscience* (*The*), 44; 'When Adam delved and Eve span', **175–6**; 'Unkind Man', **176–7**; Memento Homo Quod Cinis Es, **177–8**; Lo Lemman sweet, now may thou see, **178**; Three good brothers are ye, **178–9**; 'My truest treasure so traitorly taken, **179–80**
Riddles 4–6, 14, 25, 29, 32, **159–63**
Robert Manning of Brunne 47
'Ruin' (The) 25, 29, **159**

Saintsbury, George 85, 97, 114, 115, 116
Schlag, Evelyn 3, 57
Scott, Sir Walter 121, 123, 136
'Seafarer' (The) 16, 25, 28–9 30, 32, **153–5**
Shakespeare, Edmund 71
Shakespeare, William 16, 71, 76, 77, 82, 84, 110, 111, 122, 124
Shelley, Percy Bysshe 49
Shenstone, William 123

Sidney, Philip (Sir) 53–4, 96–7, 110
Simon of Sudbury 51
Sisson, C.H. 16
Skeat, Walter W. (Reverend) 80
Skelton, John 16, 19, 77, 86, 96, 122, 134, 140, 141
Smart, Christopher 56
Spenser, Edmund 19, 58, 77, 86, 87, 94, 96, 110, 137
Statius 85, 86, 94
Strachey, Lytton 16
Strode, Ralph 68, 89, 101
Suckling, John (Sir) 122
Swift, Jonathan 81

Tacitus 5
Tennyson, Alfred (Lord) 23
Theodore 26
Theodoric 24, 74
Thomas à Beckett 45, 104
Tolkein, J.R.R. 57
Trevelyan, G.M. 44
Trevisa, John de 45–6, 140
Tusser, Thomas 118
Tyler, Wat 51, 73, 80
Tyrwhitt, Thomas 106

Urban VI (Pope) 53

Vercelli Book (The) 25, 31
Villon, François 114, 134
Virgil 18, 82, 85, 94, 131–2, 133

Wace 110–111
Waller, A.R. 22–3, 26
Walworth, William 51
'Wanderer' (The) 25, 28, 29, 32, **156–8**
Warton, Thomas 41, 44, 71, 72, 79, 80, 92, 97, 113, 114, 116, 117, 133, 135, 137
'Widsith' 10, 24, 25, 27–8
'Wife's Complaint' (The) 29
William of Malmesbury 22
William of Wadington 47
Wood, Andrew (Sir) 119
Worde, Wynkyn de 137, 141, 142
Wordsworth, William 16, 19, 61, 64, 82, 85, 87, 115, 125
Wyatt, Thomas 106, 113
Wycliffe, John 44, 45, 49–53, 62, 64, 68, 72, 81, 88, 104, 138

Yeats, W.B. 82

INDEX OF TITLES

'A Boar's Head' 212
A Commendation of Gower, Chaucer and Lydgate (*The Pastime of Pleasure*) 470
Aeneados 437
—Prologue, Book Seven
Aeneados 425
—General Prologue
Aeneados 425
—To Know the Translator
'All night' 212
Ancient Ballad of Chevy Chase (The) 180
Ars Sciendi Mori 375

Beowulf 163
'Blow, northern wind' 206
Book of the Duchess (The) 278
—Lament and Consolation
Book of the Duchess (The) 274
—Dream
'Bring us home good ale, sir' 209
But late ago went I my heart to see 360

Canterbury Tales (*The*) 342
—The Nun's Priest's Tale
Canterbury Tales (*The*) 333
—The Wife of Bath's Tale 333
Canterbury Tales (*The*) 317
—The Miller's Tale
Canterbury Tales (*The*) 297
—General Prologue
Ceix and Alceone (*Confessio Amanti*) 267
Coercion of Swearers (*The*) 457
Confessio Amantis 272
—Supplication
Confessio Amantis 267
—Ceix and Alceone
Confessio Amantis 266
—Pygmalion
Confessio Amantis 262
—Pyramus and Thisbe

Confessio Amantis 258
—Deianira and Nessus
Confessio Amantis 247
—Tale of Florent
Confessio Amantis 245
—Prologue
Criseyde Reflects (from Book II, *Troilus and Criseyde*) 287
Criseyde's letter and the rest (from Book V, *Troilus and Criseyde*) 289

Deianira and Nessus (*Confessio Amantis*) 258
Done is a Battle on the Dragon Black 452
Dream (The) (*The House of Fame*) 281
Dream of the Rood (The) 148
Dream (*The Book of the Duchess*) 274
Dregy of Dunbar 449

Envoy (*The Regement of Princes*) 384
Envoy (The), (*The Troy Book*) 395
Example of Virtue (*The*) 462

Fall of Princes (*The*) 396
—Prologue: Dance Macabre (The)
Fall of Princes (*The*) 397
—Words of the Translator (The)
Fifteen Tokens Before Doom (*Life of Our Lady*) 392

Gawain and the Green Knight 224
General Prologue (*Aeneados*) 425
General Prologue (*The Canterbury Tales*) 297
'Green Groweth the Holly' 205

'Herefore, and therefore' 209
Hoccleve meets and talks with an old beggar (*The Regement of Princes*) 381
House of Fame (*The*) 281
—Dream (The)
House of Fame (*The*) 281
—from Proem
How Grand Amour went to geometry & what geometry is (*The Pastime of Pleasure*) 472

I have the obit of my lady dear 361
In the forest of noyous heaviness 361

Kingis Quair (The) 398
Kinmont Willie 193

Lament and Consolation (*The Book of the Duchess*) 278
Lament for the Makaris 453
'Lenten is come with love to town' 211
Life of Our Lady 392
—Fifteen Tokens Before Doom
Life of Our Lady 388
—Prologue
'Lo lemman sweet' 178
London Lickpenny 385
London thou art the Flower of Cities all 441
'Lullay, my child, and weep no more' 215

Memento Homo Quod Cinis Es 177
Merciless Beauty: A Triple Rondel 357
Miller's Tale (The) (*The Canterbury Tales*) 317
'Mother white as lily flower' 216
My ghostly father I me confess 358
'My truest treasure so traitorly taken' 179

Nun's Priest's Tale (The) (*The Canterbury Tales*) 342
Nut Brown Maid (The) 200

Passus VII (*Piers Plowman*) 239
Pastime of Pleasure (*The*) 472
—How Grand Amour went to geometry & what geometry is
Pastime of Pleasure (*The*) 470
—A Commendation of Gower, Chaucer and Lydgate
Pearl 218
Piers Plowman 239
—Passus VII
Piers Plowman 233
—Prologue
Prayer for the Plague (A) 422
Proem (*The House of Fame*) 281
Proeme (from Book II, *Troilus and Criseyde*) 286
Prologue (*Confessio Amantis*) 245
Prologue (*Life of Our Lady*) 388
Prologue (*Piers Plowman*) 233
Prologue, Book Seven (*Aeneados*) 437
Prologue: Dance Macabre (The) (*The Fall of Princes*) 396
Pygmalion (*Confessio Amantis*) 266
Pyramus and Thisbe (*Confessio Amantis*) 262

Regement of Princes (*The*) 384
—Envoy

Regement of Princes (*The*) 381
—Hoccleve meets and talks with an old beggar
'Regina celi letare' 216
Riddles Wisely Expounded 198
Robin, the Kitchie-Boy 199
Ruin (The) 159

Seafarer (The) 153
Seven Riddles 159
Sir Patrick Spence 189
Supplication (*Confessio Amantis*) 272
Sweet Willie and Lady Margery 187

Tale of Florent (*Confessio Amantis*) 247
Tale of the Uponlandis Mouse, and the Burgess Mouse (The) 399
Testament of Criseyde (The) 405
'There is no rose' 212
'This endris night' 213
Thistle and the Rose (The) 444
Thomas Hoccleve's Complaint 364
'Three good brothers are ye' 178
Timor mortis conturbat me' 217
To Know the Translator 425
Troilus and Criseyde 289
—from Book V: Criseyde's letter and the rest
Troilus and Criseyde 287
—from Book II, Criseyde Reflects
Troilus and Criseyde 286
—from Book II, Proeme
Troy Book (*The*) 395
—Envoy (The) 395
Two Married Women and the Widow (The) 442
Two Rondels: To Money and Money's Reply 363

'Unkind man' 176

Wanderer (The) 156
'When Adam delved and Eeve span' 175
When I am laid to sleep as for a stound 359
Wife of Bath's Tale (The) (*The Canterbury Tales*) 333
Wife of Usher's Well (The) 192
Words of the Translator (The) (*The Fall of Princes*) 397

'You and I and Amyas' 208

INDEX OF FIRST LINES AND EXTRACTS

A doolie season to one care-full dyte 405
A meal of words made by a moth 159
A poore widow, somdel steep in agè, 342
A strange being slipped along the waves, 163
Aesop, mine Author, makès mention 399
After that harvest innèd had his sheaves, 364
Alas! And I will tell thee why; 278
All night by the rose, rose – 212
As bright Phoebus, shein sovereign heavennès e 437
As I rose up in a morning, 216
As I went in a merry morning, 217
As the doctor Sanctus Jeronimus, 392

Be it right or be it wrong, these men among, on women do complainè; 200
Blow, northern wind, 206
Bring us home good ale, sir, bring us home good ale, 209
But as she sat alone and thoughtè thus, 287
But late ago went I my heart to see 360
By a mount on the morn merrily he rides 227

Caput apri differo 212
Cupidès son, example of goodlyhede, 289

Delight me drove in eye and earè, 223
Done is a battle on the dragon black 452

Earth out of earthe is wonderley wroghte 177

First he was founden faultless in his five wittes, 224
From spot my spirit there sprang in spacè, 220

Gabriel, that angel bright, 216
Gliding at midnight 165
Go, little book, and put thee in the grace 395
Green groweth the holly so doth the ivy 205

He spurred the steed with the spurs, and sprang on his way 225
Here is my head beaten with a hammer, 160
Herefore, and therefore, and therefore I came, 209

How that glory remains in remembrance 163
Hwaet! 149

I am not loud; where I live's not silent 160
I caught sight of a wonderful creature, 162
I find how whilom there was one, 266
I have the obit of my lady deare 361
I read a tale, and telleth this: 262
I that in health was and gladness, 453
'I woled wit at you, wise,' that worthy there said, 229
In a summer season when soft was the sun 233
'In good faith,' quoth Gawain, 'God you foryelde!' 230
In September in falling of the leafè 462
In th'oldè dayès of the King Arthour, 333
In the forest of noyous heaviness 361
It was a king, and a verray great king, 199

Laud, honour, praisings, thankes infinite 425
Lenten is come with love to town, 211
Lifte up thine eyèn, look about and see 380
Lo lemman sweet, now may thou see 178
London, thou art of towns A per se 441
Lullay, my child, and weep no more, 215

Many cliffs he over-clamb in countries strange; 226
Me thoughtè thus: —that it was May 274
My garment sweeps the world in silence, 160
My ghostly father I me confess 358
My truest treasure so traitorly taken, 179

Nad he signed himself, seggè, but three, 228
Now hearkeneth, every manner man 281
Now rides this renk through the realm of Logres, 226

O creatures ye that be reasonable, 397
O eternè god, of power infinite, 422
O have ye not heard of the false Sakelde? 193
O little booke, who gave thee hardinesse 384
O pensive hearte in the stormy pery 470
O thoughtful heartè, plunged in distress 388
O what is higher than the trees? 198
O ye folks hard-hearted as a stone, 396
Of Falsesemblant which is believed 258
Of them that written us tofore 245
Out of these blacke waves for to sail, 286

Pass over when this stormy night was gone, 381
Pearl, pleasant to princes pay, 218

Right mighty princes of every Christian region 457

She commes to the curtain and at the knight totes, 228
Since thou virtue increaseth dignity 398
So forth I went upon a craggy rocke 472
Sometimes my master miserably binds me, 161

The dubbement dear of downs and dales; 221
The GAw unbroken midled with the WYNe, 425
The king sits in Dunfermline town 189
The old king leapt up, gave thanks to God 168
The Percy out of Northumberlande, 180
The solitary man lives still in hope 156
The woeful pain of lovès malady 272
Then ruthes him the renkand rises to the Mass, 231
There is no rose of such virtue 212
There lived a wife at Usher's Well 192
There was blowing of pris on many breme horne 232
There was whilom be dayès oldè 247
This eagle, of which I have you told 281
This endris night 213
This find I writ in Poesie: 267
This verse is my voice, it is no fable, 153
Three good brothers are ye, 178
Till the knyght come him-self, kachand his blonk, 231
To learnè for to die is to han aye 375
To London once my steps I bent, 385
Truthè heard tell hereof and to Peres he sente, 239

Unkind man, give keep til me 176
Upon the Midsummer even, merriest of nightès, 442

We that are here in heavenès glory, 449
Well may I pleyne on you, lady moneye, 363
When Adam delved and Eve span, sir if thou will speed 175
When I am laid to sleep as for a stound 359
When Marchè was with variant windès past 444
When that Aprille with his showrès sootè 297
Whilom there was dwelling at Oxenford 317
Willie was a widow's son, 187

Wonder holds these walls. Under destiny destruction 159

You and I and Amyas 208
Your eyèn two will slay me suddenly, 357